uniscope. Publikationen der SGO Stiftung

Series Editor

Ingo Stolz • Sylvie Oldenziel Scherrer
Editors

International Leadership

Effecting Success Across Borders in a Boundaryless World

Springer Gabler

Editors
Ingo Stolz
Lucerne University of Applied Sciences and Arts – Business, Institute of Business and Regional Economics
Lucerne, Switzerland

Sylvie Oldenziel Scherrer
Centre for Family Entrepreneurship and Ownership
Jönköping University
Jönköping, Sweden

ISSN 2626-0581 ISSN 2626-059X (electronic)
uniscope. Publikationen der SGO Stiftung
ISBN 978-3-658-37305-4 ISBN 978-3-658-37306-1 (eBook)
https://doi.org/10.1007/978-3-658-37306-1

This Springer Gabler imprint is published by the registered company Springer Fachmedien Wiesbaden GmbH part of Springer Nature.
The registered company address is: Abraham-Lincoln-Str. 46, 65189 Wiesbaden, Germany

Preface

Leadership is a challenging job in a domestic environment. In order to be successful, the responsible actors primarily need distinct competences and experiences. International leadership is more complex, bears surprising risks, and is often exposed to new, different challenges. Well-established instruments and approaches, which hold good in domestic markets, cannot be applied internationally without verification and adaptation. Today, most companies obviously need to expand internationally, because they can no longer rely solely on their domestic success. But before going international, it is a prerequisite to study relevant theories and practical applications of international leadership.

International leadership has to deal with very diverse content, with ambiguity, uncertainty, and with the fact that external influences—macroeconomic and political components like trade or tax agreements—play an important role. International leadership can also entail aspects such as different cultures, true diversity in all dimensions, different values based on local ethical standards, unfamiliar and potentially fragile jurisdictions, as well as the risk inherent in the increasing worldwide transparency of good or bad news. All these factors can impair free and agile management, activities, and performances. But going international usually includes huge potential in various dimensions, as we know from many success stories. Furthermore, a true leader wants to engage in meaningful adventures, to satisfy his or her curiosity, to follow the instinct of creativity, and to prove that his or her ambitions result in expansion, growth, and sustainability for the company.

This publication provides broad insights into the theory of international leadership, as well as its practical application. A whole range of topics is addressed like success factors in an international project, how to understand and address the needs of foreign customers, business partners, employees, authorities, and other players, and the right time to expand further or to step back. As we all know, there is no general answer to all relevant questions and problems, and there is no single way to success. But to study and apply instruments and processes outlined in this book makes international leadership easier and can reduce nasty surprises.

Ingo Stolz and Sylvie Oldenziel Scherrer present an inspiring and very useful compendium of new theoretical content, practical cases, and key topics of international leadership today. This is the result of their intense scientific and practical work. Winning and experienced coauthors provided various chapters outlining actual, specific content.

This book presents the results of a research project in cooperation between the two editors and the foundation of the Swiss Association of Organization and Management (SGO). The board of the foundation is proud that this book is part of the “uniscope” series. We are very grateful for the perfect cooperation and express our congratulations on the fine outcome. It is our expectation that this book finds acceptance in the various communities, inspires numerous readers, and opens doors for future research.

Glattbrugg, Switzerland Markus Sulzberger
March 2022

Acknowledgments

This book is the result of our precious collaborations with the selected authors, who share with us their unique perspectives on international leadership. We feel that this book provides a novel and as yet nonexistent contribution to the field of international leadership, uniquely integrative and holistic, rigorously crafted from a leader's perspective, and from a stance of positive practice.

The joint development of the book has given us great pleasure. We would like to express our sincere gratitude first and foremost to the authors of the contributions, who so generously shared their expertise and trusted us as editors to provide a framework within which this expertise is worthwhile to be shared. Our thanks also go out to the many practitioners of international leadership, who shared their experience openly and continuously with us—and thereby inspired us to edit this volume. Also, we thank the experts who reviewed the chapters of the book and contributed to the quality assurance with their professional feedback—you know who you are. Furthermore, we want to thank the Lucerne University of Applied Sciences and Arts—Business for financing this publication, and for the trust of the university management shown toward this project. Then, we express our gratitude to the Foundation of the Swiss Society for Organization and Management (SGO), and in particular to Dr. Markus Sulzberger, who accompanied this project with great insight, interest, and commitment. We also thank Innosuisse—Swiss Innovation Agency, who supported the research project that became foundational for the creation of this book.

Furthermore, we would like to thank Mr. Peter Schmidt of Lektorat Freiburg, who did a wonderful job of proofreading and editing the texts, and Mr. Matthias Zabel, also of Lektorat Freiburg, who professionally and efficiently accomplished the final editing and layout. Finally, our thanks go out to the program managers and editors at the publishing house Springer Gabler, Ms. Monika Mülhausen and Ms. Ulrike Lörcher, for their always pleasant and competent collaboration with us.

As the publishers, we also would like to thank the readers of the book who will engage with the contributions presented, and who might continue the discussion initiated by and through this book in a variety of ways.

Lucerne, Switzerland
Jönköping, Sweden

Ingo Stolz
Sylvie Oldenziel Scherrer

Contents

Part I

Introduction

Preamble: Approach, Purpose, Structure, and Guiding Questions 1

Ingo Stolz and Sylvie Oldenziel Scherrer

This book strives to support leaders when effecting success for their organizations, by leading their teams, projects, and organizations across borders in an increasingly boundaryless world. To this end, the book offers both an academic's and practitioner's perspective, amalgamating a curated selection of established experts, seasoned leaders, and new voices. Authors were invited to showcase novel research, best practices, and business cases, for the purpose of increasing international leadership capacities of effecting success across borders in a boundaryless world. As a result, a compendium of new knowledge around the international leadership phenomenon has been created, hopefully useful for academics interested in positive practice, for leaders and experts of international and internationalizing organizations, for leaders working across borders with their teams and projects, for leaders aspiring to work internationally, and for students preparing themselves for an international career.

This book focuses on international leaders and their potential to be or become enablers of international success for and within their respective organizations. With this focus, it consistently prioritizes exhibiting the potential impact of leaders as individual agents of transformation as well as of achieving international success. Thus, the book is characterized by (1) a strong human-centered focus; (2) a strong belief in agency; and

I. Stolz (✉)
Lucerne University of Applied Sciences and Arts – Business, Institute of Business and Regional Economics, Lucerne, Switzerland
e-mail: ingo.stolz@hslu.ch

S. Oldenziel Scherrer
Centre for Family Entrepreneurship and Ownership, Jönköping University, Jönköping, Sweden
e-mail: sylvie.scherrer@ju.se

I. Stolz, S. Oldenziel Scherrer (eds.), *International Leadership*, uniscope. Publikationen der SGO Stiftung, https://doi.org/10.1007/978-3-658-37306-1_1

(3) an appreciative focus on entrepreneurial practice. Additionally, the contributions of this book situate leaders in a world characterized by both borders and boundarylessness at the same time. Please read more on our specific approach—and on our ontological, epistemological, practical, and anticipatory understanding of the international leadership phenomenon—in ▸ Chap. 2.

The contributions we curated are presented in three parts that we propose to incorporate the three core challenges of international leadership (Parts II–IV). Additionally, we have dedicated a separate part (Part V) to case studies, highlighting the "real-life" dynamics of international leadership (all case studies are derived from real events), as well as offering "teachable moments" with which the international leadership phenomenon can be hermeneutically and practically discussed and developed.

Part II of the book focuses on the aspect of *Leading International Organizations*, given that international leaders are challenged to align their respective organizations internationally—i.e. business models, strategies, resources, structures, processes, systems, partnerships, and employees. Guiding questions of this section and the respective contributions are:

- How do leaders shape and align their organizations' resources, structures, business models, processes, and systems to recognize, develop, and exploit global opportunities?
- How do leaders attend to the broader network of relationships within which their organization is embedded internationally?
- Which key capabilities and competencies do leaders need to do so? How can they be developed when lacking?
- Which approaches, interventions, and experiences have proven to be impactful when effecting organizational success across borders in a boundaryless world?

Part III highlights challenges of and solutions to *Leading International Teams*. Research clearly shows that constructive, efficient, resilient, and trusted relationships with employees and business partners are an important foundation of international leadership. Respective guiding questions of the contributions in this section are:

- How do leaders lead individuals and teams to international success? Which interpersonal leadership skills are most salient and effective for this purpose? How can they be developed when lacking?
- How do leaders account for individual differences in aspiration, motivation, and expectation across an international working context?
- How do leaders build constructive and trusting relationships across international working contexts? How do they use and take advantage of distributed intelligence within their organizations?
- How can leaders overcome the challenges of distance and maximize its advantages? Which tools can be used in what manner to accomplish this?

- Which approaches, interventions, and experiences are effective when leading international teams?

Part IV presents insights on *(Self-)Leadership with Intercultural Excellence*. On the one hand, the adaptability, effectiveness, and efficiency of international leaders is proposed to be closely related to their intercultural competencies, which have both a cognitive and a behavioral component. On the other hand, self-leadership skills have been confirmed to be very strong predictors of ultimate international leadership success. The contributions in this section therefore address the following guiding questions:

- How do leaders process, understand, bridge, and lead across cultural differences?
- How do leaders access multiple perspectives and a variety of frameworks? And how do they ultimately resolve the inherent complexity and uncertainty so as to come to a respective decision and solution on how to proceed?
- How can leaders learn to interact effectively across cultural differences?
- Which approaches, interventions, and experiences allow leaders to develop intercultural excellence?
- How do leaders compose themselves amid diverse, unfamiliar, uncertain, and ambiguous situations and contexts, so as to remain focused, resilient, and emphatic?
- Which key capabilities do leaders need to do so? How can they be developed when lacking?

In **Part V**, case studies are presented that are derived from empirically researched practice, so as to illuminate the "real-life" dynamics that occur when international leaders address and resolve their challenges of leading organizations, leading teams, and (self-) leading with intercultural excellence.

Our goal was to curate contributions that fit with the purpose and approach of the book, that promise a positive impact on leaders' capacities and capabilities of effecting success across borders in a boundaryless world, that add novelty to the discourse in the field of international leadership, that reflect both an academic and a practitioner perspective, and which in their summation shed light on the three core challenges of leading organizations, leading teams, and (self-)leading with intercultural excellence. In the light of this goal, we release you, dear reader, towards embarking on your journey of delving into the broad and deep expertise offered by the many voices elevated in this book.

International Leadership: Effecting Success across Borders in a Boundaryless World

2

Ingo Stolz and Sylvie Oldenziel Scherrer

2.1 Introduction

The ability to successfully lead organizations and teams to international success is of ever higher significance, given that global trade has "increased dramatically" (United Nations – UNCTAD 2021b, p. 6) over the last decade, reaching a record high in Q1 2021—despite the Corona pandemic (United Nations – UNCTAD 2021a). This ability to lead organizations and teams through the opportunities and challenges of internationalization is not only relevant in multinational corporations (MNCs), but ever more for leaders of small and medium-sized enterprises (SMEs) or start-ups (Baldegger et al. 2019). This is because value streams—and the corresponding entrepreneurial processes that trigger and manage them—inevitably adopt an international dimension, also in organizations that used to conduct their business rather locally or regionally in the past (Beugelsdijk et al. 2018). Thus, developing and exhibiting international leadership competencies and behaviors has become both ubiquitous and urgently in need for leaders in most business situations, in order (a) to build strategies and operations fitting with diverse market conditions; (b) to align business models, strategies, resources, structures, processes, and systems to develop and exploit opportunities also beyond the 'home' market; (c) to increase the understanding

I. Stolz (✉)
Lucerne University of Applied Sciences and Arts – Business, Institute of Business and Regional Economics, Lucerne, Switzerland
e-mail: ingo.stolz@hslu.ch

S. Oldenziel Scherrer
Centre for Family Entrepreneurship and Ownership, Jönköping University, Jönköping, Sweden
e-mail: sylvie.scherrer@ju.se

I. Stolz, S. Oldenziel Scherrer (eds.), *International Leadership*, uniscope. Publikationen der SGO Stiftung, https://doi.org/10.1007/978-3-658-37306-1_2

of diverse customer needs; (d) to reduce the risks of business transactions across borders; (e) to establish and maintain international network contacts and cooperation; (f) to conduct international business partnerships resiliently and sustainably; and (g) to increase the agility and innovativeness of organizations and teams (Stolz and Scherrer 2018). As a result, leaders in large and small companies alike are faced with the challenge of finding concrete solutions as to how to develop and exhibit the required international leadership competencies and behaviors for realizing these international opportunities.

This introductory chapter addresses the question of how leaders can effectively lead organizations, teams, and themselves across borders in a boundaryless world. The answers on the one hand serve as a lead-in into this edited volume, serving the goal of placing the arguments devised by the experts gathered within a larger discourse about international leadership in both academe and practice. On the other hand, this chapter strives to synthesize existing thought about international leadership into a new way of thinking about and practicing international leadership. As an outcome, it offers concrete solutions for developing and exhibiting international leadership competencies and behaviors on the organizational and the team level, as well as on the level of the self. To this end, first, the epistemological contexts are clarified within which international leadership is exhibited today. Second, the scope of international leadership is illuminated, encompassing organizational, team, and intra-individual perspectives. Third, concrete traits, competencies and behaviors which leaders need to develop and exhibit are derived from this scope of international leadership. And finally, we dare to invest in a prediction about which future challenges leaders will additionally encounter when leading international organizations and teams in the years to come.

2.2 The Contexts of International Leadership

First, the epistemological contexts are made transparent within which we perceive international leaders to be active in. Only before the background of this contextual information, the concrete international leadership challenges and opportunities discussed below become embedded, valid, vivid, and thereby relevant. Hereby, we would like to focus on the following aspects: (1) the simultaneous existence of borders and boundarylessness; (2) the mindset of a human-centered appreciative approach; (3) the simultaneous existence of agency and predetermination; and (4) the mindset of entrepreneurial serendipity rather than a strategic rationality.

2.2.1 Leading across Borders in a Boundaryless World

This book situates leaders in a world that is characterized by both borders and boundarylessness at the same time. On the one hand, we propose that—despite converging forces such as globalization and digitalization—national or cultural differences remain strong influencing forces and catalysts for leaders' effectuation of solutions (Zander et al. 2020). On the other hand, we acknowledge that the chain of effects on economic, societal, and organizational levels is now often operative without the impediment of national or cultural borders, therefore creating a boundaryless space of impacts within which leaders need to act. Thus, at the center of this book lies the premise that national and cultural differences as well as today's boundarylessness simultaneously influence how leaders effect success in an international realm. This simultaneity has concrete implications for the work of international leaders, because it results in increases in the number of internal and external stakeholders leaders collaborate with, in the types of boundaries they need to interact across, and in the need to simultaneously integrate local responsiveness with global coordination and cooperation (Mäkelä et al. 2020).

2.2.2 The Mindset of a Human-Centered Appreciative Approach

This book intends to explicitly exhibit the potential impacts of leaders. This means that discussions about how to trigger international business success move beyond focusing on the strategic, operational, and managerial antecedents—e.g., international strategy, business models, organizational structure, organizational systems, existing resources, sector and macro-trends, regulations, etc.–, as is often the predominant focus in international business literature. Rather, the focus additionally and rigorously shifts to the perspective of the individual leader as the nucleus of action and change, as well as to how leaders shape, react, interact, or leverage the antecedents stated above to enable the international success of the respective organization, team, or project. This book strongly invests in this shift, countering that so far "internationalisation literature has paid less attention to the role of the entrepreneurial individual (...), focusing instead on the unit of analysis of the firm" (Karami et al. 2019, p. 778).

In addition to this focus on the leader, an appreciative stance is taken, countering the tendency in the literature "that cultural differences and diversity tend to be viewed as problematic, a challenge to overcome" (Lücke 2020, p. 17). Thus, next to a strong human-centered stance, an additional appreciative focus on concrete positive solutions as brought forward by individual leaders as agents of action and change is emphasized in this book. This also entails the proposition that leaders need to adopt a mindset of appreciating their own individual power of effecting positive solutions in the context of the challenges at hand, rather than on solely identifying and characterizing the strategic, operational, and managerial antecedents which supposedly determine their actions. The chapters in this book are written by experts with this mindset, appreciating the positive solutions and success stories of international leadership as brought forward by leaders as human agents of action and change. With this collection of contributions, much-needed voices are added to the discourse about international leadership, in a field that "has continued to focus on the problems caused by diversity rather than on its potential to generate benefits and synergies" (Adler and Aycan 2018, p. 323). Thereby, the focus shifts toward *leadership potential*, an appreciative perspective in accordance with the stance taken in more recent discussions about the international leadership phenomenon (Knoll and Sternad 2021).

2.2.3 Agency and Determination

It follows from the mindset of a human-centered appreciative approach that international leaders can indeed be impactful agents of action and change within their respective contexts. Thus, this book on the one hand complies with "a pragmatist stance of seeing the world as in-the-making and therefore makeable through human action" (Read et al. 2016, p. 528). Yet, we also realize that international leaders are heavily influenced or even bound by the situations they are active in; they are predetermined by rules and customs that have been established before and which are at a leader's disposal as both antecedents and resources for action. This duality of the potential for agentic action and of predetermination means that international leaders need to master the balance of exhibiting their potential for agency while staying humble to fully discern (the often unknown) contextual forces they are supposed to be sensitive of, to accept, to react to, and to leverage. Ikegami et al. (2017) even state that staying 'foreign' is an asset, because this supposedly increases a leader's awareness of these forces. We therefore propose that international leaders act and react with a mindset of *sociomateriality*, taking into account "the constitutive entanglement of the social and the material in everyday organizational life" (Orlikowski 2007, p. 1438). This mindset emphasizes that on the one hand, "humans have agency, the ability to shape their environment" (Leonardi and Barley 2010, p. 33), but are at the same time influenced by the specific situation they are active in, meaning that "human action stems from physical causes and contexts" (p. 33). With this mindset regarding an interrelated existence of driving agency and materialistic determination, international leaders align with the notion that they are knowledgeable, skillful, and responsible agents effecting international success through their deliberative action, while also considering the contextual boundedness within which their agency shows its impact.

2.2.4 Entrepreneurial Serendipity Rather than Strategic Rationality

We propose that in essence the phenomenon of international leadership is exhibited in the form of entrepreneurial behaviors of a respective leader, rather than graspable in a linear, consecutive, or summative sequence of leadership tasks and objectives. This proposition entails that international leadership is less anchored in a rational but rather opportunistic mindset that flexibly and instinctively acts and reacts within emerging opportunities and serendipity, as a result of the high complexity and speed of internationalization processes (Andresen and Bergdolt 2017; Karami et al. 2019; Knight and Liesch 2016). Thus, successful international leaders continually create a fertile breeding ground for international opportunities to arise and to leverage (Dimitratos et al. 2016), acting "in a flow of ongoing events" (Vahlne and Johanson 2017, p. 1088) based on the realization "that continuous change characterizes any present situation" (p. 1088). This characterization of international leadership as an entrepreneurial undertaking is a departure from its traditional understanding as a more strategic and schematic business administration paradigm (Jones et al. 2011). Our understanding is therefore less about the linear and stringent implementation of strategic guidelines, but rather about quickly identifying opportunities and skillfully scaling them in collaboration with employees and partners (Sarasvathy et al. 2014). Thus, international leaders need to grapple with the questions of how entrepreneurial opportunities arise as well as how they are discovered, evaluated, and used in the international realm, and with what effects. From this perspective, international leaders need to focus primarily on the search for and production of entrepreneurial opportunities; on the process of creating, discovering, evaluating, and exploiting these opportunities; and on the people who collaboratively drive this process. This chapter, just like the whole book, is written from this entrepreneurial perspective.

2.3 The Scope of International Leadership

We generally derive the overarching definition of international leadership from Yukl's (2020) understanding of leadership—which can be characterized as an integrative approach, taking into account various perspectives on the leadership phenomenon (Mendenhall 2018)–, which he describes as "the process of influencing others to understand and agree about what needs to be done and how to do it, and the process of facilitating individual and collective efforts to accomplish shared objectives" (Yukl 2020, p. 26). Within this understanding we position international leadership, focusing additionally on the "processes and actions through which an individual influences a range of internal and external constituents from multiple national cultures and jurisdictions" (Reiche et al. 2017, p. 553) and "under the various conditions of temporal, geographical and cultural complexity" (Jeong et al. 2016, p. 290).

Based on this definition of international leadership, and derived from the integrative literature reviews of Kim and McLean (2015) as well as Bird (2018, in reference to his proposed competency distribution across three primary categories), we propose that international leadership encompasses three practice-related domains, in which successful international leaders develop and exhibit leadership competencies and behaviors: (1) leading international organizations; (2) leading international teams; (3) (self-)leadership with intercultural competence. The structure of this book is designed according to these three leadership domains, with each author expressing his/her view in relation to at least one of these domains.

The purpose of the next sections is to synthesize thought and knowledge about the leadership challenges within each of these domains, thereby providing a practice-related backdrop of leadership traits, competencies, and behaviors international leaders need to exhibit and develop.

2.3.1 Leading International Organizations

International leaders are challenged to align their respective organizations internationally—i.e. business models, strategies, resources, structures, processes, systems, partnerships, and employees (Kim and McLean 2015). This international orientation adds a cross-contextual dimension to leadership challenges at the local, regional, and national levels (Bird 2018), as leaders trigger and manage value streams in divergent markets. As alluded to above, this challenge of leading organization is at its core shaped by entrepreneurship, formulating business solutions within complexity, by quickly identifying opportunities and skillfully scaling them in collaboration with employees and partners.

Stolz and Scherrer (2018) have studied this process of opportunity identification and scaling by leaders in detail—with a special focus on the SME perspective. They concluded that the challenge of leading organizations internationally can be assigned to three phases of internationalization (*start-up; consolidation; establishment*) and seven leadership domains (risk awareness; strategy; learning organization; entrepreneurship; intercultural competence; international partnerships; market orientation)—see also ◉ Table 2.1.

When starting an internationalization effort, or when branching out to as yet unfamiliar markets, leaders typically navigate their organizations through a *start-up phase*, which involves brainstorming and initial exploration through industrious, persistent endeavor, to even realize and reflect on the options, scenarios, and opportunities of internationalization. After this initial exploration, during a *consolidation phase*, the new information gathered is condensed and developed into initial paradigms—as a foundation for idea consolidation and decision-making—and often tested in the form of a pilot. The goal of international leaders within this *consolidation phase* is to identify the best way to implement an idea, in collaboration with stakeholders both internal and external to the organization. This phase is characterized by continuous movements back and forth between intuitive action and reflective decision-making by the international leader. With the *establishment phase*, the leader steers the organization toward its transition to a consistent and focused implementation of the internationalization idea. In this phase, solutions which were previously pilot-tested and evaluated are now boldly scaled and implemented, with all organizational resources at disposal.

Depending on the characteristics and size of the organization, international leaders steer it and its employees as a whole, or they lead individual international projects through these internationalization phases.

In doing so, leaders are challenged within the following seven leadership domains:

1. *Risk awareness:* The challenge to carry out an appropriate risk assessment in order to (depending on the internationalization phase) either test small-scale versions of internationalization with error tolerance or to mobilize major resources consistently and boldly.
2. *Strategy:* The challenge to derive, focus, and implement an internationalization strategy.

Table 2.1 Enactment of international leadership when steering organizations to international success

Sub-skill	Phase 1: start-up phase	Phase 2: consolidation phase	Phase 3: establishment phase
Risk awareness	**Experiment** Use limited resources and remain flexible. Gather experience—also through occasional failure—without overly large potential losses	**Focus** Launch an internationalization pilot project and evaluate its suitability for scaling	**Raise the stakes** Make consistent as well as high-risk decisions with bold deployment of the necessary resources
Strategy	**Develop a sixth sense** Acquire a sixth sense for the opportunities of internationalization, in a quick, direct and cost-effective manner	**Develop strategy** Define SMART internationalization goals, derived from initial internationalization experiences	**Implement strategy** Motivate and empower employees and partners to achieve the internationalization goals; conduct in-depth controlling
Learning organization	**Enable intrapreneurship** Guide employees to develop their own solutions and innovative business models	**Secure resources** Delegate the working steps of the internationalization with the right assignment/resources to the right employees	**Develop ideas & skills** Equip the employees with the necessary internationalization skills and ensure that there is an exchange of knowledge and experience in the SME
Entrepreneurial spirit	**Be optimistic** Drive the internationalization with great energy and confidence in your ability to find solutions	**Be resilient** Consistently pursue the internationalization goals in accordance with your own principles—also after setbacks and when faced with a lack of information	**Be success-oriented** Rapidly identify solutions when (unexpected) problems arise in daily business; believe in long-term internationalization success
Intercultural competence	**Experience** Establish regular contact with existing and new target markets	**Adjust** Adjust to the customs of the target market: with realistic assessment of its requirements and needs	**Bridge** Reconcile your own needs with those of your international partners and customers
International partnerships	**Establish contacts** Locate and select the right international partners	**Develop trust** Establish and maintain a trusting, constructive working relationship with the international partners	**Learn from one another** Develop new ideas and skills as a result of the collaboration with international partners

(continued)

Table 2.1 (continued)

Sub-skill	Phase 1: start-up phase	Phase 2: consolidation phase	Phase 3: establishment phase
Market orientation	**Ensure customer satisfaction** Adjust the product/ service in accordance with international customer needs	**Identify distribution channels** Understand distribution and marketing channels in international target markets	**Generate volume** Ensure satisfaction with revenue and goal achievement with regard to the targeted indicators of the internationalization

3. *Learning organization:* The challenge to create an agile learning organization, so that the correct mixture of exploration, exploitation, delegation, self-management, and development takes place.
4. *Entrepreneurial spirit:* The challenge to exhibit and exemplify staying power, problem-solving orientation, improvisation skills, a clear focus, and resilience.
5. *Intercultural competence:* The challenge to gauge people with divergent cultural backgrounds both privately and professionally, to adjust to the customs and rules of other cultures and markets, and to build bridges.
6. *International partnerships:* The challenge to establish, use, and promote international partnerships and collaboration for the purpose of attaining entrepreneurial goals.
7. *Market orientation:* The challenge to understand customer/market needs and mechanisms to serve customers and markets effectively and efficiently.

Depending on the internationalization phase international leaders steer their organization through, they enact these leadership domains differently—adaptively to the requirements of a particular phase. ◉ Table 2.1 exemplifies these enactments of international leadership, depending on the internationalization phase and categorized according to the seven leadership domains.

These enactments of international leadership are semantically in compliance with leadership challenges on the organization level, as identified in prior literature review studies (Bird 2018; Kim and McLean 2015). However, with the proposition of the three internationalization phases and the seven leadership domains, these enactments become more nuanced, both from a temporal and a categorical perspective.

2.3.2 Leading International Teams

Establishing constructive, efficient, resilient, and trusted relationships with employees and business partners is an important foundation of international leadership (Bird and Mendenhall 2016). Hereby, an international leader needs to be good at leading teams, but also at being a good member of the team (Biermeier-Hanson et al. 2015). Also, the international leader needs to accommodate the circumstance that international teams are different from teams in general by both their diverse composition and their geographic as well as temporal dispersion (Maznevski and Chui 2018). Of course, the degree varies to which international teams are diverse or dispersed, based on "how many cultures are represented, how superficial and more profound cultural differences manifest themselves, and how other dimensions of diversity (e.g., gender, age, profession) interact with culture" (Adler and Aycan 2018, p. 323). Nevertheless, overarching challenges and opportunities of leading international teams within a context of diversity and dispersion can be formulated. Hereby, Maznevski and Chui (2018) have identified the challenges of diversity to be a less effective communication, an increased potential for conflict, and a tendency to a lower alignment on tasks, often invisible relationships, and logistical challenges in team management. On the other hand, the opportunities of diversity have been identified as increased creativity and innovation, more complete and comprehensive perspectives, a greater stakeholder coverage, and more objective and balanced communication outcomes.

As a result of these challenges and opportunities, international leaders need to be—according to Butler et al. (2012)—boundary-spanners, blenders, and bridge-makers when navigating their respective teams through the challenges and opportunities of diversity and dispersion. Boundary-spanning thus involves "establishing and sharing ties between multiple groups to enable the flow of information, knowledge, resources, and people" (2012, p. 241). Hereby, international leaders need to consider linguistic, cultural, and organizational boundaries (Mäkelä et al. 2020). Blending then counters the danger of forming cultural fault lines in international teams (van der Kamp et al. 2015), by a leader's simultaneous maintenance of "a group-level focus on some elements, such as developing a superordinate goal, to increase belonging (...), and an individual-level focus on others, such as developing separate relationships with each individual team member and each distinct subgroup, to retain uniqueness" (Butler et al. 2012, p. 242 f.). Also, blending is a result of building an appropriate feedback culture within the diverse and dispersed team, characterized by a high degree of source credibility and availability as well as feedback quality and delivery (Moukarzel and Steelman 2015). Finally, bridge-making creates a bond by fostering understanding and cohesion "through meaningful interaction episodes and sensemaking across cultures (...) in order to engender understanding of frames of reference and systems of meaning" (Mäkelä et al. 2020, p. 97). As a result of these enactments of boundary-spanning, blending, and bridge-making, international leaders craft identities, manage emotions, ensure psychological safety, and build trust (Lee & Schneider 2020).

Interestingly, some leadership predispositions on the team level can be considered as universal when international leaders navigate their respective teams through the challenges and opportunities of diversity and dispersion, while others are unique to specific contexts. On the one hand, House et al. (2004) as well as Park et al. (2018) empirically examined leadership predispositions that are universally observable in all contexts (but vary in expression depending on the context): being honest; being far-sighted; acting with a positive attitude; communicating clearly; evaluating and reflecting on outcomes;

identifying and solving problems; listening and providing feedback; motivating and rewarding. On the other hand, they identified that the following leadership predispositions vary in their enactment depending on the specific context: conscious use of a leader's position of power; dealing with conflict; dealing with risk; engaging employees to self-guided and self-controlled work; making information transparent; sharing and using emotions; being accessible for employees. To capture and predict these different leadership predispositions on the team level, House et al. (2014) offer the following six distinguishing characteristics—in the form of guiding questions—of how these leadership predispositions categorically differ across contexts: (1) How charismatic should a leader appear in a given context? (2) How involving? (3) How self-protective? (4) To what degree should the leader focus on individual needs? (5) To what degree on team needs? (6) To what degree should the leader promote autonomy? Thus, international leaders need to adapt themselves, depending on the conceptualization of good leadership and good team-membership prevailing in a given context.

2.3.3 (Self-)Leadership with Intercultural Excellence

The adaptability of international leaders is closely related to their basic intercultural competencies, which have a cognitive and a behavioral component. On the one hand, intercultural competence is based on a cognitive understanding of different cultural imprints in different contexts. Models such as those of House et al. (2002), Hofstede et al. (2010), as well as Trompenaars and Hampden-Turner (2012) categorize the differences of these cultural imprints. Based on their knowledge and an understanding of such models, leaders can predict which cultural self-understandings are prevalent in a given context (Andresen and Bergdolt 2017) and adapt their leadership behaviors accordingly (Browaeys and Price 2019). Yet, a purely cognitive understanding is not enough. Rather, an international leader must also find concrete solutions to diversity and dispersion in everyday work. This requires a high degree of intercultural sensitivity on their part. For example, the Developmental Model of Intercultural Sensitivity (Bennett 2018) describes the corresponding development of competencies away from resorting to the seemingly 'normal' toward the ability to flexibly adapt behaviors and contextualize them accordingly, i.e., towards "procedures that are intentionally flexible enough to work without undue cultural impositions in a range of cultural contexts" (2018, p. 6). Intercultural sensitivity is thus to be understood as a basis to "provide us with an intuitive understanding of cultural difference, and allow us to recognize previously undiscovered cultural patterns in others and within ourselves" (Shaules 2019, p. 24).

In order to identify and exhibit procedures that are flexible enough to work without undue cultural impositions—and to enact boundary-spanning, blending, and bridge-making, as presented in the section before–, Elias and Mansouri (2020) identified four domains from which leaders can derive guidance when enacting leadership with cultural competence: (1) *relational*, including enactments of interaction, dialogue, exchange, relationship, and communication; (2) *normative*, including enactments of recognition, acceptance, inclusion, and respect; (3) *transformative*, including enactments of transformation, understanding, and learning; (4) *integrative,* including enactments of sharing, social cohesion, integration, coexistence, mutuality, and reciprocity.

These types of leadership enactments with intercultural competence demand a high degree of resilience and flexibility from international leaders, because it is precisely in international contexts that predictable certainties diminish and where the need increases to deal with ambiguous situations in a goal-oriented and rapid manner (Farrar 2020). Thus, successful international leadership depends on a high degree of self-leadership. Osland (2018) speaks to these qualities of self-leadership in international leaders, anchoring her respective propositions in the Global Explorer model as established by Black et al. (1999). She states that international leaders need three qualities: *inquisitiveness*, i.e. the urge to "seek out the new rather than the comfortable" (Osland 2018, p. 74) and to "question rather than confirm" (p. 75); to *accept duality*, i.e. "embrace rather than avoid ambiguity" (p. 75); and to *exhibit character*, i.e. to "consistently demonstrate personal integrity in a world full of ethical conflicts" (p. 74).

Notably, the self-leadership category encompassed the highest prevalence amongst the competency listings when Bird (2018) systematically reviewed literature about the international leadership phenomenon. This speaks to the (intra-)personal challenges international leaders encounter and experience when leading international organizations or teams, and with intercultural excellence. Next to the self-leadership qualities identified by Osland (2018), Bird (2018) adds the need for *resilience*, i.e. the "ability to cope with the highly stressful challenges of leading across multiple time zones, large distances, myriad cultures, and widely varying national, international, political and regulatory systems" (p. 138); for *flexibility*, adapting to varied situations; and for a *global mindset*, i.e. holding the "assumption that any situation is characterized by myriad interdependencies" (p. 139).

2.4 International Leadership Traits, Competencies and Behaviors

This section is dedicated to traits as well as concrete competencies and behaviors international leaders need to hold, exhibit, and develop so as to realize the inherent opportunities of conducting business across borders in a boundaryless world. These traits, competencies, and behaviors are directly derived from the scope of international leadership—on the level of the organization, the team, and the self–, as presented in the previous section. Thus, this section addresses the following questions from the perspective of concrete practice: (1) Which traits are conducive for international leadership? (2) Which competencies are instrumental for international leadership? (3) Which behaviors contribute to successful international leadership? The answers to these questions are presented in a validated manner, drawing on and synthesizing the results of empirical (meta-)studies and reviews.

2.4.1 International Leadership Traits

The seven traits presented in this section can be considered as particularly promising for international leaders. These traits are to be understood as foundational characteristics of an international leader, on the basis of which competencies and behaviors can be exhibited, enacted, and developed.

1. *Global mindset:* Successful international leaders understand that opportunities arise beyond their immediate surroundings, because of serendipity and international interconnectedness, and they have a desire to seek and exploit these opportunities across boundaries, in collaboration with people whose opinions might be different from their own.
2. *Emotional resilience:* Successful international leadership is anchored in the willingness to resiliently endure ambiguous and even unpleasant situations, striving to search for practicable and realistic solutions despite an awareness that complex rather than simple answers are needed, thereby bouncing back quickly from potential setbacks by conceiving alternative scenarios for action.
3. *Constructive tenacity:* Despite their ability to act flexibly, successful international leaders are characterized by perseverance, persistence, and patience, derived from the realization that challenges need to be overcome before international success can materialize, and that this materialization might need time to accrue.
4. *Proactive flexibility:* International leaders see themselves as agile entrepreneurs who actively approach social situations, and who proactively, spontaneously, and creatively adapt to changing conditions, generally welcoming change as an opportunity for innovation—and ultimately for personal and economic growth.
5. *Optimistic inquisitiveness:* International leaders are motivated and able to commit to personal or professional learning steps openly, willingly, and with a positive, proactive, and open-minded demeanor, based on the realization that the unknown holds the potential for new and innovative solutions.
6. *Visionary integrity:* Successful international leaders prove to be capable of grasping even complex and ambiguous situations with a strong ethical compass, thereby defining visions of collaboration around which individuals from various contexts feel free and motivated to rally.
7. *Humble self-confidence:* While being self-confident and convinced about their high degree of self-efficacy, international leaders continually question their own point of view and the impact of their own personal and cultural imprint, with an absence of ethnocentrism and an urge to analyze, understand, and value others.

Studies have shown that these international leadership traits increase the likelihood of international leadership success. But they are far from guaranteeing it. For example, only 18% of the concrete cross-cultural competencies exhibited in practice—as measured by Bartel-Radic and Giannelloni (2017)—were explainable through the underlying traits of the respective leaders. This also implicitly means that even if international leaders do not hold all these traits, they can be successful nevertheless. This is because their success does ultimately depend on whether leaders are able to exhibit and develop the required international leadership competencies, and whether they exhibit the appropriate set of leadership behaviors in international settings.

2.4.2 International Leadership Competencies

Based on the traits presented above, successful international leaders understand to exhibit and develop the following international leadership competencies:

1. *Building cultural intelligence:* Successful international leaders can gather and interpret information, based on a general understanding of cultural dimensions and their impact on perceptions, cognitions, and behaviors. With their interpretation of the information gathered, international leaders also formulate solutions within complex systems, and communicate those solutions so that they can be understood and transferred to diverse contexts.
2. *Developing intercultural sensitivity:* Successful leadership requires the ability of the leader to understand his/her own cultural imprint and its effects, as well as to question his/her own behavior in situational terms and to adapt it to the respective context. Intercultural sensitivity also includes the ability to assess its mastery in others, so that interactions with others can be authentically adapted according to their anticipated familiarity in dealing with (cultural) diversity.
3. *Building trusted relationships:* Successful international leaders maintain a broad network both within and outside the organization. They succeed in establishing partnerships based on trust and reliability, despite geographical, cultural, and temporal distance. They can build a viable community around strategic objectives by leveraging these trusted relationships. To do so, they delegate responsibility and authority, instruct, exert control, offer support, coach, express appreciation, and award incentives, thereby energizing internal and external stakeholders in line with the contextual habits and expectations.
4. *Building savvy organizations:* International leaders can relate diverse individual and contextual needs to overarching strategic and operational objectives, and they articulate those objectives in a way that individuals in diverse contexts can understand and transfer them. For this purpose, they continuously scan their environment, trends, and risks; they balance between diverse perspectives, between detail and big picture, and between the short and the long term; they design systems, structures, and processes in line with an effective functioning of an organization on an international level; and they adapt these organizational artifacts based on changing needs.
5. *Serving diverse markets:* Successful international leaders have developed a feeling for diverse customer and market needs as well as the potentials to add value, based on a

cognitive and intuitive grasp on operations and market opportunities in the respective industry. Furthermore, they can inspire others to achieve high levels of customer satisfaction.

These competencies are the foundation for international leadership behaviors that are conducive for triggering and sustaining international success.

2.4.3 International Leadership Behaviors

Several studies (Osland 2018; Park et al. 2018; Turner et al. 2019) have shown that successful international leaders invest in the following leadership behaviors (the categorization into four aspects corresponds with Park et al. 2018):

1. *Task-oriented:* Successful international leaders invest heavily in setting SMART objectives, they communicate these objectives and expectations understandably and transparently; they merge cross-contextual predispositions and processes effectively and efficiently and simplify them when necessary; they evaluate continuously in a data-driven manner; they address problems quickly and contextually; they act as coaches in difficult and as arbitrators in conflictual situations; they encourage constructive dialogue and make decisions by taking into account the interests and needs of diverse stakeholders.
2. *Relationship-oriented:* Successful international leaders support their employees and teams in a contextually appropriate manner—by appreciating performance, initiating necessary local development measures, coordinating responsibilities and support in a decentralized manner, and by coaching and providing constructive feedback. In this way, they motivate and enable employees and partners to jointly achieve the respective internationalization objectives.
3. *Change-oriented:* Successful international leaders proactively communicate visions for future development steps, encourage innovation by using the existing international and intercultural diversity, adapt systems and structures to create a match with objectives and organizational processes, guide employees to create independent solutions, and instill an international mentality in the ranks and continuous change steps.
4. *Externally oriented:* Successful international leaders perpetually and cooperatively cultivate their networks, which are constantly expanded as a result of a prudent and foresighted monitoring of trends and opportunities in alignment with the organizational interest. With these networking behaviors, executives invest in acquiring a good sense for the opportunities of internationalization. They also regularly solicit customer input to gain a client perspective on the business.

Overall, a set of traits, competencies, and behaviors comes to the forefront, which—when exhibited and developed by international leaders—make the international success of their work more likely. These traits encompass attitudinal, competence-based, and behavioral answers to the challenges international leaders face on the level of the organization, the team, and the self. Evidently, much is asked from them. However, given our emphasis on entrepreneurship and positive agency, we propose that this set of traits, competencies, and behaviors can be developed by them while acting out and doing business, without the expectation to be perfect right from the start. This means that the traits, competencies, and behaviors presented above are to be understood less as a deterministic set of aspects that need to be complied with (in a mathematical sense), but rather as an aspirational set that provides benchmarks for international leadership action and development.

2.5 International Leadership Futures

When thinking about additional challenges international leaders will face in their daily work in the future, we see the following aspects as becoming prevalent: (1) leading over geographic distances and time without direct encounters, but rather facilitated through the use of advanced information technologies—this aspect of e-leadership is already in daily use in many organizations, and will increasingly proliferate, as a result of the mega-trends of globalization, digitization, and also sustainability; (2) leading responsibly, under the ever more careful eyes of employees, clients, policy-makers, and the public in general; (3) the challenge to aggregate and develop the right set of traits, competencies, and behaviors within an organizational context, given that the demands on international leaders are continuously increasing and encompassing not only the cognitive, but also the attitudinal, the emotional, and the spiritual. This section will discuss these additional challenges on the part of international leaders.

2.5.1 E-Leadership

Leading through and with the support of advanced information technologies (AITs) can be described as a 'new normal' (Adler and Aycan 2018; Jimenez et al. 2017; Morrison-Smith and Ruiz 2020). We are by now all accustomed to using video-conferencing tools such as Zoom or online collaboration tools such es Miro or Mural. Also, gadgets facilitating interactions in augmented and virtual realities become ever more common. Therefore, it is not surprising that a survey of 1620 individuals from 90 countries (RW3 2018) showed as early as in 2018—before the Corona pandemic and the resulting proliferation of remote online work—that 89% of respondents belonged to at least one team led with the support of AITs, and that in 48% of cases team members saw each other exclusively online and never directly. Surprisingly, however, given this new normal, 79% of respondents indicated that the speed of decision-making in such online contexts was impaired, 74% highlighted difficulties in role identification and work reliability, and 51% saw work effectiveness impaired due to communication difficulties, 48% because of impeded conflict management, 45% because of impeded trust-building; and only 15% considered themselves competent to lead adequately in the context of virtual teams (RW3 2018). So despite the growing ordinariness of online and e-leadership experiences, the question which e-leadership competencies and behaviors need to be exhibited and developed is and will remain prevalent in the years to come (Capgemini Ivent 2019). This is especially true for international organizations and teams, given that 69% of respondents indicated that their online team included individuals from at least three different cultural backgrounds (RW3 2018).

The practical opportunities and challenges of e-leadership across borders strongly and inevitably arise as consequences of the overlapping mega-trends of boundary-crossing globalization and digitization. Given this relevance and importance of e-leadership and remote online work, especially in the international realm—enabling the efficient spanning of space and time–, it is surprising that experts still identify a large gap of knowledge about what international leadership competencies and behaviors concretely look like in the specific context of e-leadership and online teams (Belitski and Liversage 2019; Caligiuri et al. 2020; Liao 2017; Oh and Chua 2018): "Unfortunately, research on diverse virtual teams lags behind the phenomenon itself" (Adler and Aycan 2018, p. 325). Given this identified gap of knowledge and the simultaneous immediate practical relevance of e-leadership for international leadership work, the future development of concepts and practice-relevant solutions specifically on this topic appears to be particularly worthwhile.

First studies in the realm of e-leadership (Antoni and Syrek 2017; Bartsch et al. 2020; Ernst and Young 2020; Herman et al. 2020; Jordan 2020; PwC 2020) indicate that successful e-leadership is characterized by: (1) clear objectives; (2) the establishment of routines; (3) the identification of appropriate communication channels; (4) the delegation of responsibility and decision-making power to employees and/or the respective local contexts; (5) the nourishment of flat hierarchies; (6) the exhibition of agile leadership techniques (design-thinking mentality, creativity techniques, balance between prototyping and scaling, transparent and rapid information management); (7) the nourishment of social interactions and emotional well-being, so as to build trust and psychological safety; (8) a proactive 'slowing down', in order to reduce the increased risk of misunderstandings in work and decision-making processes; (9) the encouragement of 'switching off', so that online work does not turn into tiring permanent availability; (10) the evaluation of technological trends so as to evaluate opportunities for further enhancing online team work. However, each of these aspects of successful e-leadership has yet to be studied from an international/intercultural perspective. Thus, it remains to be investigated how individuals from diverse backgrounds interact with AIT in e-leadership and online team contexts. For example, there is a need to explore how hierarchies and the delegation of responsibility are supposed to be concretely managed specifically in international/intercultural online teams. So far, the dominance of Western thinking and concepts is still very dominant in this realm (Chong and Fu 2020)—with the assumption that individuals from diverse backgrounds interact with AIT just as is done in 'the West'. Future research and practice need to focus on the important dynamics that evolve when e-leadership occurs across contexts, as it so often does.

Finally, within the field of e-leadership across international/intercultural distances, the focus will additionally and increasingly also shift to self-controlled systems—such as avatars, chatbots, work-tracking systems, and dashboards–, within which an embedded artificial intelligence performs leadership activities independently of a human leader (Daugherty and Wilson 2018; Zweig 2019). It is therefore increasingly important to understand e-leadership comprehensively, so that leadership processes and activities carried out by artificial intelligence can also be taken into account—in addition to or completely independent of a human leader (Antoni and Syrek 2017). In the future, research into e-leadership will therefore have to focus more on the extent to which leadership in organizations is partly taken over and carried out by virtual technologies and machine-learning, as well as how systems and individuals in diverse contexts react to and process such an interaction with artificial intelligence.

2.5.2 Responsible Leadership

International leadership becomes ever more closely linked to notions of responsible leadership, which is "not only a response to large-scale business scandals and calls for more ethical managerial conduct but also a result of changes and new demands in the global marketplace" (Stahl et al. 2018, p. 363). Next to addressing the challenges described above, international leaders are increasingly held accountable to standards of equity, ethics, corporate social responsibility, and citizenship (Elias and Mansouri 2020; Stahl et al. 2020), which entails both 'doing good' and 'avoiding harm' (Stahl and de Luque 2014). Thus, "social cohesion and intercultural contact have recently emerged as the two interlinked thematic benchmarks of the intercultural approach" (Elias and Mansouri 2020, p. 493).

Stahl et al. (2018) hereby identify four challenges for international leaders: (1) the *diversity challenge*, taking into account and balancing different stakeholder expectations; (2) the *ethics challenge*, demanding from leaders to "come up with morally imaginative solutions that align the interests of diverse stakeholders and reconcile moral differences on a higher level" (p. 370); (3) the *sustainability challenge*, grasping and addressing demands by various stakeholder groups external to the organization, or economic, social, and environmental issues, respectively; (4) the *citizenship challenge*, complying with the increasing demand that organizations engage in societal value creation beyond their immediate economic activity.

These challenges are specifically prevalent but also complex in the international realm, because conflicting paradigms that are not easily discernible and fast-evolving often need to be understood and addressed. As a consequence, the proposition has been made that international leadership needs to be thought in alignment with notions of inclusive leadership (Romani and Holgersson 2020).

2.5.3 Deep Leadership Development

Given the complex multi-dimensionality of international leadership—the necessity to lead on the level of the organization, the team, and the self; while applying the right set of competencies and behaviors; at the same time adapting to the new futures of international leadership–, the question vehemently arises of how international leadership capacities of such breadth and depth can be developed in future international leaders. Studies hereby make clear that (a) the higher the degree of depth and breadth of a respective development experience, and (b) the more comprehensive and immediate the degree of feedback to that experience, the better and more sustainably these capacities can be developed (Oddou and Mendenhall 2018). This means that (future) international leaders need to get in close contact with real-world experiences and immerse themselves in actual leadership scenarios—thus experiencing international leadership challenges and opportunities first-hand and 'live'–, while receiving both feedback on how they acted and support in reflecting about themselves and their behaviors in the situations they experienced. This sort of deep leadership development is needed because international leadership encompasses the whole person, both the cognitive and the intuitive aspects, both the conceptual and the behavioral, both the rational and the emotional, both the material and the spiritual. In order to tap into this breadth and depth of the whole person, and to develop the respective capacities, development interventions also need to involve the whole person and stimulate subsequent reflection and learning. What we are talking about in this realm are development interventions that allow for (simulated) real-life experiences and interpersonal encounters—encompassing the whole complexity, intensity, emotional affect, and relevance of a real experience—that are leveraged to stimulate learning and reflection. Such interventions are based on the premise that the "lessons learned in rigorous experiential contexts are 'sticky' in nature because rigorous experiential learning involves both intellectual and emotional memory, and thus lessons learned are learned for a lifetime" (Oddou and Mendenhall 2018, p. 233).

Osland and Bird (2018) hereby identify three types of experience-based development interventions:

1. Work assignments an individual is placed in to apply competencies and behaviors he/she has learned prior, in order to reinforce and internalize the learning;
2. Action-learning assignments that place a (prospective) leader respective to real-life problems, thus offering parallel coaching support for enabling the mastery of the respective challenges; and
3. Stretch assignments that deliberatively move individuals out of their comfort zone.

It becomes clear that these types of development interventions ideally happen in or at least near the workplace of the (prospective) international leader, but nevertheless are to be triggered and supported by didactic settings designed in parallel. Hereby, the following didactic settings have demonstrated a potential for positive and relevant learning effects in international leaders: international (job and task) assignments with coaching and mentoring support (Conger 2014); international service learning programs (Maak et al. 2020; Stolz et al. 2012); cultural 'stretch challenges' (Caligiuri and Lundby 2015); short-term international business trips (Paige et al. 2009); and experiential learning in classroom settings, in the form of transfer-oriented case studies and simulations, based on principles from cognitive behavior theory (Mendenhall et al. 2020; Osland and Vogelsang Lester 2020).

2.6 Conclusion

This chapter has made an effort to propose epistemological contexts within which we see international leaders to be active (boundarylessness across borders, appreciative human-centeredness, sociomateriality, entrepreneurial serendipity), to clarify the domains of international leadership (on the level of organization, team, and intercultural self), and to derive concrete traits, competencies and behaviors international leaders need to exhibit in practice. With this effort, a snapshot of the international leadership theme was taken, distilling current knowledge and thought into a rich but also clearly graspable theoretical and practical artifact. Despite this effort of pursuing richness and clarity, the international leadership theme remains ever-shifting and ever-changing, and therefore ever-elusive, which has also become obvious when discussing international leadership futures that will impact international leadership theory and practice in the years to come. Fortunately, excellent minds invest in this discourse, mapping the future shifts and changes, and contributing to an ever-increasing richness and clarity of this important theme. This edited volume brings together some of the most prominent names in this realm. It is now their turn—over the course of the following chapters—to take their stance on the fascinating topic of international leadership.

References

Adler, N. J., & Aycan, Z. (2018). Cross-cultural interaction: What we know and what we need to know. *Annual Review of Organizational Psychology and Organizational Behavior, 5*(1), 307-333. doi:https://doi.org/10.1146/annurev-orgpsych-032117-104528

Andresen, M., & Bergdolt, F. (2017). A systematic literature review on the definitions of global mindset and cultural intelligence: Merging two different research streams. *International Journal of Human Resource Management, 28*(1), 170-195. doi:https://doi.org/10.1080/09585192.2016.1243568

Antoni, C. H., & Syrek, C. (2017). Digitalisierung der Arbeit: Konsequenzen für Führung und Zusammenarbeit. *Gruppe. Interaktion. Organisation. Zeitschrift für Angewandte Organisationspsychologie (GIO), 48*(4), 247-258. doi:https://doi.org/10.1007/s11612-017-0391-5

Baldegger, R. J., Merkle, R. J., & Wild, P. (2019). *Swiss International Entrepreneurship Survey (SIES) 2019: Studienergebnisse zum Internationalisierungsverhalten von Schweizer KMU.* Freiburg: Hochschule für Wirtschaft Freiburg.

Bartel-Radic, A., & Giannelloni, J.-L. (2017). A renewed perspective on the measurement of cross-cultural competence: An approach through personality traits and cross-cultural knowledge. *European Management Journal, 35*(5), 632-644. doi:https://doi.org/https://doi.org/10.1016/j.emj.2017.02.003

Bartsch, S., Weber, E., Büttgen, M., & Huber, A. (2020). Leadership matters in crisis-induced digital transformation: how to lead service employees effectively during the COVID-19 pandemic. *Journal of Service Management, Ahead of print.* doi:https://doi.org/https://doi.org/10.1108/JOSM-05-2020-0160

Belitski, M., & Liversage, B. (2019). E-Leadership in small and medium-sized enterprises in the developing world. *Technology Innovation Management Review, 9*(1), 64-74. doi:https://doi.org/10.22215/timreview/1212

Bennett, M. J. (2018). Developmental model of intercultural sensitivity. In Y. Y. Kim (Ed.), *The International Encyclopedia of Intercultural Communication.* Hoboken: Wiley-Blackwell.

Beugelsdijk, S., Kostova, T., Kunst, V. E., Spadafora, E., & van Essen, M. (2018). Cultural distance and firm internationalization: A meta-analytical review and theoretical implications. *Journal of Management, 44*(1), 89-130. doi:https://doi.org/10.1177/0149206317729027

Biermeier-Hanson, B., Liu, M., & Dickson, M. (2015). Alternate views of global leadership: Applying global leadership perspectives to leading global teams. In J. L. Wildman & R. L. Griffith (Eds.), *Leading global teams: Translating multidisciplinary science to practice* (pp. 195-223). New York: Springer.

Bird, A. (2018). Mapping the content domain of global leadership competencies. In M. E. Mendenhall, J. S. Osland, A. Bird, G. R. Oddou, M. J. Stevens, M. L. Maznevski, & G. K. Stahl (Eds.), *Global leadership: Research, practice, and development* (pp. 119-142). New York: Routledge.

Bird, A., & Mendenhall, M. E. (2016). From cross-cultural management to global leadership: Evolution and adaptation. *Journal of World Business, 51*(1), 115-126. doi:https://doi.org/10.1016/j.jwb.2015.10.005

Black, J. S., Morrison, A., & Gregersen, H. B. (1999). *Global explorers: The next generation of leaders.* New York: Routledge.

Browaeys, M. J., & Price, R. (2019). *Understanding cross-cultural management* (4th ed.). Harlow: Pearson Education Limited.

Butler, C. L., Zander, L., Mockaitis, A., & Sutton, C. (2012). The global leader as boundary spanner, bridge maker, and blender. *Industrial and Organizational Psychology, 5*(2), 240-243. doi:https://doi.org/10.1111/j.1754-9434.2012.01439.x

Caligiuri, P., De Cieri, H., Minbaeva, D., Verbeke, A., & Zimmermann, A. (2020). International HRM insights for navigating the COVID-19 pandemic: Implications for future research and practice. *Journal of International Business Studies, 51*(5), 697-713. doi:https://doi.org/10.1057/s41267-020-00335-9

Caligiuri, P., & Lundby, K. (2015). Developing cross-cultural competencies through global teams. In J. L. Wildman & R. L. Griffith (Eds.), *Leading global teams: Translating multidisciplinary science to practice* (pp. 123-139). New York: Springer.

Capgemini Ivent. (2019). *Auf dem Sprung: Wege zur Organizational Dexterity.* Berlin: Capgemini.

Chong, M. P. M., & Fu, P. (2020). Global leadership: An Asian perspective. *Journal of Leadership Studies, 14*(2), 58-62. doi:https://doi.org/10.1002/jls.21702

Conger, J. A. (2014). Addressing the organizational barriers to developing global leadership talent. *Organizational Dynamics, 43*(3), 198-204. doi:https://doi.org/https://doi.org/10.1016/j.orgdyn.2014.08.006

Daugherty, P. R., & Wilson, J. H. (2018). *Human + Machine: Reimagining work in the age of AI.* Boston: Harvard Business Review Press.

Dimitratos, P., Johnson, J. E., Plakoyiannaki, E., & Young, S. (2016). SME internationalization: How does the opportunity-based international entrepreneurial culture matter? *International Business Review, 25*(6), 1211-1222. doi:https://doi.org/10.1016/j.ibusrev.2016.03.006

Elias, A., & Mansouri, F. (2020). A systematic review of studies on interculturalism and intercultural dialogue. *Journal of Intercultural Studies, 41*(4), 490-523. doi:https://doi.org/10.1080/07256868.2020.1782861

Ernst & Young. (2020). *Managing people and work remotely: Leading practices during COVID-19*. Retrieved from https://www.ey.com/en_gl/workforce-resources/managing-people-and-working-remotely-during-covid-19

Farrar, J. (2020). Intercultural knowledge and leadership skills. In Canadian-Swiss Chamber of Commerce (Ed.), *People* (pp. 18-19). Zurich: Canadian-Swiss Chamber of Commerce.

Herman, J. L., McCausland, T. C., & Bliton, D. (2020). Making a difference in the digital age: Global leadership and multiteam systems. In L. Zander (Ed.), *Global leadership: Making a difference* (pp. 126-140). Cheltenham: Edward Elgar.

Hofstede, G., Hofstede, G. J., & Minkov, M. (2010). *Cultures and organizations: Software of the mind: Intercultural cooperation and its importance for survival* (2nd ed.). New York: McGraw-Hill.

House, R., Javidan, M., Hanges, P., & Dorfman, P. (2002). Understanding cultures and implicit leadership theories across the globe: An introduction to project GLOBE. *Journal of World Business, 37*(1), 3-10. Retrieved from http://www.sciencedirect.com/science/article/B6W5M-45BXKSW-2/2/c04165554518032890af477a8f5b8fbc

House, R. J., Dorfman, P. W., Javidan, M., Hanges, P. J., & Sully de Luque, M. F. (2014). *Strategic leadership across cultures: The GLOBE study of CEO leadership behavior and effectiveness in 24 countries*. Thousand Oaks: Sage.

House, R. J., Hanges, P. J., Javidan, M., Dorfman, P. W., & Gupta, V. (2004). *Culture, leadership, and organizations: The GLOBE study of 62 societies*. Thousand Oaks, CA: Sage Publications.

Ikegami, J. J. J., Maznevski, M., & Ota, M. (2017). Creating the asset of foreignness: Schrödinger's cat and lessons from the Nissan revival. *Cross Cultural & Strategic Management, 24*(1), 55-77. doi:https://doi.org/10.1108/CCSM-12-2015-0194

Jeong, S., Kim, D., & Park, S. (2016). Leadership convergence and divergence in the era of globalization. In P. O. Pablos & R. D. Tennyson (Eds.), *Handbook of research on human resources strategies for the new millennial workforce* (pp. 286-309). Hershey: IGI Global.

Jimenez, A., Boehe, D. M., Taras, V., & Caprar, D. V. (2017). Working across boundaries: Current and future perspectives on global virtual teams. *Journal of International Management, 23*(4), 341-349. doi:https://doi.org/https://doi.org/10.1016/j.intman.2017.05.001

Jones, M. V., Coviello, N., & Tang, Y. K. (2011). International entrepreneurship research (1989–2009): A domain ontology and thematic analysis. *Journal of Business Venturing, 26*(6), 632-659. doi:https://doi.org/10.1016/j.jbusvent.2011.04.001

Jordan, J. (2020). Leading virtual teams in times of disruption. Retrieved from https://www.imd.org/research-knowledge/articles/Leading-virtual-teams-in-times-of-disruption/

Karami, M., Wooliscroft, B., & McNeill, L. (2019). Effectuation and internationalisation: A review and agenda for future research. *Small Business Economics, 55*, 777-811. doi:https://doi.org/10.1007/s11187-019-00183-4

Kim, J., & McLean, G. N. (2015). An integrative framework for global leadership competency: Levels and dimensions. *Human Resource Development International, 18*(3), 235-258. doi:https://doi.org/10.1080/13678868.2014.1003721

Knight, G. A., & Liesch, P. W. (2016). Internationalization: From incremental to born global. *Journal of World Business, 51*(1), 93-102.

Knoll, C., & Sternad, D. (2021). Identifying global leadership potential. *Journal of Management Development, 40*(4), 253-272. doi:https://doi.org/10.1108/JMD-05-2018-0158

Lee, Y.-t, & Schneider, S. C. (2020). Multicultural leadership: Keeping multiplicity alive and well. In L. Zander (Ed.), *Global leadership: Making a difference* (pp. 108-125). Cheltenham: Edward Elgar.

Leonardi, P. M., & Barley, S. R. (2010). What's under construction here? Social action, materiality, and power in constructivist studies of technology and organizing. *The Academy of Management Annals, 4*(1), 1-15. doi:https://doi.org/10.1080/19416521003654160

Liao, C. (2017). Leadership in virtual teams: A multilevel perspective. *Human Resource Management Review, 27*(4), 648-659. doi:https://doi.org/https://doi.org/10.1016/j.hrmr.2016.12.010

Lücke, G. (2020). Multicultural leadership: Keeping multiplicity alive and well. In L. Zander (Ed.), *Global leadership: Making a difference* (pp. 17-38). Cheltenham: Edward Elgar.

Maak, T., Borecká, M., & Pless, N. M. (2020). Developing socially responsible global leaders and making a difference: Global Leadership Lab social innovation projects. In L. Zander (Ed.), *Global leadership: Making a difference* (pp. 251-265). Cheltenham: Edward Elgar.

Mäkelä, K., Lauring, J., Butler, C. L., Lee, H.-J., Lücke, G., Miska, C., . . . Stahl, G. (2020). Meeting the challenge of globalization in order to make a difference: Implications for teams and team leadership. In L. Zander (Ed.), *Global leadership: Making a difference* (pp. 91-107). Cheltenham: Edward Elgar.

Maznevski, M., & Chui, C. (2018). Leading global teams. In M. E. Mendenhall, J. S. Osland, A. Bird, G. R. Oddou, M. J. Stevens, M. L. Maznevski, & G. K. Stahl (Eds.), *Global leadership: Research, practice, and development* (pp. 273-301). New York: Routledge.

Mendenhall, M. E. (2018). Leadership and the birth of global leadership. In M. E. Mendenhall, J. S. Osland, A. Bird, G. R. Oddou, M. J. Stevens, M. L. Maznevski, & G. K. Stahl (Eds.), *Global leadership: Research, practice, and development* (pp. 3-27). New York: Taylor & Francis.

Mendenhall, M. E., Burke-Smalley, L. A., Arnadottir, A. A., Oddou, G. R., & Osland, J. S. (2020). Making a difference in the classroom: Developing global leadership competencies in business school students. In L. Zander (Ed.), *Global leadership: Making a difference* (pp. 330-349). Cheltenham: Edward Elgar.

Morrison-Smith, S., & Ruiz, J. (2020). Challenges and barriers in virtual teams: A literature review. *SN Applied Sciences, 2*. doi:https://doi.org/10.1007/s42452-020-2801-5

Moukarzel, R., & Steelman, L. A. (2015). Navigating multicultural teams: A road map to feedback across cultures. In J. L. Wildman & R. L. Griffith (Eds.), *Leading global teams: Translating multidisciplinary science to practice* (pp. 169-192). New York: Springer.

Oddou, G. R., & Mendenhall, M. E. (2018). Global leadership development: Processes and practices. In M. E. Mendenhall, J. S. Osland, A. Bird, G. R. Oddou, M. J. Stevens, M. L. Maznevski, & G. K. Stahl (Eds.), *Global leadership: Research, practice, and development* (pp. 229-269). New York: Routledge.

Oh, S. P., & Chua, Y. P. (2018). An explorative review of e-leadership studies. *International Online Journal of Educational Leadership*, (1), 4–20. doi:https://doi.org/10.22452/iojel.vol2no1.2

Orlikowski, W. J. (2007). Sociomaterial practices: Exploring technology at work. *Organization Studies, 28*(9), 1435-1448. doi:https://doi.org/10.1177/0170840607081138

Osland, J. S. (2018). An overview of the global leadership literature. In M. E. Mendenhall, J. S. Osland, A. Bird, G. R. Oddou, M. J. Stevens, M. L. Maznevski, & G. K. Stahl (Eds.), *Global leadership: Research, practice, and development* (pp. 57-116). New York: Routledge.

Osland, J. S., & Bird, A. (2018). Process models of global leadership development. In M. E. Mendenhall, J. S. Osland, A. Bird, G. R. Oddou, M. J. Stevens, M. L. Maznevski, & G. K. Stahl (Eds.), *Global leadership: Research, practice, and development* (pp. 179-199). New York: Routledge.

Osland, J. S., & Vogelsang Lester, G. (2020). Developing socially responsible global leaders and making a difference: Global Leadership Lab social innovation projects. In L. Zander (Ed.), *Global leadership: Making a difference* (pp. 350-363). Cheltenham: Edward Elgar.

Paige, R. M., Fry, G. W., Stallman, E. M., Josić, J., & Jon, J. E. (2009). Study abroad for global engagement: the long-term impact of mobility experiences. *Intercultural Education, 20*(S1), S29-S44. doi:https://doi.org/10.1080/14675980903370847

Park, S., Jeong, S., Jang, S., Yoon, S. W., & Lim, D. H. (2018). Critical review of global leadership literature: Toward an integrative global leadership framework. *Human Resource Development Review, 17*(1), 95-120. doi:https://doi.org/10.1177/1534484317749030

PwC. (2020). How to lead a virtual team. Retrieved from https://www.pwc.nl/en/insights-and-publications/services-and-industries/people-and-organisation/how-to-lead-a-virtual-team.html

Read, S., Sarasvathy, S. D., Dew, N., & Wiltbank, R. (2016). Response to Arend, Sarooghi, and Burkemper (2015): Cocreating effectual entrepreneurship research. *Academy of Management Review, 41*(3), 528-556.

Reiche, B. S., Bird, A., Mendenhall, M. E., & Osland, J. S. (2017). Contextualizing leadership: A typology of global leadership roles. *Journal of International Business Studies, 48*, 552-572. doi: https://doi.org/https://doi.org/10.1057/s41267-016-0030-3

Romani, L., & Holgersson, C. (2020). Inclusive leadership for the ethical management of cultural diversity. In L. Zander (Ed.), *Global leadership: Making a difference* (pp. 235-250). Cheltenham: Edward Elgar.

RW3. (2018). *2018 trends in high-performing global virtual teams*. London: RW3.

Sarasvathy, S., Kumar, K., York, J. G., & Bhagavatula, S. (2014). An effectual approach to international entrepreneurship: Overlaps, challenges, and provocative possibilities. *Entrepreneurship Theory and Practice, 38*(1), 71-93. doi:https://doi.org/10.1111/etap.12088

Shaules, J. (2019). *Language, culture, and the embodied mind: A developmental model of linguaculture learning*. Singapore: Springer.

Stahl, G. K., Miska, C., Noval, L. J., & Patock, V. J. (2020). Responsible global leadership: A multi-level framework. In L. Zander (Ed.), *Global leadership: Making a difference* (pp. 178-201). Cheltenham: Edward Elgar.

Stahl, G. K., Pless, N. M., Maak, T., & Miska, C. (2018). Responsible global leadership. In M. E. Mendenhall, J. S. Osland, A. Bird, G. R. Oddou, M. J. Stevens, M. L. Maznevski, & G. K. Stahl (Eds.), *Global leadership: Research, practice, and development* (pp. 363-388). New York: Routledge.

Stahl, G. K., & de Luque, M. S. (2014). Antecedents of responsible leader behavior: A research synthesis, conceptual framework, and agenda for future research. *Academy of Management Perspectives, 28*(3), 235–254. doi:https://doi.org/10.5465/amp.2013.0126

Stolz, I., Fürst, M., & Mundle, D. (2012). Managing strategic corporate citizenship at Novartis. In T. Wehner & G.-C. Gentile (Eds.), *Corporate Volunteering: Unternehmen im Spannungsfeld von Effizienz und Ethik* (pp. 265-275). Wiesbaden: Springer Gabler.

Stolz, I., & Scherrer, S. (2018). *KMU zum internationalen Erfolg führen*. Retrieved from https://www.hslu.ch/de-ch/wirtschaft/institute/ibr/kompetenzen/unternehmensentwicklung-fuehrung-personal/cc-ufp-fuehrung/ibr-kmu-internationalisierung-standard-site/

Trompenaars, F., & Hampden-Turner, C. (2012). *Riding the waves of culture: Understanding diversity in global business* (3rd ed.). London: Nicholas Brealey.

Turner, J. R., Baker, R., Schroeder, J., Johnson, K. R., & Chung, C.-H. (2019). The global leadership capacity wheel: Comparing HRD leadership literature with research from global and indigenous leadership. *European Journal of Training and Development, 43*(1/2), 105-131. doi:https://doi.org/10.1108/EJTD-07-2018-0061

United Nations – UNCTAD. (2021a). *Global trade update – May 2021*. Geneva: United Nations – UNCTAD.

United Nations – UNCTAD. (2021b). *Key statistics and trends in international trade – 2020*. Geneva: United Nations – UNCTAD.

Vahlne, J.-E., & Johanson, J. (2017). From internationalization to evolution: The Uppsala model at 40 years. *Journal of International Business Studies, 48*(9), 1087-1102. doi:https://doi.org/10.1057/s41267-017-0107-7

van der Kamp, M., Tjemkes, B. V., & Jehn, K. A. (2015). Faultline deactivation: Dealing with activated faultlines and conflicts in global geams. In J. L. Wildman & R. L. Griffith (Eds.), *Leading global teams: Translating multidisciplinary science to practice* (pp. 269-293). New York: Springer.

Yukl, G. (2020). *Leadership in organizations* (9th ed.). Essex: Pearson Education Limited.

Zander, L., Mockaitis, A. I., Harzing, A.-W., Barner-Rasmussen, W., Barzantny, C., Choudhury, S. R., Davila, A., De Leon, J., Espejo, A., Ferreira, R., Giroud, A., Köster, K., Liang, Y.-K., Morley, M. J., Myloni, B., Odusanya, J. O. T., O'Sullivan, S. L., Kumar Palaniappan, A., Prochno, P., Saka-Helmhout, A., Siengthai, S., Uzunçarşılı Soydaş, A., & Viswat, L. (2020). Action intent: Getting closer to leadership behavior in 22 countries. In L. Zander (Ed.), *Global leadership: Making a difference* (pp. 54–75). Cheltenham, UK: Edward Elgar.

Zweig, K. (2019). *Ein Algorithmus hat kein Taktgefühl – Wo künstliche Intelligenz sich irrt, warum uns das betrifft und was wir dagegen tun können*. München: Heyne.

Part II

Leading International Organizations

Enacting Opportunities across Borders

3

SME Entrepreneurs as International Opportunity Seekers, Consensus Builders, and Action Takers

Sylvie Oldenziel Scherrer, Ingo Stolz, and Sheron Baumann

3.1 Introduction

With business dynamics rapidly changing, global markets are no longer the playing field of multinational corporations only. Technological advances in transportation, manufacturing, and communication have enabled SMEs access to the global arena (Dabić et al. 2020). SMEs are estimated to account for almost 95% of enterprises across the world and are widely recognized to fuel economic growth and innovation as the backbones of most national economies (Dabić et al. 2020). Despite their omnipresence, smaller businesses traditionally remained local, leaving the global arena to multinationals (Dabić et al. 2020).

However, in the last two decades, globalization has increasingly permeated SMEs' business activities. Facing globalized competition in their home markets, SMEs increasingly started to explore opportunities across borders (Baldegger et al. 2019). This process, which has been further facilitated and accelerated by technological and logistical advances, has made internationalization more accessible to SMEs (Dabić et al. 2020)

With the increase of SME internationalization activities, this topic has recently gained a lot of attention in both research and practice (Baldegger et al. 2019; Child et al. 2017; Ribau et al. 2018). Hereby, findings and experiences show that SME internationalization differs

S. Oldenziel Scherrer (✉)
Centre for Family Entrepreneurship and Ownership, Jönköping University, Jönköping, Sweden
e-mail: sylvie.scherrer@ju.se

I. Stolz · S. Baumann
Lucerne University of Applied Sciences and Arts – Business, Institute of Business and Regional Economics, Lucerne, Switzerland
e-mail: ingo.stolz@hslu.ch; sheron.baumann@hslu.ch

I. Stolz, S. Oldenziel Scherrer (eds.), *International Leadership*, uniscope. Publikationen der SGO Stiftung, https://doi.org/10.1007/978-3-658-37306-1_3

from traditional internationalization strategies pursued by multinational corporations (Carlsson and Dale 2011). Facing the high uncertainty and complexity of international endeavors with limited resources urges SMEs to tackle internationalization objectives with entrepreneurial serendipity, thus purposefully leveraging coincidences, unexpected encounters, and surprising opportunities. Consequently, many SME leaders may not rely on traditional internationalization logics, but are more likely to respond with a more effectual approach (Sarasvathy 2001), engaging in the pursuit of international opportunities in a creative and experimental way (Shepherd et al. 2021). Lacking the methods and means for a comprehensive external assessment of the international environment—as a foundation for deriving corporate strategies for internationalization–, the SME entrepreneur's personal vision on their organization—in combination with their competencies and capabilities—thereby impact internationalization much more strongly in SMEs than in larger corporations, where internationalization rather depends on rational analysis and strategic decision-making (Carlsson and Dale 2011; Child et al. 2017).

Thus, in contrast to the internationalization process of multinational organizations, SME internationalization has been shown to be a highly personal affair of the SME entrepreneur. Many SME studies have so far investigated the motives, characteristics, and competencies affiliated with SME internationalization (Dabić et al. 2020; Handrito et al. 2020). However, the roles and activities exhibited by SME entrepreneurs in the pursuit of international entrepreneurial opportunities remain largely unknown.

The present chapter therefore aims to explore *how experienced and successful SME entrepreneurs drive the internationalization process of their respective SME.* Notably, we investigate the following research questions:

1. What are the activities and interactions SME entrepreneurs engage in when pursuing international opportunities?
2. Which roles do SME entrepreneurs take on when pursuing international opportunities?

The present paper understands the SME internationalization process as the pursuit of entrepreneurial opportunities across borders (Oviatt and McDougall 2005), which encompasses the creation, evaluation, development, and implementation of entrepreneurial ideas that involve business activities at an international level. We therefore look at the entire panoply of phases an entrepreneur lives through when internationalizing, from the emergence of a first hunch to the resource-intensive implementation and manifestation of an internationalization objective. We thereby focus on understanding the SME entrepreneur's multiple and complex roles, their activities and actions amid the entrepreneurial opportunity pursuit, as well as the interactions of the individual entrepreneur with the organizational members and external stakeholders in the ongoing enactment of international opportunities.

In order to explore the entrepreneur's actions and interactions in the ongoing, iterative, and dynamic process of opportunity enactment across borders (Wood and McKinley 2010), this chapter first synthesizes current literature on SME internationalization from an international entrepreneurship perspective. Based on an explorative interview and action research study with experienced Swiss SME entrepreneurs who continuously engage in the pursuit of international opportunities, the chapter then identifies eight entrepreneurial practices for effecting success across borders and derives three key roles international SME entrepreneurs must take on. To conclude, we identify areas for future research and propose implications for practice.

3.2 Literature Review

In the past two decades, the research stream on international entrepreneurship has provided a conceptual alternative to traditional internationalization approaches, which are grounded in corporate strategy research. We consider the international entrepreneurship perspective as being particularly relevant for the present paper, because it allows to better conceptualize the creative, experimental, means- and opportunity-oriented way of internationalizing that we tend to find in SMEs.

3.2.1 Internationalizing SMEs

Studies on SME internationalization have become more prevalent over the past decade, because of the SMEs' increased presence and competitiveness in the global market (Ribau et al. 2018). Yet, despite this higher attention, significant questions regarding the internationalization processes and patterns of SMEs remain unanswered (Ribau et al. 2018). The lack of understanding SME internationalization is rooted in the prevailing focus on large multinational manufacturing firms in international business research (Ribau et al. 2018). Yet, SMEs differ considerably from large multinationals in terms of governance, strategies, competences, and resources (Dabić et al. 2020; Ribau et al. 2018). For example, while large corporations may rely on entire teams of specialists to analyze the potential of new markets, the SME entrepreneurs and their leadership team tend to take over this complex task themselves—mostly for the lack of resources. SMEs therefore often benefit from faster, less formal decision-making processes, but at the same time must base their decisions on less information. Thus, aspects like intuition and gut-feeling become very important in the internationalization process of SMEs, while they are likely to play a minor role in MNEs (Carlsson and Dale 2011).

In the current internationalization literature, these differences are primarily reflected in two contrasting theoretical perspectives: on the one hand the traditional stage models applicable for large multinational corporations, and models focusing on the entrepreneurial process of internationalizing SMEs on the other hand. The traditional view describes the internationalization process as a sequential and gradual one during which firms expand their international activities step-by-step. Typically, the stage models emphasize internationalization as an incremental and time-consuming learning process (Vahlne and

Johanson, 2017), with an inherent causality between internationalization strategy and internationalization process. This stipulated linearity and causality of traditional models may provide a sound conceptualization for internationalization processes of large corporations. However, several studies indicate that the SME internationalization process follows different patterns (Carlsson and Dale 2011; Dabić et al. 2020; Fabian et al. 2009; Ribau et al. 2018).

The entrepreneurial perspective on internationalization that has been developed over the last decade aims to address these differences and criticizes the traditional approaches for their linearity, gradation, and inherent assumption of high strategic predictability. Research clearly shows that SME internationalization unfolds in a much less gradual, less linear, and oftentimes less strategically planned way than traditional models predict (Carlsson and Dale 2011). Models with a focus on international entrepreneurship therefore look at internationalization as a pursuit of opportunities (Oviatt and McDougall 2005). The entrepreneurial perspective also takes into account the resource scarcity of SMEs, which urges them to take different avenues to internationalization—frequently characterized by the serendipity of emerging business opportunities rather than strategic planning (Jones et al. 2011). Overall, there is a consensus that this new entrepreneurial perspective on internationalization is more apt to inform SME internationalization research (Oviatt and McDougall 2005). As brought forward by Reuber et al. (2017), opportunity-based research can open new avenues to enhance our understanding of the entrepreneurial internationalization of SMEs. The question how opportunities across borders are enacted therefore lies at the center of today's international entrepreneurship research, and also of the contribution at hand.

3.2.2 The International Entrepreneurship Perspective

The international entrepreneurship research field specifically looks at the recognition, formation, enactment, evaluation, and exploitation of opportunities across national borders to create new financial, social, and environmental value through innovations, new business models and new venture creation (Oviatt and McDougall 2005). Thus, it studies "innovative, proactive, and risk-seeking behaviors across borders" (McDougall and Oviatt 2000, p. 903) intended to create new value in organizations. While corporations without doubt also engage in such behaviors across borders, and hence international entrepreneurship may today also additionally inform internationalization of multinationals, SME internationalization seems to be particularly guided by the pursuit of international opportunities.

Most international entrepreneurship studies look at the *discovery* of international opportunities and the entrepreneur's capabilities needed to identify and exploit them (Mainela et al. 2014). Accordingly, different studies stress the importance of the entrepreneur's alertness and innovativeness to international opportunities, which is often based on their prior knowledge and experiences as well as their international network (Mainela et al. 2014). Cross-cultural competence is needed to deal with cultural, historical, and national differences, and to understand how to use them as resources in the pursuit of international opportunities (Muzychenko 2008). Furthermore, the capabilities of rapid learning and knowledge accumulation allow entrepreneurs to pursue international opportunities more effectively (Tsao and Lien 2013).

However, beyond findings about competencies that help in the pursuit of international opportunities, we know little about what SME entrepreneurs actually *do* to successfully pursue opportunities across borders. Recent studies come to inconclusive results, suggesting that entrepreneurs explore and exploit international opportunities in different ways—ranging from planned strategy formation to opportunistic responses to serendipitous encounters. Nevertheless, the prevalent studies largely fail to provide rich and concrete empirical insights into SME entrepreneurs' actions and interactions in the pursuit of international opportunities (Dabić et al. 2020; Mainela et al. 2014). Particularly, few studies take a thorough perspective on the pursuit of international opportunities by SME entrepreneurs as impactful agents of internationalization. Such an opportunity-based research focus would, however, allow to study the internationalization process as a contextualized, dynamic, and heterogeneous one, and hence provide a new avenue to understanding internationalization processes in general (Reuber et al. 2017). Specifically, it allows to study the international opportunity pursuit as dynamic sequences of actions and events rather than as a linear process.

In order to respond to this call for more research focused specifically on actions and enactment (Mainela et al. 2014; Reuber et al. 2017), the present contribution builds on the multi-stage process perspective of opportunity production as proposed by Wood and McKinley (2010, 2017). Notably, their model posits that international opportunities do not only originate from the discovery of market imperfections and unique competencies, but asserts that opportunities are created via the entrepreneur's and stakeholders' actions in different phases of opportunity perception and pursuit (Wood and McKinley 2010). It further stipulates the pursuit of international opportunities as a continuous process of creating meaning, sense-making, and sense-giving in a context of high ambiguity and uncertainty (Mainela et al. 2014; Wood and McKinley 2010). Overall, we aim to contribute to a more socially embedded, dynamic, and iterative understanding of SME internationalization, which centers around the actions and interactions of SME entrepreneurs.

3.3 Methodology

As outlined above, the present paper aims to explore the actions and interactions of SME entrepreneurs when enacting opportunities across orders. Acknowledging the diverse views on how opportunities are pursued, and the lack of conceptual development of opportunity pursuit in the international context (Reuber et al. 2018), this paper builds on the *opportunity production process* as proposed by Wood and McKinley (2010, 2017). This perspective fits well with the authors understanding of SME entrepreneurs as active agents, whilst acknowledging the importance of context, since it proposes that *"entrepreneurial opportunities emerge as the result of entrepreneurs' actions that are framed by social processes and existing social structures"* (Wood and McKinley 2010, p. 66).

So as to explore the diversity and equifinality of these actions and interactions, this paper builds on a qualitative research design and follows an abductive research process. Abduction is the process in which "*empirical observations and surprises are connected to extant theoretical ideas to generate novel conceptual insight and distinctions*" (Langley et al. 2013, p. 11). An abductive approach therefore dictates a continuous iteration between theory and emerging data, to be made throughout the data collection and analysis process. In the course of this process, the empirical area is successively developed and the theory continuously adjusted as well as refined in order to develop an understanding of the underlying logic of the phenomenon, while providing a theoretical interpretation that reaches beyond description (Alvesson and Sköldberg 2009; Langley et al. 2013).

3.3.1 Data Collection

Semi-structured interviews with SME entrepreneurs were the principal means of collecting data for the present study. This type of interview aims to reconstruct an individual's subjective perspective on the theme under study and therefore allows for an in-depth understanding of the meaning attributed to international opportunities (Flick 2014). Furthermore, semi-structured interviews were selected to gather rich insights into how the process of international opportunities enactment unfolds. The interviews consisted of three sections: First, we inquired about the personal background of the entrepreneur. Second, we asked about the entrepreneurial process of internationalization from the first idea to the entry into a foreign market. And third, we focused on the entrepreneur's actions as well as interactions with internal and external stakeholders. The questions focused on activities, events, and outcomes, so as to reflect the ongoing enactment of opportunities and to reduce the potential for retrospective bias through hearsay. Follow-up questions were used to ask for clarifications, examples, and further details. In general, priority was given to the interviewees' narratives rather than sticking to the guideline. A total of eight interviews were conducted in Switzerland between January and April 2017. Typically, interviews lasted 60–90 minutes. All interviews were digitally recorded and transcribed. The interview material was complemented with archival data from internal and external sources, including websites, press releases, and social media posts. This triangulation increases the internal validity of the study and reduces the potential for retrospective bias (Santos and Eisenhardt 2005).

3.3.2 Sampling

The selection of interview partners followed a purposive sampling strategy (Patton 2014), based on the proven success of a SME when internationalizing. We focused on the owner-managers of SMEs. As outlined by Dabić et al. (2020), qualitative interviews with owner-managers of SMEs have the potential to shed light on important internationalization matters of SMEs. Entrepreneurs were selected based on their firm's official status as a "success story" of the Swiss export promotion agency. The selected SMEs employed between 10 and 30 employees; one organization employed 250 employees at the time of interviewing. Furthermore, the sample consisted of a diverse selection of startups, established firms, and long-standing family firms from different industries with different internationalization intensities and activities.

3.3.3 Data Analysis

In line with the study's abductive approach, the empirical material was analyzed in an iterative way circling back and forth between theory and empirical material (Miles et al. 2014). Dubois and Gadde (2002, 2014) propose an abductive approach of systematic combining, which stipulates the interrelatedness of different research elements and suggests that the different activities in the research process are intertwined. It allows the researcher to expand their understanding of theory, the concept, the empirical phenomenon, and the case itself by the processes of 'matching' as well as 'direction and redirection'.

Using the MAXQDA software, the analysis followed a coding cycle, first developing first-order codes adhering closely to informant terms, and eventually formulating—by seeking similarities and differences—labels for the identified categories. In line with the study's purpose to study the process of opportunity production, we used gerunds to code action and activities (Miles et al. 2014, p. 75). This coding strategy aimed to extract the entrepreneurs' actions and interactions with other stakeholders along the different phases of opportunity production (Wood and McKinley 2010, 2017). The codes were then continuously supplemented by new codes, reviewed, changed, and, in a few cases, abandoned with the primary objective to create meaningful and more parsimonious categories.

Emerging preliminary categories and results (including codes) were reviewed by a committee of SME internationalization experts (both academics and practitioners) so as to gain additional insights into the data collected as well as the categories and patterns that emerged from it. Lastly, we related the entrepreneurs' actions, activities, and interactions in their enactment of international opportunities to multiple roles an entrepreneur must take on during this process.

3.4 Findings and Discussion

In the following, we present our findings from the two research questions posed, i.e. the actions and interactions SME entrepreneurs engage in when pursuing international opportunities, and the roles they take on when doing so.

3.4.1 Part A: SME Entrepreneurs' Actions and Interactions in the Pursuit of International Opportunities

Action #1: Cultivate Innovativeness and Flexibility at Home

While we have stipulated above that the entrepreneurial process begins with the perception and conceptualization of an idea (Dimov 2007), the interviews show that entrepreneurs focus first on turning their organizations into a fertile breeding ground for international opportunities. Consequently, the interviewed SME entrepreneurs focus on cultivating their organization's innovativeness. Hereby, innovativeness is understood as the underlying force of an innovation culture, which stipulates the skills and expertise necessary to innovate, but also the 'state of mind' that is necessary to actively identify and pursue opportunities. The interviewees are therefore dedicated to creating a space for new ideas, critical questioning, continuous change, and to eliminating potential barriers to the pursuit of opportunities.

> The willingness to change—I would say that it is a basic requirement that changes are not perceived as a danger but as an opportunity. So, you need people who see the glass as half full rather than half empty. It's the mental set-up, and it does not only concern internationalization but leadership in general. (I5, 508–512)

Confined by high production costs, the Swiss context restricts SME entrepreneurs to competing through high levels of quality, innovativeness, and product/service adaptability to foreign markets. Establishing a fertile ground for innovation therefore becomes essential in order to *"develop services and products that 'can travel'"* (I2). Yet, the resulting high investments in research and development force Swiss entrepreneurs to ensure international success, because the Swiss market is too small to reach a return on its innovation investments (I2, I3, I7). Thus, a highly innovative, fast-learning, and agile organization is a necessary pre-condition for SMEs to engage in the pursuit of international opportunities. Successful SME entrepreneurs therefore invest heavily in creating and developing an organization that is ready to pursue business opportunities abroad.

Action #2: Make Traveling the World your Daily Business

While developing their organization at home, successful international SME entrepreneurs are frequently on the road to explore new markets. While traveling the world may take very different forms—from organized exploratory trips to family holidays—ideas for international opportunities seem to be popping up everywhere but in the office. Actively engaging and experiencing in the international context is described as essential to finding inspiration, developing a gut feeling for potential opportunities, and deepening existing relationships. According to our interview partners, continuous relationship building is specifically essential for exploiting international opportunities. As it is incredibly difficult for SMEs to attain a position of power in foreign markets, SME entrepreneurs invest in building and strengthening personal relationships with their internationalization partners (e.g. sales agents, distributors):

> I learnt from my father's network that the best representatives abroad were his friends. He always had a very close contact with them—also on a human level. We still have this kind of connection with many representations. Many of them have been working for us for a very long time, and we visit them often, we invite them to industry fairs, we invite to Switzerland and organize something nice. This is how we build a connection that goes beyond the subject matter. (I8, 413-418)

Ultimately, traveling means gaining personal impressions and learnings that SME entrepreneurs need to make decisions in the pursuit of international opportunities.

> I think that it is a very important point to learn that people in different countries and different cultures are different, and that you learn to deal with these differences; to be able to 'read' people from other cultures to understand whether they articulate agreement or disagreement. (I8, 354-358)

The interviewed SME entrepreneurs agreed that experiencing new contexts on the ground and engaging with people in person cannot be replaced but only complemented by digital communication. While these activities may seem time consuming and tiring, it is important to point out that successful SME entrepreneurs clearly enjoy these activities.

> The willingness is more important than the ability to internationalize. You can learn to internationalize; you can learn languages up to a certain point but what really drives the internationalization is your willingness. If you don't want to go international, it simply doesn't work. (I5, 503-508).

The individual joy of traveling, discovering, and striving to understand new cultures and new ways of working is essential for the pursuit of international opportunities.

Action # 3: Follow your Clients across the Globe

Our interviewees see their close relationships to their clients and other business partners as source for internationalization ideas. The interviewed entrepreneurs proactively and carefully follow the movements of their clients and business partners on a global scale:

> In February, I just went to Vietnam. We want to open a new branch there. We have a client in Vietnam, a big machine producer from Austria. They produce machines, which are very

> sought after in Vietnam these days, they sell extremely well, and we see that in two to three years there will be a demand for spare parts, and then we want to be ready. (I8, 164–168)

Similarly, another entrepreneur describes his industry as a *"caravan of internationalization"* (I2, 197), where innovative niche players follow the big key accounts from one international market to another. One interviewee even states that around 60 percent of their international opportunities arise through following their clients and exploiting the inherent business possibilities when doing so; and only 40 percent of the opportunities arise through exploration (I8). While it may be conceptually very interesting to scan international markets for new opportunities, developing these based on one's existing business seems to be the preferred (and easier) way to enact them (I2, I5, I8). Staying close to existing clients and attentive to the global developments of the market is therefore a key activity for internationalizing SME entrepreneurs.

Action #4: Leverage a Large Diversity of Global Connections

Our empirical material also shows that the entrepreneurs actively engage in creating a lasting and diverse network that goes beyond direct business partners. Our interviewees are primarily active in niche markets and oftentimes offer highly customized solutions. Consequently, they can hardly rely on general market statistics and industry reports to get a feeling for the potential of their internationalization ideas. Therefore, they rely heavily on trustworthy relationships with contacts from industry fairs and associations, as well as with existing clients, to get a feeling for potential internationalization ideas.

> Oftentimes, we cannot get the data that is relevant for us from official reports and statistics, because our markets are very small and very specific. Therefore, our business is a networking business—you need to go to events, conferences, and conventions of our industry. (I8, 556–559)

Increasingly, the entrepreneurs also rely on digital networks to directly seek out potentially interesting contacts and engage with them:

> Sometimes you also just sit down, and you open the internet, you go to LinkedIn, and you start looking for interesting contacts with certain search terms, and then you just reach out to them. The success rate is certainly not 100%, but also not considerably lower than 50%. That's an interesting tool to create completely new connections outside of the established paths. (I7, 565–568)

While they engage in continuous discussions with formal stakeholders such as the board of directors and the leadership team, SME entrepreneurs also seek insights and inputs from external parties in which they trust, such as family members or befriended entrepreneurs; or they reach out to role models:

> There are many entrepreneurs who are passionate about entrepreneurship and who also started small, and many of these people really enjoy supporting others, who take on the challenges of (international) entrepreneurship. For these people, it is kind of a question of honor to help shape the Swiss industry through their advice. (I2, 580–584)

Overall, the interviewees simultaneously engage in leveraging their existing network, seeking new partners for their internationalization idea, and, more generally, for creating a long-lasting and trustworthy global network. The latter in particular may demand considerable resources, and therefore becomes a matter for careful consideration: trustworthy networks depend on the right balance between giving and taking, i.e., only who is also willing to share their experiences and relevant information will be able to gain truly meaningful insights. Effective networking demands not only the careful consideration of where one wants to commit their resources for the long turn. In order to become an effective sounding board for new internationalization ideas, a network necessitates the openness to listen actively to different views and to critically reassess the status quo.

Action #5: Building Bridges

According to Butler et al. (2012), international leaders need to be bridge-builders to foster understanding and cohesion across cultures (see also Mäkelä et al. 2020). While building and leveraging their network, interviewees are increasingly confronted with multiple viewpoints from external and internal stakeholders who they need to consolidate and integrate in their decision-making processes.

The interviewees recognize that the pursuit of international opportunities can lead to severe complexity and uncertainty for employees. This implies a stringent focus on identifying pragmatic ways for finding concrete solutions across divergent perspectives.

Action #6: Improvising Internationalization Plans

The existing literature suggests that entrepreneurs often rely on the ability to spontaneously improvise when pursuing international opportunities (Dabić et al. 2020). Our empirical material indeed indicates that SME entrepreneurs rely heavily on this ability. In this context, improvisation is understood as the fusion between planning and action (see, for example, Shepherd et al. 2021).

> I think that in the beginning, planning and designing may take an important role—it would be irresponsible not to plan. However, oftentimes, the pursuit of a business opportunity—let's take Uzbekistan, but there are many countries like that—simply means to 'freestyle'. (I1, 186–191)

Entrepreneurship research also relates to this ability to 'freestyle' as *bricolage* (Baker and Nelson 2005), which emphasizes the focus on existing resources (rather than to find new ones) to create and exploit new opportunities as well as to solve problems (Baker and Nelson 2005). Concretely, this translates into creative and spontaneous mechanisms of problem-solving:

> I knew that I had to bring our prototype to our Dutch partner; they would conduct an analysis with our machine for which we were simply lacking the products. So I took the prototype, my family, and our dog on the machine—so that it looked like we were going on vacation—and thus smuggled our prototype across the border. (I3, 190–198)

The interviewees know that the pursuit of international opportunities demands quick actions and reactions, and therefore focus on finding quick, pragmatic, and sometimes also unorthodox solutions.

Action #7: Take a Well-Calculated Leap of Faith
At some point in the internationalization process, the interviewed SME entrepreneurs described taking what we labelled 'a leap of faith'. In order to exploit emerging "windows of opportunities" (Carlsson and Dale 2011), they are oftentimes obliged to take decisions based on incomplete information, to leave data analysis behind, and to trust their gut feeling.

> It is fine to run, for example, a SWOT analysis for the big picture, but at the same time you need to jump on opportunities when they emerge and where you may say 'who cares, I run with my idea because my gut feeling tells me to do it'. (I6, 662–664)

The previously described experiences—such as traveling to different places, talking to many different stakeholders—help entrepreneurs develop a sound gut feeling of whether or not they want to start acting on an idea and take a little leap of faith to bring their internationalization idea forward. Moreover, given the limited resources of SMEs, the interviewed entrepreneurs use small pilot projects to gain firsthand insights into the viability of an idea without committing too many resources, and hence without putting the financial well-being of their organizations at risk: *"I need to be able to assess the risk in order to be courageous" (I5, 458)*. Investing time and efforts into developing their gut feelings regarding an internationalization idea, as well as carefully defining the limits of their 'playground', allows SME entrepreneurs to take a leap of faith in the enactment of international opportunities.

Action #8: Commit to (or Abandon) the International Opportunity
While the previous practices of SME entrepreneurs primarily emphasized rather informal and resource-restrained approaches to internationalization, the interviewees emphasize that at some point one needs to commit to an international opportunity. This switch from testing to committing challenges SME entrepreneurs to ensure that their teams are on board and trust their decisions:

> You need to be authentic and credible—you need to know that people trust you and that they have trust in your decision, and that people don't think that you come along with yet another crazy idea. (I6, 744–750)

Thus, being able to commit quickly and courageously to an international opportunity implies that SME entrepreneurs early on develop trustworthy relationships with the decision-making committee (e.g. company owner, board of directors, leadership team) and with their employees.

3.4.2 Part B: An SME Entrepreneur's Multiple Roles in the Pursuit of International Opportunities

Having outlined the identified actions and interactions of SME entrepreneurs in developing and enacting international opportunities, we now derive three roles they take on in the pursuit of international opportunities. In the following, we present these three roles in correspondence with the actions described above.

Role #1: Opportunity-Seeker

So as to generate opportunity ideas, SME entrepreneurs are continuously on the lookout for new international opportunities. While they might not be strategically planning for the next internationalization step, they actively engage in activities that facilitate the emergence of international opportunities. They see the world through the lens of potential business opportunities, engage actively in a wide personal and professional network, and enjoy interactions with people from all over the world. At the same time, SME entrepreneurs remain strongly focused on their own organization, notably by making sure that their organization is ready to act on arising opportunities. This includes hiring and developing people, facilitating change, and fostering continuous innovation.

Role #2: Consensus-Builder

With a diverse network and new cultural settings, new internationalization ideas emerge and are developed. Oftentimes, the assessment of emerging internationalization ideas is characterized by ambiguous information and contrasting viewpoints. In order to establish clarity and consistency in this context, SME entrepreneurs actively engage in a dialogue with different players, being open to evaluate and adapt, and ultimately assess the validity of their opportunity idea. So as to produce clear support (or evidence for the lack of it), they constantly compare and adjust the beliefs and behaviors of their sparring partners and stakeholders with their own perception of an opportunity, with the ultimate objective to establish a broad consensus among their sparring partners on the viability of the international opportunity.

Role #3: Action-Taker

Having construed and invested in objectifying their own understanding, SME entrepreneurs ultimately have to start exploiting their opportunity idea. This marks the transition to a new phase in which they continuously take action so as to align their stakeholders to push toward fulfilling the inherent potential of the opportunity. This in turn implies fostering and seeking legitimacy for their idea. As SME entrepreneurs start to exploit the opportunity, they oftentimes have to take a leap of faith and commit important resources to do so.

3.5 Conclusion

The pursuit of international opportunities requires SME entrepreneurs to wear multiple hats and to accomplish complex tasks on top of their daily business. Role flexibility and responsiveness to international opportunities are without doubt essential for their internationalization success. It is oftentimes owed to this role flexibility that SME entrepreneurs are able to keep international projects alive in face of unexpected challenges and high uncertainties. Our study contributes to an enhanced understanding of the actions and interactions they invest in and the roles they play when pursuing international opportunities.

Despite this added focus, several gaps remain in the current knowledge about opportunity-driven internationalization in SMEs. First, we still know only little about successful leadership practices in the pursuit of international opportunities. Yet, these are fundamental to building a consensus among an organization's employees about the viability of an opportunity, as well as to align members to the organization's purpose. Innovative, flexible, and people-oriented organizational cultures are oftentimes fundamental to the success of highly innovative SMEs. Translating, adapting, and maintaining the organization's culture across borders will be another leadership challenge for SME entrepreneurs that is worth investigating.

Second, human capital development remains an under-researched but highly relevant theme in SME internationalization (Dabić et al. 2020). In face of scarce resources, international human capital development demands without doubt a lot of creativity from SME entrepreneurs, but in the long run, human capital will be fundamental to ensure and maintain an organization's entrepreneurial success across borders (Terjesen et al. 2016). In particular, qualitative research on international HR practices in SMEs would provide much-needed and highly relevant insights into the SME internationalization process.

References

Alvesson, M., & Sköldberg, K. (2009). Reflexive Methodology. New Vistas for Qualitative Research (2nd ed.). SAGE Publications.

Baker, T., & Nelson, R. E. (2005). Creating Something from Nothing : Resource Construction through Entrepreneurial Bricolage. Administrative Science Quarterly, 50, 329–366.

Baldegger, R., Hervé, A., & Wild, P. (2019). Swiss International Entrepreneurship Survey (SIES) 2019: Studienergebnisse zum Internationalisierungsverhalten von Schweizer KMU. Fribourg (CH): Haute école de gestion Fribourg.

Butler, C. L., Zander, L., Mockaitis, A., & Sutton, C. (2012). The global leader as boundary spanner, bridge maker, and blender. Industrial and Organizational Psychology, 5(2), 240–243.

Carlsson, E., & Dale, B. (2011). Internationalization of knowledge-intensive SMEs: The case of petroleum-related suppliers. Norwegian Journal of Geography, 1951(November). https://doi.org/10.1080/00291951.2011.623306

Child, J., Hsieh, L., Elbanna, S., Karmowska, J., Marinova, S., Puthusserry, P., . . . Zhang, Y. (2017). SME international business models: The role of context and experience. Journal of World Business, 52(5), 664–679. https://doi.org/10.1016/j.jwb.2017.05.004

Dabić, M., Maley, J., Dana, L. P., Novak, I., Pellegrini, M. M., & Caputo, A. (2020). Pathways of SME internationalization: a bibliometric and systematic review. *Small Business Economics*, Vol. 55, pp. 705–725. https://doi.org/10.1007/s11187-019-00181-6

Dimov, D. (2007). From opportunity insight to opportunity intention: The importance of person-situation learning match. *Entrepreneurship: Theory and Practice*, *31*(4), 561–583. https://doi.org/10.1111/j.1540-6520.2007.00188.x

Dubois, A., & Gadde, L. E. (2002). Systematic combining: An abductive approach to case research. *Journal of Business Research*, *55*(7), 553–560. https://doi.org/10.1016/S0148-2963(00)00195-8

Dubois, A., & Gadde, L. E. (2014). "Systematic combining"-A decade later. *Journal of Business Research*, *67*(6), 1277–1284. https://doi.org/10.1016/j.jbusres.2013.03.036

Fabian, F., Molina, H., & Labianca, G. (2009). Understanding decisions to internationalize by small and medium-sized firms located in an emerging market. *Management International Review*, *49*(5), 537–563. https://doi.org/10.1007/s11575-009-0007-6

Flick, U. (2014). *An introduction to qualitative research.*

Handrito, R. P., Slabbinck, H., & Vanderstraeten, J. (2020). Enjoying or refraining from risk? The impact of implicit need for achievement and risk perception on SME internationalization. *Cross Cultural & Strategic Management*, *27*(3), 317–342. https://doi.org/10.1108/CCSM-03-2019-0068

Jones, M. V., Coviello, N., & Tang, Y. K. (2011). International Entrepreneurship research (1989–2009): A domain ontology and thematic analysis. *Journal of Business Venturing*, *26*(6), 632–659. https://doi.org/10.1016/j.jbusvent.2011.04.001

Langley, A., Smallman, C., Tsoukas, H., & Van De Ven, A. H. (2013). Process studies of change in organization and management: Unveiling temporality, activity, and flow. *Academy of Management Journal*, *56*(1), 1–13. https://doi.org/10.5465/amj.2013.4001

Mainela, T., Puhakka, V., & Servais, P. (2014). The Concept of International Opportunity in International Entrepreneurship: A Review and a Research Agenda. *International Journal of Management Reviews*, *16*(1), 105–129. https://doi.org/10.1111/ijmr.12011

Mäkelä, K., Lauring, J., Butler, C. L., Lee, H.-J., Lücke, G., Miska, C., Pahlberg, C., Stahl, G. (2020). Meeting the challenge of globalization in order to make a difference: Implications for teams and team leadership. In E. Elgar (Ed.), *Global leadership: Making a difference* (pp. 91–107). Cheltenham, UK.

McDougall, P. P., & Oviatt, B. M. (2000). International entrepreneurship: the intersection of two research paths. Academy of management Journal, 43(5), 902-906.

Miles, M., Huberman, A. M., & Saldana, J. (2014). *Qualitative Data Analysis: A method sourcebook* (3rd ed.). Thousand Oaks, CA.: SAGE Publications Inc.

Muzychenko, O. (2008). Competence-based approach to teaching international opportunity identification: cross-cultural aspects. *European Journal of International Management*, *2*(4), 418–436.

Oviatt, B. M., & McDougall, P. (2005). Defining International Entrepreneurship and Modeling the Speed of Internationalization. *Entrepreneurship Theory and Practice*, *29*(5), 537–554.

Patton, M. Q. (2014). *Qualitative Research & Evaluation Methods. Integrating Theory and Practice* (4th ed.). Thousand Oaks, CA.: SAGE Publications.

Reuber, A. R., Dimitratos, P., & Kuivalainen, O. (2017). Beyond categorization: New directions for theory development about entrepreneurial internationalization. *Journal of International Business Studies*, *48*(4), 411–422. https://doi.org/10.1057/s41267-017-0070-3

Reuber, A. R., Knight, G. A., Liesch, P. W., & Zhou, L. (2018). International entrepreneurship: The pursuit of entrepreneurial opportunities across national borders. *Journal of International Business Studies*, *49*(4), 395–406. https://doi.org/10.1057/s41267-018-0149-5

Ribau, C. P., Moreira, A. C., & Raposo, M. (2018). SME internationalization research: Mapping the state of the art. *Canadian Journal of Administrative Sciences*, *35*(2), 280–303. https://doi.org/10.1002/cjas.1419

Santos, F. M., & Eisenhardt, K. M. (2005). Organizational Boundaries and Theories of Organization. *Organization Science*, *16*(5), 491–508. https://doi.org/10.1287/orsc.1050.0152

Sarasvathy, S. D. (2001). Causation and Effectuation : Toward a Theoretical Shift from Economic Inevitability to Entrepreneurial Contingency. *The Academy of Management Review*, *26*(2), 243–263.

Shepherd, D. A., Souitaris, V., & Gruber, M. (2021). Creating New Ventures: A Review and Research Agenda. *Journal of Management*, *47*(1), 11–42. https://doi.org/10.1177/0149206319900537

Terjesen, S., Hessels, J., & Li, D. (2016). Comparative International Entrepreneurship: A Review and Research Agenda. *Journal of Management*, *42*(1), 299–344. https://doi.org/10.1177/0149206313486259

Tsao, S.-M., & Lien, W.-H. (2013). Family Management and Internationalization: The Impact on Firm Performance and Innovation. *Management International Review*, *53*(2), 189–213. https://doi.org/10.1007/s11575-011-0125-9

Vahlne, JE. & Johanson, J. (2017) From internationalization to evolution: The Uppsala model at 40 years. J Int Bus Stud 48, 1087–1102. https://doi.org/10.1057/s41267-017-0107-7

Wood, M. S., & McKinley, W. (2010). The production of entrepreneurial opportunity: a constructivist perspective. *Strategic Entrepreneurship Journal*, *4*, 66–84. https://doi.org/10.1002/sej.83

Wood, M. S., & McKinley, W. (2017). After the Venture: The Reproduction and Destruction of Entrepreneurial Opportunity. *Strategic Entrepreneurship Journal*, *11*(1), 18–35. https://doi.org/10.1002/sej.1238

Early and Rapid or Late and Slow? 4

Path Dependency Caused by Age at Internationalization

Pascal Wild and Rico Baldegger

4.1 Introduction

The process of firm internationalization, understood as the geographical expansion of a firm's economic activities beyond a national country's border (Matlay et al. 2006), is described by two major theoretical approaches: the sequential expansion, or gradualist approach, and the international new ventures (INV) approach. In both theories, the firm's age at the time of its first cross-border activities is considered to be a key dimension. The gradualist approach describes the characteristics of a firm's internationalization as a stepwise process of mutually affecting state and change variables comprising knowledge and learning as well as building trust and commitment that lead—over time—to increased involvement in foreign market activities. This process is perceived as gradual and time-consuming and thus stands in strong contrast to the INV approach in which firms "enter a wide variety of foreign markets relatively quickly" (Meschi et al. 2017, p. 280) after (some of them even since) inception.

The two approaches derive from the empirically analyzed internationalization processes of companies from different industries. Whereas the gradualist approach originates in

P. Wild (✉)
School of Management Fribourg, Global Business Competence Center, University of Applied Sciences and Arts Western Switzerland (HES-SO), Fribourg, Switzerland
e-mail: pascal.wild@hefr.ch

R. Baldegger
School of Management Fribourg, University of Applied Sciences and Arts Western Switzerland (HES-SO), Fribourg, Switzerland
e-mail: rico.baldegger@hefr.ch

I. Stolz, S. Oldenziel Scherrer (eds.), *International Leadership*, uniscope. Publikationen der SGO Stiftung, https://doi.org/10.1007/978-3-658-37306-1_4

cross-sectoral studies of Swedish firms in the 1960s and 1970s—ranging from steel firms (Johanson and Vahlne 1977) to pulp-and-paper companies (Forsgren and Kinch 1970) and the pharmaceutical industry (Hörnell and Vahlne 1972), the INV approach was primarily detected in the 1990s while investigating ICT firms such as *Logitech* (Alahuhta 1990; Oviatt and McDougall 1994) and *Lasa Microprocessors* (Jolly et al. 1992). In the early 1990s, the ICT industry was at the beginning of its rise, and its protagonists were often internationally or globally interconnected. Thus, the entrepreneurs' international experience and their personal network also played a decisive role in the question of which international approach their firms pursue (Madsen and Servais 1997; Harveston et al. 2000; Shrader et al. 2000). However, next to specific characteristics of their industry networks, these theoretical approaches are also based on different strategic approaches and associated leadership styles prior to, during and after internationalization (Cotae 2013). The choice of market to enter, the timing of entry and the allocation of resources for such a strategic effort are, to a large extent, leadership-generated actions (Hill and McKaig 2012). Various scholars—generally arguing that the pre-internationalization phases influence the organizations' learning capacities and its agility on international markets—have contributed to this ongoing debate between the gradualist and the INV approach.

In line with the gradualist approach, Tan et al. (2007) highlight the importance of the preparation phase prior to entering international markets and consider this stage to be critical for future firm performance and survival. In this period, the firm is preparing for international performance by developing necessary learning routines (Kothari et al. 2013; Carr et al. 2010) and an adequate attitudinal commitment towards internationalization (Tan et al. 2007; Meschi et al. 2017). In contrast, Autio et al. (2000) found that as firms grow older, they "develop learning impediments that hamper their ability to successfully grow in new environments" (Autio et al. 2000, p. 919). Hence, firms need to develop knowledge through experiential learning as early as possible in their lifecycle: otherwise, they might develop "competency traps" (Cohen and Levinthal 1990, p. 136) where they find themselves unable to detect and pursue specific international opportunities. A successful internationalization process requires a certain agility, flexibility, and a high degree of collective interaction (Hambrick 1994; Meschi et al. 2017) often found in small, young firms.

This study sheds light on the crucial role of company age as a potentially decisive factor in ensuring a sound internationalization performance. It intends to demonstrate to which extent the leaders of internationalizing firms have to rely on path dependencies while pursuing their international expansion. The first research question in this chapter is thus: Which impact does organization age at internationalization—i.e. the length of time a company waits before expanding abroad—have on the speed with which foreign expansion subsequently materializes? This first question is followed by a second and third one investigating the impediments as perceived by firm management and staff while pursuing the internationalization process and caused by advanced age at internationalization. The second and third research questions are thus: Which specific weaknesses impeding internationalization success are caused by advanced age at internationalization? And which perceived impediments in the internationalization process at internationalization are a result of advanced age?

4.2 Conceptual Background

4.2.1 Internationalization

Internationalization traditionally addresses firm dynamics, which often start with the process "by which firms increase their awareness of the influence of international activities on their future, and establish and conduct transactions with firms from other countries" (Beamish et al. 1997, p. 3). It thus refers to the "process of increasing involvement in international operations" (Welch and Luostarinen 1988, p. 36) as well as a series of events and actions over time (Johanson and Vahlne 1990; Leonidou and Katsikeas 1996), generally developed and realized by the company's leadership (Cotae 2013; Colovic 2021) and the resulting path dependency (Uusitalo and Lavikka 2020). These definitions allude to the very traditional stage model of sequential expansion, i.e. the gradualist approach, according to which firms expand abroad in a slow, incremental way by gathering experiential knowledge and making a subsequent increased commitment to foreign markets (Johanson and Wiedersheim-Paul 1975; Johanson and Vahlne 1977, 1990, 2009, 2017). Oviatt and McDougall (1994, 2005) argue for emerging international new ventures (INV) to skip stages, even without sufficient experiential knowledge. Even though the INV approach has mostly been understood as an investigation into a phenomenon rather than a theoretical concept—such as the gradualist approach (Meschi et al. 2017)–, they are perceived as two distinct theories, since INV challenges the basic assumptions of the traditional gradualist approach. Johanson and Vahlne (2009) argued in their revisited Uppsala internationalization model that the phenomenon of international new ventures (INV) is consistent with the gradualist approach. They find that most of the firms attached to this phenomenon do not really have international activities (Johanson and Vahlne 2009; Rugman and Verbeke 2007), and that learning and relationship-building, which are necessary for rapid expansion, can also be in place prior to the formal founding of the firm. Nevertheless, they cite learning and relationship-building as incremental and time-consuming processes (Vahlne and Johanson 2002; Johanson and Vahlne 2009) in which the firms face a constant risk of failure (Johanson and Vahlne 1977, 1990, 2009). Many theoretical and empirical contributions that build upon the gradualist approach base their assumptions implicitly on the amplifying effects of adopting a slow and cautious pace on international survival (Chetty and Campbell-Hunt 2003) or performance (Xie et al. 2013). In light of the shortcomings of the earlier definitions, and in line with the INV approach, we understand internationalization as less stage-oriented and less constrained by the initial dynamics, but rather as a multidimensional phenomenon which affects the entire organization (Perlitz 2000).

4.2.2 Age at Internationalization

The extent, scope, and speed are inarguably key dimensions of internationalization (Zahra and George 2002). The time dimension, especially, needs careful delineation. Eden (2009) criticizes studies on firm internationalization for too frequently emphasizing its 'why', 'where', and 'how' while not paying sufficient attention to the 'when'. Yet, as George and Jones (2000) argue, any 'true' theory must explicitly include time. Similarly, Andersen (1993, 1997), Zahra et al. (2000), as well as Coviello and Jones (2004) and Jones and Coviello (2005) all call for a stronger incorporation of the role and influence of time into internationalization research. The notion of speed in internationalization has frequently been understood as the elapsed time between the company's inception and its first expansion abroad (Oviatt and McDougall 2005). More accurately, this period is defined as the internationalization age (Cellard and Prange 2008), age at entry (Autio et al. 2000), or age at internationalization (Casillas and Acedo 2013; Casillas and Moreno-Menéndez 2014). However, attempting to link the speed of completing the pre-internationalization phase, for example, to the later diversification abroad, some scholars do not provide convincing empirical insights and call for further analysis. Autio et al. (2000) found that a young age at internationalization, together with greater knowledge intensity, is associated with faster subsequent international growth. However, this study is limited to high-technology firms and leads to inconclusive results regarding what catalyzes subsequent internationalization growth, with the authors calling again for more research on the topic. Meschi et al. (2017) examine the effects of age at internationalization on the survival of French SMEs' foreign direct investments (FDI), showing that failure rates are lower for firms adopting slow and cautious expansion. However, this study is limited to a geographic expansion through FDI and to a timeframe of only about nine years. Prashantham and Young (2011) reinforce this call in their purely conceptual paper on post-entry speed, which is limited to international new ventures that rapidly expand abroad; it thus lacks an inclusive overview of all firms—a gap that our paper aims to address.

4.2.3 The Speed of Internationalization

International speed generally refers to a quotient with an indicator of time in the denominator. Depicting internationalization in line with Zahra and George (2002), Casillas and Acedo (2013) define three dimensions of speed—which have to be treated independently as they do not necessarily correlate perfectly at all times. They include the increase in sales abroad over time, the speed of increased commitment of resources to foreign activities (growth in the proportion of assets or employees in foreign markets), and growth in the breadth or dispersion of foreign international markets (number of foreign markets or cultural or physical distance in relation to the domestic market). The factors influencing speed, often with a focus on the initial trigger of internationalization, have emerged as an active stream of research (Acedo and Jones 2007; Oviatt and McDougall 2005). The following interorganizational factors have been considered to impact the speed of internationalization: social networks (e.g., Oviatt and McDougall 1994; Johanson and Vahlne 2009), international alliances and joint ventures (Yu et al. 2011; Fernhaber et al. 2009), as well as rivalry and imitation (Yu and Cannella Jr 2007). At the firm level, we find studies on the resources (Zahra and George 2002; Zahra et al. 2000), the age (Reuber and Fischer 1997; Zahra et al. 2000), and the location (Westhead and Wright 1998; Zahra and George 2002) of the company. Beyond these more structured views, other studies have acknowledged that the speed of internationalization is also affected by rather uncertain factors, which may well be accidental, dangerous, chaotic, or merely explorative (Knudsen and Madsen 2002; Mockaitis et al. 2006). Knowledge and mindsets alone may therefore not be the only and main explanatory factors. This resonates with Chandra et al.'s (2020) depiction of internationalization as an effectuation process, i.e. the result of a focus on affordable loss, opportunism, and feelings—and not as a clean, rational, calculated process. Schweizer (2012) adds "muddling through" to describe just how plannable, controllable, and anticipatory the internationalization process of SMEs is—and therefore their speed may be.

Literature on the factors influencing speed is thus broad and continues to grow. Clear-cut, empirically substantiated insights into the impact of a company's age at internationalization on its speed and success are gaps that need to be addressed.

4.3 Theory and Hypotheses

4.3.1 Age at Internationalization and Internationalization Speed

Conceptually, our hypotheses build on the broader notion of age liabilities (Cellard and Prange 2008). If early and late internationalizers are juxtaposed, distinctly different learning opportunities become apparent, leading to different capabilities. Early internationalization imprints younger firms with the dynamic capability to explore opportunities abroad (Gerschewski et al. 2020). According to Autio et al. (2000), internationalization fosters awareness of the capabilities to be developed and their eagerness to pursue international opportunities. This results in specialized capabilities for a swifter adaptation to an international business (Sapienza et al. 2006), for which early internationalizers require diametrically opposed capabilities than those needed for domestic markets. These capabilities may make the wider, more international market environment appear less foreign (Autio et al. 2000).

Both early and late internationalizers also show varying levels of inertia. Internationalization forces firms to unlearn routines in favor of new ones (Barkema and Vermeulen 1997). Because routines at younger firms are less established and less embedded, their unlearning should be less impeded and time-consuming. Similarly, other authors argue that older firms have more established routines and suffer from higher inertia (Hannan and Freeman 1984). Bettis and Prahalad (1995) posit similarly that routine embeddedness limits further organizational development—the organization's dominant logic prevails. Autio et al. (2000) apply this train of thought to the internationalization debate and likewise reason that, as a result, older firms cannot undertake internationalization efforts as dynamically.

Another pillar of age liabilities is characterized by a risky path dependency. Building capabilities for domestic markets, along with inertia to change, once again means that the future is at risk from a population ecology point of view (Hannan 1998). The organizational system tends to reproduce itself, entailing more focus and action targeted at its domestic business and at maintaining organizational routines which have served the organization well in its familiar domestic environment. As Weeks and Galunic (2002) mention, it is difficult to integrate new organizational memes, or newer ways of approaching issues, into the organization, although the changing, more international external environment may need them urgently. Knudsen and Madsen (2002) argue that the late internationalizers' accumulated body of knowledge actually has an adverse effect, as it limits growth. Based on this three-pillar train of thought on age liabilities, we posit:

Hypothesis 1: The age at internationalization is negatively related to internationalization speed.

An interesting question ensues: Would this path dependency impact internationalization speed only in the short term? Teece (2007) as well as Wang and Ahmed (2007) argue that speed is contingent upon the dynamic capabilities. Yet, Hedlund (1994) asserts that building an international organization is a complex task. According to Barkema and Vermeulen (1997), structures and control mechanisms need considerable adaptation when firms venture abroad. Previously accumulated and built resources, such as knowledge and capabilities, are often linked to managers wishing to avoid risks, decreasing the speed of reaction, increasing the cost of change and, according to Eriksson and Chetty (2003), limiting the ability to innovate. Accelerating a firm's innovative efforts is by no means risk-free, as the higher internationalization speed of late internationalizers leads to a notable exposure to internationalization liabilities when the time to adapt is limited (Vermeulen and Barkema 2002). This could materialize in a situation where companies suffer not only from inertia but also from a mismatch between available and needed capabilities. The knowledge gains of those companies that do not internationalize early on in their lifecycles tend to be incremental and slow, which is in line with the stage-wise internationalization theory (Johanson and Vahlne 2009, 2017; Vahlne 2020). Consequently, we hypothesize that the imprinting of an organization when reaching a higher internationalization age holds true for the short-term period right after the first steps abroad have been taken, but it clearly is not limited to it.

Hypothesis 1a: The age at internationalization is negatively related to internationalization speed in the short term.

Hypothesis 1b: The age at internationalization is negatively related to speed in the medium term.

Hypothesis 1c: The age at internationalization is negatively related to internationalization speed in the long term.

4.3.2 Age at Internationalization and International Learning Experiences

In both the INV and the gradualist approach to internationalization, it is assumed that knowledge and learning have an impact on international growth and success. An internationalizing firm needs to change and adapt its business model quickly and constantly in order to cope with the conditions of the foreign market (Colovic 2021). Since internationalization is often spurred and orchestrated from the highest levels of the firm's hierarchy, the leaders—from owner-CEOs to senior management and even workers with responsibilities on site at company premises—are playing a central role in this process (Chesbrough 2010; Lindgren 2012; Stieglitz and Foss 2015).

Based on the gradualist approach, Tan et al. (2007) argue that during the pre-internationalization phase, a company is exposed to various stimuli factors triggering impulses for internationalization. External stimuli factors comprise experiences and recognized opportunities from doing business domestically (Oviatt and McDougall 1994), network memberships (Johanson and Vahlne 2009; Khan and Lew 2018; Puthusserry et al. 2020), and market experiences (Johanson and Vahlne 1977). Internal stimuli include the desire of staff and senior management to achieve corporate goals and to control risks proactively (Leonidou 1998). Prior to their international expansion, exposure to these stimuli (externally as well as internally) is thought to increase the firm's experiential knowledge. Since, according to the gradualist approach, experiential knowledge plays a crucial role in increasing foreign commitment, these stimuli are believed to inspire foreign expansion (Child et al. 2017). Nevertheless, their proposition does not go beyond that of an "international readiness index" and thus does not empirically test any assumptions with regard to the firm's age prior to the internationalization process. In their study on rapidly growing ICT SMEs from India's emerging market, Puthusserry et al. (2020) found that experiential self-learning enhances the knowledge necessary for rapid SME internationalization, in particular in the post-entry phase. In line with INV, we argue that cognitive impediments to experiential learning develop in firms over time (Autio et al. 2000). Younger firms are more likely to embrace an international identity, since they can develop important relationships with foreign partners alongside domestic ones in their formative period, whereas older firms that put more effort into building a strong domestic base are more likely to continue prioritizing domestic partners (Autio et al. 2000). Bruneel et al. (2010) state that the influence of congenital learning (i.e., the management team's international learning experience prior to the start-up) decreases as internationalization increases. Schwens and Kabst (2009) show that early internationalization has a positive effect on learning from foreign partners, their routines, and best practices.

Early internationalization is largely determined by the foreign experiences of the founders (Bruneel et al. 2010; Park et al. 2015). International experience prior to start-up funding increases the likelihood of early internationalization (Kuemmerle 2002). On the other hand, domestic experience (and thus a higher age at internationalization) reduces international success, since foreign operations are seen to be more risky or costly (Eriksson and Chetty 2003). Firms tend to internationalize more slowly and thus with more perceived impediments if they do not have adequate international experience (Casillas and Acedo 2013). A younger age at internationalization thus helps them acquire better international knowledge, since young organizations are more receptive to foreign experiences. They "possess some learning advantages over older firms in terms of assimilating new foreign knowledge" (Autio et al. 2000, p. 913). In addition, they are more willing, more capable, and more aware of detecting and pursuing international opportunities. We thus formulate the following hypothesis to be tested independently of a firm's actual international experience:

Hypothesis 2: Higher age at internationalization raises the probability of lacking perceived international knowledge, thus impeding international success.

The learning capacity of INV is strongly influenced by the exposure and experience of the senior management team prior to the start-up's initiation in international markets (Busenitz and Barney 1997; Madsen and Servais 1997; Harveston et al. 2000; Shrader et al. 2000). Zahra and George (2002) as well as Knight and Cavusgil (2004) argue that the fast-paced learning of the whole organization allows an INV to internationalize early and rapidly. We base our assumptions on the notion that internationalization efforts are orchestrated by the highest levels of hierarchy (Hill and McKaig 2012) and are thus influenced by the firm's leaders. However, wc are also aware of the circumstance that leadership is the behavior of individuals in terms of communication and interpersonal influence (Posner and Kouzes 1988; Cotae 2013). It is thus not exclusively reserved for the senior management and the owner-manager but can be existent at various functional and operational levels (Zaleznik 1990; Javidan et al. 2010; Cotae 2013). We thus formulate our hypotheses for both senior management and employees in general:

Hypothesis 2a: Higher age at internationalization raises the probability of lacking perceived international knowledge among employees, impeding international success.

Hypothesis 2b: Higher age at internationalization raises the probability of lacking perceived international knowledge among senior management, impeding international success.

4.4 Methodology

4.4.1 Research Setting and Data

We relied on a quantitative research design to gather empirical evidence and to address the research question. The sample used in this study comprises a panel dataset of 609 internationalizing SMEs headquartered in Switzerland. Being a small and open economy (a so-called SMOPEC), Switzerland provides only limited domestic market potential and SMEs are dominant: they account for 99.7% of all private business entities and employ two-thirds of the local workforce (SECO 2020). Thus, international expansion is an important option for many SMEs. We focus on SMEs, since an empirical investigation of the firms' internationalization processes—whether considering INVs and born globals or internationalizing firms stepwise—requires the examination of all small and medium-sized firms that tend to be either relatively young and/or small in terms of size or resources available. The investigated firms have less than 250 full-time equivalents, and their general headquarters are located in Switzerland. In addition, they have to generate a minimum of 5% of total turnover in foreign markets in order to be classified as internationalizing firms.

We focused our analysis on internationalization through various means, starting with export and contractual modes (e.g. licensing and franchising to foreign direct investments (FDI)). A panel dataset from the SIES (Swiss International Entrepreneurship Survey) database was used to test the hypotheses and to conduct linear and logistic regressions. The SIES is a statistical survey of internationalizing firms that has been conducted every three years since 2007. Switzerland has a total of about 311,000 firms that can be defined as SMEs (Swiss Federal Statistical Office 2008). Given that about 14% of these SMEs export goods and services (Jaeger et al. 2008), the total number of exporting SMEs is approximately 44,000 companies. Initially, these SMEs were categorized according to their distribution across the different cultural, linguistic, and economic regions of Switzerland. Subsequently, maintaining the relative weight of each category, 8000 Swiss SMEs were randomly selected and surveyed—hence almost 20% of all exporting SMEs. In each of the selected SMEs, the survey targeted the CEO, with the questions specifically requiring high-level insights, which made delegation almost impossible. As an incentive, the CEOs were offered follow-up workshops where the results of the study would be discussed.

4.4.2 Measures

The major independent variable in this study is age at internationalization. It is relatively easy to conceptualize, since it comprises the period (in years) between a company's foundation and the year of its initial expansion abroad. Internationalization speed, scope, and success have no established conceptualization or measurement tradition (Casillas and Acedo 2013). As outlined in the following, this study adopts two complementary options to measure the multifaceted construct of speed and a number of points in time to distinguish between the various timeframes. The speed variable refers to the current ratio of foreign sales to total sales (FSTS) in relation to the number of years needed to achieve this level of internationalization. More precisely, the number of years refers to the internationally active years and, thus, to the period between the year of first international sales and the end of 2016, which is the survey's final year of reference. The second speed variable refers to the number of foreign countries currently being served in relation to the number of years a company has been active in international business.

In order to test the hypotheses, we relied on several points in time for a reality check and in order to gather empirical evidence. The survey inquired about the progress of internationalization within one, three, and five years after the firm's initial internationalization, the number of years of international activities, and the results at the end of 2016. Given this data availability, we used the following variables for the short, medium, and long term, and the internationalization's overall speed: first-year FSTS refers to growth in terms of foreign sales relative to total sales after one year of internationalization. The following measures are each defined accordingly, in particular third-year and fifth-year FSTS. fifth-year country addresses the number of countries served after five years of international activities. Two sub-samples were formed in order to analyze the medium- to long-term impact. Medium terms portray the first decade following the initial five years (short term) of having been active in international business, i.e. the sixth to 16th year of internationalization. Long term compiles all companies with more than 30 years of international activities. In respect of the medium-term time horizon, we define internationalization as 6th- to 16th-year FSTS and 6th- to 16th-year countries, while:

Medium term: 6th- to 16th-year FSTS = FSTS/number of years of international activities

Medium term: 6th- to 16th-year countries = number of foreign countries/number of years of international activities

In respect of the long-term time horizon, we define internationalization as >30th-year FSTS and > 30th-year countries, while:

Long term: > 30th-year FSTS = FSTS/number of years of international activities

Long term: > 30th-year countries = number of foreign countries/number of years of international activities

In respect of the entire sample, we define:

General: FSTS = FSTS/number of years of international activities

General: countries = number of foreign countries/number of years of international activities

4.4.3 Control Variables

Furthermore, we controlled for three effects: first, we introduced a control variable based on the size of the respective company. Since the previously mentioned organizational inertia may actually materialize rather in larger companies, we introduced staff size as the first control variable. Second, we also introduced Entrepreneurial Orientation (EO) as a control variable. Therefore, we used Lumpkin and Dess' (1996) five dimensional measures of EO: autonomy, innovativeness, risk-taking, proactiveness, and competitive aggressiveness. These five dimensions of the forced-choice type were measured using an 18-item scale. The respondents characterized their firm's strategic posture on a seven-point Likert scale that divided pairs of opposite statements. The statements for the dimensions proactiveness, innovativeness, and risk-taking were taken from the initial construct as developed by Covin and Slevin (1989), whereas the competitive-aggressiveness measure was taken from Lumpkin and Dess (2001) and the autonomy measure from Lumpkin et al. (2009). EO measures the firm's strategic posture in relation to process and decision-making activities, such as entering new markets (Karami and Tang 2019; Lumpkin and Dess 1996). Entering a new market requires an entrepreneurial mindset and a strategy that enhances the firm's capability to adapt to new environments (Khanna et al. 2003). A large body of knowledge reveals that EO has a positive impact on firm growth, profitability, innovation, and overall performance (Wales et al. 2013), particularly for SMEs (Tang et al. 2017; Thanos et al. 2017). Thanos et al. (2017) found that IEO stimulates the exploration and exploitation of international opportunities and that EO is particularly important for firms to tap into potential opportunities in highly hostile environments.

We also accounted for potential industry effects as suggested by Deng et al. (2013). The survey participants had to categorize their primary industry on the basis of the Swiss primary standard industry code system. These industries were included as binary dummy variables.

Specific weaknesses that have impeded internationalization success have been included in a comprehensive nine-item choice, with major impediments in the internationalization process having been included in a twelve-item choice. In both cases, the respondents had the choice of adding non-mentioned impediments in an open-ended question labeled "other". In the analysis, each item is coded as 1 if the impediment has been perceived—and as 0 if it has not.

4.4.4 Methods of Analysis

Statistically, we relied on linear regression analysis with the internationalization speed proxies as the dependent variable—as outlined above–, with age at internationalization serving as the independent variable while controlling for firm size and entrepreneurial orientation. Altogether, we investigated internationalization speed with reference to six points in time (such as stated in the hypotheses 1a to 1c): one year after initially crossing country borders, three years, five years, and six to twenty years, the period from 21 years onwards after first international expansion, and a general view of the entire sample.

A binary logistic model was fitted to the data to test the research hypotheses regarding the likelihood that higher levels of age at internationalization lead to a lack of international experience that impedes success (hypotheses 2, 2a and 2b), and which are perceived as a major impediment in the internationalization process (hypothesis 3). These hypotheses were tested while controlling for the total international experience of the organization as measured in years since it started its process of internationalization.

Logistic regression is computationally similar to linear regression but differs in that the coefficients, which are calculated by using a maximum likelihood procedure, are used to estimate the probability of the expected outcome to occur and are expressed in terms of logits. As logits are not inherently meaningful, the usual practice is to transform the coefficients into more intuitive metrics, such as odds ratios or probabilities (Menard 1995; Pampel 2000).

4.5 Results

◉ Table 4.1 summarizes the descriptive statistics. The average participating company employed 24.7 full-time equivalents and was generating slightly more than half (51.66%) of its sales abroad at the end of longitudinal data collection in 2016. On average, more than eight years passed before the first steps abroad were taken, even though age at internationalization ranged from 0 (so-called born global firms) to a maximum of 84 years of pre-international existence. On average, companies in the sample can look back on more than 23 years of international activities. Regarding the represented industries, 53.8% of the companies were active in manufacturing, while 20.4% operated in the service sector and 15.4% in the trade sector. Checks for sample selection biases based on a chi-square test for independence of group concerning the industry, size, and regional distribution confirmed that the respondents represent the original sample correctly.

Regarding the hypothesis test, ◉ Table 4.2 provides details of the linear regression analysis of the various tested models. Hypothesis 1a posits a negative impact of age at internationalization on internationalization speed in general. Based on the indicated significance levels, this study reveals the actual and significant impact of internationalization age on the subsequent internationalization speed once companies have decided to diversify geographically. Overall regression for this general model was highly significant when speed was measured with FSTS ($R2 = 0.096$, $F = 16.962$, $p < 0.001$) and significant at the 10% level when speed was measured by the number of countries per year ($R2 = 0.026$, $F = 2.482$, $p < 0.1$). Age at internationalization ($\beta = -0.675$, $p < 0.001$) had a strong and highly significant negative effect on FSTS, whereas range of internationalization ($\beta = 0.137$, $p < 0.001$) had a weaker but still highly significant effect on FSTS as well. Accordingly, we can state that the later firms start to venture abroad, the slower their international sales grow. In conjunction with the similar but less significant effects of age at

Table 4.1 Sample descriptive statistics (N = 609)

Variable	Min.	Max.	M	SD	
Staff size	1	249	24.73	40.47	General sample
Age at internationalization	0	84	8.04	15.42	
Number of years in internationalization process	0	155	23.23	19.6	
Entrepreneurial Orientation	1	7	4.0835	0.56	
FSTS at the end of 2016	5	100	51.66	35.74	
Countries at the end of 2016	1	130	14.15	19.68	
1st year FSTS	0	100	45.65	38.3	Short-term (n=252)
3rd year FSTS	0	100	48.92	35.95	
5th year FSTS	1	100	53.07	35.76	
5th year countries	1	130	9.45	14.43	
Staff size	1	166	19.35	27.93	Medium-term (n=128)
FSTS at end 2016	1	100	55.4	35.03	
Countries at the end 2016	1	85	9.66	12.12	
Age at internationalization	0	66	6.08	13.14	
Years in internationalization	0	15	11.14	2.7	
FSTS 6–10 years	0.08	14.29	5.19	3.57	
Countries 6–10 years	0.07	7.08	0.909	1.12	
Staff size	1	250	43.66	57.64	Long-term (n=134)
FSTS at end of 2016	1	100	55.76	34.7	
Countries at the end of 2016	1	66	15.17	16.48	
Age at internationalization	0	74	11.65	18.62	
Years in internationalization	31	155	49.2	21.07	
FSTS 30 + years	0.02	1.78	0.36	0.43	
Countries 30 + years	0.02	3.23	1.278	0.91	

internationalization on the average number of countries developed in the internationalization process, the core hypothesis H1 can thus be confirmed.

The analysis is then divided into different timeframes, namely short-term, medium-term, and long-term. When it comes to short-term impact, this study differentiates among the internationalization speeds portrayed by the companies one year, three years, and five years after their very first expansion abroad. ◉ Table 4.1 has revealed that age at internationalization impacts internationalization speed right after the initial steps abroad. This impact is negative and highly significant for the first year ($\beta = -1.134$, $p < 0.001$), the third year ($\beta = -0.0994$, $p < 0.001$), and the fifth year ($\beta = -0.999$, $p < 0.001$). The applied regression models are statistically significant at the marked level ($p < 0.001$), with R2 values ranging between 0.14 and 0.15 and F values of between 12.1 and 13.7. A short-term impact of age at internationalization on speed as measured by the number of reached countries within five years can also be confirmed ($\beta = -0.137$, $p < 0.1$). Therefore, hypothesis 1b can also be confirmed in respect of the internationalization speed measure,

Table 4.2 Results of the linear regression analysis

Speed of Internationalization										
Coefficients / Timeframe after first Internationalization	Short-term: 1st year	FSTS Short-term: 3th year	FSTS Short-term: 5th year	FSTS Short-term: 5th year countries	Medium-term: 6–16th year	FSTS Medium-term: 6–16th year countries	Long-term: > 30th year	FSTS Long-term: > 30th year countries	General: FSTS	General: Countries
Constant (std. error)	38.647** (23.319)	32.546 (22.567)	37.271† (22.237)	15.512* (6.452)	0.782 (2.175)	0.924 (0.847)	1.103* (16.395)	−0.155 (0.303)	50.879*** (13.289)	6.138 (7.518)
Age at Internationalization (std. error)	−1.134*** (0.0180)	−0.0994*** (0.171)	−0.999*** (0.170)	−0.137† (0.075)	−0.065** (.023)	−0.015† (0.009)	−0.022*** (0.004)	−0.010† (0.030)	−0.675*** (0.100)	−0.014† (0.007)
Size (std. error)	0.102 (0.067)	0.079 (0.059)	0.109† (0.060)	0.049† (0.029)	−0.002 (0.011)	0.014** (0.004)	0.004* (0.001)	0.004** (0.001)	0.137*** (0.037)	0.001 (0.003)
Entrepreneurial Orientation (std. error)	2.885 (5.645)	5.129 (5.460)	4.806 (5.394)	−1.434 (1.491)	1.120 (0.493)	−0.043 (0.187)	0.053 (0.107)	0.093 (0.071)	0.726 (3.193)	0.255 (0.152)
Industries	Included	Included	Included	Included	Included	Included	Included	Included	Included	Included
Model Summary										
r2	0.147	0.14	0.15	0.073	0.118	0.197	0.24	0.211	0.096	0.026
Adj. R2	0.137	0.129	0.138	0.063	0.094	0.16	0.222	0.175	0.091	0.016
F	13.703***	12.166***	12.560***	7.211***	5.306**	5.306**	12.974***	5.890**	16.962***	2.482†

†p <0.1, *p <0.05, **p <0.01, ***p <0.001

and all three hypotheses confirm the short-term timeframes. By and large, the industry does not affect these results. Slight upward or downward adjustments have to be made for the linear link between internationalization age and speed for a maximum of two industries in each of the shown models. The second control variable—the number of employees measured in full-time equivalents—shows a significant effect in the medium and long term, as summarized in ◉ Table 4.2. The results are consistently positive on the predictand variable. No significant effect has been observed resulting from the firms' strategic posture, as measured in entrepreneurial orientation, whether in the short, the medium or the long term.

Two sub-samples were formed for the analysis of the mid- to long-term impact of age at internationalization on speed and success. 128 companies in the sample fulfilled the criterion of six to 16 active years in the process of internationalization and were thus analyzed for mid-term results. 134 companies had at least 30 successive years of foreign sales and thus counted as long-term internationalization firms. The previous results repeat themselves regarding hypotheses 1c and 1d. Both additional hypotheses can be confirmed (cf. ◉ Table 4.2). A firm's age at internationalization negatively impacts the speed of FSTS growth. This holds true for the mid-term view on FSTS ($\beta = -0.065$, $p < 0.01$) and countries ($\beta = -0.015$, $p < 0.1$), which comprises the period six to 16 years after initial internationalization, as well as the long-term impact ($\beta = -0.022$, $p < 0.001$ resp. $\beta = -0.010$, $p < 0.1$) of 30 years and more.

The results from the binary logistic model are provided in ◉ Table 4.3. The logit coefficient for age at internationalization on the lack of international experience among employees and senior management (Models 1 and 2) is statistically significant and suggests that every year of company existence prior to internationalization raises the probability that lacking international experience could be an impediment for international success. Furthermore, a high age at internationalization also raises this probability (Model 3). The odds ratios for these logits were calculated by exponentiating the coefficients (e^b). The results can also be expressed as the percentage of the increase in the probability that a firm states this impediment when the independent variable is changed by one unit at a time (Ellis 2011; Pampel 2000). Since the independent variable measures age at internationalization—that is, the company's pre-internationalization years of existence–, we can state that with every pre-internationalization year, (a) the probability that international success is impeded by a lack of international experience among the employees rises by 2.5%, and (b) the probability of the same impediment, if caused by a lack of international experience by the senior management, rises by 3.6%.

Whereas the firms' pre-internationalization experience, as measured in years between a company's foundation and the initiation of the internationalization process (labeled age at internationalization) seems to raise these probabilities, we also controlled for the firms' general international experience. Effective post-international experience—as measured in years between the initiation of the internationalization process and the end date of the survey (control variable labeled organizations' international experience)—has no significant effect on the dependent variables. However, the effect of age at internationalization is

Table 4.3 Results of the logistic regression analysis

	Model 1: Lack of employees' international experience has impeded success					Model 2: Lack of senior management's international experience has impeded success					Model 3: Lack of international experience as a major obstacle in the internationalization process				
Predictor	β	Wald's χ^2	df	P	eβ (odds ratio)	β	Wald's χ^2	df	P	eβ (odds ratio)	β	Wald's χ^2	df	P	eβ (odds ratio)
Constant (std. error)	−2.636 (0.248)	113.041	1	0	NA	−2.289 (0.007)	84.1	1	0	NA	−2.732 (0.303)	81.354	1	0	NA
Age at Internationalization	0.024 (0.008)	10.414	1	0.001	1.025	0.035 (0.007)	22.654	1	0	1.036	0.024 (0.009)	7.328	1	0.007	1.025
Organizations' international experience	0.001 (0.008)	0.008	1	0.928	1.001	−0.018 (0.010)	3.666	1	0.056	0.982	−0.014 (0.011)	1.515	1	0.218	0.986
Test		χ^2	df	P			χ^2	df	P			χ^2	df	P	
Overall model evaluation Coefficient test		9.672	2	0.008			21.261	2	0			6.744	2	0.034	
Goodness-of-fit Hosmer-Lemeshow		12.226	8	0.141			5.156	8	0.741			5.861	8	0.663	
Percent correctly predicted				91.30%				90.80%				94.20%			

not particularly large. Yet small effects may be deemed important if they accumulate over time (Abelson 1985; Ellis 2011). In light of an insignificant change caused during post-internationalization years, this effect is even strengthened.

4.6 Discussion

In this chapter, we examine the impact of age at internationalization on the subsequent speed and success of internationalization, as well as on perceived impediments in the internationalization process. We provide empirical evidence that high age at internationalization negatively affects internationalization speed in the short, medium and long term. In this sense, we have confirmed that age liability is not merely a short-term effect but impacts firms even decades later. We then tested the effect of age at internationalization on a set of various perceived impediments in the internationalization process which seemed to be hindering its success. While controlling for effective international experience (as measured in years active in international markets), we found evidence that age at internationalization creates a lack of international experience among employees and senior management that adds to the negative impact on the firm's internationalization process. Academic literature has provided several arguments that enrich the discussion on long-term effects of late internationalization. A core argument refers to the acquisition of experiential knowledge and thus to the experiential learning capacity of a firm. So-called internationalization knowledge is gained through an effective accumulation of experiences on international markets (Madhok 1997; Barkema and Vermeulen 1997; Casillas and Moreno-Menéndez 2014). According to Eriksson et al. (1998), three types of knowledge are highly relevant for speed and success in internationalization projects: country-specific, institutional, and market knowledge. Since it is not so much country-specific but rather generalizable knowledge that is transferable from one country-specific experience to the next, its accumulation can foster the firm's future projects on international markets. While according to the gradualist approach, (experiential) learning is associated with a time-consuming and thus incremental process, contributions in INV often emphasize the learning advantages and flexibilities of young organizations and start-ups in particular. Based on more than 600 internationalizing firms and regardless of a firm's branch or strategic posture—as measured by the widely used concept of EO comprising relevant firm-specific elements, such as competitive aggressiveness, risk-taking, and innovativeness–, the results of our longitudinal study clearly indicate that there is long-term path dependency on speed and success connected to age at internationalization. In the same spirit, path dependency negatively affects a firm's international learning experience among senior management and staff, influencing its perceived impediments to international success. These findings scrutinize the benefits of internationalization at a higher age, such as positional advantage and legitimacy in the short or long term (Zhou and Wu 2014), trust and more resources in a variety of forms (Aldrich and Fiol 1994; Peruffo et al. 2018; Scuotto et al. 2017). In addition, they challenge the pathways of the traditional gradual approach, as described by Johanson and Vahlne (2009, 2017) and others (Vahlne 2020; Sharma and Blomstermo 2003; Zeng et al. 2013), as well as the liabilities of newness (Aldrich and Fiol 1994; Brock and Alon 2009).

4.6.1 Contributions to Theory

There are two main implications for theory in this study. The literature on stage-wise internationalization has been increasingly questioned by the emergence of more rapid internationalization processes. This literature was basically accused of no longer being timely, of being too reactive, of possibly being applied to a point in time when—decades ago—liberalization was not at today's level, which made diversification abroad more challenging. International new venture theory became the more modern theoretical foundation, complementing—if not threatening to dominate—the stage-wise logic (Autio et al. 2000). The data in this study strengthens the argument that the latter still has explanatory power—even in today's world. The majority of companies (two-thirds in this study) have not followed rapid expansion; this explains why we should not focus on 'born global' only, which—as 'odd fellows'—may be a newer and increasingly wide-spread phenomenon. We still need to devote attention and resources to studying more incremental ways of expanding abroad. This not only needs to be substantiated by investigating the factors that explore a fast—at times even precipitated—diversification across national boundaries, but also with more research on potential *versus* actual absorptive capacity, on learning and its link to routines, on routines and their links to inertia, and on the nature of this inertia. This implication of an ongoing conceptual and theoretical quest for more insights and frameworks eventually needs to lead to a better understanding of how to deal with 'balance sheets' of the assets and liabilities of newness, age, and internationalization (see Kotosaka 2011). Knowing and acknowledging individual balance sheet items differs from identifying the bottom line, for example with a force-field analysis and more advanced models.

4.6.2 Contributions to Practice

There are implications for practice as well as for individual executives and their successors—as well as for economic policies as a whole. The study at hand offers practitioners an opportunity to reflect. The faster a company internationalizes, the better the learning capacities that are at their disposal, and the sooner learning opportunities occur. Delaying expansion abroad—and thus foregoing sources of learning and adaptation to international markets—impedes the future internationalization speed and hinders its success. Based on this study's insights, the negative impact of a rather late internationalization can still be felt decades later when the environment may have changed drastically. In addition, the risk of missing experiences perceived as a major impediment literally grows with every year of focusing on home markets. Executives adopting a more conservative approach to internationalization, and potentially delaying it, may thus very well create challenges for their successors, and even successors thereafter. For a small and open economy, such as Switzerland, with a strong majority of growing and internationalizing SMEs, the results of this study bear a significant message. With regard to their behavior in foreign markets, internationalizing SMEs cannot all be lumped together. Both the executive leaders and managers themselves as well as the partners, consultants, and policy-makers are advised to become aware of the different types of internationalizing SMEs. Ultimately, they differ in terms of strategic and tactical behavior in the markets and in how they perceive and manage the problems and obstacles in international business. According to the findings of this publication, the time span between the foundation and the first internationalization steps is an important delimiting factor for such a typologization.

If opportunities can emerge only from abroad in the long term, delaying the kick-off of international learning opportunities may have clear-cut, negative, long-term repercussions. Agglomerating this effect across the majority of Swiss SMEs, Switzerland as a whole would forego substantial internationalization opportunities the later its companies embark on their initial internationalization. Universities, business schools, industry associations, banks, unions, and policy-makers should be aware of the potential for SMEs abroad, and of the downside of a high age at internationalization.

4.6.3 Limitations and Suggestions for Future Research

This study is not exempt from limitations. While the conceptualization of age at internationalization as a variable is rather straightforward, there are many other ways to measure internationalization speed. Selecting fewer measures is not uncommon (Cellard and Prange 2008). This study nonetheless leaves room for improvement and future studies, which can depict the speed of internationalization in both similar and different ways. Relying on similar ways allows for additional learning about these measures. Using different measures renders the picture of the speed of internationalization more complete. The second limitation resides in the question whether companies with a substantially higher internationalization age are not just culprits but also mere victims of their environment. Liberalization, as well as the means to internationalize more easily, has characterized the more recent past. It may well be easier to internationalize today than it was decades ago. Hence, the factor of older companies *versus* younger companies as an influencing factor of internationalization age and speed, as well as the link between these two variables, deserves further research. Additionally, we did not further analyze the predominant leadership style of the surveyed companies. As Colovic (2021) recently found out, a directive leadership in combination with a high level of business model innovation results in a timelier foreign market entry. However, by taking the concept of EO into account, we controlled our sample for the strategic posture and entrepreneurial mindset as generally implemented by a firm's leaders. Such company-level entrepreneurship that is enabling long-term success (Ferreira et al.

2011; Rauch et al. 2009) may also be helpful for overcoming the firm's path dependencies that are hindering them to enter new markets, as shown by Uusitalo and Lavikka (2020) when drawing on longitudinal case studies in the Swedish house-building sector. The impact of leadership on a firm's internationalization progress can also be affected through transactional and transformational leadership. In born global companies, a proactive and transformational leadership style that features a high work autonomy and the delegation of responsibilities to the staff does lead to a faster and more successful internationalization process (Chhotray et al. 2018). Kraus et al. (2018) argue that this also applies to traditionally internationalizing SMEs, whereas, on the other hand, in specific situations, some born global firms might also show more progressing internationalization when led with a rather responsive and transactional leadership style. So far, there is no consensus on this, and further clarification would certainly be desirable.

A reviewer of this paper made us aware that explaining other possible drivers of internationalization success could be valuable. We would like to comply with this in this section by affirming that the entrepreneurial mindset as measured by EO's five dimensions is considered as one of the most important drivers of internationalization success (Wales et al. 2019; Mostafa et al. 2005; Javalgi and Todd 2011). In a conjoint choice experiment study conducted with SME managers, Kraus et al. (2017) added the funding of the international activities in conjunction with the appropriate choice of the foreign target market and the international long-term scope to the proactive motives that are already inherent and measured by the EO concept. In general, firms gain a competitive advantage through the development and implementation of new technologies (Qian et al. 2013). Innovation certainly has positive effects on their performance, too (Rosenbusch et al. 2011; Terziovski 2010), although innovation and digitization do not necessarily have a positive impact on international performance (Baldegger et al. 2021). In this vein, the omission of performance implication from the analysis needs to be addressed as well. Performance is likely to be affected, as speed influences the capabilities being built (Kotosaka 2013). It is quite possible that the majority of the surveyed firms have good reasons for their high internationalization age and their subsequently slower internationalization speeds.

Appendix

Table 4.4 The EO strategic posture scale

In general, the top managers of my firm favor . . .		
. . . a strong emphasis on the marketing of tried and true products or services.	**1–2 – 3 – 4 – 5 – 6 – 7**	. . . a strong emphasis on R&D, technological leadership, and innovations.
How many new lines of products or services has your firm marketed in the past 5 years?		
No new lines of products or services.	**1–2 – 3 – 4 – 5 – 6 – 7**	Very many new lines of products or services.
Changes in product or service lines have been mostly of a minor nature.	**1–2 – 3 – 4 – 5 – 6 – 7**	Changes in product or service lines have usually been quite dramatic.
In dealing with its competitors, my firm . . .		
. . . typically responds to actions which competitors initiate.	**1–2 – 3 – 4 – 5 – 6 – 7**	. . . typically initiates actions which competitors then respond to.
. . . is very seldom the first business to introduce new products/services, administrative techniques, operating technologies, etc.	**1–2 – 3 – 4 – 5 – 6 – 7**	. . . is very often the first business to introduce new products/services, administrative techniques, operating technologies, etc.
. . . typically seeks to avoid competitive clashes, preferring a "live-and-let-live" posture.	**1–2 – 3 – 4 – 5 – 6 – 7**	. . . typically adopts a very competitive, "undo-the-competitors" posture.
In general, the top managers of my firm believe in . . .		
. . . a strong proclivity for low-risk projects (with normal and certain rates of returns).	**1–2 – 3 – 4 – 5 – 6 – 7**	. . . a strong proclivity for high-risk projects (with chances of very high returns).
In general, the top managers of my firm believe that . . .		
. . . owing to the nature of the environment, it is best to explore it gradually via timid, incremental behavior.	**1–2 – 3 – 4 – 5 – 6 – 7**	. . . owing to the nature of the environment, bold, wide-ranging acts are necessary to achieve the firm's objectives.
When confronted with decision-making situations involving uncertainty, my firm . . .		
. . . typically adopts a cautious, "wait-and-see" posture in order to minimize the probability of making costly decisions	1–2 – 3 – 4 – 5 – 6 – 7	. . . typically adopts a bold, aggressive posture in order to maximize the probability of exploiting potential opportunities

Table 4.5 Firmographic and internationalization scale I

When was your company established?	Year:
How many people does the company/group of companies employ at the end of XXX[a] (absolute number of full-time-equivalent employees (FTE)?	Number of employees (FTE):
When did your company first start to become internationally active (initial exports etc.)?	Year:
What percentage of total sales revenue was your company generating in foreign markets in XXX[a]?	Share of sales revenue in %:

[a] last year in 4 digits

Table 4.6 Historic internationalization scale II

Please complete the following table of your internationalization history:

	Year	Number of countries	Number of continents
After the first year of internationalization			
After the third year of internationalization			
After the fifth year of internationalization			
End of XXX[a]	XXX[a]		

[a] last year in 4 digits

Table 4.7 Impediment items

What are the specific weaknesses of your company that may have impeded your success abroad? (More than one answer possible)

❐	Insufficient specialist expertise of employees	❐	Insufficient market research
❐	Insufficient specialist expertise of senior management	❐	Insufficient familiarity with international laws and regulations
❐	Lack of international experience among employees	❐	Lack of innovation
❐	Lack of international experience among senior management	❐	Cost structures too high, product and service costs too high
❐	Products not adequately developed for the international market	❐	Other: ______________________

Table 4.8 Internationalization obstacles items

What were the major obstacles in the internationalization process? (More than one answer possible)

❐	Existing laws and regulations abroad	❐	Lack of information (foreign market, regulatory interventions of authorities, locational analysis, etc.)
❐	Cultural and linguistic obstacles	❐	No branches/subsidiaries outside Switzerland
❐	Costs of internationalization	❐	Lack of cooperation agreements with foreign companies
❐	Available time of senior management	❐	Lack of foreign experience
❐	Qualifications of own employees	❐	No unique skillsets
❐	Qualifications of senior management	❐	Lack of network
❐	Price of own products and services	❐	Other: ____________

References

Abelson, R. P. (1985). A variance explanation paradox: When a little is a lot. *Psychological Bulletin*, *97*(1): 129–133.

Acedo, F. J., & Jones, M. V. (2007). Speed of internationalization and entrepreneurial cognition: Insights and a comparison between international new ventures, exporters and domestic firms. *Journal of World Business*, *42*(3), 236–252.

Alahuhta, M. (1990). Global growth strategies for high technology challengers. ACTA PolytechnicaScandinavia. *Electrical Engineering Series No. 66*. Helsinki: Doctoral dissertation.

Aldrich, H. E., & Fiol, C. M. (1994). Fools rush in? The institutional context of industry creation. *Academy of management review*, *19*(4), 645–670.

Andersen, O. (1997). Internationalization and market entry mode: A review of theories and conceptual frameworks. *MIR: Management International Review*, 27–42.

Andersen, O. (1993). On the internationalization process of firms: A critical analysis. *Journal of International Business Studies*, *24*(2), 209–231.

Autio, E., Sapienza, H. J., & Almeida, J. G. (2000). Effects of age at entry, knowledge intensity, and imitability on international growth. *Academy of management journal*, *43*(5), 909–924.

Baldegger, R., Wild, P., & Schueffel, P. (2021). The Effects of Entrepreneurial Orientation in a Digital and International Setting. In A. C. Corbett, P. M. Kreiser, L. D. Marino, & W. J. Wales, (Eds.), *Entrepreneurial Orientation: Epistemological, Theoretical, and Empirical Perspectives (Advances in Entrepreneurship, Firm Emergence and Growth, Vol. 22)*. Bingley: Emerald Publishing Limited, 145–174.

Barkema, H. G., & Vermeulen, F. (1997). What differences in the cultural backgrounds of partners are detrimental for international joint ventures?. *Journal of International Business Studies*, *28*(4), 845–864.

Beamish, P., Morrison, A., & Rosenzweig, P. (1997). *International management – text and cases.* Homewood: Irwin: McGraw-Hill.

Bettis, R. A., & Prahalad, C. K. (1995). The dominant logic: Retrospective and extension. *Strategic management journal, 16*(1), 5–14.

Brock, D. M., & Alon, I. (2009). Internationalization of professional service firms. *International Business: Research Teaching and Practice, 3*(1), 52–70.

Bruneel, J., Yli-Renko, H., & Clarysse, B. (2010). Learning from experience and learning from others: how congenital and interorganizational learning substitute for experiential learning in young firm internationalization. *Strategic entrepreneurship journal, 4*(2), 164–182.

Busenitz, L. W., & Barney, J. B. (1997). Differences between entrepreneurs and managers in large organizations: Biases and heuristics in strategic decision-making. *Journal of business venturing, 12*(1), 9–30.

Carr, J. C., Haggard, K. S., Hmieleski, K. M., & Zahra, S. A. (2010). A study of the moderating effects of firm age at internationalization on firm survival and short-term growth. *Strategic Entrepreneurship Journal, 4*(2), 183–192.

Casillas, J. C., & Acedo, F. J. (2013). Speed in the internationalization process of the firm. *International Journal of Management Reviews, 15*(1), 15–29.

Casillas, J. C., & Moreno-Menéndez, A. M. (2014). Speed of the internationalization process: The role of diversity and depth in experiential learning. *Journal of International Business Studies, 45*(1), 85–101.

Cellard, S., & Prange, C. (2008). How do age and speed of internationalization affect foreign growth. In *Academy of Management Conference, Anaheim.*

Chandra, A., Paul, J., & Chavan, M. (2020). Internationalization barriers of SMEs from developing countries: a review and research agenda. *International Journal of Entrepreneurial Behavior & Research, 26*(6), 1355–2554.

Chesbrough, H. (2010). Business model innovation: opportunities and barriers. *Long Range Planning, 43*(2–3), 354–363.

Chetty, S., & Campbell-Hunt, C. (2003). Paths to internationalisation among small- to medium-sized firms. *European journal of marketing, 37*(5/6), 796–820.

Chhotray, S., Sivertsson, O., & Tell, J. (2018). The roles of leadership, vision, and empowerment in born global companies. *Journal of International Entrepreneurship, 16*(1), 38–57.

Child, J., Hsieh, L., Elbanna, S., Karmowska, J., Marinova, S., Puthusserry, P., & Zhang, Y. (2017). SME international business models: The role of context and experience. *Journal of World Business, 52*(5), 664–679.

Cohen, W., & Levinthal, D. (1990). Absorptive capacity: A new perspective on learning and innovation. *Administrative Science Quarterly, 35*(1): 128–152.

Colovic, A. (2021). Leadership and business model innovation in late internationalizing SMEs. *Long Range Planning, 54*(1), 1–17.

Cotae, F. F. (2013). Internationalization and leadership. *International Journal of Information and Education Technology, 3*(3), 343.

Coviello, N. E., & Jones, M. V. (2004). Methodological issues in international entrepreneurship research. *Journal of Business Venturing, 19*(4), 485–508.

Covin, J. G., & Slevin, D. P. (1989). Strategic management of small firms in hostile and benign environments. *Strategic management journal, 10*(1), 75–87.

Deng, Z., Hofman, P. S., & Newman, A. (2013). Ownership concentration and product innovation in Chinese private SMEs. *Asia Pacific Journal of Management, 30*(3), 717–734.

Eden, L. (2009). "Letter from the Editor-in-Chief: Reverse knowledge transfers, culture clashes and going international". Retrieved from https://link.springer.com/content/pdf/10.1057/jibs.2008.98.pdf

Ellis, P. D. (2011). Social ties and international entrepreneurship: Opportunities and constraints affecting firm internationalization. *Journal of International business studies*, *42*(1), 99–127.

Eriksson, K., & Chetty, S. (2003). The effect of experience and absorptive capacity on foreign market knowledge. *International business review*, *12*(6), 673–695.

Eriksson, K., Johanson, J., Sharma, D. D., & Majkgård, A. (1998). Time and experiential knowledge in the internationalization process.

Fernhaber, S. A., Mcdougall-Covin, P. P., & Shepherd, D. A. (2009). International entrepreneurship: leveraging internal and external knowledge sources. *Strategic Entrepreneurship Journal*, *3*(4), 297–320.

Ferreira, J. J., Azevedo, S. G., & Ortiz, R. F. (2011). Contribution of resource-based view and entrepreneurial orientation on small firm growth. *Cuadernos de Gestión*, *11*(1), 95–116.

Forsgren, M., & Kinch, N. (1970). *Företagets anpassning till förändringar i omgivande system. En studie av massa-och pappersindustrin*. Uppsala: Acta Universitatis Upsaliensis.

George, J. M., & Jones, G. R. (2000). The role of time in theory and theory building. *Journal of management*, *26*(4), 657–684.

Gerschewski, S., Evers, N., Nguyen, A. T., & Froese, F. J. (2020). Trade shows and SME internationalisation: Networking for performance. *Management International Review*, *60*(4), 573–595.

Hambrick, D. C. (1994). Top Management Groups: A Conceptual Integration and Reconsideration of the "team" Label. *Research in Organizational Behavior*, *16*, 171–213.

Hannan, M. T. (1998). Rethinking age dependence in organizational mortality: Logical fromalizations. *American Journal of Sociology*, *104*(1), AJSv104p126–164.

Hannan, M. T., & Freeman, J. (1984). Structural inertia and organizational change. *American sociological review*, *49*(2), 149–164.

Harveston, P. D., Kedia, B. L., & Davis, P. S. (2000). Internationalization of born global and gradual globalizing firms: the impact of the manager. *Advances in Competitiveness Research*, *8*(1), 92–99.

Hedlund, G. (1994). A model of knowledge management and the N-form corporation. *Strategic management journal*, *15*(S2), 73–90.

Hill, C., & McKaig, T. (2012). *Global Business Today*, 3rd Canadian ed. Whitby, Canada: McGraw Hill Ryerson.

Hörnell, E., & Vahlne, J. E. (1972). *The Deciding Factors in the Choice of a Sales Subsidiary as the Channel for Exports*. Uppsala, Sweden: Uppsala universitet.

Jaeger, F., Thoeni, C., Koller, J., Bernegger, U., Fauceglia, D., & Bechtold, B. (2008). *KMU-Landschaft im Wandel*, Neuenburg, Switzerland: Bundesamt für Statistik.

Javalgi, R. R. G., & Todd, P. R. (2011). Entrepreneurial orientation, management commitment, and human capital: The internationalization of SMEs in India. *Journal of Business Research*, *64*(9), 1004–1010.

Javidan, M., Hough, L., & Bullough, A. (2010). Conceptualizing and measuring global mindset: Development of the global mindset inventory. Glendale, AZ: Thunderbird School of Global Management.

Johanson, J., & Vahlne, J. E. (2017). The internationalization process of the firm—a model of knowledge development and increasing foreign market commitments. In *International business* (pp. 145–154). Routledge.

Johanson, J., & Vahlne, J. E. (2009). The Uppsala internationalization process model revisited: From liability of foreignness to liability of outsidership. *Journal of International Business Studies*, *40*(9), 1411–1431.

Johanson, J., & Vahlne, J. E. (1990). The mechanism of internationalisation. *International Marketing Review*, *7*(4), 12–24.

Johanson, J., & Vahlne, J. E. (1977). The internationalization process of the firm – a model of knowledge development and increasing foreign market commitments. *Journal of International Business Studies*, *8*(1), 23–32.

Johanson, J., & Wiedersheim-Paul, F. (1975). The internationalization of the firm: Four Swedish cases. *Journal of management studies*, *12*(3), 305–322.

Jolly, V. K., Alahuhta, M., & Jeannet, J.-P. (1992). Challenging the incumbents: How high technology start-ups compete globally. *Journal of Strategic Change, 1*, 71–82.

Jones, M. V., & Coviello, N. E. (2005). Internationalisation: conceptualising an entrepreneurial process of behaviour in time. *Journal of International Business Studies*, *36*(3), 284–303.

Karami, M., & Tang, J. (2019). Entrepreneurial orientation and SME international performance: The mediating role of networking capability and experiential learning. *International Small Business Journal*, *37*(2), 105–124.

Khan, Z., & Lew, Y. K. (2018). Post-entry survival of developing economy international new ventures: A dynamic capability perspective. *International Business Review*, *27*(1), 149–160.

Khanna, T., Palepu, K., & Srinivasan, S. (2003). Disclosure practices of foreign companies interacting with US markets. Harvard Business School Strategy Unit Working Paper, (03–081), 03–29.

Knight, G. A., & Cavusgil, S. T. (2004). Innovation, organizational capabilities, and the born-global firm. *Journal of International Business Studies*, *35*(2), 124–141.

Knudsen, T., & Madsen, T. K. (2002). Export strategy: a dynamic capabilities perspective. *Scandinavian Journal of Management*, *18*(4), 475–502.

Kothari, T., Kotabe, M., & Murphy, P. (2013). Rules of the game for emerging market multinational companies from China and India. *Journal of International Management*, *19*(3), 276–299.

Kotosaka, M. (2013). Organizational Routines Development and the Timing and Pace of Early Stage Internationalization. Available at SSRN 2204940.

Kotosaka, M. (2011). Modelling the speed: examining the different modes of internationalization by the timing and speed. Available at SSRN 1969313.

Kraus, S., Niemand, T., Besler, M., Stieg, P., & Martinez-Ciment, C. (2018). The influence of leadership styles on the internationalisation of 'born-global' firms and traditionally global-expanding firms. *European Journal of International Management*, *12*(5–6), 554–575.

Kraus, S., Mitter, C., Eggers, F., & Stieg, P. (2017). Drivers of internationalization success: a conjoint choice experiment on German SME managers. *Review of Managerial Science*, *11*(3), 691–716.

Kuemmerle, W. (2002). Home base and knowledge management in international ventures. *Journal of Business venturing*, *17*(2), 99–122.

Leonidou, L. C. (1998). Factors stimulating export business: an empirical investigation. *Journal of Applied Business Research* (JABR), *14*(2), 43–68.

Leonidou, L., & Katsikeas, C. (1996). The export development process: an integrative review of empirical models. *Journal of International Business Studies*, *27*(3), 517–552.

Lindgren, P. (2012). Business model innovation leadership: How do SMEs strategically lead business model innovation?. *International Journal of Business and Management*, *7*(14), 53.

Lumpkin, G. T., & Dess, G. G. (2001). Linking two dimensions of entrepreneurial orientation to firm performance: The moderating role of environment and industry life cycle. *Journal of business venturing*, *16*(5), 429–451.

Lumpkin, G. T., & Dess, G. G. (1996). Clarifying the entrepreneurial orientation construct and linking it to performance. *Academy of Management Review*, *21*(1), 135–172.

Lumpkin, G. T., Cogliser, C. C., & Schneider, D. R. (2009). Understanding and measuring autonomy: An entrepreneurial orientation perspective. Entrepreneurship theory and practice, *33*(1), 47–69.

Madhok, A. (1997). Cost, value and foreign market entry mode: The transaction and the firm. Strategic management journal, *18*(1), 39–61.

Madsen, T. K., & Servais, P. (1997). The internationalization of born globals: an evolutionary process?. *International business review*, *6*(6), 561–583.

Matlay, H., Ruzzier, M., Hisrich, R. D., & Antoncic, B. (2006). SME internationalization research: past, present, and future. *Journal of Small Business and Enterprise Development*, *13*(4), 476–497.

Menard, S. (1995). An introduction to logistic regression diagnostics. *Applied logistic regression analysis*, *1*, 58–79.

Meschi, P. X., Ricard, A., & Moore, E. T. (2017). Fast and furious or slow and cautious? The joint impact of age at internationalization, speed, and risk diversity on the survival of exporting firms. *Journal of International Management*, *23*(3), 279–291.

Mockaitis, A. I., Vaiginienė, E., & Giedraitis, V. (2006). The internationalization efforts of Lithuanian manufacturing firms – strategy or luck?. *Research in International Business and Finance*, *20*(1), 111–126.

Mostafa, R. H., Wheeler, C., & Jones, M. V. (2005). Entrepreneurial orientation, commitment to the Internet and export performance in small and medium sized exporting firms. *Journal of international Entrepreneurship*, *3*(4), 291–302.

Oviatt, B. M., & McDougall, P. P. (2005). Defining international entrepreneurship and modeling the speed of internationalization. *Entrepreneurship theory and practice*, *29*(5), 537–553.

Oviatt, B. M., & McDougall, P. P. (1994). Toward a theory of international new ventures. *Journal of International Business Studies*, *25*(1), 45–64.

Pampel, F. C. (2000). Interpreting logistic regression coefficients. In *Logistic Regression* (pp. 19–40). SAGE Publications.

Park, S., LiPuma, J. A., & Prange, C. (2015). Venture capitalist and entrepreneur knowledge of new venture internationalization: A review of knowledge components. *International Small Business Journal*, *33*(8), 901–928.

Perlitz, M. (2000). *Internationales Management.* 4., bearb. Aufl. Stuttgart, Germany: Lucius & Lucius.

Peruffo, E., Marchegiani, L., & Vicentini, F. (2018). Experience as a source of knowledge in divestiture decisions: emerging issues and knowledge management implications. *Journal of Knowledge Management.*

Posner, B. Z., & Kouzes, J. M. (1988). Relating leadership and credibility. *Psychological reports*, *63*(2), 527–530.

Prashantham, S., & Young, S. (2011). Post-entry speed of international new ventures. *Entrepreneurship Theory and Practice*, *35*(2), 275–292.

Puthusserry, P., Khan, Z., Knight, G., & Miller, K. (2020). How do rapidly internationalizing SMEs learn? Exploring the link between network relationships, learning approaches and post-entry growth of rapidly Internationalizing SMEs from emerging markets. *Management International Review*, *60*(4), 515–542.

Qian, C., Cao, Q., & Takeuchi, R. (2013). Top management team functional diversity and organizational innovation in China: The moderating effects of environment. *Strategic Management Journal*, *34*(1), 110–120.

Rauch, A., Wiklund, J., Lumpkin, G. T., & Frese, M. (2009). Entrepreneurial orientation and business performance: An assessment of past research and suggestions for the future. *Entrepreneurship theory and practice*, *33*(3), 761–787.

Reuber, A. R., & Fischer, E. (1997). The influence of the management team's international experience on the internationalization behaviors of SMEs. *Journal of international business studies, 28*(4), 807–825.

Rosenbusch, N., Brinckmann, J., & Bausch, A. (2011). Is innovation always beneficial? A meta-analysis of the relationship between innovation and performance in SMEs. *Journal of business Venturing*, *26*(4), 441–457.

Rugman, A. M., & Verbeke, A. (2007). Liabilities of regional foreignness and the use of firm-level versus country-level data: A response to Dunning et al. (2007). *Journal of International Business Studies*, *38*(1), 200–205.

Sapienza, H. J., Autio, E., George, G., & Zahra, S. A. (2006). A capabilities perspective on the effects of early internationalization on firm survival and growth. *Academy of management review*, *31*(4), 914–933.

Schweizer, R. (2012). The internationalization process of SMEs: A muddling-through process. *Journal of Business Research*, *65*(6), 745–751.

Schwens, C., & Kabst, R. (2009). How early opposed to late internationalizers learn: Experience of others and paradigms of interpretation. *International Business Review*, *18*(5), 509–522.

Scuotto, V., Del Giudice, M., & Carayannis, E. G. (2017). The effect of social networking sites and absorptive capacity on SMES'innovation performance. *The Journal of Technology Transfer*, *42*(2), 409–424.

SECO (2020). Die KMU-Förderung der Schweiz. Eidgenössisches Departement für Wirtschaft, Bildung und Forschung WBF. https://www.seco.admin.ch/seco/de/home/Publikationen_Dienstleistungen/Publikationen_und_Formulare/Standortforderung/Broschuren/kmufoerderung-schweiz.html

Sharma, D. D., & Blomstermo, A. (2003). A critical review of time in the internationalization process of firms. *Journal of Global Marketing*, *16*(4), 53–71.

Shrader, R. C., Oviatt, B. M., & McDougall, P. P. (2000). How new ventures exploit trade-offs among international risk factors: Lessons for the accelerated internationalization of the 21st century. *Academy of Management Journal*, *43*(6), 1227–1247.

Stieglitz, N., & Foss, N. J. (2015). Business model innovation: The role of leadership. In N. Foss & T. Saebi, (Eds.), *Business Model Innovation the Organizational Dimension* (pp. 104–122). Oxford, UK: Oxford University Press.

Swiss Federal Statistical Office (2008). Kleine und mittlere Unternehmen. Wirtschaftsstruktur: Unternehmen. https://www.bfs.admin.ch/bfs/de/home/statistiken/industrie-dienstleistungen/unternehmen-beschaeftigte/wirtschaftsstrukturunternehmen/kmu.html

Tan, A., Brewer, P., & Liesch, P. W. (2007). Before the first export decision: Internationalisation readiness in the pre-export phase. *International Business Review*, *16*(3), 294–309.

Tang, J., Tang, Z., & Cowden, B. J. (2017). Exploring the relationship between entrepreneurial orientation, CEO dual values, and SME performance in state-owned vs. nonstate-owned enterprises in China. *Entrepreneurship Theory and Practice*, *41*(6), 883–908.

Teece, D. J. (2007). Explicating dynamic capabilities: the nature and microfoundations of (sustainable) enterprise performance. *Strategic management journal*, *28*(13), 1319–1350.

Terziovski, M. (2010). Innovation practice and its performance implications in small and medium enterprises (SMEs) in the manufacturing sector: a resource-based view. *Strategic management journal*, *31*(8), 892–902.

Thanos, I. C., Dimitratos, P., & Sapouna, P. (2017). The implications of international entrepreneurial orientation, politicization, and hostility upon SME international performance. *International Small Business Journal*, *35*(4), 495–514.

Uusitalo, P., & Lavikka, R. (2020). Overcoming Path Dependency in an Industrialised House-Building Company through Entrepreneurial Orientation. *Buildings*, *10*(3), 45.

Vahlne, J. E. (2020). Development of the Uppsala model of internationalization process: From internationalization to evolution. *Global Strategy Journal*, *10*(2), 239–250.

Vahlne, J. E., & Johanson, J. (2002). *New technology, new companies, new business environments and new internationalisation processes?* Pergamon, Amsterdam, London, New York, Oxford: Elsevier Science.

Vermeulen, F., & Barkema, H. (2002). Pace, rhythm, and scope: Process dependence in building a profitable multinational corporation. *Strategic Management Journal, 23*(7), 637–653.

Wales, W., Gupta, V. K., Marino, L., & Shirokova, G. (2019). Entrepreneurial orientation: International, global and cross-cultural research. *International Small Business Journal, 37*(2), 95–104.

Wales, W. J., Patel, P. C., Parida, V., & Kreiser, P. M. (2013). Nonlinear effects of entrepreneurial orientation on small firm performance: The moderating role of resource orchestration capabilities. *Strategic Entrepreneurship Journal, 7*(2), 93–121.

Wang, C. L., & Ahmed, P. K. (2007). Dynamic capabilities: A review and research agenda. *International journal of management reviews, 9*(1), 31–51.

Weeks, J., & Galunic, C. (2002). Corporate culture and corporate gene. *Digest of Foreign Social Science, 2*, 37–40.

Welch, L. S., & Luostarinen, R. (1988). Internationalization: evolution of a concept. *Journal of General Management, 14*(2): 44–60.

Westhead, P., & Wright, M. (1998). Novice, portfolio, and serial founders: are they different?. *Journal of business venturing, 13*(3), 173–204.

Xie, X., Zeng, S., Peng, Y., & Tam, C. (2013). What affects the innovation performance of small and medium-sized enterprises in China?. *Innovation, 15*(3), 271–286.

Yu, J., Gilbert, B. A., & Oviatt, B. M. (2011). Effects of alliances, time, and network cohesion on the initiation of foreign sales by new ventures. *Strategic Management Journal, 32*(4), 424–446.

Yu, T., & Cannella Jr, A. A. (2007). Rivalry between multinational enterprises: An event history approach. *Academy of Management Journal, 50*(3), 665–686.

Zahra, S. A., & George, G. (2002). International entrepreneurship: The current status of the field and future research agenda. In M. Hitt, D.R. Ireland, S.M. Camp, & D.L. Sexton (Eds.), *Strategic entrepreneurship: Creating a new mindset* (pp. 255–288). New Jersey: Wiley-Blackwell.

Zahra, S. A., Ireland, R. D., & Hitt, M. A. (2000). International expansion by new venture firms: International diversity, mode of market entry, technological learning, and performance. *Academy of Management journal, 43*(5), 925–950.

Zaleznik, A. (1990). The leadership gap. *Academy of Management Perspectives, 4*(1), 7–22.

Zeng, Y., Shenkar, O., Lee, S. H., & Song, S. (2013). Cultural differences, MNE learning abilities, and the effect of experience on subsidiary mortality in a dissimilar culture: Evidence from Korean MNEs. *Journal of International Business Studies, 44*(1), 42–65.

Zhou, L., & Wu, A. (2014). Earliness of internationalization and performance outcomes: Exploring the moderating effects of venture age and international commitment. *Journal of World Business, 49*(1), 132–142.

Cooperation With Distributors in Arabic-Speaking Countries

5

Paul Ammann and Gerald Drißner

5.1 Introduction

In a globalized economy where products, technologies, and experiences are increasingly shared, communication and leadership styles are likely to converge. Nevertheless, this may only appear to be the case and happen only superficially, because in certain business areas, working in different geographical and cultural regions remains a challenge and is quite often a source of frustration. Specifically, with regard to the Arab business world, Western managers are either not aware of its particularities and success factors, or they simply misunderstand them.

Arabic-speaking countries[1] are important for Swiss exporters as they imported 2019 about 4% of Swiss exports, compared to 6% by China and 1% by India. The United Arab Emirates, Saudi Arabia, and Egypt are Switzerland's most important partners of the Arabic-speaking countries with regard to exports. The most important products exported from Switzerland to these countries are pharmaceutical products, watches, machines, and precision instruments.

[1]The League of Arab States has 22 members: Algeria, Bahrain, Comoros, Djibouti, Egypt, Iraq, Jordan, Kuwait, Lebanon, Libya, Mauritania, Morocco, Oman, Palestine, Qatar, Saudi Arabia, Somalia, Sudan, Syria, Tunisia, United Arab Emirates, and Yemen. (http://www.leagueofarabstates.net/ar/aboutlas/Pages/CountryData.aspx).

P. Ammann (✉) · G. Drißner
Bern University of Applied Sciences, Bern, Switzerland
e-mail: paul.ammann@bfh.ch; mail@drissner.me

I. Stolz, S. Oldenziel Scherrer (eds.), *International Leadership*, uniscope. Publikationen der SGO Stiftung, https://doi.org/10.1007/978-3-658-37306-1_5

Based on an online survey among Swiss companies and in-depth personal interviews, this study shows the most important areas of successful leadership concerning distributors in Arabic-speaking countries. They are explained via the cooperation processes with distributors, specifically, how to select, motivate, and cooperate with them on a long-term basis. Furthermore, the authors explain how cultural differences can be addressed and handled.

Management literature often lacks an analysis of the differences between Western and Arabic-speaking countries, for many reasons. One is that on the surface, the parties involved often have similar educational backgrounds and the business language is English. Although there are cultural guides for the Arab world, most of them only offer help for vacationers and refer to rather obvious differences. Nevertheless, while the differences are often subtle, the consequences may be critical to overall success. As the survey shows, dealing with cultural differences and understanding the motivation of the other person are crucial for successful leadership. This work aims to fill this gap.

This chapter will guide the reader through the key stages of successful collaboration with Arab partners. First, the authors clarify what they understand by leadership in distribution channels and elaborate on the importance and role of distributors for exporting companies. Then, four key sets of activities are analyzed: (1) selecting the distributor, (2) motivating the distributor, (3) cooperating with the distributor, and (4) dealing with cultural differences. These activities are illustrated with case studies that aim to demonstrate the practical problems and possible solutions. Subsequently, every set of activities is examined in more detail and brought to a more abstract, generally applicable level. Part 4—dealing with cultural differences—uses famous Arabic proverbs to better represent the often diffuse feeling of cultural misunderstandings that may be difficult to articulate. These proverbs are included in the analysis and provide a new perspective on this issue. At the end of each sub-chapter, the analysis is summarized in rules. These rules are listed again at the very end of this chapter as the so-called "ten golden rules" of working with distributors in Arabic-speaking countries.

5.1.1 Leadership in Distribution Channels

A distributor is a company that helps exporting companies sell their products in an export market. The two basic types of distributors are resellers and agents. A reseller buys a product from a manufacturer and sells it with a margin, while an agent mediates the sale of a product and receives a commission after the successful sale. The information in this chapter applies to both types of distributors.

Nowadays, international distributors often generate more than 90% of the annual turnover for industrial goods manufacturers (Schmitz 2007). Multiple Surveys—(e.g. DIHK, 2010 and OSEC, 2006)—confirm the great importance of distributors as success factors in international business. According to Sliwinski and Sliwinska (2016), the relationship with the distributor is the second-most important driver for sales growth in foreign

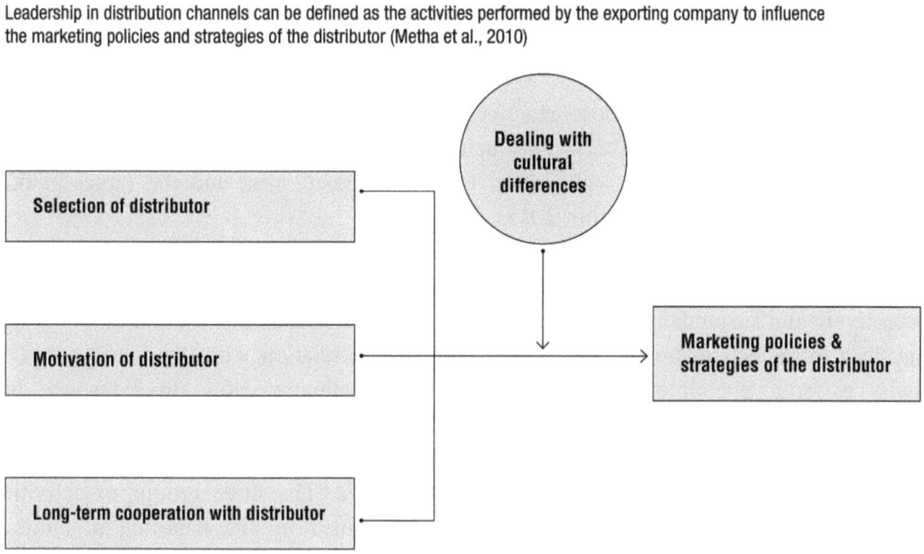

Fig. 5.1 Leadership in distribution channels

markets. The leading of distributors is thus a key task of Swiss exporters (Ammann et al. 2012).

Leadership in distribution channels can be defined as the activities performed by the exporting company to influence the marketing policies and strategies of channel partners (Metha et al. 2010). For this study, these leadership activities were divided into four subject areas (◉ Fig 5.1): (1) selection, (2) motivation, (3) long-term cooperation with the distributor, and (4) dealing with cultural differences. The distributor's marketing and sales strategies play a crucial role in such a collaboration. Ultimately, the distributors decide whether the exporter's strategies are supported or hindered in the country of export.

Choosing a distributor is in itself an important act in the context of providing leadership in distribution channels. The focus is on the question of whether cooperation with a potential distributor is likely to be possible in a way that justifies the costs and risks associated with a sales channel abroad. "Recruiting good distributors in marketing channels can improve a manufacturer's performance, and even increase its competitive advantage" (Lin and Chen 2008). Choosing a suitable distributor is also important because switching to another one can be difficult. A distributor can use his/her customer contacts against the exporter's interests if the latter wants to switch to another distributor. In case of a switch, the introductory and training costs will be incurred again. For these reasons, it is an advantage to be thorough and well-prepared from the beginning when choosing a distributor. Sources for possible new distributors in the Arabic-speaking countries are trade fairs, Switzerland Global Enterprise (S-GE)—the official Swiss organization for export promotion–, online sources, and other companies that are active in the region (Alliance

Experts 2020). Research shows that companies often are not sufficiently thorough in their search and selection of new distributors. "Some companies take less time to select an international distributor than they do to hire a clerical worker, often making the choice of international distributors almost reactively" (Bellin 2017). The decision for new distributors is made along criteria that include the potential distributors' abilities, their motivation, and strategic fit with regard to market positioning and the target market segments (Batra et al. 2016; Bellin 2015).

"Motivation" subsumes all actions of the exporting company that lead to motivating the employees of the distributor to sell the company's products in the local market as proactively and sustainably as possible. The "long-term cooperation" includes all actions that lead to the establishment of a mostly conflict-free relation with the distributor. The Swiss exporter encounters a difficult leadership challenge: How do I manage the distributor's employees? This involves managing employees of a third-party company in another country. These employees are not directly subordinate or geographically close—which makes the required leadership task a challenge. The three groups of activities mentioned above are influenced and largely determined by the handling of cultural differences between the employees of the exporter and those of the distributor.

Studies on the topic of leadership in sales channels underline the importance of trust and a high level of cooperation in the successful leadership of distributors. A worldwide study of 2006 shows: "Central to developing strategic partnerships is trust and trust-building behaviors" (Mehta et al., 2006). This study affirms that high levels of cooperation, commitment, and trust manifested on each side of the manufacturer-channel intermediary dyad are based on and form the "heart" of successful strategic alliances/partnerships. A further investigation found that greater cultural incongruences between marketing channel alliances/partners are associated with lower levels of trust, commitment, and cooperation (Anderson et al. 2020). Yli-Renko et al. (2001) emphasize that "[g]reater social interaction between an exporting firm and its distributor increases the overseas market intelligence of the former, as well as its ability to recognize and evaluate pertinent knowledge, and enhances its incentive to exchange and disseminate information". Lane and Lubatkin (1998) stress that "intensifying social interactions also facilitate the creation of relation-specific common knowledge". Likewise, Chang and Fang (2015) found:" Social interaction provides better access to, and understanding of, partner firm operations and provides more effective means of communicating with the partner firm." Johnston et al. (2012) emphasize the importance of joint actions (sales meetings or exhibitions) for further trust and collaboration between exporting company and distributor.

5.1.2 Online Survey and Personal Interviews

In order to find out the success factors of exporting companies in the four defined subject areas, an online survey and personal interviews were carried out. The questionnaire is accessible under: https://tinyurl.com/5ckm4wsy.

Companies were contacted in spring 2020 by email and were asked to take part in an online survey. Of the total of 5233 companies contacted, 17.89% opened the e-mail and 136 took part in the survey, which is a response rate of 2.6%. This value can be described as a satisfactory result. 4% of Swiss exports are sold to Arabic-speaking countries. The number of Swiss companies with export business to this region is accordingly rather limited.

In order to substantiate and scrutinize the results of the survey, personal interviews (of 45 to 90 minutes each) were carried out in August and September 2020. Four case studies were developed with the following companies: ABB, Baswa acoustic, Trafag, and USM U. Schärer Söhne AG.

5.2 The Cooperation Process with Distributors in Practice

Owing to the great importance of distributors as explained above, cooperation with them is a central task for every exporting company (Schögel 2012). This task consists of the selection of the distributor, their motivation for proactive sales, and successful long-term cooperation. We will now examine these three phases. Then, the topic of dealing with cultural differences will be discussed.

5.2.1 Selection of a Distributor

This section is about finding and choosing new distributors in Arabic-speaking countries (◉ Fig. 5.1). We begin by showing how Trafag AG proceeds when choosing a new distributor. Then the results of the survey are presented. The section is summarized in a rule with the most important insights into the selection of distributors.

5.2.1.1 Case Study: Selection of the Distributor—Trafag AG

Trafag (www.trafag.ch) is a leading global supplier of high-quality sensors and monitoring devices for pressure, temperature, and SF6 gas density. In addition to a wide range of standardized, configurable products, Trafag also develops tailor-made solutions for OEM (Original Equipment Manufacturer) customers. Trafag's pressure transmitters, pressure switches, temperature transmitters, and thermostats are used in shipbuilding, hydraulics, rail vehicles, and large engines—in potentially explosive areas, in systems for water treatment, on test stands, and elsewhere. Trafag has a broad sales and service network in over 40 countries worldwide enabling customized and competent customer advice as well as ensuring fast service.

Trafag has supplied several hundred pressure transmitters for regulating the water fountain at the Burj Khalifa in Dubai, which at its inauguration in 2010 was the tallest building in the world at 828 m. Roger Hafen works at Trafag AG in Zurich as an Area Sales Manager and is responsible for, among other regions, the Near and Middle East. Trafag works with a distributor for the Arab world in Dubai, whose owner is originally from India. The distributor employs around 60 people and is based in the free-trade zone, as that makes them independent of a local sponsor.

When looking for a partner, the image of the distributor in the target market segment plays a decisive role. The high level of competence of the employees in the technical area is also very important. “You can’t just sell Trafag products like that”, says Roger Hafen. “You first have to understand the customer’s application, find out where the customer has a problem, and how our products can generate added value for the customer.” If products are delivered that do not fit the application, problems can quickly arise. In Arabic-speaking countries, it is usually the supplier who is blamed, not the customer, which could quickly develop into an image problem. The distributor’s financial strength was also an important criterion when choosing a partner. For example, Trafag is strict when bills are not paid. “With us, a delivery block can be imposed from the first dunning level”, says Roger Hafen.

Reliability was another important criterion for choosing a distributor. In Arab countries, there is a different understanding of time. One can rely less on commitments. In Arabic-speaking countries, “soon” is a frequently used time specification. But what does “soon” mean? Weeks? Months? “Soon” could mean anything in the Arab world, but usually not what the Swiss understand. It is therefore difficult to agree on goals based on commitments. The decision of whether to work with one or several distributors in Arab countries was a challenge. Trafag is careful when granting exclusivity. If you work with several distributors, there is a risk of a ruinous price war. If you guarantee exclusivity to one distributor for a certain period, their motivation could suffer. Trafag proceeds in such a way that exclusivity is only contractually granted to the partner once they have achieved certain sales targets, which are set relatively high. Trafag always reserves the right to work with multiple partners until one emerges as the best distributor.

5.2.1.2 Survey Results: How to Select a Distributor

The three selection criteria for distributors in the Arabic-speaking countries with the most mentions are competence of the leadership, professionalism of the distributors’ employees, and a good relationship with the company’s target customers (◉ Fig. 5.2 and the Trafag case study above).

The presence of legal permits to conduct business in an Arabic-speaking country and language skills (English, French) were also often mentioned. The similarity of the corporate culture was an important condition for noticeably few respondents. This was also underlined in personal interviews, since the exporting companies want their distributors to specifically reflect and live the Arab culture internally and externally. It is noteworthy that only a relatively small number of the Swiss companies surveyed consulted other manufacturers before choosing a distributor. Correctly used benchmark interviews could certainly improve the quality of the decision—as interviewees confirmed. Other studies, e.g. Jung et al. (2013), showed a similar prioritization of the selection criteria for new distributors.

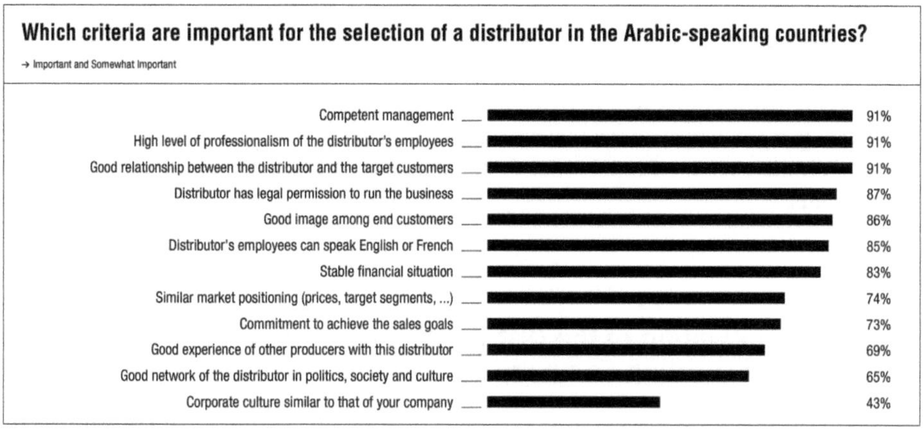

Fig. 5.2 Criteria for the selection of distributors in Arabic-speaking countries

Interview partners emphasized the importance of the appropriate person from Switzerland taking part in the negotiations. Arab managers expect an interlocutor at the same level in the company hierarchy. Distributors in Arabic-speaking countries are often family businesses (Welsh and Raven 2006), and the CEO is usually also the owner of the company: they prefer to negotiate with the exporter's CEO. In the interviews, it was stated that Swiss exporters often check whether the CEO of the distributor had studied in the USA or Europe, therefore knowing Western culture well. Another important selection criterion mentioned was that the share of sales of the exporter's product should make up at least 25% of the distributor's sales so that the product range has the necessary significance for the distributor: a small export company should therefore rather choose a small distributor. A question most distributors will ask in the negotiation process is that of exclusivity, i.e. whether the exporter would only work with one distributor in a target country (see the Trafag case study above). In this context, exclusivity means the exclusive assignment of an area or customer group to a distributor. According to the interviewees, exclusivity should only be granted with caution in order not to give too much power to the distributor. Furthermore, exclusivity clauses may be subject to anti-trust laws in some countries (Handelskammerjournal 2019). One interviewee, a supplier of standard goods manufactured on stock, pursues the strategy of working with several distributors and benefits from their competitive situation in the target country. Another one who works in the customer-specific project business has given up this strategy because the distributors fought a ruinous price war with each new project and the export company was drawn into the conflict.

▶ To summarize, we can derive the following rule:

Rule 1: A good distributor is the most important success factor for the export business. It is important to take the time to choose a well-suited distributor. Be careful when granting exclusivity! Important decision criteria are the competent management and professionalism of the distributor's employees as well as their good relationship with potential customers and the existence of the necessary legal permits.

5.2.2 The Motivation of the Distributor to Proactively Sell the Products of the Exporting Company

This section is about how distributors can be motivated to proactively sell the exporting company's products in the target country (◉ Fig. 5.1). In the beginning, the approach of Baswa AG to motivate its distributors is shown. Then the results of the survey are presented. The section closes with rules that summarize the most important insights into motivating distributors.

5.2.2.1 Case Study: Motivation of the Distributor—Baswa AG

Baswa (www.baswa.ch) employs around 40 people and manufactures sound-absorbing surfaces for walls and ceilings. The products are in use worldwide to reduce reverberation in large rooms such as lecture halls, conference centers, hotel lobbies, museums, restaurants, and many other buildings. Baswa made its entry into the Arab world with the help of well-known international architects who needed good acoustics for their projects and knew Baswa products, for example in the King Abdullah Petroleum Studies and Research Center in Saudi Arabia, says Eric Sulzer, President of the Board of Directors at Baswa. Baswa also wants to increasingly deliver to private customers who live in large villas with inadequate acoustics.

Baswa has chosen the model of a jointly financed salesperson so as to motivate the distributor for their sales. The salesperson is employed by the distributor. Wages and expenses are equally shared. This model has the advantage that Baswa has direct access to this salesperson and can therefore lead and motivate him/her very closely. There is no risk of him/her being used for other activities within the distributor. With this investment in sales, Baswa is signaling to the distributor both the importance of the market and trust in the partnership. This also has a positive effect on the motivation of the distributor.

Baswa created a job profile: it should be a woman, as building and maintaining networks is an important aspect of the job—many interior designers in Dubai are women, and women often work in the offices of local architects and entrepreneurs. The new employee should have an Arab background and experience in the construction industry. The selection process turned out to be difficult; women from Arabic-speaking countries proved to be less suitable for the job and were very demanding of a foreign employer. Finally, a woman from

Sri Lanka was hired who had been living in Dubai for more than 15 years and worked in the construction industry. Baswa is very pleased with this salesperson's proactive approach. Eric Sulzer regards the personal relationship with the distributor as very important. He is on-site two to three times a year to meet with the distributor, to present new products, and also to conduct training.

5.2.2.2 Survey Results: How to Motivate a Distributor

After the selection of a distributor, new challenges await the exporter. Numerous companies neglect the support of their distributors—with dramatic consequences for sales and growth (Zemanek and Frankel Jr. 2001). They neglect professionalization, i.e. the transfer of the knowledge necessary for sales to the distributors. Often, the distributors do not have sufficient knowledge about the products. Many Swiss machine manufacturers rate the expertise of their representatives as insufficient (Walti 2000). Furthermore, there is a one-sided mobilization that is too strongly oriented to financial factors. Looking after international distributors poses capacity problems for companies. Professionalization and motivation are important because distributors usually also sell products from other manufacturers. The exporter is thus in a competitive situation already at the distributor level.

When asked about activities that increase the motivation of a distributor, building personal relationships was mentioned most frequently (◉ Fig. 5.3). In the beginning, personal relationships must be established with appropriate employees at the distributor. The distributor's CEO is often involved in contract negotiations, but the sale is carried out by the salespeople. According to one interviewee, the relationship then also had to be built with the salespeople, as they had not been present during contract negotiations. Regular personal meetings and training courses in Switzerland and in the target country are rated as important by many respondents for the motivation of the distributor. Studies have shown the importance of training in Arabic-speaking countries: in their study, Welsh and Raven (2006) provide evidence on training methods for salespeople and retail employees in the Middle East: "Training can influence the customer orientation of salespeople in improving responsiveness, reliability, and empathy" (Welsh and Raven 2006).

The high importance of personal relationships is a challenge for exporters because building personal relationships is associated with high costs, such as trips to the target country or inviting the distributor's employees to Switzerland. A majority of companies consider fair commissions to be important, as well as the high quality of the exporter's internal processes. If the exporter expects a high level of motivation from the distributor, he/she has to ensure that they meet their deadlines, answer questions quickly, etc. The distributor must be treated like a customer.

A little more than half of the survey participants think that the distributors have to be supported in finding sales leads. The Baswa case study above shows how companies can

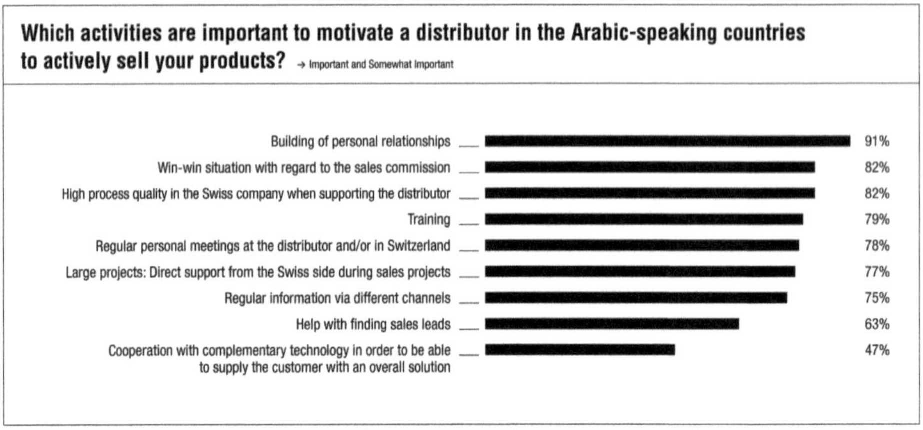

Fig. 5.3 Success factors for motivating distributors to proactive sales

get direct access to a salesperson working for a distributor. The importance of personal relationships for successful motivation was confirmed in almost every personal interview. The personality and style of the sales manager, who works with distributors and builds personal relationships, is important (see ▸ Sect. 5.2.3.3).

The promise to grant the distributor exclusivity when certain goals are achieved can also increase their motivation (see ▸ Sect. 5.2.1.2).

▶ To summarize, we can derive the following rules:

Rule 2: Personal relationships are central to motivating distributors. The supervisor/sales manager in Switzerland is responsible for this and should hold this responsibility for several years so as to be able to build long-term personal relationships. On the distributor's part, the right contact person must be identified and motivated. It is not the distributor's CEO who sells the products! Frustration tolerance, seniority, and training in dealing with cultural differences are important for a sales manager.

Rule 3: The training of the distributor's employees must be prioritized and carried out repeatedly: both in the target country and Switzerland. Digital information in the form of texts or videos on the internet or intranet is no appropriate substitute. Training is important in the areas of product knowledge and the sales process.

Rule 4: The internal processes in Switzerland should be aligned in such a way that the distributor is treated like a customer in terms of quality and adherence to deadlines. Exporters are free to make demands—but they also have to deliver. Distributors should be treated like customers with regard to delivery deadlines and the time taken to answer questions and requests.

5.2.3 Long-Term Cooperation with the Distributor

This section is about cooperation with distributors (◉ Fig. 5.1). In the beginning, the approach of USM U. Schärer Söhne AG to successfully cooperate with the distributors in the long term is shown. Then the results of the survey are presented. The section is summarized in a rule with the most important findings for long-term cooperation with distributors.

5.2.3.1 Case Study: Cooperation with the Distributor—USM U. Schärer Söhne AG

USM U. Schärer Söhne AG (www.usm.com) in Münsingen employs 400 people and offers modular furniture for the office sector in the upper price tier. At USM, Eric Berchtold is responsible for the Middle East. The company operates in Lebanon, the United Arab Emirates, Qatar, Saudi Arabia, and Egypt.

For a long-term, successful cooperation with a distributor in the Arab world, personal relationships are crucial. A good relationship with the distributor is key in the Arab world, says Eric Berchtold. Without a good personal relationship, USM would not be able to get *leads*, because the company is not there. That is why the distributor's main task is to find sales leads. In Arabic-speaking countries, you can rarely rely on numbers and data. For this reason, on-site visits should take place regularly to get an impression of what the distributor's organization looks like, who it employs, and what the showroom—very important for USM—looks like. The distributor is also regularly invited to Switzerland. He/she has to pay for travel costs (airfare) while hotels, transport, food, and entertainment in Switzerland are handled by USM.

If a distributor's showroom does not meet the agreed quality standard, this will be addressed. Criticism has to be formulated positively in the Arab world and needs to be dealt with very carefully. "If you criticize Arabs, they are often offended", says Eric Berchtold. "In Europe, we are used to very direct interactions. If something is not good, it can be clearly voiced. There, you often have to find a diplomatic path." Quality assurance also plays a major role in the control of furniture installation. This is ensured by videos of office furniture installed on-site, which the distributors send to Switzerland.

5.2.3.2 Survey Results: How to Cooperate with a Distributor in the Long Term

The quality of a long-term cooperation between manufacturer and distributor is decisive for success in a market. Shortcomings in the coordination between the manufacturer and the distributor, destructive conflicts, and dissatisfaction lead to marketing and sales concepts no longer being implemented in an optimal manner locally. Internal efficiency suffers here, as does sales effectiveness in the stores (Schmitz 2007).

Long-term cooperation with distributors in Arabic-speaking countries is described as a major challenge by a majority of the respondents (◉ Fig. 5.4). The following problems were mentioned: "The distributors do not keep their promises", "The distributors receive negative feedback from the end customers", and "The quality of the distributor's activities

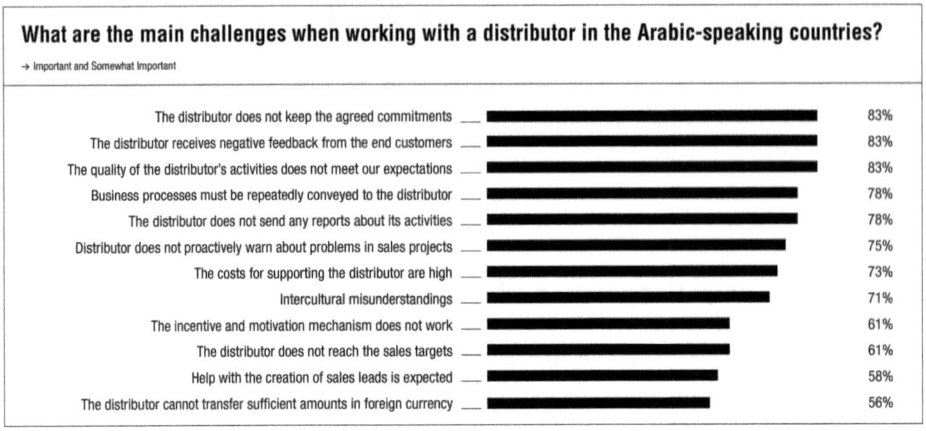

Fig. 5.4 Challenges in the long-term cooperation with distributors

does not meet our expectations". These results of the survey are dramatic and show that working with distributors in Arabic-speaking countries is anything but easy. A quote from a personal interview underlines this result: "Work under pressure is not a practice in the Arabic-speaking countries. Reaching deadlines means chasing them and staying behind them to ensure that the jointly agreed goals are achieved." Exporters also struggle with the fact that they often have to retrain employees of the distributors, and they complain about a lack of feedback on the activities of the distributor in their market. This is made even more difficult by intercultural misunderstandings (see ▸ Sect. 5.3 below). It is noticeable that while achieving sales targets is still seen as a challenge by more than 50% of respondents, this is not the most pressing challenge, as one would expect. The most important problem is that the distributors are not keeping the agreed commitments.

How do companies deal with these difficulties? Control of the distributor's activities is classified as important—in some cases, such control is possible via digital applications (see case study USM U. Schärer Söhne AG above). It is hardly surprising that the answer option "The costs of supporting the distributor are high" received many responses. Before entering the markets of Arabic-speaking countries, these expectedly high support costs must be taken into account. When it comes to ensuring the quality of the distributor's activities, the interview partners emphasized the importance of close, personal support for the distributor (see case study USM U. Schärer Söhne AG above). This view is supported by research papers (see ▸ Sect. 5.1.1 above). The sales managers play an important role in dealing with these challenges; thus, the qualities needed of such managers are described in the next section.

5.2.3.3 Important Qualities of a Sales Manager Working with Distributors

The characteristics of a sales manager in Swiss export companies have a major influence on their successful cooperation with distributors. A typical sales manager of a manufacturer in Switzerland who is responsible for distributors looks after an average of seven representatives (Belz and Reinhold 2001). With this responsibility, these employees can only make a few on-site visits. In the interviews, the frequency of visits by the sales manager to each distributor averaged twice a year.

It is very important that the sales manager can build and maintain personal relationships over the long term. Frequent changes in his/her role, however, make it impossible to do so. In the personal interviews, it was mentioned that it would be a great advantage if the sales manager was experienced in working with people from other cultures, especially in connection with Arabic culture. Many companies consider training in dealing with cultural differences to be important (◉ Fig. 5.5). The successful sales manager sees cultural differences as a positive challenge (see ▸ Sect. 5.3 below) and has a high tolerance for frustration. As one interviewee put it: "They need to be flexible, work is done differently, they need to stay calm and to compromise sometimes. They need to find the balance between the Swiss side—meaning expectations and targets—and the local side—meaning what can be achieved locally." The sales manager should also have the ability to train other people in technical and sales-related matters, as well as providing sales support on important sales projects. A certain seniority is positive for a sales manager when working with distributors in Arabic-speaking countries.

▶ To summarize, we can derive the following rule:

Rule 5: Exporters need to have a long-term perspective—success takes time. You have to provide enough capacity (time of the sales manager, training, travel expenses, etc.) to support the distributor. The real work begins after signing a new distribution agreement. Closely following up on the agreed commitments is a must. The sales managers should be trained in dealing with cultural differences—ideally, they already have such experiences. They should be able to recognize the differences between Swiss customs and the conditions in the exporting country and be able to bear them. Above all, they should be able to build long-term personal relationships with the distributor's employees.

5.3 Dealing with Cultural Differences

This section covers the topic of dealing with cultural differences between Swiss exporters and distributors in Arabic-speaking countries (◉ Fig. 5.1). In the beginning, the approach of a Swiss manager in an ABB factory in Saudi Arabia and his take on how to deal with cultural differences is presented. These are analyzed and presented based on proverbs. The section is summarized in rules with the most important insights into dealing with cultural differences.

5.3.1 Case Study: Dealing with Cultural Differences—ABB

ABB (www.abb.com) employs about 110,000 people in over 100 countries and offers products and services in the fields of electrification, robotics, automation, and motion technology.

From 2016 to 2019, Anton Tremp was the Local Business Unit Manager for High Voltage Products of ABB in Saudi Arabia, which included a production facility. In Saudi Arabia, there are cultural peculiarities that contradict typical rules and values one would commonly relate to Swiss mentality. A good example is the concept of *Barakah*, which can be translated as "blessing "and refers to the belief that closeness to God will have a more relevant impact on the result of an activity than one's own actions. What is well known and related to this concept is the expression "'in shā' Allāh", i.e. "God willing", which explicitly expresses that for the outcome, one must rely on the mercy of God. Thus, the future outcome lies in God's hands and can only be indirectly influenced by a person's closeness to God. Therefore, if a result cannot be achieved, it may not be attributed to individual actions, but rather to God's will. Foreigners who work in Saudi Arabia need to understand and positively accept the *Barakah* concept, as it would not be acceptable to directly or indirectly criticize this approach, since it would be perceived as a criticism of Islam itself.

In terms of leadership, there is quite a top-down mentality: a manager in Saudi Arabia is always right. Any form of criticism—direct or indirect—is viewed by both managers and employees as unacceptable. Even simple feedback can easily be understood as criticism, which is why employees are afraid of potential retaliation. Therefore, such an environment results in a "highly flexible approach" of subordinates toward any data, factual information, or agreements to avoid potential repercussions. At times, typically Swiss expectations are not met, which may be experienced as disturbing in the beginning; but, as Anton Tremp pointed out, it is important to understand the local "socially accepted level of dishonesty" and to adjust one's expectations while at the same time driving softly toward the necessary improvements, which are needed to manage one's business—and this is the only way to achieve sustainable improvements.

In Switzerland, efficiency is very highly valued. However, in Arab cultures, personal relationships are equally important. Building a tangible business relationship with a local partner typically requires several personal meetings to foster it before it can serve as a foundation on which to build a business. Anton Tremp mentions some of the success factors when dealing with the cultural challenges typically faced in Saudi Arabia. First and foremost, one needs to be non-judgmental in their approach, as well as flexible and fault-tolerant to start with. There is a lot that will not work in the beginning, and in such situations, the potential approaches for improvement need to be phrased free of criticism toward the local partner in the initial phase in order to avoid them losing face—not necessarily from a Swiss perspective but, more importantly, from a local perspective.

Anton Tremp also explained that for the ramp-up of the production facility, a Quality Management System according to ABB's global standards had to be built up, and, in this context, a Continuous Improvement Process (CIP) was of crucial importance. Bringing this to life in a culture where everyone was afraid of giving any feedback on how something could be improved proved to be a challenge. Therefore, as a first step, a feedback system was introduced where the local management team had to learn to openly criticize Anton Tremp himself. To start with, the team was forced to express criticism via an external person so as to ensure anonymity; all these points were openly discussed in front of the management team but still in an anonymized form. As the employees noticed that giving such feedback did not have any negative consequences, they became more open and, one-by-one, started to openly express themselves. This also improved day-to-day cooperation and commitment. In a following step, weekly CIP sessions were introduced with mandatory participation of all employees across all hierarchical levels. In these CIP sessions, the different departments had to present some of the improvements they had made, and Anton Tremp presented subjects related to leadership and soft skills, as well as the macroeconomic challenges Saudi Arabia was currently facing. Also, quarterly town hall meetings were introduced, where all employees were informed about the progress of the business. Through such open dialogue and trusted relationships, it was possible to introduce a vast range of business-related changes, being supported by the employees and consequently developing the business in line with its strategic direction. It also allowed for significant changes from a societal perspective. When Anton Tremp took over his role in 2016, there were no women in the respective workforce, but when he left in 2019, two women were part of the local management team.

Fig. 5.5 Dealing with cultural differences

5.3.2 Cultural Differences Between the Arab World and Switzerland

Over 60% of the respondents affirmed that intercultural differences are still of high importance in the age of globalization (◉ Fig. 5.5). That may come as a surprise, especially since the language of communication in upper management is English, Arab managers learn Western content at universities, and international streaming services such as Netflix are also present in Arab countries. Of those questioned, 91% stated that Western managers should receive training on cultural characteristics in the Arab world. From this, it can be concluded that intercultural differences are still of great importance in a globalized, English-speaking business world. As we will see below, the common models for culture analysis are not necessarily suitable for analyzing Arab culture.

Dutch researcher Geert Hofstede (1928–2020) was head of the Personnel Research Department at IBM Europe and began interviewing employees about their job satisfaction in the late 1960s. He noticed that employees from similar cultures gave similar answers. He weighted the statements with points (scores) and classified them into four cultural dimensions: power distance, individualism/collectivism, masculinity/femininity, and avoidance of uncertainty (Hofstede 1981). Further dimensions were added later. If two countries have a relatively similar point value in one dimension, the model suggests that people from these two countries share certain values and behavioral patterns. Hofstede's was the mostly used and applied model in studying national cultures in almost all countries of the world (Abuyassin et al. 2020). Here, the Arabs are characterized primarily by a long power distance/high hierarchy, collectiveness, and masculinity (Najm & Najm, 2015). Overall, it can be stated that Arabs follow traditional values that may be seen as conservative from a Western perspective (Khakhar and Rammal 2013). Hofstede's qualitative description of the results is helpful for identifying stark differences; however, it offers few approaches to understanding the motivation behind the action and to classify the event. International models do not tell the whole story, and they are insufficient to explain many of the decisions made by Arab managers (Najm & Najm, 2015). Dimensions that are of outstanding importance for the Arab culture, such as religion and family relationships, are often neglected, distorted, or misunderstood in the individual categories.

Nevertheless, various models have shown that similarities can be found across national borders. Halim Barakāt (1993) has identified the following characteristics, which are shared by all Arab population groups and were also confirmed in our survey: the role of the family, class structure, religious and political behavior, standards of social morality, the presence of change, and the impact of economic development on people's lives. Some of these topics will now be examined in detail.

Arab cultures have some peculiarities which people who have been socialized in the West may find difficult to deal with. Describing and comparing cultures neutrally is difficult and usually fails because of the difficult translation of terms and concepts and their perception.[2] What counts as corruption in Switzerland does not have to be understood as being corruption in Arab countries.[3]

▶ To summarize, we can derive rule 6:

Rule 6: Don't take cultural idiosyncrasies personally. The motives for action in the Arab world differ from those in Switzerland, which is why the result can trigger false feelings. A different approach to the truth does not have to be a lie or malice but sometimes happens out of courtesy or protection, which, depending on the situation, is valued higher than honesty. Anyone who judges Arab culture according to the Swiss understanding of values will take some things too personally and may fail.

5.3.2.1 Method of Classification: Arab Proverbs as Proxies

For a better understanding of the survey results, we have tried to classify the phenomena and perceived differences from the Arab point of view. To do this, we used a tool that can explain the cultural differences from society itself: proverbs are brief, memorable, and intuitively convincing formulations of socially sanctioned advice (Hernadi and Steen 1999). They are very common in the Arab world; they get to the heart of cultural peculiarities that cannot be described or measured with objective aids. We have limited ourselves to Egyptian proverbs (Abdel-Massih 1979), but these are also used in the same or a similar form in other Arab countries.

We have worked out four main challenges which are important in everyday Arab life and were discussed in our survey and interviews: (1) Personal relationships, (2) Understanding of time, (3) Dealing with criticism, and (4) Commitment to keeping promises. Arabic proverbs are presented as an introduction to each challenge.

[2]The German term for dignity (Würde), for example, can only be equated with the Arabic word *karāmah* in some respects. For Muslims, blasphemy (*kufr*) is the ultimate loss of dignity (Schroeder and Bani-Sadr 2017).

[3]A common indicator of corruption is the Corruption Perceptions Index (CPI) by Transparency International. The index ranks 180 countries and territories by their perceived levels of public sector corruption according to experts and businesspeople. Thus, the index represents perceived corruption. It is not an objectively comparable measure of the acts of corruption actually taking place. Assumed corruption, however, is also influenced by the "integrity of the media" (Philp 2006), i.e. by how transparently corruption can be reported. An objective comparison is therefore problematic. At the time of writing, the United Arab Emirates performed very well in the corruption index: 21st place—two places ahead of the USA. Switzerland ranked fourth.

5.3.3 Four Major Challenges and how to Handle Them

5.3.4 Challenge 1: Relationships

This topic is crucial, as the survey has shown (◉ Fig. 5.3). Building personal relationships is a key success factor for motivating the distributors in Arabic-speaking countries. It is therefore important for Swiss managers how personal relationships are understood and lived in this part of the world.

Selected Proverbs

- *xudd er-rafīq qabl eṭ-ṭarīq.*[4] Literally: Choose the companion before (you select) the route. Related: *ištiri el-jār qabl ed-dār.* Literally: Buy the neighbor before you buy the house. The partner you choose determines the outcome of a project. In the Western world, on the other hand, skills and facts are usually valued higher than character traits.
- *baṣalet el-muḥibb xarūf.* Literally: A dear one's onion is (as delicious as) lamb. It is not the food but the company that determines how much you enjoy a meal.
- *el-'adab faḍḍalūh 'alā el-'ilm.* Literally: Good manners are preferred to knowledge.

5.3.4.1 Characteristics of the Cultural Dimension: Relationship

The Concept of Wasta

Naming a person who acts as an intermediary between two people is common in Arab cultures.[5] For this purpose, one often uses a Wasta (Standard Arabic: *wāsiṭah*) in Arab countries, which could be translated as "mediator". A Wasta allows both business partners to save face, because they do not have to address problems directly. In North Africa, the words *ktaf*[6] and *ma'rifa*[7] are extensively used as synonyms to Wasta (Mohamed A. Ramady 2016), meaning reliance on someone's shoulders, acquaintance to bear the burden of solving a given problem, or satisfying a specific socioeconomic or ordinary personal desire. Some data from the World Bank indicates that the amount of people in the Middle East and North Africa expecting to use a Wasta is as high as 90% (Devarajan and Mottaghi 2014).

For Western managers, the use of a Wasta is often not visible, because the concept of a middleman to represent and maintain a good relationship (especially to the outside world) or to exercise power and influence does not have any meaning in the West.

---

[4] The transcription of Arabic is a problem when texts use data from both Standard Arabic and various dialects. The transcription used in this paper mainly follows the one adopted by Fischer and Jastrow in their "Handbuch der arabischen Dialekte" (1980). Regarding Standard Arabic, we use a simplified transcription which does not include case endings. Regarding Arabic proper names, we use the versions the authors themselves use.

[5] There is an Arabic proverb (quoted in Egyptian dialect): *xīr el-'umūr el-wasaṭ*, meaning: The best of all things is moderation (moderation is the best policy).

[6] The Standard Arabic word *katif* means shoulder.

[7] The Standard Arabic word *ma'rifa* may denote knowledge, acquaintance, or friend.

The Wasta is a cultural element in the Arab world and is based on human interactions. He/she is primarily used to create advantages for yourself, for example to solve bureaucratic problems or to get a job through relationships. The term Wasta could be described as referring to the behavior of ordinary or influencing individuals who, for their benefits or those of others, bypass normal and formal procedures, consequently disturbing moral stability and shaking fairness attitudes, acceptable customs, and democratic manners (Ramady 2016).

Studies have shown that the Wasta has an "entrepreneurial side" (Weir et al. 2019) that tends to be neglected in discussions. "Western businesses should regard it as a type of management and a way of doing business that is different" (Weir et al. 2019).

In a study of Qatari and Emirati culture, Solberg (2002) found that a Wasta (i.e. social connections and "string-pulling") can be used to reduce the level of uncertainty in business transactions. "Perhaps it has been too often simply assumed that the existence of social networks represents merely a distortion of 'free trade perfect competition' assumed in Western markets" (Weir et al. 2019).

The use of a Wasta influences critical decisions in organizations such as recruitment and promotion (Mohamed and Mohamad 2011). Despite the candidate's qualifications, the selection process would lean toward the candidate with the strongest Wasta.

The Swiss companies surveyed in our study had little or no experience with Wasta. However, this is mainly because most of them work with a local partner and deliver the goods "ex-works". As a result, the entire Arab import and export bureaucracy remains with the Arab partner—and with it the question of to what extent one involves a Wasta.

Family and Clan/Tribal Relationships

In Western countries these days, the focus is on the individual. In Arab countries, however, it is the family that has priority.[8] That means that the family always comes before work. Its importance is extremely high in Islam[9] and has thus found its way into the constitutions of many Arab countries.[10]

---

[8] A famous Arabic proverb sums up how to move from the inner to the outer circle: *'anā wa 'axī 'alā 'ibn 'ammī wa 'anā wa 'axī wa 'ibn 'ammī 'alā al-ġarīb:* I will side with my brother against my cousin, and I will side with my brother and my cousin against a stranger. Meaning: Blood is thicker than water.

[9] The honor of the father and mother is regulated in the Qur'an (sura 4:36; 17:23). The traditions and sayings of the Islamic prophet (Hadith) contain numerous episodes that underline the importance of family ties. For example, it is said that a Bedouin came to Muhammad and asked: "Tell me what will bring me near to the Garden and keep me far from the Fire." Muhammad replied, "Worship Allah and do not associate anything with Him, perform the prayer, pay zakat [a form of alms-giving], and maintain ties of kinship" (Hadith; *al-'adab al-mufrad* 49).

[10] While the Swiss constitution guarantees the right to marriage and the family (art. 14), Arab states go one step further: article 9 of the Saudi Arabian constitution states: "The family is the kernel of Saudi society" (Arzaqī et al. 2011). Article 10 of the Egyptian constitution of 2014 defines: "Family is the basis of society and is based on religion, morality, and patriotism" (Egyptian constitution 2014).

Those who do not belong to the family or the social network often receive different treatment. In Egypt, for example, people rarely stand in line but jostle instead; in road traffic, rules are ignored for one's benefit and the horn is sounded loudly, tourists are ripped off at markets—this behavior can be explained by the circumstance that people who do not belong to the family or one's social network are treated differently.

In business life between Arab and Western companies, the primacy of the Arab family has disadvantages for the Western partner, who therefore has to deal with increased uncertainty and unpredictability. An employer must be understanding if an Arab employee is late or absent because of family obligations. It is unreasonable to expect an Arab employee to give priority to the demands of a job if these conflict with family duties (Nydell 2018). Furthermore, Arabs do not fit easily into impersonal roles, such as the "business colleague" (with no private socializing offered or expected) or the "supervisor/employee" (Nydell 2018). Ultimately, personal contacts in the Arab world lead to more efficiency than following rules and regulations, as a study by Khakhar and Rammal (2013) has shown. In order to foster trust during the negotiations, the [interviewed] Arab managers in their study spent a considerable amount of time during the pre-negotiation stage to communicate information between the parties so as to create a somewhat informal atmosphere before beginning the actual negotiations. Arab managers even invited foreign negotiators to their private residences for an informal dinner before negotiations commenced. They believe that by creating a personal relationship, the parties would be able to negotiate in a cordial and trusting environment (Khakhar and Rammal 2013).

The Western Concept of Privacy does not Exist

The concept of privacy is much broader in the West than in the Arab world. "Western conceptions of privacy are linked to the notion of individualism and people's right to non-intrusion" (Belk and Sobh 2011).

The separation of one's professional and private lives is largely alien to Arab cultures. Information about close family members and friends is fundamental to Arabs. Those who travel are sometimes contacted several times a day by Arab friends to ensure their well-being—this can be irritating for people who grew up in the West. If a person wants to be left alone, Arabs usually assume that he/she is bothered by something and that they should therefore have people around them.[11]

In communication, Arabs are expected to find out how the interlocutor and his/her family are feeling, and to greet them. For Western interlocutors, it can be uncomfortable to be asked by unknown people about the status of their relationship and the number of children—and about the why of childlessness.[12] It is quite possible that the person you are talking to has photos of his/her family in his/her wallet or on his/her cell phone and shows them to you at the very first meeting.

[11] It is strange for Central Europeans that Arabs usually appear in larger groups. Conversely, however, Arabs would ask what is wrong with a person when they are traveling alone.

[12] There is a joke in English about this: "Name a sentence an Arab has never said before. Answer: "I'll mind my own business and won't ask any personal questions."

Wisdom comes with Age

The experience and wisdom of older people is seldom challenged in Arab countries. Rudeness and disrespect for them is socially unacceptable. In Arab societies, the patriarchal order is dominant; it begins with the sheikh who is the elder father of the tribe and hence represents the father in the large family. Accordingly, the manager also considers himself to be the father of the employees within the company (Abuyassin et al. 2020).

The expression of respect for older people and their value is also reflected in the language.[13] Even the best arguments can be invalidated by those of an elderly person. In Arab companies that have been run for several generations, this can lead to difficulties in the decision-making chain.

Bartering as Part of the Social Relationship

In our interviews, several interviewees confirmed that Arabs are better at negotiating than Central Europeans. Historically, trade has always been of great importance in the Arab world, even at the time when Islam had just come into being.[14]

In the Arab world, trade has not only an economic but also a social function. For Arabs, bartering is very different from what the West calls "negotiating". The numerous steps involved in bartering hold social meanings, the least of which is to learn about and get more acquainted with the other so as to build trust in terms of the product quality. Selling and buying are social acts (Louadi 2005) and cannot merely be described as abstract, technical actions.

Several personal meetings are needed before a business relationship can be negotiated (see case study ABB). At important meetings, care should be taken to ensure that experienced employees are sent who are not afraid to talk about private matters—as restraint and unemotional discussions can become obstacles. In the event of major difficulties with the partner, it is advisable to involve an intermediary (Wasta) so that the business relationship remains intact both formally and externally.

► To summarize, we can derive rule 7:

Rule 7: Trade has a social component and is not an abstract exchange of goods. Relationships need to be built and maintained. Situations and problems in Arab countries are often judged from a subjective point of view; data and facts become obsolete if the personal chemistry is not right.

[13] The Arabic verb for "big/get older" is *kabira*. From these so-called root letters, the word *kabīr* is derived, which can mean big, meaningful, powerful, or old. The root expresses the meaning of being/becoming great, of gaining importance (Wehr and Kropfitsch 2020).

[14] Khadīja bint Khuwaylid, Muhammad's first wife, was the heiress of a caravansery and a trade business, and Muhammad himself was also a trader (Brill, Vol. 4).

5.3.5 Challenge 2: Understanding of Time

Selected Proverbs

- *eṣ-ṣabr jamīl.* Literally: Patience is beautiful.[15] A bon mot that impatient Arabic learners often hear from their teachers (Drißner 2015).
- *eṣ-ṣabr miftāḥ el-faraj.* Literally: Patience is the key to a happy ending. Also in the meaning of "patience is the key to solution (of problems)" (Hanna and Greis 1972).
- *el-ḥelm sayyid el-'axlāq.* Literally: Patience is the master of all qualities. Intent: Patience is the greatest virtue.

5.3.5.1 Characteristics of the Cultural Dimension: Time

Sabr (Patience) as a Cultural-Religious Imperative

The Arab idea of patience goes deeper than the Western idea of accepting to wait patiently for something. In Arabic cultures, the word *ṣabr* describes not only patience but also tenacity,[16] even captivity. The significance of this conception [*ṣabr*] can hardly be conveyed with a single word in a Western European language (Brill Academic Publishers 2006). The Arabic word *ṣabr* is anchored as a concept in Arab culture due in part to having a deep meaning in Islam.

Al-Ghazālī (died 1111) describes in his work *'iḥyā' 'ulūm ad-dīn* (1096–1097; book II, fourth part) the term *ṣabr* as one half of faith (patience, perseverance). The other half is *šukr* (gratitude). The two halves support and complement each other, with *ṣabr* being the prerequisite for *šukr*.

One interviewee defined the Swiss mentality in three words: time, money, and work. Applied to the business world, one can say that the values of speed and efficiency—as represented by the Western world—meet patience and perseverance—as represented by the Arab world.

Patience is thus something to be endured in the Arab world, whatever the reasons. The insistence of a Western business partner on the execution of an order or inquiry can readily be rejected or rebuked with the term *ṣabr* in the sense of a polite imperative. Smaller milestones can help lead the managing director to the agreed goal. It is also advisable to set deadlines in such a way that a certain amount of contingency is already planned for.

---

[15] The proverb *aṣ-ṣabr jamīl* can also be found as part of a Qur'anic verse: "So be patient, [Prophet], as befits you" (sura: 70:5). According to tradition, the Islamic prophet Muhammad himself said: "None is ever given anything better and more far-reaching than patience" (Sunan an-Nasa'i 2588). The following sentence is ascribed to the second Islamic caliph, 'Umar ibn al-Khattab: "The most excellent kind of patience is the compulsion to be patient" (*'afḍal aṣ-ṣabr at-ṭasabbur*).

[16] In earlier times, the month of fasting was called *šahr aṣ-ṣabr* (literally: "month of patience"). Fasting was called *ṣabr* because it means self-restraint from food and beverage as well as sexual intercourse (Lane 1984).

▶ To summarize, we can derive rule 8:

Rule 8: Patience is a highly valued quality. Appearing on time, meeting deadlines—what is a cultural imperative for the Swiss can, with appropriate justification, be interpreted in a flexible manner in Arab cultures. Goals should be formulated in small, verifiable stages.

5.3.6 Challenge 3: Dealing with Criticism

Selected Proverbs

- *kutr el-ʿitāb yefarriq el-'aḥbāb.* Literally: Too much scolding separates loved ones. Meaning: It is wise not to over-blame others.
- *lā teḏumm walā teškur 'illā baʿda sana wesittat šuhur.* Literally: Do not censure or praise (others) except after a year and six months. Meaning: You cannot judge someone without knowing them for a long time.
- *kul illi yiʿjibak, w'ilbis illi yiʿjib an-nās.* Literally: Eat what pleases you; wear what pleases the people. Meaning: Everyone can do what they want privately; publicly one has to observe the norms—one of which is that it is frowned upon to publicly embarrass or criticize someone.

5.3.6.1 Characteristics of the Cultural Dimension: Criticism

Objective analysis suggests that Arabs exhibit both shame and guilt-oriented behavior. "What will people say?" is one of the main reasons why Arabs fear nonconformity (Bitsani 2006).

Showing Feelings

Arab culture is variably characterized as a culture of the heart, the spirit, or the faith. In contrast, Western culture is designated as being one of matter, mind, and reason. In Arab culture, however, the argument is stronger when repeated (which is a popular and valued rhetorical stylistic device) or voiced more loudly.[17] This is especially true for Egypt and parts of the Levant, but less so for the Arabian Peninsula and Bedouin culture.

Equal Law is Relative

"The Swiss claim that the world is fair," said one of our interlocutors (Eric Sulzer) in the interviews after the survey, "and if the world is not fair, then you protest." In most Western

[17] During live interviews on the news channel Al Arabiya Al Hadath, for example, interviewees sometimes get so loud that the viewer has to turn down the volume. This could indicate anger or even aggression but is usually nothing more than a rhetorical device used to add drama to the speech. This is underlined by the interviewers rarely responding to it themselves and continuing the interview normally. In everyday life, it can also happen that men pound the table.

societies, citizens assume that everyone is equal before the law and has to obey the rules. One tries to look at problems and differences objectively and to solve them. In the Arab world, people reserve the right to judge things subjectively.

Arab business people and government officials are quite ready to reconsider a decision if the personal situation of the applicant or business partner has changed. When an application is rejected by the bureaucracy, it is not uncommon to assume that this decision can be reversed if face-to-face contact is established at the highest level. A Wasta is often used for this in Arab countries (see above).

Nevertheless, the Swiss business partner should not refrain from addressing problems. At the beginning of a business relationship, criticism should be formulated in such a way that the error does not lie with the local Arab partner (see case study ABB). If possible, criticism should be formulated in a personal conversation in which the person to be criticized is not named as the cause of the problem but is involved—so they can help solve the problem.

▶ To summarize, we can derive rule 9:

Rule 9: Criticism should be voiced in such a way that the contact persons in the Arab country do not feel personally addressed and can save face. Therefore, criticism should not be communicated in public but, if possible, in a personal conversation.

5.3.7 Challenge 4: Commitment to Keeping Promises

Selected Proverbs

- *bukra fī el-mišmiš*. Literally: Tomorrow, when the apricots bloom. In the sense of: the apricot season, which is either over or a long way ahead of us (Hinds and Badawi 1986). In a figurative sense: at no point in time, never. As a proverb: when pigs fly.
- *ijrī jary el-wuḥūš ġīr rizqak matḥūš*. Literally: Run as hard as wild beasts, but you will not get more or less than what has been predestined for you. Meaning: One cannot exceed one's preordained reward, no matter how hard one tries.
- *el-bāb illi yijī lak minnuh er-rīḥ siddu wistarīḥ*. Literally: The door which brings in the wind, close it and relax. Meaning: Stay away from problems.

5.3.7.1 Characteristics of the Cultural Dimension: Commitment

Unspecific and Approximate

When Arabs say "yes", this does not necessarily mean that they know whether the cause in question can be fulfilled. Arab cultures are characterized by always giving positive answers.[18] However, this is usually nothing more than a polite answer that can be interpreted as general willingness. Often less-binding answers are chosen instead, for example "'*in shā' 'Allāh*" (God willing), to indirectly express concerns or inability. Depending on the situation, gestures and intonation could mean: yes, no, let's see, I hope, I probably won't, or I don't know yet. The prospect of a concrete result is usually not connected to this.

The situation is even stricter in cases of requests for help from family, friends, and trustworthy business partners. These should not be publicly rejected in Arab cultures, even if they are illusory or violate applicable law. One may be moving in a direction that comes close to the concept of a lie in Central European culture, but that would by no means be seen so by Arabs. For them, it is a way of expressing their courtesy.[19]

It is important for Arabs to save face. That is why it is also customary for the person seeking help not to ask about the reasons why it did not work, so as not to expose the person offering help if he/she fails.

However, misunderstandings also arise because cultural customs are not adhered to—and you may give up too quickly, break off, or offend the other person.[20]

---

[18] Tourists who ask for directions in Egypt usually get a positive answer, are explained the way, or are even taken by the hand and guided a bit. You frequently end up somewhere completely different and realize that the person actually did not know the way. From a Central European point of view, one would prefer a clear "No, I don't know"—but for Arabs, it is good manners to give help when asked for it, and to give a positive answer. The Arab helper has the feeling that he has helped—and not that he has deliberately misled someone.

[19] It takes much proper instinct to master such situations. Instead of rejecting a request immediately, you should listen carefully and express your concerns, but ultimately agree that you will try to help or get the matter done. Later, one should express one's regret and, if possible, offer an alternative. From a Central European point of view, this is inefficient and may give the other party false hopes. This is why great disappointments sometimes arise when an Arab promises help to a Central European.

[20] Sāmān Abdul Majīd, who describes himself as the personal translator of the former Iraqi dictator Saddam Hussein, gives an example of how Arab and Western cultures can misunderstand negotiating gestures and lines. In his book "Sanawāt Saddam" ("The Saddam Years", Sāmān Abdul Majīd 2007), he describes the scene when in 1993, the then US President Bill Clinton sent a friend to Baghdad on a secret mission to indicate to the dictator that he is ready for a fresh start and open to talks. Saddam Hussein was not impressed by this and gave no indications for his part but rather tiraded about the great importance of Iraq and its immortal civilization. Clinton interpreted this as a rejection and left the matter alone. Sāmān Abdul Majīd raises the question of why Saddam reacted in this way and suspects that he was afraid of "selling" himself to the Americans. Persistent bartering was a matter of honor for him. On the other hand, he was unaware that his reaction was a powerful and almost humiliating gesture after a US president had sent a personal friend.

While Saddam awaited new and concrete American signals to negotiate, Clinton saw the matter as settled. Saddam, on the other hand, was surprised that Clinton no longer sent a new envoy. In Clinton's opinion, nothing more was to be expected from the Iraqi president.

It is also part of the Arab custom that you do not accept or reject things too quickly that are offered to you.[21]

Commitment and motivation to meet goals is best achieved through a good personal relationship between the Swiss sales manager and the employees of the distributor. The aim is to ensure that they enjoy working for the sales manager and that both parties are happy to work together on a sales project.

Divine Predestination

Since divine predestination has such an important meaning in some Arab countries, especially on the Arabian Peninsula, additional proverbs are listed here.

Selected Proverbs

- *illi inkatab ʻalā el-jabīn lāzim tišūfu el-ʻayn*. Literally: Whatever is written on one's forehead (i.e. one's destiny), one's eye must see it. Meaning: One will inevitably meet one's destiny.
- *el-matʻūs matʻūs walaw ʻallaqū ʻalā ra'suh fanūs*. Literally: The unlucky person remains unlucky even if they hang a lantern above his head.
- *el-ḥaḏar māyimnaʻš min qadar*. Literally: Being cautious does not stop what fate has in store for you. Meaning: Precaution does not change your destiny.

The specific rules of Islam that regulate the everyday life of Muslims are not a major hurdle for Western companies. Less than half of the ones we surveyed see religious rules as an obstacle. One hurdle, however, is the widespread acceptance of fatalism, especially on the Arabian Peninsula, and the associated Islamic belief that God's will is ultimately laid down. In everyday parlance, the word *maktūb* (literally: "written") is used for it. This belief influences the thinking, behavior, responsibility, and motivation of Arabs (see case study ABB). In Arab countries, a failure—regardless of whether it is a personal fault or not—can ultimately be excused with God's will, and thus fate.

Hoorn and Maseland (2013) have shown that there is a connection between Protestantism and work ethic and have shown that people from Protestant societies feel more personally injured when they become unemployed than people from other societies.

In Arab societies, however, unemployment could ultimately be justified with God's will.

[21] Tourists know this situation: you want to pay a taxi driver in Cairo, ask about the price, and the driver says he doesn't want any money. If you were to say thank you now and just get out, the driver's mood would change quickly. It is a tradition in Egypt that the seller refuses the money three times for the service and the buyer insists three times on paying.

▶ To summarize, we can derive rule 10:

Rule 10: In Arab cultures, commitments do not have the same quality and probability of execution as in Switzerland. Inquiries and reassurances via third parties are important.

5.4 Summary: Ten Golden Rules for Working with Distributors in Arabic-Speaking Countries

The ten golden rules for working with distributors in Arabic-speaking countries are summarized here as they have been developed in the course of this chapter:

- A good distributor is the most important success factor for the export business. It is important to take the time to choose a well-suited distributor. Be careful when granting exclusivity! Important decision criteria are the competent management and professionalism of the distributor's employees as well as their good relationship with potential customers and the existence of the necessary legal permits.
- Personal relationships are central to motivating distributors. The supervisor/sales manager in Switzerland is responsible for this and should hold this responsibility for several years so as to be able to build long-term personal relationships. On the distributor's part, the right contact person must be identified and motivated. It is not the distributor's CEO who sells the products! Frustration tolerance, seniority, and training in dealing with cultural differences are important for a sales manager.
- The training of the distributor's employees must be prioritized and carried out repeatedly, both in the target country and Switzerland. Digital information in the form of texts or videos on the internet or intranet is no appropriate substitute. Training is important in the areas of product knowledge and the sales process.
- The internal processes in Switzerland should be aligned in such a way that the distributor is treated like a customer in terms of quality and adherence to deadlines. Exporters are free to make demands—but they also have to deliver. Distributors should be treated like customers with regard to delivery deadlines and the time taken to answer questions and requests.
- Exporters need to have a long-term perspective—success takes time. You have to provide enough capacity (time of the sales manager, training, travel expenses, etc.) to support the distributor. The real work begins after signing a new distribution agreement. Closely following up on the agreed commitments is a must. The sales managers should be trained in dealing with cultural differences—ideally, they already have such experiences. They should be able to recognize the differences between Swiss customs and the conditions in the exporting country and be able to bear them. Above all, they should be able to build long-term personal relationships with the distributor's employees.

- Don't take cultural idiosyncrasies personally. The motives for action differ in the Arab world from those in Switzerland, which is why the result can trigger false feelings. A different approach to the truth does not have to be a lie or malice but sometimes happens out of courtesy or protection, which, depending on the situation, is valued higher than honesty. Anyone who judges Arab culture according to the Western understanding of values will take some things too personally and may fail.
- Intercultural dimension "Relationships": trade has a social component and is not an abstract exchange of goods. Relationships need to be built and maintained. Situations and problems in Arab countries are often judged from a subjective point of view; data and facts do not matter if the personal chemistry is not right.
- Intercultural dimension "Time": patience is a highly valued quality. Appearing on time, meeting deadlines—what is a cultural imperative for the Swiss can, with appropriate justification, be interpreted in a flexible manner in Arab culture. Goals should be formulated in small, verifiable stages.
- Intercultural dimension "Criticism": criticism should be voiced in such a way that the contact persons in the Arab country do not feel personally addressed and can thus save face. Therefore, criticism should not be communicated in public but, if possible, in a personal conversation.
- Intercultural dimension "Commitment": in Arab cultures, commitments do not have the same quality and probability of execution as in Switzerland. Inquiries and reassurances via third parties are important.

References

Abdcl-Massih, E. T. (1979). Proverbs and metaphoric expressions. Center for Near Eastern and North African Studies, Univ. of Michigan.

Abuyassin, N., Yousif, A., Najim, N., & Alhmeidiyeen, M. (2020). The Role of National Culture in Change Management in Jordanian Firms. International Journal of Productivity and Quality Management, 31(2), 244 – 270. https://doi.org/10.1504/IJPQM.2020.110044

Alliance Experts (2020). How to start with export to the Emirates and find the right distributor?. Retrieved from https://www.allianceexperts.com/en/ten/uae-distributor-agent/

Ammann, P., Lehmann, R., van den Bergh, S., & Hauser, Ch. (2012). Going International – Konzepte und Methoden zur Erschliessung ausländischer Märkte. Zürich: Versus.

Anderson, R. E., Alex, H., Cohen, Paul F., Christ, R. M., & Dubinsky, A. J. (2020). Provenance, evolution, and transition of personal selling and sales management to strategic marketing channel management. Journal of Marketing Channels, 26(1), 28–42. https://doi.org/10.1080/1046669X.2019.1647913

Arzaqī, Jarbā', M. ibn A. al-A., & Ibn Saʿīd, I. ibn S. (2011). al-Qanūn al-dustūrī al-saūdī : dirāsah qānūniyah taṭbīqiyah. Maktabat al-qanūn wa al-iqtiṣād.

Barakāt, H. (1993). The Arab world: Society, culture, and state. Berkeley: University of California Press.

Batra G., Cheng, S., Liverman, B., & Santhanam, N. (2016). "Creating mutually beneficial partnerships with distributors". Retrieved from https://www.mckinsey.com/industries/semiconductors/our-insights/creating-mutually-beneficial-partnerships-with-distributors#

Belk, R., & Sobh, R. (2011). Gender and privacy in Arab Gulf states: Implications for consumption and marketing. In Ö. Sandıkçı & G. Rice (Eds.), Handbook of Islamic Marketing, 73–96. Cheltenham: Elgar.

Bellin, H. (2017). A Useful Toolbox for Marketing Channel Managers. Journal of Marketing Channels, 24(3–4), 204–207, https://doi.org/10.1080/1046669X.2017.1393238

Bellin, H. (2015). Picking the Right Channel to Reach Your Market. Journal of Marketing Channels, 22(3), 231–234. https://doi.org/10.1080/1046669X.2015.1071593

Belz, C., & Reinhold, M. (2001). Internationales Vertriebsmanagement für Industriegüter. St. Gallen: Thexis.

Bitsani, E. P. (2006). "Facets of Arab Culture. Implications for Business". Retrieved from https://www.academia.edu/18967603/Facets_of_Arab_Culture_Implications_for_Business

Chang, Y.-Sh., & Fang, Sh.-R. (2015). Enhancing Export Performance for Business Markets: Effects of Interorganizational Relationships on Export Market Orientation (EMO). Journal of Business-to-Business Marketing, 22(3), 211–228. https://doi.org/10.1080/1051712X.2015.1081014

Deutsche Industrie- und Handelskammer (DIHK) (2010). Going International. Erfahrungen und Perspektiven der deutschen Wirtschaft im Auslandsgeschäft. Ergebnisse der IHK-Befragung 2010. Berlin.

Devarajan, S., & Mottaghi, L. (2014). MENA Quarterly Economic Brief, July 2014: Predictions, Perceptions and Economic Reality – Challenges of the seven Middle East and North Africa Countries described in 14 Charts. Washington, DC: The World Bank.

Drißner, G. (2015). Arabic for Nerds 1: Fill the Gaps – 270 Questions about Arabic Grammar. Berlin: pochemuchka books.

Handelskammerjournal (2019, September 27). "Exklusivitätsklauseln – Zwischen zulässigem Schutz und kartellrechtlichen Schranken". Retrieved from https://www.handelskammerjournal.ch/de/exklusivitaetsklauseln-zwischen-zulaessigem-schutz-und-kartellrechtlichen-schranken

Hanna, S. A., & Greis, N. (1972). Beginning Arabic: A Linguistic Approach: from Cultivated Cairene to Formal Arabic. Leiden: Brill.

Hernadi, P., & Steen, F. (1999). The tropical landscape of proverbia: A crossdisciplinary travelogue. Style, 33, 1–20.

Hinds, M., & Badawi, E.-S. M. (1986). A dictionary of Egyptian Arabic: Arabic-English. Beirut: Librairie du Liban.

Hofstede, G. (1981). Culture's Consequences: International Differences in Work-Related Values (Expanded Edition). Newbury Park, CA: Sage Publ.

Hoorn, A., & Maseland, R. (2013). Does a Protestant work ethic exist? Evidence from the well-being effect of unemployment. Journal of Economic Behavior & Organization, 91,1–12.

Jung U., Scholz S., Hoffmann, Ch., & Sinemus, A. (2013). "The Growing Opportunity for Chemical Distributors: Reducing Complexity for Producers Through Tailored Service Offerings". Boston Consulting Group. Retrieved from https://www.bcg.com/publications/2013/process-industries-supply-chain-management-growing-opportunity-chemical-distributors

Khakhar, P., & Rammal, H. G. (2013). Culture and business networks: International business negotiations with Arab managers. International Business Review, 22(3), 578–590. https://doi.org/10.1016/j.ibusrev.2012.08.002

Lane, P. J., & Lubatkin, M. (1998). Relative absorptive capacity and interorganizational learning. Strategic Management Journal, 19(5), 461–477. doi:https://doi.org/10.1002/(SICI)1097-0266(199805)19:5<461::AID-SMJ953>3.3.CO

Lane, E. W. (1984). Arabic-English Lexicon. Cambridge: The Islamic texts Society.

Lin, J.-Sh. Ch., & Chen, Ch.-R. (2008). „Determinants of Manufacturers' Selection of Distributors". Supply Chain Management, 13(5), 356–365. https://doi.org/10.1108/13598540810894942

Louadi, M. (2005). The Arab world, culture and information technology. In St. Marshall, W. Taylor, X. Yu (Eds.), Encyclopedia of Developing Regional Communities with Information and Communication Technology (pp. 21–27). Hershey, PA: IGI Global.

Mehta, Polsa, P., Mazur, J., Xiucheng, F., & Dubinsky, A. J. (2006). Strategic alliances in international distribution channels. Journal of Business Research, 59(10), 1094–1104. https://doi.org/10.1016/j.jbusres.2006.07.003

Metha, R., Anderson, R. E., Dubinsky, A. J., Polsa, P., & Mazur, J. (2010). Managing International Distribution Channel Partners: A Cross-Cultural Approach. Journal of Marketing Channels, 17(2), 89–117. https://doi.org/10.1080/10466691003635051

Mohamed, A., & Mohamad, M. S. (2011). The effect of Wasta on perceived competence and morality in Egypt. Cross Cultural Management: An International Journal, 18(4), 412–425.

Najm A., Najm. (2015). Arab Culture Dimensions in the International and Arab Models. American Journal of Business, Economics and Management, 3(6), 423–431.

Nydell, M. K. (2018). Understanding Arabs, 6th Edition: A Contemporary Guide to Arab Society (6th Edition). Intercultural Press.

OSEC. (2006). Marktanalyse 2006. Zürich:OSEC 2006.

Philp, M. (2006). Corruption definition and measurement. In C. Sampford, A. Shacklock, C. Connors, F. Gatlung, Measuring corruption, pp.45–79. London: Ashgate.

Ramady, M. A. (Ed.) (2016). The Political Economy of Wasta: Use and Abuse of Social Capital Networking. Cham: Springer International Publishing.

Schmitz, Ch. (2007). Internationales Vertriebsmanagement für Industriegüter: Handlungsimplikationen aus dem Blickwinkel internationaler Tochtergesellschaften und Vertretungen. Wiesbaden: Gabler Edition Wissenschaft.

Schögel, M. (2012). Distributionsmanagement: Das Management der Absatzkanäle. München: Vahlen.

Schroeder, D., & Bani-Sadr, A.-H. (2017). Dignity in the Middle East. In D. Schroeder & A. Bani-Sadr (Eds.), Dignity in the 21st Century: Middle East and West (pp. 65–88). Cham: Springer International Publishing.

Sliwinski R., Sliwinska, M. (2016). Growth and internationalization of fast-growing firms. Journal of East European Management Studies, 21(2), 231–253. Retrieved from http://www.jstor.org/stable/44112764

Solberg, C. A. (2002). Culture and industrial buyer behavior: The Arab experience. Proceedings of the 18th IMP Conference de l'IMP, Dijon.

Walti, C. (2000). Vertriebsmanagement für Industriegüter, dargestellt am Beispiel der Schweizer Werkzeugmaschinenindustrie (Doctoral Dissertation, University of St. Gallen).

Wehr, H., & Kropfitsch, L. (2020). Arabisches Wörterbuch für die Schriftsprache der Gegenwart: Arabisch – Deutsch (6th edition). Wiesbaden: Harrassowitz.

Weir, D., Sultan, N., & Bunt, S. (2019) Doing Business in the Arab World: Unlocking the Potential of Wasta. In: N. Faghih (Ed.), Globalization and Development. Contributions to Management Science. Cham: Springer. https://doi.org/10.1007/978-3-030-11766-5_12

Welsh, D., & Raven, P. (2006). Family business in the Middle East: An exploratory study of retail management in Kuwait and Lebanon. Family Business Review, 19(1), 29–48. https://doi.org/10.1111/j.1741-6248.2006.00058.x

Wesley J. Johnston, Shadab Khalil, Megha Jain, Julian Ming-Sung Cheng (2012) Determinants of joint action in international channels of distribution: The moderating role of psychic distance. Journal of International Marketing, 20(3), 34-49. https://doi.org/10.1509/jim.11.0178

Yli-Renko, H., Autio, E., & Sapienza, H. J. (2001). Social capital, knowledge acquisitions, and knowledge exploitation in young technology-based firms. Strategic Management Journal, 22(6/7), 587–613. https://doi.org/10.1002/smj.183

Zemanek, J., & Frankel, R. Jr. (2001). Does the Manufacturer's Salesperson Have Power Over the Industrial Distributor? Journal of Business-to-Business Marketing, 8(4), 29–53. https://doi.org/10.1300/J033v08n04_03

6 The Curious Case of Leadership in International Branch Campuses in Higher Education

Justin Williams and Mary Gene Saudelli

6.1 Introduction

International leadership is a topic that has garnered significant interest and corresponding research efforts due to globalization of industries in both the private and public sectors. Hence, the need for adept international leadership knowledge and competencies has become increasingly important for governments, institutions, and corporations (Gelfand et al. 2007). Scholars such as Elenkov et al. (2005), Saudelli (2015), as well as Farrar and Saudelli (2022a) assert that international leadership requires different skill sets for different cultural contexts. Bhaskar-Shrinivas et al. (2005) state that cultural familiarity can influence leadership potential, too.

Many higher education institutions today publicly promote internationalization through various policies, mission statements, values, and institutional learning outcomes. While international leadership is recognized to be a subset of leadership as a broad topic, the same applies to higher education international leadership. It is logical then to recognize that international leadership in higher education is an area of study within the context of international leadership, as higher education expands its global reach. While higher

J. Williams (✉)
Dean, Faculty of Commerce and Business Administration BC, Douglas College, New Westminster, Canada
e-mail: williamsj19@douglascollege.ca

M. G. Saudelli
Faculty of Education, Community & Human Development, University of the Fraser Valley, Abbotsford, BC, Canada
e-mail: mary.saudelli@ufv.ca

I. Stolz, S. Oldenziel Scherrer (eds.), *International Leadership*, uniscope. Publikationen der SGO Stiftung, https://doi.org/10.1007/978-3-658-37306-1_6

education leadership is recognized as being complex, demanding, and unique, it also offers valuable insights into the field of international leadership and may yield transferable lessons learned for any transnational organization. Specifically, Saudelli (2015) argues that there is much to learn from higher education and higher education leadership in international contexts. Hartley (2018) further argues that significant contributions to the study of leadership behavior have emerged from that of public sector leadership. Thus, the authors of this paper assert that an inquiry into international higher education leadership provides insight into internationalization that can benefit other leadership areas.

The development of International Branch Campuses (IBCs) is one example of higher education internationalization efforts (Critchley and Saudelli 2015). A number of definitions exist for an IBC, and they are not always agreed upon by scholars and practitioners (Borgos 2016). However, the Observatory of Borderless Higher Education (OBHE) notes that IBCs have three key features: (1) a physical presence in the country, (2) offering a degree in the foreign country, and (3) the degree program being accredited (Borgos 2016). This description is problematic for non-degree granting institutions such as the Canadian College of the North Atlantic in Qatar in addition to other IBCs. For the purposes of this paper, an international branch campus will be defined as

> an educational facility-owned [one], at least in part, by a foreign institution which operates under the name of the foreign institution, where students receive face-to-face instruction to achieve a qualification bearing the name of the foreign institution. (Wilkins and Huisman 2012, p. 123)

There is a body of literature that speaks to internationalizing higher education in terms of internationalizing the curriculum (e.g. Lane 2011; Saudelli 2015; Waterval et al. 2017), but only little scholarship is available that documents leadership in IBCs, particularly since entities balance what may be very different conceptions of leadership, such as North American institutions in the Middle East. In addition, there is little scholarship that speaks to the possibilities and tensions leadership in IBCs must address, as they mediate between culture, geographic borders, and two or more leadership paradigms (e.g. conceptions of leadership in the Middle East and those in Canada). It could be argued that the IBC experience represents the penultimate higher education international experience as it touches on nearly every facet of leadership in education: power, finance, governance, program delivery, curriculum and delivery, transnational recruitment, student and faculty experience, university and college leadership, and so forth. International higher education leaders walk a fine line in their leadership competencies because they must navigate the complexities of what may appear to be dichotomous structures, interests, and practices. For this reason, research inquiring into the experiences of international higher education leaders is crucial in today's interconnected and mobilized world. This is also a reason why reflective forms of practice-based research in international higher education leadership is crucial and the valuable knowledge learned extends to international leadership in other industry areas. We need to investigate the essential elements of learning from those with lived experiences as international leaders.Both authors of this study have lived, taught, and led in international higher education for many years. They also have engaged in leadership positions in IBCs. They both articulate and envision internationalization in higher education as being important and valuable educational agendas, as well as articulating a vision of international leadership across private and public sectors. Both specifically assert that they have personally and professionally been inspired by their international experiences and value the potential of internationalizing. They assert a need for higher education to foster global civic-mindedness (Saudelli 2015), a growth mindset (Mrazek et al. 2018), and both of them believe that internationalizing through various means can provide educational spaces for these to develop. Both authors assert that their lived international leadership experiences have contributed to their respective institutions capacities with global partnerships, industry relations, and leadership discussions across a broad spectrum of contexts.

The authors also believe that IBCs offer space for the internationalisation of higher education. However, they do believe that all of these ideals do not come without experiencing tensions, cross-cultural learning, reflecting on mistakes and successes, and a recognition of profound implications of decisions. Thus, the intent of this paper is to examine their leadership experiences in IBCs in the Middle East wherein they have encountered all of these as lived experiences. Ultimately, the aim is to contribute to understanding the complexities that can be part of leadership at IBCs and bear reflection in any international leadership context. In this study, they will make specific references to their leadership and experiences in an IBC educational environment within the lens of international leadership.

6.2 Theoretical Framework and Literature Review

Leadership has been the focus of many theoretical frameworks and studies, across disciplines and contexts for some time. However, with the advent of globalization, there has been an increased interest in how leadership theory is impacted by our increasingly interconnected world. This section will first discuss prominent leadership theories commencing with a brief overview of the evolution of leadership theories. Then the focus will shift to international leadership, followed by intercultural leadership theories and literature.

6.2.1 The Evolution of Leadership Theories

Leadership plays a significant role in how individuals in an organization interact together, and how an organization performs. Many leadership models have been developed and used to interpret and explain leadership effectiveness. Generally, research in the field of leadership began in the 1950s and can be loosely divided into two time periods: 1950 to 1980 and 1980 to the present (De Vries 2010). The former period can be characterized as research conducted around structures and roles, while the latter rather focused on the effects of leadership and the development of specific and more complex ideologies around it (Raisiene et al. 2018). These latter theoretical frameworks include transformational (Bass 1985), transactional (Bass 1985), and situational leadership (Hershey and Blanchard 1969), among others.

These theories have further evolved with the recognition that the followers in an organization, often the subject matter experts, must also contribute to management decisions. This move away from trait leadership emphasized a shift in focus from "leader" to "follower". The recognition of these followers as integral members of the team with valuable insight has led to the paradigm of collaborative leadership (Raisiene 2012). These theories can further be divided into facilitative, coaching, and servant leadership (Raisiene et al. 2018). This has been supported in the literature by the recognition that the results of a group or organization represent the shared knowledge and skills of their members but also their interactions and coordination (Normore and Erbe 2013). However, as multiculturalism and internationalization have increased, leadership theories also underwent increased scrutiny, primarily based on the recognition that culture influences leader and follower behavior (Lee et al. 2020).

6.2.2 International Leadership

Over the past several decades, there has been a significant rise in international assignments as companies and institutions have expanded their global reach. Further, the increased complexity in operating internationally where management decisions may be impacted by economic, social, and political factors, as well as numerous complexities around cultural, moral, and ethical implications, has added to the complexity (Sheppard et al. 2013). This led to the study of cross-cultural leadership and the recognition that culture plays a significant role in leadership (Albert et al. 2000). The success of these international assignments, which have been prone to failure (Daniels and Insch 1998), depends on a variety of personal and institutional factors (Caligiuri and Tarique 2016). Subsequently, there is an increasing interest as international leadership realizes the gaps in the theory and knowledge base, particularly as the efficacy of leaders in international contexts has become both more challenging and increasingly important in a more connected and competitive landscape. It is generally recognized that leadership behavior plays an important role in an organization's performance (Bhatti et al. 2012).

Subsequently,research into international leadership has gained momentum with some interesting findings and validations—specifically, that national culture plays an important role in leadership behavior and that leaders tend to demonstrate a leadership style that is reflective of that culture (Dorfman et al. 2012). Naturally, the closer a leader's behavior aligns with national cultural norms and expectations on leadership, the more effective that leader is perceived. Further, while some leadership behaviors are universally appreciated, such as competence, efficiency, and proactivity, others are much more culturally specific and subject to interpretation, such as conceptions of integrity and relationships. The introduction of national cultures into leadership research has further recognized the complex nature of international leadership and the implications of follower/leader cultural value orientations (Kirkman et al. 2009).

For example, the collaborative approach to leadership (servant/coaching leadership) that focuses on building consensus may be more aligned with certain cultures and may be at odds with perceived effectiveness in others (Dorfman et al. 2012). As Fisher puts it, "leadership is in part a social construct, positioned in time and place and influenced by personality" (Fisher 2018, p. 46). Compounding the issue of international leadership is that culture may impact the perceived ethics of leaders (Ahmad et al. 2020). Kirkman et al. (2009) argue that cultural values play a significant role in follower behavior. Further, the art of effective cross-cultural leadership then requires adaptability, self-awareness, and cultural sensitivity.

Some theories have evolved as a result of international leadership per se, although some internationalization researchers have since been studying interculturalization as a basis for investigating leadership as a result of globalization and internationalization (e.g. Preskill and Brookfield 2008; Merriam et al. 2006; Saudelli 2015; Farrar & Saudelli, 2022b; Saudelli et al. 2013). Much work has been done to establish best practices in leadership; however, this should be understood as a combination of variables (Raisiene et al. 2018). In an international context, the ability to apply different leadership skills and models may be dependent on the culture, and context is essential to lead effectively. Further, it is noted that what works effectively in one context may have varying results in an alternative cultural context (Elenkov et al. 2005; Raisiene et al. 2018).

6.2.3 Higher Education Leadership

Educational leadership is recognized to be an important contributor to organizational success (Joyce 2009). Further, leadership style plays a fundamental role in the success of both the leader and the organization (Bryman and Lilley 2009). It is recognized that higher education leadership, while borrowing and learning from broader studies on leadership in general, requires a distinct set of behaviors. The changing nature of constituents, unstable funding models, and the highly accountable nature of higher education are some of the challenges faced by higher education (Davis et al. 2015). Furthermore, it is recognized that higher education leadership operates in a unique context, where power is distributed, processes are bureaucratic and often taxing, and change requires vision, perseverance, and tenacity, as well as collegiality and community. Further, the changing educational landscape, spurred by globalization, public sector rationalization, and changing student and institutional needs have promoted leadership in higher education to shift from traditional bureaucratic transactional leadership to a more collaborative, transformational model. Due to the highly complex nature of higher education, the need to adapt leadership to a more adaptive model has been recognized (Davis et al. 2015). Based on this unique context, a number of models have been proposed as suitable for higher education. Servant and distributed leadership have been identified as having congruency with higher education leadership. There is evidence that distributive leadership is effective in higher education institutions (Jones et al. 2017), as is transformational leadership (Samad et al. 2015). Pounder (2001) has identified a transformational leadership model that includes six dimensions in higher education leadership: inspirational motivation, integrity, innovation, impression management, individual consideration, and intellectual stimulation.

Kouzes and Posner's (1993) widely used transformational leadership model is slightly consolidated. The Leadership Practices Survey includes five behaviors of leaders: inspire a shared vision, model the way, challenge the process, enable others to act, and lead from the heart (Kouzes and Posner 1993). Herbst and Conradie (2011) assess leadership perceptions in higher education in South Africa using Kouzes and Posner's (1993) transformational leadership model finding that leaders rank themselves higher in competency than their followers. Lastly, transformational leadership has led to higher job satisfaction, retention, and a better work and learning environment (Scott et al. 2008).

6.2.4 Intercultural Leadership

Some research posits that the differences in leadership style and culturally dependent behaviors play a robust role in determining the effectiveness of leaders internationally (Dorfman et al. 2012; Gelfand et al. 2007). For this reason, recognition of skills and leadership characteristics will vary across cultures and in different contexts (Raisiene et al. 2018). It is argued that best practices need to be context-specific and that generic models are not always effective (Raisiene et al. 2018; Walker and Quong 2005). The success of leaders in their home context may not be representative of that in an international environment, and certain factors may moderate or shape it (Caligiuri 2006; Kim and van Dyne 2012). Further, it is recognized that the success of an organization depends largely upon its leaders to motivate their staff, which is no less true for international organizations. For this reason, the ability of expatriate leaders to manage teams cross-culturally is essential. Intrinsic in this observation is the recognition that expatriate leaders must be capable of adjusting their leadership practices across cultures and in line with host country conditions (Tsai et al. 2019).

The intention in this work is to review leadership in action in an international IBC context through two complimentary lenses: the first is culture, where we will lean on the Hofstede (1980) model; the second lens is the transformational leadership model of Kouzes and Posner (2002). Multiple environmental factors, including institutional or corporate cultures, and country-specific factors such as culture or politics play a significant role in leadership styles and effectiveness. One of the more prevalent models for understanding culture was introduced by Hofstede in 1980, based on his work with IBM (Hofstede 1980). In this model, four characteristics of a culture are introduced: power distance, uncertainty avoidance, individualism/collectivism, and masculinity/femininity. In 1988, a fifth element, long-term orientation, was introduced by Hofstede and Bond (1988). Together, these dimensions can provide a lens in which to view experiences with cross-cultural and transnational engagements. In Hofstede and Bond's (1988) model, power distance refers to the degree to which people defer to formal authority. Formal titles and hierarchy may mean more to a particular culture, resulting in less equality and more power distance. The implications for leaders are evident, and the ability to navigate within this cultural norm would likely be a moderating factor on leadership effectiveness. Individualism/collectivism refers to the level of personal freedom versus the greater collective good. Highly individualistic cultures place more emphasis on the individual and individual rights, whereas collective cultures put more emphasis on the group, be it family or otherwise, and work to support this group. The fourth dimension, uncertainty avoidance, indicates the degree to which a culture is comfortable with uncertainty. Higher levels of uncertainty avoidance in a culture would respond to change, with a degree of anxiety and concern, whereas a culture with low uncertainty avoidance would be more welcoming and accepting of change. Lastly, long-term orientation refers to the degree to which a culture values long-term goals. Here, it may be acceptable to forgo short-term rewards for a longer-term strategy and delayed but possibly higher rewards. However, a question remains: what does recognition of these cultural dimensions mean for international and transnational leadership?

Hofstede's model has been used widely as a method to measure the managerial implications (Kirkman et al. 2006). Many of these have recognized the relationship between specific cultural dimensions and their implications for leadership practitioners (Kirkman et al. 2006; Dorfman et al. 2012). The implications emerging from the GLOBE study were significant, as it represented a departure from earlier studies in its orientation. Specifically, the study posited that "the attributes and entities that differentiate a specified culture are predictive of organizational practices and leader attributes and behaviors that are most frequently enacted and most effective in that culture" (House et al. 2004). Further research has identified the implications of transformational leadership practices in their application, with specific references to power distance (Kirkman et al. 2009). Further, many factors such organizational commitment, organizational citizenship, relationship to team behavior and receptivity to leadership styles were found to be moderated by culture. Interestingly, absenteeism and turnover were not (Kirkman et al. 2009).

Kouzes and Posner's (2002) transformational leadership model (i.e. Leadership Practices Inventory or LPI) was developed based on 20 years of research which found that leadership is a collection of behaviors and practices. When grouped together, this collection of behaviors could effectively lead to extraordinary results. Kouzes and Posner's (2002) transformational leadership model identifies five behaviors that effectively shape followership behavior. The framework is based on modeling the way, inspiring a shared vision, challenging the process, enabling others to act, and encouraging from the heart.

- By modeling the way, leaders set an example of the type of behavior that is valued in an organization. Leadership by example remains a powerful tool for them.

- By inspiring a shared vision, leaders are enabled to create a compelling story of what they want to achieve. This allows them to communicate the desired outcome of their actions and provides overall direction. The shared component is important, as it gives agency to stakeholders.
- By challenging the process, leaders may inspire their colleagues to seek new ways of doing things. By supporting innovation, they encourage their colleagues to take risks and to accept challenges for improving overall organizational performance.
- The shared vision must also foster collaboration and allow individuals to feel empowered to act. This allows teammates to live the vision and to act on it.
- By encouraging from the heart, leaders genuinely encourage team members to work toward a shared goal. Recognition of individual achievements within the broader organizational context provides an opportunity to champion individual and group behaviors while reinforcing the overarching goal.

While reviewing the literature, the leadership practices inventory was used in a number of cross-cultural or international contexts. Herbst and Conradie (2011) used the model to assess the perceived effectiveness of academic leaders in South Africa. Abu-Tineh et al. (2008) used did the same to change management practices in Jordanian schoolsThey found that there was a substantial gap in understanding the cultural implications of as well as gender-based perceptions of leadership. However, while managerial actions may be shaped by culture, leadership behavior is consistent. This is supported by Posner's (2013) work, in which he argues that while general behavior may be shaped by culture, leadership behavior looks the same across cultures. Posner argues—in reference to Hofstede's (1980) cultural dimensions—that the act of leadership may be shaped by culture; however, effective leadership actions are very similar across cultures. The authors of this article, however, are not convinced of this assertion. Leaders in a transnational context must be able to navigate between cultures and to adapt their leadership style for maximum efficacy.

Posner (2013) suggests that transformational leadership practices, which may involve the perception of a more distributed leadership, may be more effective in collective as opposed to individualistic cultures. Conversely, cultures that are characterized by having higher power distance relationships may be more forgiving to or supportive of authoritative styles of leadership. The findings emerging from our cross-cultural study suggest that leaders who employ the characteristics identified in transformational leadership view their workplaces more favorably. Furthermore, and perhaps most importantly, leaders who employed the transformational leadership behaviors were viewed more effectively by their followers.

This paper investigates two higher education administrators and educational leaders who trace their experiences in IBCs in the Middle East during a time of rapid change. Informed by the theoretical models of Kouzes and Posner (2002) as well as Hofstede's (1980) cultural dimensions, the narrative will seek to elucidate the nuances of intercultural and transnational leadership in a challenging international environment, which will provide context, dimension, and nuanced relevance to the discussion of theory and models of international higher education leadership.

The guiding research question for this study is: how do these two researchers experience leadership through their roles in IBCs, and what was the impact of their leadership values in relation to their lived experiences in the Middle East? Specifically, the self-study will utilize Kouzes and Posner's (2002) leadership model which provides a framework based on the four principles elaborated upon above: modeling the way, inspiring a shared vision, enabling others to act, and encouraging the heart.

6.3 Research Methodology

In order to address the research question, the authors used a self-study research methodology (Lassonde et al. 2009) to explore the depth of our experiences, beliefs, and values as international education leaders. Self-study is a qualitative methodology for "understanding or explaining the physical or social world" (LaBoskey 2004, p. 1173). Over the last few decades, this has become "accepted as a prestigious research methodology by academia" (Alan 2016, p. 7).

The basic premise for self-study research rests with the principle that professionals continually improve their practices through systematic research (Stenhouse 1975). This principle remains true, and perhaps it is even more important today given the nature of global interaction and engagement that characterizes life in the twenty-first-century. However, while self-study has grown, there is a lack of research using this methodology to study leadership practice, particularly in leadership in international higher education, and thus, there is a gap in the literature this study addresses. As Flinn asserts, leadership in complex contexts involving the development of capacities for "sense-making, reflexivity and practical judgement" (Flinn 2018, p. 12) is imperative. Given the socio-cultural and leadership differences, the nuances of living in a different country with different mores, values, and ways of being and knowing, it can be reasonably argued that working at IBCs in the Middle East involves leading in a complex context. It can further be argued that since Flinn (2018) calls for more reflective aspects of sense-making in relation to leadership, a self-study of these two international higher education leaders is the most appropriate methodology for the guiding research question and the particularities of this study. Findings from this study can be transferred to guiding future studies of sense-making in international leadership in practice in global contexts.

With the increased interest in practitioner research, there has been a corresponding development of inquiry approaches such as participatory action research (e.g. McNiff and Whitehead 2010), the evaluation of practice (e.g. Boyd and White 2017), portrait methodology (e.g. Farrell 2002; Bottery et al. 2009), to name just a few. The self-study methodology connects with these reflective and immersive approaches, but its focus is "on one's own practice and one's own role in it, and looking more deeply to identify motivations, beliefs, and concerns around an aspect of practice" (White and Jarvis 2019). A salient aspect of self-study research is the involvement of a critical friend (Schuk and Russell 2005). According to Schuck and Russell, a critical friend "acts as a sounding board, asks challenging questions, supports reframing of events, and joins in the professional learning experience" (Schuk and Russell 2005, p. 107). In this sense, in a self-study methodology, the critical friend supports learning from experience through dialogue and feedback (Costa and Kallick 1993), and there exists a recognition that a critical friend's role is to nurture the awareness of alternate frames of reference, to ask probing questions, to challenge assumptions, to share insights, and to support an inquiry-based, reflective mindset. In this study, the authors were critical friends for each other as they engaged in dialogues about their respective and shared experiences. The critical friend role in this research thus is an aspect of methodological rigor (LaBoskey 2004), which informs our research design.

Both authors in this chapter are Canadian educators and scholars who have lived, taught, and led extensively in international higher education. Justin has lived/worked in Iran, Qatar, and Canada. Mary has lived in Turkey, Hong Kong, the United Arab Emirates, and Qatar. They met while both were members of the senior leadership team of a Canadian institution of higher education in Qatar and discovered their common interest in leadership and international education.

6.3.1 Data Collection and Analysis

Loughran and Russell (2007) see the challenging nature of this approach, because personal assumptions, judgments, and actions are challenged by the self-study researchers themselves and their critical friends. Researchers who are participants in their own study have their beliefs and actions challenged by these critical friends (Argyris and Schön 1974). They analyze their practice through Brookfield's (2017) four lenses: self, colleagues, students, and professional literature. Self-study is both challenging and illuminating, as it investigates the extent to which the participants are living out their values and beliefs about a phenomenon. It requires both sharing of experiences and scrutinizing them through a dialogue and feedback loop for meaning-making as well as potentially new or changed values and beliefs in response to examined practice (Russell 2007).

Data collection consisted of sharing storied experiences between Justin and Mary in relation to their shared experience at an IBC in Qatar during a time of profound economic change in that country and the resulting impact on their leadership. They shared experiences and engaged in virtual meetings to discuss, question, analyze, consider, and reconsider. In essence, their study began over four years ago, after both had returned to Canada and took leadership positions in different institutions in different provinces. They formed a professional bond through their time in the Middle East, which continued over the years as they went on to collaborate and communicate. The resulting sense-making of their stories, their engagement as critical friends for each other's analysis of their stories, and thinking through their shared beliefs and values as to the importance of international higher education experiences led to writing this chapter.

It is imperative that in today's interconnected and dynamically changing environment, higher education institutions are led by a leader who is able to navigate successfully through complex uncertainties. Academic leadership is generally recognized as a challenging career choice. While the reasons why a faculty member would leave their position to pursue a role that demands longer hours, less academic freedom, and little feedback are outside the scope of this chapter, the importance of academic leadership and the impact it has in academic institutions has been widely documented, e.g. by Hoff (1999), Knight and Holen (1985), Matczynski et al. (1989), as well as Meek et al. (2010). As challenging and impactful leadership already is in a domestic academic environment, the additional complexity of an international posting offers a significant increase in the degree of risk, challenge, and change.

6.4 Findings

This section will share three complex issues that we encountered as leaders in an IBC in Qatar: possibilities and tensions of budget change, leadership in a transitory international environment, and transitory/contract faculty in IBCs during a time of economic change. These sections are written from a reflective voice of the experience and the engagement of sense-making from this experience.

6.4.1 Possibilities and Tensions of Budget Change

In the Fall of 2013, Justin was working as Director of Enrolment and Student Affairs with a Canadian university operating in the Middle East, while Mary was working as Director of Teaching and Learning at the same institution commencing on January 4, 2014. Our mandate was clear: to educate local aspiring nursing professionals using Canadian faculty, curriculum, and standards to better serve the local community. The arrangement with the national government allowed us to maintain academic autonomy, ensuring that academic standards were maintained.

Our financial arrangement was more complex. The university budget was maintained through the Qatari Ministry of Finance. Each year, we would prepare our budget with input from the Senior Leadership Team (SLT) and our CFO. This budget would then be presented in person to the Minister of Finance. At that point, a decision would be made by the Minister whether to approve or deny the budget or to make changes. It was not usually a difficult experience until December 2013, when oil prices had dropped to record lows. The nation's economic forecast had been based on an oil price of more than twice of what it was in 2013. Following the lead of other nations that had slashed public sector budgets, the sense was that we had to be prepared for the worst.

It turned out that we were correct. Our CEO, along with our CFO, was instructed to reduce our current budget by a significant percentage, and the SLT was informed of this decision on January 5, 2014. We had already prepared a lean budget, and following increases in enrollment, we were hard-pressed to determine a course of action. At our ensuing SLT meeting, rather than discussing how to reduce our budgets across the IBC, it was decided that we would approach the Minister again, demonstrating rationally why we could not operate at current budget restrictions.

Already having worked in the Middle East for over six years respectively—although at different institutions and, in Mary's case, in another country –, Justin and Mary were concerned that this approach would not work and might be perceived as culturally unacceptable. Rational persuasion with evidence is the preferred form of debate in North America, where emphasis is placed on individual expertise and evidence. Competent individuals are encouraged to contribute their knowledge and share their voice in the conversation. In the Gulf region, despite there being a heavy emphasis on negotiation, power distance plays a significant role in decision-making. However, neither Justin nor Mary voiced their apprehensions for this approach at either the SLT meeting or privately with the CEO.

After approaching the Minister to request additional funding, the IBC received a communique from the Minster's office that was not supportive. It did not contain the news we had hoped for; in fact, we saw our budget further reduced by an additional significant monetary amount. In retrospect, we believe that by challenging the Minister's original budget decision, our approach of pleading our case by using rational persuasion had been perceived as a challenge and loss of face. His response was thus normal in Middle Eastern culture. Trying to change his mind may have caused him to look incompetent among his peers and might have resulted in a loss of face. Interestingly, both Justin and Mary had adapted to Middle Eastern culture to an extent that they also conformed to this cultural element by not voicing their concerns regarding this tactic at the SLT or with the CEO privately.

6.4.2 Leadership in a Transitory International Environment

In 2015, Justin moved from a faculty role to take the position of Director, Student Services and Enrolment. It was an opportunity to take on a leadership role in a top-tier Canadian university that may have not been possible, or would have taken much longer to reach, in a Canadian environment. It was an opportunity to manage a department and to learn from the leadership team.

What became apparent early in the role was that the transitory nature of managers at the branch campus had left many challenges unresolved. Of the entire Senior Leadership Team (SLT), only one had been in the position for more than two years. There were many reasons for this, including a desire to return to home country, a challenging living and work environment, and better opportunities arising back in Canada. This constant turnover in leadership created many challenges for the organization both internally and externally. In a culture-rich environment like the Middle East, the efficacy and success of an organization heavily depends on the relationships a leadership team are able to make with stakeholders.

Internally, the leadership turnover had led to a lack of organizational memory and engagement to make meaningful change, as well as to human resource issues that were not addressed adequately. From a leadership perspective, getting on board took six months, determining the issues another six months, and then dealing with these issues another year. Some substandard employees below the level of director were able to 'survive' the new leadership and continued with a new leader every two years, despite exhibiting conduct that would not have been acceptable nor would have remained unaddressed in a Canadian campus environment. As a new director, building a team, learning the processes, fixing issues, and building external relationships were a focus. Justin was new to the director role, in a new business area keen to make a difference and to improve the department.

The department he was to lead was international, with staff from Canada, Palestine, India, Egypt, and New Zealand. One of the key members in this 12-person team was the coordinator who had been in the position since the inception of the branch campus: nearly a decade. As the longest-standing departmental member, this individual held the organizational memory of the university and, most importantly, controlled the processes around enrollment as she had created them. Unfortunately, she also felt a sense of entitlement and had created a culture that was lacking in trust, one that was fraught with favoritism and bullying.

Even more challenging, whenever any new employee had entered the team, the coordinator had often been the one to orient them. Her relational culture was thus established early, in the first few months of an individual's tenure. This created an environment that had a clear pecking order and often led to decisions that were focused on maintaining the status quo rather than making decisions for the best of the students or the university.

Often, Justin would hold meetings with the group, explaining changes that needed to be made and laying out a roadmap for change. As a consultative leader, he wanted to ensure the buy-in from the team and endeavored to engage them. During the meetings, the coordinator would shake her head, display huffing sounds or eye-roll, thus intentionally demonstrating her lack of support and, in effect, undermining Justin's leadership approach. Coaching sessions ensued, where Justin would work to correct her behavior. In the sessions, however, she would deny it or act surprised. Over time, her overtly hostile behavior became less pronounced, but her subtle withholding of information and lack of compliance continued. Subtly, it became clear that with each effort to make positive change, Justin was met with a lack of compliance by the coordinator and some of her closest allies. As he moved to a more directive style, the situation seemed to improve; but in reality, it did not. She continued to undermine any efforts to change, concealed information through omission, and Justin was left with very few options.

With any challenge comes an opportunity. As we grappled with the budget cuts, it became apparent that each department would need to undertake some cuts to meet the newly reduced budget. In Justin's department, one full-time position would need to be eliminated. From a functional perspective, losing the coordinator position would be challenging as she had developed the technical elements of the department. From a cultural perspective, her removal would ultimately lead to a healthier environment. Ultimately,

Justin determined that we could survive the short-term challenges and would benefit most from a healthier culture.

6.4.3 Transitory/Contract Faculty during Economic Change

Both authors accepted contracts as educational leaders of different departments at an IBC in the Middle East. Both were aware of their roles being contract positions, just like every other faculty and staff member, as this is the norm for higher education in the Middle East. Unions and collective bargaining are illegal in Qatar, and employee rights through legislation are minimal. While civil lawsuits have occurred, instigated by employees when they felt a contractual term had been breached, both researchers are aware of instances where there was little or no recovery even when the employees won a civil or legal judgment, regardless of whether or not the institution was an IBC or a governmental or corporate institute of learning. Most institutions in the Middle East are governed by Ministries of Higher Education, which can have significant impacts on the functioning of the institution.

Given the nature of contract employment in this IBC, the role of both authors as leading and motivating faculty and staff challenges existed to guide and support people in their roles. In effect, there is little employment security even with a contract, there is often little orientation for incoming faculty and staff (confronted with a 'sink or swim' mentality), and rarely is an institutional investment made in the employee or their roles, as expectations of change and transition for the institution are inherent. This can lead to a loss of institutional knowledge, tensions from job insecurity, a loss of morale, and difficulties with maintaining highly qualified and capable faculty and staff.

After the significant budget cuts (several over the course of 2014–2016), employment reclassifications and job terminations were inevitable. Leading through employment terminations is challenging in any context, but it is exacerbated for faculty and staff who have left their home countries, brought their children to a different country, created a life half a world away, and possibly have no home to go back to when they have their permanent residency terminated. And in the cases experienced, people were given two weeks notice in the first instance, and approximately two months notice with subsequent terminations, to completely rearrange their lives and return to their country of nationality. This adds to the burden of trying to motivate faculty and staff while at the same time addressing interpersonal conflicts during a time of low employee morale.

Morale was already tense when we started, and many faculty and staff did not understand that the decisions related to whomever kept their positions, how positions were reclassified, why hiring of new faculty and staff was ongoing at a time of employment terminations, and that communications that were addressed in a fashion some saw as disturbing. Thus, the environment was tension-filled and anxious.

In March 2014, Mary was tasked with leading and co-facilitating a session of curriculum review with the faculty. Due to the already transitory nature of working in international education, the curriculum we were charged to deliver had gone through various iterations for various reasons. However, the reasoning behind decisions (institutional knowledge) was lost due to high faculty and staff turnover that can be expected when faculty positions are fixed one- or two-year-term contracts. Key information, curricular scaffolding, and course placement throughout the program had been shifted to a degree that the leadership had determined an internal review, curricular mapping, and resequencing of courses; so a discussion in relation to culturally relevant teaching and assessment practices was warranted. Mary was assigned to facilitate this task, together with two nursing colleagues. On March 31, 2014, the day after the terminations had occurred, the first of several co-facilitated sessions was expected to take place.

Mary had concerns about engaging with this activity the day after terminations but was informed to carry out as planned—'business as usual' was the message. While she understood the message and complied with the task, she was concerned about the atmosphere in the room from the events of the preceding day, which was the date chosen to deliver termination notices. Mary raised her concerns, but she was directed to proceed 'as normal'. Her insight in this regard proved to be correct. While faculty attended and were professional, with some refusing to attend in protest and with solidarity to their colleagues who were terminated, the atmosphere in the room was quiet and constrained as opposed to a free flow of ideas and potentials typical in a facilitated and collaborative curriculum review. At one point, a colleague informed the associate dean that she needed to address the group about what had happened the day before. As so much tension was present, after the first hour, all curricular work was suspended for faculty to ask questions and express opinions in relation to the terminations, the manner in which they had been done, and what would happen next to the two present SLT members, the associate dean and Mary. Faculty were angry for many reasons: the budget cuts; the fact that the session continued despite the terminations; and what they perceived as a lack of compassion and sensitivity regarding the manner in which the terminations had occurred.

Reflecting on this time, the North American values of transparency and uncertainty avoidance were at play. The message from leadership was framed with a 'business as usual' approach, but the circumstances were not usual, and lack of recognition as well as perceived insensitivity of the impact on the people who suddenly had to uproot their lives and return to Canada was perceived as dismissive and disrespectful. Thus, faculty were angry, which is not an environment conducive for curriculum renewal discussions. In retrospect, Mary realized that she did not follow her own intuition and skills as a facilitator; she had insight into the mindsets of attendees in the aftermath of the previous day and disagreed with the leadership who championed a 'business as usual' agenda. Mary placated a decision, rather than owning her voice. She should have embraced her better judgment and considerable experience in faculty development, an important leadership lesson she learned the hard way.

6.5 Discussion: Internationalizing Leadership at IBCs

Those holding international and transnational leadership positions have complex and dynamic roles with challenges and tensions beyond what may be fully recognized by the home offices of institutions. International corporate offices of organizations, much like IBCs, are—by their very nature—cross-cultural, cross-political, and cross-geographical, which has profound implications on the operations and functions, as the international organization attempts to embody the salient contributions of both the host and the guest nations. The guiding research question for this study is how these two researchers experience leadership through their roles in IBCs and what the impact of their leadership values was in relation to their lived experiences in the Middle East. The findings reveal three areas of complexity: possibilities and tensions due to budget changes; leadership in a transitory international environment; and transitory/contract faculty in IBCs in times of economic change.

In our discussion of implications for international leadership, including that in higher education, we assert that there is a need for extensive commitment to embrace, integrate, and embody intercultural competencies, wherein the leadership is charged with balancing diverse cultural aspects of employees, but also of the cultures of the host country and the guest institution. We focus our discussion on framing this recommendation through revisiting Kouzes and Posner's leadership model (Kouzes and Posner 2002): modeling the way, inspiring a shared vision, enabling others to act, and encouraging the heart.

6.5.1 Modeling the Way

According to Brzezinska, "international leadership roles are dynamic and change over time, influenced by many factors" (2020, p. 166). Pietras further posits that the most strategic international leader is creative, balancing the "internal and the external environment" (2000, p. 59). In modeling the way, international leaders must create strategies wherein they are able to demonstrate which behavior they want their followers to exhibit. However, this concept must be anchored by cultural knowledge intricately tied to context. Based on their experiences at IBCs in the Middle East, the authors of this chapter suggest that international leadership cannot simply 'learn' cultural competencies—they require a genuine recognition of cultural differences impacting the organization, and they must lead by balancing the cultures of both the host country and the guest institution. These suggestions are in line with earlier research into international leadership (Dorfman et al. 2012). The examples experienced by the authors support the recognition that leadership effectiveness is culturally based. Exemplary leadership in one culture may not easily translate into a different cultural context (Elenkov et al. 2005; Raisiene et al. 2018). Further, a recognition of cultural nuances, specifically around leadership, requires leaders to adapt to the host culture. For example, the decision to return to the Minister of Finance to request additional funding was not in line with the host country's cultural expectations on leadership and did not demonstrate the cultural adaptation Tsai et al. (2019) suggest to be necessary for cross-cultural leadership.

This adaptation requirement is especially important in times of turbulence. Leaders must recognize that their own leadership roles may have an uncertain future or demands due to the changing nature of a specific context, and they ought to be prepared to adapt. An international leader must be able to model the way of balancing the complexities of culture and a nuanced awareness of context, including the people involved in the international entity. We agree with Armstrong's statement: "The leaders of the future will have to lead with intercultural competence and with the ability to facilitate this development of competence in others" in the development of a global mindset (Armstrong 2020, p. 1). We further agree with Gupta who asserts that "cultural competency and cultural adaptability are foundational skills vital to the success of anyone working in a cross-cultural environment, domestically or internationally [and] all leaders today must possess these skills" (2009, p. 147). But we assert that international leaders must model the way of embodying a balance of cultures within a global mindset, particularly during moments of tension, strife, or situational challenges.

This balance of cultures is not unique to education, and it has broad implications for any company that is operating internationally with multiple offices (Dorfman et al. 2012). This has implications for the entire campus, as leadership in IBCs must model an approach that balances cultural conceptions of leadership for faculty, staff, and students. Adopting a 'Canadian way' at any international office campus, or any other form of nation-specific leadership, negates the opportunity for reciprocal cultural learning and, in fact, can be detrimental to the success of the organization (as noted in Mary's 'business as usual' experience). But the same applies to adopting cultural leadership ways of being and knowing of the host culture and country, (as noted in Justin's and Mary's deference to the CEO when she disclosed her decision to challenge the budget cut). Educational leaders may feel that they are culturally competent, but when we engage in international leadership experiences, our cultural competency can find itself tested, which can be particularly impactful during times of heightened difficulties. Recognizing that decisions in one culture may yield different results in a different culture (Elenkov et al. 2005; Raisiene et al. 2018) is essential leadership when operating internationaly.

This experience of challenging our mindsets highlights the need for international leaders to embrace reflection and to consider methodologies such as self-studies. Until writing this chapter as well as sharing and critiquing stories, we did not realize that both of us conformed to a cultural competency that is the norm in the Middle East but not highly regarded in Canada, nor did we realize that we had the same misgivings.

6.5.2 Inspiring a Shared Vision

Transition and change, including negative changes, are inevitable in international higher education, particularly for IBCs where all employees are contract positions with no job security, often no employment rights, and who are navigating complex socially, politically, and culturally integrated systems in an international context. Job security does not exist in international educational facilities in the Middle East, and many who go abroad recognize this (Saudelli 2015). The transitory nature of international assignments leads to many challenges as new leaders on board, who develop their vision and share the campus goals with followers every one to three years. Without clear organizational goals that are sustained over the long term, establishing and sharing a vision under each new leader will lead to constant change and poses the risk of a more transactional model of leadership as followers' commitment becomes fettered under the constant strain of new strategic directions. The development of a shared vision is also hampered by the recognition that the newly deployed leader comes with a set of ideals that may, or may not, work in this new context (Dorfman et al. 2012; Gelfand et al. 2007). In fact, the pre-supposed ideals of leadership may even prove to be a disadvantage without a deep cultural understanding of the new cultures.

When significant issues arise, it is crucial for the overall morale of the institution to know how all employees are managed, led, and engaged in, particularly in relation to their shared vision. Leadership in IBCs requires skills for navigating tensions, transitions, and change, as well as inspiring and motivating faculty, staff, and students through change. It may mean providing a space for voice, calming frayed nerves, and engaging in shared discussions regarding the vision, mission, and mandate of the institution. It often means creating spaces for engaged dialogue about how to navigate change with everyone in the institution. Adopting a 'business as usual' mindset in times of transition and change rather neglects the implications and impact of what it means to be an international citizen. It should be recognised that communicating openly with and engaging with those who are affected by the change is crucial to organisation success.

6.5.3 Challenging the Process

One of the difficulties of IBCs is the tendency to see them as bringing education to the other (Bhabha 1994), which has repercussions to thinking about internationalization through the lens of globalization (Kusch 2011; Merriam et al. 2006). However, this ideology represents a form of educational colonialism that reduces the opportunity of a global reciprocity of knowledge and knowledge sharing (Saudelli 2015). Rather, there are real strengths that can be achieved by learning from education systems and processes abroad (Critchley and Saudelli 2015). By their very nature, IBCs represent opportunities for all involved to consider new ways of thinking and integrating knowledge, as all involved are immersed in systems that represent both the host country and the guest institution. Leadership at IBCs has the unique opportunity to grow, to challenge what they think they know and do, and to explore new and alternative means for engagement in the business of higher education as a means to improve education and overall organizational performance.

Challenging the process is also about innovation, encouraging alternate views from key stakeholders, and supporting the organizational vision within the cultural context—specifically the necessity of recognizing how one can lead change within a different culture while respecting and recognizing its cultural nuances and norms (Albert et al. 2000). It also requires an understanding of the effects on both peers and followers as well as their subsequent behavior (Kirkman et al. 2009). In each of the examples provided by Justin's and Mary's narrative, opportunities occurred to challenge the process within a unique multicultural environment. However, there were subtleties that impacted the efficacy of change. In one instance, the impact was not fully recognized that layoffs would have on followers and their subsequent behavior. This also impacted the 'survivors' and possibly their organizational commitment in what was already a transitory environment, leading to a negative change in the 'individual considerations' component of Pounder's (2001) transformational leadership model.

Challenging the process in a host country also requires a deep understanding of the implications of power distance in the home country. In our example of challenging the process by meeting the Minister of Finance to request more funding, the power distance in the host country required the Minister to act in a directive, potentially punitive way by exercising his power. In this high power distance culture, the request was seen as a challenge to his formal power, leaving him no option but to react as he did, i.e. further reducing funds. Had he behaved differently than what was expected of him in this context, he would have taken the risk of appearing weak or undecided. Lastly, the perception of his leadership and competence by his followers influenced his behavior to act.

This again speaks to the need to recognize the three distinct cultures leaders in international assignments need to act in and adapt to (Tsai et al. 2019). The recognition that higher education is best suited to one form of leadership (Jones et al. 2017) is juxtaposed against the anticipated host country leadership style. This requires that leaders in this tri-culture environment are adept at navigating different leadership styles based on the context of the organizational needs.

This efficacy of leaders requires that they understand the cultural value orientations of both superiors, peers, and followers, as well as how their behavior affects each of them (Kirkman et al. 2009; Tsai et al. 2019). The ability to make change in this context can be deeply challenging and requires sensitivity and a competency in managing 'upwards' in a high power distance context.

6.5.4 Enabling Others to Act

It is interesting that both Justin and Mary did not voice their dissent at a crucial moment, which raises the question of whether or not they felt enabled to act. This is compounded by the circumstance that the campus leadership was collaborative and supportive of research on higher education leadership (Jones et al. 2017). Both have a wealth of experience in Middle Eastern contexts as well as in higher education in Canada and internationally. Both are also Canadian educators and leaders who are well-versed in the leadership values of transparency, engaging multiple voices, and collaborative approaches. Yet, they were silent in our example. While Justin and Mary have different understandings of this reaction, both agree that this lack of voice was attributed to their acculturation to a high-power distance model (i.e. the Middle East) where voice is not encouraged. However, in international higher education and, particularly, in IBCs, it is entirely possible that leadership and employees have intuitive knowledge about the context due to extensive experience, which could be valuable if people are enabled to act. This knowledge is underscored by the recognition that leadership efficacy is culturally bound (Elenkov et al. 2005; Raisiene et al. 2018).

In this case, both Justin and Mary had a wealth of knowledge about living, working, and leading in the Middle East, and both had a particular intuitive knowledge that could have benefitted the SLT and the IBC; but neither felt enabled to act, which may have been the result of them internalizing a mode of leadership that is typical in the Middle East. This is a particularly interesting finding as neither Justin nor Mary recognized at the time that they were conforming to an aspect of leadership based on adaptation during their years living in the Middle East. In fact, this represents a facet of awareness for both authors as a result of engaging in this self-study. Being a Canadian living in the Middle East for an extensive period means that some of the cultural elements may become part of the lived experiences, and thus part of an embodied way of being and knowing. Leadership in IBCs needs to be aware of the local cultural influences on their thinking and how this impacts decisions and communications. Self-study in leadership in IBCs is particularly important, as certain behaviors can come from a range of cultural influences acquired through lived experiences.

6.5.5 Encouraging the Heart

Educational leadership often espouses institutional goals of internationalization and collaboration. These appear in mission statements, shared values, and institutional outcomes. But what does this mean in terms of leadership practices? Leadership that encourages the heart creates spaces for individuals to grow, engage, and create opportunities for achievement in relation to these goals. Particularly in IBCs, there is a need to create spaces for leadership and employees to bring in their tacit wisdom, to speak to their goals, to create shared goals, to connect their goals to institutional ones, and to encourage and celebrate individuals' and team members' growth mindsets (Mrazek et al. 2018). This is true for all employees, all students, and leadership as well. Leaders may arrive at an IBC thinking they are aware of cultural differences. Many may have traveled extensively, and some may have lived in different places. Assuming a leadership position at an IBC requires a nuanced awareness of what it means to bring together what may be very different realities of leadership in practice, all of which is impacted by cultural differences (Kirkman et al. 2009). During times of tension, the cultural implications are heightened.

Enabling the heart requires a sense of humility. As Canadian leaders, we are well-versed in discussions of multiculturalism, plurality, and cultural conceptions. As educators, we believe in embracing these aspects as contributing to a thriving, democratic, peaceful society. But as Canadian leaders at IBCs, cultural awareness takes on different implications and knowledge sets. The dominant host country culture may have different values and expectations which complicate the leadership process. Educational leaders at IBCs need to open their minds, to recognize the limits of their knowledge, to be tolerant of their limitations, and to embrace a growth mindset as well as personal curiosity regarding the self, leadership practices, and diverse cultures.

6.6 Implications and Recommendations

By their very nature, IBCs are immersed in meeting the needs of what can be very different conceptions of leadership and culture. Leadership at IBCs represents people who can navigate the complexities of a convergence of cultural conceptions, which can be particularly profound in times of strife, such as with budget cuts—a more recent example being the global COVID-19 pandemic of 2020/21.

Having worked in the Middle East for nearly a decade, we came to recognize the differences between our expectations of leaders and nuanced Hofstede's (1980) dimensions of leadership to the best of our abilities. In the Arab Gulf, we quickly realized that leadership in the region had different connotations and expectations among followers than in North America. We further realized that both of us, at various times, embodied notions of leadership typical in Canada and the Middle East, respectively. Through reflection, we now recognize this as a strength.

North American culture places a great deal of emphasis on collaboration, accessibility, and engagement among group members. Many industries feature participative (Lewin 1948) or even servant leadership (Russell and Stone 2002). The importance of people, the practice of empathy, and stewardship are anchors for many forms of North American leadership. Leadership behaviors may be viewed as egalitarian and democratic, with Canada having a power distance score of 39 on Hofstede's scale (1 being the least, 100 being the highest).

Conversely, in a high-power distance environment, such as the Middle East, different expectations emerge and influence leadership behavior. In this more directive environment (Barkema et al. 2015), the management theories that work well in North America may not match expectations in the Middle East (Ramdani et al. 2014), so additional cultural adaptation will be required. Further, the actions and styles valued in Western environments—such as participative leadership, collaboration, or invitational leadership (Purkey and Novak 1996) and teamwork—may in fact be viewed as weaknesses in an environment where more directive leadership is expected by followers. They may not anticipate nor appreciate a participative leadership style and may even question the efficacy of this style of leadership (Kirkman et al. 2009). Thus, leaders must be able to pivot their leadership styles in recognition of these different cultural expectations (Tsai et al. 2019).

Justin and Mary both believe that intercultural competencies are crucial in higher education leadership. They further believe that many leaders in higher education may think they have these competencies by virtue of living and leading in a diverse society. However, both authors assert that living and working in a diverse society like Canada is not the same as leading at an IBC in a different country where the leader may have to integrate multiple cultural competencies and engage in competing or confounding conceptions of leadership, which is particularly heightened during times of change.

Perhaps most challenging for leaders is the dichotomy that may exist between the cultures of the home campus, the branch campus, and the host country—recognizing the intricacies of each culture not as a closed system but as one that is symbiotic, where each culture will influence the other. At the onset of a deployment, recognizing the different culture of each system is essential in helping leaders navigate the differing value systems and cultural norms (Kirkman et al. 2009). Conflicts are inevitable in normal workplace environments; however, the potential for misunderstandings and the underlying different cultural norms and practices in international placements are often heightened with higher stakes. Understanding and appreciating these subtle differences takes time, cultural awareness, and self-awareness for leaders who must navigate and balance both people and tasks in an intercultural assignment.

Both Justin and Mary have returned to Canada and taken leadership roles in public higher education. They identify that their experiences as educators and educational leaders in international contexts have shaped their leadership practice, their commitment to internationalization, their belief in and value of intercultural competencies, and their personal commitments to curiosity in relation to their own leadership practices. Justin identifies with a participative leadership style, which guides his leadership practices, values, and beliefs. Mary identifies with invitational leadership (Purkey and Novak 1996), which guides her leadership practices, values, and beliefs particularly in relation to advocacy and change, empathetic listening, and encouraging a growth mindset. Both identify these personal models of leadership that have developed as a result of their international experiences and collaborations, as well as the value they place on their own growth mindsets.

6.7 Conclusion

Justin and Mary spent many years in various international educational institutions—experiences they value, as these have framed their leadership practices. Through this self-study, they have realized aspects of their leadership they were not aware of, particularly that they had both embodied, at one time or another, aspects of cultural conceptions of leadership they had acquired through their international experiences. Both recognize the need to be intimately self-aware of their individual leadership styles, those anticipated by followers, and the cultural expectations of leadership. Justin and Mary assert that institutions and organizations today must embrace international partnerships, collaborations and integrations. To that end, these scholars and educational leaders recommend that organizations must learn, practice, integrate, and engage in self-studies regarding intercultural competencies in their everyday leadership practices as part of enacting international educational leadership.

References

Abu-Tineh, A. M., Khasawneh, S. A., & Al-Omari, A. A. (2008). Kouzes and Posner's transformational leadership model in practice, the case of Jordanian schools. *Leadership & Organizational Development Journal*, *29*(8), 648–660.

Ahmad, S., Fazal-e-Hasan, S., & Kaleem, A. (2020). Is the meaning of ethical leadership constant across cultures? A test of cross-cultural measurement invariance. *International Journal of Manpower*, *41*(8), 1323–1340. https://doi.org/https://doi.org/10.1108/IJM-02-2019-0079

Alan, B. (2016). Self-Study as a Qualitative Research Methodology in Teacher Education. *Journal of Qualitative Research in Education*, *4*(1), 7–25.

Albert, S., Ashforth, B. E., & Dutton, J. E. (2000). Organizational identity and identification: Charting new waters and building new bridges. *Academy of Management Review*, *25*(1), 13–17.

Argyris, C., & Schön, D. (1974). *Theory in Practice: Increasing Professional Effectiveness*. San Francisco, CA: Jossey-Bass.

Armstrong, J. P. (2020). Assessing Intercultural Competence in International Leadership Courses: Developing the Global Leader. *Journal of Leadership Education*, *19*(4), 1–19.

Barkema, H. G., Chen, X., George, G., Luo, Y., & Tsui, A. (2015). West meets East: New concepts and theories. *Academy of Management Journal*, *58*(2), 460–479.

Bass, B. M. (1985). *Leadership and Performance Beyond Expectations*. New York, NY: Free Press.

Bhabha, H. K. (1994). *The Location of Culture*. New York, NY: Routledge.

Bhaskar-Shrinivas, P. M., Harrison, D. A., Shaffer, M. A., & Luk, D. M. (2005). Input-based and time-based models of international adjustment: Meta-Analytic evidence and theoretical extensions. *Academy of Management Journal*, 48(2), 257–281.

Bhatti, Z. A., Ahmad, H. G., Aslam, A., Nadeem, U., & Ramzan, M. (2012). Leadership styles and behaviors in institutional context. *Interdisciplinary Journal of Contemporary Research in Business*, *4*(2), 744–762.

Borgos, J. (2016). Addressing Sustainable International Branch Campus Development Through an Organizational Structure Lens: A Comparative Analysis of China, Qatar, and the United Arab Emirates (4–5), 271–287. doi:https://doi.org/10.1080/10611932.2016.1237849

Bottery, M., Wong, P. M., Wright, N., & Ngai, G. (2009). Portrait Methodology and educational leadership: putting the person first. *International Studies in Educational Administration*, *37*(3), 82–96.

Boyd, P., & White, E. (2017). Teacher Educator Professional Inquiry in an Age of Accountability. In P. Boyd & E. White (Edss), *Teachers and Teacher Educators Learning Through Inquiry: International Perspectives* (pp. 123–141). Krakow, Poland: Wydawnictwo Attyka.

Brookfield, S. (2017). Becoming a Critically Reflective Teacher (2nd ed.). San Francisco, CA: Jossey-Bass.

Bryman, A., & Lilley, S. (2009). Leadership researchers on leadership in higher education. *Leadership*, *5*(30), 331–346.

Caligiuri, P., & Tarique, I., (2016). Cultural agility and international assignees' effectiveness in cross-cultural interactions. *International Journal of Training and Development, 20*(4), 280–289. doi: https://doi.org/10.1111/ijtd.12085

Caligiuri, P. M. (2006). Performance measurement in a cross-national context. In W. Bennett, C. E. Lance, & D. J. Woehr (Eds.), *Performance measurement: Current perspectives and future challenges* (pp. 227–243). Mahwah, NJ: Erlbaum.

Costa, A., & Kallick, B. (1993). Through the Lens of a Critical Friend. *Educational Leadership: Journal of the Department of Supervision and Curriculum Development, 51*(2), 49–51.

Critchley, K., & Saudelli, M. G. (2015). Helping Qatar Achieve its National Vision 2030: One Successful International Branch Campus. *Journal of Educational Thought, Special Issue University of Calgary in Qatar, 47*(2/3), 9–24.

Daniels, J. D., & Insch, G. S. (1998). Why are early departure rates from foreign assignments lower than historically reported? *Multinational Business Review*, 6(1), 13–23.

Davis, A., Dent, E., & Wharff, D. (2015). A Conceptual Model of Systems Thinking Leadership in Community Colleges. *Systemic Practice & Action Research, 28*(4), 333–353. doi:https://doi.org/10.1007/s11213-015-9340-9

De Vries, J. D. (2010). The limits of globalization in the early modern world. *The Economic History Review, 63*(3), 710–733. doi:https://doi.org/10.1111/j.1468-0289.2009.00497.x

Dorfman, P., Javidan, M., Hanges, P., Dastmalchian, A., & House, R. (2012). GLOBE: A twenty year journey into the intriguing world of culture and leadership. *Journal of World Business, 47*(4), 504–518.

Elenkov, D. S., Judge, W., & Wright, P. (2005). Strategic Leadership and Executive Innovation Influence: An International Multi-Cluster Comparative Study. *Strategic Management Journal, 26*(7), 665–682. doi:https://doi.org/10.1002/smj.469

Farrar, J., & Saudelli, M. G. (2022a). Leading International Collaborative Teams: Relationships Matter in Changing Times. In I. Stolz & S. Scherrer (Eds.), *International Leadership – Effecting Success Across Borders in a Boundaryless World.* Lucerne, Switzerland: Springer Gabler.

Farrar, J. & Saudelli, M.G. (2022b). Co-leading an international collaborative team: Relationships matter. Lucerne Switzerland: Springer Gabler for SGO Foundation (Foundation of the Swiss Society for Organization and Management)

Farrell, T. (2002). Constructivist Security Studies: Portrait of A Research Program. *International Studies Review, 4(1)*, 49–72. doi:https://doi.org/10.1111/1521-9488.t01-1-00252

Fisher, D. (2018). The essentials of international leadership. *The International Schools Journal, 37*(2), 44–53.

Flinn, K. (2018). *Leadership Development: A Complexity Approach.* London, UK: Routledge.

Gelfand, M. J., Erez, M., & Aycan, Z. (2007). Cross-cultural organizational behavior. *Annual Review of Psychology, 58*, 479–514.

Hartley, J. (2018). Ten propositions about public leadership. *International Journal of Public Leadership, 14*(4), 202–217.

Herbst, T., & Conradie, P. (2011). Leadership effectiveness in Higher Education: Managerial self-perceptions versus perceptions of others. *SA Journal of Industrial Pscychology, 37*(1) 1–14.

Hershey, P., & Blanchard, K. (1969). Life-cycle theory of leadership. *Training and Development Journal, 23*(5), 26–34.

Hoff, K. S. (1999). Leaders and managers: essential skills required within higher education. *Higher Education, 38*(3), 311–331.

Hofstede, G. (1980). *Culture's consequences: International differences in work-related values.* London, UK: Sage Publications.

Hofstede, G., & Bond, M. H. (1988). The Confucius connection: From cultural roots to economic growth. *Organizational Dynamics, 16*(4), 5–21. https://doi.org/https://doi.org/10.1016/00902616(88)90009-5

House, R. J., Hanges, P. J., Javidan, M., Dorfman, P. W., Gupta, V., & GLOBE Associates (2004). *Leadership, culture, and organizations: The GLOBE study of 62 societies*. Thousand Oaks, CA: Sage.

Jones, S., Harvey, M., Hamilton, J., Bevacqua, J., Egea, K., & McKenzie, J. (2017). Demonstrating the impact of a Distributed Leadership Approach in Higher Education. *Journal of Higher Education Policy & Management, 39*(2), 197–211. 15p. doi:https://doi.org/10.1080/1360080X.2017.1276567.

Joyce, P. (2009). Leadership and organizational effectiveness – lessons to be drawn from higher education?. *Journal of Nursing Management, 17*, 494–502.

Kim, Y. J., & van Dyne, L. (2012). Cultural intelligence and international leadership potential: The importance of contact for members of the majority. *Applied psychology: An international review, 61*(2), 272–294. doi:https://doi.org/10.1111/j.1464-0597.2011.00468.x

Kirkman, B. L., Chen, G., Farh, J.-L., Chen, Z. X., & Lowe, K. B. (2009). Individual power distance orientation and follower reactions to transformational leaders: A cross-level, cross-cultural examination. *Academy of Management Journal, 52*(4), 744–764. https://doi.org/https://doi.org/10.5465/AMJ.2009.43669971

Kirkman, B. L., Lowe, K. B., & Gibson, C. B. (2006). A quarter century of Culture's Consequences: A review of empirical research incorporating Hofstede's cultural value framework. *Journal of International Business Studies*, 36(3) 285–320.

Knight, W. H., & Holen, M. (1985). Leadership and the perceived effectiveness of department chairpersons. *The Journal of Higher Education, 56*(6), 677–690.

Kouzes, J. M., & Posner, B. Z. (2002). *Leadership challenge* (3rd ed.). San Francisco, CA: Jossey-Bass.

Kouzes, J. M., & Posner, B. Z. (1993). *Leadership Practices Inventory. A Self-assessment and Analysis* (expanded ed.). San Francisco, CA: Jossey-Bass.

Kusch, J. (2011). *Knowledge, Differences and Identity in the Time of Globalization: Institutional Discourse and Practices*. England, UK: Cambridge Scholars.

LaBoskey, V.K. (2004). *The Methodology of Self-Study and Its Theoretical Underpinnings*. In: Loughran J.J., Hamilton M.L., LaBoskey V.K., Russell T. (Eds) International Handbook of Self-Study of Teaching and Teacher Education Practices. Springer International Handbooks of Education, vol 12. Springer, Dordrecht. doi:https://doi.org/10.1007/978-1-4020-6545-3_21.

Lane, J. E. (2011). Global expansion of international branch campuses: Managerial and leadership challenges. *New Directions for Higher Education, 2011(155)*, 5–17.

Lassonde, C., Galman, S., & Kosnik, C. (Eds.) (2009). *Self-study research methodologies for teacher educators*. Rotterdam, Netherlands: Sense Publishers / Brill.

Lee, Y.-D., Chen, P.-Ch., & Su, Ch.-L. (2020). The evolution of the leadership theories and the analysis of new research trends. *International Journal of Organizational Innovation, 12*(3), 88–104.

Lewin, K. (1948). *Resolving social conflicts*. New York: Harper & Row.

Loughran, J., & Russell, T. (2007). Looking into Teaching about Teaching. *Studying Teacher Education, 3*,(1) 1–3. doi:https://doi.org/10.1080/17425960701279768.

Matczynski, T. J., Lasley, T. J., & Haberman, M. (1989). The Deanship: How faculty evaluate performance. *Journal of Teacher Education, 40*(6), 10–14.

McNiff, J., & Whitehead, J. (2010). *You and your action research project*. Abingdon, UK: Routledge.

Meek, V. L., Goedegebuure, L., & De Boer, H. (2010). The changing role of academic leadership in Australia and the Netherlands: who is the modern dean? In V. L. Meek, L. Goedegebuure, R. Santiago, & T. Carvalho (Eds.), *The changing dynamics of higher education middle management* (pp. 31–54) (Higher Education Dynamics, no. 33). Dordrecht: Springer. doi.org/10.1007/978-90-481-9163-5_3

Merriam, S. B., Courtenay, B. C., & Cervero, R. M. (Eds.) (2006). Global issues and adult education: Perspectives from Latin America, Southern Africa, and the United States. San Francisco, CA: Jossey-Bass.

Mrazek, A. J., Ihm, E. D., Molden, D. C., Mrazek, M. D., Zedelius, C. M., & Schooler, J. W. (2018). Expanding minds: Growth mindsets of self-regulation and the influences on effort and perseverance. *Journal of Experimental Social Psychology*, *79*, 164–180.

Normore, A. H., & Erbe, N. (2013). Collective efficacy: Interdisciplinary perspectives on international leadership. In A. H. Normore, & N. Erbe (Eds.), *Collective Efficacy: Interdisciplinary Perspectives on International Leadership (Advances in Educational Administration, Vol. 20)*. Bingley, UK: Emerald Group Publishing.

Posner, B. Z. (2013). It's how leaders behave that matters, not where they are from. *Leadership & Organization Development Journal*, *34*(6), 573–587.

Pounder, J. S. (2001). New leadership and university organisational effectiveness: Exploring the relationship. *Leadership & Organization Development Journal*, *22*(6), 281–290.

Preskill, S., & Brookfield, S. (2008). Learning as a Way of Leading: Lessons from the Struggle for Social Justice. San Francisco, CA: Jossey-Bass.

Purkey, W. W., & Novak, J. M. (1996). *Inviting school success: A self-concept approach to teaching, learning, and democratic practice* (3rd ed.). Belmont, CA: Wadsworth Publishing Company.

Raisiene, A. G. (2012). Sustainable development of inter-organizational relationships and social innovations. *Journal of Security and Sustainability Issues*, *2*(1), 65–76.

Raisiene, A. G., Pulokiene, A., & Valickas, A. (2018). Examining Leadership Characteristics in International Multilaterals. *Montenegrin Journal of Economics*, *14*(3), 189–198.

Ramdani, B., Mellahi, K., Guermat, C., & Kechad, R. (2014). The efficacy of high performance work practices in the Middle East: evidence from Algerian firms. *International Journal of Human Resource Management*, *25*(2), 252–275.

Russell, R. F., & Stone, G. A. (2002). A review of servant leadership attributes: developing a practical model. *Leadership & Organization Development Journal*, *23*(3),145–157.

Russell, T. (2007) How experience changed my values as a teacher educator. In T. Russell J. Loughran (Eds.), Enacting a pedagogy of teacher education, 182-192. Values, relationships and practices. Abingdon: Routledge.

Samad, A., Reaburn, P., Davis, H., & Ezaz, H. (2015). Towards an Understanding of the Effect of Leadership on Employee Wellbeing and Organizational Outcomes in Australian Universities. *The Journal of Developing Areas*, *49*(6), 984-999.

Saudelli, M. G. (2015). *The balancing act: International higher education in the 21st century.* Rotterdam, Netherlands: Sense Publishers/Brill.

Saudelli, M. G., Mogadime, D., & Taber, N. (2013). A conversation with Sharan Merriam: Impact of Globalization for Adult Education and Higher Education. *Brock Education Journal Special Issue*, *23*(2), 3–10.

Schuk, S., & Russell, T. (2005). Studying teacher education: A journal of self-study, critical friendship, and the complexities of teacher education. *Studying Teacher Education*, *1*(2), 107–121.

Scott, G., Coates, H., & Anderson, M. (2008). Learning Leaders in Times of Change: Academic Leadership Capabilities for Australian Higher Education, https://research.acer.edu.au/higher_education/3.

Sheppard, J.G., Sarros, J. C., & Santora, J. C.(2013). Twenty-first century leadership: international imperatives. Management Decision. London, *51*(2), 267–280. doi:https://doi.org/10.1108/00251741311301812

Stenhouse, L. (1975). *An introduction to curriculum research and development.* London, UK: Heinemann.

Tsai, C., Carr, C., Qiao, K., & Supprakit, S. (2019). Modes of cross-culture leadership adjustment: adapting leadership to meet local conditions and/or changing followers to match personal requirements? *The International Journal of Human Resource Management*, *30*(9), 1477–1504.

Walker, A., & Quong, T. (2005). Gateways to International Leadership Learning: Beyond Best Practice. *Education Research and Perspectives*, *32*(2), 97–121. doi:https://doi.org/10.2276/0311-25433.32.2.3588

Waterval, D., Tinnemans-Adriaanse, M., Meziani, M., Driessen, E., Scherpbier, A., Mazrou, A., & Frambach, J. (2017). Exporting a Student-Centered Curriculum: A Home Institution's Perspective. *Journal of Studies in International Education*, *21*(3), 278–290. doi:https://doi.org/10.1177/1028315317697542

White, L., & Jarvis, J. (2019). Self-study: a developing research approach for professional learning. *LINK Journal*, *4*(1) 1-5. Retrieved from https://www.herts.ac.uk/link/volume-4,-issue-1/self-study-a-developing-research-approach-for-professional-learning

Wilkins, S., & Huisman, J. (2012). The international branch campus as transnational strategy in higher education. *Higher Education*, *64*(5), 627–645.

International Leadership and the Fight Against Corruption

7

Christian Hauser

7.1 Introduction

Today, foreign corruption is considered legally and ethically reprehensible, but for a long time it was common practice in international business transactions (Hauser 2019a). One consequence of this supposed normality of corruption was that most OECD countries regarded corrupt payments abroad as a legitimate means, provided these facilitated domestic companies in acquiring or retaining business abroad. This circumstance was brought about by the fact that in most OECD countries, these payments were fiscally deductible (Gerstner and Hauser 2019). It was not until the late 1990s that a social, political, and, subsequently, legal awareness emerged of the need to fight corruption in international business (Becker et al. 2013). This led to a paradigm shift, finding expression in the efforts to establish the OECD Convention on Combating Bribery of Foreign Public Officials in International Business Transactions, which came into force in 1999. Along with other international conventions, this measure had a knock-on effect in all OECD countries, which in turn enacted strict anti-corruption laws to sanction corruption in international business (Hauser 2019a; Bahoo et al. 2020). The current state of affairs is that both natural persons and legal entities can be prosecuted if they engage in corrupt practices, both abroad under the place of offence principle and in their home country. The criminal sanctions for foreign corruption range from fines and imprisonment to (permanent) exclusion from business tenders ("blacklisting"). The consequence of these punitive measures is deterrence and a

C. Hauser (✉)
PRME Business Integrity Action Center, University of Applied Sciences of the Grisons, Chur, Switzerland
e-mail: christian.hauser@fhgr.ch

I. Stolz, S. Oldenziel Scherrer (eds.), *International Leadership*, uniscope. Publikationen der SGO Stiftung, https://doi.org/10.1007/978-3-658-37306-1_7

new international business standard, as internationally active companies must comply with the applicable anti-corruption rules in order to avoid legal liabilities (Gerstner and Hauser 2019).

However, a legal paradigm shift is not yet sufficient to eradicate corruption, especially because some actors continue to place perceived (short-term) economic gains above legal and ethical considerations. In fact, given the latest corruption scandals, it seems that not much has changed despite all the new national laws that have come into force since the early 2000s, as corruption is still widespread around the globe (Becker et al. 2013). Recent cases of well-known companies like ABB, Alstom, Daimler, EADS, Ericsson, Goldman Sachs, Ferrostaal, MAN, Novartis, Siemens, or Walmart show that corruption is still a major challenge in international business practice, which needs to be addressed by internationally active business leaders (Gerstner and Hauser 2019). In addition to large companies, foreign corruption also affects commonly unknown and less-noticed small and medium-sized enterprises (SMEs), as evidenced by the finding that corruption is not correlated with firm size (Hauser and Kronthaler 2013).

Against this background, the question arises as to which contributions international leaders of large corporations and SMEs can offer in order to combat corruption. In the global fight against corruption, internationally active business leaders are challenged in a particular way. Largely, this is due to their high level of legal and ethical responsibility within the company, and as such, they are tasked with carrying out the necessary measures to uncover, sanction, or, in the best case, prevent corrupt behaviour on behalf or against the company. However, if international leaders fail to fulfil their responsibilities, they can either willingly or unwillingly promote corruption in international business transactions.

Therefore, this article first describes combatting corruption as a leadership task and, in this context, discusses the concept, importance, and limitation of ethical leadership in the fight against corruption. The second section is devoted to a selection of direct and indirect management tools leaders can apply in an international context to mitigate and manage corruption risks. Finally, the third section discusses the context in which international leaders act to prevent corruption, specifically the organisational culture and the influence they have upon it.

7.2 The Fight Against Corruption as a Leadership Task

7.2.1 Recent History and Principles of Leadership in the Fight Against Corruption

International markets have undergone massive changes over the past decades. In particular, the ability of companies to expand internationally has emerged as a key factor in today's global economy. However, as the opportunities for international expansion grew, so did the challenges, without all companies realising it. Developing new international markets is a highly demanding task, as it is not just about economics but also about the political and socio-cultural conditions in which business takes place. These conditions can be quite different from those in the home country of the company doing international business. For example, international growth markets are often geographically located in regions where there is both historically and currently a high risk of corruption (Hauser and Kronthaler 2013). Goertzel (2005) notes that while the roots of corruption lie in part in regional or national historical traditions, they are also rooted in psychological, economic, and political circumstances that are global in nature and cannot be confined to one part of the world. Thus, corruption continues to be one of the most significant challenges for internationally active business leaders.

Corruption is defined as the abuse of power in order to gain a private advantage, which, however, is not justified. In this respect, bribery, illegal gratuities, economic extortion, and conflicts of interest come into consideration (Hauser 2019a). The principal-agent model can be utilised to better illustrate corruption: it occurs when agent A betrays the interests of his/her principal P by pursuing his/her own interests, by accepting or trying to accept an undue advantage from a third party. The conditions for corruption are met when P has entrusted A to act on his/her behalf, and A has a certain discretionary power in this respect but uses this discretionary power for his/her own benefit and to the disadvantage of P. According to the principal-agent model, corruption can be reduced or avoided by minimizing the discretionary power of the agent or by improving the environment in which discretionary power is granted and exercised, thereby increasing confidence in the way discretion is practised (Carr 2017).

The normalisation of corrupt practices in organisations usually takes place in three stages in which social practices play a key role: in the first step, corrupt practices are institutionalised by allowing them to become routine; in the second step, they are legitimised by those who engage in corrupt practices by arguing that these actions are socially acceptable, thus rationalising corruption; finally, the third step perpetuates corruption by teaching new members of the organisation to accept corruption practices and to act corruptly themselves (Ashforth and Anand 2003; Anand et al. 2005).

In 1977, the United States of America enacted the Foreign Corrupt Practices Act (FCPA), which prohibits individuals and companies from engaging in corrupt business transactions abroad. In this regard, the US became pioneers in the implementation of anti-corruption legislation. Two decades later, the OECD adopted its so-called Anti-Bribery Convention. Currently, the anti-corruption legislation in place across all OECD countries is based on this Convention as well as on several additional international agreements which have since been adopted (Becker et al. 2013; Bahoo et al. 2020). However, the mere existence of legislation does not necessarily mean that corruption is eliminated. There are circumstances where judicial systems are weak or ineffective, or the authorities can be indifferent to the issue of corruption (Bahoo et al. 2020). In the United States, for example, the FCPA was initially merely understood as a moral obligation. Nevertheless, US prosecutors have successfully pursued cases of foreign corruption against both domestic and international companies, particularly in the last two decades, resulting in prison sentences and fines amounting to several billion US dollars.

Companies operating in foreign markets face considerable pressure from corruption, and this threat should not be underestimated. This affects, for example, companies seeking to conclude contracts or to establish a joint venture. In addition, internationally active companies are particularly prone to corrupt behaviour if there is a high level of bureaucracy and corporate regulation in the target country, and if taxes for foreign companies are high (Frei and Muethel 2017). Corruption is not limited to large companies but can affect enterprises of any size and age (Hauser and Kronthaler 2013). It has been observed in entrepreneurship literature that a corrupt context in a company's operating environment plays a major role in hindering legitimate business. If corruption is prevalent and accepted in a company's surroundings, then entrepreneurs may build the business model on corrupt practices, regardless of company demographics (Castro et al. 2020). Especially companies whose goal is to conquer international markets through their innovations—as is often the case with SMEs and so called born globals—are seen to be particularly opposed to corruption, because corruption facilitates the circumvention of regulations and keeps inferior goods in the market which lack innovative qualities. Thus, corruption forces companies that strive to achieve a competitive advantage through their innovation to unfairly compete against poorer goods. On the other hand, a recent study suggests that corruption may also promote innovation, since corruption can speed up the innovation process by circumventing timely regulatory delays (Krammer 2019). For this reason, Castro et al. (2020) consider the relationship between innovation and corporate corruption to be still under-researched. In the context of start-ups, Goel (2012) reports that previous research has found only a weak correlation between corruption and their regulation. Goel's own research, however, has found that higher levels of bureaucratic hurdles for company formation—which includes time for registering a start-up, licensing, property registration, and taxation—lead to more corruption. In their research on the reasons why small business owners in the post-Soviet Union, Central Eastern Europe, and Western industrialized countries engage in corruption, Tonoyan et al. (2010) found that the low efficiency of financial and legal institutions and their lack of enforcement encourage corruption, as well as the perception that illegal business activities are perceived as largely normal. Hauser and Kronthaler (2013) investigated how often internationally active Swiss SMEs are confronted with corruption, how often they make informal payments under the table when requested to do so, and what the amounts of these payments are. Their results show that in the case of foreign corruption, company size and ownership structure do not have a significant impact on a firm's corruption risk. At the same time, the large number of companies that pay bribes abroad reveals that internationally active SMEs are also directly affected by corruption risks and must take appropriate preventive measures. Combating corruption is therefore a leadership task for executives in both internationally active large companies and SMEs. The following remarks are therefore aimed at executives from both internationally active large companies and SMEs.

7.2.2 Ethical Leadership as a Prerequisite for Fighting Corruption

In a company, the senior and middle managements occupy a central role in the fight against corruption. In the sense of "ethical leadership", business leaders should exemplify corporate values that are directed against corruption, and they should create and implement anti-corruption commitments (Bussmann et al. 2017). Thus, one way to counter corruption in organisations is to exercise leadership in such a way that corruption does not arise in the first place. Ethical Leadership should therefore strongly and visibly highlight ethical and moral principles that focus on the management personnel.

Ethical leadership is associated with qualities such as trust, role model, integrity, competence, and experience. In concrete terms, this means that international leaders are expected to create, control, and improve all conditions to prevent corruption in their respective organisations. The concept of ethical leadership places trust in the leader in the foreground and is based on social responsibility as well as on disclosure, transparency credibility, accountability, and honesty (Belasen 2016a). This includes sharing information with the public in the interest of transparency, communication tools to mobilise staff and stakeholders, codes of conduct, and ethics. Primarily, ethical leadership develops its impact through the interconnection of the above-mentioned areas: transparency and credibility through external communication, the public image, and reputation; credibility and accountability refer to compliance with codes of ethics and rules of conduct. Furthermore, accountability and honesty are the prerequisites for ethical behaviour and moral values. Belasen thus assumes that honesty and transparency strengthen the social identity and public image of the organisation and, as such, allow it to appear responsible and responsive. Ethical leaders ensure that, due to their self-regulation, the members of an organisation also learn from this behaviour. Ethical leadership thus triggers ethical mindfulness in others (Belasen 2016a). In turn, this leads to the requirement that leaders communicate their ethical commitment, for example in the form of the so-called "tone from the top". This implies that the senior leaders of a company are committed to anti-corruption norms and values and thus forms a role model of which behaviour is appropriate in legal and ethical terms. It is therefore the responsibility of the senior leaders to provide middle managers and employees with a consistent standard for dealing with anti-corruption. The decisive aspects here are consistency, unity, absolute commitment, and clear public positioning. The "tone from the top" is thus the clear message of the senior leaders that corruption is prohibited and that the ban is enforced within the framework of a compliance programme (Bussmann et al. 2017; International Chamber of Commerce 2019).

Belasen (2016b, 206) lists six requirements a leader should embody in order to become an ethical leader:

1. They must clearly define roles, goals and expectations of employees and leave no room for interpretation. Because, unclear statements create uncertainty, doubt, and, in extreme cases, fear.

2. Denial, blame, excuses, and scapegoats should not be accepted. If something goes wrong, beware of the 'victim mentality'.
3. A trusted leader must hold department heads, team or project leaders accountable by encouraging them to raise problems as they arise, rather than waiting.
4. Trusted leaders identify the obstacles to success, both within themselves and their departments.
5. Trusted leaders set milestones and metrics to make performance measurable.
6. Trusted leaders find a balance between process and results. This means that employees should be responsible for the standards and processes that precede the results, and not just for the results themselves.

7.2.3 Limitations of Ethical Leadership in Fighting Corruption

If the leader acts as a role model, he/she carries a great responsibility, as moral behaviour is focused on the leader, and ideally, he/she must be devoid of error.

Jung et al. (2017) contrast the thinking of the leader as a role model with the structural level of the organisation, i.e., if the leader acts as a role model, he/she is the instance that prevents corruption, and less so organisational structures such as rules and regulations. As according to Jung et al., one assumes that leaders always act correctly under these conditions. However, morally correct actions do not always have to lead to the prevention of corruption, because every action can have unforeseen consequences that make it a possibility. Moreover, it is impossible to say whether leaders act in a morally acceptable way or do so only because it is expected of them. Thus, the conclusion is that it is not sufficient to shift the responsibility for anti-corruption onto the international leaders alone, and that the leaders with high levels of integrity shown as a role model, creating a copycat effect, can hardly remain the only measure to prevent corruption. While international leaders can act as strong role models, they must also be able to rely on formal structures that necessarily complement their efforts to prevent corruption.

Furthermore, Jung (2017) pleads for a new understanding of leadership as an organisational disorder. In turn, this should help combat corruption by redefining the leadership role, which has so far been understood as a moral authority. Jung views corruption as structurally embedded and occasionally systemic in organisations (normalised). So instead of introducing and monitoring systems of rules in an organisation to prevent corruption, leadership consists of questioning established routines, i.e. by disturbing them in order to activate a critical awareness. In doing so, Jung highlights that the power of leaders, which the ethical leadership model is based on, is limited by the self-referentiality of organisations. This means that within the organisational system, decisions are made on the basis of others which have been previously made, thus replicating the established decision-making precedent. Now, international leaders are faced with the challenge of operating within the limits of this self-referentiality whilst also accepting that their effectiveness is limited. Jung argues that ethical leadership overemphasises the role of international leaders, thereby ignoring other central decision-making premises (e.g. different personnel, communication channels, and decision-making programmes), such as the circumstance that decisions made in a decentralised manner can be assessed as being of integrity, yet the system-emergent consequences no longer exist. Therefore, this type of dividing labour within an organisation can lead to the suppression of morality because the leader behind a decision cannot always appropriately assess its consequences. The reason is that in this way, responsibility is distributed, as it were, over a number of individual decisions, and as such they are neutralised. Corrupt actions are thus no longer recognised as such. For leaders in an internationally active organisation, this means in practice that they must refrain from perceiving their organisation as a smooth system; instead, they must view corruption as an event that is likely to occur in their business environment. Furthermore, they should be aware that "morality" is not an all-encompassing category for preventing corruption but is limited and constrained by the form of organisation. Moreover, this limits the leadership's ability to intervene against corruption. However, should it occur, it will give leaders the challenging opportunity to learn from the situation and ask themselves, for instance, how corruption has come about and what can be done about it. This learning process, Jung argues, is better than an error-avoidance culture that in a very predictable way only leads to the members of an organisation seeking to hide their mistakes.

Furthermore, the "tone at the top" does not always necessarily have to be meant or perceived positively but can also be in the service of corruption, for example when international leaders use their position of power to promote corruption (Starnawska 2016), or when they abuse their high social status or position to do so by disregarding laws for their own benefit (Kirchler 2011). A further complication is that leaders who have acted corruptly often lack the insight that they did so, because they view this behaviour to be at the service of achieving the company's goals and thus transform it into something that is supposedly positive (Kirchler 2011). It follows that the senior leaders themselves must be subject to control in order to prevent corrupt behaviour.

7.3 Direct and Indirect Management Tools and the Fight Against Corruption

7.3.1 Direct Management Tools

Direct management instruments are used to exert a direct influence on employees, for example in the form of appraisal interviews, target agreements, the delegation of responsibility and/or tasks, or through praise and criticism (Thommen and Achleitner 2006). This part describes as to which role job rotation and the dual control principle, target agreements and appraisal interviews can play in the fight against corruption.

7.3.1.1 Job Rotation and the Principle of Dual Control

Job rotation should be considered if key personnel work in areas of the company where the risk of corruption is high (International Chamber of Commerce 2019). These areas include, for example, the purchasing and sales departments in subsidiaries in emerging markets with a high level of corruption. Job rotation minimises the opportunities for corrupt behaviour and prevents corruption from becoming normalised (Litzcke et al. 2017; Osrecki 2017). A higher risk of corrupt behaviour arises when close relationships with other companies and their representatives develop over many years, or when bias arises due to such relationships. In order to prevent or at least impede the development of such relationships and ultimately corruption, the personnel concerned can be rotated by transferring them (in multinational companies also internationally), by changing the entire team, or by changing the distribution of business. However, rotation measures need not be perceived by the employee as harassment or control, but instead as a protective action since they may be at risk of corruption (Stierle and Siller 2014). However, job rotation can also be a disadvantage, namely when an employee in a specific function is difficult to replace due to his/her special skills. In such cases, however, this person can be more intensively and strictly supervised and subject to more stringent controls. In an international context, this control can be carried out, for example, with the help of mobile control stations (Stocker 2001). These have the advantage that they assess the respective local conditions more objectively and impartially and are not personally acquainted with the staff that need to be assessed or checked.

Closely related to job rotation is another key consideration, namely how to deal with people in the company who have acted corruptly and thus shown no respect to the principles of ethical leadership. One clear option is dismissal, but not all forms of corruption might justify such a drastic measure. Thus, there are also possibilities to link incidents of corruption on a smaller scale, for example the possibility of self-denunciation (Stocker 2001). Thereby, the individual concerned is given the opportunity to lessen the potential disadvantage they may encounter on the labour market if he/she leaves the company. If the person remains in the company, a transfer is a potentially appropriate measure.

Stierle and Siller (2014) recommend additional corruption prevention measures such as the four-eye principle or full transparency for highly specialised staff. Another means of internal control is the principle of dual control. In other words, employees of equal rank or superiors control another employee or support him/her if he/she is in danger of becoming susceptible to corruption. This principle does not necessarily understand control as a top-down relationship, but instead views it as a partnership. The person being monitored in this way should not be given the impression that he/she is being watched or even spied on by an undefined authority, but should be encouraged to bring up their own behaviour in order to avert harm to the company and to themselves as early as possible (Stierle and Siller 2014).

7.3.1.2 Target Agreements and Performance Reviews

Agreements on objectives are a means of steering and regulation within an organisation as well as in connection with the prevention of corruption, because they can be transferred into a mode of self-regulation. Furthermore, they are useful for the person concerned and the leader when the path to the goal is clear and seems desirable (Stierle and Siller 2014). However, if employees feel overburdened by the target agreements—for example because they have to achieve a certain turnover or contribution margin targets—this in turn could result in them being tempted to act corruptly in order to achieve the goals, at least in this way. The corruption-related aspect of target agreements must be taken into account by international leaders, e.g. when defining growth targets for a subsidiary in a foreign market or in the course of budget planning by questioning the targets with regard to their achievability and plausibility (Stierle and Siller 2014; Castro et al. 2020). In addition, excessive demands can also occur when managers and/or employees are faced with schedules and deadlines that cannot be met, for example in the execution of an international project. Therefore, such circumstances create pressure, which might lead to the impression that this can only be counterbalanced by corrupt behaviour. Thus, it is necessary for international leaders to be aware that excessive demands and pressure can create a motive for corrupt behaviour, and they must take appropriate steps to mitigate this risk (Hauser 2019b, 2020).

Employee appraisals are one way of exploring an employee's susceptibility to corruption. The Global Fraud Study 2012 by the Association of Certified Fraud Examiners lists the following red flags that are typical of employees who are prone to corrupt behaviour: they live beyond their means, have financial difficulties, have an unusual closeness to vendors or customers, are unwilling to share tasks, have family or relationship problems, are more irritable and suspicious than average. It is the task of international leaders to recognise such red flags, for example during employee appraisals, and, if necessary, address them at an early stage (Stierle and Siller 2014).

7.3.2 Indirect Management Instruments

Indirect management instruments do not exert a direct influence on employees. They relate either to the international leader him-/herself, if he/she acts as a role model (see first section), or to the tasks of the leader, for example when he/she selects suitable personnel, assembles teams, or ensures regulated work processes and a constructive working atmosphere, as well as shaping the working environment.

7.3.2.1 Personnel Selection (Recruitment, Promotion)

In the context of corruption prevention, personnel selection is of central interest as the risk of corruption in the company depends not least on the composition of the company's workforce. Thus, a skilful selection of personnel, especially for leadership roles, plays an important role in the fight against corruption.

Recent research has shown that professionals with strong Machiavellian traits are a poor premise. Companies should be careful when recruiting personalities with such a “the end justifies the means” attitude of character, as these have a stronger tendency to see corruption as a legitimate tool to achieve business goals. Another precautionary measure is to observe those employees who work in an environment prone to corruption and who have many years of experience in international business. Both factors have been identified as high-risk for condoning corruption due to a certain copycat effect. People who frequently experience corruption eventually consider it normal business practice and no longer problematise it as ethically and legally reprehensible. Such actions at the employee and management level can quickly lead to the normalisation of corruption in the company (Hauser et al. 2021). The process of taking on new staff as a corruption prevention measure can thus already include criminal records information, and the psychological susceptibility of the potential employee to corruption or his/her tolerance of corrupt behaviour can be questioned in the job interview (Stierle and Siller 2014).

Similarly, promotions are comprised of a twofold effect: on the one hand, a promotion can be used, among other things, to explicitly reward an employee for his/her anti-corruption efforts; on the other hand, it also has an internal organisational signal effect since it indicates to the staff the type of behaviour that is rewarded by the organisation. In this way, it is not only leaders but also co-workers who can become role models and induce other employees to behave in the same way, so they can be rewarded, too.

7.3.2.2 Personnel Development and Training

Regular training of employees is considered one of the most effective means of preventing corruption, as such action minimises the risk of employees becoming involved in corrupt behaviour (Hauser 2019b, 2020; Bendahan et al. 2015; Hauser et al. 2021).

The content of such training should inform participants as to the applicable international anti-corruption standards and their application at the national level. Participants should also be familiarised with the company’s anti-corruption policies as well as internal compliance rules and regulations. Such practice is implemented so as to ensure that the compliance rules and regulations are known by the employees when performing their day-to-day business. Discussions of case studies on corruption according to defined instructions, in conjunction with a reminder of the ethical and legal framework, also helps raise awareness of corrupt behaviour (Hauser 2019b). In order to check the transfer of knowledge and experience, participants should take tests, since this enables the company to comply with its documentation obligation, while at the same time they are able to confirm their participation in and awareness of the company’s anti-corruption policy (Becker et al. 2012).

In a study based on a survey of 200 business professionals, Hauser (2019b) presents the conclusion that education correlates positively with the probability of refusing to justify corruption. At the same time, however, training methods must become more specific in order to eliminate the grey areas between ethics and compliance (Castro et al. 2020). Hauser (2020) therefore suggests such training concepts that favour understanding, dialogue, and critical reflection, especially because it has been shown that there is a mismatch between compliance knowledge and the actual actions of persons in everyday business life. In anti-corruption training, therefore, sufficient time should be allowed to convey the learning content in the necessary detail. In addition, it must be avoided that the participants are given the impression to have wasted their time. This is the case if they do not recognise the relevance of the training content in their everyday work. So as to avoid this, there must be consistency, i.e. by ensuring that what is learned is consistent with daily business practice. A further success factor for anti-corruption training is the legitimacy of the source, i.e. the competence, credibility, and authenticity of the training provider, as well as a measurement of the effectiveness and impact of the training programme (Hauser 2020). The impact of training can be enhanced by pedagogical measures such as experiential and action learning. Guided learning is a particularly common approach, but it forces the learner into a passive role, as he/she is mainly confronted with frontal teaching, whereas experiential and action learning have a greater chance of success. Action learning means that the course participants organise the learning process themselves and develop problem-oriented solutions, while experiential learning in turn dispenses with learning goals but assumes that knowledge is collected in the course of daily work and is therefore better internalised (Hauser 2020). The consequence of such training is not only an increased awareness of the existence of corrupt behaviour, but also an increase in the loyalty of the employee to the company (Tang et al. 2015). In this context, leadership development should also be considered, because it can change corporate cultural values effectively through the process of monitoring and shaping behaviour. The prevention of corruption should therefore be integrated into leadership development programmes, too (Stierle and Siller 2014).

In the context of self-regulation, the International Chamber of Commerce (2019) recommends that the persons responsible for compliance in an organisation conduct properly documented as well as regular training of leaders and employees on anti-corruption policies and known corruption risks.

7.3.2.3 Control and Incentive Systems

As discussed above, the clear commitment of senior leaders is of central importance in the fight against corruption, and this must be non-negotiable and unwavering under all circumstances. If this clear commitment is present, the company must implement further anti-corruption measures in order to reduce the risk of corruption and to prevent legal liability. These measures should be taken at three levels, which complement each other: measures for prevention, detection, and response (Stierle and Siller 2014).

Measures for corruption prevention include corresponding guidelines. Such company-wide standards are, for example, corporate mission statements or management guidelines. A corporate mission statement formulates the company's principles with regard to its desired goals and behaviour, with the intention that all parts of the company adhere to them (Thommen and Achleitner 2006).

Furthermore, the implementation of rules and standards provides a significant and preventive contribution to avoiding corrupt behaviour in an organisation. Similar to a corporate mission statement, a code of conduct can also help shape the conduct guidelines in a company in such a way that corruption is prevented (Becker et al. 2012). A code of conduct expresses, for example, that an organisation strictly distances itself from any corrupt behaviour and also expects employees to act in a non-corrupt manner; moreover, it suggests ethical ways to behave in certain situations which occur in day-to-day business. Since employees are generally confronted with corporate mission statements and codes of conduct as part of their process of joining the company, this allows them to influence and control their attitudes and behaviour from the outset. Simultaneously, new employees are confronted with the consequences and implications of corrupt behaviour, which is particularly important in countries where giving or accepting gifts is not considered corrupt behaviour. In addition, according to Becker et al. (2012), a code of conduct should define the correct way of dealing with business partners and authorities. It should also be extended to supply chain partners. This supplier code of conduct should include the written commitment of partners to comply with legal and internal company regulations and to carry out regular checks in business areas exposed to corruption (Becker et al. 2012).

Preventive controls can also be exercised with the help of a risk checklist as proposed by Stierle and Siller (2014). It is used for the self-assessment of employees and differentiates, for example, between factors inherent in the system and task-specific ones. System-immanent factors include, for instance, the concentration of tasks on individual employees, the number of external contacts, the extent of the scope for personal decision-making, or the influence on processes by other company divisions. Task-specific factors include, for example, controls, markets, trade fairs, and the like. Currently, employee self-assessment is frequently utilised by international leaders to assess the level of risk of corruption in specific areas of a company. If the risk is high, the affected business area must be regulated, supervised, controlled, and documented more intensively.

Incentive systems, in turn, have the characteristic that they motivate employees to refrain from corrupt behaviour because the requirement for their behaviour is linked to a target. This target could be a bonus payment, for example, which is paid out if the employee acts with integrity in corruption-prone situations, or a positive employee assessment (Becker et al. 2012), which under favourable conditions even leads to a promotion.

The Hanoverian Corruption Scale (HKS 38) can serve as a further control measure. It focuses on attitudes rather than personality dimensions, offers the opportunity to proactively tackle corruption in companies, and aims to identify corruption risks in different areas of the company. The scale contains 38 cognitive, affective, and conative items to measure attitudes towards corruption. The HKS is implemented as an anonymous employee survey (Litzcke et al. 2017).

Corporate anti-corruption measures should also make possible the systematic uncovering of corruption. Therefore, even the first signs of corrupt behaviour should be recognised, which can in turn be achieved if there is an independent confidential contact point within the company or externally. Those who provide the contact point with information must, of course, be guaranteed anonymity and protection from retaliation. In addition, employees could be contractually obliged to report cases of corruption. Moreover, random checks can be carried out by internal audits. These should especially cover those areas of the company that are at risk of corruption. Of particular effect are unannounced inspections and spot checks as well as the complete documentation of all business transactions. Further internal control measures to detect corruption include the creation of a compliance officer to monitor compliance with laws and regulations (Becker et al. 2012).

Besides internal controls, external controls are also conceivable. Stierle and Siller (2014) distinguish between sovereign, statutory, and voluntary audits. While sovereign audits are primarily carried out by state authorities (financial administration, cartel authorities, courts of auditors, local government audit offices), whose purpose is to uncover corruption offences, statutory audits are often carried out by auditing companies. Voluntary audits are conducted by business consultants, lawyers, tax advisers, or experts and are also designed to prevent or detect corruption. The advantage of external audit bodies is that they are perceived by company employees as an objective and non-corruptible entity, which is not necessarily the case for audits by internal persons or bodies.

Within the framework of anti-corruption measures, lawyers, management consultants, experts, etc. can be involved in drafting service and business instructions, conducting trainings, risk and vulnerability analyses, carrying out the implementation and management of a whistle-blower system, etc. Internal steering and audit bodies, in turn, should include decision-makers from HR, the legal department, risk management, internal audit and controlling, as well as compliance officers. Additionally to the control measures aimed at internal personnel, further control measures should also be extended to third parties, such as suppliers or sales representatives.

This leads to the next step in the potential response to corruption cases. One possibility is to warn of personal consequences which might follow ethically and legally reprehensible behaviour such as bribery or fraud. In other words, such a warning communicates within the company that corruption will not be tolerated under any circumstances, and so creates a deterrent effect. These consequences consist of dismissal, termination, warning, termination agreement, or extraordinary dismissal at the levels of labour or civil law, for example in actions for damages (Becker et al. 2012).

7.3.3 Limitations of Management Tools for Fighting Corruption

Formal rules and standards cannot fully prevent corruption. Anechiaro and Jacobs (1996) conducted a multi-year qualitative case study to examine the effects of an anti-corruption strategy in New York City. The strategy described in the study was initially successful because it was based on undercover investigations and caused city officials to behave in the desired manner, namely to act strictly according to the formal rules of their organisation. However, the study found that such action did not lead to measurably less corruption. Rather, this strict practice produced a number of side effects that limited the effectiveness of the municipal administration, namely a slowdown in decision-making processes and inadequate leadership. The latter manifested itself in that central management positions lost their power because they were subject to increased control—thus not only leading to a diffusion of power within the organisation but eventually to a lack of clarity regarding who was ultimately responsible for strategic decisions. The consequence of these effects was over-bureaucratisation, and the monitoring process became an end in itself. A further consequence was the "adverse selection" of staff. This term referred to the effect of well-trained staff leaving the organisation due to the minimum of discretionary powers they were now facing. They no longer saw an opportunity to use their creativity and act professionally within such a strict formal framework. In this way, the organisation lost valuable staff. In addition, members of the organisation used payphones to make business calls in order to avoid being targeted by surveillance and to complete tasks as quickly as possible. Thus, so as to ensure the efficiency of the organisation, decisions were transferred to the invisible sphere, which is why the authors concluded that transparency measures can paradoxically lead to a distinct lack of transparency.

Furthermore, a lack of transparency can allow an organisation to become more flexible, but this in turn carries the risk that ordinary corruption will grow because people act for personal gain. Strict transparency measures can make individual breaches of rules more difficult, but stricter controls can lead to even more far-reaching breaches, as it can be argued that they were committed for the benefit of the organisation. Therefore, if the members of an organisation comply with individual rules, this does not mean that the organisation as such also acts in accordance with the rules. In more general terms, it can be said that formal rules and measures have their limits, and international leaders who act against corruption must be aware of this (Osrecki 2017).

7.4 Organisational Culture

7.4.1 How International Leaders Should Perceive Organizational Culture

In addition to ethical leadership as well as direct and indirect management tools, the organisational culture plays a major role in the likelihood of corruption occurring in a company. If, for example, a competitive culture prevails, this can encourage rule violations and corrupt activities. Thus, the organisational culture creates a context which, in turn, can have a significant impact on the occurrence of corruption (Castro et al. 2020). International leaders are therefore called upon to help shape organisational culture in order to curb or prevent corrupt activities. However, this point of view includes the premise of an organisational culture as a blank canvas to start from. In reality, in many cases, it is already established at the time an international leader takes over, including the subcultures in the various subunits of the organisation (Ashforth and Anand 2003). To increase the challenge, these organisational cultures and subcultures differ internationally and might include more or less corrupt behaviour which is considered normal. Thus, besides the explicit code of conduct, there is an implicit one that differs in every country where the company is doing business. Therefore, it is the task of a successful international leader in the context of fighting corruption to know the company's organisational cultures and subcultures, their implicit values, and how they shape the corruption-related behaviour of organisational members.

7.4.2 Importance of the Organisational Culture in the Fight Against Corruption

Bussmann et al. (2017) describe organisational culture as a central factor influencing the effectiveness of an anti-corruption programme. It is important to note that while each company has its own culture, including national or regional subcultures with implicit codes of conduct, a corporate guiding culture that promotes integrity is a prerequisite for fighting corruption. Bussmann et al. define this guiding culture as one of success. By this, they mean those business behaviours which lead to success in a company. If the culture of success promotes personal integrity, then successful employees deal with colleagues and business partners in an open and transparent manner; they do not act on their own interest and do not neglect the company guidelines. In this regard, the national and regional subcultures of success should not be underestimated (Ashforth and Anand 2003). Ethical leadership, as described above, can influence corporate culture and subcultures, especially when practised throughout a sufficient period of time and both authentically and credibly.

In the international context, it should be noted that culture is characterised by national, regional, or local influences. With reference to the theoretical discussion of corruption in anthropology, Castro et al. (2020) point out that companies may not attach sufficient importance to creating their own corporate culture, which carries the risk that this gap may be filled by the local culture outside the internationally active company, thereby making it extremely difficult or even impossible to enforce anti-corruption standards within it. In other words: the national or regional code of conduct, which may be more or less tolerant towards corruption, takes over as soon as the company fails to install a strong company-related value system. The solution to this problem lies in taking local cultural standards into account when developing anti-corruption policies and programmes, namely by paying close attention to how corruption-friendly or corruption-hostile the respective culture is outside the company. Thus, it is important to consider that the corporate culture is not only defined by the leadership and the employees but also by their external environment. For example, the amount and value of gifts considered as normal within business transactions differ greatly from nation to nation (Gerstner and Hauser 2019). In this way, a company cannot be regarded as a self-contained system, as it also depends on its environment. This includes external partners, i.e. suppliers, sales partners, or agents, as well as customers. Cooperation with such external partners is, however, accompanied by a high risk of corruption, which confronts a company with the task of carrying out analyses and research in the course of the selection process of suitable partners, especially if they are foreign partners. Once they have been recruited, they should give a written commitment to comply with both legal and internal company regulations (Becker et al. 2012).

7.4.3 Shaping the Organisational Culture by the International Leaders

If corrupt practices occur in a company, the task falls to international leaders to change entrenched habits and practices. To achieve this, corrupt behaviour must be sanctioned through a new cultural framework that has to be defined clearly. However, especially in international business, this poses a legal and ethical challenge for leaders to confront the company's internal policies and principles with its respective national convictions and to then subsequently correct them (Castro et al. 2020).

According to Bussmann et al. (2017), components of such an integrity-promoting corporate culture are the ethical behaviour of the senior management, the leadership behaviour of the direct superior, and the culture of success of a company. The aim of such a culture is to create an ethical and legal awareness among employees as to which business practices should be regarded as corrupt, so that corrupt actions do not occur in the first place. A corporate culture promoting integrity can reduce the risk of corrupt behaviour on behalf or against the company, positively influence informal social controls, and promote a positive speak-up culture. Appropriate training measures can ensure that this awareness is created or maintained.

Stierle and Siller (2014) stress the importance of a balanced relationship between control and a culture of trust, which must be established by international leaders in the interests of the company. If the culture of trust is low and the control systems are deficient, an organisation takes the highest risk. Even in such a situation, the right balance must be found to compensate, which cannot be the case if the company gives preference to control, which can lead to a loss of trust and a culture of mistrust. The reverse is also possible: if control is abandoned in favour of increased trust, this can lure into corrupt behaviour or otherwise become damaging to business. This balance could be achieved through active ethics and value management based on incorruptibility and transparency. If ethical rules are accepted over a longer period of time (for example, because a company has ethics awareness programmes), they become incorporated into the organisational culture.

7.5 Conclusion

The paradigm shift concerning foreign corruption—thus labelling it as a crime and making prevention mandatory—has put pressure on international leaders since the late 1990s (Gerstner and Hauser 2019). As a result of the legal and ethical demands placed on them or created by themselves, international leaders act as role models through their own behaviour: if corruption is scientifically defined as the abuse of power, their role model should reflect the justified use of power (Rogow and Lasswell 1963; Hauser 2019a).

However, the competence of international leaders to act also enables them to create the structures that prevent corruption in their company: they need to take preventive measures, which may consist of behavioural guidelines, training, or the appropriate selection of partners and personnel. Moreover, international leaders need to successfully implement measures that uncover corruption in the company, for example through control mechanisms. Finally, they need to respond to cases of corruption by sanctioning corrupt behaviour (Becker et al. 2012). However, such actions are easier in theory than in practice. The challenges arise in a special way in an international context, for example, when internationally active companies come into contact with other cultures where corrupt behaviour is deemed normal. Obviously, the fight against corruption is then a combination of the measures mentioned above, including ethical leadership with all its implications on the one hand and an organisational culture including value-related intercultural competences on the other.

Regarding the future of dealing with corruption in an international context, Bahoo et al. (2020) call upon international leaders to improve operational efficiency and performance as well as to design the organisational structure of their company in such a way that corruption is eliminated. In order to achieve this, it is necessary to question and expand current management theories to address the issue of corruption in international business apart from the economic and cultural factors discussed so far. Researchers and international leaders should acquire precise knowledge of the implicit codes of conduct of the subcultures involved in business strategies, which might include a certain tolerance towards practices of granting and obtaining undue personal advantages, in order to successfully prevent and counteract corruption in the future.

Acknowledgement The author would like to gratefully acknowledge writing assistance by Ernst Grabovszki.

References

Anand, V., Ashforth, B. E., & Joshi, M. (2005). Business as usual: The acceptance and perpetuation of corruption in organizations. *Academy of Management Executive*, *19*(4), 9–23.

Anechiaro, F., & Jacobs, J. B. (1996). *The pursuit of absolute integrity: How corruption control makes government ineffective*. Chicago, IL: University of Chicago Press.

Ashforth, B. E., & Anand, V. (2003). The Normalization of Corruption in Organizations. *Research in Organizational Behavior*, *25*, 1–52.

Bahoo, S., Alon, I., & Paltrinieri, A. (2020). Corruption in international business: A review and research agenda. *International Business Review*, *29*(4), 1–24.

Becker, K., Hauser, C., & Kronthaler, F. (2013). Fostering Management Education to Deter Corruption: What Do Students Know About Corruption and Its Legal Consequences? *Crime, Law and Social Change*, *60*, 227–240. doi: https://doi.org/10.1007/s10611-013-9448-8.

Becker, K., Hauser, C., & Kronthaler, F. (2012). *Korruptionsrisiken erfolgreich begegnen: Strategien für international tätige Unternehmen*. Chur, Switzerland: HTW Chur Verlag.

Belasen, A. T. (2016a). Introduction: Corruption and Destructive Leadership. In A. T. Belasen & R. Toma (Eds.), *Confronting corruption in business: Trusted leadership, civic engagement* (pp. 1–29). New York and London: Routledge Taylor & Francis Group.

Belasen, A. T. (2016b). Deception and Failure: Mitigating Leader-Centric Behaviors. In A. T. Belasen & R. Toma (Eds.), *Confronting corruption in business: Trusted leadership, civic engagement* (pp. 183–216). New York and London: Routledge Taylor & Francis Group.

Bendahan, S., Zehnder, C., Pralong, F. P., & Antonakis, J. (2015). Leader corruption depends on power and testosterone. *The Leadership Quarterly*, *26*(2), 101–122.

Bussmann, K.-D., Niemeczek, A., & Vockrodt, M. (2017). Die Bedeutung der Unternehmenskultur für wirksame Antikorruptionsprogramme—Ein Vergleich von Deutschland, China und Russland. In S. Jung, S. Friedrichs, A. Armbruster, H. Horstmann, F. Osrecki, I. Carr, R. Linssen, M. Meyer, I. Voigt, K.-D. Bussmann, A. Niemeczek, M. Vockrodt, A. Suchanek, E. M. Entschew, J. K. Rennstich, K. W. Rennstich, D. Kos, S. Litzcke, & M. Hermanutz (Eds.), *Management—Ethik—Organisation: Band 3. Antikorruption und Leadership* (pp. 113–134). Göttingen: V&R unipress.

Carr, I. (2017). Anti-Corruption and CSR. In S. Jung, S. Friedrichs, A. Armbruster, H. Horstmann, F. Osrecki, I. Carr, R. Linssen, M. Meyer, I. Voigt, K.-D. Bussmann, A. Niemeczek, M. Vockrodt, A. Suchanek, E. M. Entschew, J. K. Rennstich, K. W. Rennstich, D. Kos, S. Litzcke, & M. Hermanutz (Eds.), *Management—Ethik—Organisation: Band 3. Antikorruption und Leadership* (pp. 67–86). Göttingen: V&R unipress.

Castro, A., Phillips, N., & Ansari, S. (2020). Corporate Corruption: A Review and an Agenda for Future Research. *Academy of Management Annals*, *14*(2), 935–968.

Frei, C., & Muethel, M. (2017). Antecedents and Consequences of MNE Bribery: A Multilevel Review. *Journal of Management Inquiry*, *26*(4), 418–432.

Gerstner, M. B., & Hauser, C. (2019). Geschäftsberichterstattung zur Anti-Korruptions-Compliance börsennotierter Unternehmen mit Sitz in Deutschland und Frankreich. *Betriebswirtschaftliche Forschung und Praxis*, *71*(1), 55–79.

Goel, R. K. (2012). Business regulation and taxation: effects on cross-country corruption. *Journal of Economic Policy Reform*, *15*(3), 223–242.

Goertzel, T. (2005). On corruption, leadership and development in Latin America. *Psicología Política*, *31*, 77–102.

Hauser, C. (2020). From Preaching to Behavioral Change: Fostering Ethics and Compliance Learning in the Workplace. *Journal of Business Ethics*, *162*(4), 835–855.

Hauser, C. (2019a). Reflecting on the role of universities in the fight against corruption. *RAUSP Management Journal*, *54*, 4–13. doi: https://doi.org/10.1108/RAUSP-09-2018-0080

Hauser, C. (2019b). Fighting Against Corruption: Does Anti-corruption Training Make Any Difference? *Journal of Business Ethics*, *159*(1), 281–299.

Hauser, C., & Kronthaler, F. (2013). Neue Märkte, neue Risiken: Empirische Evidenz zum Korruptionsrisiko für den international aktiven Mittelstand. *Zeitschrift für Betriebswirtschaft*, *83*, 37–60. doi: https://doi.org/10.1007/978-3-658-04092-5_3

Hauser, C., Simonyan, A., & Werner, A. (2021). Condoning Corrupt Behavior at Work: What Roles Do Machiavellianism, On-the-Job Experience, and Neutralization Play? *Business & Society*, *60*(6), 1468–1506.

International Chamber of Commerce (2019). *Principles on Combating Corruption for Business Associations and Chambers of Commerce*. Paris. Retrieved from https://iccwbo.org/content/uploads/sites/3/2019/06/icc-principles-on-combatting-corruption-web.pdf

Jung, S. (2017). Antikorruption durch Ent-Moralisierung und Ent-Heroisierung—Für ein neues Verständnis von Führung als organisationale Störung. In S. Jung, S. Friedrichs, A. Armbruster, H. Horstmann, F. Osrecki, I. Carr, R. Linssen, M. Meyer, I. Voigt, K.-D. Bussmann, A. Niemeczek, M. Vockrodt, A. Suchanek, E. M. Entschew, J. K. Rennstich, K. W. Rennstich,

D. Kos, S. Litzcke, & M. Hermanutz (Eds.), *Management—Ethik—Organisation: Band 3. Antikorruption und Leadership* (pp. 43–66). Göttingen: V&R unipress.

Jung, S., Friedrichs, S., & Armbruster, A. (2017). Antikorruption und Leadership—Ein Essay zu einem problematischen Zusammenhang. In S. Jung, S. Friedrichs, A. Armbruster, H. Horstmann, F. Osrecki, I. Carr, R. Linssen, M. Meyer, I. Voigt, K.-D. Bussmann, A. Niemeczek, M. Vockrodt, A. Suchanek, E. M. Entschew, J. K. Rennstich, K. W. Rennstich, D. Kos, S. Litzcke, & M. Hermanutz (Eds.), *Management—Ethik—Organisation: Band 3. Antikorruption und Leadership* (pp. 7–18). Göttingen: V&R unipress.

Kirchler, E. (2011). *Wirtschaftspsychologie: Individuen, Gruppen, Märkte, Staat* (4th ed.). Göttingen: Hogrefe.

Krammer, S. M. (2019). Greasing the wheels of change: Bribery, institutions, and new product introductions in emerging markets. *Journal of Management, 45*(5), 1889–1926.

Litzcke, S., Linssen, R., & Hermanutz, M. (2017). Neue Perspektiven für Führung mit der Hannoverschen Korruptionsskala (HKS 38). In S. Jung, S. Friedrichs, A. Armbruster, H. Horstmann, F. Osrecki, I. Carr, R. Linssen, M. Meyer, I. Voigt, K.-D. Bussmann, A. Niemeczek, M. Vockrodt, A. Suchanek, E. M. Entschew, J. K. Rennstich, K. W. Rennstich, D. Kos, S. Litzcke, & M. Hermanutz (Eds.), *Management—Ethik—Organisation: Band 3. Antikorruption und Leadership* (pp. 217–236). Göttingen: V&R unipress.

Osrecki, F. (2017). Korruptionsbekämpfung durch transparente Organisationen—Die unbeabsichtigten Nebenfolgen eines populären Konzepts. In S. Jung, S. Friedrichs, A. Armbruster, H. Horstmann, F. Osrecki, I. Carr, R. Linssen, M. Meyer, I. Voigt, K.-D. Bussmann, A. Niemeczek, M. Vockrodt, A. Suchanek, E. M. Entschew, J. K. Rennstich, K. W. Rennstich, D. Kos, S. Litzcke, & M. Hermanutz (Eds.), *Management—Ethik—Organisation: Band 3. Antikorruption und Leadership* (pp. 19–42). Göttingen: V&R unipress.

Rogow, A., & Lasswell, H. (1963): *Power, Corruption and Rectitude.* Englewood Cliffs, NJ: Prentice-Hall.

Starnawska, S. E. (2016). Banking failures and unethical leadership. In A. T. Belasen & R. Toma (Eds.), *Confronting corruption in business: Trusted leadership, civic engagement* (pp. 275–307). New York and London: Routledge Taylor & Francis Group.

Stierle, J., & Siller, H. (2014). *Praxishandbuch Korruptionscontrolling: Konzepte, Prävention, Fallbeispiele.* Berlin: Erich Schmidt.

Stocker, L. (2001, November 28). Job-Rotation soll Korruption unterbinden. *Die Welt.* Retrieved from https://www.welt.de/print-welt/article489823/Job-Rotation-soll-Korruption-unterbinden.html

Tang, Y., Qian, C., Chen, G., & Shen, R. (2015). How CEO hubris affects corporate social (ir)-responsibility. *Strategic Management Journal, 36*(9), 1338–1357.

Thommen, J.-P., & Achleitner, A.-K. (2006). *Allgemeine Betriebswirtschaftslehre* (5th rev. ed.). Wiesbaden: Gabler.

Tonoyan, V., Strohmeyer, R., Habib, M., & Perlitz, M. (2010). Corruption and Entrepreneurship: How Formal and Informal Institutions Shape Small Firm Behavior in Transition and Mature Market Economies. *Entrepreneurship Theory and Practice, 34*(5), 803–831.

Part III

Leading International Teams

Intercultural Work Settings: Which Competences for Managers, Leaders, and Teams?

8

Pia Stalder

8.1 Introduction

To the present day, the professional landscapes have become global, complex networks of relationships. Growing mobility, digitization, and rapidly changing markets turn many—if not most—contexts into "intercultural" systems where people need to be creative and have to negotiate new forms of collaboration and cohabitation. Individuals and groups involved in those negotiation processes are challenged by "in-between" situations as well as by the volatility, uncertainty, complexity, and ambiguity (VUCA) they bring along. Managers, leaders, and employees with different backgrounds, experiences, values, beliefs, and views have to be able to connect and cooperate despite their diversity. The diversity of team members and the growing transboundary collaboration open up new opportunities. At the same time, they raise numerous managerial questions. The diversity of team members has been shown to be generally positive for group creativity and innovation (see, e.g., Amabile and Kurtzberg 2001; Milliken et al. 2003), but it remains a double-edged sword in organizations (Carter and Phillips 2017). Being successful in the professional context today necessarily implies spanning multiple boundaries: national, cultural, disciplinary, physical and, above all, cognitive hurdles. The VUCA environment we are living in definitely calls for collaboration in teams because:

P. Stalder (✉)
School of Engineering and Management Vaud (HEIG-VD), University of Applied Sciences of Western Switzerland (HES-SO), Yverdon-les-Bains, Switzerland
e-mail: pia.stalder@heig-vd.ch

I. Stolz, S. Oldenziel Scherrer (eds.), *International Leadership*, uniscope. Publikationen der SGO Stiftung, https://doi.org/10.1007/978-3-658-37306-1_8

> Organizations are facing more and more complex challenges that can no longer be solved by creative individuals only. They need 'teams' with diverse skills, ideas and knowledge to creatively solve these challenging issues. (Chompunuch et al. 2019, p. 1)

Inclusive and effective transboundary team collaboration is more important than ever. Strong intercultural competences are the conditio sine qua non for entrepreneurial success. They concern the whole workforce. In this article, we look at the necessary individual and collective competences for managers, leaders, and team members. The questions we address here are the following:

- How can we successfully collaborate across borders?
- Which competences are key?
- What can we learn from theory and practice to further develop our competences as managers, leaders, and team members?

The goal of this article is to shed more light on the subject of intercultural competences needed for today's work settings, which challenge all of us. We have a look at the following items:

- The theoretical concepts underlying the topic of intercultural collaboration in general and the competences for successful team interactions in particular;
- A selection of intercultural managers' best practices; and
- Some methods that help promote these competences among staff members.

As for the structure of the chapter, there are three sections. In the first part, we lay the theoretical foundation of the topic and present our view of its conceptual cornerstones. In the second one, we take a glimpse at best practices compiled through qualitative interviews we have conducted with managers—in Switzerland and abroad—about their strategies in intercultural work settings. In the third and last section, we address the subject of learning and training methods that can help enhance intercultural competences. Here, we also present different methods we use in our own practice. This final section is closed by a synthesis—in the form of a model—which summarizes our conception of the process of intercultural competence development.

8.2 Theoretical Approach to Intercultural Management and Competence

International collaboration is indispensable for giving answers to questions that are no longer of local but also of global concern. Today, transboundary collaboration is essential for developing—political, economic and, above all, social—solutions that are sustainable and benefitting for all of us. We need to know *how* to collaborate across boundaries—not only national but, above all, cultural and psychological ones. It is the broad diversity of people, their experiences, knowledge, and skills that drive creativity as well as innovation and add value for our wellbeing. The challenge for managers, leaders, and employees is to find suitable ways of collaboration. They need to be able to navigate in "intercultural waters" and to co-construct shared cultures.

The theoretical cornerstones of our topic are complex. There is a myriad of definitions of management, leadership, culture, and competence. The goal of this first section is to lay the theoretical foundation of the topic. We clarify here *our* view of these concepts. We set out by describing what we understand by "management" and "leadership". In a second step, we open the perspective on "intercultural management". Here, we first address two core concepts: "culture" and "intercultural communication". In the third and last part, we look at the individual and collective competences that are key for transboundary collaboration.

8.2.1 Management and Leadership

The challenge of management in the globalized and virtualized world we live in is to lead with intercultural excellence. Collaboration in transboundary, intercultural networks requires more responsible leadership than ever. Management and leadership go together. Neither is superior or inferior to the other.

The English verb "to manage" is derived from the Italian "maneggiare": to hold in the hand, to handle, to control. According to Pettersson's research (2005), there are also French influences which are attributed to the contemporary meaning of the verb, namely from "manège", which means small arena, i.e. a place where a horse is led by hand. In addition, the word "management" is associated with "ménage", which signifies household in English (see Pettersson 2005, for the full etymological trajectory of the word). To put it simply, management starts from our home. It refers to keeping our household. Management is generally defined as a process consisting of five functions: planning, organizing, staffing, *leading*, and controlling. In our view, Allen (2018) gets to the heart of it: We "manage things" and "lead people".

Leading is an essential function of management. Ciulla (2014, p. XV) states that "leadership is not a person or a position. It is a complex moral relationship between people based in trust, obligation, commitment, and a shared vision of the good". According to Schein and Schein (2018), contemporary leadership is "humble leadership", which, in particular, refers to leaders who accept shifting roles. Jordans, Ng'weno and Spencer-Oatey refer to the Global Leadership Fellows Programme by the World Economic Forum (2022) for describing the "modern" leader: Today, leaders are required "who have the vision and values, the character and competence, to shape the future while also balancing the polarities between short- and long-term goals" (2020, p. 22). We need "dynamic, engaged and driven individuals who possess a high degree of intellectual curiosity and service-oriented humility, ... entrepreneur[s] in the global public interest with a profound sense of purpose regardless of the scale and scope of the challenge" (Jordans et al. 2020, p. 22).

To summarize, acting as a leader does not require any managerial position, whereas a manager definitely needs leadership skills. Management can be seen as a "science" (plan, structure, analyze, control) (Pierre 2020),[1] while leadership is more of an "art" (vision, connect and build relationships, inspire, motivate, persuade) (see also Surbhi, 2018).[2] For inclusive, effective collaboration in teams, the essence of this art is, according to Schein and Schein (2018, p. 3), to build "personal cooperative, trusting relationships as in friendships" while also taking into account feelings and emotions.

In conclusion, management, and leadership are closely interrelated. We view leadership as a key function of management. For us, managers' and leaders' main business today is the "art" of establishing and maintaining solid relationships across physical and mental borders (Stalder 2014b).

The individual and collective key competences we are talking about in this chapter not only apply to managers and leaders but to all of us. Collaborative success depends essentially on the quality of the interactions among people in social networks which, today, span the entire globe. In order to succeed, we need strong "intercultural competence" in all our functions. In management science, this notion has been of interest since the 1950s (Bolten 2018, p. 188), and it is in the focus of the following sub-sections.

8.2.2 Intercultural Management: From Culture to Competence

In the past, management was mainly associated with planning, structuring, dividing, delegating, directing, and controlling tasks (e.g. Taylor 1911; Fayol 1916/1970). Today, it is no longer only about technical-strategic competences but also very much about solution-oriented, relationship-based, and dynamic interactions in real and virtual networks.

Intercultural management has emerged from the observation that people do not organize themselves in the same way everywhere (cf. Cloet et al. 2018). There are different "cultures", in other words: different ways of communication, cohabitation, and collaboration. Before we open the perspective on the literature in the field of intercultural management research, it is important to clarify the concepts at the heart of this managerial approach, i.e. "culture" and "intercultural communication".

8.2.2.1 Culture and Intercultural Communication

The culture concept is understood here in its broad, and not in its narrow sense. The narrow sense reduces it to artistic products or performances and to national or ethnic belonging.

---

[1]In this sense, Pierre (2020) understands "management" as the "analysis of the conditions of an organization's efficiency" (author's translation of the original quote "analyse des conditions d'efficacité d'une organization").

[2]See, e.g., the Management Study Guide (n.d.) for comprehensive comparative summaries of the differences between the two concepts.

Our broad understanding of the culture concept is based on North American anthropologists' research (e.g. Sapir 1921/2001; Kroeber 1952/1972; Kroeber and Kluckhohn 1952; Hall 1976/1979), on the work by Cuche (1996/2001), Wicker (1997), Rivera (1997/2000), Giordano (2003, 2008), Kilani (2009) or Pretceille (2012). We define cultures as *forms of organization*, negotiated and co-constructed by individuals and groups in their daily interactions (Gohard-Radenkovic and Stalder 2013). Cultures are dynamic systems: we organize, structure and thereby simplify our ways of living and working together. Thus, individuals and groups are active "culture engineers" (Stalder 2018, 2019b, 2019c). As for "interculture", this concept is understood as the creation process of new cultures in contact situations (Beneke 1995). People involved in those negotiation processes are challenged by "in-between" situations and by the uncertainties they bring along. By an "interculture", we mean a physical and psychological space where individuals with different allegiances and experiences meet and (have to) negotiate common forms of organization, i.e. cultures (see also Stalder 2014b, 2017).

Management forms and strategies cannot simply be transferred from one company or group to another. Working and living together are strongly context-, team-, individual-, and task-bound. Intercultural collaboration is complex and places high communicative demands, especially on people in leadership functions. In our view, broad and solid communication skills are the core of intercultural competence.

We call "intercultural communication" verbal, para-verbal, and non-verbal interactions between people who are in the process of negotiating new forms of organization. These people have complex identities composed of different affiliations. Today, intercultural communication is no longer understood as just interacting with people from different nationalities. It is about diversity in a much broader sense: age, gender, discipline, experience. Unfortunately, in practice, "interculturality" is still mainly associated with national or linguistic allegiances and seen as a problem. Intercultural communication situations can indeed be unsettling. People on the intercultural stage find themselves in uncharted territory. Familiar strategies no longer work. New paths have to be explored and taken together. However, intercultural encounters have many beneficial aspects: if perceived positively and managed well, they broaden horizons, instill learning processes, and foster creativity as well as innovation.

These central cornerstones of knowledge set, we can move on to the topic of intercultural management.

8.2.2.2 Research on Intercultural Management and Definitions

8.2.2.2.1 Research on Intercultural Management

There are countless research papers and publications—both theory- and practice-oriented ones—on this subject on the market today. A good overview of the various study and research trends in the field of intercultural management is provided by Spencer-Oatey and Franklin (2009), Barmeyer and Franklin (2016), as well as by Bolten (2018) in his introduction to intercultural business communication.

In the field of intercultural management, there are mainly two approaches: researchers conduct either quantitative and comparative cross-cultural studies or qualitative in-depth fieldwork.

Widely known figures who have taken the quantitative approach include Kluckhohn and Strodtbeck (1961), Hofstede (e.g. 2001), Trompenaars (1994), House et al. (2004), Schwartz (2011), Trompenaars and Hampden-Turner (2020) as well as Meyer (2014/2015)—and, see also the Globe Project (SFU Beedie School of Business n.d.). These pieces of work have resulted in a number of cultural value and behavior "dimensions" (Hofstede 2020)[3] or "scales" (Meyer 2014/2015)[4] representing key areas that managers need to be aware of when it comes to interactions across national borders. These publications offer interesting insights into different cultural expectations of people from other nationalities.

Nevertheless, as we have seen above, culture goes far beyond nationality. We must not reduce individuals to their national belonging. Their identities are made of multiple allegiances and constantly change. When looking for guidance and practical information in view of interactions on the international stage, the reader of this type of publication must be aware of the (over-)generalizing character of these research results. It is necessary to adopt a critical stance and to avoid jumping to rapid conclusions. The individual interpretation of those "dimensions" or "scales" cannot be taken for granted. There is no general recipe that works in any interaction and in any context. Cultures do not meet; individuals meet, with all the complexity of their identity and of the experiences that shape it. It is important to add here that there is no universal method or model to manage intercultural collaboration. Interactions always take place in unique settings. The individuals involved have their own background, experiences, values, and needs. Their behavioral responses always depend on the situation and are not predictable.

Other pieces of research are based on qualitative data collected through field observations and "thick descriptions" (Geertz 1973/2000) of people's verbal, para-verbal, and non-verbal behavior, via interviews, audio-, and video-recordings, among others

[3]E.g. Hofstede's six dimensions (2020 - www.hofstede-insights.com/models/national-culture/): (1) Power Distance Index (PDI); (2) Individualism versus Collectivism (IDV); (3) Masculinity versus Feminity (MAS): in the business context, Masculinity versus Femininity is related to "tough versus tender" cultures; (4) Uncertainty Avoidance (UAI); (5) Long-Term Orientation versus Short-Term Normative Orientation (LTO); (6) Indulgence versus Restraint (IVR): Indulgence stands for a society that allows relatively free gratification of basic and natural human drives related to enjoying life and having fun. Restraint stands for a society that suppresses gratification of needs and regulates this by means of strict social norms.

[4]Following in the footsteps of her predecessors' work, Meyer (2014/2015, p. 16) focuses in her practice-oriented book on eight "scales": (1) Communicating: low-context versus high-context; (2) Evaluating: direct negative feedback versus indirect negative feedback; (3) Persuading: principles-first versus applications-first; (4) Leading: hierarchical versus egalitarian; (5) Deciding: consensual versus top-down; (6) Trusting: task-based versus relationship-based; (7) Disagreeing: confrontational versus non-confrontational; (8) Scheduling: linear time versus flexible time.

(e.g. Chevrier 2003/2006; D'Iribarne 1989; Chanlat 1990; Mutabazi and Pierre 2008; Stalder 2010, 2013, 2016a, b, 2019b, 2019c). In our own research—at the crossroads of anthropology, sociology, linguistics, and intercultural pragmatics—we privilege the inductive and qualitative approach. In our view, it renders well the contextual, relational, and individual subtleties to be considered when interacting on the international stage.

Both types of research and publications are most valuable sources of learning and development for those who wish to enhance their intercultural competences.

8.2.2.2.2 Definitions of Intercultural Management

But what exactly do we mean by intercultural management here? According to Bolten (2018, p. 137), "intercultural management [. . .] goes beyond comparative cultural issues and addresses concrete interactions". For him, "cultural diversity is not to be overcome, but to be understood as an opportunity for the construction of synergetic scenarios for action, which would not be achieved by a suppression or a 'best-of-both' synthesis of existing potentials" (Bolten 2018, p. 137; cf. also Page 2017). Mutabazi and Pierre define intercultural management as

> a managerial approach whose policies and practices are structured around mutual recognition between actors from different cultures [. . .], linked by a regular process of interaction and exchange, and driven by a team spirit characterized by mutual respect, learning and enrichment around a project and constantly shared and revised objectives. (2008, pp. 137–138)

Nevertheless, intercultural management is more than an "approach". In Sauquet's view (2014)—who conceptualizes intercultural management in terms of "intercultural intelligence"—it is both, a "posture" and a "method": "Intercultural intelligence is a posture that encourages us, by scratching behind appearances, to try to discover what can explain people's behavior" (p. 109). At the same time, it is the "method of exploring our differences and of taking them into account in our social relationships at work" (Sauquet 2014, p. 109). For Pierre (2020), intercultural management is the "discipline of 'voluntary astonishment' and of 'suspension of any judgement'". It aims at "getting to know ourselves and each other better" (Pierre 2020). For us, intercultural management

> encompasses the processes of questioning, developing and organizing forms of cooperation between individuals of different backgrounds who need to work together in heterogeneous and complex geographical, political, economic, historical and above all socio-cultural spaces (Stalder and Agbobli 2021).

Finally, for some years now, there has been a tendency towards the use of a new vocabulary in our field. Researchers, trainers, and practitioners are increasingly resorting to the concepts of "intercultural intelligence" (Sauquet 2014; Sauquet and Vielajus 2014) or "cultural intelligence" (e.g. Salih 2020; Toth 2020; Rüth and Netzer 2020). This specific type of "intelligence" is considered as the most powerful "tool" for dealing with intercultural situations. (Inter)cultural intelligence is understood as the ability to recognize and understand how cultural differences influence behavior. According to Toth, "cultural intelligence, or ICQ, introduces us to a wide range of approaches to common sense [...] and gives us strategies not only to help us tolerate them but to make the most of our differences" (2020, p. 11).

From our point of view, (inter)cultural intelligence is an integrative component of intercultural competence. We do not single it out; the new wording seems somewhat limiting to us. As we will show in the next sections, the competences for interacting on the international stage go far beyond "intelligence".

8.2.2.3 Individual and Collective Competences for Managers, Leaders, and Teams

Cultural complexity in the professional context is no longer the exception, but has become the rule. In our work settings, we all have more and more contact, face-to-face and virtually, with people of different origins, experiences, education, expectations, perspectives, value definitions, and interpretations. Today, business is interdisciplinary, international, and intercultural. In such an environment, intercultural competences are definitely crucial. Their promotion among managers, leaders, and team members is a fundamental prerequisite for sustainable success—socially, politically, economically, and ecologically.

Effective intercultural management and leadership that also drive teams' performances require global identity and openness to cultural diversity (Ang et al. 2006; Shokef and Erez 2008; Fotso et al. 2018; Abadir et al. 2019).

Adopting global perspectives as well as co-constructing common cultures and shared allegiances are key for managers and leadership (Gandolfi 2012; Reiche et al. 2017). Armstrong takes it a step further: "The leaders of the future will have to lead with intercultural competence and with the ability to facilitate this development of competence in others" (Armstrong 2020, p. 1).

We definitely share Armstrong's view: Intercultural competence is not only managers' and leaders' business. It concerns all of us. In order to collaborate with intercultural excellence and to further develop our competences, it is important to look at their components: what do we understand by "competence" and, more specifically, by "intercultural communication competence"? Which elements is it composed of? The next paragraphs shall answer these questions.

Competence is the combination of knowledge, will, and ability (Le Boterf 2010). Bolten (2018) describes it as the interaction of self-competence, social competence, professional competence, and methodological competence; for him, "action competence" is the synergetic result of the interdependence of these four partial competences. For Le Boterf, managers need to be able to "take initiatives and decisions, negotiate and arbitrate, make choices, take risks, react to breakdowns, innovate and take responsibilities" (2010, p. 63).

Being competent therefore means to know 'what to do', 'what to say', 'to whom', 'when', 'where', and 'how'.

Competent behavior has individual and collective dimensions. According to Le Boterf (2010, p. 67), "to act with competence means knowing to interact with others; one cannot be competent alone". And "collective competence is a process of emergence and a compositional effect. It results from the quality of the cooperation between individual competences" (Le Boterf 2010, p. 205). Le Boterf identifies ten "cooperation indicators" (2010, pp. 207 ff.). We only mention a selection of them here. The members of a group cooperate if they

1. Build, from their individual representations, compatible representations of the problems to be solved, the situations to be dealt with, the objectives to be achieved (shared situation awareness). The particular challenge for managers and leaders is to work for the convergence of individual reference frames toward common frames.
2. Communicate effectively using a common language.
3. Have "recognizable" behaviors that enable each member to anticipate and evaluate the possibilities of cooperation with others. Also, they must "know how to silence their ego": "It is not only necessary to assert one's genius, but also to listen to the other, to try to understand them, to put oneself in their place, to give them space" (2010, p. 210).
4. Synchronize their reasoning and the progress of their actions.
5. Act by making and implementing decisions that they have agreed upon.
6. Accept the existence of conflicts and know how to make compromises, arrangements, negotiations, and regulations.
7. Transcend their divisions—disciplinary, sectoral, geographical—and implement inter-disciplinary and inter-sectoral approaches.

Those collective competences are key in intercultural contexts where team members have not yet consolidated their collaboration cultures. As stated above, intercultural situations can trigger uncertainty, confusion or conflicts. Managers, leaders, and team members need to co-create psychological safety and trust. Therefore, intercultural communication competence is fundamental. According to Chen and Starosta,

> intercultural communication competence can be conceived of as the ability to negotiate cultural meanings and to execute appropriately effective communication behaviours that recognise the interactants' multiple identities in a specific environment. (1996, pp. 358–359)

They differentiate three dimensions in their model:

1. The cognitive dimension encompasses knowledge discovery and intercultural awareness (self-consciousness, cultural awareness)
2. The affective dimension involves attitudes, personality traits, motivation, and intercultural sensitivity (self-conception, self-reliance and reliability, open-mindedness, observation, and non-judgmental attitude)
3. The communicative and behavioral dimension relates to intercultural adaptability and ability (message skills, adequate self-disclosure, management skills) (Chen and Starosta 1996, pp. 358–359)

In theory, we can find many lists of interculturally relevant characteristics for successful interactions among people with different backgrounds. Bolten (2018, p. 188)—in reference to Ruben (1976), Triandis (1977), Fritz et al. (2000) or Deardorff (2006), see also Keup (2010)—mentions the following:

- Tolerance for ambiguity
- Empathy
- Adaptability
- Self-aware and self-oriented role behavior
- Cultural awareness
- Open-mindedness
- Respect for cultural differences

Especially in view of the contemporary globalization and the ongoing digitization trend, three further aspects should be added (see also Bendell 2018):

- High observational capacity
- Resilience
- Renunciation

In conclusion, we strongly agree with Toth (2020): intercultural communication competence begins with self-knowledge, open-mindedness, and flexibility. Managers, leaders, and team members need to be able to shift perspectives. In other words, intercultural competence starts where individuals and groups manage to apply the *Platinum Rule*® (by Alessandra, quoted in Toth 2020, p. 9): "Do onto others as they would like to be done on them", instead of the widely-known *Golden Rule:* "Do onto others as you would like them to do on you".

The theoretical foundation being laid, we now move on to practice. In the next section, we open the perspective on a selection of intercultural communication strategies experienced managers use in the field.

8.3 Practical View of Intercultural Management: Insights from the Field

How do experienced managers and leaders enhance collaboration in international and intercultural work settings? Which communication strategies do they use? In our own, mainly qualitative fieldwork in international settings, we are interested in strategies that help promote cooperation between people who have different affiliations. In terms of methodology, our approach is interdisciplinary. We work at the crossroads of socio-anthropology, psychology, linguistics (in particular pragmatics), and management sciences. By now, we have interviewed more than 100 internationally working managers about their strategies and methods. The data is collected from individuals who hold management positions in private companies, foundations, umbrella associations, research and training institutions as well as governmental or non-governmental organizations.[5]

We explore how the managers perceive their work contexts and, in particular, which strategies they use to interact successfully with their colleagues and teams. Over the years, a comprehensive repertoire of strategy descriptions has emerged which they apply in their professional environment (see, e.g., Stalder 2010, 2016a, b, or also 2019a and 2019b).

Ideally, practice- and theory-building are strongly interconnected. In the field of intercultural management, this is increasingly the case. When looking at the strategies described by the managers we have interviewed, there is more and more consensus between the practitioners' perceptions and the competences highlighted in theory (cf. Sect. 8.2.2.3). The strategies described by our interviewees range, for example, from "paying attention", "questioning oneself", "expressing interest", "being open", "self-restraint", "finding a common language", "team training", "making expectations explicit", "paying attention to status and role", "defending territory" to "finding consensus" and "using humor". The difference between practice and theory is that the practitioners' observations and reflections, particularly when collected through qualitative interviews, reveal very rich insights, as they are the result of "thick" descriptions (Geertz 1973/2000) of situations, relationships, and tasks. They add value to the theory in the sense that they make us aware—and beware—of the complexity and dynamics that are so characteristic of interculturality. Qualitative interview results also raise consciousness for the fact that there is no unique method, model or strategy that works as a magic wand or recipe in international work settings. In the following sections, we give insight into a selection of strategies described by managers in the field.

8.3.1 The Benefits of Positive Attitudes

For Nadia, head of a science promotion agency in India, who we interviewed about her strategies for intercultural management, a positive attitude towards diversity is key. In her view, we need to go beyond differences instead of considering them as disruptive factors. She relies on curiosity, respect, and the recognition of skills. What is important to her is not

[5]The interviews normally last between 30 and 90 min and are audio-recorded. They are conducted in English, French, Spanish, German or Swiss German—depending on the language skills and preferences of the informants and of the respective interviewer. The recordings are transcribed partly or in full while using common transcription conventions (e.g. Mondada 2005). The interview protocol includes questions such as: How do you deal with diversity in practice? What do you see as the main challenges when it comes to managing diversity? What are the key strategies, models or tools you have experienced and would recommend to a young manager? Can you translate the key tool(s) among all you have just mentioned into a metaphor? See Stalder (2010, 2016b) for more details on the research methodology.

only self-restraint (cf. Le Boterf 2010) but also courage and openness. Nadia underlines that she always tries to analyze the situations she observes by asking many questions to the colleagues involved, as well as by seeking advice from people she trusts and who are more familiar than herself with the specific context in which she is working. When asked to translate her main strategies into a metaphor in order to visualize and summarize them, it is the kaleidoscope that springs to her mind:

> I have just seen a kaleidoscope in front of me. So I think, you have to, you must not be a one-dimensional person. You should have mental openness, [in the sense] that many things can be, and see that primarily as an opportunity, not as a deterrent or obstacle.[6]

8.3.2 Physical and Psychological Mobility

For Brian, team head in the packaging section of the pharmaceutical industry, physical mobility was an eye-opener. Before coming to the headquarters of his employer in Basel, he had worked in London for several years. Very often, when receiving mails or calls from colleagues in Switzerland, he could not make much sense of the questions he was asked. But mobility changed his perspective:

> You can see things from the other side, from the other perspective. In the UK, I would sit there in the UK, maybe I would get a phone call from Basel, and there would be somebody asking me something I considered to be a stupid question. And I just didn't understand why they would want to know this. Of what use is that for you? Why is that so important for you?

Moving to Basel opened his mind. He learned to adopt other points of view and raised his cultural awareness.

For Li, a Chinese manager also working in the Swiss pharmaceutical industry, "thought process is very difficult to manage". It may hinder the development of collective competences, in particular the synchronization of individual reasonings and the co-construction of shared representations.

To sum this up, intercultural competence not only implies "physical" mobility but also "psychological" mobility, in other words, the capacity to access other people's ways of thinking. In our view, it is such physical and psychological mobility that can considerably help break down the barriers Rod, an American manager working in Switzerland, was talking about in our interview:

> But I think that we really need to break down some cultural barriers by educating folks if we want to move forward in interacting with the Chinese. [. . .] And if you can level, if you can level the cultural differences—not, not saying we ought to be the same, but at least knock down

[6] All quotations have been translated by ourselves from Swiss German, German and French.

the walls, the barriers that we have that make it unclear to us what is on the other side. If we understand what is on the other side, then things are leveled. You can, you know how to approach each other, you know how to talk to each other.

8.3.3 Arrangement of Time and Space for People to Meet

The two following statements illustrate well the importance of individual and collective competences differentiated in theory. According to Sylvie, a French product manager working in Basel, it is key to take into account colleagues' personalities:

> I think that the personality of each individual is very important in this kind of multicultural situation. [. . .] Because people don't have the same way, don't have the same openness, don't have the same ability to listen, don't have the same desire to get to know others.

For Eric, head of research in the pharmaceutical industry, it is essential to work on a team's collective competence:

> There is no doubt that teams need time to get to know each other better, and probably more in a multicultural environment than in a monocultural environment. And it's true, regular face-to-face meetings, or lunches or breakfasts, or in the evening, or when you go beyond the professional context, are in my opinion opportunities precisely to get to know others better and to communicate better with them. That's right, that's the first thing.

The implicit recommendation for managers and leaders here is that they should arrange time and space for individuals and teams to meet, in formal as well as informal contexts.

8.3.4 Climb and Sail "Across the Globe"

Intercultural collaboration is not a walk in the park. Misunderstandings, controversies, rivalries, and conflicts are social practices inherent to interculturality. It is not the goodwill of the various parties involved that avoids intercultural divergencies. It is "necessary to question the meaning given by the individuals concerned to their actions, given the fact that man [is an] active builder of sociability" (Giordano 2008, p. 161). In this sense, for Peter, CEO of an international textile company with its headquarters in Switzerland, intercultural collaboration is like climbing a mountain. He evokes the iconic Swiss mountain, the Matterhorn, as an illustration of his management strategy. He uses it for building shared representations and for enhancing collective competences. In particular, the Matterhorn is the picture he shows to new employees so as to explain the company's strategy: "Everyone knows the Matterhorn, and everyone is able to understand it, because people know that we are climbing it." The following is the corresponding excerpt of the interview translated from Swiss German:

> PETER: M-hm, I always show our employees, the new employees, our strategy by the means of the Matterhorn. INTERVIEWER: The Matterhorn? PETER: The Matterhorn, the Matterhorn in the form of a picture, that's our strategy. And everyone knows that, and everyone understands that, because, somehow, they know that we're climbing the Matterhorn.

This example reminds us of the fact that getting people to work together and achieving common goals is hard work. Climbing the Matterhorn involves hazards: abrupt weather changes, rock falls, slippery ridges.

Sophia, director of a federal foundation in the German-speaking part of Switzerland, describes her main strategy for intercultural collaboration with a sailing metaphor:

> Yes, just, simply, sailing. [...] You know where you want to go, but the wind keeps turning and you always have to look, to redirect and to readjust the exposure of your sails.

We close this sub-section with Barbara's point of view. She is the CEO of a large international manufacturer of multifunctional tools. Her description encompasses—literally and figuratively—all the previous ones. While talking, she refers to the mobile globe on her desk. For Barbara, when it comes to intercultural collaboration, "the first question to be asked is the one of our own position, and then that of others". She continues:

> The globe is a good example: you can turn it, you realize, 'oh', 'poah', I'll probably have to turn a bit myself here, too. You see here also the different starting position. Some countries are close to the sea, others have lots of mountains. So, well, if you're asking for a picture [that illustrates my strategies], I'd say the globe is not a bad one.

Barbara finishes by stressing that the image of the globe is certainly more appropriate than that of the road map, as the latter is two-dimensional only, and that intercultural management is more complex than that.

To sum this up, we consider these insights into managers' practices as "mirror images" of theory. Pictures, figures and metaphors like the kaleidoscope, the Matterhorn, or the Globe are useful in intercultural communication: They help visualize problem spaces and build the common ground that is necessary for collaboration. In our view, these mirror images are not only inspiring but also make it clear to us that intercultural collaboration is a never-ending adventure we undertake together. It is not a business of just goodwill. There are conflicting dimensions and risks: we are all different and do not, a priori, share exactly the same objectives. Not all of us envisage the same paths. Intercultural management means confrontation: with oneself, with others. It starts with good observation skills as well as a readiness to question existing cultures and to negotiate new forms of organization together. To paraphrase Giordano (2008): We are all actors of sociability, which is the foundation of any common project. Intercultural communication and management competences do not come from goodwill or from reading books—we need to practice and to question the status quo. The insight into the variety of approaches and into a selection of methods that we will provide in the third and last section of this chapter may give some guidance for further learning and competence development.

8.4 Intercultural Competence Development: Which Methods?

The goal of intercultural management and leadership is, among others, to recognize cultural diversity, to contribute to the acceptance and non-violent handling of it, and to connect people across multiple boundaries by encouraging the exchange of experiences, inclusion, and fairness. As we have seen, competence has individual and collective dimensions. It does not only concern managers and leaders but all staff members. However, there is a specific task that is incumbent on managers and leaders: that of going beyond the development of their own competences and to promote them among their team members (cf. Armstrong 2020). In other words, managers and leaders need not only to acquire intercultural competences themselves but also to take action for enhancing the development of these same competences in their teams.

In this last section, we address the subject of learning and training methods. Here, we also present different methods we use in our own practice. The section is closed by a synthesis—in the form of a model—which summarizes our conception of the process of intercultural competence development.

8.4.1 Some Paths for Action

There are many means to enhance intercultural competences of individuals and teams in professional contexts. Keup (2010, pp. 262 ff.), for example, mentions the following ones:

- Assessment centers and tools (for better self-knowledge, analysis of potential, identification of specific learning, and development needs, see, e.g., the "Global Fitness Development Profiler"[7] or the "Intercultural Development Inventory ®"[8])
- Foreign language training
- On-boarding and welcome days (for fostering inclusion and corporate cultures)
- Country-specific trainings and coaching (for staff sent abroad)
- Cross-cultural awareness trainings (for bilateral collaboration projects) and also

[7] The "Global Fitness Development Profiler" (GF-DP) has been developed at the University of Warwick under the supervision of Helen Spencer-Oatey. It is an indicator tool that reveals planning and development information in relation to "global fitness".

[8] The Intercultural Development Inventory® (IDI)—developed under the supervision of M. R. Hammer—is an assessment tool for building cultural competence in organizations and schools.

– Preparation and integration trainings for expatriates and their families

One of the most comprehensive overviews and collections of methods for intercultural learning, training, and coaching we have come across so far and can thus recommend to the interested reader is the "Handbuch Methoden interkultureller Weiterbildung" edited by Leenen (2019). It is an extremely rich and well-documented piece of collective work by experts, which covers the following:

– Broad theoretical foundations for intercultural learning (definition of key concepts, teaching and learning processes, didactic-methodical action)
– Detailed methodological approaches and "building blocks": e.g. case-based methods (like critical incidents), self-assessments, and other test procedures, simulations, presentations and
– A myriad of teaching and learning media (ranging from the use of pictures to different types of films, such as specific intercultural training films, documentaries, reports, film clips with contemporary witnesses, explanatory films, advertising films, or film clips from cabaret and comedy—all these media types come along with examples and access references)

Learning games (e.g. Diversophy®)[9] and assessment tools coupled with face-to-face as well as with online training and coaching activities by certified professionals (e.g. "Global DISC"®)[10] should also be added to these lists.

Last but not least, there are professional networks of international experts in intercultural communication and management, which associate individuals, higher education institutions, and private company members who are all active in the fields of mentoring, coaching, training, and research. These networks regularly organize practice- and/or research-oriented events. With its national organizations in different regions of the world, the Society for Intercultural Education, Training and Research (SIETAR) may serve us as an example here.

[9] Diversophy's games open our mind and contribute to the development of our intercultural communication competences. There are more than 100 games on doing business, interacting with people from various countries, and belonging to diverse cultures. The games address the perspectives and skill sets required to work in diverse contexts and environments.

[10] "Global DISC" is a tool that allows us to better understand how personality type and cultural background impact our behavior and communication style. It strongly supports the development of our self-knowledge—values, needs, norms, behavior, preferences (work, cohabitation, etc.)—and our capability of connecting with other people who have different experiential, educational, and cultural backgrounds. Developed by Csaba Toth (2020 ff.), "Global DISC" consists of (a) an online questionnaire, (b) a personal report (for reflection and learning), and (c) the "Quest", which is an interactive coaching application aiming to expand the users' "comfort zone" and to enhance behavioral flexibility as well as reflection.

In the next sub-sections, we give an insight in two selected methods we use in our own practice for contributing to the enhancement of intercultural communication competence: the "Culturoscope" and the "Plastic Mediation".

8.4.2 The Culturoscope

Sauquet and Vielajus (2014) have developed the "Culturoscope". This is a tool that facilitates an approach to the invisible dimensions of our diversity and of our cultures. It is a guide in the form of a grid that consists of 130 questions for analyzing contexts, representations, and cultural practices which are likely to explain other people's ways of behaving and interacting. In the authors' terms, the questions

> make up a sort of non-exhaustive but very broad checklist, which expatriates may find useful to consult whenever an operation, a project or a negotiation presents unexpected difficulties that are thought to have a cultural origin. The idea is not to answer these questions alone, but to research and have certain things explained by people with a good knowledge of local cultures (Sauquet 2014, p. 111).

This checklist covers 15 major themes (linked to world visions, identity and status, professional and organizational cultures, language, and communication issues) upon which actors in intercultural encounters "may stumble or lead to the observation of common visions and reflexes" (Sauquet and Vielajus 2014, p. 19). In our professional practice, we use the Culturoscope as a repository for asking solution-oriented questions in intercultural work settings, in individual and team coaching sessions, as well as in trainings. The Culturoscope promotes a change of perspective, reflexivity, openness, flexibility, and, thus, intercultural competence.

8.4.3 "Plastic Mediation": A Method for Intercultural Coaching

A powerful method to develop intercultural communication competence is, in our view, the coaching of individuals and teams. We understand coaching as the professional accompaniment by a *certified* trainer or coach with intercultural experience. Team leaders and staff are supported in raising awareness of cultural differences and their effects on cooperation. Coaching contributes to the analysis of complex systems and situations. It means empowerment and contributes to the improvement of collaboration dynamics by making visible the diversity of perspectives, thinking styles, and behavioral patterns.

In our own practice (individual and team coaching, training, consulting, and R & D), we use a method we call "plastic mediation" (cf. Stalder 2014b).[11] This is a useful method for visualizing complex social systems. Plastic mediation is a creativity technique based on all kinds of materials and artefacts (wooden cubes and sticks, glass beads, play figures, symbol cards, modeling clay, Playmobil© and animal figures, Post-its® and moderation cards, etc.). These materials play the role of "mediators". Plastic mediation is thus a work technique that helps give (tangible, visual, and communicable) forms to thoughts, to visible and invisible boundaries of complex social systems.

In a coaching, consulting, or training session, the participants are invited to use the "mediators" to illustrate the situation they are struggling with and wish to change. The "mediators" are the key agents of the method and help overcome internal or external obstacles—both visible and invisible—of one's individual or collective organization. The method facilitates raising awareness, a change of perspective, resource identification, and multiplication. It enhances the individuals' and the teams' problem-solving capacity.

When working with an individual or a team in a coaching session, the participants are invited, for instance, to use the "mediators" for illustrating the status quo of the situation they seek to clarify. They choose figures or cubes to show and explain their situation, concerns, views, and goals. The figures and artefacts are place holders for the "actors" on the coachees' "stage". The coach supports the process, in particular by asking questions, which helps cross boundaries.

We have recently used the method in the context of a consultation mandate. Eleven associations committed to the same cause, but operating in different language regions and cantons of Switzerland, they wanted to think about possibilities to federate. In this case, the plastic mediation method helped define the starting point of the discussions and clarify the goal of the meeting. Figure 8.1 shows the illustration of the group's line-up:

The figures in the picture represent the different associations. In the middle of the circle, the participants placed the "salt box", which was chosen as the symbol for their goal of the consulting session. The participants' aim was to *define the common denominators and identify the maximum of possible, meaningful cooperation.* Based on this visual starting point, a list of the common denominators was elaborated before passing on to shaping the collaboration possibilities.

Plastic mediation promotes self-awareness and self-positioning in relation to the different systems in which an individual or group is moving. It is a practical method to change perspectives, which is essential for tackling intercultural collaboration challenges.

[11] The plastic mediation method is originally based on the Compad®. This was a learning material box marketed by the Schulverlag publisher. It is unfortunately out of edition today. However, similar pieces of material can be bought individually so as to compose personal sets of artefacts.

Fig. 8.1 Group line-up

8.4.4 Synthesis: Attempt at an Observation and Reflection Model

In summary, we can neither be competent by ourselves nor develop our competences without interacting with other people. The VUCA environment and the challenges we face (the COVID-19 pandemic may serve us as an example) cannot be solved by individuals on their own. Global task forces with strong intercultural competences are necessary to find and implement sustainable solutions that are beneficial for all of us. In our view, we can progress by

- Observing, reflecting, and practicing transboundary collaboration
- Actively questioning and listening
- "Scratching behind appearances, to try to discover what can explain people's behavior" (to recall Sauquet's words, 2014, p. 109)
- Being goal-oriented while remaining open-minded and flexible

As a synthesis, we present a circular "observation and reflection model" (Fig. 8.2). It may stimulate the development process of managers', leaders', and teams' intercultural competences. The model is inspired by the "reflective circle" of Palmer et al. (1994). It shall encourage us to take time, pay attention to our emotions, and to have a closer look at situations, relationships, and tasks—not on our own, but together.

The process starts with listening to our feelings when in a specific situation. Emotions and somatic markers[12] are the triggers of the observation process. The broad context, the

[12]For theoretical insights, see the research and publications by Damasio (e.g. 2018). For more practical guidance, see, e.g., Storch (2014).

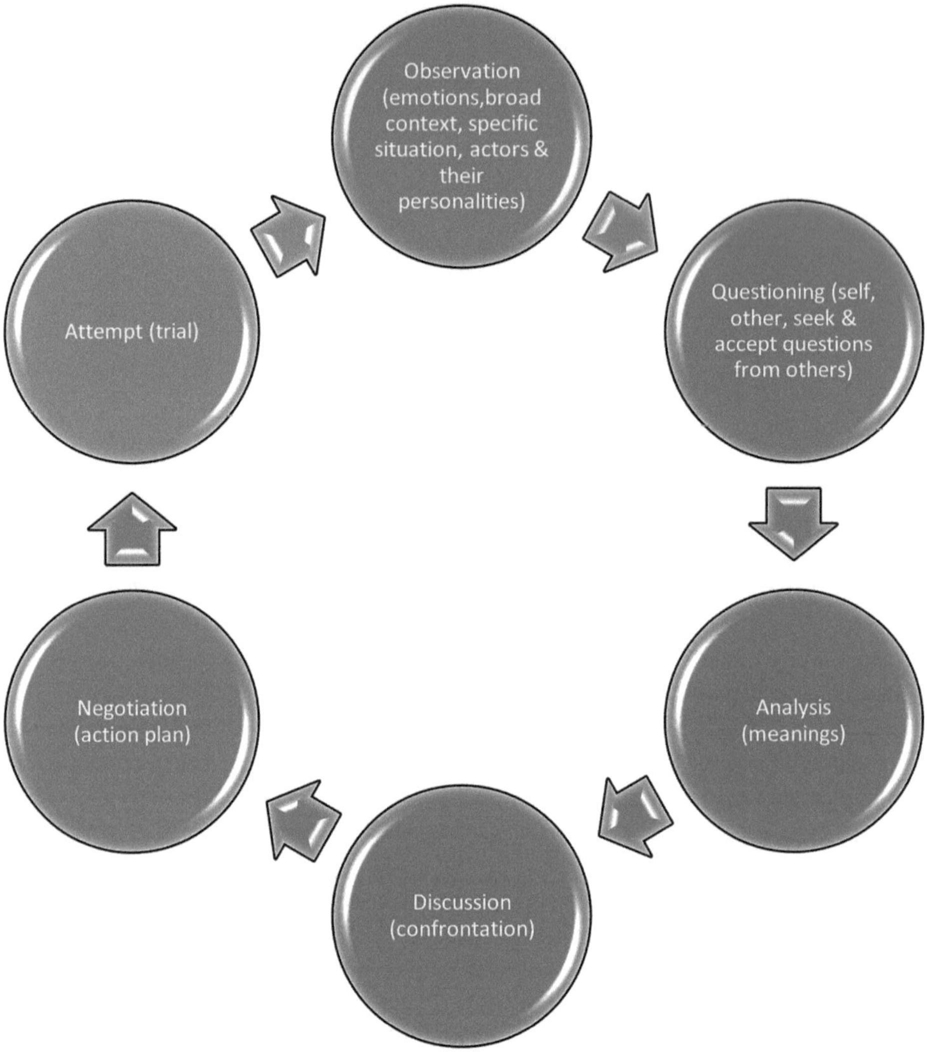

Fig. 8.2 Observation and reflection model

specific situation, and the actors involved (their allegiances, their background, their expectations, and their needs—see *Platinum Rule*® in Sect. 8.2.2.3) have to be considered. The "plastic mediation" method may help here. The next step is the—extensive—questioning phase: we question ourselves (What is going on here? What's my impression and view of the situation or the problem here?) and the other actors involved (first, people we trust—see Nadia's example in Sect. 8.3.1—and then the other players, too). In addition, we let others question and challenge us. The next steps are the analysis (What is the meaning of the situation for me, for the others, for all of us?), the confrontation and discussion of the results (What is the situation? What can we learn?), the negotiation of a new action plan (if necessary), and its trial phase. Sauquet and Vielajus' Culturoscope (see Sect. 8.4.2) can serve as a useful guide for navigating through all the stages of this circular model.

8.5 Conclusions

Today, managers and leaders are necessarily *global* actors. They need to recognize, appreciate, and rely on diversity. Management and leadership mean, in essence, "bridge construction"—across multiple boundaries. People in management and leadership positions are facilitators of individual and collective efforts to achieve common goals. Their "matter" is "relationship", which is made out of recognition, trust, psychological safety, commitment, shared vision-building, and the implementation of common goals. Managers and leaders not only need to cultivate their own intercultural competences. The particular task incumbent on them is to instill these same competences in all staff members. Intercultural competence concerns all of us.

The aim of this contribution was to give an insight into the subject of communication and management competences for intercultural work settings. We have not only tried to shed some light on the theoretical concepts and discussions related to this topic, but also to provide insights into practice. The objective is to give some guidance for the further development of managers', leaders', and teams' intercultural competences. We hope that the definitions, the shared practice, and the selected ideas for taking (further) action to enhance intercultural competences have the expected effect of inspiration.

References

Abadir, S., Batsa, E., Neubert, M., & Halkias, D. (2019). *Leading Multicultural Teams in Agile Organizations*. Retrieved from https://ssrn.com/abstract=3507635

Allen, T. (2018). "What is the difference between management and leadership?". Retrieved from https://www.forbes.com/sites/terinaallen/2018/10/09/what-is-the-difference-between-management-and-leadership/?sh=478780a874d6

Amabile, T. M., & Kurtzberg, T. R. (2001). From Guilford to creative synergy: Opening the black box of team-level creativity. *Creativity Research Journal, 13*(3–4), 285–294. https://doi.org/10.1207/s15326934crj1334_06

Ang, S., van Dyne, L., & Koh, C. (2006). Personality correlates of the four-factor model of cultural intelligence. *Group & Organization Management, 31*(1), 100–123. doi: https://doi.org/10.1177/1059601105275267

Armstrong, J. P. (2020). Assessing intercultural competence in international leadership courses: Developing the Global Leader. *Journal of Leadership Education, 19*(4), 1–20.

Barmeyer, Ch., & Franklin, P. (2016). *Intercultural Management. A Case-Based Approach to Achieving Complementarity and Synergy*. London: Palgrave.

Bendell, J. (2018). Deep Adaptation. L'Adaptation radicale: un guide pour naviguer dans la tragédie climatique. Rapport de recherche *IFLAS*, n° 2, 27 Juillet 2018. Retrieved from https://www.lifeworth.com/deepadaptation.pdf

Beneke, J. (1995). Der Gebrauch des Englischen in Handel und Wirtschaft. In R. Ahrens, W.-D. Bald, & W. Hüllen (Eds.), *Handbuch Englisch als Fremdsprache (HEF)* (pp. 61–64). Berlin: Erich Schmidt.

Bolten, J. (2018). *Einführung in die interkulturelle Wirtschaftskommunikation*. Göttingen: Vandenhoeck & Ruprecht.

Bollinger, D. et Hofstede, G. (1987). Les différences culturelles dans le management. Comment chaque pays gère-t-il ses hommes? Paris: Ed. d'Organisation.

Carter, A. B., & Phillips, K. W. (2017). The double-edged sword of diversity: Toward a dual pathway model. *Social and Personality Psychology Compass, 11*(5), 1–13.

Chanlat, J. F. (1990). *L'individu dans l'organisation: les dimensions oubliées*. Laval/Paris: Presses de l'Université de Laval.

Chen, G.-M., & Starosta, W. J. (1996). Intercultural Communication Competence: A Synthesis. In *Communication Yearbook, 19*, 353–383.

Chevrier, S. (2003/2006). *Le management interculturel*. Paris: PUF.

Chompunuch, S., Ribiere, V., & Chanal, V. (2019). *Team Creativity: Systematic Literature Review*. Paper presented at The ISPIM Innovation Conference – Celebrating Innovation: 500 Years Since daVinci, Florence, Italy on 16–19 June 2019. This publication is available to ISPIM members at www.ispim.org.

Ciulla, J. B. (Ed.) (2014). *Ethics, the heart of leadership* (3rd ed.). Santa Barbara, CA: Praeger.

Cloet, P. R., Guénette, A. M., Mutabazi, E., & Pierre, Ph. (2018). *Le défi interculturel. Enjeux et perspectives pour entreprendre*. Paris: L'Harmattan.

Cuche, D. (1996/2001). *La notion de culture dans les sciences sociales*. Paris: La Découverte.

D'Iribarne, Ph. (1989). *La logique de l'honneur*. Paris: Seuil.

Damasio, A. (2018). *Im Anfang war das Gefühl: der biologische Ursprung menschlicher Kultur*. München: Siedler.

Deardorff, D. K. (2006). The identification and assessment of intercultural competence as a student outcome of internationalization. *Journal of Studies in International Education, 10*(3), 241–266. doi: https://doi.org/10.1177/1028315306287002

Fayol, H. (1916/1970). *Administration industrielle et générale. Prévoyance–Organisation–Commandement–Coordination–Contrôle*. Paris: Dunod.

Fotso, G. B., Edoun, E. I., & Mbohwa, C. (2018). Business Enablers and Organisational Performance: Challenges and Opportunities. *Proceedings of the 2018 International Conference on Internet and e-Business* (pp. 94–98). ACM.

Fritz, W., Möllenberg, A., & Chen, G.-M. (2000). Measuring intercultural sensitivity in different cultural contexts. Working paper, No. 00/11, Institut für Marketing, Technische Universität Braunschweig.

Gandolfi, F. (2012). A conceptual discussion of transformational leadership and intercultural competence. *Revista De Management Comparat International, 13*(4), 522–534.

Geertz, C. (1973/2000). *The Interpretation of Cultures*. New York: Basic Books.

Giordano, Ch. (2008). L'insoutenable innocence de l'interculturel. In A. Gohard-Radenkovic & A. J. Akkari (Eds.), *Coopération internationale: entre accommodements interculturels et utopies du changement* (pp. 161–170). Paris: L'Harmattan.

Giordano, Ch. (2003). Préface. De la crise des représentations au triomphe des préfixes. In A. Gohard-Radenkovic, D. Mujawamariya, & S. Pérez (Eds.), *Intégration des "minorités" et nouveaux espaces interculturels* (pp. XI–XVII). Bern: Peter Lang.

Gohard-Radenkovic, A., & Stalder, P. (2013). Pour en finir avec la conception ordinaire de la notion de culture. *Universitas, 1*, 53–54.

Hall, E. T. (1976/1979). *Au-delà de la culture.* Paris: Éditions du Seuil.

Hofstede, G. (2001). Culture's consequences: Comparing values, behaviors, institutions and organizations across nations. London: Sage.

Hofstede, 2020 is the reference to the following website, information "Retrieved December 1st, 2020 from https://www.hofstede-insights.com/fi/product/compare-countries/

House, R. J., Hanges, P. J., Javidan, M., Dorfman, P. W., & Gupta, V. (Eds.) (2004). *Culture, leadership, and organizations. The GLOBE study of 62 societies.* London: Sage.

Jordans, E., Ng'weno, B., & Spencer-Oatey, H. (2020). *Developing Global Leaders. Insights from African Case Studies.* Cham: Springer/Palgrave Macmillan.

Keup, M. (2010). *Internationale Kompetenz. Erfolgreich kommunizieren und handeln im Global Business.* Wiesbaden: Gabler.

Kilani, M. (2009). *Anthropologie, du local au global.* Paris: Armand Colin.

Kluckhohn, F. and Strodtbeck, F. (1961). Variations in Value Orientation. New York: Harper Collins.

Kroeber, A. L. (1952/1972). *The Nature of Culture.* Chicago, IL/London: The University of Chicago Press.

Kroeber, A. L., & Kluckhohn, C. (1952). Culture: A critical review of concepts and definitions. *Peabody Museum of American Archeology and Ethnology Papers, 47.*

Le Boterf, G. (2010). *Construire les compétences individuelles et collectives.* Paris: Editions d'Organisation.

Leenen, W. R. (Ed.) (2019). *Handbuch Methoden interkultureller Weiterbildung.* Göttingen: Vandenhoeck & Ruprecht.

Management Study Guide (n.d.). "Leadership and Management – Relationship & Differences". Retrieved from https://www.managementstudyguide.com/leadership-management.htm

Meyer, E. (2014/2015). *The Culture Map. Decoding How People Think, Lead and Get Things Done Across Cultures.* New York, NY: PublicAffairs.

Milliken, F., Bartel, C., & Kurtzberg, T. (2003). Diversity and Creativity in Work Groups: A Dynamic Perspective on the Affective and Cognitive Processes That Link Diversity and Performance. In P. Paulus & B. Nijstad (Eds.), *Group Creativity* (1st ed.) (pp. 32–62). Oxford University Press.

Mondada, L. (2005). *Chercheurs en interaction. Comment émergent les savoirs.* Lausanne: Presses polytechniques et universitaires romandes, Collection Le Savoir suisse.

Mutabazi, E., & Pierre, Ph. (2008). *Pour un management interculturel. De la diversité à la reconnaissance en entreprise.* Paris: L'Harmattan.

Page, S. E. (2017). *The Diversity Bonus. How Great Teams pay off in the Knowledge Economy.* Princeton, NJ: Princeton University Press.

Palmer, A., Burns, S., & Bulman, C. (1994). *Reflective practice in nursing: The growth of the professional practitioner.* Boston, MA: Blackwell Scientific.

Pettersson, D. (2005). Guide pratique du coaching interne. Des collaborateurs heureux dans des entreprises performantes. Paris: Gualino.

Pierre, Ph. (2020). "En quoi le management interculturel peut-il être utile demain?". Retrieved from https://www.youtube.com/watch?v=o59WDiIvqns

Pretceille, M. A. (2012). Quelle anthropologie pour quel enseignement?. In F. & B. Fracciolla (Eds.), *Anthropologies, interculturalité et enseignement-apprentissage des langues. Quelle (s) compatibilité(s)?*, (pp. 19–34). Bern: Peter Lang.

Reiche, B. S., Bird, A., Mendenhall, M. E., & Osland, J. S. (2017). Contextualizing leadership: A typology of global leadership roles. *Journal of International Business Studies, 48*(5), 552–572.

Rivera, A. (1997/2000). Culture. In R. Gallissot, M. Kilani, & A. Rivera (Eds.), *L'imbroglio ethnique* (pp. 63–82). Lausanne: Payot.
Ruben, B. D. (1976). Assessing communication competency for intercultural adaptation. *Group & Organization Studies*, *1*, 334–354.
Rüth, R., & Netzer, T. (2020). The key elements of cultural intelligence as a driver for digital leadership success. *Leadership, Education, Personality: An Interdisciplinary Journal*, 2:3–8, 1–6.
Salih, A. M. (2020). *Cross-Cultural Leadership: Being Effective in an Era of Globalization, Digital Transformation and Disruptive Innovation*. New York: Routledge.
Sapir, E. (1921/2001). *Anthropologie. Tome 1. Culture et personnalité*. Paris: Editions de Minuit.
Sauquet, M. (2014). L'intelligence interculturelle: une posture et une méthode. *Revue économique et sociale* (bulletin de la Société d'Etudes Economiques et Sociales), *72*(2), 107–112.
Sauquet, M., & Vielajus, M. (2014). *L'intelligence interculturelle. 15 thèmes à explorer pour travailler au contact d'autres cultures*. Paris: Charles Léopold Mayer.
Schein, H., & Schein, P. (2018). *Humble Leadership. The Power of Relationships, Openness & Trust*. Oakland, CA: BK Publisher.
Schwartz, S. H. (2011). Values: Individual and cultural. In F. J. R. van de Vijver, A. Chasiotis, and S. M. Breugelmans (eds), Fundamental questions in cross-cultural psychology (pp. 463-493). Cambridge: Cambridge University Press.
SFU Beedie School of Business (n.d.). Globe 2020. Retrieved from https://globeproject.com/
Shokef, E., & Erez, M. (2008). Cultural intelligence and global identity in multicultural teams. In S. Ang & L. van Dyne (Eds.), *Handbook of cultural intelligence: Theory, measurement, and applications* (pp. 177–191). New York, NY: M.E. Sharpe.
Spencer-Oatey, H., & Franklin, P. (2009). *Intercultural interaction. A multidisciplinary approach to intercultural communication*. Basingstoke: Palgrave Macmillan.
Stalder, P. (2019a). Mentoring zur Förderung der interkulturellen Managementkompetenz im Betrieb. Theorie und Praxis. Unpublished thematic paper.
Stalder, P. (2019b). Funo? Humour, émotion et créativité au sein d'équipes interculturelles. In F. Berdal-Masuy (Ed.), *Emo-langages: Vers une approche transversale des langages dans leurs dynamiques émotionnelles et créatives*, Revue TIPA (Travaux interdisciplinaires sur la parole et le langage), *35*. Retrieved from https://journals.openedition.org/tipa/
Stalder, P. (2019c). Creativity in Intercultural Teams: Which Indicators, Facilitators and Competencies? In *IACCM-IESEG Conference Proceedings*, Paris, 31/10.–02/11/19, pp. 9–27. Paris: IÉSEG School of Management.
Stalder, P. (2018). Management interculturel: entre théorie et anarchie. In P. R. Cloet, A. M. Guénette, E. Mutabazi, & Ph. Pierre (Eds.), *Le défi interculturel. Enjeux et perspectives pour entreprendre* (pp. 141–149). Paris: L'Harmattan.
Stalder, P. (2017). Management interculturel: entre théorie et anarchie. In Cloet, P. R., Guenette, A. M., Mutabazi, E., & Pierre, Ph. (Eds.), *Le défi interculturel. Enjeux et perspectives pour entreprendre* (pp. 141–149). Paris: L'Harmattan.
Stalder, P. (2016a). Berne, Bucarest, Delphes. Aperçu d'une hybridation de démarches et méthodes pour appréhender le lien entre la diversité et l'innovation en Suisse. *Recherches qualitatives, Hors-série*, *20*, 416–432. Retrieved from http://www.recherche-qualitative.qc.ca/documents/files/revue/hors_serie/HS-20/rq-hs-20-stalder.pdf
Stalder, P. (2016b). 'J'existe, car je me souviens'. La réflexivité au profit du management interculturel. In P. Banon & C. Blons-Pierre (Eds.), *Didactique du français langue étrangère et seconde dans une perspective plurilingue et pluriculturelle* (pp. 241–257). Bern: Peter Lang.
Stalder, P. (2014a). Strike Season? Gestion des diversités linguistiques et culturelles dans les réunions en milieu professionnel international. *Les Cahiers de l'Acedle, Recherches en didactique des langues et cultures*, *8*(4), 1–15.

Stalder, P. (2014b). La médiation plastique pour le développement des compétences de communication en milieu professionnel international: Compad®, Playmobils® & Cie. In P. Stalder & A. Tonti (Eds.), *La médiation interculturelle: représentations, mises en œuvre et développement des compétences* (pp. 177–195). Paris: Editions des archives contemporaines.

Stalder, P. (2013). Management international: développer les compétences en innovant les formations. In X. Yang & L. Zheng (Eds.), *Culture et management* (pp. 215–223). Paris: L'Harmattan.

Stalder, P. (2010). *Pratiques imaginées et images des pratiques plurilingues. Stratégies de communication dans les réunions en milieu professionnel international.* Bern: Peter Lang.

Stalder, P., & Agbobli, C. (2021). La compétence interculturelle et l'humour comme stratégie dans le contexte du management interculturel. *Langages*, *222*, 77–94.

Storch, M. (2014). *Das Geheimnis kluger Entscheidungen: von Bauchgefühl und Körpersignalen.* München: Piper.

Surbhi S. (2018). "Difference Between Leadership and Management". Retrieved from https://keydifferences.com/differencebetween-leadership-and-management.html

Taylor, F. W. (1911). The Principles of Scientific Management. New York, London: Harper & Brothers.

Toth, C. (2020). *Uncommon Sense in Unusual Times.* E-Book. Retrieved from https://www.amazon.fr/Uncommon-Sense-Unusual-Times-opportunities-ebook/dp/B085MMVHNF/ref=sr_1_4

Triandis, H. C. (1977). Subjective culture and interpersonal relations across cultures. In L. Loeb-Adler (Ed.), Issues in cross-cultural research [Special Issue]. *Annual of the New York Academy of Sciences*, *285*, 418–434.

Trompenaars, F. (1994). Riding the Waves of Culture. Understanding Diversity in Global Business. New York: IRWIN Professional Publishing.

Trompenaars, F. and Hampden-Turner C. (2020). Riding the Waves of Culture. Understanding Diversity in Global Business. London: Nicholas Brealey Publisher.

Wicker, H.-R. (1997). From complex culture to cultural complexity. In P. Werbner & T. Modood (Eds.), *Debating Cultural Hybridity, Multi-Cultural Identities and the Politics of Anti-Racism* (pp. 29–45). London: Zed Books.

World Economic Forum (2022). Global Leadership Fellows Programme. Retrieved June 2nd, 2022 from https://www.weforum.org/communities/global-leadership-fellows

9 Co-leading an International Collaborative Team: Relationships Matter

Jillaine Farrar and Mary Gene Saudelli

9.1 Background

UFV is a mid-sized Canadian university in British Columbia that is partnered with HSLU-W in Lucerne, Switzerland. The School of Business (SoB) at UFV and the Lucerne School of Business (HSLU-W) both value the importance of international experiences for participants as meaningful and important in contemporary higher education. Formally, the relationship between these two institutions has existed for over a decade, and one of the learning events associated with internationalising is titled *International Leadership—Vancouver as the Asian-Pacific Gateway* (VILW). During this event, executive-education participants from HSLU-W travel to Vancouver and attend a series of visits to government, industry, and academic engagements for the period of 1 week. Canadian participants from the SoB at UFV also attend all of these events with participants from HSLU-W.

As educational leaders, both researchers involved in this study are passionate about international experiences and learning in higher education: We agree that "individual intercultural educators can make a significant difference in the intercultural learning of education abroad students (both incoming and outgoing), and the impact may not be fully

J. Farrar (✉)
Lucerne University of Applied Sciences and Arts – Business, Institute of Business and Regional Economics, Lucerne, Switzerland
e-mail: jillaine.farrar@hslu.ch

M. G. Saudelli
Faculty of Education, Community, & Human Development, University of the Fraser Valley, Abbotsford, BC, Canada
e-mail: mary.saudelli@ufv.ca

I. Stolz, S. Oldenziel Scherrer (eds.), *International Leadership*, uniscope. Publikationen der SGO Stiftung, https://doi.org/10.1007/978-3-658-37306-1_9

realised until well after they have left the classroom" (Jackson 2015, p. 98). Moreover, we strive to connect practice and theory throughout the week because we believe that "simply providing cultural information can seem shallow, but focusing on more abstract goals such as awareness can seem vague and detached from real life" (Shaules 2019, p. 205). Ultimately, we want participants to experience cultural information through real-life, immersive involvement in an international experience.

In 2018, Mary Gene Saudelli was promoted to Associate Dean in the Faculty of Professional Studies, which houses the SoB at UFV. In February 2019, Mary contacted Jillaine Farrar, Co-Head CAS International Leadership at HSLU-W and vice-president at SIETAR Switzerland (Society for Intercultural Education, Training and Research). Later, we connected to discuss the planning for the upcoming VILW scheduled for October 2019. What began as two educational leaders in two different countries planning an international event became a relationship of camaraderie, trust, and appreciation of mutual beliefs in relation to leadership and international reciprocity in learning. Through our collaboration, we discovered a mutual appreciation for the complexities of relationships in higher education, as well as across geographical and cultural collaborations.

This qualitative research study explores the following research question: What can be learned about international leadership through an exploration of collaborative co-leadership of the VILW for 2019, 2020, and 2021? Our purpose with this research is to consider how our relationship has formed and evolved, what this means for our continued partnership with our institutions, and how reciprocity and appreciation in international higher education can be mutually rewarding institutionally, professionally, and personally across borders in this boundaryless world. Our purposes are to edify the following:

(a) How sharing life histories with each other and reflecting on how our international competencies have shifted over time have contributed to co-leading our international team.
(b) How our aspirations and expectations regarding international experiences impacted our collaboration and our relationship as international citizens and leaders.
(c) How we were able to maintain our relationship and our collaboration across geographical contexts.

Using the intercultural citizenship theory (Byram 2008, 2014), this study contributes to the knowledge base regarding resilient and relational teams as well as international collaborative co-leadership. Readers will learn the following: the value of deep analysis of life histories as a background for relational dynamics that emerge in collaborative and international teams; the value of individual and dialogical reflection for collaborative co-leadership; and the value of using a duoethnographic methodology to explore international and collaborative co-leadership.

9.2 Theoretical Framework and Literature Review

Leadership as a construct has been well researched and theorised. Important leadership theories have been presented, such as: distributed leadership (e.g. Gronn 2011; Uhl-Bien 2006), invitational leadership (e.g. Novak 2002; Purkey and Novak 1996), authoritative leadership (e.g. Dinham 2007), and so forth. Leadership competencies have also been thoroughly researched and categorised in terms of skills, such as: ethics, nurturing growth, communication, self-organising, and efficiency (e.g. Giles 2016). However, leadership has been underexplored in relation to international and cross-national collaborative co-leadership, particularly in the context of higher and executive education. We believe this is a substantial gap in both theory and leadership. The theoretical framework guiding this study is the intercultural citizenship theory (Byram 2008, 2014; Deardorff 2015, 2020; Killick 2013), which is:

> ... viewed as the extension of citizenship beyond national borders, through recognition of the global scale of social relations, the need to respect and value diversity, and participation in and responsibility to communities at multiple levels from the local to the global. (Baker and Fang 2020, p. 3)

Intercultural citizenship theory involves conflating two central theoretical concepts: interculturalisation, due to the rapid flow of global movement, and global citizenship, which involves the recognition that we are all part of a global community and belong to that community as citizens (Saudelli 2015). Global citizenship is not about neglecting national citizenship but rather expanding it to recognise that our world is interconnected. As we work together to resolve global issues, engaging in the difficult questions of today requires effective intercultural communication, appreciation of differences (Saudelli 2015), and effective international leadership skills.

As leaders and employees continue to seek ways of learning to live and work together successfully across borders, understanding intercultural awareness, international leadership, and trust within international partnerships have become essential to successfully navigate the waters of international business and international educational leadership. The goal of this literature review is to illustrate the interrelations of these topics and to provide a basis for the authors' reflections on their international collaborative co-leadership. Fundamental to this is the underlying concept that culture learning changes us and helps build bridges of intercultural understanding (Shaules 2019, p. 4)—and thus intercultural competence, which is increasingly raised by educational institutions, corporate entities, and governments as "a central capability for the 21st century" (Hammer 2011, p. 474). Surprisingly, as noted by House et al. (2014), "although there are compelling reasons for understanding the influence of societal culture on leadership and organizational processes, only during the past two decades has there been an increased interest in studying leadership in multiple cultures (including non-Western cultures)" (p. 2). We rely on these and the other views presented in this literature review to frame *educational leadership competencies* and *intercultural competencies* as integral to the nature of the international collaboration between HSLU-W in Switzerland and UFV in Canada in the area of executive education. To this end, as global educational leaders in their respective institutions, the authors Farrar and Saudelli posit that leadership is crucial to ensuring positive, global engagements across boundaries, which involves intercultural and global citizenship competencies in order to facilitate impactful global learning for participants. We believe international and cross-national collaborative co-leadership involves communication beyond one's personal lenses (intercultural competence) as well as trust and flexibility in the relationship.

9.2.1 Intercultural Competencies

Intercultural competencies have been well researched, particularly in higher education studies. Alred et al. (2006) emphasise that being intercultural involves:

> Questioning the conventions and values we have unquestioningly acquired as if they were natural; experiencing the Otherness of Others of different social groups, moving from one of the many in-groups to which we belong to one of the many out-groups that contrast with them; reflecting on the relationships among groups and the experience of those relationships; and analysing our intercultural experience and acting upon the analysis. (p. 1)

Thus, the focus of intercultural competencies should be to facilitate the increase in skills, the acquisition of knowledge, and the honing of attitudes that will engender individuals to become intercultural speakers. Alred et al. (2006) further assert the urgency for people to build these attributes due to global developments which "necessitate a thoughtful and systematic approach to intercultural citizenship education" (p. 3).

If "there are no obvious a priori grounds for claiming that a particular behavioral phenomenon is universal based on sampling from a single subpopulation" (Henrich et al. 2010, p. 61), there are also no grounds for assuming that the perspectives of one's own culture can be applied to other cultures, as supported by Deardorff's (2015) editorial on the future of intercultural research. She notes, "if a key element of intercultural competence is in seeing from others' perspectives, it becomes imperative that scholars indeed examine this concept from a wide variety of perspectives" (Deardorff 2015, p. 3)—particularly those that embody critical reflection as a methodology (Deardorff 2020, p. 9).

In their seminal work on intercultural sensitivity, Hammer et al. (2003) state that Bennett's developmental model of intercultural sensitivity (DMIS) "constitutes a progression of worldview 'orientations toward cultural difference' that comprise the potential for increasingly more sophisticated intercultural experiences" (p. 421). They go on to explain that "three ethnocentric orientations, where one's culture is experienced as central to reality (Denial, Defense, Minimization), and three ethnorelative orientations, where one's culture is experienced in the context of other cultures (Acceptance, Adaptation, Integration), are identified in the DMIS" (Hammer et al. 2003, p. 421). The theoretical framework of the "Intercultural Development Inventory (IDI) was constructed to measure the orientations toward cultural differences" (Hammer et al. 2003, p. 421) explained in the DMIS, albeit with "Adaptation" being the final orientation in the "Intercultural Mindset" of the "Intercultural Development Continuum" (Hammer 2011, p. 475).

Browaeys and Price (2019) suggest identifying cultural values by plotting them on a cultural profile (p. 169). Although this does not offer the check-and-balance questions of the IDI, when overlapped with the country profile of one's business partner, it does provide an initial awareness of where issues may arise when working together. In a country-level analysis, this is similar to Meyer's (2014) culture mapping and Hofstede's (1998) view that "managing multinationals means accepting national culture differences and managing organizational culture differences" (p. 7) on which his county comparison tool is based. Where Browaey and Price's (2019) cultural profile differs from the country-level analysis, the possibility rises to identify individual nuances, such as in one's own relationship with time or hierarchy, which could, for example, have been influenced by having lived in multiple countries. In addition, it does not allow for cultural plurality within an individual, community, or country, thus creating space for generalisations or misattributions to occur.

In his influential work of analysing language, culture, and the embodied mind, Shaules (2019) states that "intercultural experiences provide us with an intuitive understanding of cultural difference, and allow us to recognize previously undiscovered cultural patterns in others and within ourselves" (p. 24). He further explains that "intuitive knowledge is developed through experience and pattern recognition—a process that can be both helped or hindered by conscious analysis and conceptual thinking" (Shaules 2019, p. 24). For deep learning to occur, there needs to be a "combination of analytic and intuitive processes" (Shaules 2019, p. 24). In a closer analysis of deeper learning and related experiential opportunities, he emphasises that "foreign travel and intercultural experiences are more deeply meaningful when they go beyond intellectual understanding or superficial cultural contact" (Shaules 2019, p. 25). Thus, it is not just the intercultural contact that is important but the meaning and deep learning about culture that can be a focus with international experiences.

What participants actually take along from their intercultural and international experiences may only surface in their consciousness when faced with real-life business decisions. This is supported by Jackson (2015) who states that education-abroad students have significant intercultural encounters, which may not be fully recognised until later in their careers (p. 98). Furthermore, the actual development of intercultural citizenship, although positively perceived by participants, has been found to be uneven during study abroad (Baker and Fang 2020, p. 1). Indeed, this is not surprising, as activating newfound intercultural and international leadership knowledge requires a context in which to use it, the flexibility to be able to employ it within organisational constraints, the trust and social capital to try things out, and the willingness as well as the ability to consciously adapt to situations and cultures.

The willingness to learn about other cultures and to be open to new information is key in international business. In order to maximize cross-cultural learning, Chwialkowska (2020) purports the "importance of getting out of one's comfort zone" (p. 1). Looking at the importance of intercultural knowledge and leadership skills for SMEs in both Switzerland and Canada aiming to expand their businesses globally, Farrar (2020) states that "a big part of making progress in the business world is making the best decisions possible with the information available" (p. 18). The complexity of making such decisions is underscored by Crossman and Clarke's (2010) findings which suggest that stakeholders highlight the connection between international experiences and career-oriented outcomes, such as "the forging of networks, opportunities for experiential learning, language acquisition and the development of soft skills related to cultural understandings, personal characteristics and ways of thinking" (p. 599). International study-abroad experiences as part of executive and higher education can provide opportunities for individuals to forge networks, engage in cross-cultural communication, and encounter intercultural knowledge through direct exposure to and immersion in lived experiences 'out of the comfort zone'.

9.2.2 Impact of Short-Term Intercultural Experiences

Going abroad for longer periods does not necessarily equate with an increase in intercultural competence and international leadership skills. Making a genuine effort to learn about a culture for however short a period can lead to an increase in intercultural awareness, including the understanding of commonalities and differences. Looking at short-term programmes abroad versus full single-semester study abroad, Potts (2020) confirms participants' perceptions of the positive impact of several short-term study-abroad programmes in terms of their employability skills. For some, this perception was reported as being higher than for those who participated in a single long-term programme. However, in her research on the impact of study-abroad programmes on participants' lives, Dwyer (2004) found that "more is better" in relation to "the duration of a study abroad experience" (p. 161).

In their research on "linguistic exchange activities and their impact on intercultural competence and the motivation to learn languages", Heinzmann et al. (2015) reported that "findings regarding duration suggest that a stay of 1–2 weeks is not particularly useful for the development of intercultural competence or motivation" (p. 40). Although these findings are specifically relevant for the language stays evaluated by the authors, they cannot be juxtaposed to the learning events associated with internationalising the VILW. While English is the language of communication during the preparation period prior to this week, during the actual week and throughout the post-week assignment, this language exposure can be considered an added benefit to the intercultural and international leadership content.

Studying participants reaping the benefits of well-structured short-term study-abroad programmes, Donnelly-Smith (2009) shares that faculty, administrators, and directors generally "agree that students get the most out of short-term programs that are highly structured, require ongoing reflection, and include in-depth experience working or studying with host country participants" (p. 3). This is concurrent with Vertesi (2015), who states that "significant changes in attitudes, openness and intercultural perspective can occur even with a short period away" (para. 10).

9.2.3 Global Citizenship Competencies: Trust, Flexibility, and Dedicated Boundary Spanners

Schreier et al. (2020) studied international partnerships emergence and form in the context of Swiss and Thai small and mid-sized enterprises (SMEs). They remarked on the importance of trust in international partnerships, and how it can be developed ex ante, i.e. given in the early stages of a relationship—and/or ex post, i.e. developed over time. Although there is still a "relative absence of research exploring how cultural differences influence the formation and development of international trustworthy partnerships" (Schreier et al. 2020, p. 5), the gap has been identified (Mainela et al. 2014, p. 121). Trust is essential in successful network relationships because it can help secure insider positions in foreign networks (Johanson and Vahlne 2009). Potentially, numerous individuals could span the boundaries between organisations and forge trust; but, as Vanneste (2016) suggests, "dedicated boundary spanners" play a key role in this as they are "more closely involved in the interorganisational relationships" and "interact more frequently than other employees" (pp. 13–14).

Flexibility and open-mindedness towards other cultures are important for international leadership and citizenship. Equally important is having trustful relationships in which you can broach sensitive topics and difficult conversations in addition to considerations of viable alternative solutions to projects potentially affected by unknown factors, such as the pandemic in 2020 and 2021. Reflecting on how education systems have been disrupted as a result of COVID-19, MacIntyre et al. (2020) speak of the uncertainty that currently exists in global and local educational contexts. They further indicate that "responses to COVID-19 may be rewarding those teachers who show greater flexibility" (p. 23). Hence, for those who engage in global networking and create global opportunities, a mindset is required that is adaptable, flexible, and open-minded. Further, Levin and Kurtzberg (2020) advocate for sustaining networks while working virtually and using tools such as video-conferencing, because one's "undivided attention is a gift to others and will bolster relationships when you aren't able to interact in person" (section 5, para. 1). Thus, trust, flexibility, and engaging personally by using available tools can make a difference in international, collaborative co-leadership.

Current literature identifies many benefits of creating international experiences in higher and executive education. What is less clear is what is involved in collaboration and co-leadership across geographic boundaries for these international experiences. This study addresses this gap in the literature. Farrar and Saudelli use their own biographies as sites for learning in this duoethnographic research study. While as scholars and educational leaders, we recognise that narrative forms of qualitative research remain, as Pinnegar and Daynes (2007) note, on the "margins of academic work" (p. 28), we also argue that "it offers sound methodological tools to the researcher who seeks to pay closer attention to the diversity of human experience" (McAlpine 2016, p. 16). In their research on managing relations across cultures, Spencer-Oatey and Kádár (2021) emphasize the need to acknowledge "personal histories" (p. 5) while exploring "how cultural identities and cultural patterning can affect the dynamics of interaction" (p. 6). In this duoethnography, we explore multiple perspectives related to our collaborative leadership and planning of the learning event, as we dialogue and question ourselves as well as our processes in relation to intercultural citizenship theory, study abroad, leadership, and internationalisation.

9.3 Research Methodology

This duoethnography explores the following research question: What can be learned about international leadership through an exploration of a 2-year time frame of collaborative co-leadership of the VILW for 2019, 2020, and 2021? Given this research question, a duoethnographic, qualitative methodology (Sawyer and Norris 2013) is appropriate. Duoethnography is a somewhat new qualitative research methodology that emanates from two narrative research approaches: Pinar's (1975, 2003) landmark concept of "currere", which is the framework for studying autobiographical reflections on educational experiences, engages in a storytelling approach to the research methodology. According to Norris et al. (2012), duoethnography is a collaborative, dialogical, rigorous methodology. Duoethnographers centre themselves as both researchers and participants in their studies (Sawyer and Norris 2013), thus interpreting meaning and "seeking critical tension, insights, and new perspectives" (p. 4) through their dialogue of their stories. This research method honours dialogic meaning-making with the researchers often transformed and empowered through research studies (e.g. Krammer and Mangiardi 2012; Lund and Veinotte 2010; Sawyer and Liggett 2012; Seidel and Hill 2015).

A duoethnographic approach is most appropriate for this study for multiple reasons. In a duoethnographic study, as collaborators share their stories, life histories, beliefs, and values, a key concept of "narrative unity" (Sawyer and Norris 2013, p. 10) emerges through dialogue focused on inquiry themes and questions. Duoethnography draws from traditions such as: ethnography with "thick descriptions" (Gertz 1973) of the sites of study; autoethnography with the emphasis on self-evaluation, description, and interpretive analysis (Chang 2008); and narrative inquiry with an emphasis on understanding storied experiences (Clandinin and Connelly 2000). The difference between duoethnography and these other methods of study is that duoethnography inquires about the ways in which individuals build and construct both narrative unity and disunity. As researchers dialogue and make their stories explicit, thus constructing, deconstructing, and reconstructing their storied experiences within the dialectic, critical conversations progress and a growth in perspectives emerges. Imagination, new ways of perceiving the stories, beliefs, and values, as well as new stories emerge. In duoethnography, the aim is "to seek not categorical conclusions but rather exposure, transformation, and uncertainty" (Sawyer and Norris 2013, p. 11) by "critically juxtaposing their stories" (Roth 2005, p. 3). As such, the stories, life histories, beliefs, and dialogues of the researchers as participants frame the analyses.

In this duoethnography, the authors as researchers will "juxtapose their life histories in order to provide multiple understandings of a social phenomenon" (Norris et al. 2012, p. 1). These life histories are in essence stories of experiences the researchers use to reflect and reconceptualise their life history as well as their shared experiences and collaborations. According to the prominent scholars Higgins et al. (2018), the result is an awareness and potentially a "reformation of researcher/educator beliefs, values and ways of knowing as a result of thinking and writing about research in participatory ways" (p. 75). To achieve this, in this duoethnography, the researchers' ethnographies present their stories as texts "side by side, creating a hybrid text of alternating alliances promoting rigorous study as partners jointly reflect on, and (re) conceptualize, their life stories" (p. 75).

In this duoethnography, the authors present their stories by integrating significant aspects of their life histories as they engage in the joint planning of an international event involving their two respective universities and faculties. They then dialogue with each other about their stories, in essence using the dialogue to function "as a mediating device that assists researchers in examining the frames that they use to situate meaning" (Sawyer and Norris 2013, p. 4). First, the researchers engaged in a personal reflection and created vignettes of their experiences as academics who have crossed international borders to live, teach, and research in one or more settings different from those they lived in previously. In the case of Mary, over a 14-year period, she left her Canadian teaching career to live and teach in Turkey, Hong Kong, the United Arab Emirates, and Qatar. In 2016, she returned to Canada and accepted a position at UFV in British Columbia. Jillaine was born and raised in British Columbia, Canada, but left in 1989 for Switzerland, where she still lives, teaches, and researches. Both authors are highly involved in creating international educational experiences for participants at their respective universities. One of those experiences involves their collaborative co-leadership of the VILW for the Lucerne University of Applied Sciences and Arts executive-education participants at the School of Business, Institute of Business and Regional Economics.

Mary and Jillaine did not know each other prior to co-leading the planning of the VILW. After they will have documented their stories, they will engage in several critical dialogues to nuance each other's life-history experiences and shared experiences with planning the VILW events for 2019, 2020, and 2021. Thus, data collection and analysis in this qualitative study are storied, comparative, and reflective (Saldaña 2012). Themes are analyzed by using axial and interpretive coding procedures of engaging and reviewing each other's stories, as well as their responses to the reflective inquiry for overlapping themes and principles. Then, themes and principles will be further codified, looking for values, beliefs, and changes in relation to conceptions of collaboration and leadership. These themes are further analysed through a dialogue that elicits and explores the core of these ideals for these two international educational leaders. Thus, this research study presents emergent and reflective theorizing about collaborations in international higher-education leadership.

9.3.1 The Process of Reflection: Appreciative Inquiry Framework

Research that involves reflection needs a framework to guide systematic analysis. Appreciative Inquiry (AI) is a strengths-based framework for reflective inquiry (Stavros et al. 2015). AI can be used by individuals, teams, organisations, or at the societal level. In each case, it helps people move towards a shared vision for the future by engaging others in strategic innovation and reflective thought. AI represents a "fundamental shift in the overall perspective taken throughout the entire change process to 'see' the wholeness of the human system and to 'inquire' into that system's strengths, possibilities, and successes" (Stavros et al. 2015, p. 97). In his research on building social capital by using an AI mindset, Calabrese (2006) explains that "mutuality moves beyond the quid pro quo of transactional relationships into the context of transformational relationships where actions occur in each party's best interest without the demand for reciprocation" (p. 174). As educational leaders and collaborators, we naturally gravitated to an AI framework as it aligns with our views and experiences of internationalisation.

AI is not a research method but a mindset and model of reflective inquiry. According to Cooperrider and Whitney (1999), the core principles of AI are: Constructionist, Simultaneity, Anticipatory, Poetic, and Positive. This means that educators and scholars who examine their work in internationalisation, leadership and collaboration must consider, reflect, and dialogue using these principles. Accordingly, the first principle is constructivist, which is described as representations of reality that are socially created through dialogue and language (Cooperrider and Whitney 1999). The second principle is simultaneity, or inquiry that creates change through meaningful and probing questions. The third principle is poetic: the choices we make regarding what we study. "Teams and organizations, like open books, are endless sources of study and learning. What we choose to study makes a difference. It describes—even creates—the world as we know it" (Perrakis & Scientific Partners n.d.). The fourth principle is anticipatory, or the images of the future that inspire action. "The more positive and hopeful the image of the future, the more positive the present-day action" (Cooperrider and Whitney 1999, p. 24). The fifth principle is positive: Positive questions lead to positive change. "Momentum for [small- or] large-scale change requires large amounts of positive affect and social bonding" (p. 25). As the researchers shared each other's life histories and engaged in their collaborative co-leadership of the VILW event (and further throughout this duoethnographic study), they followed these five principles of AI as they engaged in dialogical reflection into their international and collaborative approaches to co-leadership.

9.3.2 Limitations

Limitations of this study involve the typical limitations of any qualitative study. While illuminating, they are not intended to be generalizable. They represent the stories and meaning making of these two researchers, who came together in a collaboration, a shared co-leadership experience, and a duoethnographic research study. This research generates the proposition of theory, as opposed to positivistic assertions or cause-and-effect predictions. The purpose is to nuance the meaning of their shared experience to them, which may have resonance with others going through similar experiences, if not replication.

9.4 Our Stories

Given the nature of this study as a duoethnography, this section will use a storied approach to present Jillaine's Story, sharing some of her beliefs and values learned from crossing geographic borders, and then present Mary's Story by detailing some of her beliefs and values learned from crossing geographic borders. We will then proceed to share our story of collaboration and co-leadership in the planning of VILW for 2019, 2020, and 2021.

9.4.1 Jillaine's Story

The intercultural is an important part of my life, both privately and professionally. I have been teaching intercultural communication and English for Business to adults in Switzerland and internationally, in both higher education and corporate settings, for over two decades. My experiences as a qualified Intercultural Development Inventory (IDI) administrator have contributed to my belief in the importance of facilitating cooperative actions aimed towards intercultural growth and leadership development.

As vice president of SIETAR Switzerland, I am proud to have been involved in the strategising and planning of the successful 2020 congress on inclusion and intercultural topics, which had to be shifted to the online mode in autumn 2020 in a dispersed format due to the pandemic. The congress was suddenly accessible by the world and scholarships, made possible by congress sponsors, and evened the playing field for everyone who wanted to attend, regardless of their financial means. This is personally and professionally relevant for me as it is my way of giving my experience back to international and local communities. I have had the opportunity to learn from so many experts over the years who willingly shared their knowledge with me. Volunteering as a SIETAR Switzerland mentor and taking on the elected role of vice president has meant that I can help those newer to the field. My hope is that when they are well-established in their careers, they will consider doing the same, but this is just a hope and not an obligation.

My first experience with teaching was in Vancouver, Canada, where I grew up. While I was taking my initial Teaching English as a Foreign Language (TEFL) programme, I was a volunteer tutor for college participants who needed to prepare for their academic studies in English. Freshly married to a Swiss man who had been offered his dream job, I then moved to Switzerland. We had agreed to try living in Switzerland for 3 years. That was 31 October 1989. I am still living in Switzerland now and consider this my home. Earning my master's degree from the University of Manchester in the United Kingdom, the only geographically close (by Canadian thinking) degree programme of interest to me that I could access at that time in English added another layer of cultural experiences to my educational pathway. Crossing geographic borders in order to learn, live, and work has provided me with many opportunities to embody lived experiences interculturally. I have certainly made a considerable number of faux pas, but have turned these into learning experiences important for my growth mindset. These are what Joseph Shaules repeatedly referred to as "Oz Moments" in the Brain, Mind and Culture Masterclass I attended in autumn 2020 through the Japan Intercultural Institute. These situations may initially appear to lack any particular importance, but they are vivid memories. The name originates from The Wizard of Oz film, when Dorothy unexpectedly finds herself in a new place with new ways of doing things. Analysing these experiences highlighted for me how theory and practice go hand in hand to trigger deep cultural learning.

In addition to the Canadian and Swiss cultures, I have had the privilege to interact with many other cultures thanks to my position as Head of the Exchange Program, lecturer in the taught-in-English degree programmes, and Co-Head CAS International Leadership at the Institute of Business and Regional Economics, a part of HSLU-W. It is with the latter that I have the honour of working on the VILW with Mary Gene Saudelli. Interestingly, prior to my first contact with Mary, I had been told by a very dear, now retired colleague at UFV, John Potts, that he trusted her completely and therefore I should, too. This was a real-life ex-ante trust situation, where one 'gives' trust right at the beginning of a relationship because of the trust a common contact has explicitly stated, and I often refer to this in my lessons. Mary and I have now established ex-post trust, which is a natural outcome of working together well and, in our case, has facilitated further international activities, such as co-authoring this research study, and developed into a true friendship. This illustrates a fundamental value for me with regards to successful international collaboration. Not only is there potential for the relationship built on trust to evolve and become a reciprocal friendship, there is also an excellent scaffolding for future collaborations in business, within the universities and in research. Relationships matter.

9.4.2 Mary's Story

I spent most of my life dreaming of multiple worlds far away, people I could meet, lessons I could learn. Through my years as an undergraduate, I took courses in culture, geography, religion, and linguistics, always thinking about a chance to visit the incredible people and places I studied. When I began my career as an educator, I felt like the whole world was now mine to experience, and I did. Every vacation began with a question: "Where do I want to go now?" I spent months backpacking through Europe, bartered in the souks (markets) in North Africa, snorkelled in the Caribbean, climbed the Great Wall of China, and appreciated museums, restaurants, and local people in every location along the way. But the time came when travelling as a tourist was not enough anymore. I needed to live as a participating member of society in places different from what I had known. I took a sabbatical from my position in Canada for a year-long teaching position in Istanbul, Turkey. One year later, I resigned from my position in Canada and continued in Istanbul for another year. Then I accepted a position in Hong Kong, embarked on a master's degree, and lived in another new environment. A few years later, I was offered and accepted a position at a governmental college in Abu Dhabi in the United Arab Emirates (UAE), and after another few years, transferred to Dubai (UAE). I simultaneously began a PhD, and by the time I was in Dubai, I was in the data collection and comprehensive examination period of my studies.

At my faculty position in Dubai, I was also in the role of curriculum team lead. Looking back, I often point to this period of time as one of the greatest professional experiences in my life for a number of reasons. First, Dubai as an Emirate and a city was undergoing significant and rapid change. It was an incredible mix of diverse people (i.e. Emiratis who are the citizens of the Emirates and the Indigenous peoples of the UAE, expatriates, tourists to Dubai) and a rapidly changing social, political, and economic context. The UAE is also an Islamic and Arab region, and all aspects of a learning life must embrace this as a norm. Thus, the focus of curricula across the institution was on women, leadership, change, culture, Emiratisation (emphasis on Emiratis in leadership positions), Islam, interculturality and internationalisation, all of which became the subject of my PhD.

At the Higher Colleges of Technology (HCT) with a particularly diverse international team of faculty, I realised the salient learning that comes from leaving your comfort zone to experience real change. I realised how building relationships and learning about each other in this context were the starting points to any and all endeavours. At HCT, the curriculum redesign involved collaboration from faculty as well as from the private and public sectors, as the programme was trans-disciplinary, experiential, and transformative. The curriculum involved team-teaching, task- and project-based learning, as well as the integration of themes of empowerment, feminism, global civic mindedness, and leadership. The faculty with whom I worked were both Emirati nationals and people from across the globe, many holding citizenships in multiple countries. The diversity of perspectives as we designed and delivered the curriculum was captivating. The approach among all of us, and with participants, was premised on relationships and building trust, and time spent learning about each other was central to beginning any endeavour. To me, this is the power of international education, the power of diversity, and the power of relational collaboration across cultures, disciplines, geographies, nationalities, networks, ways of being, ways of doing, and ways of knowing—it all came together during this phase of my life.

Now I am Associate Dean in the Faculty of Professional Studies (FPS) at UFV in Canada, a role I assumed on October 1, 2018. The FPS consists of the Schools of Business, Social Work, and Computing, as well as the Departments of Teacher Education, Adult Education, Child Youth and Family Studies, and Information Studies. Across these Schools and Departments, my portfolio has three main areas: faculty development, internationalisation, and Indigenisation. This involves working across the faculty to support new programme development, curriculum reviews, international opportunities and learning, as well as Indigenisation across curriculum and learning. For me, this means the integration across disciplines of opportunities for diverse and empowering learning experiences, in addition to embodying an agenda conducive to valuing multiple worldviews, diverse ideas, reciprocity of learning, and approaches, as well as ultimately, in my view, building lasting relationships among people who value global civic-mindedness. Relationships matter.

9.4.3 Our Story, Mary's and Jillaine's Collaboration in the VILW

We, Jillaine and Mary, already knew of each other before we first met in person or interacted through digital tools. Just after Mary had begun her role at UFV, a colleague, John Potts, requested a meeting to discuss the VILW partnership with HSLU-W in Lucerne, Switzerland. Jillaine was a friend of his and his contact in Switzerland. The upcoming VILW was scheduled for September 29 to October 4, 2019. As Mary was new in the role, she felt it was a good time to look at the plans and organisation of VILW with a vision to refresh and consider new ideas. John suggested that he could connect Mary with Jillaine in Switzerland. During our collaboration, and throughout our research study, three themes evolved: aspirations and expectations through relationship-building; honesty, openness, and listening as co-leaders of an international collaboration; and maintaining the relationship and planning over time.

9.4.3.1 Aspirations and Expectations Through Relationship-Building

After John had introduced us to each other via e-mail, we scheduled the first of many digital synchronous video chats. The first few digital interactions focussed on getting to know each other and discovering that we had both experienced leaving all we knew to embrace life in a different social, cultural, political, and geographical context—not as tourists, but as participating members of society. We shared stories of our experiences, the kind of stories we could both fully appreciate given the nature of our lived experiences.

For example, Mary shared the story of the Emirati graciousness in the UAE and how she once had to navigate the complexity of refusing the gift of a Lamborghini car from a student's family in an Arab culture. Gift-giving is an important part of Arab graciousness, which is welcoming and sincere. As an educator,, Mary has been given tokens of appreciation, such as flowers or chocolates in the past, feeling pleasantly grateful. She had never lived in a wealthy country like the UAE, nor had she ever encountered the great respect for teachers that is a part of Arab culture. Thus, when her appreciative student attempted to give her the generous gift of a luxury car, she was utterly overwhelmed, uncertain, and worried about the extravagance of the gift. Mary was also aware that refusing a gift in this culture was considered offensive, so she did not know how to handle the situation. Mary went to the Emirati leadership in the institution and asked for advice and intervention. She was shocked when asked: "And you do not wish to accept?" That was when Mary realised that in this gracious culture, the gift was truly intended to be just that: a gift. Ultimately, the Emirati leadership managed the situation in a manner that was culturally appropriate, explaining to the student and her powerful father that Mary could not accept the generous gift but that she was humbled and appreciative of their thoughtfulness.

Jillaine shared an anecdote from the beginning of her career in Switzerland. She was proudly lecturing in her first full-time bachelor's degree class 20 years ago as a part-time lecturer when, as was the norm, she received an unannounced visit from her superior. He, now retired, is someone she considers a friend as well as a very respected professional colleague, but at that time he was clearly a superior, whom she hardly knew. After he had monitored her lesson for the entire session from the back of the room, they met in his office for debriefing and feedback. He said something to the effect of: "Ms Farrar, your lesson was very well prepared, you had very good rapport with the students, everyone was there and clearly learning, there were no problems, except" (here her heart stood still) "we do not use first names with the bachelor students." In her cultural naivety back then, she argued that she was teaching English for Business and that the culture in the classroom was a part of this. It was made clear to her that this was Switzerland, not Canada. She had a learning experience about fitting into institutional cultures while still trying to integrate the essential intercultural aspects with the English-for-Business teaching she was doing at the time. They compromised, which turned out to be a communality with the Swiss and Canadian cultures, with Jillaine using first names for that full semester and surnames with future bachelor students.

Through our sharing of these stories and our corresponding dialogue of the cultural implications, we realised that we share values and beliefs that impact our co-leadership of the VILW. We now realise that we are both continuing our own intercultural learning. We cherish our experiences living international lives, where uncertainty, worry, and mistakes are part of the value of these lived experiences. This has led to a dialogue of how both of us appreciate the value of a growth mindset from exploring beyond individual comfort zones of life, and how we both believe that higher education students need these kinds of international educational experiences as part of their learning. Although aspirational, this was a shared commitment to what we could achieve when managing the design of our VILW, how we would work together with our respective teams, and what we wanted this experience to look like. We consider ourselves international citizens, international educators, and international leaders. We share aspirations and expectations related to learning from our international experiences.

As we continued to engage, our interactions shifted to discussions of our upcoming Vancouver Week. Jillaine spoke of the history of the programme (9 years in running at that time), and Mary shared her thoughts on her review of the previous 2 years of the programme as well as her desire to give it a refresh with a contemporary vision. The theme throughout the previous years had been *Vancouver as the Asian-Pacific Gateway*, which was to be maintained due to stakeholder expectations, but Mary felt that sustainability and environmentalism could be woven throughout this main theme. During our discussion, it was decided to bring into the international experience aspects of government, education, and industry as being interconnected and integral to the concept of sustainability: a facet of education where the UFV School of Business has specific expertise.

As brainstorming continued, we realised we were generating a new story for our VILW—one that reflected the aspirations and expectations we value as international higher-education leaders. Moving forward, Mary indicated that she would bring together the planning team at UFV to engage in the further brainstorming and planning of the refreshed approach to the VILW. Both of us agreed that Mary would be the primary point of contact with the planning team, in order to avoid confusion and to streamline collaboration. Possibly we also just wanted to continue speaking to each other regularly as we collaborated on this exciting annual event.

9.4.3.2 Honesty, Openness and Listening as Co-leaders of an International Collaboration

The planning of an event such as the VILW involves many people, many meetings, and many details. Mary held frequent meetings with the planning team (which included John Potts who graciously volunteered his time and energy) which presented ideas, possibilities, and connections. During the brainstorming sessions with the planning committee at UFV, various options and network connections were explored, from an industry visit to the Vancouver Port Authority to attendance of a session at the Cultural Centre in Whistler, British Columbia. The planning committee had a vast network of connections throughout BC, and we wanted to bring a new angle to the event. The planning committee welcomed the integration of industry, government, academics, and culture. On a monthly basis, Mary openly shared all of the team's ideas with Jillaine for her thoughts. Jillaine shared her opinions on these ideas honestly with a nuanced awareness of the circumstances of the participants attending this event, their industry experiences, and their engagement with their graduate learning. Interestingly, almost all of our communications were via scheduled, synchronous digital video chat, rather than e-mail. Jillaine's feedback was discussed with Mary, who took note of the distinctive lens Jillaine shared as a Canadian and Swiss national.

Listening carefully to Jillaine's contributions, and sharing these openly with the working group, allowed for a revision process of reciprocity and intercultural learning across the international team. Jillaine shared her embodiment of Swiss cross-cultural aspects such as time management, professionalism, structure, and discourse. Moreover, she shared nuanced understandings regarding cultures: Swiss, Swiss-German, and Canadian. We shared our cross-cultural thoughts regarding feminism as well as trends about women in graduate schools and industry, cultural blunders, and the ease with which these may happen, as well as micro-aggressions that can occur.

Mary also travelled to Lucerne, Switzerland, and spent some time immersed in Swiss culture, which was integral for her to thinking through the planning of the VILW. This was the first time we met in person, although we felt we already knew each other well. Jillaine had made arrangements for scheduled events while Mary was on campus at HSLU-W. Mary delivered presentations about full-semester exchange opportunities at UFV, about British Columbia, and the executive programme, VILW. Furthermore, she met with the primary leaders involved in the institutional partnership with UFV. Mary felt honoured to have met the principles and to have been received graciously by them, even though she knew some discussions could directly address issues of non-reciprocal agreements, especially at the executive level. Specifically, while HSLU-W had paid to send executive participants to UFV in Canada, UFV had not reciprocated equally by sending participants to Lucerne. This was raised, and Mary openly acknowledged and expressed her desire to change this inequity, sharing ideas to encourage Canadian students to go to Lucerne—and receiving feedback on those ideas. At the bachelor's level, exchanges had already become reciprocal, which was considered a positive achievement.

In discussions, Jillaine, with her nuanced awareness of Swiss culture, shared and deconstructed the interactions for which Mary had engaged. This was integral as Mary not only learned important cultural considerations impacting their collaboration from a Swiss cultural perspective, but she began establishing relationships with the leaders at HSLU-W. This led to Mary's idea to include in the VILW programme a lunch event with the President of UFV and to invite the Mayor of Abbotsford, BC to attend, thus extending the relationship of our two universities, our communities, our collaboration, and our co-leadership of collaborative teams.

Ultimately, the revision and refresh of our VILW was a success due to the brainstorming, honesty, openness, and efforts of the collaborative international team, including the planning team at UFV. As usual at the end of the week, we debriefed immediately with members of the planning team, this time including Prof. Dr. Ingo Stolz, who attended the VILW for the first time in 2019. This debrief explored each event, each speaker, the schedule, the timetable, and all of the interactions, including anonymous participant feedback. Our debriefings were an exercise in honesty, openness, and listening from all who are committed to the reciprocity of learning through international experiences. Feedback was specific, operational, and did not stray from difficult conversations, but we all approached these talks with honesty, integrity, and goodwill due to the relationship that had been established. Relationships matter.

9.4.3.3 The Relationship Continues as Co-leaders and Collaborators

Following the success of the VILW 2019, we maintained our relationship across the digital space. When 2020 planning began, the world correspondingly became more complicated with reports of an emerging pandemic. Would participants be able to travel across geographical boundaries in September 2020? How about 2021? Suddenly, a limitless world was rife with boundaries, restrictions, and confusion across every aspect of daily life. In March 2020, We scheduled a video conference call to catch up with each other and to discuss the ramifications of COVID-19. In a brainstorming session with the planning team, we discussed options for the VILW and whether a quality experience could be arranged digitally to fulfil the needs of the participants and the universities within such a short planning time. Ultimately, the Vancouver Week 2020 was postponed for 1 year due to federal quarantine and travel restrictions.

The two of us embarked on this duoethnographic study of our lived experiences with planning the VILW, an effort mired with complex decisions of how to create a profound learning experience in a boundaryless world, while dealing with a pandemic. Throughout the summer of 2020, synchronous chats continued as we shared our stories, interrogated our perceptions, explored values and beliefs, and engaged in this research. We soon realised that we shared many commonalities beyond being international citizens and educators, both personally and professionally. While leadership and culture were important mutual interests, as are the ways we continually strive to support others in their intercultural and international leadership journeys. In fact, dealing with a pandemic heightened those beliefs and values significantly. Indeed, relationships do matter.

9.5 Implications and Discussion

The findings of this duoethnography highlight several important implications for international collaborations and leadership. Readers have learned the following: the value to be derived from the deep analysis of life histories as a background for relational dynamics that emerge in collaborative teams; the value of individual and dialogical reflection for collaborative co-leadership; and the value of using a duoethnographic methodology to explore international and collaborative co-leadership.

9.5.1 Life Histories and Relational Dynamics in Collaborative Leadership: Trust in a Boundaryless World

In our collaboration, planning began early in February 2019 and started with our relationship, intuitively rather than as an expressed agenda. While it started with an introduction by John Potts via e-mail, almost all of our conversations took place via video chat, though not for any reason we determined at the time; and they began with stories of introduction, which meant primarily sharing life histories right from the beginning of the collaboration. We agree with Levin and Kurtzberg (2020) who stress the importance of sustaining networks while working virtually and specifically state: "Keeping your own and your organization's ties positive and productive through periods of sustained virtual work will allow these valuable interpersonal networks to survive and even thrive" (section 5, para. 2). In our findings, we determined that there are two important considerations: First, while e-mail is a valuable tool, for collaborative relationships to form and build across a boundaryless world, personal interactions via synchronous video chat were crucial to share personal life histories as we did. It is unlikely that interaction via e-mail would have resulted in the same personal and deep communication. Second, building and maintaining trust in the interaction opens up space for complicated and difficult conversations to occur.

When crossing cultural and geographic borders, trust can enable an insider position in a foreign network (Johanson and Vahlne 2009, p. 1417). Trusting each other meant that we had this insider position in both of our university contexts. As Schreier et al. (2020) point out in the context of SME international network development, "trust in new partners needs to emerge and develop" (p. 91). They further found that "network relationships are based on mutual trust, knowledge as well as knowledge exchange, and commitment towards each other" (p. 102). We found this to be present due to the planning of the VILW, the planning as a result of the pandemic, and through this research study, which allowed space of our cultural lens to contribute to our planning processes.

In the first few interactions, we endeavoured to learn about the aspirations and expectations we each have in our partnerships, collaborations, and relationships as international citizens and educators. The effort we engaged contributed to the trust we had for and with each other. While the relationship may have begun with an ante-trust situation, it evolved to become a relationship of post-trust, professional trust, and friendship trust. The trusting, collaborative relationship created the space for a level of honesty and open dialogue that contributed to the brainstorming, planning, and feedback process of leading international teams for the VILW 2019. As we had both traversed the globe living and learning along the way, we openly discussed the various lenses we bring to our international collaborations: a Canadian lens, a Swiss lens, and an international lens. This perspective is supported by Spencer-Oatey and Kádár (2021) who note that cultural encounters are considered co-constructed but highlight that their approach takes this a step further as it "combines acknowledgment of personal histories with the dynamics of interaction" (pp. 5–6).

In these moments, we ensured time zone differences were accommodated: Some conversations occurred early in the morning and some in the evening, but we treasured these times as opportunities for like-minded global leaders to build a mutually respectful relationship with each other, valuing time, effort, stories, and ideas. This is noteworthy as it ties in with Shaules's (2019) work on how cultural understanding, from the neurocognitive perspective, includes reading patterns and interpreting situations (p. 30). Interestingly, while interculturalists can be insightful about culture without having studied cultural concepts, it is also possible for them to study cultural concepts and "have only shallow intercultural insights" (Shaules 2019, p. 30). Empathy and trust are a part of this. Although empathy, i.e. sharing and feeling for others, is universal in human psychology, it is not necessarily automatic in all situations (Zaki 2014, p. 1608; Shaules 2019, p. 37), or across all cultural interactions and situations (Saudelli 2015). We find this relevant because while it is not realistic to think we can erase our cultural biases, we can seek to understand how we function, how others function, and how we can function together. We concur with Shaules (2019) that understanding cultures can be conceptual or deep (p. 30). Moreover, we believe that a judicious mix of both conceptual and deep learning are essential, and therefore, educators collaboratively co-leading international experiences need to integrate this into intercultural learning opportunities and international leadership programmes.

9.5.2 Individual and Dialogical Reflection in Collaborative Co-leadership

The need for open communication, active listening, valuing the various cultural lenses brought to the collaborative process, and engaging in constructive debriefing and feedback cannot be underscored enough. As leadership continues to encounter difficult decisions and circumstances in a boundaryless world, there will be increasingly complex times when difficult conversations must happen. While we refer to them as "difficult conversations", they, in fact, do not need to be difficult at all if the leaders embrace them as with a mindset of AI (Stavros et al. 2015).

In this study, we have naturally gravitated to an appreciative approach in relation to the collaboration and our knowledge, skills, and international cultural competencies, which helped guide us through any moments when difficult conversations occurred. As we engaged in our co-leadership over the last 3-plus years, our dialogues, even the difficult ones, embodied all principles of AI (Gohain 2020; Srivastva and Cooperrider 1999; Stavros et al. 2015). The result was our professional relationship, initially based on collaboration, trust and respect, ultimately an international friendship. Further, through our stories, we discovered our mutual beliefs in the necessity of international collaboration, intercultural competencies, and leadership. Thus, we assert that an AI framework is a means to approach the complexity of international, intercultural citizenship efforts (Byram 2008, 2014; Deardorff 2015, 2020).

This study highlights the value of reflection in international leadership: individually and dialogically. We began as two like-minded educational leaders who live international lives and value the learning that comes with a boundaryless world. We recognize the importance of how our relationship formed, evolved, and strengthened through our analysis of our reflections. Reflecting on our lived leadership experiences, including our collaborative co-leadership, provided new insights to both of us. We discovered more about each other personally, in terms of our beliefs in relation to intercultural competencies, our leadership, and commonalities beyond our professions as scholars and leaders in internationalisation.

9.5.3 Duoethnographic Research Methodology and International Collaborative Co-leadership

This study demonstrates the importance of duoethnographic studies (Norris et al. 2012) in leadership and international education particularly as we move forward as a global community to unite and resolve issues that have a global scope and which requires a mindset of global citizenship. There is a demonstrable gap in the literature of leadership and internationalisation as explored through duoethnography or other forms of reflective research. These co-researchers, co-leaders, and collaborators shared their life histories and systematically analysed their stories to come to a deep and meaningful vision of their relationship. Duoethnography goes beyond reflection as a form of research methodology (Norris et al. 2012); it offers a systematic means of studying life histories, relationships, co-leadership, and collaborations in a boundaryless world. As global citizens and global leaders, duoethnography offers a method for deep awareness—not only for the individuals involved in the study but from the communication of different ways of being, different ways of knowing, and different ways of leading, all of which contributes to a global mindset (Saudelli 2015). Education for intercultural citizenship postulates that learners can, in addition to learning active citizenship in their own country, acquire the knowledge and skills necessary to act in a community which is multicultural as well as international and comprises more than one set of cultural values, beliefs, and behaviours (Alred et al. 2006).

It is because relationships matter in a boundaryless world that we specifically identify the importance of intercultural training. We agree with Vouillemin (2020) who states that "cultural training is an aspect of management training, not an extension of language training, although understanding something about the language and even speaking it is important in avoiding misunderstandings and communication breakdown" (p. 10). There were many moments when a communication breakdown or a misunderstanding could have negatively impacted our collaboration and planning for the VILW, but both of us are interculturally open-minded due to having lived international experiences, making mistakes along the way, and consciously learning from them. Ultimately, we have thrived from living, learning, and leading in a boundaryless world.

9.6 Conclusions

This study uses a duoethnographic methodology to edify the collaboration of two international educational leaders over a 3-year period of time, encompassing the planning of an international event, the VILW, as well as both institutional and national responses to a global pandemic. They discovered that ultimately, relationships matter in collaboration and co-leadership—with trust, honesty, intercultural awareness, and personal interactions framing how their relationship developed. Both authors believe even more fervently in the need for global collaboration, global leadership, and embracing cross-cultural competencies in order to be effective global citizens and leaders. In a boundaryless world, relationships matter.

References

Alred, G., Byram, M., & Fleming, M. (2006). Education for intercultural citizenship: Concepts and comparisons. *Languages for Intercultural Communication and Education, 13*, 86–105. https://doi.org/10.21832/9781853599200

Baker, W., & Fang, F. (2020). 'So maybe I'm a global citizen': developing intercultural citizenship in English medium education. *Language, Culture and Curriculum, 33*, 1–17. doi: https://doi.org/10.1080/07908318.2020.1748045

Browaeys, M. J., & Price, R. (2019). *Understanding cross-cultural management* (4th ed.). London: Pearson.

Byram, M. (2014). Twenty-five years on – from cultural studies to intercultural citizenship. *Language, Culture and Curriculum*, 27(3), 209–225. https://doi.org/10.1080/07908318.2014.974329

Byram, M. (2008). *From foreign language education to education for intercultural citizenship. Essays and reflections.* North Somerset, UK: Multilingual Matters Ltd.

Calabrese, R. L. (2006), Building social capital through the use of an appreciative inquiry theoretical perspective in a school and university partnership. *International Journal of Educational Management, 20*(3), 173–182. doi: https://doi.org/10.1108/09513540610654146

Chang, H. (2008). *Autoethnography as method.* London, UK: Routledge.

Chwialkowska, A. (2020). Maximizing cross-cultural learning from exchange study abroad programs: Transformative learning theory. *Journal of Studies in International Education, 24*(5), 535–554. https://doi.org/10.1177/1028315320906163

Clandinin, J. D., & Connelly, F. M. (2000). *Narrative inquiry: Experience and story in qualitative research.* San Francisco, CA: Jossey-Bass.

Cooperrider, D. L., & Whitney, D. A. (1999). *Positive revolution in change: Appreciative inquiry.* Corporation for Positive Change. Oakland, CA: Berrett-Koehler Publishers.

Crossman, J. E., & Clarke, M. (2010). International experience and graduate employability: Stakeholder perceptions on the connection. *Higher Education, 59*(5), 599–613. https://doi.org/10.1007/s10734-009-9268-z

Deardorff, D. K. (2020). Manual for developing intercultural competencies. *Routledge focus on environment and sustainability.* UNESCO. London, UK: Routledge.

Deardorff, D. K. (2015). Intercultural competence: Mapping the future research agenda. *International Journal of Intercultural Relations, 48*, 3–5.

Dinham, S. (2007). "Authoritative Leadership, Action Learning and Student Accomplishment". Retrieved from https://research.acer.edu.au/research_conference_2007/3

Donnelly-Smith, L. (2009). Global learning through short-term study abroad. *Association of American Colleges and Universities: Peer Review, Fall 2009, 11*(4), 1–7. Retrieved from https://www.aacu.org/peerreview/2009/fall/donnelly-smith

Dwyer, M. M. (2004). More is better: The impact of study abroad program duration. *Frontiers: The Interdisciplinary Journal of Study Abroad, 10*(1), 151–163.

Farrar, J. (2020). Intercultural Knowledge and Leadership Skills. *People: Honoring the people who make our businesses and community. Canadian-Swiss Chamber of Commerce*, 18–19. Retrieved from https://canswiss.ch/wp-content/uploads/2020/06/Booklet-2020_BD-basse-d%C3%A9finition-pour-le-site-web_DEF.pdf

Gertz, C. (1973). *The interpretation of cultures: Selected essays.* New York: Basic Books.

Giles, S. (2016). The most important leadership competencies, according to leaders around the world. *Harvard Business Review*. Retrieved from https://hbr.org/2016/03/the-most-important-leadership-competencies-according-to-leaders-around-the-world

Gohain, T. T. (2020). Appreciative Leadership: Bringing Out the Best of All Worlds!!!. In S. Bhattacharya & T. Chakraborty (Eds.), *Appreciative Inquiry Approaches to Organizational Transformation*. IGI Global: India. doi: https://doi.org/10.4018/978-1-5225-9675-2.ch011

Gronn, P. (2011). Hybrid configurations of leadership. In A. Bryman, D. Collinson, K. Grint, B. Jackson, & M. Uhl-Bien (Eds.), *Sage Handbook of Leadership* (pp. 435–452). Thousand Oaks, CA: Sage.

Hammer, M. R. (2011). Additional cross-cultural validity testing of the Intercultural Development Inventory. *International Journal of Intercultural Relations, 35*(4), 474–487. https://doi.org/10.1016/j.ijintrel.2011.02.014

Hammer, M. R., Bennett, M. J., & Wiseman, R. (2003). Measuring intercultural sensitivity: The intercultural development inventory. *International Journal of Intercultural Relations, 27*(4), 421–443. https://doi.org/10.1016/S0147-1767(03)00032-4

Heinzmann, S., Schallhart, N., Müller, M., Künzle, R., & Wicki, W. (2015). *Linguistic exchange activities and their impact on intercultural competence and the motivation to learn languages.* Freiburg, Switzerland: University of Teacher Education Lucerne, funded by the Research Centre on Multilingualism. Retrieved from http://www.zentrum-mehrsprachigkeit.ch/en/content/linguistic-exchange-activities-and-their-impact-intercultural-competence-and-language

Henrich, J., Heine, S., & Norenzayan, A. (2010). The weirdest people in the world? *Behavioral and Brain Sciences, 33*(2–3), 61–83. doi: https://doi.org/10.1017/S0140525X0999152X.

Higgins, M., Morton, A., & Wolkenhauer, R. (2018). (Re)conceptualizing preservice teacher supervision through duoethnography: Reflecting, supporting, and collaborating with and for each other. *Teaching and Teacher Education, 69*, 75–84.

Hofstede, G. (1998) Think Locally, Act Globally: Cultural Constraints in Personnel Management. In W. Weber, M. Festing, & P. J. Dowling (Eds.), *Management and International Review*, Special Issue. Wiesbaden: Gabler Verlag. https://doi.org/10.1007/978-3-322-90989-3_2

House, R. J., Dorfmann, P. W., Javidan, M., & Sully de Luque, M. F. (2014). *Strategic leadership across cultures: The GLOBE study of CEO leadership behavior and effectiveness in 24 countries.* Thousand Oaks: Sage.

Jackson, J. (2015). Becoming interculturally competent: Theory to practice in international education. *International Journal of Intercultural Relations, 48*, 91–107. https://doi.org/10.1016/j.ijintrel.2015.03.012

Johanson, J., & Vahlne, J. E. (2009). The Uppsala internationalization process model revisited: From liability of foreignness to liability of outsidership. *Journal of International Business Studies, 40*(9), 1411–1431.

Killick, D. (2013). Global citizenship, sojourning students and campus communities. *Teaching in Higher Education, 18*(7), 721–735. doi: https://doi.org/10.1080/13562517.2013.836087

Krammer, D., & Mangiardi, R. (2012). The hidden curriculum of schooling: A duoethnographic exploration of what schools teach us about schooling. In J. Norris, R. D. Sawyer, & D. Lund (Eds.), *Duoethnography: Dialogic methods for social, health, and educational research* (pp. 41–70). London, UK: Taylor and Francis Group.

Levin, D. Z., & Kurtzberg, T. R. (2020). Sustaining employee networks in the virtual workplace. MIT Sloan Management Review. *Issuefrontiers* (Summer 2020). Retrieved from https://sloanreview.mit.edu/article/sustaining-employee-networks-in-the-virtual-workplace/amp

Lund, D. E., & Veinotte, C. (2010). Researching a social justice course in a charter school: A duoethnographic conversation. *Education: Exploring Our Connective Educational Landscape, 16*(2), 1–19. Retrieved from http://www.ineducation.ca/article/researching-social-justicecourse-charter-school-xfduoethnographic-conversation

MacIntyre, P. D., Gregersen, T., & Mercer, S. (2020). Language teachers' coping strategies during the Covid-19 conversion to online teaching: Correlations with stress, wellbeing and negative emotions. *System, 94*, 1–13. https://doi.org/10.1016/j.system.2020.102352

Mainela, T., Puhakka, V., & Servais, P. (2014). The Concept of International Opportunity in International Entrepreneurship: A Review and a Research Agenda. *International Journal of Management Reviews, 16*(1), 105–129. https://doi.org/10.1111/ijmr.12011

McAlpine, L. (2016). Why might you use narrative methodology? A story about narrative. *Eesti Haridusteaduste Ajakiri. Estonian Journal of Education, 4*(1), 32–57. https://doi.org/10.12697/eha.2016.4.1.02b

Meyer, E. (2014). *The culture map: breaking through the invisible boundaries of global business.* New York: Persus Books Group.

Norris, J., Sawyer, R. D., & Lund, D. (2012). *Duoethnography: Dialogic methods for social, health, and educational research.* London, UK: Taylor and Francis Group.

Novak, J. M. (2002). *Inviting educational leadership.* Toronto, ON: Pearson Education.

Perrakis & Scientific Partners (n.d.). "Appreciative inquiry". Retrieved from https://markosperrakis.eu/appreciative-inquiry/

Pinar, W. (Ed.) (1975). *Curriculum theorizing: The reconceptualists.* Berkeley, CA: McCutchan Publishing Corporation.

Pinar, W. F. (Ed.) (2003). *International handbook of curriculum research* (2nd ed.). Mahwah, NJ: Lawrence Erlbaum Associates.

Pinnegar, S., & Daynes, J. G. (2007). Locating Narrative Inquiry Historically: Thematics in the Turn to Narrative. In D. J. Clandinin (Ed.), *Handbook of narrative inquiry: Mapping a Methodology* (pp. 3–34). Thousand Oaks, CA: Sage Publications. https://doi.org/10.4135/9781452226552.n1

Potts, D. (2020). Short stays revisited. *EAIE Forum*, Summer 2020 (pp. 40–42).

Purkey, W. W., & Novak, J. M. (1996). *Inviting school success: A self-concept approach to teaching, learning, and democratic practice* (3rd ed.). Belmont, MA: Wadsworth Publishing Company.

Roth, W. M. (2005). *Auto/biography and auto/ethnography: Praxis of research method.* Rotterdam, the Netherlands: Sense Publishers/Brill.

Saldaña, J. (2012). *The coding manual for qualitative researchers* (2nd ed.). Thousand Oaks, CA: Sage.

Saudelli, M. G. (2015). The balancing act: International higher education in the 21st century. Rotterdam, the Netherlands: Sense Publishers/Brill.

Sawyer, R. D. & Norris, J. (2013). *Duoethnography: Understanding Qualitative Research.* Toronto, ON: Oxford University Press.

Sawyer, R. D., & Liggett, T. (2012). Postcolonial education: Using a duoethnographic lens to explore a personal curriculum of post/decolonization. In J. Norris, R. D. Sawyer, & D. Lund (Eds.), *Duoethnography: Dialogic methods for social, health, and educational research* (pp. 71–88). Walnut Creek, CA: Left Coast Press.

Schreier, C., Scherrer, S., Udomkit, N., & Farrar, J. (2020). Trustworthy small and medium-sized enterprise network partners: Small and medium-sized enterprise partnerships in the international entrepreneurial process. *Global Business Review, 21*(1), 88–107. doi: https://doi.org/10.1177/0972150919850414

Seidel, J., & Hill, L. (2015). Thinking Together: A Duoethnographic Inquiry into the Implementation of a Field Experience Curriculum. *Education, 21*(2), 49–64.

Shaules, J. (2019). *Language, Culture, and the Embodied Mind.* Singapore: Springer. https://doi.org/10.1007/978-981-15-0587-4

Stavros, J., Godwin, L., & Cooperrider, D. (2015). Appreciative inquiry: Organization development and the strengths revolution. In W. Rothwell, R. Sullivan, & J. Stavros (Eds.), *Practicing*

Organization Development: A guide to leading change and transformation (4th ed.) (pp. 96–116). Wiley. doi: https://doi.org/10.1002/9781119176626.ch6

Spencer-Oatey, H., & Kádár, D. Z. (2021). Intercultural politeness: managing relations across cultures. Cambridge University Press. doi: https://doi.org/10.1017/9781316810071

Srivastva, S., & Cooperrider, D. L. (1999). *Appreciative management and leadership: The power of positive thought and action in organizations*. Brunswick, GA: Crown Custom Publishing.

Uhl-Bien, M. (2006). Relational leadership theory: exploring the social processes of leadership and organizing. *Leadership Quarterly, 17*, 654–676. doi: https://doi.org/10.1016/j.leaqua.2006.10.007

Vanneste, B. S. (2016). From interpersonal to interorganisational trust: The role of indirect reciprocity. *Journal of Trust Research, 6*(1), 7–36. doi: https://doi.org/10.1080/21515581.2015.1108849

Vertesi, C. (2015, August 15). Can you build a global perspective in your students with only a short-term stay? *EAIE Blog*. Retrieved from https://www.eaie.org/blog/can-you-build-a-global-perspective-in-your-students-with-only-a-short-term-stay.html

Vouillemin, D. (2020). Business cultural training in a globalised economy. *Training, Language and Culture, 4*(1), 33–43. doi: https://doi.org/10.22363/2521-442X-2020-4-1-33-43

Zaki, J. (2014). Empathy: A Motivated Account. *Psychological Bulletin, 140*(6), 1608–1647. https://doi.org/10.1037/a0037679

An Exploration of Humanistic Leadership Practices in a Multicultural Work Environment

10

Christopher Vohrer

10.1 Introduction

The global footprint, the international and intercultural workforce in different locations all over the world as well as further plans for international expansion are top agenda points of the executive management and the board of directors in many multinational companies and conglomerates. This is independent of their respective industry. Such a goal can be achieved by expanding to new locations, by entering new markets, by acquiring other companies and by setting up internal shared service centres in low-cost regions. One factor all these different strategies have in common is that the leadership model needs to be adjusted when working with international and intercultural teams. The key management needs to embrace such changes if it wants to be successful. During the COVID-19 pandemic, this aspect has even gained in importance. With business travel having been reduced to an absolute minimum and the majority of collaboration now being done virtually, there is increased scrutiny on leadership and good ways of collaboration.

In recent years, much research about international leadership has been conducted. However, there is more need for investigation, especially on the specific facets of the particular leadership skills needed in Singapore (Peus et al. 2015). This will be even more crucial when considering the increased importance of Singapore as a business hub for the Southeast Asian region for many globally operating companies. Over the past few years, Singapore has constantly achieved top rankings as being one of the most innovative economies around the globe (Global Innovation Index 2020). In addition, in 2019,

C. Vohrer (✉)
PwC Switzerland, Zurich, Switzerland

I. Stolz, S. Oldenziel Scherrer (eds.), *International Leadership*, uniscope. Publikationen der SGO Stiftung, https://doi.org/10.1007/978-3-658-37306-1_10

Singapore ranked as the most competitive economy worldwide, which further highlights the country's prominent position in the globalised world (World Economic Forum 2019).

In order to continue to be successful in collaborating across borders, international leadership is one if not the key factor. Various leadership models have been established and much research has been done on this issue. However, there is no "one model fits all" approach given the multitude of regions and cultures as well as the ethnic composition of any given population. Furthermore, the economic model of the respective country as well as the political situation play important roles for determining the leadership model that needs to be applied.

This article focuses on international leadership, in particular on the aspect of how leaders deal with European/Western teams and how they need to change their leadership styles in practice when guiding teams that include, or exclusively consist of, Asian members.

The collaboration for this research project was characterized by extensive project work with one of the globally leading firms within the professional services industry. In this context, the Asian team members resided in Singapore. The teams consisted mainly of ethnic Chinese Singapore citizens—many of whom had held Malaysian or Chinese citizenship before—but also of Malay and Indian Singaporeans. Malaysian and Indonesian nationals with a Chinese background or mainland Chinese were also part of the investigated teams.

The spotlight will therefore be on Singapore. As this city state has a strong Chinese influence given the ethnic composition of its population, a number of characteristics relating to Chinese culture and mentality will be considered for the analysis. The cultural history as well as the political and economic situation of Singapore will also be analysed in this paper. The theoretical research results on Chinese-Singaporean and Western leadership models will be put into context by sharing practical examples and experiences made when working extensively with such teams. This is based on the author's own experiences over several years in Singapore. Further explanations will be provided on how these collaborations were successful—or, if they were not, what the reasons were for failure.

The key skills needed from a practical viewpoint will be outlined in more detail, and an analysis will show the experiences made during various collaborations, including the parameters that had to be changed during the process. Subsequently, an overview will be given of the biggest challenges as well as of the pitfalls to be avoided from the beginning. The last section will include the lessons learned from these experiences and to what extent they have influenced the author's leadership style in practice—as well as how this can be translated into virtual intercultural project work that is now becoming increasingly important. In a separate section, the experiences will be shared that were made while virtually leading international cross-border project teams.

10.2 Singapore's Cultural Background and Economic Environment, Its Political and Educational System

In order to find the right approach to dealing with international teams, it is vital to understand certain characteristics in a team's backgrounds. The following are the main points (which are not necessarily conclusive) that should be considered when dealing with teams in Singapore that mainly consist of people with an ethnic Chinese background.

Singapore has a population of around 5.69 million and a gross domestic product (GDP) of USD 372.1 billion, which is around half of the Swiss GDP (The World Bank 2020a). Out of these 5.69 million residents, almost 40% do not have a Singaporean citizenship. There are 520,000 permanent residents and 1.64 million employment pass or work permit holders who are officially considered to be non-residents. This reduces the number of official residents to about 4 million (National Population and Talent Division 2020).

Singapore's cultural background is strongly influenced by Chinese culture, given that almost three quarters of its inhabitants are of Chinese ethnicity, due to a wave of immigrants from mainland China in the early twentieth century (IndexMundi 2020). As a result, the second and third generations of these immigrants now form the majority of the Singaporean workforce. Based on Hofstede's cultural framework as applied to China, their cultural values have a strong impact on workplace behaviour and on the extent to which cultural mores and attitudes influence people's work; this model can be applied to all countries with an ethnic Chinese majority (Hofstede et al. 1991).

The political systems of Singapore and the People's Republic of China are similar and different at the same time. It is important to understand this when working with teams in Singapore due to their constitution and when looking at Hofstede's research results. One striking similarity is that both countries have always been governed by the same party since their foundation. China has been led by the Chinese Communist Party since 1949. Singapore has been run continuously by the People's Action Party (PAP) since 1965.

However, the two political systems are fundamentally different. What Singapore implemented after achieving self-government in 1959 is considered to be a meritocracy. This system presumes that people with innate and demonstrated talents will be an elite (Bellows 2009). Singapore has a high-income economy that provides one of the world's most business-friendly regulatory environments (The World Bank 2019). Besides, Singapore also tops the global ranking for human capital development. This is reflected in the ongoing provision of education for their workforce (The Human Capital Index 2020). A strong indicator for the country's high educational level is that Singapore was one of the top-performing countries in the latest 2018 PISA survey (OECD 2019).

Comparatively, the People's Republic of China is the only Communist-party-led member state of the G20 group of major economies. China's state and society are dominated and controlled by the Communist Party, with the clear commitment to maintain a permanent monopoly on power. There is no tolerance for those challenging the party's right to rule the country (Lawrence and Martin 2012). After China started opening up to the world and reforming its economy in 1978, the economy has grown substantially. This includes bringing more than 850 million people out of poverty. Today, China is an upper-middle-income country. However, there are still lags in labour productivity and human capital. Although income inequality has lessened over the last decade, it remains at a fairly high level (The World Bank 2020b).

10.3 Working with International Teams in a Globalised World

What does working with international teams mean today in the context of a globalised world? Large globally operating companies are usually present in all major global jurisdictions, including Singapore which is used as a Southeast Asian business hub by many. However, not only larger corporations have a global footprint these days, but also medium-sized and even small companies are often internationally present due to requirements by their clients and customers.

The collaboration, project and team work investigated for this paper refer to teams that are based in Singapore, are composed of members from various ethnic backgrounds and have been established for certain projects, collaborations or engagements. These teams are working in the professional services industry (consulting, advisory, tax or audit), each with one of the globally leading firms in that area.

Leadership is being executed in different ways. One leader has been living in Singapore for several years, managing and leading international teams within the given political, economic and cultural environment. This is definitely the most valuable approach and thus preferred by the author, as the leader can be on site and therefore close to the team.

Another leadership model the author will shortly reflect on in a separate section—and which is considered the most challenging one—is managing cross-border teams whose members have remained in their home countries, with the leader being located elsewhere. Here, leadership has been executed during regular site visits and permanent contact through electronic communication systems like video meetings and telephone conferences. Especially during the COVID-19 pandemic, usage of electronic communication tools was unavoidable. This was the only possible way of communication given the health risk in face-to-face meetings, the closure of borders and the extremely limited possibilities of travelling to almost any country.

10.4 The Western Humanistic Approach to Leading Teams

Many researchers hold the view that a leader cannot be successful if he/she totally ignores humanistic values in their leadership. This behaviour might work in a short run but will not be long-lasting. For long-term success and to become an exceptional leader, it is key to communicate values and to always treat employees with respect. This includes embracing diversity in all its forms: talents, cultures, one's personal background, ideas and nationalities as contradictory views must be seen as chances for innovation and development, not as a risk to any existing behaviour. In order to form a more humanistic and effective organisation, the theory claims that six widely accepted cornerstones need to be implemented (Peus 2012), which will be elaborated upon in the following.

Responsibility

A manager should be aware of their responsibility and be self-reflective in their actions towards their subordinates. This is not limited to the people you manage or work with but even extends to clients, suppliers, local communities and the environment. As we can see in current discussions, the sustainable use of natural resources has climbed to the top of the agenda in many companies. Putting this into practice means being open, honest and reliable in all decisions and behaviours. One's impact on others needs to be considered in addition to giving constructive feedback and to not undermining the trust of one's staff. There will always be situations in which it is impossible to align business interests and those of different stakeholder groups, but the leader needs to be aware of this. All of this has to be considered to come up with a fair decision.

Communication

Communication with one's team should also be an important principle of a humanistic leader. A leader needs to have values they stand up for and behave accordingly. What do you want to be known or remembered for? What do you want people to say about you? These questions help managers find out the values they stand for. They must be communicated to the teams clearly. The leader's behaviour must be consistent with these values even under pressure. On the job, this means that communication needs to be constantly repeated, with a focus on what and how one communicates.

Vision

A real vision or goal needs to exist to make a team aware of the organisation strategy or of the ambition of an assignment. People need to know how their daily work and commitment is embedded in the overall picture. A feeling of contribution towards a greater goal needs to be provided by the leader to their team members. This should include an inspiring vision of the future. In many cases, meaningful work is more important to the staff than compensation or status. A leader needs to reflect on whether this has been communicated in the past or if the message was more focused on economic indicators like profits or cost-cutting.

Fairness

Another very important touchstone is fairness. In the humanistic leadership model, fairness consists of four areas. The first part is *distributive fairness*. This stands for a distribution of outcomes that honours the employee's contribution to a project. Many leaders still distribute outcomes equally among all team members. When it comes to acting on the distribution of the outcomes, it needs to be applied consistently and comprehensively. Furthermore, the downsides also need to be distributed equally. Due to the limitation of resources, a manager cannot always achieve distributive fairness and must aim to achieve *procedural fairness*.

For this goal, rules—including but not limited to resource allocation—need to be defined upfront and in a transparent manner in order to get all team members on board. Procedural fairness also means that even if the team members are not directly involved in the decision-making process, they are granted a voice to express their opinions and to feel heard. *Informational Fairness* is the third crucial area here. No matter if good or bad news, employees need to be informed about them above and beyond their scope of work. This ensures predictability and helps in times of change. People need to feel that they have been informed honestly, transparently and comprehensively. Information must be provided clearly with the necessary respect and appropriateness. It is key to treat all people in the team with the same integrity and respect regardless of their grades and positions. Being tough on the issue but soft on the person is crucial here. This *fairness on an interpersonal level* is the fourth pillar.

Growth

The fifth principle is growth, in which the leader must know the skills, interests and goals of their employees. The topic of personal growth is a fundamental concern for human beings. It is important to be aware of every team member's different aspirations, goals and plans in order to help them individually in getting there. Knowing what they want to learn and develop is essential in order to be able to take care of them. Acting as a coach or mentor, the challenge is to provide individualized consideration and support. All this needs to be considered when distributing work among individuals. A leader must support their efforts and involve employees during the whole change process.

Role Model

The last criterion a humanistic leader needs to apply is to be a role model. When managers act as a good role model, their employees will follow them, thus being more involved, motivated and dedicated. For the leader, this means to present their own authenticity at work to the team, to interpret data as objectively as possible and to act with the awareness that team members are watching them. The leader's behaviour must be aligned with what they advocate. A culture needs to be established in which people are not afraid of challenging the leader's opinion and to give honest and constructive feedback. Asking subordinates to do more than you do yourself is not the behaviour of a role model and should therefore be avoided; thus the leader must always be willing to take the hardest step or to make the greatest sacrifice. In order to be an effective role model, the leader needs to know their values and live them accordingly (Peus 2012).

10.5 The Chinese Approach to Leading Teams

But does the Asian and especially the Chinese leadership model require the same leadership skills as a Western model so as to be successful, such as the humanistic leadership principles described above?

In order to get more insights into the Chinese leadership style that is widely used in Singapore, Hofstede's model of leadership (Hofstede et al. 1991) is used here. The field study was conducted from 1967 to 1973 with more than 100,000 IBM employees participating in more than 50 countries.

Hofstede's model consists of five dimensions. The first dimension used is *Power Distance*. The Chinese culture appreciates and accepts inequality within a team, which is a very different perception compared to the humanistic leadership principle. But at the same time, the leader's use of power should be moderated by a sense of obligation. This is similar for all countries with strong Chinese influence.

The *Individualism* index shows that Chinese culture focuses on collectivism. The "keeping face" concept of the collectivist family is very important here. "Losing face" equals being humiliated. Face is "lost" when through their action, the individual or someone close fails to meet the essential requirements placed upon them. Another factor was the proclamation of the Chinese Communist Party under Mao Zedong, who identified individualism and liberalism as being responsible for selfishness and aversion to discipline. As a result, a leader needs to carefully consider this dimension in cases like giving negative or even constructive feedback, as this could also be seen as "losing face". As a solution in practice, feedback should be given on a one-to-one basis and not in front of the entire team or when someone else is able to observe the conversation.

With regard to the "masculinity versus femininity" dimension, Chinese culture tends very much towards the direction of masculine poles, which is strongly associated with the opportunities of high earnings, recognition and the option of promotion when doing a good job, as well as the need for a challenging job. Setting this in the contrast to the necessary vision in a humanistic leadership model, in which meaningful work often counts more than status or pay, one can easily see the cultural difference in principles.

Hofstede's fourth dimension is *Uncertainty Avoidance*. This index shows that China has one of the lowest uncertainty avoidance scores. The reason for this is the cultural acceptance of conformity, especially in the context of "losing face"; Chinese employees tend to obey laws, regulations and social rules. For a work environment, this means that subordinates need a strong leader who gives them clear guidance rather than expecting them to make decisions themselves.

The fifth universal dimension, based on the "Chinese Value Survey" and considered an essential addition, was included in 1991 and labelled *Long-term versus Short-term Orientation*. Many of the values included in this dimension can be found in the teachings of the Chinese intellectual Confucius. Ranking number 4, China is one of the most long-term-oriented cultures. In Chinese culture, it is more important *that* something works than investigating the reason *why* it works. Chinese politics has always been oriented long-term, e.g. the policy of the one-child family rule by looking more than a generation ahead. Translating this into the business world means that there is a tendency towards thinking big and extremely strategic. In Chinese business and culture, challenges and problems are usually solved over a long time and not as fast as possible as Western business leaders tend to do.

Twenty years after adding the fifth dimension, Minkov unravelled another closely correlated dimension and helped redefine it: the *Indulgence versus Restraint* dimension. China ranks very low in this dimension, which reflects that one's actions are restrained by various social norms and prohibitions within Chinese culture. In addition, the enjoyment of leisure activities, spending and similar types of indulgence are seen in a negative light. In practice, this means that aggression is encouraged to the extent that it does not impinge thinking for the group one values. In other words, this is some kind of balancing act for Chinese team members (Hofstede et al. 1991).

According to another research, Chinese leaders are expected to regard ethical considerations higher than profit achievement. A leader should be a role model and a source of inspiration for his/her staff by being persuasive and not coercive. The promotion of internal harmony and being a personal example by strengthening equality and a simple life also play a role here (King and Zhang 2014). This is very similar to the role model cornerstone described in the humanistic leadership approach. The most relevant leadership style in China is the paternalistic one, combining a strong authority with a compassion for support, guidance and care for one's team. Paternalistic leadership is strongly based on Confucian teachings and therefore has a high value for teamwork in Chinese culture. This also underpins the long-term orientation that includes certain Confucian principles (Peus et al. 2015).

When comparing the Western leadership model to a leadership style in societies with a strong Chinese cultural influence, it becomes obvious that there are fundamental differences that need to be addressed when working with such teams—but also a number of similarities that can be applied consistently. The following sections will investigate this in more detail from a practical point of view.

10.6 Leadership Skills Required to Start Leading and Working with International Teams

After having identified the differences between Western and Chinese leadership skills that are required for leading international teams according to academic research, this section will give more practical insights based on experiences made by the author and elaborates on what is needed in general to start working and leading international project teams.

The first step when it comes to working with teams consisting of members from different cultural, ethnic and/or geographical backgrounds is to be open-minded and ready to adapt. This is relevant even for teams whose members feature only minor geographical differences, like Germany and Switzerland. Without this mindset, long-term success cannot be achieved and sustained. This is especially important when moving to a new environment and thus getting out of one's own comfort zone. When moving to a Chinese-dominated country like Singapore, it is extremely important to integrate and be part of the local culture, even more so outside the business environment. Learning more about the local culture and knowing what is important for the people will demonstrate respect for one's subordinates. This can happen through small gestures like knowing some basic Chinese or being considerate about certain traditions during Chinese New Year, which is one of the most important public holidays in Chinese culture. In Singapore, for example, the exchange of two mandarin oranges after arriving at someone else's household represents the wish of good luck and prosperity for the counterpart.

Even when working with teams across borders, it is crucial to have certain knowledge of the cultural, economic and political background of the country the team is located in or originally comes from. This may require some preparation but helps avoid the most embarrassing situations from the beginning and demonstrates the necessary respect for the people.

Being flexible in adapting to new circumstances is a must for an effective leader in an international environment. Displaying a mindset of Western superiority will make collaboration fail from day one. A leadership style that purely nurtures itself from the idea of trying to turn the situation at hand into a more familiar one will not be successful in the long run.

However, it is also important to remain authentic and be yourself. This is similarly described in humanistic leadership value communication. Changing one's leadership style without being completely convinced of the foreign ways of managing things will not work either. Your team will realise very quickly that you do not have faith in this way of leadership—and you will easily lose their trust.

The last point that should be considered is to involve a local co-leader. This is especially crucial in crisis times like the COVID-19 pandemic when the leader cannot be on site and communication is done only virtually. Someone is needed on-site who can be fully trusted and who acts as an advisor to the leader as well as an ambassador of the team. With the establishment of a local co-leader, one does stay aware not only of the team atmosphere but also of the whole situation in the region at large. However, roles and responsibilities need to be clarified beforehand so as to avoid any conflicts between the leader and the co-leader.

10.7 Practical Examples of Successfully Leading International Teams

In this section, a few practical examples will be outlined that helped me successfully lead an international team while living in Singapore. As explained in the second section, the Singapore culture and political system is structured in a way that people who have proven their talents in the business community are considered to be part of the elite. Achieving this is a goal for almost all local Singaporeans—everything else is subordinated to this goal. The very diverse teams mainly consisted of Singapore citizens, Malaysians and Indonesians, all of whom had a Chinese background; but there were also mainland Chinese. In addition, Singaporeans with a Malay or Indian ethnic background were also of the team members. With this team composition in mind, the Western and Chinese leadership models can be directly compared to first-hand experiences made in Singapore.

One of the first observations the author made was the cultural differences within the teams. The three main ethnic groups in Singapore are Chinese, Malays and Indians, and an external leader needs to carefully consider all their backgrounds. These can be of a religious, cultural or traditional nature. For example, it is very important for Malays, who are usually Muslims, to follow their religious diet requirements. Taking care of all the different needs from the beginning helped a lot in forming a strong team where everybody felt valued and taken care of, regardless of their background. A good way of achieving this is to have a kick-off meeting and ongoing status meetings, so as to listen to them and to understand their needs. In order not to disadvantage any team members, one offer that proved to be very successful was to ensure that everyone chose one weekday on which to leave earlier, without having to explain this in detail. This was not an easy task in the professional services industry, due to constant time pressure and successive deadlines. So this needs careful planning as well as the full commitment and support of the leader. This is very different to working with Western teams, which already do have a clear view and expectations in terms of their work-life balance. In the West, this is a significantly differentiating factor against competitors.

Before moving to Singapore, you may be told various stories about working there. One of these stories the author heard was that the people in Singapore work extremely long hours, similar to many other Asian countries like China or Hong Kong. After the first few weeks and working long hours myself from time to time, I noted that my team members were always in the office, too. Due to the hierarchical system, it is expected not to leave work before the most senior person does so. From the leader's point of view, this was not necessary, and I openly discussed with the team that whenever someone finalised their tasks, there was no need to stay and wait for the superiors to leave as well. The team was quite surprised about this offer, but agreed to this approach and largely made use of it; yet it was still difficult for some to take this step and leave earlier than the superior.

It can be useful to appoint a local spokesperson who regularly communicates with the manager but is also an ambassador for the team—someone who can raise the team's issues to the leader. This proved to be a very successful leadership method. Given the different seniority levels within the team as well as their mindset of always following hierarchical orders, this helped give everyone the opportunity to raise their voice to the leader anonymously. This way, many issues could be resolved at a very early stage. A permanently good team atmosphere evolved, and efficiency increased significantly since they could now discuss problems that might otherwise not have been communicated.

This goes hand in hand with an open team discussion about the projects, taking them along the journey, explaining clearly what the objective of the project is and how it can be reached together. Knowing the broad vision and conveying that the team contributes to a greater goal is in line with the principles of a humanistic leader. The first experience was that they needed instructions on what had to be done but failed to see the overall strategy and the path to reaching the goal together. Asking for their input and their ideas on how to do things differently allowed them to develop a feeling for their own contribution to completing the project successfully. This was a relatively new experience for them. It is not uncommon in Chinese culture for a team to get clear instructions on what everybody has to do. This goes hand in hand with Hofstede's research results that Chinese tend to obey laws, regulations and rules (Hofstede et al. 1991). However, after finishing these tasks, there was no proactive approach to asking for and taking on new responsibilities. This was a significantly inhibiting factor for efficiency. Getting the team members actively involved from day one thus helped increase efficiency drastically and made them feel valued at the same time.

The feedback culture in Western teams is often very straight and communicated in a transparent manner, with the whole team being present. With a leader who does not know how important it is in Southeast Asia not to "lose face", issues are inevitable (Hofstede et al. 1991). Uttering direct criticism or giving negative (or even constructively critical) feedback to a particular team member in front of the whole team might result in this person "losing face". In such a situation, it is extremely difficult to regain the trust of this individual. Any individual feedback or performance rating needs to be communicated in a one-on-one meeting with the respective person, but never in front of the whole team. When working in the environment of a leading professional services firm, this is a key area that needs to be considered, as the team members cooperate in constantly changing compositions and will receive feedback at the end of each project from their respective leader.

In 2019, more than 90% of Singapore citizens were owning their own property (Singapore Department of Statistics 2019). Material possessions are very important for the residents and are expected by their families. This is in line with the political system that encourages the development of elites in Singaporean society. This causes the conflict situation that employees are extremely committed in their job, as they want to move up the career ladder as quickly as possible, while their loyalty to a particular employer is very limited. If there are other work opportunities that will offer a higher remuneration, people tend to leave a workplace for the competitor very easily. For a leader to manage this situation in the best possible way, it is important not to take advantage of this commitment, since this may result in a burnout; instead, it is crucial to create a balanced atmosphere. Simultaneously, the employees need to be involved in the company's strategy and vision of the project and the company in order to offer a strong career path—which again is in line with the humanistic leadership principles. That helps strengthen loyalty to the firm, to its leaders as well as to its teams. As a result, the staff turnover rate decreases.

Staff loyalty as we know it from Europe is something one should not expect in a Chinese business environment. In order to establish it, to build a relationship with your team and to thus be a successful leader, you need to work on their loyalty every day. This requires much more than just fulfilling your leadership tasks during working hours. In a mainly Chinese-dominated societies like Singapore, your colleagues at work are in almost all instances also your friends. This means that the team not only works together but also spends much time together outside of office hours. As a leader, you need to become part of this team, as well as invest time to get closer to them and to break down their hierarchical mindset. Making efforts like joining them for dinner or drinks on a Friday night is helpful to build a relationship, to understand the different needs of the individual team members and to learn what is important to them.

It is still a goal and actually a dream of many Southeast Asians, especially Singaporeans, to spend a number of years abroad. Offering your team the opportunity to go on an international assignment will improve their motivation significantly and let them feel the appreciation of their superior. When a project comes to an end or when certain milestones have been reached, it is very important that the leader supports the individuals in making this happen. Without doing so, the leader will be considered as not being trustworthy, and his/her team will not follow him/her in the future.

As mentioned in a previous paragraph, hierarchies and job titles are extremely important in Chinese culture, compared to academic qualifications. Such degrees are often not considered for employing someone as they are assumed for certain staff levels or leadership positions, even though this is often not the case. Following the given hierarchy, however, is extremely crucial so as not to pass someone over. For a successful team, this needs to be obeyed strictly. This experience can be linked directly to the most relevant Chinese leadership styles according to academic research: the paternalistic leadership that combines strong authority with support, guidance and care for the team (Peus et al. 2015).

An important success factor is also to align the client's expectations. If the counterpart's main contact or manager is originally not of the same cultural background as the team members, the plan how to run a project needs to be discussed and aligned upfront. This way, a lot of expectation gaps can be closed from the beginning and both sides have a common understanding of the project plan.

10.8 Analysis

10.8.1 Experiences and Reflections Made During Project Work with International Teams

An analysis of the most important experiences and reflections made during collaborations with international teams is provided in this section.

One of the experiences while working with Chinese-dominated teams in Singapore was that decisions were made in a much faster way than is known in Western countries. This is a striking difference to Europe. The administrative hurdles are taken extremely efficiently, avoiding unnecessary steps from the beginning. This is certainly one of the reasons why Singapore is one of the most innovative economies around the globe (The Global Innovation Index 2020), and the most competitive economy according to latest reports (World Economic Forum 2019). This is also reflected in decisions made within companies, which are fast and very opportunistic. However, Singaporean leaders always stick to regulations, which results in them ranking top in the Corruption Perceptions Index 2019 (Transparency International 2020). Therefore, teams need to be flexible to adapt to fast-changing circumstances. Such business behaviour is needed to successfully cope with the rise of the Chinese economy, given the almost double-digit annual growth rates in China over the last 30 years. Furthermore, China was Singapore's top trading partner in 2017. From 2013 to 2017, Singapore was China's top foreign investor, with US$4.8 billion in 2017 alone (Enterprise Singapore 2021).

As described in the previous paragraph, business in Asia is changing rapidly and continuously. This requires teams, and especially their leaders, to also adapt to these changes in their leadership style. Task allocation and collaboration plans change steadily. The leader needs to be open-minded and ready to change things so as to be able to bring a project to a successful completion. However, this is not only necessary for a project and its parameters, but the teams also need to change constantly. An alternative plan needs to exist at any time in order to reallocate tasks and/or responsibilities. Given the circumstance of very short notice periods of 4 weeks or less, this is a common issue leaders will face and need to resolve.

Working remotely has become the so-called "new normal" since the COVID-19 pandemic has hit the world in March 2020. Businesses have realised that things can also be done without being together on-site and seeing each other on a regular basis. Already 10 years ago, while working in Singapore, the remote working model had become very common in Asia, using certain fully qualified team members remotely, i.e. without shared service centres. This is mostly practised in the fast-growing economies in Southeast Asia, like Malaysia, Indonesia and the Philippines. The experience of working remotely with such teams was extremely positive for me. The main success factors are the eagerness of the people, their positive attitude towards taking on new opportunities and the excellent academic qualifications of the individuals.

After having worked with international teams in Singapore for several years, one of the constant reflections is that there are always things a leader has not considered. Even with a good preparation, many years of experience and close interaction with the teams, it is almost impossible to avoid surprises. As variously mentioned, it is very important in these cases to react fast and to make the necessary changes immediately. This helps ensure that the collaboration becomes a success story.

How can relationships be created with international teams? This reflection is very different from working with Western teams. In Singapore's Chinese-dominated business environment, bonding with the team is not only done while working together; it is much more important to establish a team spirit outside normal working hours. This can be done through regular lunches or dinners with the team, but also on weekends by joining the members for other social activities. A leader participating in such gatherings will have a very different standing, instead of being seen as a purely foreign leader who just wants to follow his/her own way of doing things. Many Western leaders do not really consider this point, which may mark them as being arrogant, presumptuous and unwilling to adapt.

10.8.2 Adjustments of the Leadership Principles That Proved Successful

As seen in the highlighted theoretical approaches and the described practical experiences, there is no single perfect leadership model that can be applied at any case when working with international teams. This section describes some examples of changes made to a leadership strategy that helped make collaborations successful and long-lasting.

One of the adjustments made was reconsidering priorities. At the start of the collaboration, the focus was on taking the team through the process, with explanations of why certain things work and others don't. It was quickly noted that this was not of highest importance for the team members. Their interest was rather that things work throughout the project and they can be reliably planned. With this in mind, the whole approach of leading the team based on the Western approach had to be changed in order to adapt to the priorities of Chinese cultural thinking in Singapore (Hofstede et al. 1991).

With a clear project plan on how things could be done—and without considering how a team led by a local leader would have done things—it quickly became clear that the team was quite surprised that everything was done in a totally different manner than they would have done it. After realising this, an open discussion started, with the objective of seeing how they would do things differently, as well as considering local requirements; as a result, an adjusted project plan was established taking into account the best features of both sides. The team really appreciated this flexibility to adopt their views and to listen to their ideas. This approach, which was strongly based on the humanistic leadership model, was new to them. At the same time, the team members also realised that some of the planned points were the better solutions to reach the goal. This helped the team learn and widen their horizon as well.

One parameter that may initially sound minimal is simply the timing of doing things or of having meetings. While it is quite common to have early morning meetings in Switzerland or Germany, this is not at all the case in Asia. After setting up the first meetings at 7 or 8 a.m. in the morning, it was obvious that this was not appreciated by the people required to attend. When discussing this with the team, they explained that their daily routines, in line with their cultures, started later, and it was agreed to shift the daily update meeting to 10 a.m. In contrast to this, late night meetings after dinner, at 8 or 9 p.m., were not an issue for any team member, as they were used to late work in their daily routines. This would not be looked upon favourably in a Western business environment, but a leader working in an Southeast Asian environment is required to adapt to such circumstances.

10.9 Leadership Learnings

Every successful leader who has been working abroad or with international teams on projects would have changed his/her mindset and leadership style after making the kind of experiences elaborated upon above. Some of the experiences the author made in Singapore, the learnings and the implemented changes are outlined in this chapter.

One of the key points every leader learns, after having been involved in an international assignment or project, is to become more open-minded. This happens in connection with the new culture(s) one gets to know, as well as by adapting to how different people manage situations in business or personal life. Developing an awareness of these differences is definitely a result of such collaborations. The open mindset as well as seeing the benefit of doing things in another successful way makes these leaders more open to trying new things and pushing forward with any kind of diversity initiatives.

An understanding of different ways towards achieving the very same things helps these leaders implement this in their daily work routine. Combining the best approaches from two or more cultural groups is a way to improving efficiency and to scrutinising old structures. Any team will certainly acknowledge this. The mindset required to continuously reinvent yourself is essential in today's constantly changing world. Especially in a rapidly changing business environment that is driven by technological developments or digitalisation, this is key to being successful.

When spending several years in Asia, the collaboration and guidance of international teams for more than a decade—but also working with globally operating clients—change the business behaviour of each leader. Of equal or even higher importance is the personal development of the leader and the experiences he/she makes outside their work environment. This might be one of the requirements for promotion to the next leadership role. It is expected from the executive management of many reputable and internationally operating companies that their key talents and future leaders spend at least a couple of years abroad to get the skills (both personal and business) needed to be a successful international leader. A central recommendation is to take on such opportunities whenever they occur, as they might not come up that often, and not to be afraid of getting out of one's own comfort zone.

▶ Get to know different people from various countries and backgrounds. Experience new cultures and understand the roots for certain actions. Try new things and see how these new approaches work. All this will translate into much more confidence in leading a diverse team. Trust in the people you are working with will definitely be higher than before—as compared to a one-dimensional leader having experiences with only of one kind of working style, mindset, geography, cultural background and education.

The last learning point from my experiences is that you will never be a successful leader if you focus only on business-related matters, especially when working in a Chinese-dominated society. Particularly when relocating to a new country like Singapore or when starting to work with these teams, this is crucial for being successful. This can concern very small details like joining the team during an afternoon tea break or for dinner.

10.10 Challenges and Pitfalls to Avoid in Order to Be a Successful Leader

When starting to work with international or intercultural teams as a leader, one will inevitably face a number of challenges and pitfalls (especially) at the beginning of the collaboration. The most common ones are explained in this chapter and can be used as a starting kit by other leaders.

External factors are often not considered to the necessary extent. In countries with extreme weather conditions, like the heat and humidity as well as the occasional haze that is common in Singapore, these factors need to be seriously considered for work planning. Likewise, in China, especially in the greater Beijing area, the ongoing air pollution and the resulting smog is a serious issue that also impacts business life. In other Asian countries like the Philippines, typhoons regularly hit the country, resulting in power and internet outages. All this needs to be considered when planning a collaboration, and the team needs to be supported in these situations so as to ensure their safety and wellbeing.

Working in a new country or on an international project will never take the planned path. Flexibility and adaption to new or amended circumstances are needed to make such a project a success. Grimly sticking to the original plan will not get you the results you wanted and is thus never a good option.

Establishing a trustful relationship with the team is one if not *the* key factor to lead successfully. As it is much easier to do this from the beginning than to fix upcoming issues in the course of a collaboration, the full focus needs to start from day 1. In order to achieve this, as much involvement as possible is required from the leader early on. Experience shows that if this is not done from the start, the project will become extremely challenging and demanding, for both the leader and the team.

You will always face problematic situations you are not prepared for. It is crucial to also discuss these issues with other leaders and, if possible, especially with those who are familiar with the respective cultural and business environment. This helps you draw the right conclusions and bring the team back on track.

Finally, honesty is key from day 1. Preaching something but not practicing it as a leader will not fulfil the principle of a role model and is very contradictory to the principles a humanistic leader needs to follow. The team will not be happy to go the extra mile for a leader who is not authentic, and they will not have faith that this manager takes the right decisions to reach to overall goal.

10.11 Virtually Leading International Cross-Border Project Teams

Another practical experience the author has made in the past relates to managers who are working with international teams that are not based in the same jurisdiction or time zone. This is a very common setting in today's business world with the increased setup of shared service centres. In order to make such collaborations a success, a clear code of behaviour needs to be defined upfront. This starts with regular calls or video conferences. Equally important is the agreement of a core time of 'presence' when both the leader and the team members are available; this is to ensure that the team members are not strictly following the same working hours as the leader, even if they are based in a different time zone. Assuming and forcing the team to just adapt to the time zone of the leader would not show the necessary consideration, respect and appreciation for the team. During normal times, physical site visits are a key factor that should not be underestimated. Even with the COVID-19 experiences in mind, this should not be considered as unnecessary. A strong long-lasting relationship, a team spirit and bonding can only be created if the whole team gets together face to face.

All the above experiences are related to working with international teams in their home country. But how does a leader need to behave and interact with an international team that is based in Europe or any other Western country (e.g. United States, Australia or Canada). These challenges are different from but of similar nature to working in the team members' home country. In such a situation, the leader needs to support the team in integrating in the social, cultural and economic environment in the country he/she is based in. This is crucial for the team to anticipate what Western customers as well as other local team members are expecting. However, in order to foster diversity—something that all internationally operating companies are aiming for—it is also important that the international team members can still be themselves and live their culture as much as possible and are not under pressure to change their behaviour and habits completely. As this work model will become increasingly important after the positive experiences made during the COVID-19 pandemic, it is worthwhile to focus on leadership in this context as well as to further develop and improve it.

10.12 Singapore's Influence on the Author's Leadership Practices and How This Translates into Virtual Intercultural Project Work

To what extent did the daily practices of the author change after the influence of several years spent in Singapore, and can this be translated into virtual intercultural project work, which is a very contemporary issue during and after the COVID-19 pandemic?

There are two topics that have strongly influenced and changed the author's leadership style based on the experiences gained while working with intercultural teams on projects in Singapore. One radical change was the open mindset within the teams, their willingness to recognize and accept ongoing changes as well as the preparedness to manage different views. A key driver for this is the cultural and ethnic variety in the melting pot of Singapore, having worked with three different ethnic groups: Chinese, Malay and Indian. Another driver is the variety of the religious backgrounds, which are even more diverse than ethnicity, composed of free thinkers, Christians, Muslims, Hindus, Buddhists and Taoists. It is impressive to see how coexistence is managed by the Singapore government, but it is similarly inspiring to see how business leaders manage this in their companies and teams, too. The author's leadership practice was influenced significantly by this experience in that he is now willing to create extremely diverse teams, thus going beyond the differences experienced in Singapore. He now has a very advanced approach as he has realised that such team compositions are effective; they can be even more beneficial and thus contribute to adding value to the company. The author implements this in his daily work to the maximal extent possible. Given the traditionally international environment in Switzerland, this is easily done.

The other important influence is to make the local team members aware of how to deal with clients or team members in Singapore and the wider region. This is not only done by considering the economic importance of this part of the world—China could become the largest economy in the world as early as 2024 (World Economic Forum 2020)—but the sheer size of the qualified workforce in this region will further increase in the near future. Both factors result in an increased number of interactions with both clients and team members in this part of the world.

10.13 Conclusion

Looking at all the theoretical models, combined with the practical experiences made in Singapore, every leader can learn many things from working on projects with international teams. It could also be shown that in general, the six humanistic leadership principles are applicable to working in a Chinese-dominated society like Singapore. As it has been outlined, certain amendments due to local circumstances need to be made, but following these leadership principles is a recommended starting point for any leader.

Taking on the opportunity of an international assignment is the best option to learn the skills required for leading international teams. As this article has focused on leadership in Singapore, this is very important for the future. Given the global trend of increasingly shifting economic power to Asia, especially to China, more emphasis needs to be put on how teams from these jurisdictions have to be led. Rather sooner than later, this needs to be extended to the fast-growing economies of India and Indonesia that will play very important roles in the near and mid-term future.

The experiences are strongly based on the time the author spent in Singapore in one of the globally leading firms in the professional services industry. Therefore, this might not be representative for all Chinese-dominated countries, for all industries and enterprises; but it provides a good first overview for leaders based on day-to-day experiences.

Due to the reasons outlined in this paper, leading international teams will become even more prominent in the future. It is a great opportunity for leaders to widen their horizon, both professionally and personally, and to benefit from new approaches to leading successfully.

References

Bellows, T.J. (2009). Meritocracy and the Singapore Political System. *Asian Journal of Political Science, 17(1)*, 24–44.

Enterprise Singapore (2021). *China Market Profile*. Retrieved from https://www.enterprisesg.gov.sg/overseas-markets/asia-pacific/china/market-profile

Hofstede, G., Hofstede, G.J., & Minkov, M. (1991). *Cultures and organizations: Software of the mind* (Vol. 3). London: McGraw-Hill.

IndexMundi (2020). *Singapore Demographics Profile*. Retrieved from https://www.indexmundi.com/singapore/demographics_profile.html

King, P., & Zhang, W. (2014). Chinese and Western Leadership Models: A literature review. *Journal of Management Research, 6(2)*, 1–21.

Lawrence, S.V., & Martin, M.F. (2012). *Understanding China's Political System*. Washington: Congressional Research Service.

OECD (2019). *PISA 2018 Results – Combined Executive Summaries*. Retrieved from https://www.oecd.org/pisa/Combined_Executive_Summaries_PISA_2018.pdf

Peus, C. (2012). Giving wings to your leadership style. *IESE Insight, 13*, 20–27.

Peus, C., Braun, S., & Knipfer, K. (2015). On becoming a leader in Asia and America: Empirical evidence from women managers. *The Leadership Quarterly, 26*, 55–67.

Singapore Department of Statistics (2019). *Households*. Retrieved from https://www.singstat.gov.sg/find-data/search-by-theme/households/households/latest-data

The Global Innovation Index (2020). *Who will Finance Innovation?* Retrieved from https://www.globalinnovationindex.org/gii-2020-report#

The Human Capital Index (2020). *Human Capital in the Time of COVID-19*. Retrieved from https://openknowledge.worldbank.org/handle/10986/34432

The National Population and Talent Division (2020). *Population in Brief 2020*. Retrieved from https://www.population.gov.sg/files/media-centre/publications/pib-2020-final.pdf

The World Bank (2020a). *World Bank Open Data*. Retrieved from https://data.worldbank.org/

The World Bank (2020b). *The World Bank in China*. Retrieved from https://www.worldbank.org/en/country/china/overview

The World Bank (2019). *The World Bank in Singapore*. Retrieved from https://www.worldbank.org/en/country/singapore/overview

Transparency International (2020). *Corruption Perceptions Index 2019*. Retrieved from https://images.transparencycdn.org/images/2019_CPI_Report_EN_200331_141425.pdf

World Economic Forum (2020). *China could overtake the US as the world's largest economy by 2024*. Retrieved from https://www.weforum.org/agenda/2020/07/largest-global-economies-1992-2008-2024/

World Economic Forum (2019). *Global Competitiveness Report 2019*. Retrieved from http://www3.weforum.org/docs/WEF_TheGlobalCompetitivenessReport2019.pdf

Developing Global Leadership in Africa

11

Addressing Young Leaders' Ambitions for a People- and Community-Oriented Approach

Eva Jordans, Maria Derakhshan, Zoe Rutter, Santie de Villiers, and Bettina Ng'weno

11.1 Introduction

There is a growing interest in leadership and leadership development in Africa. This is evident from the increase in available literature on the topic over the past decade. For example, a search on publications from 2010 to 2019 in the "Business Source Complete" database generated 1328 returns (for peer-reviewed articles), three times more than in the previous decade.

In his introduction to a volume on "Leadership in Post-Colonial Africa" in the *Palgrave series on African Leadership*, Jallow states that "while some studies highlight in graphic

E. Jordans (✉)
Vierhuizen, The Netherlands
e-mail: Jordans@leadership.one

M. Derakhshan
The London School of Hygiene & Tropical Medicine, London, UK
e-mail: maria.derakhshan@lshtm.ac.uk

Z. Rutter
Centre for Targeted Protein Degradation, University of Dundee, Dundee, UK
e-mail: zrutter001@dundee.ac.uk

S. de Villiers
Department of Biochemistry and Biotechnology, Pwani University, Kilifi, Kenya
e-mail: s.devilliers@pu.ac.ke

B. Ng'weno
African American and African Studies, University of California, Davis, Davis, CA, USA
e-mail: bngweno@ucdavis.edu

I. Stolz, S. Oldenziel Scherrer (eds.), *International Leadership*, uniscope. Publikationen der SGO Stiftung, https://doi.org/10.1007/978-3-658-37306-1_11

detail the extent of leadership failure in postcolonial Africa, others show that good leadership has flourished in Africa" (2014, p. 2). For example, Banda (2014) describes the leadership failure of Dr Hastings Kamuzu Banda in Malawi, whereas good leadership is analysed by Ciulla (2013) regarding Nelson Mandela of South Africa, and Pailey (2014) analyses Ellen Johnson-Sirleaf of Liberia.

Jallow further indicates that most research on leadership in Africa has focused on political leaders. He concludes that "there appears to be a critical mass of civic leaders whose stories need to be studied and shared" (2014, p. 2). Furthermore, a focus on women's engagement in leadership and management in Africa reveals their marginalisation (Nkomo and Ngambi 2009), even though there are women leading in all sectors of the society. Studies on youth in leadership roles in Africa are very rare and mostly recent, such as Balogun et al. (2019).

Several authors indicate the need for a leadership transformation in Africa. Amah states that "the need for a new style of leadership in Africa is obvious from the drive for leadership development in Africa (for example African Leadership Academy, African Leaders Initiative, and Mo Ibrahim Prize for Achievement in African Leadership)" (2019, p. 78). Leadership scholars have also insisted that Africa needs a new crop of leaders if the continent is to survive and grow (Achebe 1983; Kumuyi 2007). For example, Kumuyi (2007) concludes that a new form of leadership directed at the common good is required. In a review of women and leadership in West Africa, Steady concludes that "a consensus emerged that suggested a desire for change; from male-dominated ideologies of dominance, hierarchies, violence, wars, and a propensity for intransigent dictatorships to centralizing values of motherhood such as nurturance, compassion, protection, and peace" (2011, p. 239).

Recent empirical research on leadership in several African countries reported in the book *Developing Global Leaders: Insights from African Case Studies* (Jordans et al. 2020) also revealed a desire for a leadership transformation. In this book, African leaders expressed a desire and a need for transformational types of leadership and new leadership paradigms. This was particularly true for youth and women leaders who are challenging behavioural and cultural conventions regarding leadership. The new paradigms centred on the following themes: (1) non-hierarchical leadership, i.e. a dissatisfaction with high hierarchy practices; (2) the importance of a leader's humane or people orientation; and (3) community-oriented leadership practices with key characteristics of being a good leader, including integrity and doing good. The African youth especially criticised the unequal societies that have been built through corruption and expressed a desire for communal strategies to help others and to pull up society as a whole. Integrity relates to the concept of ethics, which can be seen "to encompass the means by which social relationships are regulated such that an individual's wants, needs, aspirations and rights are balanced against those of another" (Clement 1996, quoted by Ladkin 2017, p.15). People and community orientation both link to the concept of Ubuntu which features widely in the literature on leadership in Africa. Its meaning can be explained as "you are who you are because of how you relate to others around you". The concept links to the notion of servant leadership, such as presented by Greenleaf (2010) and explained as a leader who shares power, puts the needs of the employees first and helps people develop and perform as best as possible (Sendjaya and Sarros 2002). These two concepts feature widely in the literature on leadership in Africa (e.g. Gaylord 2004; Hailey 2008) and are connected to the history of humanistic thinking among African leaders (Jallow 2014; Metz 2018). Leadership training in Africa thus needs to take into account Ubuntu—or the communal aspects of leadership.

Literature on experiences with leadership development in Africa (rather than the notion of leadership itself) is very limited. Modisane (2018, p. 13) speculates that the lack thereof mirrors the dearth of human resource development in research institutions in Africa. Jordans et al. (2020) document a gap between the importance leaders in Africa attach to leadership development and the frequency with which they experience this.

Most of the limited leadership development research in Africa has focused on leaders in the education sector, particularly in South Africa. There, both gender and race present women leaders with a dual marginalisation (Mabokela 2003; Moorosi 2014). In her study of women administrators at South African universities, Mabokela (2003, p. 143) concludes that women identify strategies at the individual level to create more supportive environments, such as the support and mentoring of other women. They also see the need to create a network of support with other women administrators within and beyond their institutions so as to avoid loneliness and isolation. Serpell (2011) has likewise documented how group-based learning improves social intelligence and agency amongst pupils in rural Zambia. Recorded by Moorosi (2020), narratives of three women leaders in education from Botswana, Lesotho and South Africa suggest that processes of becoming a leader are influenced by early socialisation as well as values and attributes. A strong perception of who they are instils a sense of agency that facilitates 'leaderful' actions. Moorosi concludes that women leaders' experiences of leader identity are an important ingredient of leadership development.

Pérezts et al. (2020) analyse an executive education course in South Africa, Kenya and Egypt in 2016, 2017 and 2018, respectively. Taking its inspiration from the African context, the course design was based on an experiential learning approach. Within the course, the 'ME (individual)—WE (organization)—WORLD (country) framework' connects participants' dreams for themselves to a network of relationships. The individual-level issues cannot be disconnected from the other two, meaning that they are always relationally constructed and experienced. Such a shift away from an organization-centric perspective to leadership development, as Giacalone and Thomson (2006) argue, could help integrate a vision of the self (identification) with a view of others and the world (inspiration). Bolden and Kirk's study of an Africa-wide leadership development programme has likewise highlighted the interconnectedness between self, community and leadership; they conclude that "leadership begins with accepting and taking up one's role within a community (or social) context" (2005, p.13).

Very few studies analyse the impact of leadership development initiatives. An exception is the evaluation of a programme for staff at universities in Ghana, Uganda and Tanzania as described in Mouton and Wildschut (2015). They state that "the most frequently identified change [as a result of the programme] in leadership across the three countries was the adoption of participatory styles of leadership [...], especially in terms of involving staff and sometimes students in their decision-making" (p. 100).

Several authors point to the need for adapting leadership development to African contexts (Jordans et al. 2020; Zoogah et al. 2015; Iwowo 2015, 2019). Iwowo states that "in the absence of a local indigenous conceptual framework that facilitates leadership development practice, local frameworks in which a leadership theory is applied must be adapted to global leadership development interventions as well as to the specific socio-cultural context" (Iwowo 2015; Skype interview with Mrs. Iwowo on 11 July, 2019).

Against this background, a contextualized leadership development programme in Kenya that set out to address young people's leadership transformation ambitions is analysed in this chapter. The aim is to answer two questions:

- How was the leadership training contextualised to the Kenyan context to support desired leadership transformation?
- To what extent did it succeed? Was the impact of the training indeed a leadership transformation?

11.2 Theoretical Framework

The theoretical framework that was used to design and evaluate the pilot training seminars consisted of three elements. Both the Interpersonal Circumplex (IPC) and the Leadership Circumplex that was derived from the IPC were used to analyse and discuss leadership transformation. The third element, Bird's global leadership competency framework, was used to contextualise and structure the seminars. This section further describes these elements.

Interpersonal Circumplex (IPC)

Many interpersonal domain researchers, both early and contemporary, see the interpersonal domain as having a two-dimensional circumplex structure, notably Sullivan (1940, 1953), Leary (1957), Wiggins (1996) and, more recently, Locke (2000, 2019). The IPC is typically defined with reference to a vertical *agency* dimension that concerns the degree of pro-activeness (also termed dominance, power, status) and a horizontal *communal* dimension that concerns the degree of affiliation and connection to people (also called friendliness, warmth, love).

Leadership Circumplex

Redeker et al. (2014) have proposed that the same fundamental concepts as in the IPC can be applied to leadership, focusing on the interactional styles leaders may have with their followers. The leadership circumplex shown in Fig. 11.1 depicts the perceptions of the

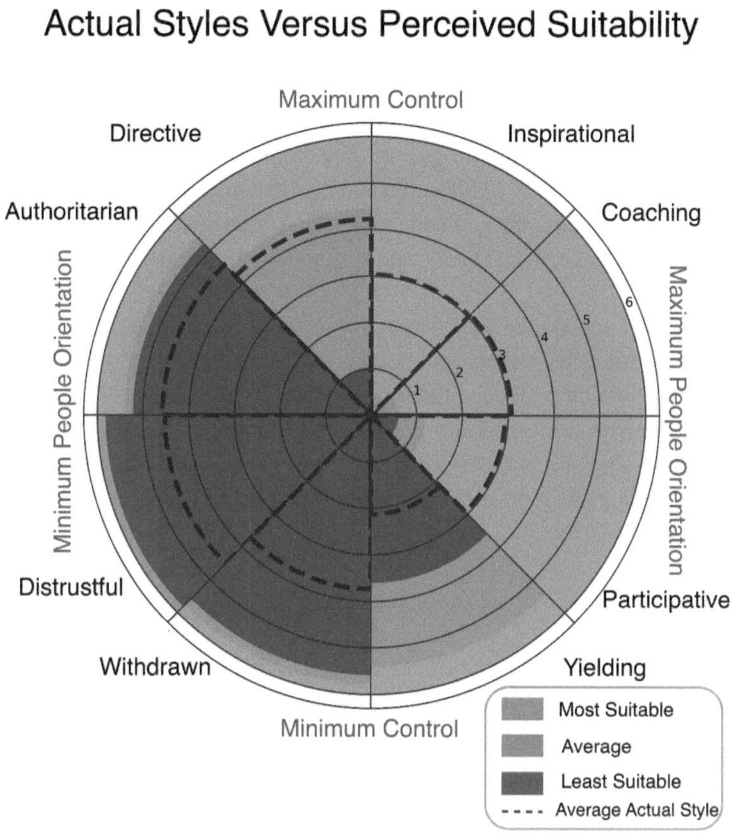

Fig. 11.1 Actual leadership styles versus perceived suitability in Kenya (n = 30) (Mutooni et al. 2020, p. 226)

actual types of leadership experienced in Kenya, as well as people's perceptions of their suitability and hence any necessary changes. The most commonly experienced styles, which are also perceived as least suitable, are typified by non-communal behaviour, such as authoritarian and distrustful styles, and the desire is to move towards more suitable styles with maximum people orientation/communion, such as coaching and participative styles, followed by styles that are maximum control/agency, such as inspirational and directive.

Global Leadership Competencies

Bird states that "from the early 1990s forward, a growing number of scholars have studied global leaders and attempted to delineate the competencies that are critical to their success" (2013, p. 80). Reviews of this literature (Bird and Osland 2004; Mendenhall and Osland 2002) found over 160 competencies that influence global leadership effectiveness. Bird (2013, p. 95) 'pruned' these 160 competencies down to 15, each of which reflects a complex, multifaceted construct that spans pre-dispositional, attitudinal, cognitive, behavioural and knowledge aspects. The consequent framework of global leadership competencies was broadly categorised into three parts:

- Managing self: inquisitiveness, global mind-set, flexibility, character, resilience
- Managing people and relationships: valuing people, cross-cultural communication, interpersonal skills, teaming skills, empowering others
- Business and organizational acumen: vision and strategic thinking, leading change, business savvy, organizational savvy, managing communities

The agency dimension links to Bird's first category of—managing self. The communion dimension links to his two categories of competencies: managing others and organization/community. Coincidentally, Bird's three groups of competencies correspond with two models used in African leadership development programmes (Pérezts et al. 2020; Bolden and Kirk 2005). It also aligns to leadership identity theory that, according to DeRue and Ashford (2010), comprises three elements: individual internalisation, relational recognition and collective endorsement.

11.3 Methodology

This research reports on the design, implementation and impact of a pilot delivery of leadership development seminars. Training participants were selected from among MSc scholarship students at Pwani University, a state-run university in Kilifi, Kenya. This setting was an effective way of targeting young leaders who had not yet benefited from leadership development training and were willing as well as able to participate in this pilot. Two UK PhD students, Maria Derakhshan and Zoe Rutter, were undertaking their Professional Internship for PhD Students (PIPS[1]) at Pwani University in early 2020 and facilitated the seminars. Being students themselves and in a similar age group helped create an informal, open atmosphere, quickly developing mutual trust between the facilitators and the students. The first group consisted of eleven students (seven male/four female) of the MSc in Bioinformatics. Most were from Kenya, one was from Tanzania and one from Uganda. The second group was composed of ten students (six male/four female) of the MSc in Immunology, all of them Kenyans. Participant selection was thus driven by the students' actual participation in the pilot seminar series.

Kirkpatrick's (1996) four-level model of evaluation was used to design the data collection (Fig. 11.2).

[1]Studentships were organized through the 'science students development network in Africa—ssDNAfrica' (http://ssdnafrica.acaciaafrica.org) and funded by the Biotechnology and Biological Research Council (BBSRC).

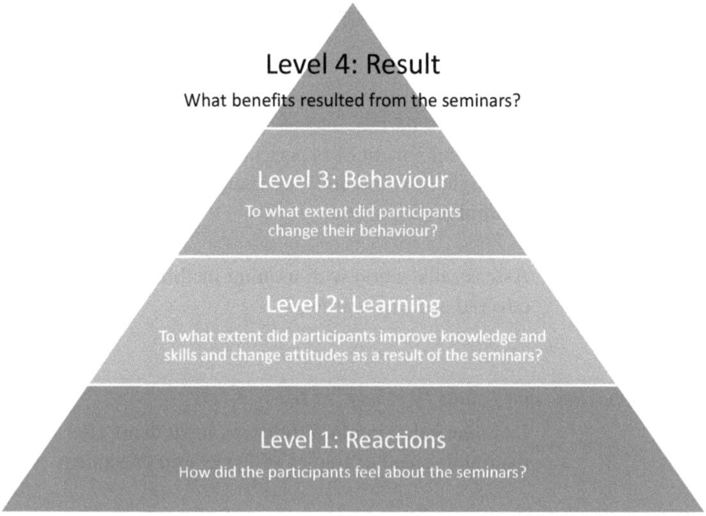

Fig. 11.2 Adapted version of Kirkpatrick's (1996) four-level model of evaluation

Reactions and Learning Reactions and learning were observed during the seminars by the facilitators. Seminar participants (n = 20; one participant did not return the survey) also completed an online evaluation survey shortly after completing the seminar series, which focused mostly on gauging their immediate reactions and primary learning outcomes. The quantitative results were compiled and the qualitative comments analysed. The results are reported in Sect. 11.5.

Training Impact To gain more insight into the long-term impacts of the training on behaviour and results, students (n = 16, five participants did not return the survey) completed a second online 'impact' survey questionnaire 1–2 months later, which focused on changes in their behaviour and resulting effects. This survey was followed by in-depth qualitative interviews another 4 months later, which were conducted with eight students who had volunteered to give interviews (six male/two female; five from the first group, three from the second group). In addition, interviews were held with five university lecturers (one male/four female), who, although not facilitated the training themselves, were in a position to observe the impact of the training on the participants and to reflect on this training within the university environment. The quantitative results were compiled and the qualitative comments analysed. The results are reported in Sects. 11.6 and 11.7. Table 11.1 summarises the data collection methods and their purpose.

Table 11.1 Data collection methods, key purpose and evaluation levels

Data collection method	Key purpose	Kirkpatrick's level
Training evaluation: reactions and learning (see Sect. 11.5)		
Observations during the training sessions	Assess enjoyment of experiential learning Highlight how opinions are shaped by socio-cultural environment	Level 1: Reactions Level 2: Learning
Evaluation survey shortly after completing training	Assess satisfaction with training methods, material covered and key learnings	Level 1: Reactions Level 2: Learning
Training impact: behaviour and results (see Sect. 11.6)		
Impact survey	Examine behavioural differences in students after the training and examples of leadership enactment	Level 3: Behaviour Level 4: Result
Qualitative interviews with students and lecturers	Further probe students' behavioural changes and the impact	Level 3: Behaviour Level 4: Result

11.4 Leadership Training Contextualisation

In this section, we look at how leadership training was designed and implemented to support the desired leadership transformation in the Kenyan context.

As a first step, a seminar on "Developing Global Leadership in Africa" was organised for students and lecturers at Pwani University in January 2020. Discussions during the seminar indicated participants' desire for a leadership transformation towards (1) a less hierarchical, (2) a more people-oriented and (3) a more communion-oriented leadership approach. The seminar concluded with a leadership training needs assessment and prioritisation.

The content of the six training seminars was based on the transformation ambitions noted above. This was then linked to the 'nested' global leadership competencies of Bird (2013), with Managing Self taken as the starting point, followed by People and Relationships and then the wider Organization/Community. Table 11.2 details the six training sessions[2] and shows how these are linked to the transformational themes and leadership competencies.

---

[2]The first seminar series was composed of six 3-hour face-to-face seminars and two clinics over a 4-week period. The second group attended two three-hour face-to-face seminars and then participated in four redesigned online self-study seminars as necessitated by COVID-19 lockdown restrictions.

Table 11.2 Linking the training sessions to transformational themes and global leadership competencies

Training session	Transformational themes	Bird's nested global leadership competencies
1. Personality Type and Motivation 2. Leaders' Attributes	Leaders' attributes: Adaptability Integrity Doing good Candidness Decisiveness	Managing Self
3. Leadership Styles & Diversity 4. Communication & Presentation Skills 5. Giving Feedback & Conflict Resolution	Hierarchy: Cross-cultural perceptions/power People orientation	Managing People and Relationships
6. Diversity, Career Planning & Peer Mentoring	Community: Doing good at level of Business/Community	Business and Organizational Acumen

Individual personality and leaders' attributes were chosen as a starting point for the seminar series so as to provide the foundation and the context that ultimately underpins the next two groups of competencies and themes: managing people and relationships as well as business and organizational acumen. The leadership training addressed the following specific competencies (Bird 2013):

- Managing Self: inquisitiveness, flexibility, character, resilience
- Managing People and Relationships: valuing people, cross-cultural communication, interpersonal skills, teaming skills, empowering others
- Business and Organizational Acumen: leading change

By focusing in the seminars on the three global categories of competencies, a focus on self, relationships and the community was ensured.

Adapting to the Kenyan Context The approach towards leadership development in Africa is often largely influenced by Western leadership development frameworks and material. In order to move beyond this, the seminars used and adapted material suitable to the Kenyan context, as well as an experiential learning approach.

Localized Material Mainstream leadership training material was adapted and combined with (1) case studies and research findings from a leadership case study on Kenya (Mutooni et al. 2020), (2) role play scenarios for the specific context of Kenyan students so that they could understand and relate to them, and (3) proverbs, stories, videos and visuals from various sources in Kenya and East Africa.

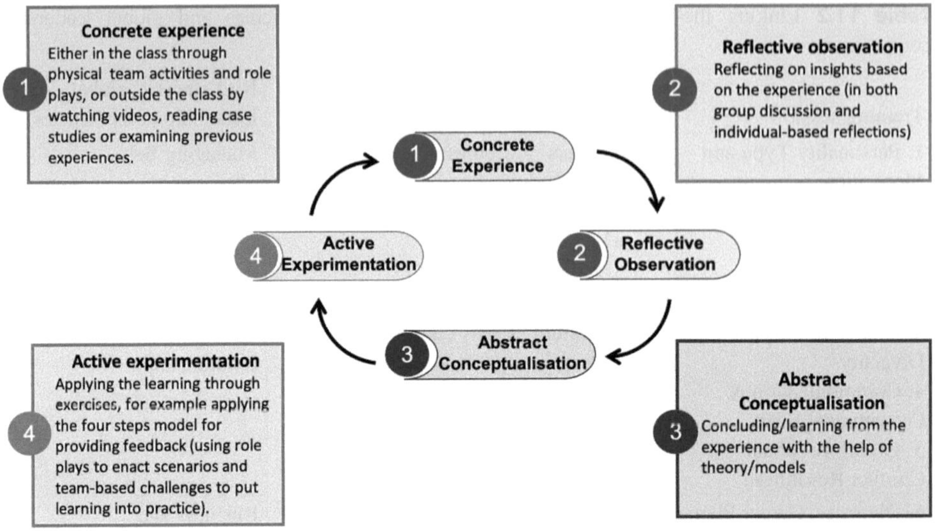

Fig. 11.3 The application of the Kolb learning cycle (2014, p. 113) to the leadership training seminars

Experiential Approach Crucial in terms of contextualisation was the use of an *experiential learning approach* centred around reflections on participants' own leadership experiences from Kenya, Uganda and Tanzania. Each session was designed based on the steps in the learning cycle of American educational theorist Kolb (1984), who states that "learning is the process whereby knowledge is created through the transformation of experience" (p. 38). His theory presents a cyclical model of learning consisting of four stages as shown in Fig. 11.3.

Training methods were selected based on the experiential learning cycle:

- Concrete experience: reading and discussing selected personal experiences from Kenyan leaders, participating in fun exercises such as drawing themselves as a leader, or interactive team assignments such as building a tower out of straws.
- Reflective observation: contributing reflections on their own leadership experiences in an open environment that aimed to promote knowledge sharing and collaborative learning, as well as thought-provoking exercises where students held in-depth conversations in pairs or groups of three.
- Abstract conceptualisation: reading background material, presenting and discussing conceptual models.
- Active experimentation: enacting role plays and completing exercises.

In order to enhance learning, students were also required to complete short preparation work before each session, in the form of responding to questionnaires, watching videos and reading material. Each session started with a group-based recapitulation of key learnings from the previous session.

11.5 Evaluation: Reactions and Learning

The evaluation of reactions and learning (levels 1 and 2 in Kirkpatrick's framework, 1996) was based on observations during the training sessions and the evaluation survey immediately after the seminars finished.

Observations during the training sessions: the method of discussing topics in small groups of two or three followed by one student reporting back to the group was a new experience for many students and took time for them to adjust to. At the start of the seminars, students were more hesitant to participate in in-depth discussions. As the seminars progressed, the participants adapted to this method and a number of insightful discussions took place in which students freely shared their opinions. By doing so, it was evident that the social-cultural context heavily influenced their opinions, with key participant comments centred on the themes of doing good, respect and hierarchy, tribalism, gender and age roles.

A notable finding was students expressing their belief that 'doing good' was an integral leadership attribute, in line with the findings of Jordans et al. (2020). For example, one student drew himself pushing an elderly person in a wheelchair as a demonstration of leadership (Fig. 11.4). Explaining his picture, he said: "*This is me pushing an old man in a wheelchair because he is unable to walk and do things for himself. This demonstrates leadership because I am leading by example; we should do things for other people who need help.*" The student then went on to link his drawing to his personality: "*I have a feeling personality trait and I make decisions based on emotions.*"

To facilitate a discussion on hierarchy, students were shown a picture of the Zambian Livestock minister Hon. Michael Katambo kneeling while talking to president Lungu, who was seated on a chair, and asked what their reactions were. One student from Uganda said: "*I see this as normal behaviour, in Uganda people lie on the floor for important leaders to walk over them, it is a sign of respect.*" This was discussed in the group, and while some students agreed that it is important to show leaders respect in this manner, others thought this was too extreme and followers should be treated more as equals. In addition, the leadership circumplex was used as a framework for discussing leadership styles.

An example of a topic that split opinions in the group was women in leadership roles. Some of the male students had strong opinions that high leadership roles should be filled by men, arguing that women were not able to do these jobs along with family responsibilities. Whilst most of the women in the group strongly disagreed with this, one female student did agree that men are more suited to leadership roles. After a group discussion, most agreed that there is a stereotype in Africa about leaders being older males, which is based on old traditions, and that they are more likely to be respected than young leaders or women. Around half of the group agreed that younger adults and females are just as capable of

Fig. 11.4 Student holding a picture he drew as his interpretation of good leadership

taking up leadership roles at higher levels and that this change needs to happen. One particular exercise demonstrated differences in leadership between men and women, when students were asked to build a tower of straws in two teams. The group with the highest share of women (4 out of 5) built a taller tower than the other group, which consisted only of males. In the winning group, the members first discussed and planned their strategy and then assigned person-specific tasks. This outcome is in line with the findings of Mutooni et al. (2020, p. 231) that in Kenya, women leaders are perceived to be better at people management or people-oriented leadership styles.

Evaluation survey: this survey was designed to assess student satisfaction with the training sessions. On a scale from 1 to 5, the overall satisfaction rating was very high on average (4.8/5), with 75% of students rating the seminars at 5/5 and 25% rating them at 4/5.

Some reflections on the training contents and methodology by students were as follows:

> The content was relevant. The facilitators were practical and realistic in their examples. (Evaluation survey, first group)

> Giving feedback was one of my favourite topics where I really never thought of giving feedback to a higher authority, but now I even know how to go about it. I liked the activity on how to give feedback to your supervisor . . . it really got me thinking. (Evaluation survey, second group)

These comments illustrate that the approach towards contextualisation was successful and resulted in high satisfaction. The training helped students develop skills to implement their desired leadership transformation. The next section describes how they then applied these insights in practice.

11.6 Impact by Behaviour and Results

The extent to which the training succeeded in contributing to the desired leadership behaviour and results in terms of transformation (levels 3 and 4 in Kirkpatrick's 1996, framework) was assessed through an impact survey and qualitative interviews. Distinct impacts were observed for each of Bird's (2013) global leadership competencies levels:

1. Managing Self: change in perspective on leadership, increased confidence and proactive volunteering for leadership roles
2. Managing others: increased ability to apply desired leadership skills
3. Organization/Community: broad-reaching impact on organization and students' lives

These results are detailed below, with examples provided by participants and lecturers.

11.6.1 Impact 1: Managing Self: Change in Perspective on Leadership, Increased Confidence and Proactive Volunteering for Leadership Roles

The impact survey and interviews suggested a change in participants' perspectives on leadership. At the beginning of the series, some students believed that you are born a leader and some people are born followers. Our results indicate that their perspectives had changed after completing the course. They now see leadership as a contextual relationship instead of a one-way process, challenging their idea of what a leader is and how personality differences and diversity affect leadership, on the side of both the leader and the followers, also for women and youth leaders. An example:

> Understanding my personality. It helped me understand that we are not the same, and therefore as a leader, I should be able to appreciate and accommodate everyone. (Impact survey, first group)

After completion of the seminars, the students were aware that leadership skills can be developed by anyone and can be applied to various aspects of life. An example:

> I learned that people can develop leadership skills, you are not born a leader.(Interview with female student, group 1).

As a result of the increased confidence and new skills they had gained, many participants started to proactively look for opportunities to function in leadership roles after the seminars. The following example illustrates this:

> The career planning session encouraged me to become a mentor. I now mentor two undergraduate students and have meetings with them to help drive their ambitions in science. I have also obtained my own mentor who I look up to in the field of bioinformatics. I have also been able to come up with my career roadmap plan for myself. Thank you. (Group 1, male student)

One male lecturer has also noticed a change in some students' behaviour as a result of the seminars. He explains:

> One student I interact with attended the leadership seminars. He was very enthusiastic about the course. Since he attended the seminars, he now deliberately wants to go out to offer leadership, which he would not have thought of before.

11.6.2 Impact 2: Managing Others: Increased Ability to Apply Desired Leadership Skills

Although personally favouring more people-oriented leadership styles, initially the students saw leadership more as authoritarian and directive from past experiences and agreed that this is the most common type of leadership in Kenya. Learning about the different types of leadership styles and applying them to different situations in role plays provided the students with the skills to choose and apply appropriate leadership styles to real-life situations. Students related these new perspectives to changes in their own behaviour, particularly demonstrating increased skills in mentoring other students, consulting others and resolving conflicts.

> I learned about the different types of leadership styles. Before the session, I only knew of a dictator-type leadership style with a strict hierarchy (Authoritarian and Directive); but during the seminars, I learned about other leadership styles such as coaching and participative. I am the first-born child in my family and have to take care of my siblings at home (especially being at home due to COVID-19). What I learned from the course helped me with this. Instead of just telling them what to do I involved them in discussions and I believe this worked well and led to less conflict. (Interview with female student, group 2)

When asked to rate the impact of the training sessions on leadership skills on a scale of 1–5, the rating turned out to be overall high with at least 4.6/5 for all skills, showing the largest positive impact on students' communication skills and motivating others and also high ratings for leadership styles, giving presentations and giving feedback.

Interviews with two class representatives (one from each group) suggested that the leadership training resulted in a reflection on their own leadership styles. They were spokespersons for the class and contact persons between teaching staff and the students, so they have to ensure that all arrangements around all class issues are effectively communicated to the entire class. The class representatives described themselves as inherently using an authoritarian leadership style. They were mirroring what they saw from current leaders, even though in the seminar and course, all participants expressed that they would prefer a more collaborative, people-orientated approach. One reflected as follows:

> This workshop has taught me to be more open to people's opinions and feelings and to try to accommodate everyone's ideas, especially my classmates'. Unfortunately, I used to make decisions myself, which was an inappropriate style of a good leader. The course gave me an insight, too, that culture and history affect our (African) leadership styles and diversity. In most cases in Africa, it has been believed that leaders should be middle-aged or old men. (Class representative, group 2).

The training thus gave these students the confidence and skills to transform towards a more collaborative leadership style. This highlights the importance of enabling participants to embrace their own leadership, to connect to themselves and to empower themselves to develop and apply a range of leadership skills.

11.6.3 Impact 3: Community: Broad-Reaching Impact on Organization and Students' Lives

The impact survey questionnaire further demonstrated that the training had a positive impact on various aspects of students' lives, most notably in relationships with family and friends, work place/study and community (Fig. 11.5). This impact is likely to be a result of the behavioural changes described above.

Participants reflected on what has had the strongest impact on them, for example:

> Conflict management. This is an issue we face at our homes, in the society and even at our work place. (Impact survey, participant group 1)

The following extract from an interview indicates that one participant found that with an increased agency and assertiveness, she was able to apply the new skills of conflict management and providing feedback towards a research supervisor:

> The sessions on giving feedback, conflict resolution and communication skills helped me address a problem I had with my research supervisor. I was busy with university work, including online classes, and my research supervisor gave me a lot of reading materials to prepare for my research project. I was able to effectively communicate to my supervisor that I appreciated the reading materials, but I was struggling to balance reading those with the work I already had. (Female student, group 2)

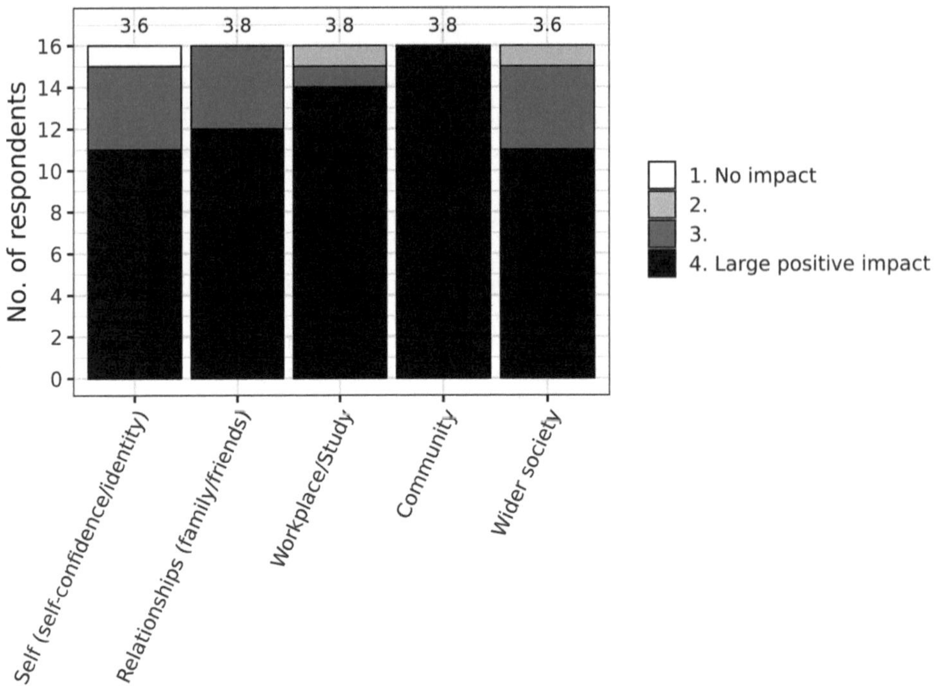

Fig. 11.5 Impact of seminars on students' lives (n = 16). The average rating of the impact for each social context is given above each bar

We conclude this section with a detailed example of a female student from the first group, who describes her evolvement during the course of the seminars, afterwards showing evidence for all three impacts described above.

11.6.4 From Fluttering Flag to Winner

The behaviour of one female student and her attitude towards leadership changed drastically during the course of and the seminars. In the first session, she drew herself as a flag in the 'draw yourself as a leader' exercise, describing how she felt like a flag being blown around by life, insisting that she was born to follow and unable to see herself as a leader.

This student described herself as a strong introvert and thought that with this characteristic, she was more suited to be a follower. Furthermore, she had strong opinions about males being more suited for leadership roles, which seems a reflection of society's perception of female leaders. This student really embraced the seminar series, listening carefully, contributing to group discussions and applying the skills she had learned in the role play scenarios. When interviewing this student 7 months after the completion of the course, it became apparent how her perspectives and actions in relation to leadership had changed from not believing in herself as a leader to opting for a leadership opportunity shortly afterwards—and then successfully leading a large group in an international bioinformatics internship. Her story in her own words:

> I used what I had learned from the leadership seminars and applied it to a virtual bioinformatics internship I took part in. The internship involved participants from around 15 countries. I was elected the leader of my group, which involved guiding the group through the various tasks. Before the leadership training, I didn't think of myself as a leader, I always thought I was a follower. The training made me realise that people are not born leaders and that you can build your leadership skills. (Impact 1)
>
> I used what I had learned during the leadership styles section of the course to choose the appropriate leadership style for our group to achieve success. I used aspects of a coaching leadership style, as some of the group members had less experience with bioinformatics and needed help with tasks. I also used a participative leadership style, which allowed individuals to contribute to the team. (Impact 2)
>
> During the internship, I applied what I had learned in the conflict resolution section of the seminars. At one stage in the internship, I was the leader of around 30 people, and we had to write a proposal and prepare a manuscript. A member of the group was making changes to the shared documents the group did not agree with, and they were complaining about this individual. I made a phone call to this person and explained the reasons why they shouldn't be doing it and suggested that they should share the comments to the group and we can discuss if it should be added to the documents. This seemed to resolve the conflict well. Before the leadership seminars, I might have just sent them an e-mail, which could have been taken the wrong way and the individual may have dropped out of the course. (Impact 3)
>
> At the end of the internship, there was a competition, and the remaining five groups had to present their work via a Zoom call. I used what I had learned in the leadership seminars to prepare good slides, keep to time and communicate well. I also considered the feedback I got from the presentation I did during the leadership seminars. I was chosen by my group to present our work to the judges. And we won the competition! (Impacts 2 and 3)

Although at first hesitant to be a leader—due to cultural notions about female leaders and her introvert personality—it is instructive that through her increase in agency, this participant volunteered for a leadership role shortly afterwards. She then deliberately chose leadership styles that were people- and community-oriented, such as coaching and participatory ones, to build a team from a diverse group of people. She applied the conflict resolution skills to achieve her desired goal. She opened herself up to feedback and used it to win a competition. Her story tells us that she has learned to build success through newly acquired skills that allowed her to flexibly enact the kinds of leadership she desired. Her initial self-perception as a fluttering flag also implies the attribute of adaptability, another important characteristic of leadership. The success of leading teams and ensuring results through the use of people-oriented leadership styles then contributed to her further increase in confidence and individual agency.

On the basis of analysing the impact of the training and the specific impacts identified, we can conclude that the leadership training contributed to the desired leadership transformation for those students who participated. Central in this successful transformation is the dynamic between the two dimensions of the IPC and the leadership circumplex, starting with strengthening individual agency and then focusing on leadership in relationships and community.

11.7 Future Training and University Perspective

The importance of leadership development was broadly felt in the training. One of the student participants indicated this importance for university students:

> I strongly believe that the leadership training is important. I think it would be great to have had training earlier on, and I think it is high time the university incorporates seminars like these into the curriculum and delivers them to undergraduate students. I believe that if students are exposed to these trainings, they might deal with hardships better, for example in their handling of student strikes. It would help students appreciate the diversity in society, deal with quarrels and resolve conflicts. (Group 1, male student)

Interviews with lecturers indicated they are likewise convinced of the importance of leadership development. A female lecturer, and initiator of the seminar series, explains:

> This is very important. Young students are at a formative stage of their life, and at Pwani somehow in a disadvantaged position compared to students in the West—more and broader skills, especially a good grasp of soft skills, will make them more competitive, also internationally.

In this context, all lecturers also consider the importance of their role as mentors, too. A female lecturer explains:

> My role as mentor and role model is important, but I view it broader than that, I also need to ensure that I create space for them, create opportunities for them such as these seminars, that I make things happen, that I am an instigator.

Going forward, the university management as well as many members of the academic staff are very enthusiastic about incorporating this leadership training at Pwani University. There are several initiatives and ideas on how these seminars could be integrated into the curriculum. At the time of writing (October 2021), a "Training of Trainers" course had been conducted for lecturers and recent graduates who jointly facilitated the leadership seminars for two groups of students in late June/July 2021, with a further series being planned for early 2022, possibly with the help of visiting PhD students under the PIPS programme. Another possibility to further develop leadership skills currently being considered is the use of some of the experiential learning approaches in the regular technical curriculum, such as discussion in pairs or small team work and assignments as well as presenting to the larger class.

11.8 Discussion and Concluding Comments

This chapter has analysed and reported on a leadership training programme conducted in Kenya, with a focus on the process of contextualisation and its impact on leadership transformation. Here we discuss the practical and theoretical implications of the study.

Regarding contextualisation, we conclude that the training was successfully tailored to the Kenyan context by adapting training material, using case studies as well as visual materials from the Kenyan context, and by adopting an experiential learning approach. This enabled students to reflect on and discuss their own opinions, experiences and typical situations in Kenya, and to apply critical thinking to abstract leadership concepts before re-affirming their learning through practical activities. Group work and role plays were especially appreciated, as they offered opportunities to practise and apply leadership skills. Based on our findings, this is likely to have led to increased confidence, enabling the participants to apply these skills more easily in real life. This is in line with the findings of Bolden and Kirk (2005). We also suggest that part of the success of the training sessions was the approach to first establish participants' needs and desired leadership styles, thus enabling a tailored training experience directed towards those styles. As a result, participants then have a stronger vested interest in putting into practice these styles of leadership. This finding resonates with documented changes by Mouton and Wildschut (2015).

When reviewing the training through interviews several months later, distinct impacts were observed for three competencies levels: (1) Managing Self: changes in perspectives on leadership, increased confidence and proactive volunteering for leadership roles; (2) Managing Others: an increased ability to apply desired leadership skills; and (3) Organization/Community: a broad-reaching impact on organization and students' lives.

The documented training sessions are unique, as they were designed for the specific context of MSc students in Kenya. The empirical data are limited to the students who attended the leadership seminars. As such, the findings are specific to this context and these students. We may, however, assume that other young leaders in Kenya will also need contextualised support to put their leadership transformation ambitions into practice. The lack of readily available role models, confidence and skills (Jordans et al. 2020) is likely to require contextualized tools for successful leadership transformation. The documented impact from this study provides evidence that rather than just formulating an abstract ambition, participants experienced transformation towards their desired new leadership paradigm.

Amidst a dearth of analytical studies on leadership development and its impact in Africa, this analysis contributes to a general understanding of how leadership development can be contextualised to a particular culture and setting. The use of adapted and localised materials combined with the use of an experiential learning approach can be transferred and applied to other contexts and situations in Kenya, to other countries in Africa and also beyond. If accompanied by a documenting of the contextualisation process and a detailed impact analysis of these programmes, this would contribute to broader insights and gradually build a body of knowledge on contextualised leadership development in Africa as well as beyond.

From a theoretical point of view, our new insights into international leadership and its development demonstrate the relevance of distinguishing between the two dimensions Agency and Communion that underlie the IPC and leadership Circumplex. These two dimensions relate to different skills and impacts. Increased individual agency has been seen to result in an increase in self-confidence, deeper insight into their own personality as well as that of others and a proactivity in career planning. An increase in the Communion dimension leads to an appreciation of diversity, to improved communication and conflict management skills as well as an effective use of leadership styles that are people-oriented. This dimensional perspective resonates with the frameworks used in African leadership development programmes (Pérezts et al. 2020; Bolden and Kirk 2005) and also with the three levels of leaders' identity recognized by DeRue and Ashford (2010) which was analysed in an African context by Moorosi (2014).

A new insight documented in our analysis indicates the importance of taking as a starting point the increase of individual agency, which then enables the taking up of leadership roles and subsequent growth through applying communion-oriented competencies. In areas where few leadership roles models are present, leadership agency cannot be assumed. International leadership discourse and practice would benefit from contextualizing leadership development based on insights into this dynamic.

References

Achebe, Ch. (1983). *The trouble with Nigeria*. Enugu, Nigeria: Fourth Dimension Publishing Company Ltd.

Amah, O. (2019). *Globalisation and Leadership in Africa. Developments and Challenges for the Future*. Cham, Switzerland: Palgrave MacMillan.

Balogun, F., Obamwonyi, H., & Falade, T. (2019). *From Resilience to Transilience: Interrogating Ideas on Youth Agency and Social Innovation in Nigeria. A Literature Review Article*. LEAP Africa, Lagos, Nigeria. Retrieved from https://www.researchgate.net/publication/336618083_From_Resilience_to_Transilience_Interrogating_Ideas_on_Youth_Agency_and_Social_Innovation_in_Nigeria_A_Literature_Review

Banda, P. (2014). How the Cold War Sustained Bad Leadership in Malawi, 1964–1994. In B. G. Jallow (Ed.), *Leadership in Post-Colonial Africa* (pp. 27–44). London, England: Palgrave MacMillan.

Bird, A. (2013). Mapping the content domain of global leadership competencies. In M. E. Mendenhall, J. S. Osland, A. Bird, G. R. Oddou, M. J. Stevens, M. L. Maznevski, & G. K. Stahl (Eds.), *Global leadership: Research, practice, and development* (pp. 119–142). New York: Routledge.

Bird, A., & Osland, J. S. (2004). Global Competencies: An introduction. In H. W. Lane, M. L. Maznevski, M. E. Mendenhall, & J. McNett (Eds.), *The Blackwell Handbook of Global Management. A Guide to Managing Complexity* (pp. 57–80). Oxford, MA: Blackwell.

Bolden, R., & Kirk, P. (2005). *Leadership in Africa: Meanings, Impacts and Identities*. Conference paper from 'Studying Leadership: Future Agendas', the 4th International Conference on Leadership Research. Lancaster University Management School, 12–13 December 2005. Retrieved from https://www.researchgate.net/publication/29811042

Ciulla, J. (2013). Chapter 11: Essay: searching for Mandela: the saint as a sinner who keeps on trying. In D. Ladkin & C. Spill (Eds.), *Authentic Leadership. Clashes, Convergences and Coalescences.* New Horizons in Leadership Studies series (pp. 152–175). Cheltenham, UK: Edward Elgar. https://doi.org/10.4337/9781781006382

Clement, G. (1996). Care, Autonomy and Justice: Feminism and the Ethic of Care. Boulder, CO: Westview.

DeRue, D., & Ashford, S. (2010). Who will lead and who will follow: A social process of leadership identity construction in organizations. *Academy of Management Review*, *35*(4), 627–647.

Gaylord, R. (2004). African humanism, ubuntu and black South African writing. *Journal of Literary Studies*, *20*, 3–4.

Giacalone, R., & Thomson, K. (2006). Business ethics and social responsibility education, shifting the worldview. *Academy of Management Learning and Education*, *5*(3), 266–277.

Greenleaf, R. (2010). Servant leadership. In G. R. Hickman (Ed.), *Leading organizations* (pp. 87–95). Thousand Oaks, CA: Sage Publications.

Hailey, J. (2008). *Ubuntu: A Literature Review*. Paper Prepared for the Tutu Foundation, London. Retrieved from https://www.coursehero.com/file/37161128/UbuntuLiteratureReviewpdf/

Iwowo, V. A. (2019). Skype interview on 11 July 2019.

Iwowo, V. A. (2015). Leadership in Africa: rethinking development. *Personnel Review*, *44*(3), 408–429. https://doi.org/10.1108/PR-07-2013-0128

Jallow, B. (2014). Leadership in Colonial Africa: An Introduction. In B. Jallow (ed.), *Leadership in Postcolonial Africa: Trends Transformed by Independence*. London, UK: Palgrave MacMillan.

Jordans, E., Ng'weno, B., & Spencer-Oatey, H. (Eds.) (2020). *Developing Global Leaders: Insights from African Case Studies*. Palgrave Studies in African Leadership. London, UK: Palgrave MacMillan.

Kirkpatrick, D. (1996). Great ideas revisited. *Training & Development*, *50*(1), 54–57.

Kolb, D. A. (2014). *Experiential Learning: Experience as the Source of Learning and Development*. Second edition. Upper Saddle River, NJ: Pearson Education Ltd.

Kolb, D. A. (1984). *Experiential Learning: Experience as the Source of Learning and Development*. Englewood Cliffs, NJ: Prentice-Hall.

Kumuyi, W. F. (2007). The case for servant leadership. *New Africa*, *467*, 18–19.

Ladkin, D. (2017) A Practice-Based Approach to Developing Ethically Responsible Leaders. In S. Kempster, A. Turner, & G. Edwards (Eds.), *Field Guide to Leadership Development* (pp. 15–28). Cheltenham, UK: Edward Elgar.

Leary, T. (1957). *Interpersonal diagnosis of personality: a functional theory and methodology for personality evaluation*. New York, NY: Ronald Press.

Locke, K. D. (2019). Development and Validation of a Circumplex Measure of the Interpersonal Culture in Work Teams and Organizations. *Frontiers in Psychology*, *10*. Retrieved from https://www.frontiersin.org/article/10.3389/fpsyg.2019.00850

Locke, K. D. (2000). Circumplex scales of interpersonal values: Reliability, validity, and applicability to interpersonal problems and personality disorders. *Journal of Personality Assessment*, *75*(2), 249–267. https://doi.org/10.1207/S15327752JPA7502_6

Mabokela, R. (2003). "Donkeys of the University": Organizational Culture and Its Impact on South African Women Administrators. *Higher Education, 46*(2), 129–145. Retrieved from http://www.jstor.org/stable/3447463

Mendenhall, M., & Osland, J. S. (2002). *An overview of the extant global leadership research.* Symposium presentation, Academy of International Business, Puerto Rico.

Metz, T. (2018). An African theory of good leadership. *African Journal of Business Ethics, 12*(2), 36–53.

Modisane, K. (2018). Finding the niche to reposition leadership in Africa's developing economies for the global highway: review of literature on leadership development programmes—methods and techniques. *Human Resource Development International, 21*(1), 12–23. https://doi.org/10.1080/13678868.2017.1326220

Moorosi, P. (2020). Constructions of Leadership Identities via Narratives of African Women School Leaders. *Frontiers in Education, 5*(86). doi: https://doi.org/10.3389/feduc.2020.00086

Moorosi, P. (2014). Constructing a leader's identity development through a leadership development programme: an intersectional analysis. *Educational Management Administration & Leadership, 42*(6), 792–807. doi: https://doi.org/10.1177/1741143213494888

Mouton, J., & Wildschut, L. (Eds.) (2015). *Leadership and management: Case studies in training in higher education in Africa.* Cape Town, South Africa: African Minds. Retrieved from http://www.africanminds.co.za/leadership-and-management-case-studies-in-training-in-higher-education-in-africa/

Mutooni, K., Ng'weno, B., & Jordans, E. (2020). Changing Leadership Perceptions: Leaders in the Private Sector in Kenya. In E. Jordans, B. Ng'weno, & H. Spencer-Oatey (Eds.), *Developing Global Leaders: Insights from African Case Studies* (pp. 211–257). Palgrave Studies in African Leadership. London, UK: Palgrave MacMillan.

Nkomo, S., & Ngambi, H. (2009). African Women in Leadership: Current Knowledge and a Framework for Future Studies. *International Journal of African Renaissance Studies – Multi, Inter- and Transdisciplinary, 4*(1), 49–68.

Pailey, R. N. (2014). Patriarchy, power distance, and female presidency in Liberia. In B. G. Jallow (Ed.), *Leadership in post-colonial Africa* (pp. 175–196). Palgrave MacMillan.

Pérezts, M., Russon, J., & Painter, M. (2020). This Time from Africa: Developing a Relational Approach to Values-Driven Leadership. *Journal of Business Ethics, 161*(4), 731–748. https://doi.org/10.1007/s10551-019-04343-0

Redeker, M., de Fries, R. E., Rouckhout, D., Vermeren, P., & Filip, D. F. (2014). Integrating leadership: the leadership circumplex. *European Journal of Work and Organizational Psychology, 23*(3), 435–455. doi: https://doi.org/10.1080/1359432X.2012.738671

Sendjaya, S., & Sarros, J. (2002). Servant leadership: Its origin, development, and application in organizations. *Journal of Leadership & Organizational Studies, 9*(2), 57–64.

Serpell, R. (2011). Social Responsibility as a Dimension of Intelligence, and as an Educational Goal: Insights from Programmatic Research in an African Society. *Child Development Perspectives, 5*(2), 126–133.

Steady, F. C. (2011). Conclusion: Mothering the Nation and Humanizing the State. In F. C. Steady (Ed.), *Women and Leadership in West Africa* (pp. 237–241). New York, NY: Palgrave Macmillan. https://0-doi-org.pugwash.lib.warwick.ac.uk/10.1057/9781137010391_9

Sullivan, H. S. (1953). *The interpersonal theory of psychiatry.* New York, NY: Norton.

Sullivan, H. S. (1940). Conceptions of modern psychiatry: The first William Alanson White Memorial Lectures. *Psychiatry*, 3(1), 3–17.

Wiggins, J. S. (1996). An informal history of the interpersonal circumplex tradition. *Journal of Personality Assessment*, *66*(2), 217–233. https://doi.org/10.1207/s15327752jpa6602_2

Zoogah, D., Peng, M., & Woldu, H. (2015). Institutions, Resources and Organizational Effectiveness in Africa. *The Academy of Management Perspectives*, *29*(1), 7–31. doi: https://doi.org/10.5465/amp.2012.0033

Emergent Leadership in Multicultural, Global, and Virtual Teams 12

Lessons from Global Enterprise Experience's Virtual Mobility Program

Pierre Sindambiwe and Michel Ndahimana

12.1 Introduction

How do ordinary team members in spontaneous global teams in less structured, multicultural, global, and virtual teams without power and authority become global leaders? This chapter provides answers to this question.

Emergent leaders working in multicultural, global, and virtual teams are characterized by their traditional roles as leaders, like working with a clear structure, authority, and responsibility. However, there has been an increase in online jobs, meetings, and discussions. Very little is known about emergent leadership among peers working in an environment which has a less static structure, power, and authority while sharing the responsibility for reaching a common goal in contests or group assignments. Leadership in these groups may be concentrated on focusing on performance or on monitoring the behavior of team members (Carte et al. 2006). The more these groups become globalized—with multicultural members living in different time zones and interconnecting in a virtual mode—the more interesting becomes the emergence of leadership . As this is a situation rarely faced in real life by organizations, few examples exist of international students working in management and doing projects online.

P. Sindambiwe (✉)
Jönkoping International Business School, Jönköping University, Jönköping, Sweden

Berlin Study Center, Arden University, Coventry, UK

M. Ndahimana
College of Business and Economics (CBE), University of Rwanda, Kigali, Rwanda

I. Stolz, S. Oldenziel Scherrer (eds.), *International Leadership*, uniscope. Publikationen der SGO Stiftung, https://doi.org/10.1007/978-3-658-37306-1_12

Contrary to the ordinary organization, a virtual team usually disperses immediately after their common goal has been met. In a virtual environment, team leaders are appointed or elected with less power, as they can neither assign tasks to suit other members' capabilities nor sanction volunteering members. Even if members are removed from a team, this has little or no impact on their careers, since the team is not their organization. Therefore, learning from real-life examples is essential for understanding the emergent leadership phenomenon in the online sphere.

Experiences of leadership emerging among peers in online programs is increasing because not only has life gone global, but the current pandemic is also shifting most activities online. These online activities are less structured, and those who attend meetings or conferences come from all over the globe.

We know that the physical location of team members is important as it affects emergent leadership's perceptions in terms of the use and interpretation of communication in virtual teams (Charlier et al. 2016). A virtual group's members firmly believe in leadership which is provided by someone who acts as a mediator, at least more so than the one who directs or monitors them (Sutanto et al. 2011, p. 435). We also know that leadership style in such self-managed teams yields better results if the leaders exhibit leadership competencies rather sooner than later; because the more time passes, the less the identification of the group members, which may impact their performance (Carte et al. 2006). Hanson et al. (2012) as well as Jarvenpaa and Leidner (1999) focus on challenges like the fragile and temporary trust faced by virtual teams. They have identified the challenges, but we also need to understand the factors for emergent leadership in a virtual working environment and the competencies expected from a leader by the participants in virtual interactions. This is complicated because these teams work without meeting face-to-face or in a group, and there is more than just one cultural background to manage.

However, the focus of this chapter is not on the challenges emergent leaders face but on the factors, strategies, and competencies they use for overcoming these challenges.

This chapter examines individual reports of selected "highly commended peer-leaders" from the virtual mobility project of the Global Enterprise Experience (GEE) in order to capture leadership emergence over time. Candidates emerged from among hundreds of peers who took part in GEE's annual contest. The chapter investigates peer-leaders' reports which provide solutions to the challenges the teams faced during teamwork. It uses qualitative and narrative approaches to analyze the data in the reports. This helps understand the way in which global leadership emerges and the characteristic behavior of emerging global leaders through coded narratives regarding the challenges faced and strategies adopted.

12.2 Literature Review

Existing literature studies leadership in multicultural or virtual teams but always within defined organizations working with a clear structure, like virtual groups with software systems and social networks (Sutanto et al. 2011)—a situation with social structures, or rules and resources where people interact through technology (Charlier et al. 2016). However, comparatively much less is known about leading an unstructured global team and the associated challenges as well as leadership strategies for overcoming these challenges.

Studying emergent leadership in global virtual teams is essential because of situations like the COVID-19 pandemic era and its aftermath, which does not provide the option of working together in physical locations or traveling for meetings, as has been done in the past; instead, nearly all meetings are now held in a virtual setting. In addition, contrary to the traditional leadership style, it is hard to know how a virtual team environment may influence leadership practices or behavior and trustworthiness in emergent leadership in virtual teams (Tyran et al. 2003, p. 183).

Those who primarily assume a mediating rather than a directing or monitoring role are seen as emergent leaders (Sutanto et al. 2011, p. 421). Another category of emergent leaders consists of those members who send longer messages than others but are not necessarily experts in the field (Yoo and Alavi 2004).

One stream of literature states that the more effective emergent leaders in virtual collaborative settings are not necessarily the official ones.

Another stream of literature—like the recent systematic review by Hanna et al. (2021)—tracks and categorizes the emerging leadership construct. At the group or team level, there are a few variables like the team network's centrality, team dispersion (or co-location), virtuality, social cues, and gender representation, which moderate the leadership's emergence construct, while other variables like a shared team vision as well as the quantity and quality of team communication mediate in it.

At an individual level, the antecedents of the emergence of leadership include individual traits, demographics, state, and behavior (Hanna et al. 2021). The principal individual traits include agreeableness and conscientiousness in emergent leaders, creativity, self-efficacy, self-esteem, and emotional stability. Major individual demographic variables include gender, age, educational level, economic status, and race. Significant individual state variables include attitudes toward leadership, identifying with the team, self-concept, status, identification with the leadership role, leader (anti-)prototypicality, and task ability. The variables of principal individual behavior include the amount of attention given to the team, a promotive voice, self-monitoring, self-promotion, teamwork, and traditional team behavior like being considerate and task-oriented. Some other individual factors moderate the emergence of leadership such as an emergent leader's cognitive abilities, one's desire to lead, dominance, and prosocial motivation.

Another stream of literature focuses on the outcomes of emergent leaders for the team. These include individual factors like self-identification with a team, behavior, role, typicality,, network centrality, status, and peer-relations, which mediate the leadership emergence process instead of predicting or moderating leadership emergence variables (Hanna et al. 2021). However, literature related to the outcomes of leadership emergence for the team is not the focus of this chapter.

By concentrating on individual antecedents, Hanna et al. (2021), Auvinen et al. (2021), Hanson et al. (2012), González-Anta et al. (2021), as well as Jarvenpaa and Leidner (1999) call for expanding the field by looking at contextual and situational issues like the likelihood and personality composition of emergent leaders. This appeal is the focus of this contribution which, however, does not feed on the theoretical lens of a functional, identity-based model or on relational models as suggested, or on other theories like the behaviorally-based leadership theory (Misiolek and Heckman 2005), as it prefers a qualitative method for investigating this phenomenon.

12.3 Methodology

This chapter investigates peer-leaders in Global Enterprise Experience (GEE) projects because their functions are spontaneous as compared to team leaders who are appointed. It helps understand the concept of emergent leadership in virtual mobility over time. The chapter examines individual reports of "highly commended global peer-leaders", having been selected from many others who took part in the GEE virtual mobility project. Peer-leaders' reports provide solutions to the challenges faced while executing teamwork. Groups are highly heterogeneous as they can incorporate students from all continents. Reflexive reports contain a lot of information about personal achievements, challenging circumstances, and strategies used to cope with the situation, which will help trace competencies of the best emerging global leaders. Every year, GEE attracts hundreds of students worldwide, places them in highly heterogeneous groups, with one of them acts as the leader who can be assisted by anyone in the team. That assisting capacity characterizes a peer-leader.

The GEE project links participants from several countries and all continents; data originates from peer leaders coming from Brunei, Cameroon, China, Colombia, Indonesia, Italy, Nepal, the Netherlands, New Zealand, Nigeria, the Philippines, Rwanda, the UK, and the USA. Victoria University runs this contest in New Zealand to create future global leaders capable of working in partnerships across cultures, worldviews, and levels of wealth and poverty. As far as possible, it is ensured that the team members come from five continents making it a global and multicultural environment. They meet and work online via a medium they agree on under the precondition that they complete the project within 3 weeks. So the teams have 3 weeks to meet online, choose a project, to research, design, and make a business proposal for a profitable product or service that addresses a specific topic, including sustainable development goals (SDGs). This makes it a temporal and virtual team.

Contrary to Erez et al.'s (2013) student project (where the evaluation was done in the middle of the program), in the case of GEE, no direct interventions are made by its project coordinators, making it a less structured and spontaneous environment that reflects today's times where most meetings and teamwork is done online via Zoom or similar platforms due to the COVID-19 pandemic. This is challenging since we do not know much about the competencies needed by emerging leaders in virtual and self-directed teams (Ziek and Smulowitz 2014).

In a GEE project, the team's goal is to work on a project and to win the contest as a team. Usually, hundreds of teams participate in the contest. Not only are the team reports evaluated to award the best team, but individual reflexive reports are also evaluated to rank the greatest and most highly commended leaders as well as emerging peer-leaders. Those who exhibit unusual behavior as individuals are not necessarily leaders of the winning teams. Six best team leaders out of more than 100 participants are identified every year to be nominated as *global leaders*. Besides official group leaders, since 2016, another category of leaders has also been nominated: *peer global leaders*.

This chapter focuses on the latter category of peer-leaders. In order to assess peer-leadership, GEE uses participants' reflections, their feedback to other colleagues, and team members' assessment of the candidates. According to the project coordination website,

> ... peer-leaders are skilled at supporting the leader or stepping into a leadership vacuum, role modeling creativity, professionalism, strategic thinking, are hard-working, and pick up some of the leadership roles. Evidence for peer-leadership came from their journal, invitation to be a peer-leader by the team leader, comments from team members in their journals, peer-leadership challenges faced and overcome, and the quality of the team report. (Global Enterprise Experience 2021)

During 2016–2020, a total of 27 global peer-leaders were identified, and the first one among them was awarded. In 2016, only three instead of the usual six global peer-leaders were selected. During these years, peer-leaders emerged from all continents.

The names of the participating peer-leaders were coded to ensure anonymity. Editing was done wherever necessary for spelling, grammar, punctuation, sentence structure, and writing style, since many of them were not native English speakers. Whenever we write "he" or "she" in this chapter, this refers to the gender of the respective pseudonym. Names have been changed, and the pseudonymization code is only known to the authors.

In this chapter, we analyze the reflexive reports of all 27 peer-leaders who emerged over the last 5 years of the competition.

This article adopts a qualitative approach with a narrative research design for the study. We also conducted a thematic analysis of the reports. According to Stalker (2009), the narrative design has broadly been adopted since the postmodern era in the 1990s as an interdisciplinary source of data. A narrative design application provides for a meaningful telling of events chronologically and allows for identifying people's context, temporality, and how they witness their life experiences and actions. A narrative analysis in the form of expressive and naturalist methods assesses the structure and themes to be investigated. It can equal a case study investigation that helps build a theory (Boje 2009). We use a theme analysis for categorizing observed behavior as well as for reading documents and transcripts that inform the researchers' interpretations (Boje 2009).

Data was coded into first-order categories, second-order themes, and aggregate dimensions to identify challenges, motives for taking up leadership roles, strategies, and characteristic behavior of emerging leaders in less structured, multicultural, global, and virtual teams. The data analysis followed an iterative process because the first-order coding informed the process, which was discovered in the course of coding and forced us to go back and generate more codes based on the emerging themes. Codification and analysis were done concurrently and influenced each other. Until data saturation was reached, codification focused on the challenges, issues, and situations faced by peer global leaders, as well as the strategies adopted by them as they narrated them in their reports.

12.4 Findings

12.4.1 Challenges of Team Reluctancy, Individual Responsibility, and Leaders' Inactivity Calling for Potential Leaders' Attention

Our findings show that ordinary participants stepped in as leaders due to the challenges the virtual teams had to face. These challenges included inactive leaders, group inactivity in terms of lack of communication, and slowness of team members.

Inactive Leaders

Team members were less organized due to a lack of initiative by the leader. "With everybody's disappointment, the team leader, although collaborative and responsive, rarely played his leading role; he never joined the WhatsApp group and did not take any initiative in the project" (Bright-P20171257). In another case, the appointed leader was absent. This was a common challenge that called for emergent leaders to do their duty. "The original team leader did not take the lead, and after a week I decided to take some initiative and try to get everybody together. This is where my journey as the team leader started" (Chelsea-P20201394). In such a situation, only brave, engaged, and responsible members have the courage to take the lead.

Group Inactivity and Slowness

Another situation that calls for people to take the initiative is a generalized lack of activity or communication within the team. "Our group didn't do well in the beginning. People just said hello to each other, and there was no more" (Agnes-P20192211). The members became silent, inactive, and rarely responded to the team's common goal. For responsible members, this was a difficult situation, especially when coupled with the leader's inactivity. Then, the potential leader in the team saw this as a call for him/her to do something to save the situation. "To be honest, the first week of our project was not an easy one. Some team members did not respond to Georgia's (the leader's) messages" (Anne-P2016422).

Even when a team does work, it sometimes only works slowly. People are reluctant to fight for its primary goal, which is frustrating for motivated members. Lack of feedback or member participation is a common feature in slow teams. "I was surprised when one week went by and some members did not reply to an e-mail from our team leader" (Durie-P2018624). From the point of view of some committed members, this was a result of team members' irresponsibility or lack of a common goal when joining the group. Nevertheless, as slowness is not inactivity, people do end up working—at least a few start working and the group can move ahead. This can go along with many disagreements which slow down the whole process. "My team was very late to agree on a business idea, and there were daily arguments on what we all thought would be a winning idea" (Daniel-P2016979).

12.4.2 Triggers Pushing Potential Leaders to Action: Worries of Collective Failure

The challenges of inactive leaders, group inactivity in terms of lack of communication, and the slowness of team members that call for potential leaders' attention provide external stimuli. As individuals, potential leaders have their personal motives that explain why some take the initiative when others are reluctant or indifferent to the situation. The triggers include feelings of concern about the collective failure of the team, a sense of individual responsibility, and individual eagerness of emergent leaders to contribute to the team's accomplishments.

Concerns About Collective Failure of the Team
A feeling of collective shame brings about an identity conflict, and one may fight for the team or maintain a distance until the other members realize that they need to be part of the team. "I must confess it was discouraging at this point, I did not feel I was part of a team" (Elias-P20161275). Among this team, this ignited a certain feeling of guilt in terms of not giving enough to get the team out of the current situation, especially when it was moving forward slowly and the potential leader realized that his/her effort was missing. "A member stepped up to support the leader and helped get us on a common platform to communicate and get started. I also thought, 'Next time there is such a situation, I will step up to take the lead' (which I did later)" (Kaiser-P20201937). In other words, emergent leaders can develop an inner feeling about their own lack of responsibility or not contributing enough, so they decide to move forward and contribute.

Sense of Individual Responsibility
Instead of waiting for other team members to act, their sense of responsibility does not allow potential leaders to close their eyes vis-à-vis the situation. They feel they must do something. This impulse comes from within: "If nobody takes the responsibility in your group, you should learn to take the initiative so that our discussion goes well" (Agnes-P20192211).

A significant aspect for potential leaders is that they do not do this for themselves or by themselves but think of it as teamwork and strive to involve others by doing something themselves. "Ten days passed; the situation did not change much. I started thinking that it was impossible to get all the members involved" (Anne-P2016422). This sense of responsibility is shared with all members to share collective responsibility for their work. To do so, leaders start by contributing themselves as an example and sharing their contributions with the group. "We had lost most of the time in the first half just coming to an idea, so when I felt that it was late, I made a proposal for a new idea in a new area" (Amy-P2018838). Potential leaders admitted that this perception comes instantly due to the feeling that the group was left behind and that something needed to be done.

Individual Eagerness Among Emergent Leaders to Contribute to the Team's Accomplishment

It starts with an individual's own pressure to contribute to his/her team's success. They desperately want something to happen instead of doing nothing when the situation demands a contribution. "During the first days of GEE I was extremely insecure if I could come up with some ideas which were creative enough to convince my team members" (Dennis-P2018435). This sense of responsibility goes hand in hand with contributing to the team's goal. The concern about collective responsibility pushes emergent leaders to take the initiative. "I felt worried about it (the situation), but at the same time I got an idea for our business plan" (Agnes-P20192211). Eagerness is an inner driver in an emergent leader, pushing team productivity and a desire for accomplishment.

12.4.3 Ice-Breaking and Acting to Contribute and Save the Situation

The challenges listed above (having an inactive leader, group inactivity in terms of lack of communication, and the slowness of team members), together with personal motives and triggers in potential leaders, push them to step in as leaders (a sense of individual responsibility and individual eagerness of emergent leaders to contribute to the team's accomplishments), which leads to the final act of leadership. Now the emergent leaders move to take action.

These actions include breaking the silence to boost communication and group activities, taking an initiative to deal with the team's slowness, and tackling the official team leader's passivity.

Breaking the Silence to Boost Communication and Group Activities

In every group, achieving the intended goals starts with proper communication among the team members. Involving peers in what has been happening or what has to happen requires taking the lead. In this case, any communication platform connecting a group's members can shed light on what has been missing and the responsibility each member should take to benefit the team as a whole. "Since communication started on a rocky footing, I decided to create a Facebook group. Besides creating a group communication platform, I also thought about the time zones everyone was living in" (Davidson-P20192173).

Once a sense of community in terms of having communication platforms is achieved, an emergent leader encourages the proper sharing of ideas and puts the group on the same page. He/she may initiate or motivate the rest of the group to overlook the weaknesses in the past and to learn from the group's failure or poor performance. "When it comes to being silent, I broke the ice by putting forward my idea loudly to encourage all the members of the group to take a proactive approach [...], everyone in our group agreed with me" (Agnes-P20192211).

Breaking the silence may not seem to ease the situation. However, inculcating a culture of timely communication among the group members may encourage them to occasionally go the extra mile. This is because some members may not agree with what is presented to them, while others react instantly to a given situation as long as they are given a push. An emergent leader must actively participate in improving communication within the group. "Therefore, I decided to send a message, proposing ideas for our concept and asking how we wished to proceed, yet no one replied except for Amelia (the team leader). Amelia teamed us up, divided the task, and gave us a deadline" (Ben-P20171107). Another emergent leader, after observing inactivity among some members, opted to assume full responsibility of deputizing the group's inactive leader. "Since there was radio silence from the leader for the first few days, I stood in and took charge and sent out the first introductory e-mail, leading to a quick response from the leader" (Daniel-P2016979).

Taking an Initiative to Deal with the Team's Slowness

Making an effort to get the team a wake-up call may generate both positive and negative reactions. For example, as an active team member, she may want to see positive reactions from others, which would lead to a rapid transformation of the group. She tested the readiness of each member and collected their feedback at an individual level. "All these issues pushed me to write to everybody privately, especially our team leader; some replied back while others did not" (Durie-P2018624).

Furthermore, a group leader has to feel ashamed if his/her group mates are not performing up to certain standards. However, after several reminders and almost minimal reactions, it becomes inevitable that an emergent leader takes the initiative as he/she has to comply with deadlines: "I took the initiative to get the project started and tried to get the other members involved" (Basco-P20192528). Eventually, taking the lead yielded results, like in the case of Amy: "I set the deadlines for tasks that were essential to get the group started, and everyone was very supportive" (Amy-P2018838).

Dealing with the Team Leader's Passivity

Having a silent leader leads to paralysis in the group. Being an active member of the group, one would volunteer to deputize as the team leader and prepare the proposal to share it with the rest of the team. "As our leader was initially extremely silent and passive, I took the initiative. I started organizing Google docs, schedules, deadlines, and dividing tasks" (Dennis-P2018435). This was an opportunity for the team leader to assess the attributes that were likely to induce the members to get more involved in the team's activities. "I decided to write directly to the team leader about my ideas, as well as expressing my worries about the lack of response from other team members" (Elias-P20161275). Initiating regular communication with the team leader resulted in tangible results;

Davidson was motivated to see that the team leader's absence energized him to prevent the group from collapsing. As an emergent leader, he stood up to boost the morale of the team. "I decided to approach my leader to discuss some issues directly. We both made a lot of effort in the group chat and noticed that another team member was also very motivated" (Davidson-P20192173).

12.4.4 Group and Individual Resistance to Co-leadership Initiatives

Even though emergent leaders take steps and action to move their teams forward, they face resistance that is different from other challenges, as members may resist the non-appointed leaders. These challenges include cultural and language barriers, different opinions, communication tools slowing down a team's performance, as well as a low level of participation and persistent absenteeism.

Cultural and Language Barriers

Handling laziness and inactive members in a team is a challenging task. Managing people with different cultural backgrounds with different interests is not easy. This is challenging throughout the project. "Bringing different cultural backgrounds, time zones, interests, mindsets, and personalities together in one group can be extremely challenging" (Dennis-P2018435). Cultural differences were identified as a source of disagreement among members with different cultural backgrounds. Coming from different continents and countries which share both similarities and differences triggered the need to adopt a particular way of dealing with people. This attribute enabled the peer-leader to bring people whom he/she believed to have cultural differences on board and start working as a team. "It was sometimes difficult for me to communicate clearly with the girls from China since I didn't want to be too direct as our cultures are opposite on that matter" (Chelsea-P20201394). Negotiating, Google translator, and brief summaries assisted in bridging the communication gap between members who were not fluent in English and native English-speakers. "I still struggle about what sentences are appropriate for people from different cultural backgrounds. I fear that I might come off as too strong or commanding" (Amy-P2018838).

Difference of Opinion and Communication Tools Slowing Down the Team's Performance

Misunderstandings in terms of communication, projects to be undertaken, and who should play what role also emerged. "Because the same color might be gold for someone while it might be yellow for someone else" (Amy-P2018838). Ultimately, differences in opinion also led to delays in achieving project goals. "With everyone being from different countries, cultures, and presenting different ideas, there were some clashes. One case in particular occurred when everyone agreed to do our fish farmers project in Rwanda, whereas one member wanted to follow his own suggested idea" (Fleming-P2017603).

There was a need for brainstorming, for generating ideas to achieve the team's ultimate goal. Afterwards, it was identified that although the team members agreed with the idea, there was a need to impart information about different tasks that were to be assigned to them. "I think the issue was language and that she was afraid to admit she didn't understand everything" (Chelsea-P20201394).

Level of Participation and Persistent Absenteeism
Some members were on board from the beginning, and some were active while others were passive. Communicating with team members did not automatically result in generating more commitments and positive reactions about content and outcomes among group members. "However, I would also have liked to see commitment by some team members in terms of content and outcomes, as some members did not participate despite efforts to communicate with them and include them" (Basco-P20192528).

Working in a team involves total commitment by individual participants. Lack of commitment by some members results in disappointment and endless complaints on the part of others. Despite several reminders to the slow participants, they made no further efforts, leading to poor team performance. "We had to deal with the laziness and passivity of some of our team members until the end of the project" (Dennis-P2018435). Though the team leader gave all team members their parts to play, some remained passive to the extent that the leader got frustrated. Even using all communication platforms to reach inactive members and to remind them to fulfill their obligations was in vain.

12.4.5 Strategies Against Resistance and Challenges from Team Members

Initially, emergent leaders faced resistance besides the initial challenges that called for interventions. The above-mentioned resistances were due to cultural and language barriers, differences in opinion, communication tools slowing down a team's performance, as well as a low level of participation and persistent absenteeism. Emergent leaders strived to manage these, bearing in mind that they were not the official leaders. Therefore, they had to negotiate the team's performance. The strategies they used included helping the team by coordinating and sharing experiences for improving performance, mobilizing and engaging all members to deal with participation and communication differences, collaborating with the official leaders, saving the team from a dire situation, and self-sacrificing as well as putting the interests of the group before one's own interests when it came to team performance.

Helping the Team by Coordinating and Sharing Experiences for Improving Team Performance
Taking the lead and developing a business plan is a possible strategy to get inactive group members on board. This helped Agnes contribute to improving team performance. "To solve this problem, I wrote a business plan and put it in our communicating group so that

everyone knew how to write their own parts" (Agnes-P20192211). Approaching inactive participants was seen as the responsibility of active members. "I personally messaged everyone who was inactive in the initial days to check if they were facing any problems" (Dyanthe-P20202262). An emergent leader helped the other team members get acquainted with the group's tasks. He talked to everyone so as to share the assigned roles and to find out how every group mate could play a role in achieving their goals. "I decided to use this opportunity to have conversations with every team mate [. . .], alerting the team if they had trouble with anything" (Brown-P20191347).

Mobilizing and Engaging All Members to Improve Participation and to Eliminate Communication Differences

Building a team also involves individual commitment. This leads to building resilience. "I started encouraging team members to work together to deliver as a team. I helped out every time someone didn't know how to go on, trying to be as patient and motivating as possible" (Dennis-P2018435). Engaging team members does not require focusing on problems but instead involves providing suggestions that are based on research findings. Seeking the views of team members also helps build ownership of the idea to carry on as a team. "I tried to achieve this by constantly asking team members' opinions on the different ideas, after which they felt the need to answer instead of assuming the question was for someone else" (Brenda-P2018924).

Collaborating with Official Leaders

Communication platforms with team leaders improved communication between emergent leaders and the officially appointed team leaders. They had regular consultations on what was to be done and how a final decision could be taken. "I regularly kept in touch with all the team members to get updated on their progress and offered help if needed" (Dyanthe-P20202262).

A strong partnership between the team leader and the emergent leader yields tangible results that promote mutual consultations and consideration in the successful completion of a team's goals. This also generates harmony: "To help the team, I sent an outline to the leader so that she could edit it and propose it to the team" (Anne-P2016422). Any team's success relies on team members sticking together. After realizing that the team leader could not achieve this alone, Fleming volunteered and deputized her. However, he needed her cooperation and comments to confirm the correctness of things to be done. The workload couldn't be handled by her alone without the team leader's support. "I know how stressful being a team leader can be, and I can't imagine how much more stressful it is for an international project, so I decided that I should support the team leader where possible" (Fleming-P2017603). So the team leader's support contributed to bringing everyone on board. Afterwards, the team leader acknowledged Fleming's work and appointed him as a co-leader.

As an emergent leader who was later appointed to co-lead with the team leader, Anne regularly gave up the time allocated to her other businesses and concentrated on researching her areas and project. "Thus, I could make some minor changes while I was preparing for my thesis defense. After the defense, I worked on the final revisions of the draft" (Anne-P2016422). Fleming also experienced pressure due to sacrificing his spare time for the team. "This meant that my time was restricted, my stress was high, sleep suffered, and my anxiety constantly came back" (Fleming-P2017603).

12.4.6 Emergent Leaders' Behavioral Response, Character, and Attitudes

Emergent leaders are concerned about the collective failure of the team, they have a sense of individual responsibility and an eagerness to contribute to the team's accomplishments. They face resistance and invent strategies to cope with the challenges. They can lead the process without being official leaders. That shadow status helps them adopt strategies for helping the team by coordinating and sharing experiences for improving team performance. The adopted strategies reveal the character of an emergent leader when working with the official one. This is directly related to the challenges encountered in the leadership process. There is resistance because of cultural and language barriers, differences in opinions, and communication tools slowing down the team's performance, as well as a low level of participation and persistent absenteeism. Therefore, resistance requires a strategy but is also related to an emergent leader's behavior that differentiates him/her from ordinary members or ordinary leaders.

Empathy and Total Cross-Cultural Inclusion

This behavior is adopted to cope with differences. The leader does everything possible to ensure that no one feels excluded. "I did my best to include everyone as much as possible. I called people by name to ensure that everybody heard me and had the opportunity to share their opinions" (Chelsea-P20201394). Total inclusion involves people's ideas and treating all these ideas as valuable for sticking together. "I did not categorize some of the ideas as bad, as this would make the person uncomfortable and prevent him/her from bringing up ideas later on" (Brenda-P2018924). Instead, the leader learns how to accommodate all ideas even if he/she disagrees personally. "I utilized the strengths I brought to the team such as being open to ideas during the creativity process [. . .], appreciating members' opinions even when they differed from mine. I remained committed to the group's agreed decision" (Kaiser-P20201937).

Emerging leaders also go in for direct contact with team members. "I thought her part was excellent. Therefore, after learning that a direct approach is effective, I complimented her in a personal text" (Davidson-P20192173). This was a common strategy among committed emerging leaders. "I also took out time to appreciate members' contributions personally (which I rarely did before)" (Kaiser-P20201937).

Tolerance and Flexibility

Times of disappointment require self-control so as not to showing one's feelings to the team. "I praised them and told them to keep up their good work to keep them motivated. This was also to avoid conflict or dissatisfaction in the team" (Dickson-P20192370). Managing emotions requires flexibility and tolerance from peer-leaders, and putting yourself in other members' shoes before judging them. "Though there were team members who did less than the others, I made myself think that they might be facing some difficulties, so I did not criticize or blame them" (Dickson-P20192370).

Handling regional differences and minding your language were other challenges. "When I sent someone a message, I checked the regional clock so as not to disturb him/her. [. . .] I used different ways to encourage people; for example, if they had no time, I told them not to worry because we were in different time zones" (Agnes-P20192211). As a result, Dyanthe changed his manners when he started putting other people's interests ahead of his own, which was rewarding. "I have become more considerate of others' situations and their views. I have also learned to put the team's interests before my own interests. I saved the team members' names along with their regional time on WhatsApp so I wouldn't disturb them at the wrong time" (Dyanthe-P20202262).

12.4.7 Self-Discovery, Leadership Development, and Pride in the Outcomes of Leadership Initiatives

Emergent leadership is the path people take to make a difference. At the end of the path, the question is: to what extent was the process beneficial, and to whom? We paid attention to emerging leaders' testimonies on the outcomes of the process in order to understand this aspect.

Initially, people acted because of the required task and the challenges they faced in fulfilling the task. However, the outcome might not be the task's only achievement. Evidence from peer-leaders' journals shows that the achieved result was not only to having got things done, but that this outcome of the leadership initiative had also been valuable for them as a path to self-discovery. It was beneficial for the doers because they moved ahead facing resistance and challenges which ignited their potential. Learning from the strategies they applied to overcome the challenges was also essential, as this experience made and shaped their behavior.

The benefits thus achieved include learning and self-awareness, leadership development and self-identification as a leader, as well as the satisfaction of having made a personal contribution to the team and its members' accomplishment as an outcome of a leadership initiative.

Learning Process and Self-Awareness as an Outcome of a Leadership Initiative

"Some people learn from their mistakes over time. I feel terrible that I lost patience, especially with someone younger than me" (Brandon-P2017696).

"But now, after several meetings, I am quite comfortable with it. I have learned to keep calm and articulate my thoughts clearly when things go wrong" (Dyanthe-P 20202262). Self-development requires experience: "This is not only a great lesson in communication, but it also helped me realize that I cannot get everything right the first time, and sometimes I have to try a few times" (Eloy-P20191031).

Peer-leaders learned a lot from the virtual teams. "I learned to take initiatives, guide the group, and work with people from around the globe in different time zones who were young and busy" (Amy-P2018838). For instance, a participant observed different leadership styles and how team members viewed their leaders differently: "Taking a step back and observing other leadership styles and discovering how other team members felt towards their leaders was a new insight for me" (Daniel-P2016979).

Leadership Development and Self-Identification as a Leader

GEE exposure transformed participant Brown into somebody else as far as global collaborations are concerned: "It taught me that in our own little spaces, global collaborations are possible if you are willing to work with different people for a common goal. [. . .] Thank you, the GEE team, for helping shape me into a global leader" (Brown-P20191347). GEE virtual teams required high levels of determination. "Now I move ahead determined to become a global leader, challenging my own progress alongside helping my teammates to grow, lead, and learn" (Kaiser-P20201937). This determination leads to more learning and leadership development which focuses on collaborative efforts and peer contributions: "I want to say that I believe that this influenced my behavior a lot. It made me think more of the collective [. . .], not just for a good report, but for everyone to be and feel involved every step of the way" (Chelsea-P20201394).

Pride in One's Personal Contribution to the Team and Its Members' Accomplishments as an Outcome of a Leadership Initiative

The effort Fleming put in showed how his contribution to the group's performance led to a feeling of pride: "I'm not saying that I did anything that drastically changed an outcome, but I would like to believe that I helped" (Fleming-P2017603). Working hard with strict deadlines meant that the job got done and the effort was not wasted. "The work is far better than perfect. [. . .] I am glad I did this as it empowered and allowed the other team members to contribute and get a final report. If they had to start from a blank canvas, it would have been hard—it often is for everyone" (Eloy-P20191031). Gladness about getting things done and influencing other team members were common feelings among emergent leaders. Being part of a team set an example of what an individual can achieve if he/she put in effort, commitment, concentration, and courage. "By trying different approaches to motivate and inspire people, supporting someone else's leadership, and realizing my own strengths and ability to do this, I was glad I stepped up as a leader" (Eloy-P20191031). The team welcomed the team leader to retake the lead. When the concerns were gone, the appointed leaders surfaced again and took back the lead. "At that time, I felt happy because we were with our team leader, the one who was supposed to lead us in the process" (Durie-P2018624).

12.5 Conclusion, Discussion, Contributions, and Suggestions for Future Research

This chapter has discussed how ordinary team members in spontaneous global teams perform in less structured, multicultural, global, and virtual teams without power and authority to emerge as renowned global leaders. Answering this question is necessary because of the growing need to work virtually due to the ongoing pandemic life experience. Emerging and excelling in such an unstructured new world requires a particular pattern which is as yet unknown. This chapter has used Global Enterprise Experience's virtual mobility project to understand how global leaders emerge in a virtual environment. In GEE's project, groups comprised of students from all over the world are formed and leaders are appointed. Among other aims, the program traces the leadership emergence known as "peer-leadership". The first series of conclusions addresses the emergent leaders' motives. They are pushed by internal and external stimuli. Understanding these stimuli is important, as this explains why some individuals take the initiative to lead, while others are reluctant. The internal stimuli include a feeling of concern for the collective failure of the team, a sense of individual responsibility, and an individual eagerness among emergent leaders to contribute to the team's accomplishments. The external stimuli that push an emergent leader to act are the appointed leader's as well as group inactivity, and the slowness of team members.

The second conclusion concerns the process of leadership activity. It is divided into three phases: initiative, resistance, and the leadership's response to resistance. Understanding this process is vital for determining the status of the leader who acts without power over others. Emergent leaders take initiatives to break the silence so as to boost communication and group activity, and they deal with a team's slowness, including the team leader's passivity. They face cultural and other challenges emerging from different opinions and language differences, as well as persistently low levels of participation. However, they mobilize and engage members by coordinating and sharing their experiences, as well as collaborating with the official leader while they make sacrifices and put the interests of the group before their own when it comes to team performance.

Another conclusion deals with the behavior that characterizes emergent leaders and helps differentiate them from ordinary members and ordinary leaders. They exhibit empathy and total cross-cultural inclusion as well as tolerance and flexibility. They accompany emergent leaders across the leadership process and permit them to navigate it.

The last series of conclusions deal with the outcomes of the leadership process for the emergent leaders themselves. Intuitively, the outcome is the accomplished task, i.e. team performance. However, this chapter found more outcomes that were beneficial for emergent leaders. At the end of the process, they are proud of their learning process, self-awareness, leadership development, and self-identification as leaders.

These findings contradict Mockaitis et al.'s (2009) findings, who concluded that geographical dispersion does not affect a virtual team's performance.

Our findings show that working in geographically spread-out teams virtually requires special skills of volunteer and emergent leaders, but not of the team as such. This chapter supports Misiolek and Heckman (2005) regarding the importance of the behaviorally based leadership theory and emergent leadership in a virtual setting. Our study has identified that the individual sentiment for feeling responsible for collective achievement helps an emergent leader during the leadership process. Our study also looked into leadership competencies developed as an outcome of the exercise. Like Zander et al.'s (2012), this study also found that an emergent leader's role is important in the entire process.

One contribution of this chapter is that it helps the academic community understand how global leadership emerges in a less structured, multicultural, and virtual environment during a pandemic, which has established virtual education and virtual mobility as a way of student exchange. Knowing the emerging role of future leaders among students within popular global teams working in a virtual environment also helps educate policymakers in planning the needed improvements in the curricula and the content for desired future leaders. It also helps team leaders in managing multicultural teams by learning and developing appropriate competencies needed for this position.

This study contributes to the emergent leadership literature, especially to "shared leadership". It responds to recent calls for conceptual clarification and operationalization of emergent leadership (Auvinen et al. 2021), as well as to the call for a better understanding of how personality composition influences the well-being of virtual teams (González-Anta et al. 2021)—for example, in terms of sex and gender and how they influence (Lanaj and Hollenbeck 2015; Schneier 1978) the emergent leadership process also as personality composition (Hoch and Dulebohn 2017). This need has been felt to determine to what extent emergent leadership is interconnected with gender issues. There is also a need to incorporate a situational or contextual analysis that influences emergent leadership (Hanna et al. 2021). Our study addresses all these issues by looking at virtual teams that are less observable, especially at the group level, so as to understand the context or group factors that lead to emergent leadership and its development. Understanding the motives and strategies of peer or emergent leaders vis-à-vis their group situation increases our knowledge about shared leadership, whereby emerging leaders with no formal leadership roles can influence other team members and nurture responsibility among their peers to focus on achieving a common goal (for shared leadership, see also Hanna et al. 2021, p. 82). This chapter shows that emerging leaders take initiates to get involved in the group's activities in cases of group inactivity and/or resistance while having the common goal of winning a competition. Individual traits and characteristics also play a part, but involvement is more important because emergent leaders do not start as leaders-to-be and would not have taken the initiative if the appointed leaders had done their jobs properly and if team members had cooperated with them. In virtual teams, in most cases, multiple leaders emerge instead of just one (Ziek and Smulowitz 2014). Our study also shows that peer-leaders emerge and influence the team's performance without necessarily replacing or taking over the role of the appointed leader, but they complement each other if the official leader is still present.

Future research can look at how individual stimuli in emergent leadership are linked to individual behavior. This chapter has focused on antecedents and put less emphasis on the outcomes for the team. Future research could focus on team outcomes besides emergent leadership.

References

Auvinen, E., Huhtala, M., Rantanen, J., & Feldt, T. (2021). Drivers or Drifters? The "Who" and "Why" of Leader Role Occupancy—A Mixed-Method Study. *Frontiers in Psychology, 12*, 475.

Boje, D. M. (2009). Narratives Analysis. In A. J. Mills, G. Durepos, & E. Wiebe (Eds.), *Encyclopedia of Case Study Research*, 591–594. London: Sage Publications.

Carte, T. A., Chidambaram, L., & Becker, A. (2006). Emergent leadership in self-managed virtual teams. *Group Decision and Negotiation, 15*(4), 323–343.

Charlier, S. D., Stewart, G. L., Greco, L. M., & Reeves, C. J. (2016). Emergent leadership in virtual teams: A multilevel investigation of individual communication and team dispersion antecedents. *The Leadership Quarterly, 27*(5), 745–764.

Erez, M., Lisak, A., Harush, R., Glikson, E., Nouri, R., & Shokef, E. (2013). Going global: Developing management students' cultural intelligence and global identity in culturally diverse virtual teams. *Academy of Management Learning & Education, 12*(3), 330–355.

Global Enterprise Experience (2021). "Winners". Retrieved from https://geebiz.org/index.php/winners

González-Anta, B., Orengo, V., Zornoza, A., Peñarroja, V., & Gamero, N. (2021). Sustainable Virtual Teams: Promoting Well-Being through Affect Management Training and Openness to Experience Configurations. *Sustainability, 13*(6), 3491.

Hanna, A. A., Smith, T. A., Kirkman, B. L., & Griffin, R. W. (2021). The Emergence of Emergent Leadership: A Comprehensive Framework and Directions for Future Research. *Journal of Management, 47*(1), 76–104.

Hanson, D., Ward, C., & Chin, P. (2012). Leading virtual teams across national and cultural boundaries. *International Leadership Journal, 4*(3), 1–17.

Hoch, J. E., & Dulebohn, J. H. (2017). Team personality composition, emergent leadership and shared leadership in virtual teams: A theoretical framework. *Human Resource Management Review, 27*(4), 678–693.

Jarvenpaa, S. L., & Leidner, D. E. (1999). Communication and trust in global virtual teams. *Organization science, 10*(6), 791–815.

Lanaj, K., & Hollenbeck, J. R. (2015). Leadership over-emergence in self-managing teams: The role of gender and countervailing biases. *Academy of Management Journal, 58*(5), 1476–1494.

Misiolek, N. I., & Heckman, R. (2005, January). Patterns of emergent leadership in virtual teams. In *Proceedings of the 38th Annual Hawaii International Conference on System Sciences* (pp. 49a–49a). IEEE.

Mockaitis, A. I., Rose, E. L., & Zettinig, P. (2009). The determinants of trust in multicultural global virtual teams. In *Academy of Management Proceedings*, Vol. 2009, No. 1 (pp. 1–6). Briarcliff Manor, NY: Academy of Management.

Schneier, C. E. (1978). The contingency model of leadership: An extension to emergent leadership and leader's sex. *Organizational behavior and human performance*, *21*(2), 220–239.

Stalker, L. L. H. (2009). Narratives. In A. J. Mills, G. Durepos, & E. Wiebe (Eds.), *Encyclopedia of Case Study Research,* 594–596. London: Sage Publications.

Sutanto, J., Tan, C. H., Battistini, B., & Phang, C. W. (2011). Emergent leadership in virtual collaboration settings: A social network analysis approach. *Long-Range Planning*, *44*(5–6), 421–439.

Tyran, K. L., Tyran, C. K., & Shepherd, M. (2003). Exploring emerging leadership in virtual teams. In C. B. Gibson & S. G. Cohen (Eds.), *Virtual teams that work: Creating conditions for virtual team effectiveness* (pp. 183–195). San Francisco, CA: Jossey-Bass.

Yoo, Y., & Alavi, M. (2004). Emergent leadership in virtual teams: what do emergent leaders do?. *Information and Organization*, *14*(1), 27–58.

Zander, L., Mockaitis, A. I., & Butler, C. L. (2012). Leading global teams. *Journal of World Business*, *47*(4), 592–603.

Ziek, P., & Smulowitz, S. (2014). The impact of emergent virtual leadership competencies on team effectiveness. *Leadership & Organization Development Journal*, *35*(2), 106–120.

Part IV

Leading with Intercultural and Intrapersonal Excellence

13 Effective Leadership across Cultures

Achieving Intercultural Excellence

Mesut Akdere and Kris Acheson

13.1 Introduction

Organizational leaders, as the most essential drivers of mission, policy, and practice, need a particular mindset and skillset in order to be effective in their roles. During times of organizational prosperity or crisis, stakeholders (including employees and shareholders) rely on leaders for motivation, direction, and accountability. In a strategically connected world of global business, leading others effectively and efficiently requires additional knowledge, skills, and attitudes beyond traditional leadership competencies that work well in localized contexts. Furthermore, technological advances are forcing contemporary organizations to adopt new methods, such as different means of communication and new forms of human-machine cooperation, in order to remain competitive and to survive. As a result, effective leaders are becoming increasingly vital in the organizational context. Leadership is considered "a process whereby an individual influences a group of individuals to achieve a common goal" (Northouse 2019, p. 5). Engaging successfully in this complex process in a culturally and generationally diverse work setting thus demands intercultural competence (IC) of today's organizational leaders (Akdere and Hickman 2018). In this chapter, we define *intercultural* as being inclusive of but not limited to interaction across national differences, since much recent scholarship expands the term to ethnic, gender, linguistic, socioeconomic, generational, religious, and other aspects of culture that do not align neatly with national borders (Jameson 2007). IC is vital whether the application is international in scope or involves local cultural diversity. The capacity for

M. Akdere (✉) · K. Acheson
Purdue University, West Lafayette, IN, USA
e-mail: makdere@purdue.edu; kacheson@purdue.edu

I. Stolz, S. Oldenziel Scherrer (eds.), *International Leadership*, uniscope. Publikationen der SGO Stiftung, https://doi.org/10.1007/978-3-658-37306-1_13

IC is especially important if leaders are to attend to the varying needs of their followers and motivate them to reach their full potentials. Without IC, leaders will not have the ability to influence followers throughout the depth and breadth of their organizations as they will not be able to thoroughly understand and connect the diverse motivational and attitudinal needs of their followers who are culturally different from themselves.

We believe there is a significant gap in the existing literature on leadership theories and approaches commonly applied in today's organizational settings, as the theoretical underpinnings associated with leadership do not incorporate a dimension for IC. In this chapter, we explore leadership theories and practices through the lenses of intercultural excellence within the context of an interconnected world. Our chapter first provides an overview of the various leadership theories and approaches, followed by an introduction to models of the components of IC (Deardorff 2009) as well as of its development and maintenance (Acheson and Schneider-Bean 2019). We then shift our focus to concrete recommendations on how leaders lacking IC can learn to interact more effectively with their followers who come from different cultures. Within this section, we examine via organizational case studies how effective leaders process and bridge across cultural differences as part of their daily work to develop and foster an organizational culture that values and supports all organizational members, including those who are ethnic, generational, racial, and gender minorities. In each section, we also provide prompts to help readers apply recommendations through individual reflection or group discussion. We conclude our chapter by calling for a reexamination of existing leadership theories and the development of new models that would theoretically incorporate and empirically identify IC as part of the leadership processes.

13.2 Theoretical Frameworks

Myriads of scholars from a wide range of fields (e.g., management, psychology, communication, and more) have theorized human developmental processes. Models of development, however, often exist in disciplinary silos, uninformed by discussion in relation to other relevant constructs. In this section, therefore, we intend to synthesize various frameworks from leadership and intercultural studies by bringing them into conversation with each other to begin to build a theoretical foundation for leading with intercultural excellence.

13.2.1 Leadership Development

As a result of globalization and technological advances in organizations, the field of leadership has evolved from early stages that emphasized the trait approach to leadership in the early twentieth century into cultural approaches to leadership in the twenty-first. The trait approach focuses on innate qualities and characteristics of great societal influencers

(Stogdill 1948), while more recent frameworks tend to emphasize skills and abilities leaders can intentionally develop (Katz 1955). In addition, the current leadership literature includes many major theories of leadership, including:

- The behavioral approach, which focuses on the actions leaders perform and the ways in which they treat their followers (Blake and Mouton 1964);
- The situational approach, in which leaders flexibly adapt to the demands of different contexts (Hersey and Blanchard 1969);
- The path-goal theory of aligning leaders' styles with the characteristics of followers, making pragmatic decisions based on organizational goals (House 1971);
- The leader-member exchange theory that highlights the transactional relationship between leaders and their followers (Dansereau et al. 1975);
- Transformational leadership, which aims to change and transform people and the organization through participatory processes (Burns 1978);
- Authentic leadership, focusing on the level and extent of the genuineness of leadership as well as encouraging mindfulness and the development of self-awareness in leaders (George 2003);
- Servant leadership, which places leaders in a role of service and prioritizes the needs and goals of followers (Greenleaf 1970);
- Adaptive leadership that underlines the role of leaders in change management and emphasizes encouraging followers to engage in adaptation processes (Heifetz 1994);
- Leadership ethics, which incorporates a concern for ethical behavior into leadership decision-making and communicative processes (Trevino 1986);
- Team leadership that aims to maximize small group outcomes and effectiveness, often within diverse teams (Larson and LaFasto 1989);
- Shared leadership that recommends flatter power differentials between leaders and teams so as to increase each member's leadership capacity (Bergman et al. 2012); and
- Theories of gender and leadership that highlight barriers and challenges experienced by women in the leadership pipeline, as they are significantly underrepresented in the ranks of organizational leaders while experiencing significant issues in both becoming a leader and leading that are unique as compared to their male counterparts (Chemers 1997).

With the advances in technology and its impact in the workplace, leadership phenomena are evolving as well. Technology enables the globalization of industries and corporations, resulting in increased diversity within these settings and thus expanding the scope of leadership in traditional organizational contexts because of the greater reach of leaders through technology to diverse followers, local or otherwise. While technology is an enabler for leadership to involve broader followership, it can also erect barriers to understanding and communication across cultural differences, resulting in miscommunications as leaders would be missing contextual cues in the constrained virtual contexts which technology provides. Therefore, while leadership continues to exist in dual modalities of the workplace (physical and virtual), the demand for interculturally competent leaders is growing to not only tackle the need for working with a more diverse followership, but also for working with such followers through non-traditional work contexts that require additional knowledge, skills, and abilities to lead.

The world of business is increasingly more connected, so both employees and leaders frequently find themselves in work situations in which they need to interact with those who are culturally different. For leaders, intercultural excellence is a mandate that goes beyond familiarity with the cultures of their customers and also encompasses their followers (Hickman and Akdere 2018). Thanks to globalization, today's leaders (both domestic and international) need to lead followers who come from many different cultural backgrounds (Steers and Osland 2019). Existing leadership theories and approaches tend not to include this emerging organizational context, which creates a significant gap in leadership practice and research. While organizational culture is perceived to be a significant space of interaction for leaders (Hughes et al. 2019; Manning and Curtis 2018; Western 2019), the role of IC in fostering an inclusive and cohesive culture that enables the organization to thrive needs to be further explored and addressed through empirical research, especially considering that "leadership is not just the province of people at the top" but "can occur at all levels and by any individual" (Bass and Riggio 2006, p. 2). As Schedlitzki and Edwards (2018) point out, various current issues in leadership practice focus on the exploration of culture, gender, followers, ethics, and authenticity, among other things. Incorporating intercultural excellence into the fabric of leadership will enable emerging and experienced leaders to address some of these issues by equipping them with much-needed knowledge, skills, and abilities to effectively navigate and lead in multicultural organizational contexts and environments.

13.2.2 Intercultural Competence Development and Maintenance

Although scholars are far from having a consensus on even a single definition of IC, one common way to define the concept is the ability to communicate effectively and appropriately in intercultural situations (Deardorff 2006). Developing this capacity leads to an improved understanding of culturally different others, as well as to an increased effectiveness in bridging cultural diversity through mindful adaptation. IC is therefore considered a key business skill for individual success within globalized industries, since employees are increasingly called upon to interact successfully with diverse co-workers, clients, and suppliers (Lévy-Leboyer 2007). Many scholars and practitioners (i.e., trainers and coaches) see IC as inherently developmental in nature. That is, the construct is a set of interrelated competencies that—with a combination of exposure to learning catalysts (such as experience in multicultural teams) or work as an expatriate plus intentional and reflective processing of those potential learning opportunities—can lead to improvement over time. In other words, IC is an inherently learnable capacity rather than a static personality trait (Hammer 2015).

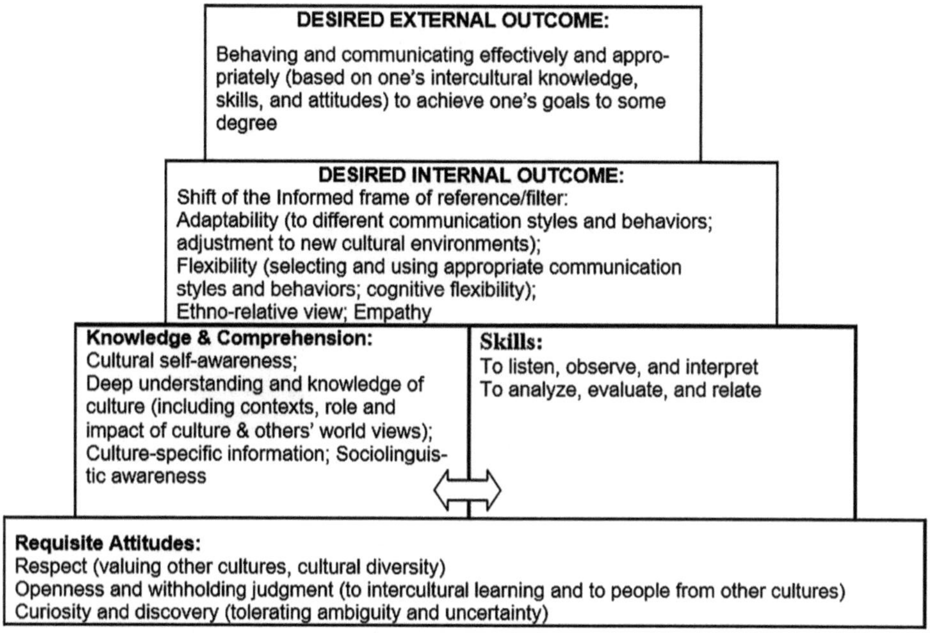

Fig. 13.1 Deardorff's (2006) pyramid model of intercultural competence

Importantly, as a collection of competencies, IC includes components across affective (attitudes), cognitive (knowledge), and behavioral (skills) domains of learning (Spitzberg and Changnon 2009). One way to visualize these components of IC lies within a pyramid structure, as illustrated in ◉ Fig. 13.1, where foundational attitudes such as cultural curiosity and openness to interacting across differences enable the construction of knowledge: of the self, of specific other cultures, and of generalized frameworks for cultural comparisons (Deardorff 2006). In turn, this knowledge and various skills of cultural discovery (e.g., observing, analyzing) help build internal outcomes such as perspective-taking and flexibility, as well as eventually the external outcomes of adaptation that impact relationships.

Another popular developmental model of IC is the Intercultural Development Continuum (IDC). Based on empirical evidence from a widely used proprietary psychometric instrument called the Intercultural Development Inventory, or IDI (IDI, 2021), the IDC model (Hammer 2009) posits five stages on a developmental spectrum, ranging from more monocultural perspectives such as denial and polarization to the more multicultural orientations of acceptance and adaptation, with minimization between the two ends of the spectrum as a transition stage.

In essence, the IDC represents a developmental journey with denial (an orientation that recognizes observable cultural variation but not deeper differences), the natural or naïve state of humanity. Individuals may move into other orientations throughout their lives, but such a development is not guaranteed either through simple exposure to cultural diversity

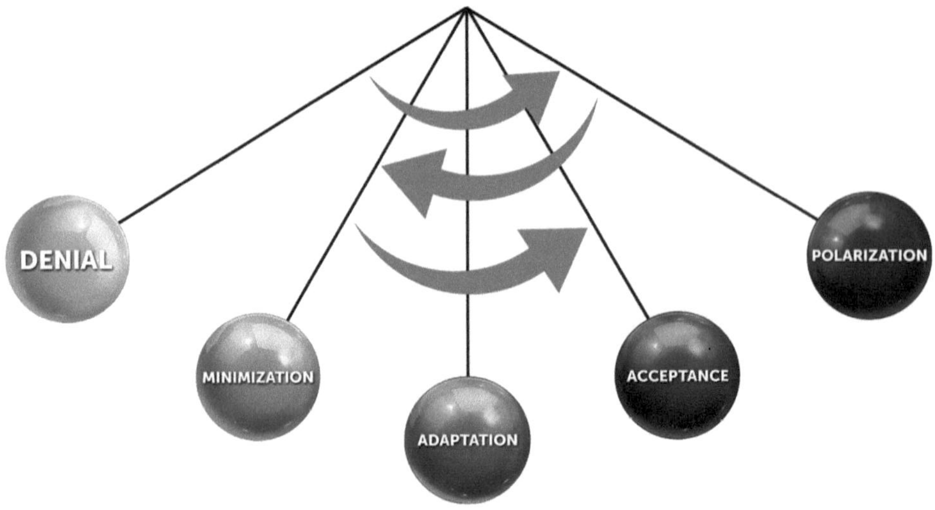

Fig. 13.2 The pendulum metaphor for IC development (Sundae Bean, LCC, 2020)

or via a desire to gain capacity. While generally considered useful for understanding the subjective experience of difference, the IDC has garnered a number of critiques (Witte 2014). Most recently, Acheson and Schneider-Bean (2019) noted the linearity of the model as problematic since IC can be both multifaceted in the moment and unstable in the long term. These authors analyze the IDC in the case of expatriate lived experiences, visualizing the developmental stages on a pendulum instead of along a unidirectional arrow. They arrange the five developmental stages of the IDC, from Denial to Acceptance, on a pendulum that swings between too much focus on similarity and too much focus on difference, with a balance between these extremes represented by the Adaptation stage (see ◉ Fig. 13.2).

Rather than a linear and unidirectional developmental process followed by expatriates in the long term, the pendulum emphasizes to what extent lived experiences of this development are unstable and context-dependent. As illustrated in ◉ Fig. 13.2, a pendulum is set into motion by change, for example, by moving into an unfamiliar context:

> This defensive reaction to a new environment is often the result of the loss of local knowledge and skills, so the more dramatic the change/the loss, the more extreme the swings of the pendulum are likely to be... Swings can be large-scale, moving you for a significant period of time to a previous orientation, or minor, shifting you from moment to moment between narrow-minded focus on similarity or difference. (Acheson and Schneider-Bean 2019, pp. 51–53)

The pendulum model also details how and why such fluctuations occur—through the metaphor of magnets that pull one towards too much emphasis on cultural similarity, or towards too much emphasis on cultural difference. Furthermore, the metaphor of anchors is

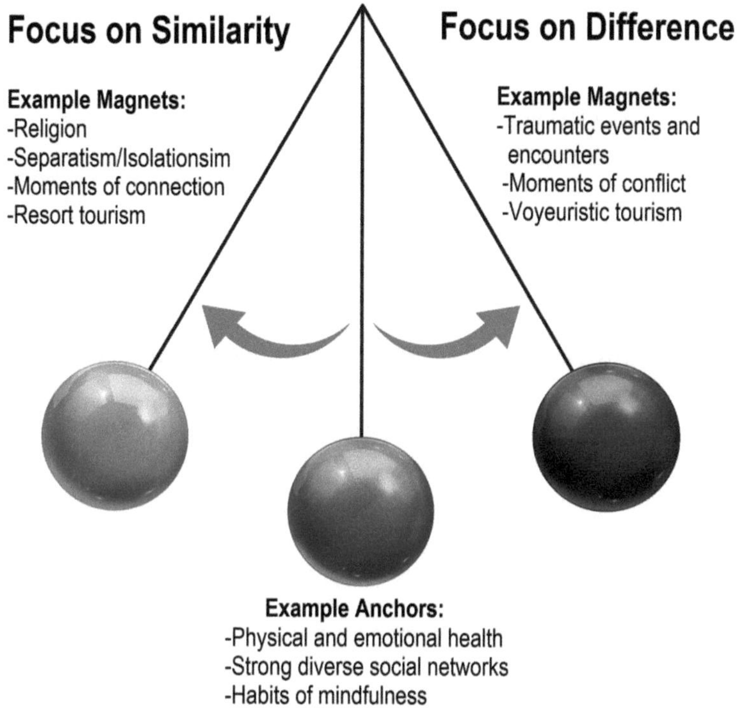

Fig. 13.3 Magnets and Anchors on the IDC Pendulum (Sundae Bean, LCC, 2020)

used to illustrate how we can both reactively counter the pull of magnets in order to stabilize the pendulum and proactively prevent swings from occurring. ◉ Fig. 13.3 depicts magnets and anchors that operate as forces on the pendulum. As an example, note that tourist lifestyles are listed as magnets on both sides:

> A hotel-and-guided-tour type of cultural experience might buffer us from local customs and blind us to significant cultural differences (pulling towards similarity); on the other hand, the exoticisation of foreign cultures that undergirds much tourism – that is, the performance of local rituals as a spectacle for the enjoyment of visitors rather than for their original purposes and the commodification of cultural artifacts as souvenirs – can encourage us to frame the world as us vs. them (pulling towards difference) (Acheson and Schneider-Bean 2019, p. 53).

Among other advantages, this reimagining of the IC developmental process emphasizes the fluctuating nature of IC, which better reflects the actual lived experiences of culture-crossers. In addition, the model marks the relationship between global and local aspects of IC (that is, those that are and are not transferable between distinct cultural contexts). Unlike conceptualizations of IC as being universally applicable regardless of linguistic ability, local cultural knowledge, power dynamics, and other important contextual factors (e.g., the concept of cultural intelligence), or as being specific to a very particular setting (e.g., Spanish language skills that do not help with communicating in, say, Vietnam), the pendulum "offers a realistic sense of the partial/temporary shifts in effectiveness across difference that is likely to occur when we enter new cultural territory, carrying with us some global competencies and lacking some local ones" (Acheson and Schneider-Bean 2019, p. 56). Two additional benefits of the model are that it demonstrates the necessity of the purposeful maintenance of IC after its initial development, and that it alleviates the shame and frustration of the inevitable swings on the pendulum we all experience in response to changing circumstances.

13.2.3 Synthesizing Leadership with Intercultural Models

You may already have noticed some points of overlap between the models of leadership and IC as presented here, for example a movement away from trait-based understandings to skills-based developmental frameworks. They may even be considered mutually dependent; one cannot lead well in a diverse environment without a certain level of IC, and the same knowledge, attitudes and skills that support success in interactions across cultures contribute to effective leadership.

One point we would like to make to bring the models into conversation with each other is that some models of leadership may be more or less popular or appropriate in different cultural contexts, depending on the values prevalent for those cultural groups. Consider that

- More task-oriented cultures that are pragmatic and prioritize problem-solving to achieve desired results may prefer a path-goal model, while on the other end of the spectrum more relationship-oriented cultures that emphasize cultivating and maintaining interpersonal relationships might prefer the transactional approach of leader-member frameworks;
- More collectivistic societies that define identity via group membership and highly value group harmony may gravitate naturally to servant leadership instead of a more individualistic approach such as behavioral leadership that focuses mostly on leaders themselves;
- More low-power distance cultures where organizational members are less comfortable with hierarchies might find themselves better suited to shared leadership models than high-power distance cultures;
- Situational or adaptive models seem more appropriate in cultures where fatalism is a predominant philosophy, whereas transformational leadership, which actively pursues intentional change, is better aligned with cultures that value will power and agency.

Secondly, some models of leadership lend themselves more naturally to intercultural excellence. Leadership frameworks that focus on mindfulness (e.g., authentic) and those that emphasize flexibility (e.g., situational and adaptive) are particularly well-aligned with effectiveness across cultural boundaries because self-awareness and adaptive communication skills constitute components of IC. However, as with ethics—which theoretically could and should be embedded in all leadership models–, the capacity to lead a diverse followership is an applicable skill no matter which framework for leadership is in play.

13.3 Leading with Intercultural Excellence

In this section, we leverage real-world organizational cases to illustrate a set of recommended practices for leading with intercultural excellence. For each case, we suggest a reflection or dialogue prompt to encourage leaders towards developing these practices by transferring knowledge from their own past experiences and strategically planning for their future leadership roles.

13.3.1 Negotiating "Third Culture" Spaces with Inclusive Norms

2020 was the year of diversity statements in the United States. Salesforce, for instance, released a statement committing to increasing its US representation of Black employees by 50% and to double its number of Black employees in leadership positions within three years (Zaveri 2020). Some may criticize such statements as publicity stunts or engagement in corporate social responsibility only for the sake of branding and company image. Natasha Lamb, managing partner of Arjuna Capital, pointed out in a recent Reuters article that "the rush of corporate concern belies the reality of workforce inequity," with women and people of color underrepresented in most organizations and even further minoritized in leadership positions (Kerber et al. 2020, np).

However, while recent horrific world events and the resulting social justice movements may be providing the impetus to work on issues of equity, diversity, and inclusion, organizations actually have many good reasons to focus their efforts in these areas. Scholars frequently find that having diverse management teams supports increased productivity and profit. For instance, McKinsey and Company's (2018) "Delivering through Diversity" reported that the top 25% most diverse management teams among public companies were 21% (for gender diversity) to 33% (for ethnic diversity) more likely to exceed industry means in returns. Paul Block of Merisant explained how this productivity is driven by the innovation that diversity supports: "People with different lifestyles and different backgrounds challenge each other more. Diversity creates dissent, and you need that. Without it, you're not going to get any deep inquiry or breakthroughs" (Groysberg and Connolly 2014, np).

Still, throwing together people with different perspectives is not always productive. Yielding innovation from diversity rather than conflict alone requires intentional efforts to be inclusive of those differences. When Pinterest leadership recently found themselves in the news over allegations of racial and gender discrimination by former employees, their solution was to adopt workplace culture recommendations (Dickey 2020). Pinterest management formed a committee, commissioned an external workplace environment review, interviewed over 350 former and current employees, and accepted recommendations towards building a more inclusive workplace. In giving voice to members at all levels of the organization and, more importantly, from a number of cultural perspectives, Pinterest illustrates what scholars sometimes call a "third culture" approach to the development of a shared set of group values and norms for behavior (Casmir 1993). In essence, third culture building in most organizational settings comprises a dominant culture laying aside their claim to rule-making and inviting minoritized voices to the table so as to negotiate a shared set of expectations. This model of culture construction in a diverse workforce aligns well with principles of situational, adaptive, and team leadership models and illustrates the adaptive capacity of IC in action, synthesizing many of the frameworks presented above.

Technology is an important factor in this discussion, because communication technologies may create true third culture virtual spaces for interaction where neither party is visiting or hosting the other. Yet, on the other hand, the speed of communication facilitated by modern technology can discourage the reflection and planning that would enable more adaptive communication forms in diverse teams; firing off an e-mail, text, or group message without thought to the preferred communication styles of others can be counter-productive, for instance, even while these platforms support connectivity both globally and locally. Finally, there is the risk of technology distancing us empathetically from others even as we work to create third culture spaces across cultural and geographical barriers. The double-edged sword of technology must therefore always be considered in this endeavor.

Reflection/dialogue prompts: In your organizational setting, which signs point to the need for more third culture spaces? Who would leaders need to invite to the table in order to negotiate a third culture? Which concrete steps could you take in your current or future roles to leverage this approach so as to create more inclusive workplaces and thus more effective organizations?

13.3.2 Making Intercultural Competency Development a Priority for Professional Development

Salesforce, mentioned above, is not alone in setting high goals for increasing diversity. Starbucks has promised that 30% of its US corporate as well as 40% of its US retail and manufacturing workforce will be composed of BIPOC (Black, Indigenous, and People of Color) employees by 2025 (Haddon 2020). As we have seen in the previous case, though, hiring a diverse mix of people is no guarantee for business success. In fact, diversity hiring efforts must be paired with attempts to create the kind of inclusive environment in which employees thrive, as well as a commitment to equity in promotion practices so that diverse hires make their way up the ranks into positions of leadership. For this reason, Starbucks has also mandated anti-bias training for its executives.

The problem with this approach is the limited evidence of the effectiveness of such training. Learning outcomes of diversity training are often assumed rather than measured (Shepherd 2019), and where effectiveness *is* evaluated, most workshops and courses are found to be insufficient (Bezrukova et al. 2012). In fact, required programs such as Starbucks' mandatory anti-bias training can backfire because the requirement itself may be resented either passively or actively (Dobbin and Kaley 2016). If professional development is so vital but *en masse* mandatory diversity training is ineffectual, then what is the solution? We argue that those interested in leading with intercultural excellence must seriously and continuously invest in intrinsically motivated and individualized professional development for themselves and others. The numbers support this claim: A recent study by the Korn Ferry Institute (Zes and Landis 2013) found that self-awareness, one of the key components of IC, impacts companies' bottom lines, with employee self-awareness strongly correlated to corporate financial performance. The Institute briefing recommends regular 360-degree feedback evaluations of managers in order to increase self-awareness and to reduce "blind spots".

This commitment to continual improvement is certainly an expectation of the upper management in some organizations. Merck, Nissan, General Mills, Telstra, and ABB North America are all exemplars that evaluate managers' performance based on their inclusion efforts, such as mentoring others and developing more mindfulness about equity issues (Groysberg and Connolly 2014). Likewise, Google's Project Oxygen implemented a comprehensive manager training program in the early 2000s that was so demonstrably successful in yielding statistically significant performance boosts that Google soon expanded it to employees on the lower strata of the corporation (Garvin 2013). These efforts are reflective of the many skill-based models of leadership in which leaders develop capacities deliberately rather than relying on innate abilities and character traits (e.g., the behavioral approach and authentic leadership, among others). In addition, consider how phenomena such as globalization and digitalization are transforming workforces towards Industry 4.0 (Sima et al. 2020). As societies and organizations change, adaptive and transformative models of leadership point to the need for leaders to continually upskill themselves as well as their followers in order to be successful. Developmental models of IC are also applicable here, especially the Pendulum (Acheson and Schneider-Bean 2019). This model emphasizes that not all capacities are transferable across changing contexts, thus demanding continual attention to learning about oneself and culturally different others, as well as the most effective ways to bridge the two.

Avenues for increasing intercultural excellence in leadership through professional development include individual activities such as support from a mentor, executive coaching, expatriate experiences, and informal learning opportunities. Group activities are also options: mandated or voluntary group trainings, peer learning groups or 'communities of practice', and formal leadership development cohorts. These group approaches, however, must be organized with care so as to ensure buy-in from trainees, to effectively utilize active-learning techniques, and to appropriately design training for factors such as background knowledge, aptitude, and motivation. For these reasons, while being costlier, individualized approaches often yield a greater return on investment (Dearborn 2002).

Reflection/dialogue prompts: How committed are you as a leader to life-long learning? Which avenues of IC professional development seem most feasible for you and your team, given your organizational context? Which arguments can you articulate to gain the resources you would need to accomplish this professional development in the short and long term as part of your leadership journey?

13.3.3 Practicing Self-Care to Maintain Emotional Resilience

In a 2014 study for the Australian National Health Commission, PriceWaterhouseCoopers documented the importance of organizational attention to the mental health of its members, finding that initiatives and programs that fostered an emotionally resilient workplace culture averaged a return on investment of US$ 2.30 for every dollar spent (PriceWaterhouseCoopers, 2014). In contrast, organizations not making this investment in mental health had higher healthcare costs, absenteeism, and turnover among employees, all of which lowered productivity. As with life-long attention to professional development discussed above, the Pendulum model also advocates self-care as a way to anchor leaders within their adaptational capacities (Acheson and Schneider-Bean 2019). Consistently practicing self-care can help prevent regression to earlier developmental stages such as denial—that is, retreating from cultural differences—or polarization—e.g., treating culturally different others with contempt when leaders are faced with traumatic events or over time become too exhausted to function effectively.

Interestingly, a generational difference in valuing self-care and work-life balance is often evident, with millennials and Gen Z employees placing greater emphasis on working 'smarter, not harder', preferring telework options as well as casual workplace environments, and placing greater value on their lives beyond their careers (Parker 2007). We see that double-edged sword of technology at play here, too: Telework may allow us to forgo a daily commute, but it also makes us increasingly (perhaps unreasonably) accessible by cell, which could be detrimental to self-care and family life. With younger generations beginning to dominate the workforce, corporations in some industries are under increasing pressure to care for their employees' mental and physical health by designing high-quality work experiences. Thus, Glassdoor now rates companies on their work-life balance (Stansell 2020). Some top-rated companies are, as might be expected, hip young tech companies such as Slack and Zoom where many employees may not even work in traditional physical 'brick-and-mortar' workplaces. Others may provide 'perks' that are particularly attractive to young job hunters, such as napping or meditation spaces; complementary massages, snacks and beverages, as well as fitness center memberships; and organized social activities such as sports teams and book clubs (North Dakota Young

Professionals Network 2013). Yet surprisingly, some that made Glassdoor's list are not only well-established organizations but also inherently high-stress environments. Take, for example, St. Jude's Children's Hospital, which is a childhood cancer treatment center focusing on terminal illnesses such as Acute Lymphoblastic Leukemia. Pediatric oncology has an extremely high incidence of emotional exhaustion and career burnout (Roth et al. 2011), and yet St. Jude's was number 13 on Glassdoor's list for best work-life balance during COVID-19. How do successful organizations encourage self-care and emotional resilience, even with emotionally demanding missions and during stressful times like a global pandemic?

The American Psychological Association defines emotional resilience not as the avoidance of trauma or adversity but as the capacity to (a) bounce back and (b) learn from sources of stress (2012). WellRight (2020) recommends that corporations implement employee wellness programs and offer resources to encourage both emotional and physical self-care. Some solutions are intrapersonal (e.g., mindfulness training and relaxation techniques like yoga and meditation), while others are interpersonal (e.g., team-building activities to establish stronger social connections). Even activities that appear to waste time—like challenging yourself to small fitness tasks, playing games, watching animal videos on social media, and connecting with a friend—can boost physical, mental, emotional, and social aspects of resilience (McGonigal 2012). All of these approaches are supportive of IC maintenance in the Pendulum model, and they also align well with leadership models such as adaptive, transformational, and ethical leadership, particularly when we not only practice self-care ourselves but encourage others to follow our lead.

Self-care is particularly salient to theories of gender and leadership, since women often experience more tension between responsibilities at work and at home (Emslie and Hunt 2009). Paradoxically, a large-scale meta-analysis of data across 34 countries found that while organizational work-life balance initiatives are more often aimed at women, men seem to benefit most from such efforts, perhaps because they tend to find it more culturally acceptable to engage unapologetically in self-care or more highly value leisure time (Noda 2019). These issues make it imperative for organizations to focus on gender-specific leadership support, as PepsiCo has modeled by systematically promoting women to director, chief officer, and board positions and then strategically supporting the success of those female leaders through mentoring, flexible family leave, and other support programs (Beba and Church 2020).

Reflection/dialogue prompts: In which situations as a leader have you demonstrated the most and the least emotional resilience? How attentive are you to self-care? Which habits should you cultivate in yourself and in those who follow your example that would support better work-life balance and sustainable productivity?

13.3.4 Inspiring Trust and Motivating Followership

As leadership should be considered central to an organization, and not only at the top, trust should be at the heart of all dyadic relationships between leaders and followers. Without trust in the leader by their followers and vice versa, the leadership process is impaired. In the case of leaders, trust is a must for their relationship with the followers (Middlebrooks et al. 2020). We see trust noted in many contemporary leadership theories and approaches, including transformational leadership (Braun et al. 2013; Kelloway et al. 2012; Zhu et al. 2013), authentic leadership (Agote et al. 2016; Clapp-Smith et al. 2009; Wong and Cummings 2009), leader-member exchange theory (Hirvi et al. 2020; Gottfredson et al. 2020; Legood et al. 2021), and servant leadership (Chan and Mak 2014; Sendjaya and Pekerti 2010; Miao et al. 2014), among others. Yet, most people find it more difficult to build trust across cultural boundaries (Kwantes and McMurphy 2021; Luo 2002; Saunders et al. 2010). These barriers to trust are sometimes complicated across the spectrum of spaces common in current business practice—that is, physical, hybrid, and virtual.

Defined as "a psychological state comprising the intention to accept vulnerability based upon positive expectations of the intentions or behavior of another" (Rousseau et al. 1998, p. 395), trust within the leadership context is considered both trust in the specific individual holding the leadership role/position and trust in general organizational leadership (anyone perceived as a leader among the senior leadership of an organization). This is generally a bi-directional concept: "The establishment of a view of trust (reciprocal and recursive) between the players is a determining factor for the growth of co-players and the productiveness of every relational system" (Godard and Lenhardt 1999, p. 104). Yet, in leadership studies, this reciprocity is expected to be initiated and established by organizational leaders. Moreover, while building trust among in-group followers can be easily accomplished, establishing trust with out-group members can be challenging for leaders. Minoritized and underrepresented organizational members typically find themselves in the position of out-group members (Dover et al. 2020), raising barriers to trust-building, no matter whether minoritized individuals are operating in leader or follower roles. Without the ability to interact with culturally different others (i.e., lacking IC), building trust with all organizational members thus becomes a daunting and impossible task for leaders. In this process, IC can serve as a catalyst to establish trust among followers, which, in turn, enables leaders to articulate persuasively their vision, mission, goals, and values to all organizational members.

As the ways of business change and the gig economy takes over the marketplace, the need for IC among organizational leaders of both traditional and non-traditional markets becomes more evident than ever, because leaders often find themselves working with employees from around the world (Javidan and Zaheer 2019). Such an environment is challenging for trust-building. Recently, a number of scandals challenged public trust in Uber due to widespread harassment and discrimination towards minority-identity employees (Frei and Morriss 2020) as well as hostile attitudes among the senior leadership towards women (Taylor and Goggin 2019). Similar organizational issues have surfaced in other multinational global technology companies such as Google, Facebook, LinkedIn, and Reddit. Despite many leadership development efforts in today's organizations, a lack of focus on interculturally competent leaders continues to impact both individual leadership practices and organizational diversity and inclusion efforts (Cherkowski and Ragoonaden 2016). IC is a solution to this issue because it enables leaders with the ability and skills to move away from their ethnocentrism to an ethno-relative perspective, enabling them to overcome their biases through cultural self-awareness. Interculturally competent leaders are well-positioned to evoke trust in their followers and to lead inclusive transformations of the organizational culture to better foster effective teamwork.

Effective communication and expressions of empathy are key factors in leaders' successful trust-building. Today's leaders will need to achieve this not only through traditional leadership approaches but also by factoring in the contemporary technology-enhanced work environments that may solely rely on non-physical virtual platforms for conducting daily work. Interculturally competent leaders strive to connect personally with all employees (not only their in-group members). In order to address the rampant workplace injuries at Tesla plants, which were reported to exceed the industry standard by 30%, CEO Elon Musk expressed his commitment to the wellbeing and safety of his employees. He demonstrated empathy and authenticity when he shared in an e-mail to all company employees that it broke his heart whenever a member of Tesla was injured at work (Boitnott 2017). Musk welcomed direct communication from employees who had problems and involved himself personally in addressing safety issues, which communicated care to his followers and built trust in his staff that he deeply felt his responsibility for their wellbeing. Leaders following Musk's example must take care to show care and empathy towards all followers without excluding out-group members. Since caretaking for in-group members comes more naturally, a real risk is to unintentionally exclude followers who are culturally different.

As part of the trust-building process, the ability to listen and consider various viewpoints in leadership practice is vital yet often ignored by leaders. IC enables them to effectively listen and to successfully incorporate different perspectives into organizational decision-making, thus creating a vision for shared leadership that is especially crucial in multicultural organizations. For example, in high-functioning teams, with IC, leaders must establish trust through understanding the cross-cultural formation of their teams and by structuring them for success (Molinsky and Gundling 2016). In such teams, followers feel empowered and motivated when they feel that their opinions matter to their leaders. With reference to the Pendulum of the IC model illustrated earlier (Acheson and Schneider-Bean 2019), it is important to balance a focus on similarity and difference in trust-building. Too much emphasis on similarity (denial or minimization of cultural differences) will leave followers feeling that their differences went unseen and unheard by a leader, while too much emphasis on difference (polarization) may leave team members feeling judged—neither perception is conducive to trust-building.

It is important to note that establishing trust in this way is necessarily proactive, not reactive. In other words, it must be done consistently and habitually, not as a reaction to a crisis. Like resilience, trust must be cultivated before it is needed. Leaders must incorporate IC as part of regular leadership skillset and mindset development, which will then enable them to lead with intercultural excellence when their work with a diverse followership demands these skills and attitudes (Hieker and Pringle 2021). There is no point of mastery beyond which this developmental journey becomes unnecessary. Given the changing nature of the world of work and the impact of technology in transforming organizations, leadership processes will always demand new approaches, additional knowledge, and continued attention to leader IC development.

Reflection/dialogue prompts: In which past or potential future situations has/will trust across cultural differences become an issue for your leadership? As a leader, which attitudes and attributes do you believe are critical for fostering trust, especially with out-group members? What is one concrete habit you could cultivate to foster more trust across the full range of diversity in your organizational context?

13.4 Conclusion

This chapter lays out a case for the need to incorporate IC development as part of leadership theory and practice in order to effectively manage contemporary organizations and their diverse members. In his germinal work on leadership, Burns (1978) suggested that leadership principles "can be identified that to a marked degree transcend national cultural borders, that these principles constitute both model values and end values" (p. 431). We propose that IC development be considered as a core leadership value, no matter which approach to leadership one prescribes to. Just like in earlier calls for incorporating ethics into the core of leadership (Northouse 2019), IC should be synthesized through a more holistic approach to leadership development and growth in which it becomes embedded within leadership theories, models, and recommended practices. Organizational leaders should be encouraged to develop their cultural awareness and to learn respect for other cultures in order to more effectively lead employees from any cultural background.

The current corona virus pandemic has rapidly transformed organizations and the workplace through remote work and digital technologies, showing us very clearly that we have become more interconnected through technology. Leaders must be prepared for an even more technology-driven future. Effective leadership practices should therefore strive for intercultural excellence in the age of technology—human-machine interfaces and other technological advances that continue to shape intergenerational communication, global team collaboration, and organizational communication relying heavily on virtual platforms. In the face of these new norms, existing leadership theories and practices should be revisited so as to assess and determine their applicability and utility for fostering organizational cultures that are "high-performing, collaborative, innovative, customer-focused, entrepreneurial, results-oriented, transparent, or trusting" (Leetaru 2019, p. 22). We are just beginning to scratch the surface of the demands that will be placed on future leaders. IC can help us dig deeper and prepare for a rapidly changing world.

References

Acheson, K., & Schneider-Bean, S. (2019). Representing the intercultural development continuum as a pendulum: Addressing the lived experiences of intercultural competence development and maintenance. *European Journal of Cross-Cultural Competence and Management*, *5*(1), 42–61. https://doi.org/10.1504/EJCCM.2019.097826

Agote, L., Aramburu, N., & Lines, R. (2016). Authentic leadership perception, trust in the leader, and followers' emotions in organizational change processes. *The Journal of Applied Behavioral Science*, *52*(1), 35–63. https://doi.org/10.1177/0021886315617531

Akdere, M., & Hickman, L. (2018). My kingdom for time to reflect: Developing global leaders through critical self-reflection. *Annual Refereed Proceedings of the Academy of Management.*

Bass, B. M., & Riggio, R. E. (2006). *Transformational leadership* (2nd ed.). Mahwah, New Jersey: Lawrence Erlbaum Associates, Publishers.

Beba, U., & Church, A. H. (2020). Changing the game for women leaders at PepsiCo: From local action to enterprise accountability. *Consulting Psychology Journal: Practice and Research*, *72*(4), 288–302.

Bergman, J. Z., Rentsch, J. R., Small, E. E., Davenport, S. W., & Bergman, S. M. (2012). The shared leadership process in decision-making teams. *The Journal of Social Psychology*, *152*(1), 17–42. https://doi.org/10.1080/00224545.2010.538763

Bezrukova, K., Jehn, K. A., & Spell, C. S. (2012). Reviewing diversity training: Where we have been and where we should go. *Academy of Management Learning & Education*, *11*(2), 207–227. doi: https://doi.org/10.5465/amle.2008.0090

Blake, R., & Mouton, J. (1964). *The managerial grid: The key to leadership excellence*. Houston, TX: Gulf Publishing Company.

Boitnott, J. (2017). The power of emotional intelligence is on full display with Elon Musk, Jeff Bezos, and Ursula Burns. *Inc. Best Workplaces*. Retrieved from https://www.inc.com/john-boitnott/3-ceos-who-are-using-emotional-intelligence-to-expand-their-business.html

Braun, S., Peus, C., Weisweiler, S., & Frey, D. (2013). Transformational leadership, job satisfaction, and team performance: A multilevel mediation model of trust. *The Leadership Quarterly*, *24*(1), 270–283. https://doi.org/10.1016/j.leaqua.2012.11.006

Burns, J. M. G. (1978). *Leadership*. New York: Harper & Row.

Casmir, F. L. (1993) Third-culture building: A paradigm shift for international and intercultural communication. *Annals of the International Communication Association*, *16*(1), 407–428. doi: https://doi.org/10.1080/23808985.1993.11678861

Chan, S. C. H., & Mak, W. (2014). The impact of servant leadership and subordinates' organizational tenure on trust in leader and attitudes. *Personnel Review*, *43*(2), 272–287. https://doi.org/10.1108/PR-08-2011-0125

Chemers, M. M. (1997). *An integrative theory of leadership*. Mahwah, NJ: Erlbaum.

Cherkowski, S., & Ragoonaden, K. (2016). Leadership for diversity: Intercultural communication competence as professional development. *Teacher Learning and Professional Development*, *1*(1), 33–43.

Clapp-Smith, R., Vogelgesang, G. R., & Avey, J. B. (2009). Authentic leadership and positive psychological capital: The mediating role of trust at the group level of analysis. *Journal of Leadership & Organizational Studies, 15*(3), 227–240. https://doi.org/10.1177/1548051808326596

Dansereau, F., Graen, G., & Haga, W. J. (1975). A vertical dyad linkage approach to leadership in formal organizations. *Organizational Behavior and Human Performance, 13*(1), 46–78.

Dearborn, K. (2002). Studies in emotional intelligence redefine our approach to leadership development. *Public Personnel Management, 31*(4), 523–530. doi:https://doi.org/10.1177/009102600203100408

Deardorff, D. K. (2009). Implementing intercultural competence assessment. In D. K. Deardorff (Ed.), *The SAGE Handbook of Intercultural Competence*, 477–491. Thousand Oaks, CA: Sage.

Deardorff, D. K. (2006). The identification and assessment of intercultural competence as a student outcome of internationalization. *Journal of Studies in International Education, 10*(3), 241–266.

Dickey, M. R. (2020). "Pinterest says it will adopt workplace culture recommendations." Retrieved from https://www.msn.com/en-us/money/careersandeducation/pinterest-says-it-will-adopt-workplace-culture-recommendations/arBB1bYXdl#:~:text=Pinterest%20says%20it%20will%20adopt%20workplace%20culture%20recommendations,the%20company%20wrote%20in%20a%20blog%20post%20today

Dobbin, F, & Kaley, A. (2016). Why diversity programs fail. *Harvard Business Review*. Retrieved from https://hbr.org/2016/07/why-diversity-programs-fail

Dover, T. L., Kaiser, C. R., & Major, B. (2020). Mixed signals: The unintended effects of diversity initiatives. *Social Issues and Policy Review, 14*(2), 152–181. https://doi.org/10.1111/sipr.12059

Emslie, C., & Hunt, K. (2009). 'Live to work' or 'work to live'? A qualitative study of gender and work-life balance among men and women in mid-life. *Gender, Work & Organization, 16*(1), 151–172. https://doi.org/10.1111/j.1468-0432.2008.00434.x

Frei, F., & Morriss, A. (2020). Begin with trust. *Harvard Business Review*. Retrieved from https://hbr.org/2020/05/begin-with-trust

Garvin, D. A. (2013). How Google sold its engineers on management. *Harvard Business Review*. Retrieved from https://hbr.org/2013/12/how-google-sold-its-engineers-on-management

George, B. (2003). *Authentic leadership: Rediscovering the secrets to creating lasting value*. San Francisco: Jossey-Bass.

Godard, A., & Lenhardt, V. (1999). *Transformational leadership: Shared dreams to succeed*. Paris: Palgrave Macmillan.

Gottfredson, R. K., Wright, S. L., & Heaphy, E. D. (2020). A critique of the Leader-Member Exchange construct: Back to square one. *The Leadership Quarterly, 31*(6), Art. 101385. https://doi.org/10.1016/j.leaqua.2020.101385

Greenleaf, R. K. (1970). *The servant as leader*. Westfield, IN: Greenleaf Center for Servant Leadership.

Groysberg, B., & Connolly, K. (2014). "Great leaders who make the mix work." Retrieved from https://hbr.org/2013/09/great-leaders-who-make-the-mix-work

Haddon, H. (2020). "Starbucks ties executive pay to 2025 diversity targets." Retrieved from https://www.wsj.com/articles/starbucks-ties-executive-pay-to-2025-diversity-targets-11602680401?reflink=desktopwebshare_permalink

Hammer, M. R. (2015). The developmental paradigm for intercultural competence research. *International Journal of Intercultural Relations, 48*(1), 12–13.

Hammer, M. R. (2009). Solving problems and resolving conflict using the intercultural conflict style model and inventory. In M. A. Moodian (Ed.), *Contemporary Leadership and Intercultural Competence*, 219–232. Thousand Oaks, CA: Sage.

Heifetz, R. A. (1994). *Leadership without easy answers*. Cambridge, MA: The Belknap Press of Harvard University Press.

Hersey, P., & Blanchard, K. (1969). Life cycle theory of leadership. *Training and Development Journal, 23*(1), 26–35.

Hickman, L., & Akdere, M. (2018). Guided critical self-reflection for intercultural leadership development: A research proposal. *Proceedings of the Academy of Human Resource Development International Research Conference in the Americas*.

Hieker, C., & Pringle, J. (2021). *The future of leadership development: Disruption and the impact of megatrends*. Cham, Switzerland: Springer Nature.

Hirvi, S. K., Laulainen, S., & Taskinen, H. (2020). Trust as a multidimensional phenomenon in LMX relationships. *Journal of Health Organization and Management, 35*(1), 17–33. https://doi.org/10.1108/JHOM-12-2019-0349

House, R. J. (1971). A path goal theory of leader effectiveness. *Administrative Science Quarterly, 16*(3), 321–339.

Hughes, R., Ginnett, R., & Curphy, G. (2019). *Leadership: Enhancing the lessons of experience* (9th ed.). New York: McGraw-Hill Education.

IDI, LCC (2021). *The roadmap to intercultural competence using the IDI*. Retrieved from www.idiinventory.com

Jameson, D. A. (2007). Reconceptualizing cultural identity and its role in intercultural business communication. *International Journal of Business Communication, 44*(3), 199–235.

Javidan, M., & Zaheer, A. (2019). How leaders around the world build trust across cultures. *Harvard Business Review*. Retrieved from https://hbr.org/2019/05/how-leaders-around-the-world-build-trust-across-cultures

Katz, L. (1955). Skills of an effective administrator. *Harvard Business Review*. Retrieved from https://hbr.org/1974/09/skills-of-an-effective-administrator

Kelloway, E. K., Turner, N., Barling, J., & Loughlin, C. (2012) Transformational leadership and employee psychological well-being: The mediating role of employee trust in leadership. *Work & Stress, 26*(1), 39–55. doi:https://doi.org/10.1080/02678373.2012.660774

Kerber, R., Coster, H., & McLymore, A. (2020). U.S. companies vow to fight racism but face critics on diversity. *Reuters*. Retrieved from https://www.reuters.com/article/us-minneapolis-police-companies-insight/u-s-companies-vow-to-fight-racism-but-face-critics-on-diversity-idUSKBN23H1KW

Kwantes, C. T., & McMurphy, S. (2021). Contextual influences on trust and trustworthiness: Anetic perspective. In C. T. Kwantes & B. C. H. Kuo (eds.), *Trust and trustworthiness across cultures: Implications for societies and workplaces*, 1–15. Cham, Switzerland: Springer.

Larson, C. E., & LaFasto, F. M. J. (1989). *Sage series in interpersonal communication, Vol. 10. Teamwork: What must go right/what can go wrong*. Thousand Oaks, CA: Sage.

Leetaru, L. (2019). The wrong ways to strengthen culture. *Harvard Business Review*. Retrieved from https://hbr.org/2019/07/the-wrong-ways-to-strengthen-culture

Legood, A., van der Werff, L., Lee, A., & Hartog, D. D. (2021). A meta-analysis of the role of trust in the leadership- performance relationship. *European Journal of Work and Organizational Psychology, 30*(1), 1–22. doi:https://doi.org/10.1080/1359432X.2020.1819241

Lévy-Leboyer, C. (2007). CQ: Developing cultural intelligence at work. *Personnel Psychology, 60*(1), 242–245.

Luo, Y. (2002). Building trust in cross-cultural collaborations: Toward a contingency perspective. *Journal of Management, 28*(5), 669–694. doi:https://doi.org/10.1177/014920630202800506

Manning, G., & Curtis, K. (2018). *The art of leadership* (6th ed.). New York: McGraw-Hill Education.

McGonigal, J. (2012). Building resilience by wasting time. *Harvard Business Review*. Retrieved from https://hbr.org/2012/10/building-resilience-by-wasting-time

McKinsey & Company (2018). "Delivering through diversity." Retrieved from https://www.mckinsey.com/~/media/mckinsey/business%20functions/organization/our%20insights/delivering%20through%20diversity/delivering-through-diversity_fullreport.ashx

Miao, Q., Newman, A., Schwarz, G., & Xu, L. (2014). Servant leadership, trust, and the organizational commitment of public sector employees in China. *Public Administration, 92*(3), 727–743. https://doi.org/10.1111/padm.12091

Middlebrooks, A. E., Allen, S. J., McNutt, M. S., & Morrison, J. L. (2020). *Discovering leadership: Designing your success*. Thousand Oaks, CA: Sage.

Molinsky, A., & Gundling, E. (2016). How to build trust on your cross-cultural team. *Harvard Business Review*. Retrieved from https://hbr.org/2016/06/how-to-build-trust-on-your-cross-cultural-team

Noda, H. (2019). Work-life balance and life satisfaction in OECD countries: A cross-sectional analysis. *Journal of Happiness Studies, 21*(4), 1325–1348. doi:https://doi.org/10.1007/s10902 019-00131-9

North Dakota Young Professionals Network (2013). "Best place to work and best place to intern awards." Retrieved from http://www.prweb.com/releases/2013/2/prweb10403307.htm

Northouse, P. G. (2019). *Leadership: Theory and practice* (8th ed.). Thousand Oaks, CA: Sage.

Parker, C. C. (2007). *Generational differences in work life balance attitudes*. Unpublished thesis, The State University of New York at New Paltz, New Paltz. Retrieved from https://dspace.sunyconnect.suny.edu/bitstream/handle/1951/43099/Parker%20thesis121807.pdf?sequence=1

PriceWaterhouseCoopers (2014). Creating a mentally healthy workplace: Return on investment analysis. Retrieved from https://www.headsup.org.au/docs/default-source/resources/beyondblue_workplaceroi_finalreport_may-2014.pdf

Roth, M., Morrone, K., Moody, K., Kim, M., Wang, D., Moadel, A., & Levy, A. (2011). Career burnout among pediatric oncologists. *Pediatric Blood & Cancer, 57*(7), 1168–1173. https://doi.org/10.1002/pbc.23121

Rousseau, D. M., Sitkin, S. B., Burt, R. S., & Camerer, C. (1998). Not so different after all: A cross-discipline view of trust. *Academy of Management Review, 23*(3), 393–404.

Saunders, M., Skinner, D., Dietz, G., Gillespie, N., & Lewicki, R. (2010). *Organizational trust: A cultural perspective*. New York: Cambridge University Press.

Schedlitzki, D., & Edwards, G. (2018). *Studying leadership: Traditional and critical approaches* (2nd ed.). Thousand Oaks, CA: Sage.

Sendjaya, S., & Pekerti, A. (2010). Servant leadership as antecedent of trust in organizations. *Leadership & Organization Development Journal, 31*(7), 643–663. https://doi.org/10.1108/01437731011079673

Shepherd, S. M. (2019). Cultural awareness workshops: limitations and practical consequences. *BMC Medical Education, 19*(1), 14. https://doi.org/10.1186/s12909-018-1450-5

Sima, V., Gheorghe, I. G., Subić, J., & Nancu, D. (2020). Influences of the Industry 4.0 revolution on the human capital development and consumer behavior: A systematic review. *Sustainability, 12*(10), 4035. https://doi.org/10.3390/su12104035

Spitzberg, B. H., & Changnon, G. (2009). Conceptualizing intercultural competence. In D. K. Deardorff (Ed.), *The SAGE Handbook of Intercultural Competence*, 2–52. Thousand Oaks, CA: Sage.

Stansell, A. (2020). Burning out? These are the highest rated companies for work-life balance during COVID-19. Retrieved from https://www.glassdoor.com/research/companies-work-life-balance/#

Steers, R. M., & Osland, J. S. (2019). *Management across cultures: Challenges, strategies, and skills* (4th ed.). New York: Cambridge University Press.

Stogdill, R. M. (1948). Personal factors associated with leadership: A survey of the literature. *The Journal of Psychology*, *25*(1), 35–71. doi:https://doi.org/10.1080/00223980.1948.9917362

Sundae Bean, LCC (2020). "A new metaphor for intercultural competence development." Retrieved from https://www.sundaebean.com/wp-content/uploads/2018/12/pendulum_guide01.pdf

Taylor, K., & Goggin, B. (2019). 49 of the biggest scandals in Uber's history. *Business Insider*. Retrieved from https://www.businessinsider.com/uber-company-scandals-and-controversies-2017-11

The American Psychological Association (2012). "Building your resilience." Retrieved from http://www.apa.org/topics/resilience

Trevino, L. K. (1986). Ethical decision making in organizations: A person-situation interactionist model. *The Academy of Management Review*, *11*(3), 601–617. https://doi.org/10.2307/258313

WellRight (2020). "Helping employees strengthen emotional resilience." Retrieved from https://www.wellright.com/blog/helping-employees-strengthen-emotional-resilience

Western, S. (2019). *Leadership: A critical text* (3rd ed.). Thousand Oaks, CA: Sage.

Witte, A. (2014) *Blending spaces: Mediating and assessing intercultural competence in the L2 Classroom*. Boston: Walter de Gruyter.

Wong, C. A., & Cummings, G. G. (2009). The influence of authentic leadership behaviors on trust and work outcomes of health care staff. *Journal of Leadership Studies*, *3*(1), 6–23. https://doi.org/10.1002/jls.20104

Zaveri, P. (2020). Salesforce plans to double its number of Black leaders in the US by 2023. Retrieved from https://www.businessinsider.com/salesforce-double-black-leaders-employees-racial-justice-2020-7

Zes, D., & Landis, D. (2013). "A better return on self-awareness." Retrieved from https://www.kornferry.com/content/dam/kornferry/docs/article-migration/KFI-SelfAwareness-ProofPoint-6.pdf

Zhu, W., Newman, A., Miao, Q., & Hooke, A. (2013). Revisiting the mediating role of trust in transformational leadership effects: Do different types of trust make a difference? *The Leadership Quarterly*, *24*(1), 94–105. https://doi.org/10.1016/j.leaqua.2012.08.004

The Emergence of Chinese Global Executives 14

A Transvergent Perspective of Leadership

Xinhua Wittman and Yuan Qin

14.1 Introduction

Since the opening up of China's borders some 40 years ago, the country has been able to transform its economy from an underdeveloped one to become the second-largest in the world. The role played by Chinese business elites in China's unprecedented economic growth over the last few decades cannot be overlooked, as effective leadership and management are crucial factors in economic advancement. With China's rising presence in every facet of world affairs, along with the fast pace of its enterprises' globalization, there is a growing interest in studying this phenomenon of economic growth, in terms of both understanding China in general and learning about the Chinese way of doing business in particular. From bold moves in international mergers and acquisitions to enterprising start-ups, the world has seen how Chinese executives[1] often exhibit a unique style or set of characteristics of leadership and management—a style that deviates from the MBA school of thought prevalent in the West as much as it does from the Confucian doctrine which is deep-rooted in Chinese culture.

[1] In the context of this study, the term "Chinese executives" means Chinese nationals who have spent their formative years in China and hence can be regarded as having their core values formed by Chinese culture.

X. Wittman (✉) · Y. Qin
Executive Education of the Faculty Business, Economics and Informaticsm, Swiss Chinese Case Study Center, University of Zürich, Zürich, Switzerland
e-mail: xinhua.wittmann@execed.uzh.ch; yuan.qin@execed.uzh.ch

I. Stolz, S. Oldenziel Scherrer (eds.), *International Leadership*, uniscope. Publikationen der SGO Stiftung, https://doi.org/10.1007/978-3-658-37306-1_14

According to the United Nations Conference on Trade and Development (UNCTAD, as cited in Reuters 2021), by attracting USD163 billion in Foreign Direct Investment (FDI) in 2020 (inflow), China surpassed the United States, becoming the world's largest recipient of FDI. Meanwhile, Chinese enterprises have been investing heavily abroad, too: FDI outflows (USD163 billion) ranked fourth worldwide in 2019 (UNCTAD n.d.). In light of the increasing integration of Chinese businesses into global networks, more and more Chinese executives are taking on international assignments—either as expats working for Chinese outbound investment ventures or as host country nationals for foreign organizations operating in China.

The purpose of this chapter is to examine the key leadership elements of Chinese executives who work in a highly convergent, high-tech environment with divergent cultural contexts. We borrow the concept of "transvergence" to chart their prevailing leadership qualities from three perspectives—those of dynamics of *glocal* context, personal traits, and skills approach. We have selected three case studies based on Chinese business leaders so as to sustain our proposition of transvergent leadership—a consolidation of diverse elements which cannot be traced back solely to either the traditional Confucian philosophy or the management rationality driven by Western ideas. Rather, our field research will show "a wider and deeper confluent transvergence of problem-solving abilities within changing international, economic and business parameters" (Mackinnon 2005, p. 392). The backgrounds of the protagonists in the three cases share some similarities: they are Chinese nationals, born and raised in China, where group-oriented (Eastern) culture, hierarchical structure, and relational governance are predominant. All of them have also studied in European countries, where individual-oriented (Western) culture is dominant (Ralston 2008), and have later taken on leadership roles in complex, dynamic, and intercultural[2] environments where contractual governance is the norm and a flat organizational structure in companies is favored (Mackinnon 2008). By analyzing the case studies, we aim to shed light on the transvergent characteristics of effective Chinese leaders and to convey an understanding of where their influences stem from.

In the following, we will briefly review the literature of two leadership theories and the debates relating to intercultural leadership from different perspectives, namely divergence, convergence, cross-vergence, and transvergence. We will then outline our research propositions developed for the present study. Thereafter, we will present and analyze the three case studies with a focus on the leadership styles of Chinese executives from the transvergent perspective. Each case narrative will illustrate how the individual Chinese executives have dealt with leadership challenges. The intercultural background and the dynamic environments under which our case protagonists act/react will help explain the distinctiveness of Chinese business leaders and why it is important to understand it.

[2]"Intercultural" describes a deep understanding of different cultures, emphasizing interactions and mutual exchanges between people across cultures.

14.2 Literature Review

Since the present paper aims to study the important elements attributed to Chinese global executives through a leader-centered lens, two theories, namely the *traits leadership theory* and the *skills approach* from the abundant leadership models, are applied in our research framework.

14.2.1 Traits Theory

The *traits approach* of leadership is among the earliest of systematic leadership studies. It assumes that leaders can differentiate themselves from non-leaders on the basis of a special set of personal characteristics or traits they possess. Those traits were thought to be inherent to the leaders and remain with them in a stable manner (Zaccaro 2007). However, researchers later paid attention to the influence of situations on leadership, and the traits theory maintains its initial focus on the critical role of personal traits in the effectiveness of leadership until today (Germain 2012). Through decades of research in the twentieth century, especially studies of prominent leaders, a long list of typical character traits of successful leaders have been identified. The common core traits include self-confidence, intelligence, ambition, perseverance, assertiveness, emotional stability, creativity, and motivation (Fleenor 2006). Though the traits theory provides important criteria for effective leaders, it fails to explain why the same leader is successful in a given situation but fails in another context. As traits were considered to be innate and largely fixed psychological structures, leadership training and development become irrelevant (Northhouse 2013, p. 32).

14.2.2 Skills Approach

Unlike the traits theory, which regards leaders as born as such, the *skills approach* emphasizes leadership competencies as both innate and acquired. At the heart of this model, leadership effectiveness is attributed to both personal traits and competencies. Based on research from the mid-twentieth century up until more recent studies, skills that are important for effective leadership include: technical, i.e. problem-solving skills; human, i.e. social skills; and conceptual skills, i.e. ideas including vision and strategic plans (Yammarino 2000; Northhouse 2013, pp. 44–46). The Chinese translation of "leadership" is "the abilities to lead" or "leading ability", which implies a set of personal skills and strategies that are learned, trained, and accumulated along the career trajectory.

14.2.3 Intercultural Leadership

Both the *traits theory* and the *skills approach* are helpful to identify the most relevant personality traits and qualifications a leader should possess. However, those qualities have mainly been validated in relatively static, monocultural environments. Inspired by Hofstede's seminal work of 1980 on culture's consequences in work-related values, scholarly research began to pay attention to the influence of national cultures on leadership behaviors. Subsequently, cross-cultural[3] leadership has grown to become an important sub-domain in leadership studies. By illustrating culture-specific leadership styles, cross-cultural leadership research has shown that some leadership traits and skills are universally effective, while others are culturally contingent (Dorfman and House 2004). The comparative studies of similarities and differences lead to scholarly debates on convergence and divergence.

Under the forces of globalization, are organizations becoming more similar worldwide, or are they maintaining their dissimilarities due to distinctive national cultures? This question has puzzled scholars as well as managerial practitioners for years (Adler and Gundersen 2007).

In intercultural management literature, the debates over the effects of globalization on managerial practices of leaders in a globalizing business environment (Mackinnon 2005) can be looked at from four perspectives: convergence, divergence, cross-vergence, and transvergence.

The convergence school argues that the gap between Eastern and Anglo-Saxon management styles has been narrowing along with market deregulation and industrialization and that "managers in industrialized nations will embrace the attitudes and behaviors common to managers in other industrialized nations despite cultural differences" (Gupta and Wang 2004, p. 47). Researchers who advocate divergence maintain that an individual's values and beliefs are largely influenced by the person's national culture, and that organizational culture is bound to societal culture (Hofstede 1980; Adler and Jelinek 1986).

In contrast to the two polar extremes of convergence and divergence, the cross-vergence school of thought provides a hybrid perspective by arguing that individuals or firms can take the best features of different cultures and integrate them into a unique value set as a result of the dynamic interaction of combined influences from the sociocultural and economic ideologies dimension (Guillén 2000; Ralston 2008). Ralston, Holt, Terpstra, and Kai-Cheng define cross-vergence as:

> Cross-vergence occurs when an individual incorporates both national culture influences and economic ideology influences synergistically to form a unique value system that is different from the value set supported by either national culture or economic ideology. (2008, p. 12)

[3]"Cross-cultural" compares and stresses differences across cultures.

A study by Ralston et al. (2008) on the sociocultural and business ideological impact on work values in four distinct countries supports the cross-vergence perspective. The conceptualization of cross-vergence also finds a strong echo in the fusion leadership theory (Vu and Gill 2019) as well as the hybrid leadership model (Gronn 2009; Tian 2021). Both perspectives stress the hybridity of blending cultural values in an adaptive or emerging response to the contextual dynamics characterized by multiculturalism, interconnectedness, and ever-changing global environments. Nonetheless the limitations of the cross-vergence perspective should not be overlooked. A random and senseless hybridization destroys both independence and the identity of the organization (Gupta and Wang 2004). The firm has to constantly decide whether to cross-verge with the Anglo-Saxon, the German, or the Confucian model, and may end up with a confusing mix that is stuck in the middle without any distinctive advantage (p. 4).

To overcome the weaknesses of the aforementioned models, the transvergent concept defined by Gupta and Wang (2004, p. 47) emphasizes the "reinterpretations" and "reapplications" of a company's history or an individual's national culture to "fully tap the opportunities inherent in globalization as well as localization"—an "integrated, original, and distinct perspective". Mackinnon also differentiates transvergence from cross-vergence:

> Transvergence occurs when an individual incorporates both national and non-national culture influences synergistically to form a unique value system, that is simultaneously locally responsive and globally integrative, controlling strategic adaptation to economic exchange. (2005, p. 76)

Mackinnon (2005) has observed in his study that Chinese management can adapt to contractual governance of the Anglo-Saxon model and simultaneously maintain the relational government while doing business with other Asian cultures, indicating that "a Western interpretation of Chinese strategy is feasible" (p. 76). However, he also stresses the importance of strategy consistency and of being "locally responsive and globally integrative" in the transvergent adaption process.

14.3 Research Propositions and Framework

Scholarly opinions have underpinned the persistent influence of culture on leadership behavior (Erez and Earley 1993; Scarborough 1998; Koopman et al. 1999). While cultural values are formed in childhood and remain relatively stable after at the age of about ten (Hofstede 1991, 2010), it is plausible to assume that leadership behavior can be attributed to those cultural values. In light of an uninterrupted Chinese history, the core of Chinese culture has been largely preserved and can still be traced back to Confucianism (Li et al. 2017). Nevertheless, the 30-year legacy of planned economy and the following 40-year exposure to Western values have made a remarkable impact on contemporary Chinese

Layers of mental programing

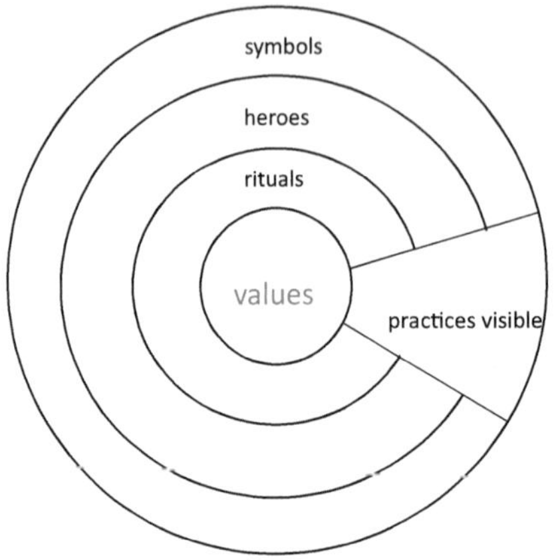

	Traditional	Contemporary
Symbols	Dragon, lantern, dress code etc. to symbolize power, wealth and luck	5G, mobile phone, all kinds of high-tech applications to symbolize modernity
Heroes	War warriors, scholars including poets and painters who achieved highest level of imperial examination	Returnees who got an academic degree from the West, changemakers, entrepreneurs, innovators
Rituals	Important to obey tradition and to show respect for hierarchy and elders	Less important to follow tradition, but still showing respect for hierarchy and elders
Values	Collectivism, familyism, and extended familyism	Collectivism, familyism

Fig. 14.1 Authors' manifestations of the evolution of Chinese culture

society. We use the "Layers of Mental Programming" model (◉ Fig. 14.1) constructed by Hofstede (1991) to illustrate our proposal on the evolution of Chinese culture: the closer the cultural elements are to the core, the less has been changed.

With the introduction of business and management programs in Chinese universities in the 1980s, leadership education and research have become very attractive. The most comprehensive study of GLOBE project across 160 countries in collaboration with more than 500 researchers revealed that traditional Chinese norms, planned economy ideologies, and Western thoughts are the major forces shaping Chinese leadership (Dorfman and House 2004). According to its survey results, besides the universally validated leadership characteristics—such as integrity, inspiration, administrative competence–, Chinese managers possess some unique traits which can be readily tracked back to their cultural influences. Moral leadership, human concern (empathy), conformity, reciprocalism, and paternalism are the striking differences in comparison with Western leaders. In their contribution of Chinese researchers to the GLOBE study, Fu, Wu, Yang and Ye concluded:

> Though traditional values are still highly respected, and constantly pull back China's organizational leaders and urge them to conform to the traditional values, their internal desires to become competitive and the external pressure to do so are all pushing them toward modern Western ideologies, encouraging them to challenge the norms. (2007, p. 891)

Proposition 1 Chinese global executives possess leadership traits and skills that are influenced by Chinese cultural tradition, Western management practices, and contemporary socio-economic developments.

Despite the durability and relevance of Confucius philosophy in today's Chinese society, what about the values held by Chinese executives who have studied and worked in Western institutions? In a comparative study of Chang and Lin (2008), no significant differences in terms of personal values and leadership behavior were found between Taiwanese nationals with Anglo-Saxon cultural experience and those without. However, correlations between personal values and leadership behavior show a profound divergence. Their findings demonstrate that the leadership behavior of Taiwanese leaders with Anglo-Saxon cultural experience is less related to the personal values identified than is the case for the behavior of Taiwanese leaders without foreign cultural experience.

Proposition 2 Chinese global executives with international experience incorporate both national and non-national cultures into their leadership practices, i.e. in a rather transvergent position.

Besides personal traits and skills, what else would be needed to become a great leader? Without the battlefield at Austerlitz, there would be no Napoleon as we acknowledge him today. In our opinion, the right timing in the right battlefield is also important, for a commander to demonstrate his/her heroic charisma. While at the heart of transvergence is a locally responsive and globally integrative dialectic, we adopt the term *"glocal"* to characterize the nature of contextual dynamics on both the organizational and the individual level. The contextual dynamics in the course of *glocalization* is an opportunity as well as a touchstone for global leaders.

Proposition 3 Chinese global executives operate under *glocal* and intercultural contexts.

In order to validate our research propositions of the emergence of Chinese global executives, three dimensions are essential for the transvergent leadership framework, as shown in ◉ Fig. 14.2. We focus on identifying the unique personal traits backed by Chinese traditional values that are essential for effective leadership; a better understanding of what skills Chinese executives have gained is also important given the ever-changing business environment. In the many facets of a *glocal* context, what are the most challenging aspects that need to incorporate both a national and a non-national culture to be dealt with synergistically. Guided by the Transvergent Leadership framework, we conducted a field study by means of semi-structured and open-ended interviews with three Chinese executives.

14.4 Research Method

Although the transvergent strategic perspective in dealing with globalization has been proposed by Gupta and Wang as early as 2003, there is a lack of empirical evidence to support this proposition. To prove our research propositions around the question of how

Fig. 14.2 Transvergent leadership framework

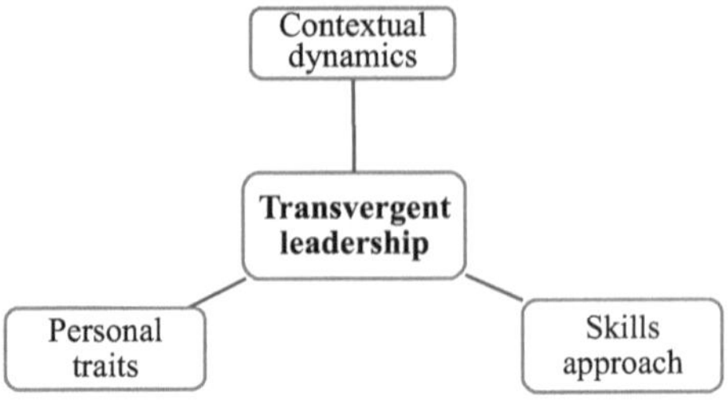

Chinese executives incorporate cultural values from both the East and the West in dealing with managerial issues in different business environments, we adopted an exploratory and heuristic research method in the form of multiple case studies. These are used because we want to replicate the transvergence leadership framework in different business contexts. To that end, we purposefully selected three Chinese executives from diverse backgrounds who interact with different national cultures and business environments. ◉ Table 14.1 provides an overview of the backgrounds of the three interviewees in our case study.

We used semi-structured interviews to collect our data. To start the conversation, we asked them to tell us some stories from their childhood, their family backgrounds, their relationships with parents and friends, how they got the job, and why they do it. We then asked our interviewees open-ended questions such as: "What are the differences between communicating with your headquarters (in Europe) and your local (Chinese) employees?"; "Could you please share some incidents about intercultural conflicts that emerged in your career, and how did you resolve them?"; "How do you lead a culturally diversified team?"; "How do you think your overseas education has influenced your current leadership style?" We then transcribed the interview records and sent the transcripts to the corresponding interviewees for review and additional input as well as, if necessary, corrections.

We combined both deductive and inductive coding to analyze our data. Deductive coding was applied for the reason that one research objective was to validate our propositions in the transvergence leadership framework, while inductive coding was adopted to explore possible new elements that were not considered in the literature. We compiled a list of codes in the three dimensions of our framework based on previous research prior to data collection so as to serve as the coding guideline. The guideline codes were assigned while the researchers read through the case; where none of the pre-compiled codes fit with the narrative, a new code was assigned. In order to minimize biased analyses, the two researchers coded three cases separately and the results were cross-examined and discussed until the researchers reached a consensus.

14.5 Field Study and Discussion

In this section, we will present the three field-researched cases. At the end of each case, we will analyze and discuss them based on our transvergent leadership framework.

Table 14.1 The business environment under which the three protagonists act/react

	Industry	Business environment
Case 1: Dr. Guangjian Yu	Swiss multinational company, subsidiary in China Manufacturer for electronic instruments	Headquarter: Free market economy, task focus, global integration Subsidiary: Government-visible hand, interpersonal relationships prevail, local responsiveness
Case 2: Dr. Zhenzhong Su	Start-up in Switzerland Navigation and drone technology	Market economy, rule of law Global integration Local responsiveness
Case 3: Jerry J.[a]	Multinational company, subsidiary in China Heavy electrical equipment and automation technology	Headquarter: Free market economy, task focus, global integration Subsidiary: Government-visible hand, interpersonal relationships prevail, local responsiveness

[a]At the request of the interviewee, all names and the organization in the third case are anonymized

14.5.1 Case 1: Managing Director of a Swiss Company's Subsidiary in China—Finding the Right Balance

Born in a small city in southern China, Dr. Guangjian Yu began his student life during the ten-year Cultural Revolution period in China. He continued with his Master's degree studies when China began its open-door policy and economic reforms. Inspired by the advanced technologies brought to China by Western companies in the early 1980s, Yu went to study in Germany for his PhD. Through hard work and determination, he obtained his doctoral degree from the University of Duisburg in the difficult "double E" major, i.e. electrical engineering, in 1992. Right after graduation, Yu joined the Swiss-based and family-owned instrumentation and process automation company Endress+Hauser in 1993. Soon after that, in 1994, he took the initiative and asked the company to send him to China to help set up the company's new subsidiaries there. Dr. Yu remained in China and worked as the managing director of the company's Chinese subsidiaries until his recent retirement.

In the beginning, it was not an easy sell at the company's headquarters in Basel to entrust a young, freshly minted Chinese engineer to be completely in charge of developing its business in the Far East. When Yu was first hired by Endress+Hauser, he was in a team based in Germany that supported the company's business in China. Yu worked hard, was always the first in and last out at the office, and quickly proved his value and loyalty to the company. Back then, two Chinese nationals were on the team, but he was the only one who had the necessary Chinese language skills coupled with a solid technical background. When he traveled with his non-Chinese colleagues to exhibitions and trade fairs in China, local company representatives favored Yu over his *"laowai"*[4] colleagues—partially

[4]*Laowai*, which literally means "old foreign" in Chinese, is an informal slang word for non-Chinese nationals.

because it was more convenient for them to communicate directly in Chinese rather than through an interpreter, but also because they perceived Yu, with his overseas doctorate, as a respectful and trustworthy expert. Yu often had to take so many questions at these events that he would actually lose his voice by the end of the day.

In his more than two-decade career at Endress+Hauser, Yu traveled frequently between China and Europe, overseeing the company's operations in China while reporting to its headquarters in Switzerland. Speaking of leadership across cultures, he stressed the importance of finding the right balance and adapting his leadership style to different contexts. This can be well illustrated by how Yu handled his duties with straightforwardness in two different countries.

At the Endress+Hauser headquarters, Dr. Yu was used to communicating with his European colleagues and superiors in a frank and open manner. Yu said:

> Klaus Endress (owner and former CEO of Endress+Hauser) and I were quite close in private. He trusted me a lot, so did the executive board. I had a lot of direct communication with them. There's this family spirit in Endress+Hauser. That's the reason why I could always tell the truth. I knew they would always back me up.

Yu also tried to bring this family spirit to the company's Chinese subsidiaries. He knew nearly every employee in China by name and always left his door open to encourage employees to approach him with their concerns and questions. At Endress+Hauser China, the traditional superior-subordinate hierarchy which is common in Chinese companies was far less visible.

In global executive meetings or C-level gatherings, Yu kept communication low-context, since he understood that clear and direct messages were efficient and effective, and nobody would take anything personally. Sometimes he would openly confront Endress+Hauser's manufacturers in Europe when he found the inferiority of their products or delayed deliveries were a problem. He would do so in front of all board members, and his candor was highly appreciated at headquarters. However, he seldom directly criticized his co-workers in China, particularly junior-level employees. *"Criticism has to be gentle and subtle here in China. Nobody should feel like they're losing face"*, he explained.

For management to get feedback from employees, a staff survey was conducted every two years at the Chinese subsidiaries so that the leadership of the company could get a sense of the workplace environment. According to Yu, this survey benefited the entire organization as it helped maintain a positive relationship between different managerial levels, and it avoided the "big boss culture", as he referred to it. Employees were encouraged to express their views openly and to participate in internal discussions, even on such delicate issues as the bonus system or yearly sales and other targets:

> When we set a target for the year, we discuss with salespeople how it can be achieved. This discussion is not always easy, but we insist on having one rather than presenting ready numbers. Our yearly target is therefore always a result of a long discussion between

salespeople and managers. This way, our management processes are more transparent, more personal, and not arrogant.

In Dr. Yu's case, he strived for an "open and constructive communication"—a corporate value of Endress+Hauser—for the company's Chinese subsidiaries, but translated the "openness" into a Chinese context. Indeed, cultural values influence communication styles (Gudykunst et al. 1996). "Cultural individualism-collectivism has a direct effect on communication because it affects the norms and rules that guide behavior in individualistic and collectivistic cultures" (Gudykunst et al. 1996, p. 511).

In individual-oriented cultures, such as Switzerland, people tend to adhere to low-context communication styles—"being dramatic, dominant, animated, relaxed attentive, open, friendly, contentious, and impression-leaving"–, while in group-oriented cultures, such as China, people tend to adhere to high-context communication styles—"being indirect, inferring meaning, interpersonal sensitivity, using feelings to guide behavior, and using silence" (Park and Kim 2008, p. 47). Yu tended to be more straightforward and bold in voicing his dissatisfaction in low-context cultural settings. He encouraged his subordinates in China to adopt a similar commutation style and to approach him with matters for discussion and suggestions. However, he also compromised his forthrightness when it came to criticism in high-context cultural settings to save face for his employees in China.

Additionally, Yu's ultimate goal was to encourage transparency in the traditionally hierarchical Chinese culture while remaining consistent with the corporate culture of Endress+Hauser. His pragmatism and ability to adapt within a dynamic, intercultural context helped him succeed in finding the proper balance between being an effective leader of his team in China while also maintaining a smooth relationship (by way of healthy communication) with headquarters in Switzerland.

14.5.2 Case 2: CEO of a High-Tech Swiss Company—The Making of a Successful Start-Up

Born in 1986, Dr. Su Zhenzhong grew up a single child, which became common for a whole generation in China after the country implemented its one-child policy in 1979. But he had a large extended family, as his grandfather had had eleven children. *"That part helped me a lot. Early in my childhood I learned how to negotiate with cousins and network with others"*, he says. Su's parents were former factory workers who lost their jobs when the country opened itself up to global competition, and they later struggled to make ends meet, working odd, sometimes difficult jobs. Brought up in a disadvantaged home where he had less than other kids he knew, Su says: *"I was a little shy as a child and understood life means working hard"*, although his childhood did not lack support from his parents. Su still remembers his parents' proud smiles when he scored the highest grade in the junior high school entrance exam, the top in the whole country. Su remained a dedicated pupil in school and was later able to attend Wuhan University in Hubei province, which is one of the top universities in Asia for geophysics/geomatics engineering. After graduating, employment choices were plenty in China, given the university's reputation. Su easily found a job in China and planned on staying there. Then, the opportunity from abroad came knocking.

One of Su's professors from Wuhan University, Professor Jiang Weiping, had been visiting the University of Stuttgart and thought it a good idea to propose for Su to continue his studies in Germany. Without hesitation, Su did so and completed his Master's study there in 2009.

At the University of Stuttgart, Su learned that the ETH in Zurich was one of the top technical universities in the world. That led him to apply for a PhD position there. He was accepted, which is how he came to Switzerland.

During his PhD studies, Su worked on navigation positioning technology. He preferred working on applications as opposed to theoretical work but never thought about founding a company. He was happy with his PhD project, where he was using GNSS/GPS positioning technology to monitor rockfalls and landslides, which could be a life-saving technology for people living in alpine areas.

But an encounter with a fellow Chinese entrepreneur piqued Su's curiosity. This entrepreneur (Li Xiang, CEO and founder of Zurimed) told him that what Su was working on was an emerging technology and could have real market potential. He further encouraged Su to take the entrepreneurial route. As Li had launched his own business from the ETHZ pioneer fellowship program, and with the support of Venturelab, Su also began to pay attention to the workshops and seminars on start-ups offered by the ETHZ and Venturelab, as well as following the trends in the application of the technology he was working on.

Su's interest in taking the entrepreneurial route grew and he became involved in the founding of a Chinese tech company, which he did not end up joining because he wanted to finish his PhD studies. But the process was helpful in that he got to know the whole drone development community in China.

Armed with his technology and the knowledge of what the industrial needs were for the type of tech he was developing, Su entered competitions like the European Satellite Navigation Competition at the end of 2015 and won two prizes for his start-up idea, including the top prize in the Swiss Region and European Space Agency space solutions competition, out of 500 competitors. During his ETHZ pioneer fellowship program in 2016/17, though, Su developed only a GPS-based navigation system and soon found that this was a difficult market to pursue, since it was glutted. He almost gave up.

But then Su spoke with colleagues at the Innovation and Entrepreneur Lab (ieLab) at the ETHZ, who were developing a computer-vision-based navigation system for drones. They realized that if they merged their ideas and technologies, they would have a unique selling point for the market—an offering that was and continues to be in high demand.

In 2017, during the fourth year of his PhD studies, and with the support of the innovation grants from the start-up competitions he had entered, Su founded Fixposition, a tech start-up which provides reliable and highly accurate navigation solutions for autonomous machines such as self-driving cars, robots, and drones, at the ETH incubator lab along with his colleagues. In July 2018, just about one year after its founding, Fixposition released its first product. By March 2019, the company had eight customers, and in July the same year opened its first office in China. At the moment, Fixposition's main customers are drone manufacturers in China, but the company also has products for autonomous vehicles and robots and hopes to expand into other regions and market sectors as well.

The mission of the start-up is to simplify autonomous navigation applications and to increase the reliability of precise positioning while also expanding its availability. Some early revenue was generated by the NAV-RTK product, which is a centimeter-accurate differential GNSS RTK positioning and navigation package for industrial and commercial drones. The company is now focusing on their new disruptive product VISION RTK, which is a deep fusion of computer vision, inertial sensor, and GNSS technology, built for autonomous robots. At the moment, the main market for Fixposition is in autonomous robots and industrial drone navigation.

Fixposition's potential has drawn the attention of various investors, and the start-up secured CHF 3.35 million of capital in a seed round just two years after its founding. By 2020, as CEO of the company, Su was already leading a team of 18 people from diverse cultural backgrounds at Fixposition's Zurich headquarters.

When asked about his leadership style, Dr. Su said:

> I grew up in China. I have benefited from Chinese culture a lot, the good side being working hard, being persistent, but also I have some of the downside of our culture, I would say. At the beginning, I was trying to always be a little bit dominating. If I think that's a good idea, that's the right decision, that's a good way to go, before I always start with in a sort of way that I throw the decision on the table, and then tell everyone 'Hey, that's the decision. Do it!' I found it's not working at all, and also maybe that's not the best way to lead a company. With the help from our new chairman Daniel Ammann and my team, I have now switched more to this 'getting people involved'. Then I found something very interesting. We do one-to-one talks with our people. I asked them how they would appreciate the leadership for the decision-making. They say: 'If you get us involved, even though in the end, my proposal is not considered, I feel respected, because I was part of the decision discussion. Eventually we need to make a decision, maybe that's not my proposal, but that's fine, because I feel like I'm part of it, I'm involved, I'm respected. Eventually I might even support a decision which is not my own proposal.' That's how I see leadership works here.

Trained as a technologist, Su did not know much about being a CEO. According to the learning curve as he has experienced it, he has had to play different roles during the evolution phases of his company. In the initial phase of a start-up, when you have just the idea and one or two people (often the founders themselves) trying to get things moving, you need to carry on all-around tasks, and you must be the major doer to ensure things happen.

Then, as things progress and more people join the company, you become more of a project leader. Afterward, when the start-up becomes established with about ten or more employees, the CEO transitions into yet another role—that of devising business strategy, making sure the right people get hired, raising capital and marketing the business to potential customers or investors. Gradually, as things progress and the company expands, you are less caught up in the details and become more of a manager, Su says.

According to Su, scaling up your team means delegating your responsibilities wisely to others as the company grows and your role changes. This requires smart hiring practices. *"As a CEO, always hire people who are smarter than you in their respective field"*, he says. Hence, he entrusted a Swiss graduate from the University of St. Gallen with a major in business administration as the company's COO. Dr. Su gave him full autonomy to deal with human resources (HR) and matters related to public relations. *"We use everyone's strength and expertise, and work as a team with respect to each other. Hierarchy has no role here to play."* Thanks to the COO's good management, the company has a very low staff turnover. Even during the COVID-19 crisis, *"we have not had a single one [employee] being infected, and we could continue to be as productive as in normal times because our COO has well informed every staff member of the protective measures and applied strict hygienic rules within the company"*, said Su.

Currently, Su has significantly reduced his role in product development and has delegated those tasks to others. His focus is now on selling the company's products and raising capital for the venture. *"The important thing for a CEO is that you have to be present. If you just send sales people to potential customers, those customers won't really take them seriously. They simply won't believe them. But if the CEO goes, the effect would be different"*, he says. This is especially true with matters of technology where the CEO has tech expertise like Su himself.

Su thinks the CEO needs not only to adapt to the dynamic development of a start-up, but also to remain consistent. That means representing the company and being its main driver in moving forward.

Belonging to a younger generation, Su realized that in order to lead a culturally diverse company in Switzerland, he had to apply the essence of the Chinese Gen Y's values as well as traditional Chinese culture while at the same time removing their ineffectual elements. "Growing up in a controlled environment and coming to adulthood in an open and fast-changing world" (WARC, 2016), the Gen Y cohort in China are characterized as "upbeat, open-minded, creative, self-centric, self-boasting, non-cooperative" (Liu and Zhao 2008, p. 613).

In a small-sized tech start-up targeting the global market, where efficiency and close collaboration are crucial to the survival of the company, dominating the decision-making and adopting the traditional hierarchical organizational structure is neither the best way to motivate employees nor a good fit for the current development of Su's company. Therefore, he had to adapt his cultural values to the "societal and organizational culture" (Gupta and Wang 2003, p. 69) of his host country, Switzerland. Tapping into his education in both East and West, and his cultural experiences in both places, Su, by taking a 'trial and error' approach, managed to become a leader of a competent and motivated team in a culturally diverse working environment.

14.5.3 Case 3: General Manager of a Multinational's Subsidiary in China—Being Ready for Adaptation

Jerry joined the Chinese subsidiary of a Swiss-based Fortune 500 company in 1998. Although he was only an inexperienced recent-graduate with a Bachelor's degree from a lesser-known university in an underdeveloped inland city in China, he managed to convince the HR of this Swiss multinational corporation to hire him by being proactive and demonstrating his high level of motivation during the interview process.

Alongside the strong growth of the company's business in China in the early 2000s, Jerry quickly climbed the corporate ranks to reach a senior executive position in the company's China branch. He did so with his ability to learn quickly, his devotion to the job, and his outstanding performance. Jerry was one of the young local talents in China who got an early chance to work with senior managers from Western countries, where he was actively involved in a global business environment, using Chinese wisdom, efficiency, and speed to support the business's development and help everybody out. Soon he was sponsored by the company to study for an MBA and, in the meantime, was sent for both long-term and short-term assignments to various countries, such as the United States, Sweden, India, Australia, and Switzerland. During his stay in Switzerland, Jerry also registered for a MAS program offered by the University of Zurich, though he already had a Master's degree: *"I want to understand local culture and update my knowledge."* He used his free time in the evening and weekends to study while continuing to work full time.

The frequent international business trips and long-term stints abroad allowed Jerry to observe and experience different national cultures and business systems. When dealing with the cultural issues that arise in an international team, depending on the circumstances, he was able to adapt different cultural frames with ease and to incorporate the "strong points" of various cultures.

As the COVID-19 pandemic halted most of the world's economic activities in 2020, China, where the outbreak had first begun, surprisingly was one of the first countries to show signs of recovery as a result of its stringent oversight measures. The company's manufacturing sites in China, which Jerry is in charge of, also implemented very strict preventive policies to ensure continued production, as their products were in high demand during the outbreak. They set up a checkpoint at the entry to the facilities and used infrared thermometers, also dubbed "thermometer guns" in China, so as to measure each employee's body temperature every morning. Employees with fever, one of the main symptoms of the coronavirus, would not be allowed to enter. Temperature screening at the entry and exit point of business sites and public areas was ubiquitous in China during the COVID-19 outbreak and was considered by Chinese authorities to be an effective way to contain the spread of the virus. By taking those measures, production was not affected at the factories supervised by Jerry.

As the pandemic grew more serious in Europe, Jerry also became increasingly anxious, since one part of the product he was responsible for is produced in one of the company's factories in Germany. If production in Germany were to be stopped due to an outbreak, this could have had a detrimental effect on the whole production process. Therefore, Jerry immediately contacted his German colleagues and asked whether they were in need of support from the Chinese team, which could provide them with infrared thermometers to check their employees' temperatures before entering the production facility. His kind suggestion, however, was politely turned down for the reason that the use of such measures is considered a breach of privacy and would not be accepted by the factory employees in Germany.

Thanks to Jerry's years of experience with Western cultures, he immediately realized that there was little room for compromise when it comes to privacy issues in Germany. His quick response was to seek out a domestic partner in China who was able to produce substitute parts to avoid the potential risk of a production suspension in Germany—even though he was also aware that this could jeopardize the operational planning of and damage his relationship with the company's factory in Germany.

The dilemma was a familiar one to Jerry. Back in 2005, he had been sent by the company's headquarters to the United States for an international assignment. One day, when he opened a file with employee data sent from his HR colleague Ann, he found that in the "Age" column of the file, all entries had been filled in with "90". Jerry was confused. How could it be possible that all employees in the company were 90 years old? Jerry called Ann for clarification: *"Ann, I think there is a mistake in your HR system. I found all employees in your file are aged 90!"* To his surprise, Ann explained to him that the number "90" displayed in the "Age" column was written on purpose, as age is classified as personal information in the United States and the employer is obliged to protect the privacy of their employees. However, in the HR system of the company's Chinese subsidiaries, one can find very extensive information about each employee: age, address, political affiliation, marital status, ethnicity, etc. This information is not considered to be private in Chinese workplaces, and even the employees know a lot of the information among each other.

That was when Jerry learned that privacy is highly valued in Western cultures. So he then used that knowledge while being assigned to the company's headquarters in Switzerland where he was sure to pay special attention to privacy issues both in his professional and personal life, which he said saved him a lot of miscommunication problems.

Another example that shows how Jerry incorporated both Eastern and Western philosophies and business practices synergistically can be found in his mediation of a conflict between his Swiss colleagues and Chinese government officials when he was assigned to headquarters in Switzerland. On a Monday morning, one of the company's VIP customers from China, who happened to be visiting in Switzerland, asked whether Jerry and someone else from headquarters would be able to have dinner with a delegation of government officials from the province where the VIP customer's factory was located. The dinner would have to be the following Friday, the only time that the delegation was available. Usually in China, when it comes to business dinners, the more important a customer, the higher the rank of the representatives from the company who are to join the dinner. By doing this, a host gives *mianzi*—the face—to the guest and demonstrates his/her sincerity and respect. Therefore, on the same day, Jerry went to Urs, the head of the Global Business Unit at headquarters, and asked:

> Urs, we got an important delegation from China visiting us this coming Friday. The delegation is our biggest customer's local government. This customer bought more than 1 million USD worth of products from us last year and would like to have a dinner with you on Friday.

Urs replied:

> Jerry, thank you very much for coordinating this visit. However, I already promised my family we would be dining together, I need to be at home on Friday. Apart from that, these officials are not our customer.

To solve the problem, Jerry told Urs:

> Urs, I understand that it's very important for you to spend time with your family on Friday, but we need to have an important representative to show up. I will schedule the dinner an hour earlier, and you just come to say hi and give a toast. Then you can go back home for the family gathering. What do you think of this proposal?

In the end, Jerry's plan worked out well: the guests were very pleased to meet an important executive from the company headquarters, while Urs was still able to go back home for his family dinner. In fact, the delegation was at ease after the early departure of Urs because they could speak Chinese at the table and eat and drink in a relaxed manner without having to worry about Western etiquette. It was a great event for both the hosts and the guests!

In our last case, when it comes to privacy, Jerry showed respect to the value of privacy at the company's factory in Germany; but he also turned to a Chinese partner who was able to produce substitute parts, at the risk of potential damage to his relationship with the German factory, to reduce lead times. The transvergent approach employed by Jerry helped the company gain a competitive advantage. Similarly, he internalized both Eastern and Western values and sought out a creative way to solve the conflict of priorities between his Swiss colleague and the Chinese delegation. His ability to adapt to a complex and multicultural working environment as well as to a flexible leadership style have enabled Jerry to win over his employer and co-workers.

14.6 Discussion and Concluding Remarks

This paper is a study of the leadership characteristics of three Chinese executives who have educational and professional experiences in both China and the West. Through the three case studies, we illustrate how Chinese executives have taken advantage of personal traits and skills acquired in China, as well as their cultural immersion during their stays in Europe, and integrate synergistically both Eastern and Western values into their daily management in an intercultural context. From a transvergent leadership perspective, we have identified some unique elements in each of the three dimensions in the transvergent leadership framework, as shown in ◉ Fig. 14.3.

In the dimension of personal traits, we found that persistence, an ethos of working hard, and continued learning are shared characteristics from the three interviewees. As for the dimension of skills approach, all of them stressed the importance of having an education and work experience in both China and the West. Equipped with intercultural knowledge and soft skills, the key to effective leadership is adaptation and pragmatism. All three protagonists of our case studies have embraced the opportunities given to them by globalization. The contextual dynamics featured in the *glocal* context—especially the blending of relationship vs task focus as well as vertical vs horizontal orientation in the organizational settings—offered an exciting learning experience and at the same time enabled them to stand out as global leaders.

With the rise of globalization, Chinese executives are increasingly in demand for filling leadership positions. Our study shows that an executive's ability to incorporate cultural values from both the East and the West in managerial tasks in an adaptable manner is essential, but this is only one part of the whole picture. In order to be an effective global

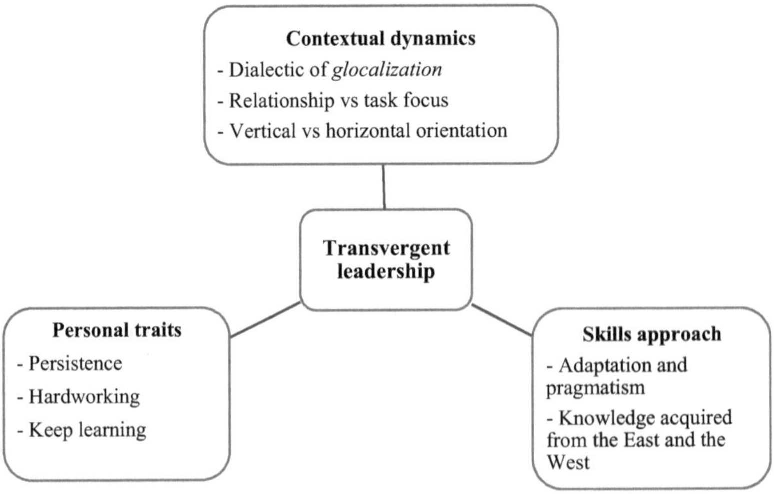

Fig. 14.3 Transvergent leadership of chinese global executives

leader, one needs to possess traits such as hard work and continued learning in a fast-changing environment. We believe that the three-dimensional transvergence framework can adequately describe the leadership characteristics of contemporary Chinese executives. The business world has seen how the development of Chinese leadership is evolving along the lines of learning, adopting, and adapting, which opens up new avenues in academic and applied research. Though the case study approach provides multi-faceted and in-depth explorations of real-life problems, we need to combine rigorous quantitative research and insights from case studies to draw any generalized conclusions.

References

Adler, N. J., & Gundersen, A. (2007). *International dimensions of organizational behavior.* Boston, MA: Cengage Learning.

Adler, N. J., & Jelinek, M. (1986). Is "organization culture" culture bound? *Human Resource Management, 25*(1), 73–90.

Chang, H. W., & Lin, G. (2008). Effect of personal values transformation on leadership behaviour. *Total Quality Management, 19*(1–2), 67–77.

China was largest recipient of FDI in 2020: Report. *Reuters* (2021, January 25). Retrieved from https://www.reuters.com/article/us-china-economy-fdi-idUSKBN29T0TC

Dorfman, P. W., & House, R. J. (2004). Cultural influences of organizational leadership. In R. J. House, P. J. Hanges, M. Javidan, P. W. Dorfman, & V. Gupta, (Eds.), *Culture, leadership, and organizations: The GLOBE study of 62 societies* (pp. 51–73). Thousand Oaks, CA: Sage Publications.

Erez, M., & Earley, P. C. (1993). *Culture, self-identity, and work.* Oxford, UK: Oxford University Press on Demand.

Fleenor, J. W. (2006). Trait approach to leadership. *Psychology, 37*(1), 651–665.

Fu, P. P., Wu, R., Yang, Y., & Ye, J. (2007). Chinese Culture and Leadership. In J. S. Chhokar, F. C. Brodbeck, & R. J. House (Eds.), *Culture and leadership across the world: The GLOBE book of in-depth studies of 25 societies* (pp. 877–907). Mahwah, NJ: Lawrence Erlbaum Associates.

Germain, M. L. (2012). Traits and skills theories as the nexus between leadership and expertise: Reality or fallacy?. *Performance Improvement, 51*(5), 32–39.

Gronn, P. (2009). Hybrid leadership. In K. Leithwood, B. Mascall, & T. Strauss (Eds.), *Distributed Leadership According to the Evidence* (pp. 17–40). New York: Routledge.

Gudykunst, W. B., Matsumoto, Y., Ting-Toomey, S., Nishida, T., Kim, K., & Heyman, S. (1996). The influence of cultural individualism-collectivism, self construals, and individual values on communication styles across cultures. *Human Communication Research, 22*(4), 510–543.

Guillén, M. F. (2000). Corporate governance and globalization: is there convergence across countries?. *Advances in International Comparative Management, 13*, 175–204.

Gupta, V., & Wang, J. (2004). The transvergence proposition under globalization: Looking beyond convergence, divergence and cross-vergence. *Multinational Business Review, 12*(2), 37–57.

Gupta, V., & Wang, J. (2003). Globalization And Convergence-Divergence Debate: Strategic Perspectives For Emerging Markets. *Journal of Business & Economics Research* (JBER), *1*(2), 69–76. https://doi.org/https://doi.org/10.19030/jber.v1i2.2974

Hofstede, G. (2010) The GLOBE debate: Back to relevance. *Journal of International Business Studies, 41*, 1339–1346. https://doi.org/https://doi.org/10.1057/jibs.2010.31

Hofstede, G. (1991). Empirical models of cultural differences. In N. Bleichrodt & P. J. D. Drenth (Eds.), *Contemporary issues in cross-cultural psychology* (pp. 4–20). Lisse, the Netherlands: Swets & Zeitlinger Publishers.

Hofstede, G. (1980). Culture and organizations. *International Studies of Management & Organization, 10*(4), 15–41.

Koopman, P. L., Den Hartog, D. N., & Konrad, E. (1999). National culture and leadership profiles in Europe: Some results from the GLOBE study. *European Journal of Work and Organizational Psychology, 8*(4), 503–520.

Li, J., Wang, Y., & Wu, F. (2017). Leadership and leadership development in China. In A. Ardichvili & K. M. Dirani (Eds.), *Leadership Development in Emerging Market Economies* (pp. 73–91). New York, NY: Palgrave Macmillan.

Life is complicated for China's Gen Y. (2016, May 27). *WARC.* Retrieved from https://www.warc.com/newsandopinion/news/life-is-complicated-for-chinas-gen-y/36792

Liu, L., & Zhao, E. (2008). China's Generation Y: New trend-setter in the workforce. In *2008 4th International Conference on Wireless Communications, Networking and Mobile Computing*, 1–4. doi: https://doi.org/10.1109/WiCom.2008.1678

Mackinnon, A. (2008). Chinese strategy: is it crossverging, converging or transverging to Western systems? *Management decision, 46*(2), 173–186.

Mackinnon, A. (2005). Relating cultural change to strategic adaptation: an interpretation of modern Chinese management. PhD thesis, Middlesex University. Middlesex University Research Repository. Retrieved from https://eprints.mdx.ac.uk/10744/1/568378.pdf

Northhouse, P. G. (2013). *Leadership: Theory and practice* (6th Edition). Thousand Oaks, CA: SAGE Publications.

Park, Y. S., & Kim, B. S. K. (2008). Asian and European American cultural values and communication styles among Asian American and European American college students. *Cultural Diversity and Ethnic Minority Psychology, 14*(1), 47–56. https://doi.org/https://doi.org/10.1037/1099-9809.14.1.47

Ralston, D. A. (2008). The cross-vergence perspective: Reflections and projections. *Journal of International Business Studies, 39*(1), 27–40.

Ralston, D. A., Holt, D. H., Terpstra, R. H., & Kai-Cheng, Y. (2008). The impact of national culture and economic ideology on managerial work values: A study of the United States, Russia, Japan, and China. *Journal of International Business Studies, 39*(1), 8–26.

Scarborough, J. (1998). *The origins of cultural differences and their impact on management.* Westport, CT: Greenwood Publishing Group.

Tian, Q. (2021). *Glocalization and the Development of a Hybrid Leadership Model: A Study of Chinese University Presidency.* New York: Routledge.

United Nations Conference on Trade and Development (n.d.). Foreign direct investment: Inward and outward flows and stock, annual. Retrieved from https://unctadstat.unctad.org/wds/TableViewer/tableView.aspx?ReportId=96740

Vu, M. C., & Gill, R. (2019). "Letting go of the raft" – the art of spiritual leadership in contemporary organizations from a Buddhist perspective using skilful means. *Leadership, 15*(3), 360–380.

Yammarino, F. J. (2000). Leadership skills: Introduction and overview. *Leadership Quarterly, 11*(1), 11–35.

Zaccaro, S. J. (2007). Trait-based perspectives of leadership. *American psychologist, 62*(1), 6.

"A Corporate's Character Is its Fate" 15

Character and Ethical Leadership in Multicultural Systems

Michael Fürst

15.1 Introduction

In times of economic and societal changes that are typically characterized by high levels of complexity, ambiguity, and ethical disruption, leadership and a virtuous character in business and society seem to be high in demand and on top of the priority list. These changes are caused by numerous factors, one of which seems to be connected to more pronounced and more loudly voiced expectations of society toward business and its role in a well-governed, fair, and equitable society. Obviously, such societal expectation of business forcefully questions the (for a long time predominant) economic ideology that the business of business is business and that societal factors and institutions are only exogenous behavioral restrictions to an economy. Such a theoretical position eventually neglects the role of a company as a responsible collective actor in society. Academic scholars such as Josef Wieland, however, argue that a firm is a social cooperative project of multiple stakeholders to invest and use their resources under the conditions of economic competition. It is a contractually constituted form that enables organized cooperation within the firm as well as with relevant stakeholders outside of it. Although this does not result in a normative determination regarding the purpose of the company, it implies a linkage to the normative legitimacy of corporate objectives and business activities. This

We borrow and adapt this from Heraclitus, Fragments B119: "Man's character is his fate".
Disclaimer: When not otherwise indicated, this chapter represents the personal opinion and perspective of the author and not of the affiliated organization.

M. Fürst (✉)
UCB Farchim S.A., Bulle, Switzerland

I. Stolz, S. Oldenziel Scherrer (eds.), *International Leadership*, uniscope. Publikationen der SGO Stiftung, https://doi.org/10.1007/978-3-658-37306-1_15

embraces the desirability and necessity of corporate contributions to social welfare and progress beyond legal requirements. The social character of an enterprise, its nature, and its purpose are thus defined as endogenous—for economic reasons–, because otherwise transactions and any cooperation cannot be managed successfully.

Whereas—in the past—this debate about the normative foundation of a company and the business-society nexus has been predominantly focused on avoiding harm to society that might be caused by business activities, the above-mentioned understanding of the firm and the most current debates are focused much more on the positive contributions business should provide to environmental and societal problems—and, in a more fundamental sense, which role a firm should have in modern societies (Fürst and Schotter 2013; Fürst 2014b, 2017).

Fundamentally this means a complete shift in the debate about the purpose of business in society, and, de facto, not just investors such as BlackRock but also many companies are now trying to rethink and reconsider what purpose they might have in societies in which the horizon of expectations is changing to a considerable extent. However, finding this purpose-oriented place in the tectonics of modern societies, filling it with meaning, and setting up the right governance in a company requires character and ethical leadership skills that unfortunately have not been trained at business schools nor have they been systematically incentivized and cultivated in business. Additionally, there seems to be a limited understanding of what a virtuous character in the corporate context actually means and whether character is something that can be only attributed to individual actors, or also to collective ones such as companies. The latter is linked to the discussion whether collective actors have an ethical responsibility *as an entity*, or whether ethical responsibility can only be worn by the individual actors within an organization (French 1979; Soares 2003; Wieland 2006).

This situation leads to a gap in the availability of specific leadership skills that are required in business to tackle some of the biggest challenges of humankind—just think about the enormous challenges underlying the 17 Sustainable Development Goals–, which desperately need ethical leadership with the related awareness, willingness to contribute, and the specific skills to purposefully deliver. It sometimes becomes even worse since it appears that some companies do seem to believe that managing this business—society nexus and defining the purpose of a firm—does not require any specific skills but can be managed by any experienced leader who has developed an ambition to do good, irrespective of whether the selected people have any education, specific expertise, or experience in this. To be slightly provocative: Ambition does not substitute skills, experience, and expertise. And ethical leadership does not mean to simply have bold ambitions to engage in social or environmental issues—as well-meant as such an intent and ambition may be–, it rather requires the willingness to have a thorough (theoretical) understanding of corporate responsibilities and ethics, to deeply connect with practical societal and ethical problems, to professionally reflect on those jointly with affected stakeholders, and, most importantly, to have the specific experiences, skills, and capabilities that are needed to address or solve those problems, most often by collaborative means with others. Only then, if the ambition and willingness to lead is paired with the required knowledge and skills, will the journey toward a more sustainable, inclusive, and equitable economy eventually find its right direction and realize the promise it bears. This is a challenging task in itself, but it becomes even more difficult if we consider that business is conducted in systems that are defined by cultural diversity between and within, e.g., geographies, life styles, organizations, belief systems, religions, etc., to name just a few.

Based on the above problem statement, this paper tries to explore potential theoretical answers to how ethical leadership can be developed, how it is connected to terms like character and virtues (i.e. the willingness and ability to behave ethically), how perception mechanisms with regards to ethical problems work, and how purpose-oriented decision-making processes in a company need to be structured by purpose-driven leaders in order to systematically allow all members of a company to behave in sync with its purpose. This discussion around the character and the virtues of leaders needs to be seen in the context of a globalized and multicultural world in which ethical leadership is often surrounded by nothing less than high levels of ethical ambiguity or even conflict in which an agreement on what "good" or "ethical" means is not an easy objective to accomplish.

This is connected to discussions around ethical incentive structures that need to serve to accomplish the purpose of the business and to support the emergence or manifestation of moral imagination[1] within a company to ethically manage situations of tough choices, as well as to create superior solutions for the challenges at the intersection of business and society. All of this needs to be linked to a better practical understanding of how ethical leadership can be developed, trained, and sustained within sometimes harsh business realities where ethical and cultural differences are the norm rather than the exception and where tough choices do not lean toward romantic ethical ideals of the purpose of business or purposeful leadership.

In the attempt to find answers to the above-mentioned issues, we will start by analyzing what ethical character in business means, how it can be developed and nurtured, how it connects to the concept of ethical leadership, and how this eventually needs to be linked to the figure of a collective actor and its character that can be defined and described.[2]

So let's start with an examination how ethical character can be defined and described.

15.2 Some Background to the Debate on Character and Leadership

Traditionally, discussions in ethics (and thus also in business ethics) have focused to a considerable extent on individual actors and the virtues they possess or display in their behavior. With this focus, philosophy and ethics have developed criteria and analytical frameworks that allow to distinguish, evaluate, and legitimize economic decisions and

[1] The term moral imagination has been coined and described by Patricia Werhane, see (1994, 1998, 1999; Werhane and Moriarty 2009) et al.

[2] This and the following chapters to a considerable extent specifically refer to the work of Josef Wieland (Wieland 2014b).

specific behaviors that consider legitimate interests of stakeholders or from a procedural point of view, and build on discursive practice to find consensus on issues around fairness, equality etc. (Ulrich 2008). Some theories and conceptions in business ethics have given attention to incentive structures at the macro-level, information asymmetries in typical dilemma situations such as the prisoners dilemma or how economic rationality can be aligned with ethical considerations to create win-win situations, based on specific policy choices and regulatory regimes (Homann and Suchanek 2005). One specific strain of research has been (and is being) focused on the internal governance structures that allow companies and their employees to take ethical decisions systematically. These governance structures are the enabling elements for ethical decision-making and elevate ethics from a concept that is focusing on individual actors to the collective actor who can own ethical virtues (Wieland 2004).

Some other research foci have been directed toward questions around how individuals do form an opinion on ethical choices and how they make judgments on what to be ethical or unethical. This was accompanied by an attempt to in-depth analyze the emotional and motivational forces that would lead to a certain kind of conduct and, with regard to our particular topic, to specifically deviant behavior (Wieland 2014b).[3]

In their analyses, some scholars focus on the cultural dimension of economic activities, i.e., they observe an increasing importance and relevance of cultural issues in economic activities. According to them, culture represents itself as a dimension that draws through all parts of life—including the economy. Hence their hypothesis is that on the one hand, ethical responsibilities and sustainability in themselves represent cultural challenges within an economic system, and on the other hand, companies via their strategies make cultural offerings to society which contain moral or ethical viewpoints and positions. Specifically, Reinhard Pfriem and Thomas Beschorner are working on such a concept within the business ethics debate that primarily aims to be application-oriented in its design and seems to be relevant in an economy in which the cultural dimension is gaining increasing importance (Pfriem 2008; Beschorner 2013).

However, what seems to be a missing piece in the research efforts existing so far is a more fundamental and in-depth analysis of the interplay in the development of the individual and organizational virtuous character, which of course assumes that organizations as collective actors can "possess" something like a character, be virtuous, and have ethical responsibilities.[4] This development question, and the interplay between the individual and the collective level is of particular importance in the context of leadership, since developing a virtuous character is primarily driven by exercise, practice, and routine that can be established in business transactions but not by theoretical studies

[3]Wieland refers in this article to Trevino et al. (2006).

[4]Peter French (1979) has extensively worked and written about this. In the business ethics debate, Josef Wieland may be the most prominent researcher who builds his Governance Ethics on the concept of an ethical responsibility of a collective actor. We will refer to this at a later point in the article.

(Wieland 2014b).[5] Ethical decision-making in business as a sign of good character and virtuous leadership is "praktiké"—to say it in Aristotle's terms—and needs to be trained in order to be developed, maintained, and sustained. This is even more important in a highly diverse globalized economy in which ethical values and the idea of virtuous behavior are often ambiguous in real situations of tough choices and beyond academic seminars. Peter French would argue that organizations are intentional actors that have moral agency since they have internal corporate decision structures (CID) that express idiosyncratic organizational strategies, goals, plans, incentive structures, systems, and processes that inform, standardize, and enforce aligned decision-making of individuals (French 1979). These CIDs with their normative positions would then express the character of the collective actor and allow the individual actor to constantly train and exercise individual decision-making in line with the key ethical or normative positions of their organization. In multicultural settings and situations with high levels of cultural diversity, these CIDs are the signpost that guides decision-making and avoids actions to go beyond the normative guardrails, which would eventually misrepresent the corporate character.

One distinction needs to be drawn in order to develop a modern understanding of moral character and leadership, as Wieland very lucidly explains: In pre-modern societies, ethical direction and orientation were provided and decisions were taken based on hierarchical considerations, i.e., a person at the top of a hierarchy held the status to lead and decide (Wieland 2014b). The moral character or the virtues of individual persons historically are the focal point of ethical reflection and discourse; this individual person is embedded in a hierarchically stratified society in which the individual has to display character and virtuous behavior (Tugendhat 1993).[6] In modern, functionally differentiated societies, status is not the main reference point anymore, but systems and individual actors have a role and an accountability to fulfill certain requirements and to perform against those accountabilities. This means that the leaders in an organization are not expected to display good conduct and moral character because they want to earn status as a respected person in society, but because they have an accountability to be ethical leaders and functional representatives of an organization with good character that also expects a moral character from individual decision-makers where this expectation is codified and processed via the CID. This different allocation mechanism of ethical expectations is based on a changed societal context in which the addressee of moral-economic expectations and discourse is not the founder, the entrepreneur, or the manager as an individual actor but the company as the collective one (Wieland 2003, 2005a). Ethics and integrity in business transactions are not related anymore to the entirety of an individual actor's lifestyle but to the systematic management of risks and the assurance of a values-based and ethical conduct of the collective actor. This implies a categorical shift with regard to the allocation of ethical

[5] Josef Wieland refers to the work of Aristotle (2014b).

[6] According to E. Tugendhat, the way of being is congruent with the traditional term of character, and a good character typically corresponds with the term virtue.

accountability from individuals to organizations. Three distinct questions in the context of ethical leadership and character then need to be considered: (1) What constitutes and defines ethical conduct and good character of leaders as agents of a corporate actor? (2) What constitutes an ethical character of a collective actor as the new focal point of ethical discourse and reflection? (3) How do these two dimensions intersect with each other on a managerial level (e.g. training and development, incentive structures, etc.) to help the collective actor accomplish its corporate purpose and be a good corporate citizen?

In this section, we want to investigate these three questions, which requires us to give specific attention to the interplay between the moral character of the collective actor that is materially expressed in its governance structures[7] and the influence this governance has on the character and conduct of individual actors.

Now why is this interplay important? We can assume with some confidence that rational analysis, well-structured decision-making processes, and well-designed economic incentive structures do influence behavior but of course need to be complemented by something else in order to achieve good conduct. All of these elements have a certain power to motivate a person to behave in line with ethical expectations and standards. However, we need to recognize that rational arguments and rational decision-making structures have limited motivational power. They only work if they are accompanied by moral incentives, the upbringing and the basic moral education of a person, empathy, a sense of belonging to a moral community, and the willingness to live a virtuous life as well as the capabilities to do so.[8] These are all important preconditions for a positive ethical outcome (Wieland 2006; Tugendhat 1993; Joas 2013).[9] From an ethical leadership perspective, this alignment is of particular interest since leadership development in this context means, on the one hand, to foster and maintain the willingness of leaders to behave ethically and to manage a company with the ultimate objective to accomplish its purpose, as well as, on the other hand, to develop organizational structures and systems (governance) that manifest, develop, and train the capabilities or the "ethical muscle" of leaders to behave in line with what we would call an ethical character. Furthermore, ethical leadership also means that managers develop the capabilities to use ethical governance structures in an appropriate way, as well as to invent and implement new governance structures in order to build ethical support structures across a company which are of particular importance in systems of high cultural diversity. As early as 1994, Lynn Sharp Paine emphasized this by stating:

[7]Peter French (1979) would refer to these governance structures as the CID of an organization.

[8]This means to have the skills and capabilities to not just have the intention and the will to be virtuous, but also the capabilities to realize ethical intentions.

[9]This follows the theoretical conception of a virtue that is defined as the individual willingness (intention, conviction, sympathy) and ability (ratio, reasoning, wisdom, knowledge, prudence, organizational governance) to virtuously behave.

> Managers who fail to provide proper leadership and to institute systems that facilitate ethical conduct share responsibility with those who conceive, execute, and knowingly benefit from corporate misdeeds. (Paine 1994, p. 106)

In 2002, she became even clearer about the risk to ethical conduct if the institutionalizing effort was not undertaken or failed:

> In the absence of an active effort to build and maintain a positive set of organizational values, the values of individuals are left to the corrosive forces of indifference. (Paine 2002, p. 8)

However, Paine also clearly pointed to the fact that the development and the use of such governance structures are intertwined with the first element of a virtuous character: the intention to follow ethical principles and to take ethical decisions[10]:

> Moreover, only someone who cares to use the tools, who recognizes when they are appropriate and who wants to do what they recommend will benefit from careful instruction in how to use them. (Paine 1991, p. 72)

In the context of a multicultural environment in which organizations often operate today, and the considerable levels of cultural diversity within many organizations, Paine's caution about the corrosive forces of indifference is particularly relevant. This is because indifference toward different cultural heritages, positions, worldviews, etc. can obviously not just cause personal harm but also create risks at the organizational level. This does not mean that cultural differences should be overcome by some sort of cultural universalism or should be simply maintained, since these differences are immutable. It rather means that the organizational set of values and ethical worldviews—enshrined and expressed in the organizational governance structure or CID of the collective actor—is a net of coherent convictions that are being made transparent and are therefore a frame of reference for decision-making as well as a starting point for dialogue on the meaning and applicability of specific norms. For Richard Rorty (1998), such aspiration or quest for coherence is nothing more than an expression of rationality and pragmatism as well as an attempt to generate influence for one's own position, (a) without trying to simply refer back to existing certain cultural or ethical norms that are superior to others, or (b) without assuming that cultural differences can be easily leveled with the goal to find new universal, superior norms. This concept of a coherence of ethical norms, positions, and behavior at the individual and organizational level is a fundamental characteristic of virtuous leadership and should be a constitutional element of leadership development activities. *Creating* such coherence—strategically and operationally—is far from simple, given that this requires a recognition that the principal agreement to an ethical norm does not necessarily mean an agreement as to what the concrete application of this norm means in different circumstances or cultures.

[10] See also Wieland (2014b).

It also requires specific discursive skills of leaders to have such ethical dispute or dialogue with numerous, sometimes very diverse stakeholders with the aim to find some ethical consensus in terms of the application of ethical standards. Additionally, the development of a governance structure that allows to institutionalize such a coherent approach on ethical norms and values throughout the organization and relevant processes is also a capability that most leaders unfortunately have not learned at business schools; it hence needs to become a fundamental element of any leadership development strategy in an organizational context.In all this, the interdependence and necessary resonance between the "instrumentation" (Wieland 2014a) of ethical rules and principles, as well as the character of the leaders of an organization, is a crucial fundament for accomplishing a company's purpose as well as the ethical conduct of the corporate actor.[11] This necessary amalgamation of these two dimensions can already be found in the works of Adam Smith that explained that ethical judgments about what is right cannot be purely deduced from ethical rules, since this would require unjustifiable simplifications of the overly complex reality; but it additionally requires character as well as the capability for practical ethical judgment (Tugendhat 1993, p. 230).

Given that character plays such an important role in the context of ethical leadership, we will now further describe two important dimensions of character that will then allow us to discuss a perspective on ethical leadership development in more detail.

15.3 The Development Aspect of Character

One important question in this context—as posed by Josef Wieland (2014b, p. 382)—is whether the concept of character is of a static nature or dynamic and hence open for development. This question is of relevance because it either closes or opens the debate as to how ethical leadership can be trained and developed by positively shaping character.

The static nature of character assumes that the fundament of each individual person's character is built in early childhood and is barely susceptible to change. Character would then not be something of a malleable nature, and learning related to the definitional elements of character would logically be impossible. Such understanding of the genesis of character would have enormous consequences for the recruitment, development, and training work in an organization, for a simple reason: If in this static conceptualization, a good character is something a person possesses and brings into an organization as an asset, staffing and recruitment processes would need to be very targeted and precise in terms of identifying people with the right character; this would allow almost no failure since the organization would have no chance to further develop the character of their staff and leaders after having hired them. Consequentially, companies would have to fatalistically

[11] Ernst Tugendhat (1993) also makes the point that morality is best assured if it is based on a combination of ethical rules ("Regelethik") and virtues.

cope with the situation that they hired a certain number of people who most likely have a negative character and hence a tendency for unethical or deviant conduct.

Additionally, as discussed before, moral standards and ethical norms are in reality often differently interpreted and understood in different cultures; as a result, such a static nature would cause considerable problems for companies operating in multicultural environments because the ethical sensitivity toward such diversity as well as the willingness and ability to understand and adapt to a potentially diverging understanding of ethical principles and norms could barely be trained or improved—or not at all.

A dynamic interpretation of character-building and development assumes (Wieland 2014b), however, that this can happen as a result of practical learning processes that take place over a certain period of time and can be purposefully initiated and driven by organizations.

This development process of an individual's character is closely correlated with organizational and societal institutions, since these are constitutional elements of economic and social transactions and exchange, and hence practice. They are an element of the CID or organizational governance and hence a target for interventions from HR or ethics departments that want to develop and shape the character of their members. The virtuous element of the character develops its orientation from this dynamic interplay of these dimensions, as well as the behavioral principles that emerge from moral sanctions and incentives as well as the wish to be a member of a moral community.[12]

In the past, an individual actor had limited options to freely decide whether she or he wants to belong to a specific community with its distinct cultural and ethical norms which then also become the main reference point for building and further developing one's own character. In modern societies, however, the increased levels of contingency and available options for discretionary choices have a considerable influence on the bonding of individual actors to specific values, groups of other human beings, or institutions (Joas 2013). People experience a real increase in possible courses of actions and choices, which is even higher when taking place in various multicultural settings. This does not mean that the good character of an actor is under constant threat to become corroded[13] because of its systematic confrontation with normative offerings and choices that are being provided by a huge variety of different communities and are not necessarily in sync with traditional values or ethical standards. What it means, though, is that the bonds or ties to specific values and virtues that are an element of good character can only be sustained as a kind of "dynamic stability" (Joas 2013, p. 140). This requires constant reflection, negotiation,

[12]For further elaboration of this emergence and the constitution of moral requirements as a rational or prudential must, see Tugendhat (1993) or Stemmer (2000).

[13]Richard Sennett (1999) became well-known for his hypothesis of the corrosion of character that is, i.a., caused by the negative influence of capitalistic institutional settings that are forcing individuals to completely adapt to the flexibility needs of modern capitalistic systems as well as the fragmentation and disintegration of traditional societal systems. Hans Joas (2013) shows very lucidly in his analysis that this negative idea of corrosion is most likely too simplistic in its assumptions and conclusions.

discourse, and empathy with other actors, as well as specific procedures that help develop a shared understanding of what specific values and ethical norms do mean in a dynamic, diverse, and contingent society (Joas 2013; Wieland 2005b).

15.4 Understanding the Meaning of Individual and Corporate Character

In this section, we will move to a deeper level in our analysis with the aim to describe in some more detail what character specifically means at the level of an individual as well as a corporate actor. To begin, we will investigate the meaning of the term 'individual character'.

As we have already alluded to in an earlier section, character is the result of a dynamic process in which the acceptance of social and moral norms as well as a sense of belonging to moral communities become important elements of a person's being and behaving and in which she or he learns to emotionally relate to other beings and to display empathy toward them. Tugendhat (1993) explains in his lecture on virtues that the mechanism of self-binding and commitment to moral rules can then be described as a good character. This good character emerges as a result of learning that is stimulated by applying ethical principles and values as well as by experiencing the results of this application. However, since learning is not a one-way street, this experience can also be of a negative nature and therefore weaken the principally positive nature of a character an individual person has. Central definitional elements of a good character are integrity, honesty, fairness, adherence to commitments made, respect, and self-awareness (Paine 1991; Wieland 2014b). The character to recognize the moral dimension and moral challenges in an economic transaction as well as the skills to use values and ethical principles as the basis for decision-making requires "moral imagination" (Dunham and Werhane 2005; Werhane 1998). In this sense, moral imagination is an element of a virtuous character, since it relates back to the constitutional elements of virtues, which are the willingness and the ability to behave virtuously. Werhane describes three stages of this development: (a) reproductive imagination, (b) productive imagination, and (c) creative imagination.[14] The first stage refers to a person's perception and awareness of a specific moral issue—specifically to the contextual factors affecting the person. At the second stage, a person is able to reframe an issue from different perspectives and to consider new possibilities within the role she or he has. At the third stage, a person has the capabilities and skills to develop morally acceptable or preferable solutions to an ethical challenge. This entails that the solutions are not determined by contextual factors but rather include the perspectives a rational and moral person

[14] The first publication by Werhane on the topic of moral imagination dates to our knowledge back to 1994 and has since then be reprinted or further developed in a number of other publications (Werhane 1998, 1999; Werhane and Moriarty 2009; Dunham and Werhane 2005).

would take (Werhane 1994, p. 22). All three stages can be subject to leadership development strategies and activities. These strategies need to reflect the already described tensions that can arise or already exist in multicultural settings in which ethical agreements are not a given and where moral imagination needs to embrace a diversity of values, views, and opinions.

Moral imagination allows to take a development perspective on moral awareness and behavior, and is hence closely connected to the concept of a dynamic character, as described by Wieland (2014b). It is a concept that allows for a positive perspective since the term 'moral imagination' in itself conveys a message about the possibility to successfully form an image of potential solutions to ethical problems. Both—the development perspective and the positive connotation—build a bridge to a discussion about leadership development that, however, needs to be intentional in terms of integrating such a development goal into respective leadership development programs. This means that the development of a moral imagination will not happen by accident but is the result of a strategic choice of senior management with regard to enabling and fostering ethical conduct:

> Managers can foster more ethical performance, . . . within their organizations by encouraging the development and exercise of moral imagination by their employees. (Dunham and Werhane 2005, p. 11)

In intercultural settings or in a globalized economy, it is of essential importance to develop a common understanding of the meaning and underlying principles of a good character in order to allow, establish, and process successful economic transactions. In a complex and globalized economy, managers are fundamentally expected to master a variety of different languages—economic, moral, technical, social ones (Wieland 2005a, p. 107). These skills that allow managers to generate and stabilize polylingual discourse, to speak the "moral language", and to display social competencies cannot just be expected as a pre-existing condition (Palazzo 2006, p. 32). Although we agree with Donaldson and Dunfee—as a baseline assumption—that individual actors generally "bring with them the underlying senses of what is right and wrong" (Donaldson and Dunfee 1999, p. 27), it is not a given that this basic ethical orientation will come to bear in situations of tough choices if the governance structure—or the corporate character, as we will see later—fosters and further maintains this ethical basis. Specifically in situations of moral ambiguity because of cultural differences, the individual ethical character or ethical orientation will not suffice as the sole guarantor of ethical conduct. On the other hand, if this basic moral orientation or virtuous character of individual actors does not exist, institutions at the corporate and societal level remain empty (Palazzo 2006).[15] From this we can conclude that morality can become an integral part of systems and organizations if these offer the opportunity and individual actors bring the willingness, commitments, and capabilities to display their

[15]Palazzo (2006) illustrates this by pointing to many thinkers in political theory and political philosophy, such as Habermas, Dahrendorf, Rousseau, de Tocqueville, etc.

ethical character as well as to operate with ethical excellence. Building on what Wieland has described, we can see five distinct factors that have an influence on the development of a person's individual character[16]:

1. **Awareness** of the potential moral dimension of a specific transaction or challenge. This awareness does already exist or has been learned and trained.
2. **Perception** of a concrete moral dimension, including the ability to make sense of it.
3. **Acceptance** that an ethical challenge requires specific behavioral choices that are in line with internal values and ethical principles.
4. **Commitment** to take action as an expression of an ethical character in order to address an ethical challenge.
5. **Capabilities and skills** to execute the commitment and to systematically change the ecosystem so as to enable further ethical actions.

A dynamic interpretation of character-building and development assumes (Wieland 2014b), however, that this needs to happen as the result of practical learning processes that take place over a certain period of time and can be purposefully initiated and driven by organizations. However, developing and improving one's character in this sense cannot be done with the classical classroom type of trainings, since these lack the required experiential and practical dimension; hence it is recommendable to consider practical or experiential learning instruments as more promising and appropriate (Stolz et al. 2012).

All the above-mentioned factors are—in a dynamic concept of character—subject to development activities and hence exist within the remit of the training and leadership development activities of a corporate actor. Typically, accountability for such activities is with the Human Resources function that needs to develop a strategic and structured approach on this training and development task in order to build the factors of character mentioned before. We should understand that character—and specifically the related capabilities—is not a commodity but a specific asset that needs to be socially and economically valued. With its constitutional dimensions, character has to be a non-negotiable element of a leader's profile, i.e., all five development elements need to be professionally engrained into all steps and processes of the Human Resources value chain, just like functional or managerial skills are engrained in these processes as well.

[16]With regard to the first four factors, we refer here to Wieland. In-depth research on perception mechanisms and moral awareness can be found in Fürst (2005, 2014a).

15.5 Governance, Culture and Corporate Character

We have seen the importance of the individual character and the ability for moral imagination as an element of ethical leadership and entrepreneurial activity. However, as alluded to a number of times, excellence in ethical leadership can only be realized if the individual character is properly embedded in an organizational culture and a governance structure that build the backbone for good conduct. Such values-based governance (Wieland 2004, 2014a, 2014b; French 1979) allows that transactions with a moral and economic dimension (Fürst 2005) can be effectively and efficiently managed as well as successfully completed. This argument primarily refers to the policies and procedures by which a company meets its societal role—namely the provision of goods and services, and notably not the maximization of shareholder value (Drucker 1973; Heracleous and Lan 2010)[17]—by adhering to ethical standards that companies are measured against. However, ethical and economic performance emerges when ethical and economic leadership based on individual character as well as ethical and corporate governance merge as an expression of the corporate character.

All this opens up a number of different avenues for discussion as to how the corporate and the individual character intersect, how they recursively reinforce each other, how organizational development needs to be seen in the perspective of creating and maintaining the corporate character as an expression of good governance, and how leadership development needs to be conceptualized and institutionalized in order to foster, develop, and strengthen he character and ethical skills of the individual actor within the organization. Of specific relevance is the ability of the management population to transfer ethical awareness and orientation into managerial practice and ethical language that can lead and guide employees as well as relevant other stakeholders. Although it seems like an obvious need, this transfer is not a given, as many practical examples illustrate in which ethics is dissected from the managerial problems, or where ethical criticism is countered with legalistic or narrow economic arguments.[18] In a globalized economy in which the agreement on ethical principles on a theoretical level can easily be found, but where the application of ethical principles is far less obvious and much more ambiguous, leadership development means that organizations need to establish governance mechanisms that allow to build a coherent understanding of the ethical principles the organization stands for and to train managers and leaders on speaking a common moral language that defines the identity of the collective actor. Such a coherent set of values and a distinct moral language structure the perception and interpretation of the world, and thus decisions and behaviors. This

[17]The work of Peter Drucker may serve as an important reference here. More recently, see the short but instructive remarks of Heracleaous et al. titled "The myth of shareholder capitalism".

[18]For a list of examples, see Palazzo (2006).

sense-making is based on cultural patterns, values, or identity semantics of social entities.[19] Perception processes are based on existing values and cultural patterns that describe social entities and define their identity. Such a constructed perceptual process is indispensably and closely linked to the self-description and self-observation of social systems (Fürst 2005; Japp 1996; Douglas and Wildavsky 1982). A process of "sense-making" emerges in organizations, which can be described as a method to search, analyze, and interpret critical changes and subsequently enables individual to take "rational" decisions within the given cultural and institutional framework (Weick 1995). "Sense-making" in the context described here is the construction of an organization's identity and institutionalized self-description; it entails processes that can enable an individual as well as collective actors to perceive ethical and societal challenges in a coherent manner and to develop relevant business strategies to address these challenges. The beliefs and values of a distinct social unit are defined and described in this organizational culture which also enhances internal reliability:

> Organizational cultures can codify the organization's understanding of itself and its environment, and thereby clarify the organization's belief and goals for members. (Sorensen 2002, p. 80)

Distinct institutions represent cultural determinants from the perspectives of systems theory and institutional economics. These determinants shape specific behavioral dispositions and constitute an environment that provides individuals with a certain degree of reliability and safety, as they understand what is expected and how they should decide from an ethical, legal, or economic point of view. The establishment of distinct institutional settings (values, morals, interpretation patterns, policies, etc.) leads to the emergence of a kind of "collective mind" (Weick and Roberts 1993) that represents perception, interpretation, and behavior patterns of individual as well as collective actors and thus determines the perception and selection of distinct opportunities.Belief systems work like glasses, i.e. on the one hand, they allow for distinct perceptions of issues and sharpen the view on these, but on the other hand, they literally tune out issues and realities that are outside of scope. In the context described here, the relevant belief systems work like sustainability glasses, meaning that an organization is enabled to perceive societal challenges as existing as well as relevant and to subsequently develop appropriate strategies and social business models to manage these challenges successfully and sustainably.

In conjunction with theoretical considerations in the New Institutional Economics and Organizational Economics, we can say that each company owns an organization-specific "shared mental model" (Denzau and North 1994) that represents and determines patterns of

[19] See the work of Weick on the topic of "sensemaking in organizations" (Weick et al. 2005; Weick and Roberts 1993; Weick 1995).

perception and behavior (Schlicht 2008).[20] Institutionalization means in this context that a consensus on behavioral expectations exists in each organizational entity. Establishing perception routines as a crystallization of cultural patterns is a central process in the context of leadership development. As a collective actor, a company maintains and conveys perception patterns by its own cultural preferences and institutional settings; the task is to establish organizational governance and learning so that societal challenges can be seen through such sustainability glasses, so they can be interpreted in a coherent manner with the goal to find ethical solutions to ethical issues.

This line of argument is based on the assumption that the world is understood only through a construction process and that this in turn is differentiated and determined through different cultural types. Leadership development can only succeed if value systems exist in the organization that shape specific perceptual patterns, and if such a social entrepreneurial venture is within the "zone of acceptance" (Barnard 1938) of a collective actor. This informal institutional setting is to be strengthened by establishing distinct formal governance structures that encourage and incentivize the desired behavior. The informal and formal institutional layers work reciprocally and reinforce the intended pattern of perception in a recursive process. It is known from the risk research done in cultural sociology that the perception bias of an organization is processed by using the distinction of accepting and rejecting information. Information which fits into the framework of values or of the cultural setting is perceived as acceptable, whereas information that is not compatible with the specific organizational bias and thus is outside the "zone of acceptance" is typically rejected. The permanent repetition of accepting or rejecting information culturally solidifies perceptual episodes into perception patterns of a collective actor (Japp 1996).

To summarize, we can say that institutional settings, values, and cultural patterns shape the positive or negative perception of information. This means that specific governance structures of an organization that are part of a leadership development strategy should enable its members to recognize the ethical dimension of managerial issues and to successfully engage in and solve such issues (Stolz et al. 2012). This is about the design of the context and about "choosing preferences by constructing institutions" (Wildavsky 1987), p. 1).

Hence, the formation of character takes place as an interplay of these different levels as a dynamic process without knowing whether the results will be as expected, i.e., a prediction of a positive determination is not possible. Governance structures are the obvious expression of corporate character and display the willingness as well as the capabilities of an organization to behave in line with its moral commitments.

---

[20] Schlicht (2008, p. 14) references (Isaac et al. 1991): "... firms and other institutions provide institutional frames which activate certain types of behavior rather than others."

15.6 Character, Leadership and Ethical Conduct

In this chapter, we try to amalgamate the analysis from the previous chapters and describe in more detail how the characters of the individual and the collective actor relate to the theme of leadership, as this topic obviously has a strong relevance with regard to enabling and ensuring ethical conduct. As we have seen, the willingness and ability of an individual actor to systematically reflect and to professionally deal with ethical conflicts, different cultural dispositions and traditions—as to what the application of an ethical principle or value means in a situation of tough choice—is an expression of character. Taking decisions in situations of tough choices or dilemma situations is particularly challenging and requires a strength of character, since these situations cannot be solved but only managed in the best possible manner. Deciding on conflicts of interests or on conflicting values is different, as rationale decision algorithms can be applied that are guided by governance elements such as value management systems, Codes of Ethics, policies, incentives structures, etc. They all have the goal to guide, channel, restrain behavior and preventively activate good conduct—but also to stimulate innovation that is based on breaking up with established but unethical behavior that is now recognized to not be longer acceptable or in line with future-oriented ethical principles. From an organizational perspective, these governance elements have the objective to safeguard the ability of an organization to behave in line with its corporate character and to accomplish its business objectives in line with ethical values and principles that find a positive echo in societal discourse and are aligned with societal expectations. Bearing that in mind, the character of a collective actor represents an important structure that constitutes a supporting individual motivation, as a result increases the likelihood of successful ethical transactions, and intensifies the functional effect of the individual character (Wieland 2004; French 1979).

Of course, this is a reciprocal relationship, i.e., the collective actor is also dependent on the willingness of the individual actor to behave virtuously in order to accomplish their organizational ethical principles and economic goals. In this sense, the individual and the corporate character relate to each other as reinforcing constituents and simultaneously operating elements of good conduct (Fürst 2014a). Leadership development aims to create a cadre of ethical leaders who display the foundational elements of good character that have been described above These leaders (a) lead by example, (b) proactively communicate a position and point of view that others would ethically deem desirable, and (c) establish and maintain an ethical governance.

Such a development effort will only lead to results if the strategy is simultaneously focusing on training the "ethical muscle" of leaders to take ethical decisions and at the same time develop their understanding, competence, and skills to create an organizational character by building an organizational ecosystem or governance that works in conjunction with individual ethical ambitions and skills across all different hierarchical levels of an organization. This needs to result in higher levels of awareness and reflection about the ethical and economic interest of relevant stakeholders, in the ability to differentiate legitimate from non-legitimate interests, and eventually to decide according to the company's own ethical principles and expectations of society at large, as well as, even more importantly, affected stakeholder groups.

In a globalized economy that is often ambiguous in terms of ethical expectations and cultural norms with an impact on business transactions, such an awareness and skills set is the fundament for business leaders to formulate ethical positions on a considerable variety of different issues that are affecting a business but cannot just be solved or addressed by applying narrow economic codings, principles, or language. This development task also needs to include the transfer of these skills to the wider management population and to influence their creative capabilities. Leaders who develop such character and take the transfer of such a diverse skills set seriously display "leadership excellence".[21] The definition of excellence in leadership is then—according to Wieland—the result of the interplay between motivation and structure, the generation, activation, and integration of formal (e.g. policies, values management systems, etc.) and informal governance structures (e.g. company culture), as well as the alignment with societal standards (Wieland 2014b, p. 390). How important leadership and organizational structures are can be illustrated when looking at the "fuzzy logic" of values (Wieland 2014b): In theory, it is relatively easy to agree on the abstract meaning of ethical values and principles. It is, however, not necessarily clear how these values and principles should be applied and which practical consequences have to be drawn from such norms in a specific situation that is sometimes defined by disagreement rather than agreement.

Ethical behavior that is derived from moral principles is very often anything but self-evident, even when the norms seem to be absolutely clear in theory or on an abstract level. What a locally acceptable moral decision in such dilemmas requires is on the one hand the capability to jointly develop a concrete proposal with regard to what results from ethical norms in an empirical context of a concrete local application. On the other hand, it requires the emotional and cognitive willingness to behave ethically and to take responsibility for a local decision. The truth of the matter is that in most situations, the willingness to take responsibility for the application of an ethical norm in a local situation also implies to accept negative effects, since these are situations of tough choices or dilemmas in which ideal solutions can never be created or achieved for systematic reasons.

From an ethical leadership point of view, this means that leaders need to systematically engage in a dialogue to actually debate and determine in which way a specific situation where two ethical norms are in conflict needs to be managed with the aim to have a morally preferable situation. The development of a moral character and leadership quality is not a static condition but a constant development process with the final objective to generate an economic and societal value for the stakeholders involved. As already mentioned earlier,

[21] We borrow this term from Josef Wieland (e.g. 2014b) and the comprehensive literature he has published on this topic.

character is nothing that a person inherits or that stays unchanged over time—it is a dynamic asset companies need to develop and evolve so as to benefit from the economic and ethical value virtuous behavior can generate.

Leadership development needs to consider a number of topics: First and foremost, the focus of the development activities needs to change from just paying attention to how leaders can avoid unethical conduct or deviant behavior of their own or of the organization, to also developing and training the skills of leaders to promote and enable ethical conduct or to develop positive contributions of business to societal problems—both arising from the moral imagination a leader should own. In practical terms, this means that leaders have a responsibility for avoiding negative effects on society that are caused by corporate activities, even if these are carried out within the existing legal framework. Secondly, leaders need to own the awareness and skills to enable their companies to work together with other stakeholders within innovative and cooperative frameworks in order to solve societal problems. Therefore, it is imperative to integrate the concept of the positive social impact into the leadership development strategies and activities of global companies that have an enormous influence in societal debates and can positively shape governance in a globalized economy. The aim of such a development effort is then (a) to create a corporate character and a way of being that enables corporate leaders to specifically target societal problems and to create such positive contributions, and (b) to foster cooperation between business and society, as well as through the creation of purpose-driven and impact-oriented business solutions. As mentioned before, this means that leaders do not just need to develop this awareness and the skills but also the governance for the collective actor that allows the execution of good corporate conduct at the corporate level and in a sustainable mode.[22] These training and development activities need to address a number of important topics, such as moral imagination; the application of ethical principles in ambiguous situations and dilemmas; the development of perception mechanisms in the organization that will help establish shared mental models (Fürst 2005, 2014a); an incentives structure that prevents unethical conduct, enables ethical behavior, and stimulates positive contributions to societal problems; and lastly the ability to find ethical consensus in a multicultural setting in which the agreement on ethical issues is not necessarily a given but needs to be built through ethical discourse and the quest for ethically preferable solutions.

15.7 Individual and Corporate Character in a Globalized, Multicultural World

In previous chapters, we have discussed the interconnectedness and interplay between the individual and the corporate character as well as the mechanisms that are required to enable ethical conduct within organizations as well as between organizations and related

[22] We have already argued for this enrichment of the business ethics debate on the social dimension in previous articles (Fürst 2011, 2014b, 2017; Fürst and Schotter 2013).

stakeholders. An additional layer of complexity comes into play when we discuss this in the context of a globalized, multicultural world and economy in which mutual benefit can only arise if different stakeholders with sometimes very diverse cultural backgrounds cooperate and work toward a jointly agreed goal. When we refer to cultures in this context, we go beyond the cultural differences one can find between countries or regions but also include industry-sector-specific cultures, company cultures, and specific community cultures that can, e.g., manifest themselves along choices of lifestyles, demography, gender, religious orientations, etc. All of this can have an impact on the efficiency and effectiveness of a specific transaction that has to be managed.[23] The individual and corporate actors now need to invest their individual resources into "transaction-specific communities" (Wieland and Baumann-Montecinos 2019) or projects that can only become effective and productive if the involved parties can find commonalities and an ethical baseline that will then be sustained over time as part of a joint journey of learning. Besides what has already been discussed before, we need to further analyze which factors actually contribute to the creation of these commonalities and which leadership competences are required in a globalized context. In focus here are "pro-social skills such as empathy or inclusive rationality that can be attributed to all humans and that pave the way for the emergence of a transaction-related community in concrete cooperation projects" (Wieland and Baumann-Montecinos 2019, p. 13).

Inclusive rationality in a multicultural setting or transaction cannot be successfully built on the assumption that an agreement on abstract values would be sufficient to create this commonality just because stakeholders would agree with the universal meaning of these values. Solutions to ethical disagreements and tensions rather requires discourse and an attempt to create a local, context-specific or "thick" understanding or interpretation of values that different stakeholders can temporarily agree on.[24] To successfully manage this discourse and to create such agreement requires character from individual actors and for the corporate actor and its leadership development programs this means that respective programs and activities need to establish systems, processes—or more generally—the governance structures (or CID) that allow to learn how to establish this temporary commonality. From a theoretical perspective, we have argued that a virtuous character establishes itself through interactions and practicing; any leadership development activity that aims to develop such virtuous character needs to provide a platform and a structure for learning by practicing, which then allows to establish valid, "thick" normative principles that become routines in behavior within a transcultural community. The sustained effectiveness of these jointly developed and agreed normative principles is dependent on the existence of moral awareness, shared perception patterns, the trained skills to manage

[23]This wide scope is the rationale for Josef Wieland calling it transcultural leadership, since the culture concept cuts across numerous different cultures that have to be managed simultaneously (Wieland and Baumann-Montecinos 2019).

[24]We refer here to the Michael Walzer's (1994) distinction of "thick" and "thin" cultures.

ethically challenging situations, and to establish a supportive ecosystem that enables community members to apply the norms as well.

Given the dynamic developments in modern societies, it seems obvious, though, that the previously described situation cannot be thought of as an equilibrium that can be established once and then just be maintained. It is rather a situation of permanent change driven by heterogeneity in which real character and leadership manifests itself in the mastery to understand and manage this heterogeneity through constant learning and the solutions-oriented application of normative principles, without ignoring that morals and values have a disputatious dimension that needs to be considered. Hence this mastery is not about deducing irrevocable normative principles and fundamental definitions of values, but about applying the basic elements of character—willingness and ability to behave ethically—in order to constantly seek a real-world solution to a real-world ethical problem. This solution-seeking journey is not limited to avoiding negative impacts on relevant stakeholders, but, as illustrated earlier and elsewhere, needs to be strongly oriented toward innovation and value-creation opportunities (Fürst 2011, 2014b, 2017). The importance of leadership in this journey has been described by Chester Barnard in "The Function of the Executive":

> The limitations imposed by the physical environment and the biological constitution of human beings, the uncertainties of the outcome of cooperation, the difficulties of common understanding of purpose, the delicacy of the systems of communication essential to organization, the dispersive tendencies of individuals, the necessity of individual assent to establish the authority for coordination, the great role of persuasion in securing adherence to organization and submission to its requirements, the complexity and instability of motives, the never-ending burden of decision—all these elements of organization, in which the moral factor finds its concrete expression, spell the necessity of leadership, the power of individuals to inspire cooperative personal decision by creating faith. (Barnard 1938, p. 259)

We agree with Josef Wieland that companies are relational networks into which stakeholders invest their resources so as to enable more efficient transactions, economic cooperation, and joint value creation. The implication of such a conceptualization is that cultural competences as described above are a resource that can be possessed by either individual actors or corporate actors. Leadership then means to create voluntary followership in diverse cultural communities, to mobilize these intangible resources without having formal or directive authority over the stakeholders that own them, and to enable the most productive allocation of these resources into value-creating opportunities which are—to be very clear—a result of cooperation and not leadership itself, although leadership is required as the "indispensable fulminator of its forces", as Chester Barnard (1938, p. 259) clearly pointed out. To a community, leaders create a sense of belonging with reciprocal dependencies that arise and persist in local situations and local transactions. They display character that has a motivational power for their followers; they create meaning and a sense of purpose; and they can productively relate and tie organizational strategies to societal expectations and discourse. This ethical dimension of character and leadership is a key ingredient for the endurance of organizations that are dependent on the "morality by which they are governed" (Barnard 1938, p. 259).A leadership concept that is built on the premises that leadership entails virtuous character then has transformational power, since it is not just based on a one-way leaders-to-followers relationship, but systematically integrates a reciprocal relationship that can reinforce ethical conduct in both ways:

> Transformational leadership occurs when one or more persons engage with others in such a way that leaders and followers raise one another to higher levels of motivation and morality. (Burns 1978, p. 20)

References

Barnard, C. I. (1938). The Functions of the Executive. Boston: Harvard University Press.

Beschorner, T. (2013). Kulturalistische Wirtschaftsethik. Grundzüge einer Theorie der Anwendung. Zeitschrift für Wirtschafts- und Unternehmensethik, 14(3), 346–377.

Burns, J. M. (1978). Leadership. New York: Harper.

Denzau, A. T., & North, D. C. (1994). Shared Mental Models: Ideologies and Institutions. Kyklos, 47(1), 3–31.

Donaldson, Th., & Dunfee, T. W. (1999). Ties that Bind. A social contracts approach to business ethics. Boston: Harvard Business School Press.

Douglas, M., & Wildavsky, A. (1982). Risk and Culture (1st ed.). Berkeley: University of California Press.

Drucker, P. (1973). Management: Tasks, Responsibilities and Practices. New York: Harper Paperbacks.

Dunham, L., & Werhane, P. H. (2005). Moral Imagination: A Bridge Between Ethics and Entrepreneurship. Darden Graduate School of Business, Working Paper No. 00-04.

French, P. (1979). The corporation as a moral person. American Philosophical Quarterly, 16(3), 207–215.

Fürst, M. (2017). Just When You Thought It Couldn't Get Worse, You Hear: "The Business of Business Is Business" – Some Reflections on a Self-Fulfilling Prophecy and Alternative Perspectives on the Purpose of Companies. In J. Wieland (Ed.), Creating Shared Value -- Concepts, Experience, Criticism (pp. 55–77). Cham: Springer International Publishing.

Fürst, M. (2014a). „Ich sehe was, was Du nicht siehst!" Das Problem der Risikowahrnehmung als vernachlässigte Dimension in der Compliance-Forschung. In J. Wieland, R. Steinmeyer, & St. Grüninger (Eds.), Handbuch Compliance Management (2nd ed.) (pp. 501–526). Berlin: E. Schmidt.

Fürst, M. (2014b). Opening the Door to Opportunities: How to Design CR Strategies that Optimize Impact for Business and Society. In C. Weidinger, F. Fischler, & R. Schmidpeter (Eds.), Sustainable Entrepreneurship (pp. 265–268). Heidelberg: Springer.

Fürst, M. (2011). Nachhaltig Wert schaffen durch soziales Unternehmertum. Corporate Citizenship, Governanceethik und die Theorie der Firma im Kontext moderner Gesellschaften. In M. Fürst, St. Grüninger, M. Schmiedeknecht, & S. Pforr (Eds.), Verantwortung in der globalen Ökonomie gestalten (pp. 249–278). Marburg: Metropolis.

Fürst, M. (2005). Risiko Governance. Die Wahrnehmung und Steuerung moralökonomsicher Risiken. Marburg: Metropolis.

Fürst, M., & Schotter, A. (2013). Strategic integrity management as a dynamic capability. In T. Wilkinson & A. Thomas (Eds.), Strategic Management in the 21st Century (pp. 1–35). Westport: Praeger.

Homann, K., & Suchanek, A. (2005). Ökonomik eine Einführung. Neue ökonomische Grundrisse. Tübingen: Mohr Siebeck

Heracleous, L. & Lan, L. L. (2010). The Myth of Shareholder Capitalism. Harvard Business Review 88 (April): 24

Japp, K. P. (1996). Soziologische Risikotheorie. Funktionale Differenzierung, Politisierung und Reflexion. Weinheim: Juventa.

Joas, H. (2013). Glaube als Option. Zukunftsmöglichkeiten des Christentums. Freiburg, Basel, Wien: Herder.

Karl E. Weick, Kathleen M. Sutcliffe, David Obstfeld (2005) Organizing and the Process of Sensemaking. Organization Science 16(4) 409-421 https://doi.org/10.1287/orsc.1050.0133

R. Mark Isaac, Deborah Mathieu, Edward E. Zajac (1991) Institutional framing and perceptions of fairness. Constitutional Political Economy 2(3) 329-370 https://doi.org/10.1007/BF02393135

Paine, L. S. (2002). Bad people don't have a monopoly on bad deeds: taking an organizational approach to ethics. The Federal Bank of Boston, Regional Review, 12 (Dec. 2001), 6–8.

Paine, L. S. (1994). Managing for organizational integrity. Harvard Business Review, 72 (2), 106–117.

Paine, L. S. (1991). Ethics as Character Development: Reflections on the Objective of Ethics Education. In R. Freeman (Ed.): Business Ethics: The State of the Art (pp. 67–85). New York: Oxford University Press.

Palazzo, G. (2006). Die Rückkehr des Individuums in die Governanceethik. In J. Wieland (Ed.), Die Tugend der Governance (pp. 31–50). Marburg: Metropolis.

Pfriem, R. (2008). Vom Sollen zum können Wollen. Auf dem Wege zu einer kulturalistischen Unternehmensethik und Unternehmenstheorie. In A. G. Scherer & M. Patzer (Eds.), Betriebswirtschaftslehre und Unternehmensethik (pp. 65–84). Wiesbaden: Gabler.

Rorty, R. (1998). Human Rights, Rationality, and Sentimentality. In R. Rorty: Truth and Progress (pp. 167–185). Cambridge: Cambridge University Press.

Schlicht, E. (2008). Consistency in Organization. Journal of Institutional and Theoretical Economics, 164(4), 612.

Sennett, R. (1999). The Corrosion of Character. New York: W. W. Norton

Soares, C. (2003). Corporate Versus Individual Moral Responsibility. Journal of Business Ethics 46, 143–150.

Sorensen, J. B. (2002): The Strength of Corporate Culture and the Reliability of Firm Performance. Administrative Science Quarterly, Vol. 47, No. 1, pp. 970 – 91.

Stemmer, P. (2000). Handeln zugunsten anderer. Eine moralphilosophische Untersuchung. Eine moralphilosophische Untersuchung. Berlin: Walter de Gruyter.

Stolz, I., Fürst, M., & Mundle, D. (2012). Managing strategic corporate citizenship at Novartis. In Th. Wehner, G.-C. Gentile (Eds.): Corporate Volunteering im Spannungsfeld von Effizienz und Ethik (pp. 250–260). Wiesbaden: Springer.

Trevino, L. K., Weaver, G. R., & Reynolds, J. S. (2006). Behavioral Ethics in Organizations: A Review. Journal of Management, 32(6), 951–990.

Tugendhat, E. (1993). Vorlesungen über Ethik (Wissenschaft). Frankfurt a. Main: Suhrkamp.

Ulrich, P. (2008). Integrative economic ethics: Foundations of a civilized market economy. Cambridge: Cambridge University Press.

Walzer, M. (1994). Thick and Thin: moral argument at home and abroad. Notre Dame: University of Notre Dame Press.

Weick, K. E. (1995). Sense-Making in Organizations. Thousands Oaks: Sage.

Weick, K. E., & Roberts, K. H. (1993). Collective mind in organizations: Heedful interrelating on flight decks. Administrative Science Quarterly, 38, 357–381.

Werhane, P. H. (1999). Moral Imagination and Management Decision-Making. New York: Oxford University Press.

Werhane, P. H. (1994). Moral imagination and the search for ethical decision-making in management. The Ruffin Lectures in Business Ethics. Charlottesville, VA: The Darden School, University of Virginia.

Werhane, P. H. (1998). Moral imagination and the search for ethical decision-making in management. Business Ethics Quarterly, Volume 8 (1), pp. 75–98

Werhane, P. H., & Moriarty, B. (2009): Moral Imagination and Management Decision Making. Business Roundtable Institute for Corporate Ethics. Retrieved from http://www.corporate-ethics.org/pdf/moral_imagination.pdf

Wieland, J. (2014a). Governance ethics: Global value creation, economic organization and creativity. Heidelberg, New York: Springer.

Wieland, J. (2014b). Moralische Charakterbildung, Leadership Excellence und Corporate Character. Wirtschafts- und Unternehmensethik, 15(3), 376–397.

Wieland, J. (2006). Die Tugend der Governance. Reflexion und Kritik, 22, 12. Retrieved from http://www.htwg-konstanz.de/KIeM-Working-Paper-Series.2850.0.html

Wieland, J. (2005a). Governanceethik und moralische Anreize. In: Beschorner, Th., König, M., Schumann, O.J. (Hrsg.): Wirtschafts- und Unternehmensethik. Rückblick, Ausblick, Perspektiven. München/Mering: Hampp, S.251-280.

Wieland, J. (2005b). Normativität und Governance. Gesellschaftstheoretische und philosophische Reflexionen der Governanceethik. Marburg: Metropolis.

Wieland, J. (2004). Die Ethik der Governance. Marburg: Metropolis.

Wieland, J. (2003). Die Tugend kollektiver Akteure. In J. Wieland (Ed.), Die moralische Verantwortung kollektiver Akteure (pp. 22–40). Heidelberg: Physica.

Wieland, J., & Baumann-Montecinos, J. (2019). A Competence-based Approach to Transcultural Leadership – Introduction to a Research Program. In J. Wieland & J. Baumann-Montecinos (Eds.), Transcultural Leadership and Transcultural Competence (pp. 11–20). Marburg: Metropolis.

Wildavsky, A. (1987). Choosing Preferences by Constructing Institutions: A Cultural Theory of Preference Formation. American Political Science Review, Volume 81, Issue 1, March 1987, pp. 3–21.

"Worthy of Trust": What a Leader Should Do in Order to be Considered a Trusted Leader

16

Nuntana Udomkit and Claus Schreier

16.1 Introduction

Globalization and the fast-paced changes of the twenty-first century have led to external and internal challenges in the field of international management and leadership. For many firms, internationalization would seem an inevitable path to follow. Therefore, they will have to deal with businesses they may never have dealt with, or which they hardly know. Moreover, they will more likely have to deal with a diverse workforce and its corresponding diversity in terms of gender, age, ethnicity, nationalities, education, languages, cultures, beliefs, and norms.

The term VUCA (an acronym for volatility, uncertainty, complexity, and ambiguity) is being commonly applied to twenty-first century business environments (Gläser 2020). This VUCA-shaped business environment has shaken our sense of stability. It has affected the level of trust within organizations, has complicated the leadership decision-making process, and has affected the leaders' ability to steer a business through these diverse and ambiguous situations (Burke et al. 2007; Huntsman and Greer 2019). Moreover, in extreme situations such as crisis management during the Covid-19 pandemic, trust in leaders is tremendously important; it helps stabilize turbulence, uncertainties, and complexity and ensures that a leader continues to have a considerable managerial impact.

The concept of trust has been discussed throughout a wide range of literature, from philosophy to sociology, psychology, politics, law, leadership, management, and business

N. Udomkit · C. Schreier (✉)
Business Administration Division, Mahidol University International College, Mahidol University, Salaya, Nakhon Pathom, Thailand
e-mail: nuntana.udo@mahidol.edu; claus.sch@mahidol.edu

I. Stolz, S. Oldenziel Scherrer (eds.), *International Leadership*, uniscope. Publikationen der SGO Stiftung, https://doi.org/10.1007/978-3-658-37306-1_16

administration. From a business perspective, trust has proven to be one of the key elements for a successful partnership and for motivating productive working relationships (Bigne and Blesa 2003; Brenkert 1998; Child and Hsieh 2014; Gambetta 1988). Trust between international business partners facilitates network development and evokes positive emotions such as a sense of security in a situation of vulnerability; it can also help reduce uncertainty. Perceived trustworthiness can also reduce transaction costs and correlates with wider information-sharing (Child and Hsieh 2014; Dyer and Chu 2000).

Baldoni (2008) has emphasized that leaders who cannot inspire trust cannot truly lead. Many successful business leaders have also confirmed the importance and necessity of building trust. For example, Jack Welch, the former CEO of General Electric, has stated that

> Leaders establish trust with candor, transparency, and credit.
> (Quoted in Severson n.d.)

Dara Khosrowshahi, the current CEO of Uber, emphasized the importance of trustworthiness when connecting with his team in the following statement:

> The higher up in the chain of command you are, the harder it is to really know what's going on, so you have to discover the right information out of your people. You have to be great at reading body language and asking questions. You have to engender trust to get to the real stuff. Leaders who are disconnected with reality are the ones who fail.
> (Quoted in Chchrazi 2017)

Marc Benioff, Chair and CEO of Salesforce, shared his insights on trust:

> Trust is the glue that holds successful relationships between companies and their stakeholders together ... Nothing is more important than the trust we have with our employees, our customers, our partners with our industry and our local communities – all of our stakeholders. We operationalize the idea of trust. We want to have it, and we don't want to lose it ... We realize that if our customers don't trust us, they're not going to continue to invest with us. And trust can also relate to employees. Employees aren't going to stay with our company if they don't trust us. You can actually put trust at the top of your corporate policies and operationalize it.
> (Quoted in Salesforce n.d.)

It goes without saying that trust is an invaluable asset of both an individual person and organizations. Although many competent leaders can be found in workplaces out there, the hard reality is that not all of them are trustworthy. This chapter aims at unveiling the traits that denote the trustworthiness of a leader. We will begin with exploring the existing literature on the constituents of trustworthiness, after which the interview background will be explained. The last part will deal with the key findings obtained from the interviews.

16.2 Constituents of Trustworthiness

A number of inter- and intra-firm trust studies have been conducted to explore the constituents of trust. Blomqvist and Ståhle (2000) defined trust as an actor's expectation of the other party's competence, goodwill, and behavior. Along the same lines, Frankel (2005) viewed trust as the reasonable belief that trusted persons (Amadeo 2020) tell the truth and (Ambrose and Schminke 2003) keep their promises.

McKnight and Chervany (2001) identified four categories of trust characteristics, namely benevolence, integrity, competence, and predictability. By the same token, Dyer and Chu (2000) indicated that inter-firm trust is based on three interrelated components: reliability, fairness, and goodwill/benevolence. More recently, Frei and Morriss (2020) emphasized that trust is a foundational leadership concept:

> People tend to trust you when they believe they are interacting with the real you (authenticity), when they have faith in your judgment and competence (logic), and when they feel that you care about them (empathy).

Udomkit et al. (2019) proposed three components of trust, namely competence and professionalism, honesty and integrity, and empathy and caring. They stated that competency is a basic requirement for trust formation when starting a business, and has to be consistent throughout time. Honesty and integrity as well as empathy and caring are viewed by business partners as resulting in a higher level of trust. This is in line with Blomqvist's (1997) findings that in a business context, both the competence and goodwill levels are necessary traits for trust to develop. Possessing the relevant competence (technical capabilities, skills, and know-how) is also a necessary antecedent and basis for trust in professional relationships in a business context. The existence of goodwill (moral responsibility and positive intentions towards the other party) is also deemed a necessary trait before the trusting party undertakes a potentially vulnerable position.

Green and Howe (2011) looked at how trustworthiness is measured. They quantified trust and developed a self-assessment that measures an individual's "trust quotient" which is composed of four attributes, namely: credibility (what you say and how credible you are to others), reliability (your actions and how reliable you appear), intimacy (how safe people feel about sharing their ideas with you), and self-orientation (a personal focus, e.g. from the viewpoint of yourself or others). They concluded that credibility, reliability, and intimacy improve trustworthiness, whereas too much self-orientation will lower the degree of trustworthiness.

Zenger and Folkman (2019) analyzed over 80,000 "360-degree" reviews and found three elements that predict whether a leader can be trusted—by focusing on direct reports, peers, and other colleagues. These are (Amadeo 2020) positive relationships, (Ambrose and Schminke 2003) consistency, and (Bies and Moag 1986) good judgment/expertise. Since trust is an important asset in any organization, they believe that therefore, it is worth investing time and effort into building it up by focusing on these three elements. A leader must be able to create positive relationships with other people and groups, as well as being well-informed and knowledgeable. They must understand the technical aspects of their work, as well as having in-depth experience. Last but not least, a leader must walk their talk and carry out what they say they will do.

16.3 Diversity and Trust-Building

As a consequence of globalization, as well as of international expansion, firms have to deal with a vast diversity in their workforce in terms of gender, age, ethnicity, nationalities, education, languages, cultures, beliefs, and norms. Previous research has proven that diversity can be a source of competitive advantage, an invaluable asset to a firm, if it is managed properly. It can bring about synergies, creativity, and increase opportunities for knowledge and innovation (Saxena 2014; Frei and Morriss 2020). Frei and Morriss (2020) discussed the challenges of creating an atmosphere of trust that allows diverse team members to bring their unique perspectives and experiences to the table. However, they also pointed out "the pitfall of the common information effect", namely that

> [a]s human beings, we tend to focus on the things we have in common with other people. We tend to seek out and affirm our shared knowledge, because it confirms our value and kinship with the group. Diverse teams, by definition, have less common information readily available to them to use in collective decision-making.

As a consequence, diverse teams could end up underperforming homogenous teams if the differences between members are not managed well (Frei and Morriss 2020).

These findings are supported by a study conducted by Schreier et al. (2019) that examined required competencies for managing workforce diversity in Swiss-based multinational enterprises. They found that the ability to build relationships and to create "an atmosphere of trust" are the most important traits that diverse team members would expect to see in their leader. Other competencies also stand out: knowledge/skills necessary for the job/position; the ability to set clear structures, yet allow team members the freedom to work and make own decisions; awareness of their strengths and weaknesses; a willingness to learn/improve; fair judgment in evaluating themselves as well as others; open-mindedness; empathy; and supporting any changes needed for the team.

Interestingly, Schreier et al. (2019) highlighted the gaps in the expectations of the required competencies from the perspectives of managers and team members—so as to ensure the success of the team. Managers mentioned a wider spectrum of leadership and intrapersonal skills, namely, an understanding of their strengths and weaknesses, a willingness to learn and continuously improve themselves, the ability to evaluate themselves as well as others in a fair manner, empathy, a tolerance for other people's opinions, and self-confidence in allowing and supporting any changes needed for the team. The team members, on the other hand, regarded general business skills as being important management soft skills. They expected their leaders to have both good mentoring and coaching skills. They emphasized that the leaders should also be aware of their own strengths and weaknesses, and that they ought to create an atmosphere of trust. They stressed that their manager must have the ability to build relationships and trust in order to foster a team spirit within the team, to approach and promote inclusivity, and to have empathy. From a team members' perspective, managing relationships and building an atmosphere of trust are the most important traits a manager needs to possess (Schreier et al. 2019).

16.4 The Emphasis on Moral and Relational Traits

Literature on leadership has shed light on hidden, but critical traits of trusted leaders. Besides competency, there are ethical/moral traits as well as relational parts that constitute trust.

Warren Buffett advises leaders to weigh integrity above all traits. He stated:

> We look for three things when we hire people. We look for intelligence, we look for initiative or energy, and we look for integrity. And if they don't have the latter, the first two will kill you, because if you're going to get someone without integrity, you want them lazy and dumb...
>
> When you hire someone with integrity, it makes it hard to question a person's decisions. And colleagues and co-workers of such hires will quickly see them as dependable and accountable for their actions, which is a laser path to developing team trust.
>
> (Quoted in Schwantes 2020)

The Cambridge Dictionary defines integrity as "the quality of being honest and having strong moral principles that you refuse to change". It is a quality of honesty, fairness, openness, transparency, and inclusiveness (Gambetta 1988; Frankel 2005; Wicks et al. 1999). Highly trusted leaders honor their word, do what they say, and remain consistent. If they fail to do so, they are honest about it, they accept, apologize, and improve (Huntsman and Greer 2019).

Fairness has also been shown to be an important moral quality desired in trusted leaders (Ambrose and Schminke 2003; Dirks and Ferrin 2002; Huntsman and Greer 2019). Dirks and Ferrin (2002) noted that perceived fairness in leaders' practices or decisions will influence the level of trust in their leadership. They can be judged through different dimensions, such as fairness of outcomes and pay or promotion (Folger and Konovsky 1989), by their consistent application of policies and procedures (Konovsky and Pugh 1994), and by how fairly members are treated at an interpersonal level (Bies and Moag 1986).

Interrelated with fair judgment, highly trusted leaders are open and receptive to different opinions and feedback (Flinchbaugh 2019). Trusted leaders facilitate dialogue and are great listeners. They can justify and communicate the rationale behind their decisions rather than hiding or manipulating situations. Flinchbaugh (2019) and Hurley (2012) emphasized how important highly trusted leaders' ability is to explain the "why" behind their decisions, and to communicate the reasons behind the decisions openly and honestly. This will help create a mutual or better understanding, which can build up trust—even if they disagree with the leaders' decisions.

Besides moral traits, much of the research found important relational characteristics in highly trusted leaders—such as being mindful in their dealings with people, as well as being able to listen, look, contemplate, pause, and tolerate—as prerequisites for discussing, agreeing, or disagreeing and responding with empathy (Brower et al. 2000; Colquitt et al. 2011; McAllister 1995; Whitener et al. 1998).

Studies show that leaders engaging in benevolent behaviors influence the extent to which they engender trust (Brower et al. 2000; Mayer et al. 1995; Whitener et al. 1998). Benevolence commonly refers to the degree in which members consider a leader to demonstrate genuine care and authentic concerns (Burke et al. 2007). Leaders must show consideration and display sensitivity towards members' needs, interests, and welfare, as well as refraining from exploiting others for their own personal benefit. Leaders should be able to step into someone else's shoes and understand their perspective (Brower et al. 2000). Highly trusted leaders develop a closer relationship with their team members—based on goodwill, knowledge about the technical aspects of the job, and being receptive to members' ideas or suggestions (Whitener et al. 1998).

A confirmation of the importance of the benevolence trait in highly trusted leaders can be found in thc rcscarch of Huntsman and Greer (2019) on the antecedents of trust in leadership in high-risk and high-stress jobs. They highlighted that the personnel of fire departments trust leaders who form social exchanges and relationships with members based on emotional support, assistance, role-modeling, goodwill, competence, and demonstrating cooperative behavior.

16.5 Our Interview Setting

We interviewed five international Chief Executive Officers and Managing Directors of successful international firms, who shared their experiences and views on the trustworthiness traits of a trusted leader.

Leader 1 is the CEO and a founder of an international legal consulting firm.
Leader 2 is the Managing Director and a founder of a global investment firm.
Leader 3 is the South East Asia Managing Director of an Austrian multinational firm.
Leader 4 is the Asia Regional Director of a leading American global sourcing firm.
Leader 5 is a partner of an international management consulting firm.

Their ages range from 50 to 65, and they all have extensive experiences with working in and leading international teams across the world for more than 25 years. Four of them are expatriates. The interviews were conducted in Bangkok, Thailand.

To avoid self-bias, instead of asking questions about their team or their organizations, we inquired about their trusted leaders. In this way, we were able to obtain the characteristics of trusted leaders from the experiences and judgments of CEOs/MDs who have ascended their career ladders to the top of their professions, have dealt with numerous levels of hierarchies, and experienced a wide range of team diversity. We focused on only three key open-ended questions:

Is trust important? Can it be built, or it is more intuitive?
Who was your best boss? What made him/her so special?
Do/did you trust him/her? What are the reasons why your trust/trusted him/her?

The next part highlights the key points that were drawn from the experiences of the five leaders.

16.6 Take-Away Points

16.6.1 No Trust, no Real Motivation for Collaborations

All five leaders emphasized the importance of trust and the urge to build up trust so as to drive their organization forward. Leader 3 shared his experiences and challenges of being an expatriate and of being posted in China and Southeast Asia.

> Being an expatriate posted or doing business abroad, no matter how good and competent you are, at the start, you are just regarded as an alien. It is important that a leader is able to build a trusting environment within the team. If there is no trust, it is impossible to develop real motivation for future collaborations.

16.6.2 To Gain Trust, you Have to Give Trust (to the Right Person)

When asked "Who was your most trusted leader? What was special about him/her?", the first thing every respondent mentioned was that they were given opportunities and challenging responsibilities by their leaders, which made them feel trusted. They felt that their leaders were confident in their competence to deliver their jobs. They felt they were being empowered and given the chance to prove themselves, while at the same time developing themselves. Leader 3 commented:

> What was so special about him is that he gave me many opportunities. He gave me his trust and believed I was capable of carrying out these tasks. He took a risk with me. He allowed me to do the work in my own way, and so I wanted to prove myself to him. It was a wonderful feeling, very empowering, I was full of energy. I was given an assignment to explore China back in

> 1990, at a time when Europeans were looked upon as aliens in China. The first assignment to set up an operation in China led to opportunities to expand the business to other locations in Asia. Now we have operations all over the world. I am proud to have played a part in the company's growth.

Similarly, leader 2 stated:

> I was given opportunities to grow, along with challenging responsibilities. I was always the one who was selected to explore new market opportunities in the real estate industry all over the world. I was able to get connected to key people. It was fun.

And leader 5 shared with us that

> I was empowered by him, given challenging jobs and responsibilities, and was allowed plenty of room to manage the various projects. He was always there to step in and fix bottlenecks whenever I needed it.

Trusted leaders observe and understand their team's strengths and weaknesses. In responses to the questions "How did your trusted leader spot you? What made him/her believe in you?", leader 2 responded:

> I don't know. I guess he was impressed by my level of energy, and also my prominent background in the area of real estate.

Likewise, leader 5 stated:

> I really have no clue. But he seemed to know all my key strengths and assigned work that could fit in with them. That made my work a lot of fun.

16.6.3 Trusted Leaders Have Self-Awareness of their Strengths and Weaknesses and Continuously Improve Themselves

Trusted leaders must have, and consistently demonstrate, their competencies in their jobs. This includes technical knowledge to get the job done, an ability to deal with complexity, strategic thinking, planning, and administering, as well as a wider spectrum in the area of leadership (for example, the ability to coach and mentor, to motivate and empower the team, to delegate work, and to be a role model), interpersonal competence (for example, to be approachable and empathetic), as well as intrapersonal competence (for example, to be emotionally stable, to possess integrity, and an ability to deal with ambiguity).

We entered into a conversation with leader 2 about the fact that nobody is perfect. So we asked him if it was presumptuous to expect everything from one's leader? We also asked him how to deal with the competency gap in the era of fast-pace changes? Leader 2 shared his experience in Box 16.1 about how he deals with the competency gap within his company. He emphasized that it is important for leaders themselves to be aware of their own strengths and weaknesses, and to have a willingness and the courage to learn as well as continuously improve themselves.

Box 16.1 How to Deal with the Competency Gap?

> You need to have a good radar that can detect what comes in, what goes out, what is good, and what is bad. Nowadays technology changes so fast; there are many new products that are good for business, such as data analysis tools. We have to keep on learning, to keep up to date.
> So what do I do with the gap? I think competency gaps will always be there. Within a firm, people have different backgrounds, skills, and personalities. So a competency gap, in my opinion, is not a major problem as such. But it definitely requires the management's attention to understand and manage the ramifications. They should not ignore it.
> Regarding expectations from the team, I don't think there will be any leader who has all the competencies the team might expect. Nobody is perfect. We all have our strengths and weaknesses. Therefore, it is of utmost importance that we are receptive, open-minded, and have a self-awareness of our own strengths and weaknesses—that we acknowledge them and make an effort to improve.
> A simple solution for me is to consult, seek help, and get advice from the team or experts in the field. It is fun to learn new things, that can only lead to improvements. From my perspective, people can be trained in the required business/technical skills, so gaps are easy to fix. But a leadership spirit takes time to develop. However, at the management level, I don't compromise with things like honesty and integrity. As a boss, you have to be fair and do the right thing. We need to have, keep, and nurture good and competent people. As a CEO, it is my job to plan ahead in order to decide how to move the company forward for the next ten years, and always be ahead of the game. I need a good team to assist me in doing so. It would be impossible for me to do it on my own.
> Interview, Leader 2

16.6.4 Trusted Leaders Have Not Only an Intelligence Quotient, but also a Moral Quotient and an Emotional Quotient

It has been pointed out to us that a number of competencies is an important foundation and a prerequisite for a leader to build up trust. However, the traits that make a difference between competent and trusted leaders are underlined by the ethical dimension (integrity and honesty) and the relational dimension (benevolence and caring). Highly trusted leaders are equipped with an intelligence quotient, a moral quotient, and an emotional quotient.

Leader 2 explained:

> I think what constitutes trust in the boss varies. That depends on your respective level of management. When I was a junior, to me, a good boss was an expert in their field who had

> business competency – as much as I expected a boss/supervisor to be knowledgeable, and able to give me guidance and advice when I need it.
>
> When I was in middle management, this was at a time when many of my supervisees had better technical knowledge than I did. A good boss has to know how to manage, co-ordinate, motivate, and empower the team. Also, bosses have to be aware of their strengths and weaknesses and seek out the expertise from the relevant team members.
>
> With regard to the top management positions, I think they have to have good judgment and be a role model that represents the firm's values and work ethics.
>
> Now that I am the boss myself, I always give my staff opportunities, just like I was given by my former boss. If they do not want to seize the opportunity, or if it does not work out, that is not the end of the world. Perhaps it is not the right time, nor the right job, nor the right people. I am trying my best to help my people grow to a level they can achieve.

Leader 3 described the characteristics of his trusted boss in the following way:

> He is stable and able to control his emotions. I have never seen him in a bad mood in any meeting, he is always very open. He tries to find the best solutions, but he is not a micro-management person. He allows us freedom to work in our own way. He keeps his word, is authentic and fair. He has good judgment, but I would not say that I agree with all of his decisions – I do agree with most of them. For the few ones I don't agree with, I can accept his reasons.

Leader 5 shared his views on the characteristics of his trusted boss:

> He is open-minded, a great listener, authentic, empathetic, and mindful. He does what he says, he keeps his word. He is a great coach, I learnt so much from him.
>
> There were, however, few occasions when things didn't work out as planned. He took responsibility as a leader, and he never blamed others, but looked for a way to fix it.

16.6.5 Consistency Counts

It is important to note that our initial trust may be generated by a gut feeling at any first meeting. Trust should not be given blindly. The combination of competencies, integrity, and benevolence has to be proven as being genuine and consistent. Trustworthiness does not come from the first impression, nor a gut feeling; it has to develop with consistency over time.

Leader 1 highlighted the following:

> Trust should not be subjective but rather objective. It should be based on historical data. It is like a process where the bank must check our creditworthiness before granting us a credit card. In some circumstances, we might start with a subjective approach, using our gut feeling or going by our first impression. But we have to turn it into an objective approach as soon as possible.

Leader 3 stated:

> Trust is something for which you have to be in there long enough to feel it. It has to be built gradually without any shortcuts.

Trust levels can be depleted or even terminated if there is no evidence to confirm granted trust. The quality of trustworthiness always requires a solid back-up by evidence of past records. Leader 4 explained:

> Trust has to be proven by consistency. In business, it is shown by the consistency in their past performance record. So it goes down to their reliability, honesty, empathy, and thoughtful behavior towards others.

16.7 Conclusion

Most of us start our careers by being led and part of a team. Only few can climb up the ladder to become a leader. Not all leaders are competent, and only a few competent ones are highly trusted leaders, so these are rare and distinctive. They are leaders who can make a difference, especially in a VUCA environment.

Highly trusted leaders must be competent in their jobs and have to be equipped with the ethical components of integrity and benevolence; these traits have to be demonstrated with consistency. Trusted leaders must be genuine, truthful, and authentic. Trusted leadership is generous, building up team confidence and strengthening their team, and it is meaningful when it develops potential and becomes effective.

Assessments and judgments as to whether or not leaders are trustworthy are made explicitly and implicitly all the time by the people surrounding them. The combination of competencies and their ability to deliver their commitments, their integrity, and benevolent behavior have to be both persistent and consistent enough to build up confirmation and confidence in their trustworthiness. Trust cannot be asked for. Leaders have to take action to generate it, and it requires consistency over time. As Jack Welch (quoted in JWMI 2020) stated: "Leadership, very simply, is about two things: 1. Truth and trust. 2. Ceaselessly seeking the former, relentlessly building the latter".

Acknowledgement The authors deeply appreciate the generous provision of time by the five interviewed leaders and the experiences they shared with us. The interviews were invaluable, constructive, and fruitful. We do hope that in one way or another, their shared experiences will be beneficial to the readers.

References

Amadeo, K. (2020). "Cultural Diversity in the Work Place". Retrieved from https://www.thebalance.com/cultural-diversity-3306201

Ambrose, M. L., & Schminke, M. (2003). Organization Structure as a Moderator of the Relationship between Procedural Justice, Interactional Justice, Perceived Organizational Support, and Supervisory Trust. Journal of Applied Psychology, 88, 295–305. http://dx.doi.org/https://doi.org/10.1037/0021-9010.88.2.295

Bies, R. J., & Moag, J. F. (1986). Interactional justice: Communication criteria of fairness. In R. J. Lewicki, B. H. Sheppard, & M. H. Bazerman (Eds.), Research on negotiations in organizations (Vol. 1, pp. 43–55). Greenwich, CT: JAI Press.

Bigne, E., & Blesa, A. (2003). Market orientation, trust and satisfaction in dyadic relationships: a manufacturer-retailer analysis. International Journal of Retail & Distribution Management, 31(11), 574–590.

Blomqvist, K. (1997). The many faces of trust. Scandinavian journal of management, 13(3), 271–286.

Blomqvist, K., & Ståhle, P. (2000). Building organizational trust. 16th Annual IMP Conference, Bath, UK (pp. 7–9).

Baldoni, J. (2008). "How Trustworthy Are You?" Harvard Business Review. https://hbr.org/2008/05/how-trustworthy-are-you

Brenkert, G. G. (1998). Trust, morality and international business. Business Ethics Quarterly, 8(2), 293–317.

Brower, H. H., Schoorman, F. D., & Tan, H. H. (2000). A model of relational leadership: The integration of trust and leader-member exchange. Leadership Quarterly, 11, 227–250.

Burke, C. S., Sims, D. E., Lazzara, E. H., & Salas, E. (2007). Trust in leadership: A multi-level review and integration. The Leadership Quarterly, 18(6), 606–632.

Chehrazi, S. (2017). "Expedia CEO Shares the Critical Traits to Develop by Age 30". Retrieved from https://www.entrepreneur.com/article/293231

Child, J., & Hsieh, L. H. (2014). Decision mode, information and network attachment in the internationalization of SMEs: A configurational and contingency analysis. Journal of world Business, 49(4), 598–610.

Colquitt, J. A., LePine, J. A., Zapata, C. P., & Wild, R. E. (2011). Trust in typical and high-reliability contexts: Building and reacting to trust among firefighters. Academy of Management Journal, 54(5), 999–1015.

Dirks, K. T. & Ferrin, D. L. (2002). Trust in Leadership: Meta-Analytic Findings and Implications for Research and Practice. Journal of Applied Psychology, 87(4), 611–628. http://dx.doi.org/https://doi.org/10.1037/0021-9010.87.4.611

Dyer, J. H., & Chu, W. (2000). The determinants of trust in supplier-automaker relationships in the US, Japan and Korea. Journal of International Business Studies, 31(2), 259–285.

Flinchbaugh, J. (2019). "The 4Cs of Building Trust". Retrieved from https://www.industryweek.com/leadership/article/22027350/the-4cs-of-building-trust

Folger, R., & Konovsky, M. A. (1989). Effects of procedural and distributive justice on reactions to pay raise decisions. Academy of Management Journal, 32(1), 115–130.

Frankel, T. (2005). Trust and honesty: America's business culture at a crossroad. Oxford University Press.

Frei, F., & Morriss, A. (2020). "Begin with Trust: The first step to becoming a genuinely empowering leader". Harvard Business Review. Retrieved from https://hbr.org/2020/05/begin-with-trust

Gambetta, D. (Ed.) (1988). Trust: Making and breaking cooperative relations. Oxford: Blackwell.

Gläser, W. (2020). "Where does the term 'VUCA' come from?". Retrieved from https://www.vuca-world.org/where-does-the-term-vuca-come-from/

Green, C., & Howe, A. (2011). The Trusted Advisor Fieldbook: A Comprehensive Toolkit for Leading with Trust. Hoboken, N.J: Wiley.

Huntsman, D., & Greer, A. (2019). Antecedents of Trust in Leadership: A Multilevel Perspective in the Fire Service. International Fire Service Journal of Leadership & Management, 13, 19–33.

Hurley, R. (2012). The trustworthy leader: The first step toward creating high-trust organizations. Leader to Leader, 2012(66), 33-39. https://doi.org/https://doi.org/10.1002/ltl.20047

JWMI (2020). "How to Build Trust and Grow as a Leader". Retrieved from https://jackwelch.strayer.edu/winning/how-to-build-trust-grow-as-a-leader/

Konovsky, M. A., & Pugh, S. D. (1994). Citizenship behavior and social exchange. Academy of Management Journal, 37(3), 656–669.

Mayer, R. C., Davis, J. H., & Schoorman, F. D. (1995). An integrative model of organizational trust. Academy of Management Review, 20(3), 709–734.

McAllister, D. J. (1995). Affect- and cognition-based trust as foundations for interpersonal cooperation in organizations. Academy of Management Journal, 38, 24–59.

McKnight, D. H., & Chervany, N. L. (2001). Trust and distrust definitions: One bite at a time. In Falcone, R., Singh, M., Tan, Y. H. (Eds.), Trust in Cyber-societies. Lecture Notes in Computer Science, 2246 (pp. 27–54). Springer, Berlin, Heidelberg.

Salesforce (n.d.). "A Conversation with Marc Benioff and Hiromichi Mizuno". Retrieved from https://www.salesforce.com/news/stories/salesforce-chair-and-ceo-marc-benioff-discusses-trust-and-stakeholders-at-the-milken-institute-conference/

Saxena, A. (2014). Workforce Diversity: A Key to Improve Productivity. Procedia Economics and Finance, 11, 76–85. https://doi.org/https://doi.org/10.1016/S2212-5671(14)00178-6

Schreier, C., Udomkit, N., & Capone, R. (2019). A Study on Competencies for Managing Workforce Diversity: Evidences from Multi-National Enterprises in Switzerland. ABAC Journal, 39(3), 1–16.

Schwantes, M. (2020). "Warren Buffett: Integrity Is the Most Important Attribute to Hire For. Ask 7 Simple Questions to Find It". Retrieved from https://www.inc.com/marcel-schwantes/warren-buffett-hiring-top-talent-characteristics.html

Severson, D. (n.d.). "The 8 Rules of Leadership by Jack Welch". Retrieved from https://www.inc.com/dana-severson/these-8-simple-rules-of-leadership-from-jack-welch-are-more-important-now-than-ever-before.html

Udomkit, N., Ensslin, V., & Meinhold, R. (2019). Three Stages of Trust Building of International Small and Medium-Size Enterprises. Global Business Review, 21(4), 1–12. https://doi.org/https://doi.org/10.1177/0972150919856990

Whitener, E., Brodt, S., Korsgaard, A., & Werner, J. (1998). Managers as initiators of trust: an exchange relationship framework for understanding managerial trustworthy behavior. Academy of Management Review, 3(23), 513–530.

Wicks, A. C., Berman, S. L., & Jones, T. M. (1999). The structure of optimal trust: Moral and strategic implications. Academy of Management review, 24(1), 99–116.

Zenger, J., & Folkman, J. (2019). The 3 Elements of Trust. Harvard Business Review. Retrieved from https://hbr.org/2019/02/the-3-elements-of-trust

Part V

International Leadership Case Studies

SME Internationalization: Exploration of Unknown Territories by Strategically Seizing Serendipity

17

Claus Schreier and Nuntana Udomkit

17.1 Entrepreneurship: Seize Opportunities and Gain Experience

Frank Wilson has been an entrepreneur for quite a long time and describes himself as a lifelong SME entrepreneur. During his school days, he turned his hobby into a business. With several of his friends, he bought all the components that were necessary to assemble loudspeakers, putting them together on weekends and selling them to an extended circle of friends. This is not to say that constructing and selling loudspeakers generated a regular income, but at least it earned Frank enough money for all of them to expand their CD collection.

No doubt, selling self-made loudspeakers to friends was not about "profit maximization", since sometimes they had to be sold even below production costs. Instead of gaining an "financial profit", it was more about keeping the costs of the components low by purchasing them in East Asia. A "stop-loss" (instead of "profit maximization") strategy kept the young entrepreneur in this venture. Finally, in retrospect, the economic success of the loudspeaker venture was less important for Frank than the business experience he was able to gain.

Nowadays, Frank makes his living in the cosmetics industry, because he realized its potential rather coincidentally and seized arising opportunities. His uncle, a well-known dermatologist in Central Switzerland, explained to him that many mass-produced skin creams do not contain a substantial degree of active substances which protect against skin

C. Schreier · N. Udomkit (✉)
Business Administration Division, Mahidol University International College, Mahidol University, Salaya, Nakhon Pathom, Thailand
e-mail: claus.sch@mahidol.edu; nuntana.udo@mahidol.edu

I. Stolz, S. Oldenziel Scherrer (eds.), *International Leadership*, uniscope. Publikationen der SGO Stiftung, https://doi.org/10.1007/978-3-658-37306-1_17

aging. Furthermore, people who have sensitive skin tend to suffer from allergies and skin rashes because of the preservatives in traditional mass-market products. In order to help his patients, his uncle therefore developed a skin cream based on his own anti-aging formula; he believed the specific ingredients to be very effective against skin aging without the negative effects for those suffering from skin allergies.

Frank's gut feeling told him that his uncle's skin cream could be a commercial success. He invested some time into research about skin creams, interviewed dermatologists, and gathered information about existing products. It quickly became clear to him that the skin areas around the eyes in particular need special protection, constituting a skin-cream niche market with specific challenges and opportunities. When the muscles around the eye slacken with age, so-called "periorbital dark circles" develop. Only if the body's own collagen and elastin structure remains intact and so-called free radicals are intercepted, the natural aging process of the corresponding muscles can be slowed down or even stopped to some degree. In addition, the skin around the eyes is usually very thin and gets increasingly thinner with age; if conventional preservatives are applied, an allergic reaction is likely to occur.

Frank and his uncle discussed which additional active ingredients needed to be added to his existing skin cream to be effective as an eye cream. They concluded that the existing anti-allergenic base of the cream needed to be kept intact, because the sensitive skin around the eyes meant doing away with perfume, parabens, paraffin, and, of course, aluminum. However, in order to serve the special needs of the skin areas around the eyes and the eye-ring muscles, the existing formula was supplemented with a specially prepared variety of peptides. As a result, the eye cream "NatureYou" was born.

17.2 Internationalization: A Matter of Strategy

Seven years after establishing "NatureYou", Frank looked back at some of the ups and downs of this venture. The start had been much harder than he had expected. No bank had granted him a start-up loan, and venture capital institutions could not be convinced of the potential of the "NatureYou" business idea. Without considerable financial support from family and friends, Frank's personal trusted social network, "NatureYou" would now not exist. In other words, Frank faced a lack of capital, and instead of expecting a profit for himself, he wondered at the beginning how long he could hold out and whether he had any prospects of actually ever earning any money with "NatureYou".

Despite the funding worries in the early phase, "NatureYou" was growing slowly but steadily and quite soon had twelve full-time employees. Meanwhile the one-product start-up had become a company with a slightly wider range of skin and eye creams. A "NatureYou" day cream—with its UV filter and active ingredients against pigment spots on the one hand and a night repair cream with retinol and a vitamin complex on the other hand—completed the successful eye cream offer. In order to bring all his products to the market, Frank had mostly been relying on direct sales via internet, which increased the profit margins for "NatureYou". Thereby, Frank was also closer to his customers and their needs. For him, customer needs always come first. Satisfied customers and their feedback have always been of more appeal to him than the return on investment. Frank's customer focus may thus help secure his company's success, but an entrepreneur can also have sleepless nights if the profit and liquidity needs of the organization are neglected.

In addition, Frank was active in the Central Switzerland SME Business Network Association. He took every opportunity to present his business to other SME owners and also provided them with potential ideas and advice. During one of these exchanges, Frank had a conversation with another entrepreneur, Dietmar Junker, who told him that he had been in a similar situation few years ago. Everything was going well for Dietmar, and his company was making a relatively solid profit. He told Frank that at some point one needs to answer the question of how to professionalize one's business so as to ensure the company's long-term success. How to transform the company from a start-up which depends heavily on the entrepreneur's personal actions and involvement into a professionalized organization of a certain sustainable size to ensure its long-term survival independently of the founder.

A question closely related to the long-term survival of the company is how far it can grow and whether the business should be internationalized for this goal; because by now, globalization has become a viable option for SMEs, too. Of course, "NatureYou" also had options to professionalize as well as internationalize, and Dietmar's advice was that since Frank already largely used digital direct sales, his potential international customers were only a mouse click away; so why don't you offer your successful range of creams on the global market?

After the conversation with Dietmar, internationalization suddenly seemed to be a very logical next entrepreneurial step to Frank in order to ensure the long-term survival and growth of "NatureYou". Up to now, the option of growth and internationalization had never occurred to him. Everyday business had distracted him from considering where he would like to steer "NatureYou" to in the long term.

17.3 Internationalization: Just another Business Opportunity the Entrepreneur Seizes Upon?

Should "NatureYou" internationalize? Frank couldn't get this question out of his mind. So he called Michael Hartman, his "wing man" since he founded "NatureYou"—a trusted colleague and friend. Even though Frank is the sole owner and final decision-maker of the company, he takes advantage of an unofficial but trusted "sounding board", which allows him to discuss and reflect business matters he perceives as relevant. Michael is a regular practitioner in this sounding board and had also been the main driver behind Frank's decision to strategically position "NatureYou" by utilizing a direct marketing approach via internet—recognizing that distributors would charge very high margins, which would result in "NatureYou" skin creams being unnecessarily expensive for end users.

Frank told Michael that he would like to discuss significant strategic changes: "NatureYou" should go international. Michael, who was very familiar Frank's spontaneous initiatives, responded immediately: "Frank, I think that you are on the right track, we should plan out more where we want to steer 'NatureYou' to in the future. Our products are doing well with our existing regionally focused and relatively small but loyal customer basis, no doubt about that. But at any time, the company is run on a day-by-day basis while customer demand is fluctuating sometimes unpredictably. We react when the unexpected happens, such as with promotions and discounts, but what we need to do is to more proactively develop markets so as to create more overall demand. We need to drive 'NatureYou's' future more actively and strategically, and going international might be the right strategic move."

At first, Frank didn't feel comfortable with what he was hearing. He didn't feel that "NatureYou" just reacts to the unexpected. From his perspective, there was no need to make major changes, apart from taking advantage of a good opportunity if it arose. Of course, Frank was aware that organizational development, including going international, should be approached strategically from a planning point of view. On the other hand, too much planning obstructs one's view on the big picture and, in the worst case, results in failure to seize the opportunities that arise spontaneously.

Meanwhile, Michael went on talking about prospective proceedings on the basis of solid strategic planning, instead of simply relying on gut feelings about merely assumed opportunities. At the same time, he stressed the need to bear in mind that they would lose on a larger scale if something went wrong with the international expansion.

Frank had always been proud of his gut instincts and liked to tell others that he had set up "NatureYou" without a business plan. If he were to reflect on his "success", it would probably be based on how he would embody entrepreneurship, namely "courageously seizing opportunities, utilizing networks, and finding comrades-in-arms who strongly and firmly push in the same direction". Objectively speaking, he believed he had achieved a lot with this approach.

Frank felt that he needed some time for himself in order to reflect on the situation. He agreed with Michael that they couldn't make such a far-reaching and impactful decision right away. Frank suggested for both of them to contemplate more about whether and how they should approach the potential internationalization of "NatureYou"—sticking with the entrepreneurial mindset that had made them successful so far, or with a stronger focus on the strategic planning process. Maybe determining the future path of "NatureYou" would require bringing these different perspectives together.

17.4 A Strategic Approach Finds its Way into the Organizational Development of "NatureYou"

For the next few days, Frank couldn't stop thinking about internationalization. Intuitively he knew that "NatureYou" was limited in terms of its domestic demand and growth potential. This was a small niche-focused company compared to the major cosmetic brands. SMEs like "NatureYou" just cannot compete with the marketing and brand power of the global industry giants. Frank realized that "NatureYou" very quickly gets into an existence-threatening situation if the domestic SME experienced problems with its products due to changes in customer preferences. Frank sensed that the growth question had been up in the air for a long time and that he had successfully ignored it so far, in the hope that opportunities would arise in the future.

Michael Hartman was also worried. He admired Frank for his intuition and his flair for anticipating the right timing. He had watched Frank discuss situations that required important decisions amongst a large number of stakeholders. He knew that Frank wouldn't allow himself to be confused by many different perspectives; he uses partial information and puts it together like a puzzle to form a coherent overall picture that allows him to come to a decision. Michael admires this "holistic-gut-feeling" approach, but at the same time it remains totally peregrine to him. As a graduate economist, Michael prefers to proceed in a "strategic and planned" manner by analyzing the alternatives and evaluating them using various criteria. He then selects the most promising strategy and scenario from his point of view. Surprisingly, what seems to be a contradiction between Michaels's and Frank's respective methods has almost always led to quite similar results—two different entrepreneurial approaches led to the same goals; but the question is whether that would also be the case if "NatureYou" went international.

To Michael, it has long been clear that "NatureYou" ultimately doesn't generate enough profit to be able to invest the amount of money needed for research and the development of new products to serve the zeitgeist. Further development of all current products would also be too expensive, as the home market is too small to justify such an investment. Therefore, Michael realized that the time had come for "NatureYou" to set up a continuous strategic management system and to consider internationalization as a strategic growth option. Furthermore, he was convinced that in principle, the necessary knowledge of what to do was available within the company—but that they also needed help to capitalize on this wealth of knowledge. It seemed logical to him to hire a consultant for a while in order to question and discuss the strategic options and growth alternatives.

17.5 The Outsider's Perspective: Establishing a Systematic SME Development Process

A week after their first meeting, Michael Hartman and Frank Wilson meet again to review the internationalization plans of "NatureYou". The following is a description of how their conversation went:

Frank: "I think we should talk about the alternatives we want to consider for the future path of 'NatureYou'. Over the past few years, we have been focused on the founding process and getting the existing business on a secure path to the best of our knowledge and belief. We have succeeded in doing so, and now is the time to think more about the future, about opportunities to grab and treats to manage. I agree that we cannot just rely on the hope that additional opportunities will arise in the domestic market for the future growth and prosperity of the company."

Michael: "I see it the same way, we should proceed strategically and analyze the various options we have in order to then decide, based on concrete criteria, how we want to lead 'NatureYou' into the future. Let's clarify which way we want to go. I suggest that we get outside support—someone with an objective view on our SME, who can and should ask probing questions, and who would be able to help us. What do you think about this idea?"

Frank didn't really like the idea of calling in a consultant for helping them with the upcoming development towards internationalization possibilities and alternatives. He considered the consultant fees to be completely overpriced and ultimately "wasted money". For him, consultants were something for managers who cannot or do not want to make decisions themselves. But was "NatureYou" and thus himself now in such a situation, was he shirking a decision?

Frank: "Michael, you know I'm not a fan of external consultants. But I understand your argument, and a consultant may be able to advise us on a few ideas and provide us with an innovative point of view to help us make the right decisions. Let's set a budget that we are willing to spend on a consulting service. If this consultant helps, that's great; otherwise we just accept the wasted costs. But I don't want to have any of these 'smart' advisors in our company for an unlimited period of time."

Michael, who had recently completed an MBA program at a renowned university, suggested hiring his MBA lecturer, Andrea Bucher, who taught strategic and international management and at the same time provided strategy consulting services and workshops for SMEs in the context of internationalization. Frank agreed to Michael's idea.

17.6 Strategic Internationalization Paths and Defining Target Markets

Andrea Bucher, who has strategically advised a large number of SMEs, invited Frank, Michael, and some other "NatureYou" stakeholders of Frank's choice to strategy workshops. She asked the participants to analyze and define the assets, capabilities, and core competencies of "NatureYou". An in-depth analysis of the existing Central Switzerland market and the competitors provided a solid insight into the opportunities and risks "NatureYou" faced. Furthermore, Andrea guided them through the process of compiling strengths and weaknesses of the organization, then used the results—in combination with market knowledge already acquired in a SWOT analysis—to come up with options for various strategic initiatives.

The various further workshops reinforced Michael's and Frank's belief that "NatureYou" could only justify and shoulder the necessary future investments to develop and upgrade their skin cream portfolio for both the local and potentially the international markets if the organization reached a critical size. While they discussed potential growth strategies, it turned out that a wider national focus wouldn't entirely solve "NatureYou"'s size problem; and while analyzing their customer base, they realized that "NatureYou" already supplied its skin creams beyond the Central Switzerland region. Internationalization increasingly crystallized as a rationally justified and logical strategic path for "NatureYou".

Andrea Bucher explained various alternative internationalization strategies and encouraged the participants to reflect on the "NatureYou" context for each alternative. Frank, as the main decision-maker, founder, and owner realized that an additional one-on one-coaching with Andrea had helped him become familiar with a traditional export strategy for the existing "NatureYou" products, as a first meaningful internationalization step. Andrea gave the team the task of analyzing various potential international markets with regard to their opportunities and risks for "NatureYou". Gradually, based on solid alternative market analysis as well as on "NatureYou"'s strengths and weaknesses, the pilot export market of Dubai emerged as a suitable first market step in their move to internationalization.

The strategic analysis of Dubai highlights, among others, that the business-friendly governance, the free movement of capital, and a high level of internal security make the Emirates an attractive business location for even further internationalization steps in the future. Dubai is the most important trade hub in this middle-eastern region, as a market the size of the EU population opens up from there. Furthermore, the Dubai State Economic Development Agency is known for its support to new companies willing to enter the market.

What was also of importance for "NatureYou" is that the high income level of Dubai residents promised good sales opportunities of "NatureYou"'s quite high-priced skin creams—and the annually 14 million high-spending tourists who value Dubai as a shopping hub further increased sales probabilities. In Dubai City, where 85% of the three million inhabitants of the emirate live, the distribution costs for "NatureYou" were quite low. In addition, Swiss quality and luxury products are particularly popular in the United Arab Emirates, despite or perhaps even because of the high price levels.

Convinced by the analysis done by the team, Frank was confident giving a green light for Dubai as "NatureYou"'s international pilot. The next step was to work out a suitable entry strategy. In order to minimize the risk for "NatureYou", and to maximize the chances of success, the project team suggested to look for an experienced sales and distribution partner in Dubai.

Michael was very satisfied with the progress and the methodical approach. The "NatureYou-Dubai" project was accelerating quickly and in a focused manner. The Dubai State Economic Development Agency was extremely professional and provided initial, promising contacts. Following on the defined "action plan", "NatureYou" set up a booth at an annual cosmetics fair in Dubai. The fair proved to be very successful for "NatureYou"—a "lucky punch". The sales company proposed by the Economic Development Agency was very interested in the "NatureYou" skin cream products. It offered to organize the FDI approval for Dubai—and the United Arab Emirates (UAE) at large—and to initiate marketing for Dubai as well as for the other UAE emirates. Ultimately, as a first internationalization step, "NatureYou" successfully implemented the strategic plan developed for Dubai. One can speak of it as a success story even if the sales figures in Dubai were not yet within a range in which "NatureYou" actually earned money there. Undoubtedly, "NatureYou" gained the relevant knowledge on how to strategically perform internationalization steps, and once the full potential of the United Arab Emirates was raised, Frank was optimistic this step could be the game changer they had been waiting for from a profit perspective.

Either way, Frank was extremely satisfied with the successful market entry in Dubai, and thus the consultant's systematic and logical approach satisfied him. He was certainly very glad that he had followed Michael's advice.

17.7 Internationalization: A Social Network Constructivism Task

Frank really enjoyed the strategy workshop lessons and the coaching Andrea Bucher had given them. He also communicated and discussed "NatureYou" going international on his social networks whenever and wherever possible. So it was no surprise that he let his long-time golf partner Rolf Enderson know about his plans over a round of golf.

Frank: "Rolf, 'NatureYou' is entering the international market. With the help of a consultant from university, we have analyzed and evaluated several alternatives and eventually chose Dubai. At first, I was skeptical, as I was not familiar with Dubai at all. I have no networks or contacts in Dubai who could provide me with information about the market there. Perhaps adopting a really systematic approach with the assistance of external expertise can make internationalization work for an SME? What do you think?"

Rolf: "I understand the dilemma. How can you enter an unknown market without experience and trustful partnerships? If you make the wrong decision, this can be fatal for an SME. I really don't know much about Dubai. Ultimately, however, it is success that counts. Have you ever thought about going to Asia with "NatureYou"? The greater Asia region is certainly not an easy market to succeed on, but I have personally made very good experiences in Thailand. The country is characterized by a growing middle class with steadily rising incomes. Thailand is not just the land of smiles, but also a hub for design, fine arts, as well as cosmetics in Southeast Asia; creams from Korea, for example, are extremely popular in Thailand according to a friend of mine who is living and working there. 'NatureYou' has great cosmetic products, so why shouldn't it be successful in Thailand, too? What works in Dubai should also work in Thailand, don't you think?"

As already a couple of times before, Rolf thus inspired Frank and activated his entrepreneurial spirit for opportunities. Frank grew very interested in the idea of going to Thailand with "NatureYou". He would have liked to have a second international pillar besides Dubai, and Asia was a growth region everyone was talking about. In addition, he could literally "feel" this Thailand venture might work. Frank had been to Thailand several times as a tourist and was very impressed by the country and its people. During those visits, he had not seen Thailand as a potential business location, but Rolf had already awakened his interest. Nevertheless, was it really a smart idea to venture into both markets, Dubai and Thailand, nearly simultaneously? Frank's entrepreneurial spirit and intuition came to force and he asked himself what he had to lose if he continued to pursue the coincidently popped-up Thailand option.

17.8 Internationalization by Leveraging Trusted Networks

Frank, who was looking forward to meeting Rolf again, didn't have to wait long to meet his golf and business friend. They had been supporting each other for many years, providing each other with relevant information, business opportunities, and friendly advice. The relationship between them was based on experiences they had made together and on the resulting mutual trust; along with other business partners, the two formed a business network in its "best sense".

Frank: "Rolf, do you really think 'NatureYou''s cream assortment could be successful in Thailand? The friend you told me about—the one who lives and works in Thailand–, would he be a possible contact person for me? A potential business partner to figure out possibilities?"

Rolf: "Frank, I think Matthias Keller could be a valuable contact person for you. I've known him for a long time, we were in the military together, I would call him a friend I can trust. He is 'cut from the same cloth' as we are. As far as I know, he is a member of the Thai Chamber of Commerce and the Rotary Club of Bangkok. I'm pretty sure he could prove to be a valuable business partner for you. I will establish the contact and you can discuss the matter with him."

Rolf gave his friend Matthias Keller a personal call and quickly established the contact between Frank and him. The first contact with him turned out very promisingly for Frank. He found out that Matthias was married to a Thai woman, whose family is specialized in importing all types of goods and products from Europe. Matthias held a senior management position in the company. An opportunity to leverage within a trusted network seemed to be opening up.

17.9 SME Internationalization Based on Personal Relationships and "A Gut Feeling"

Frank felt he needed to meet Matthias personally, since he did not want to make a decision about a business partner without first meeting him in person. Matthias agreed to meet in Bangkok for a personal talk at the famous Oriental Hotel.

After just a few hours of small and business talk, Frank and Matthias came to an agreement. Both were "old-school entrepreneurs" and, as Rolf Enderson had assumed, "cut from the same cloth". Together, the two businessmen agreed to seize the opportunity and give "NatureYou"'s skin creams a try in Thailand. They set out a financial and organizational conceptual framework that was intended to ensure a successful market entry and, at the same time, remained within a cost range. Matthias was to receive distribution rights for "NatureYou" in the long run, and in return, he would take care of FDI approval, customs procedures, and the various sales activities. If the set minimum turnover that was agreed upon by both of them was not reached within two years, the business relationship could be terminated by either side. Frank agreed to make a certain number of his skin creams available as promotion and advertising samples and furthermore promised to provide the creams on a "cost-price basis". Matthias would utilize his company's network and sales organization to open the doors for "NatureYou" in Thailand.

The contracts were not yet legally formulated, but the chemistry between the two future business partners seemed to match. Frank was very optimistic that a business partnership with Matthias would lead to a win-win situation, which, to a certain extent, was a great leap of faith on his part. But his gut feeling confirmed that he was on the right path, flanked by a stop-loss strategy regarding the overall investment.

17.10 Many Roads Lead to Rome, but which One Is the Most Effective and Efficient?

After a few months, it turned out that "NatureYou"'s business activities in both Dubai and Thailand were developing promisingly. Frank took into account that "NatureYou" still had quite a way to go to generate a sustainable profit in both markets. However, he was already thinking about entering other markets in Asia. In addition, Michael and Frank sketched a plan that included the development of a whitening cream for the new markets as soon as sales opportunities allowed.

Regarding further internationalization steps, in case the two international pilot markets fulfill profit expectations, Frank was wondering which steps he should take next. Should "NatureYou" even start producing its skin creams in Thailand? Should he dare to make a direct investment in a Southeast Asian country? Should he wait for opportunities such as the Thailand move and look for allies in his network to conquer further markets, or should he—as Michael had suggested—initiate a permanent strategic management process for internationalization within his team? Would the use of substantial funds for a well-planned internationalization strategy be justified, as in the case of Dubai? Would it make sense to hire a full-time strategy expert or would the help of consultants suffice? Would he need more advice from trusted sources in the future, just to be on the safe side? Or should he maybe just combine both internationalization approaches he had applied recently, "strategically helping fortune perform"?

Frank drew up a preliminary conclusion on the internationalization of "NatureYou" so far. Without the strategic workshops, the in-depth analysis, and discussions with the team, they would not have taken the Dubai step. The Dubai endeavor was the ice-breaker, and the Dubai experience had been so promising that Frank, according to his temperament, had eagerly undertaken the Thailand opportunity. He decided that having a strategic planning approach, along with strategic decision-making as well as combined with entrepreneurship and exploiting opportunities, is not mutually exclusive but rather a complement to each other.

Further Questions on This Case:

1. How would you describe the alternative pathways of "NatureYou"'s internationalization? Would you relate your answers to concrete examples as exhibited in this case? Is there a path you would prefer?
2. Was Frank Wilson just lucky with his internationalization of "NatureYou"? Do you believe a "rude awakening" will soon follow?
3. What characterizes Frank Wilson's entrepreneurial activity? To what extent do you think his way of making strategic decisions is typical of SMEs?
4. What do you think about the importance of "social networks" and "trust" for SMEs in general—and in the context of SME internationalization in particular?
5. Are SME entrepreneurs less inclined by nature to implement strategic planning before undertaking internationalization than MNE managers? If so, why do you think so?
6. Is there a common, or even superior, pathway on which SMEs internationalize their business? Is "NatureYou" a role model for SME internationalization? What do you think about the preliminary conclusion Frank had drawn from the internationalization of "NatureYou" so far?
7. If Frank Wilson had asked you how to "seize opportunities" to internationalize "NatureYou", what would your advice have been? Do you think one of the approaches taken in this case is more or less superior than the other one? What would be your preferred pathway of internationalization?

From Zero to Sales

18

Developing and Implementing an International Sales Strategy in Competitive Consumer Markets (Case Study)

Sebastian Huber

18.1 A New Customer in Australia

On a pleasant Tuesday morning in May of 2018, Andreas stands in his warehouse in Zollikofen—a pleasant village at the outskirts of the Swiss capital city of Bern—and marvels at his luggage collection. It is simply the best in high-tech travel gear the industry has to offer. The black carbon suitcases are indeed his baby: a stroke of genius followed by years of hard work and relentless innovation supported with millions of seed investment at the best technical research institute of the country. All the effort had led to a carbon-fabric shell so sturdy and tough; a man could stand on the ultralight suitcases without them even showing the slightest dent. As CEO of the company in its seventh year, it is now Andreas's challenge to get these perfectly engineered products into the hands of happy customers around the world!

But daydreaming about his products is not the reason why Andreas visits his warehouse today. He's here to assemble a starter package of products to be shipped to a new customer in Sydney, Australia. After weeks of negotiating the prices and shipment terms, the Australian luggage shop owner placed an order in an e-mail to him last night. So Andreas drove down to the warehouse this morning to put a total of six suitcases onto a palette, printed the customs and shipping documents, then called his logistics service, and had the package on its way to the other side of the globe as soon as this afternoon. He can't wait to

S. Huber (✉)
Institute of Business and Regional Economics, Lucerne University of Applied Sciences and Arts – Business, Lucerne, Switzerland
e-mail: sebastian.huber@hslu.ch

I. Stolz, S. Oldenziel Scherrer (eds.), *International Leadership*, uniscope. Publikationen der SGO Stiftung, https://doi.org/10.1007/978-3-658-37306-1_18

reply to his new customer with the shipment number as confirmation of the order being on its way.

As Andreas walks along the aisle to collect one or two pieces of each size of the carefully packaged suitcases, he catches himself thinking back to yesterday's photo op. With a student friend of his son, they had met at the Bern local airport and then carefully maneuvered his Rover pick-up van onto four of the suitcases to demonstrate just how strong these products are. The photos came out ultimately cool, and he will place them on the company's social media feed later today. He smiles at the thought that this type of guerilla marketing is just about his thing. And great fun, too!

18.2 Back to Reality

Just before lunch, Andreas returns to his office at Bern Technopark, an innovation hub and office building for start-ups, from where he operates the company. He clarifies all details with his logistics provider who is going to collect the shipment from the warehouse the same evening. His mood, however, changes as he starts to prepare the quarterly sales numbers for the board of directors meeting at the end of the week. Once again, he has only sold very few pieces of luggage to dealers, who have sold even smaller quantities to final consumers. The order from Sydney will not change much about that, unfortunately. The value of all items still stored in his warehouse remains a huge burden and will once again raise concerns by Peter, the company's owner and president of the board. Obtaining his support and financing much-needed activities in sales promotion and marketing is going to be a tough discussion.

With his background as a trained engineer, Andreas longs to scale up production, which would dramatically reduce unit costs, make the company profitable, and allow for pricing the collection at a much more competitive level. Andreas has invested much of his time and energy into finding the right production partner—first in Slovakia, then in China—who could reliably manufacture and assemble the high-end suitcases to his quality standards (cf. Fig. 18.1). Having set up the machinery and production line with much of Andreas's own know-how and oversight on site, his production partner is now ready to ramp up production as soon as Andreas gives him the go-ahead. But with all the merchandise still piled up at the warehouse, there is no way of thinking about producing more quantities anytime soon. In one way or the other, Andreas must get sales going if this venture is to continue.

As Andreas scans the agenda of the upcoming board meeting, he recalls a consulting project on the topic of internationalization of his company which is soon to start in a partnership with a team from a nearby university. Could this project be set up in such a way to help him accelerate his international sales efforts? Maybe such support could convince Peter to invest the additionally needed cash and time to win the next round of distribution partners and develop the company's marketing and branding.

Fig. 18.1 Luggage production and warehouse (courtesy of company records)

Conversationally, Peter and other senior members of the board are known for their firm belief that a good product does all the selling it needs by itself. So long as the product is superior in quality and functionality to others in the market, customers will be convinced by just holding it in their hands and testing it. Andreas, however, has learned the hard way that this is not true for the highly competitive suitcase market which is dominated by global giants such as Samsonite, Rimova, and Tumi (cf. Fig. 18.2). His distribution partners need marketing support, and final consumers have to be made aware of the brand and its products. A few times, Andreas has convinced Peter to invest in marketing and sales activities, such as exhibiting at the Baselworld tradeshow where he met that luggage retailer from Sydney. A fixed budget or personnel resource for sales and marketing, however, is out of the question for his board of directors, so the entire task remains on Andreas's shoulders. So more often than not, he works out low-budget guerilla tactics like yesterday's photo shoot.

The ringtone of his mobile phone disrupts Andreas in his thoughts. On the phone—coincidentally—is his contact from university, Roland, who calls to align with Andreas on the next steps for their project. They have not spoken for a while, so Andreas enthusiastically tells Roland of his new customer in Sydney. On his end, Roland also reports some progress: the team has evaluated options for their project and acknowledged that Andreas's company is already successfully internationalized for its production and logistics. What is lacking—and thus should be the project's focus—is their international sales and business development efforts, Roland concludes. And for that, he has found a suitable expert in Daniel, a member of his team whom he would like to introduce to Andreas.

To Andreas, these are fantastic news, so he excitedly accepts Roland's proposal. Anticipating his shareholder's likely reluctance to further investments into sales and marketing, he suggests to Roland that he and Daniel should join the board meeting on Friday, present their project idea, and directly obtain the mandate and support of the board

Fig. 18.2 A tough competition landscape—luggage retail (courtesy of company records)

of directors. Roland is delighted by the invitation, confirms his availability, and Andreas finishes the call with a light spirit. Could he win over the board's support, and might this project even pave him the way to international business success?

18.3 Navigating the Board Meeting

The board of directors meets on Friday morning in a rather dull room adjacent to Peter's private garage in Langenthal, near Bern. Andreas knows the setting well and anticipates that Peter is going to show his car collection to the two guests at the board meeting, Roland and Daniel. And while he does so, Andreas sets up the projector and laptop for the meeting.

Setting a positive note, Andreas starts the meeting by showing pictures from the recent photo shoot at Bern airport, then introduces the two academic guests and their project. Daniel presents a few slides on the approach and focus of the project along with the objectives and plan of action to reach them. In the discussion, it becomes painfully obvious that the rigid analytics applied to the engineering of the company's products has been lacking in its sales and marketing approach. Acknowledging that, a discussion erupts on how to position the brand and company in the future. In contrast to other options of licensing or technology supply, the board confidently confirms to keep following its strategy to cover the full value chain from innovation, technology, and production all the way through to marketing and distribution of the final product (cf. Fig. 18.3).

Contentedly, Andreas notes that the board implicitly agrees to a more thorough analysis of the marketing and sales activities while confirming that both those domains remain in his responsibility and will not be delegated to a third-party distribution partner. All the same, his quarterly numbers will soon be up on the screen, but he does not yet understand how Daniel intends to proceed with increasing international sales. And can Peter be convinced to invest additional cash? The numbers come up and draw long faces around the table. Peter questions Andreas on what has come from his exhibition at Baselworld 2 months ago, so Andreas shares a list of contacts from his sales pipeline stretching all around the world. To

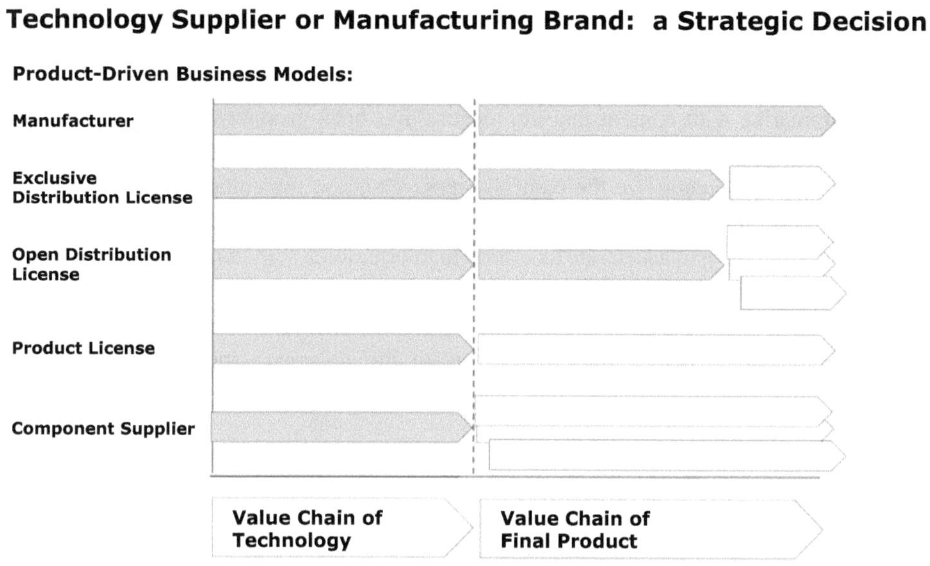

Fig. 18.3 Business model scope (adopted from Abele, 2013, p. 90). (Abele, T. (Ed.) (2013). Suchfeldbestimmung und Ideenbewertung: Methoden und Prozesse in den frühen Phasen des Innovationsprozesses. Springer)

Andreas's surprise, the two guests from university intervene: Daniel suggests to first run a thorough analysis on past sales activities before taking any more decisions. In his view, the company needs to understand which markets are performing and which point-of-sales (POS) types are successful. Describing the successful cases, strengths and weaknesses of the company along with the opportunities and threats in the international luggage market will lead to an international sales SWOT[1] for the company. Daniel insists that only then strategic options can be developed.

The board falls silent for an awkwardly long moment. On the one hand, both Andreas and Peter are familiar with pragmatic, yet analytical approaches to solving problems. However, it has not occurred to them that sales and business development could be approached the same way. What is more, both gentlemen are aware that consenting to this approach implies to invest time and effort into an analysis which diverts attention from following up on promising sales leads. It is Peter who first speaks and simply agrees to the suggestion, probably due to the sheer lack of alternatives—or so Andreas guesses. He quickly throws all his support behind the idea and presses for a stringent timeline to

[1]Often attributed to Albert Humphrey of the Stanford Research Institute in the late 1960s, a SWOT (strengths, weaknesses, opportunities, and threats) analysis is a framework used to evaluate a company's competitive position and to develop strategic planning. A SWOT analysis assesses internal and external factors as well as current and future potential.

produce results for his next quarterly report. If sales numbers cannot be immediately lifted, Andreas needs an action plan for the remainder of the year, the sooner the better.

Taking an afternoon train back to their campus after the board meeting, Roland and Daniel summarize with content that the meeting has been productive and that they have been able to support Andreas with a tangible project proposal supported by his board. At the same time, they recognize the painfully tense situation the company and its board of directors are in. Stripped of cash locked in a warehouse full of finished merchandise, the company is struggling to accelerate its efforts in international sales and distribution. Even if their project produces a solid analysis and tangible proposals for growing the business internationally, the company might simply not have enough of its own resources to implement the suggested actions and to create the necessary momentum to become profitable.

18.4 Crunching the Numbers

A few days later, Daniel receives a long e-mail from Andreas with lots of attachments. He has asked for recent sales data along with Andreas's contact lists of customers as well as for prospective distribution partners. From the board meeting, Daniel has taken the impression that Andreas—like so many other entrepreneurs in love with their product—is spreading his efforts across way too many countries and aspirational contacts in hope for random success without really understanding what might work to sell his luggage—and what does not.

Andreas's e-mail includes an address book of almost 170 contacts, along with a more exclusive list of 24 POS that are already in a contractual relationship with him, and another 40 prospects from his sales pipeline. Daniel begins by classifying each commercial partner (cf. Fig. 18.4) and prospect (cf. Fig. 18.5) with regards to the POS type (luggage retailer, department store, online shop, outlet, etc.) and the county in which it operates. The numbers tell a very clear story: 13 out of today's 24 POS are located in Germany and Switzerland—as are another 22 of the 40 prospects. The other POS are scattered across 13 countries, with another 25 countries in Andreas's prospect pipeline. Even from the long list in Andreas's address book, almost half of the contacts are from Germany and Switzerland. Raising an eyebrow as he goes through the data, Daniel notices prospects from Vietnam, Lebanon, Nigeria, and Romania, which to him are surprisingly unusual countries for distributing a high-end luggage item. He is going to ask Andreas at the next occasion what his intentions for these markets are.

Second, Daniel scans the unit sales numbers that Andreas was so concerned with sharing at the board meeting. For Daniel's analysis, Andreas has added to each contact the 5-month year-to-date sales of 2018. On the classification by country and POS type, Daniel runs the sales numbers. They are consistent with distribution reach: Switzerland and Germany are by far the most important distribution markets, generating two-thirds of sales

Number of Contracted POS by Country and Type (as of 2018)									
	TYPE	Department Store	Accessories Retail	Luggage Retail	Fashion Retail	online	Mall	B2B	B2C
COUNTRY		0	5	7	0	1	1	5	5
Switzerland	8		1	1				2	4
Germany	5			3				1	1
Austria	1			1					
UK	1							1	
Denmark	1		1						
Spain	1			1					
Russia	1						1		
Turkey	1							1	
USA	1					1			
Mexico	1		1						
China	1			1					
Korea	1		1						
Australia	1		1						

Fig. 18.4 Country-channel analysis based on contracted relationships (2018 company data)

Number of Prospective POS by Country and Type (as of 2018)									
	TYPE	Department Store	Accessories Retail	Luggage Retail	Fashion Retail	online	Mall	B2B	B2C
COUNTRY		4	10	12	0	1	0	4	1
Switzerland	12	2	3	4				2	1
Germany	10	2	1	4		1		2	
Austria	2		1	1					
Italy	1			1					
Turkey	1		1						
China	1		1						
Singapore	1			1					
Hong Kong	1		1						
Korea	1		1						
Japan	1			1					
Australia	1		1						
BeNeLux	2		1			1			
Dubai, UAE	1			1					
Nigeria	1		1						
Romania	1		1						
Greece	1		1						

Fig. 18.5 Country-channel analysis based on prospective distribution partnerships (2018 company data)

in 2018 thus far. Notably, Andreas's most recent success in Australia shows prominently on Daniel's overview chart as well.

Further looking for the success stories and best practices in the numbers, Daniel reiterates his analysis by type of POS—once again finding alignment between the number of POS per type and the sales per type—, with specialized travel gear retailers and accessories stores dominating Andreas's customer and prospect lists. Notably absent are department stores, travel retailers at airports, and e-commerce channels, all of which are much more difficult to win over but offer great multiplication effects through their networks. Daniel copies his pie charts into a slide deck and writes back to Andreas that he's ready with the numbers for a workshop to develop the international sales SWOT.

18.5 Not Just Any SWOT

Andreas enters the university building on an afternoon in early June with quite some curiosity on which news the figures might reveal. As an engineer, he is used to trusting the data and taking numbers very seriously. He is also desperate for a cup of good coffee and relieved when Daniel greets him with the invitation to start with a chat at the coffee machine. Coffee in hand and overlooking the old town from the university terrace, Daniel asks Andreas how countries like Vietnam and Romania have made it to his prospect list. Shrugging his shoulders, Andreas acknowledges that in order to distribute his luggage collection, he follows any and all international sales opportunities at this point, knowingly stretching his resources and risking the high-end positioning of the brand.

As Daniel presents his analysis back in a meeting room, Andreas is struck by the clarity and brutality of the figures. He somehow knew that he was putting a lot of time and effort into international distribution, but it had never been so obvious to him where the true opportunities lie: Germany and Switzerland are his most important and most prospective markets. More to himself, he sadly comments that the glitz and buzz of international business might have been an aspiration, but in order to bring his company to profitability, he would need to put his money where his mouth is and focus on his most promising markets. Furthermore, he agrees that the absence of POS networks, such as department stores and travel retailers, remains a challenge to be addressed.

Daniel notes the slight consternation in Andreas's voice and turns their attention to the next item on the workshop agenda: classifying and describing POS success stories. This is where Andreas swiftly recovers his enthusiasm as he tells stories, shows pictures, and shares the sales successes of partners and distributors from his network. Just on his way this afternoon, he had stopped at one of his most enthusiastic partners in Switzerland only to be fascinated how that partner sells luggage products in the strangest environment of an apparently random assortment of other luxury items and accessories. Catching on to Andreas's excitement, Daniel groups the POS into (a) those with success due to tangible efforts; (b) those with apparently random success and little to no effort; and (c) POS that have not yet shown significant sell-through results. Directly projecting his digital notes to a wall, Daniel documents the activities and actions for each successful POS. He will later compile these into a prioritized list of potential marketing activities which Andreas is going to use for supporting his partners and driving sales.

Exhausted from all the talking and afternoon heat in their meeting room, the two agree to finalize their notes via e-mail and to compile their results into a sales SWOT from which they are going to derive potential strategic options for Andreas and his board of directors to decide upon. Knowing that Andreas has some promising sales activities scheduled with a partner at Vienna airport in the weeks ahead, Daniel offers to prepare his draft of the SWOT analysis for when Andreas is back in Switzerland.

18.6 Pondering Strategic Options

Swiss summer is in full swing when Andreas and Daniel meet for lunch in a conveniently located conference hotel near the Olten train station in late June. Waiting for their main course, Andreas shares some stories from the "sales push" at Vienna airport. Hurried transfer passengers from China were huddling by his product presentation stand only to ask "How much?" whenever he presented one of his suitcases to them. The sales assistant supporting him in the promotion repeatedly complained that products had a tough stance if their branding did not pull people into a POS. So Andreas is full of questions on how a new sales strategy will emerge to create the necessary buzz around his products.

Taking their coffee to the meeting room, Daniel switches back to their strategic journey with a pile of post-its in four colors for each of the SWOT dimensions, which he had extracted from their last workshop notes: yellow for opportunity, orange for threat, green for strength, and blue for weakness. On a big wall, Andreas and Daniel label, then group the colorful post-its into pairs, generating combinations of strengths and threats, opportunities and weaknesses, and many more, leading to a long list of strategic options to be prioritized (cf. Fig. 18.6). Intuitively most appealing to Andreas are the opportunity-strength combinations where the company can seize a market opportunity by playing on its strengths. But are these also the most viable and promising options? Can the company sustain the required investment, and how fast will these actions materialize? Going back and forth between strategic statements and the current market realities, a controversial discussion emerges between the two—pondering options, grouping similar ideas, comparing timelines and investment volumes between options.

Separating the grain from the chaff, the two agree on a condensed list of just about ten strategic directions, some combining opportunities and strengths but also measures to address where the company weaknesses are challenged by threats from the market. Without losing any time, Andreas is eager to share this strategy with his board of directors so as to obtain backing for his strategic action plan. Daniel, however, throws in a word of caution and recommends to first simplify the strategic narrative, to outline a tangible action plan for the next 3 years, and to interlace that into a sales scenario that should lead the company to break-even and into profitability. The challenge is to bring the strategic directions into alignment with the current, actual distribution network and sales numbers, then to show how a strategic choice will lead from today's status quo to the agreed objectives. Confident that they are sharing enough common understanding on the way forward, the two agree to keep working on their action plan in an exchange of e-mails while Andreas is going to schedule a next board meeting for mid-July. In the afternoon sun, Andreas and Daniel head back to the train station in uplifted spirits, looking forward to the conceptual work ahead of them.

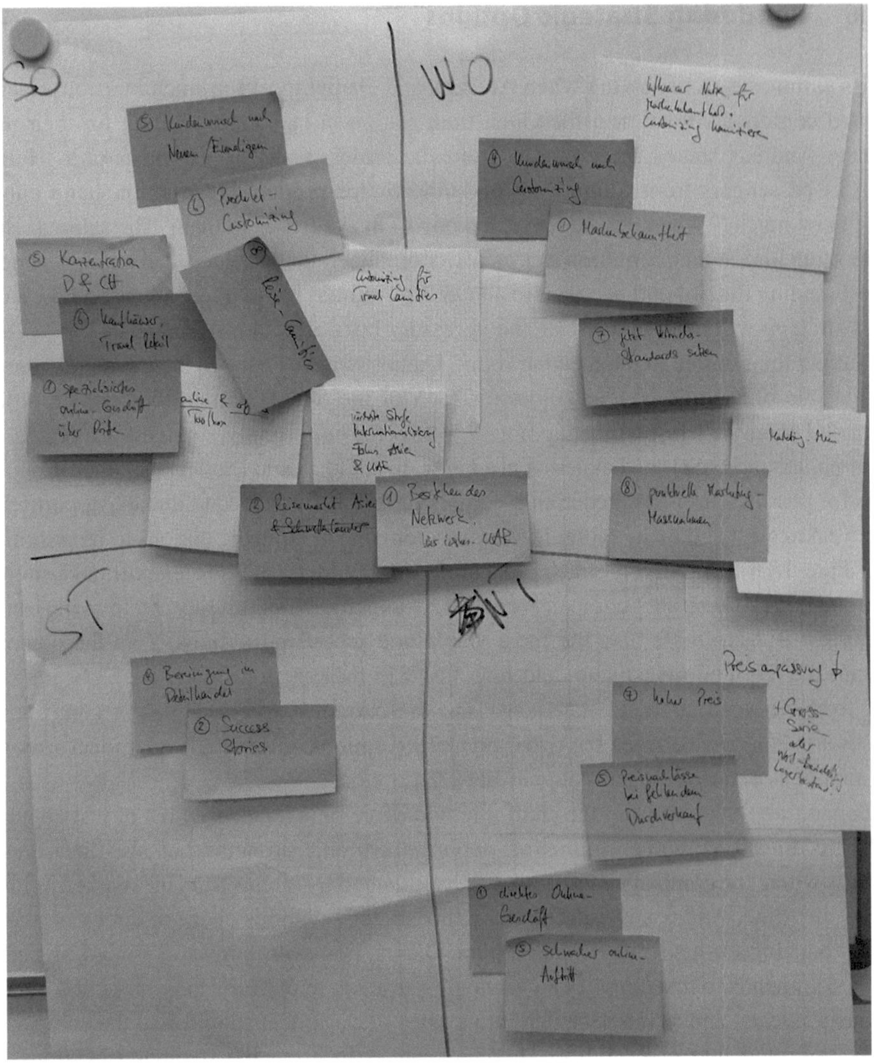

Fig. 18.6 Developing strategic options (workshop flipchart)

18.7 Taking Tangible Action

The clear morning air of July 19th offers a pleasant view of the snow-covered Alps in the distance as Andreas and Daniel sip at their coffee in the large meeting room of Bern's Technopark where today's board meeting is scheduled. Over the past weeks, the two have developed a strategic narrative in five chapters which they look forward to presenting and discussing with the board today: (1) a snappy yet blunt analysis of the status quo with

(2) current sales success stories, followed by (3) the updated SWOT analysis and leading to (4) five strategic avenues that are then translated into (5) tangible sales numbers for the 3 years ahead. A concluding slide of the presentation shows three board decisions for immediate action that Andreas is most edgy about. They include a commitment to adjust market prices of the assortment while investing time and resources into a marketing and sales initiative for Germany and Switzerland still this year.

Everything is ready when Peter arrives: the presentation printouts nicely bound for each meeting participant, the projector switched on with slides on the screen, and coffee with a few refreshments on the table. Andreas starts by welcoming everyone and recognizing the benefits from a thorough analysis on the sales and marketing activities. Daniel then summarizes the status quo: an organization torn by spreading its sales and marketing activities across way too many countries and POS, while only a handful of them in Germany and Switzerland are truly successful. He also points at the risk of further dispersing resources if all new contacts and markets were to be followed up with equal priority. From the sales SWOT, he then outlines the five strategic avenues: some for more short-term impact, others along a more long-term choice of positioning the brand in the competitive luggage market. No immediate controversy erupts at this point as Peter refrains from objecting to these analyses and observations, being curious to discover how they will translate into tangible actions.

Daniel continues to outline the 2018–2021 sales strategy, in which he recommends to focus on the most promising markets and dedicated acquisition of POS chains such as department stores, travel retail, and e-commerce in Germany and Switzerland. For Andreas and Peter, that will mean to put their global aspirations on hold, to roll up their sleeves, and to actively recruit as well as pursue the more challenging yet more promising distribution channels. Making existing and new POS in those two markets successful is the second priority, requiring the support of a dedicated marketing campaign which includes a POS locator tool on the company's updated website, support materials, and co-op marketing activities with the support of Andreas on-site at his distribution partners.

Working with sell-in and sell-out estimates from 2018 to 2021, Daniel then outlines a plan with an increase of sell-through in existing POS and showing the addition of other POS to the distribution network (cf. Fig. 18.7). Given successful performances in Germany and Switzerland, the company would only expand to the United Arab Emirates in 2020 and to China in 2021, following preferences and some personal contacts from the board of directors and Andreas himself. Showing moderate growth in adding POS, the sales numbers appear to be quite dynamic since over time, each POS would improve its sell-in and sell-out performance thanks to dedicated marketing support. Knowing that the numbers were going to be ambitious and depend on the launch and implementation of a successful marketing campaign, Andreas glances with curiosity at Peter who seems to take the numbers confidently at face value and almost impatiently waits for the 2018 action plan as well as the decisions requested from the board today.

So without further ado, Andreas takes the lead and outlines his immediate three-step action plan for board approval: (a) the immediate development of a marketing campaign

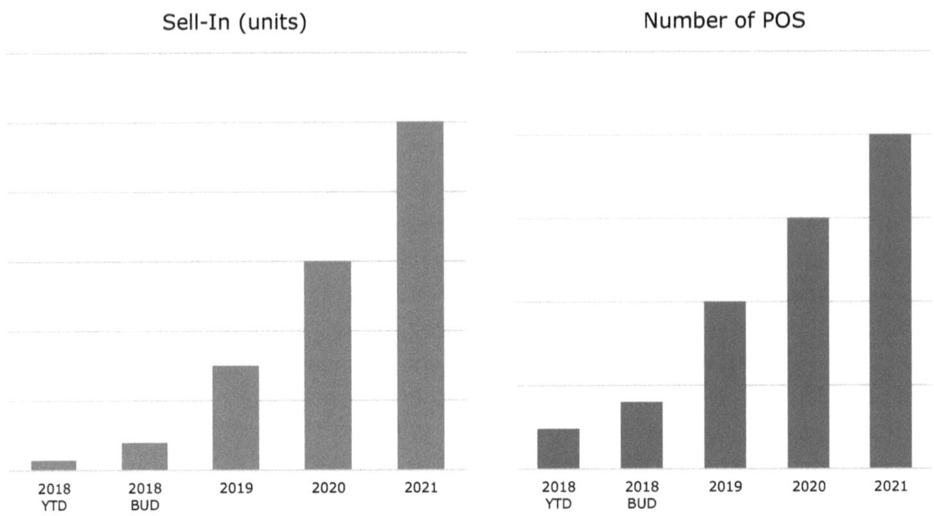

Fig. 18.7 Projections on sales and POS (2018 company data, explicit numbers omitted for confidentiality)

still for implementation before the all-important Christmas shopping period in November; (b) an adjustment in value of the merchandise on stock and a reduction of end-consumer pricing as per August 2018; as well as (c) developing a full financial plan based on the agreed strategic direction for the next 3 years.

With high expectations, Andreas looks over at Peter: will he chip in additional cash to support this effort in financial and human resources to lift the brand to the next level, even if it means postponing his global aspirations for the company to the longer term?

Possible Assignment Questions and Points for Further Discussion

- From reading the case, how would you describe the company's overall profile and international business outlook in your own words?
- Which international leadership behaviors and subsequent decisions can you detect within the case study?
- Scrutinize the strategy process along five steps: (1) internal and external situation analysis; (2) developing strategic options; (3) providing decision-making rationale; (4) implementation; and (5) evaluation. Is this an appropriate approach for this case? If not, how else could the protagonists have proceeded?
- If you were a member of the board, how would you evaluate Andreas's proposal? How would you argue for/against (a) the investment into sales and market; (b) a price reduction of the assortment; and (c) a focus on market development in Germany and Switzerland for the near future?

- Describe and assess the company's leadership approach to decision-making on its internationalization efforts.
- Resource constraints aside, how would you judge and evaluate further expansion into additional market and territories?
- Specifically considering e-commerce, what strategy and which specific players would you consider for this product category and brand?
- Often referred to as "buying growth" or "buying sales", the short-term investment into a distribution channel, POS types or specific partners and markets can quickly outweigh the incremental sales and profits generated there. Do you consider this case to be at risk of "buying sales"? And if so, how can that be avoided?

Leading Leadership Development

19

Designing and Sustaining the Next Generation Scientist Program

Henri Michel Yéré, Goonaseelan Colin Pillai, Akiko Nathalie Keller, and Ingo Stolz

19.1 A Blow to the Core

And then—all of a sudden—the room went quiet. Colin and Henri[1] quickly looked at each other and at their colleagues in the core team, before their eyes moved slowly across the faces of the 20+ people in the room, to assess the impact of the words that had just been

The case study contains real anecdotes that occurred in multiple separate incidents over the course of the program. They have been written, dramatized, and condensed in a way to illustrate leadership behaviors exhibited by the stakeholders involved.

[1] All names with an asterisk (*) are anonymized, with titles, country of origin, and event settings

H. M. Yéré (✉)
University of Basel, Basel, Switzerland
e-mail: h.yere@unibas.ch

G. C. Pillai
CP+ Associates GmbH, Binningen, Switzerland
e-mail: colin@cpplusassociates.org

A. N. Keller
Novartis Pharma AG, Basel, Switzerland
e-mail: akiko.keller@novartis.com

I. Stolz
Lucerne University of Applied Sciences and Arts – Business, Institute of Business and Regional Economics, Lucerne, Switzerland
e-mail: ingo.stolz@hslu.ch

I. Stolz, S. Oldenziel Scherrer (eds.), *International Leadership*, uniscope. Publikationen der SGO Stiftung, https://doi.org/10.1007/978-3-658-37306-1_19

spoken. They truly went to the core! Of all people, it was Richard* who seemed exasperated and shared his feelings with the group:

> I am very disappointed with Julia's* performance, even though I know from experience how young scientists from Africa are being poorly trained in this day and age. She does not even know the most basic sets of experimental procedures needed in her field ...! How am I to continue working with her under those conditions, can you tell me? Besides, I have more important things to do than to take care of such an intern, let me tell you now ...

Colin, Henri and the Core Team knew—just like everybody—that this was not just a negative testimony about the work performance of an intern. This was a potential blow to the legitimacy of the program which, though still in its infancy, had been designed after extensive stakeholder consultation and was now being nurtured and passionately implemented. Up until Richard's* outburst, the team had been at ease. Even more than that. As the mentors took turns to discuss the specific situation of each of their respective interns, they all provided glowing reports and impressive progress. The room was filled with collective pride, hearing that the interns for whom they were ultimately responsible were developing well within and as a result of their program. How rewarding! It was amid this feel-good atmosphere that Richard*, a respected scientist in the company, originally from Nigeria, impugned his intern, Julia*, a medicinal chemistry doctoral student from Malawi. Colin and Henri immediately understood that they needed to intervene, addressing the situation so as to ensure that the Next Generation Scientist program remained on track for its broader goals that went beyond the obvious short-term plan of capacity development. This was neither the first nor last time the program was challenged.

19.2 The Next Generation Scientist Program (NGS)

The Next Generation Scientist program, organized by Novartis and the University of Basel (NGS), was designed as a 3-month immersive learning program for talented and motivated young research scientists on the Masters, PhD, or early post-doctoral level from low- and middle-income countries (LMICs). While attending the program, the interns are mentored by Novartis scientists, working on a jointly agreed-upon scientific research project. The interns additionally participate in a leadership development program designed to enhance their decision-making and communication skills. According to reporting in BMC Medical Education (Pillai et al. 2018), the annual program had trained more than 140 scientists and clinicians from 25 LMICs over the previous 7-year period.

Having grown up in South Africa and Côte d'Ivoire respectively, both Colin and Henri felt passionate about working for an organization that supported a program such as NGS,

altered so as to avoid association with specific participants in the program. All other names—and the respective personal information—are real and are mentioned with permission.

allowing them to apply their professional skills in a way that directly benefited their continent of origin. Together with Marcelo Gutierrez and Fareed Mirza, two scientists with family links to the Philippines and the Indian subcontinent, the program was supported scientifically and administratively by Sandra Felix, Fernando Romero, Rita Michel, and Akiko Keller during its formative years. Indeed, many members of the diverse and global Core Team who worked on the NGS program over the years viewed it as a "personal calling" rather than just a job, and they were personally invested in the goals the NGS program pursued. They knew firsthand about the disproportionately low number of skilled scientists in LMICs, specifically in relation to the high disease burden that affected many of these countries. They were privileged to contribute to the development of future scientists who would practice in global settings. For many of the Core Team members, this was a path on which they felt able to help support science and health in LMICs, while at the same time contributing to an increased awareness within the company of healthcare challenges in LMICs.

19.3 A Unique Implementation Program to Support Diversity and Inclusion (D&I)

By inviting scientists from LMICs and pairing them with experienced scientists at Novartis, the NGS program pursued the following goals:

- to help foster interns' personal and professional development;
- to help educate and train motivated scientists and clinicians who plan to contribute toward strengthening healthcare systems in their home countries;
- to help interns facilitate knowledge transfer to their wider scientific communities upon returning home after the program;
- to establish and maintain a global network of future leaders in LMICs; and
- to increase the volume and quality of healthcare research in previously under-served parts of the world.

For Novartis, a crucial element of the program was to help expose scientists and other associates to healthcare systems and challenges in LMICs via their mentees. In addition, the NGS program was seen to provide an opportunity to establish strategic partnerships with academic and research institutions in parts of the world for which Novartis was developing medical solutions but did not always have a strong local presence. Furthermore, Colin, Henri, and the Core Team were passionate about the NGS program, because it was designed according to deep convictions they held individually:

- the more diverse the perspectives are in a given research context, the stronger is the scientific output;

- leaders need to learn to trust in the power of diversity as a precursor of creativity and innovation; that scientists not only need research skills but also soft skills in order to bring their work to full fruition;
- transformation always begins with shifting individual minds;
- scientific leaders first and foremost need to learn about themselves, in order to enable themselves to consciously manage their personality, their energy, and also their biases within the complex research processes they navigate.

Finally, based on experiences of their own respective career paths, both Colin and Henri were convinced that being a good leader necessitates the ability to manage a crisis and to identify, whenever possible, ways to convert such situations into opportunities for learning or other advantages. They understood firsthand that this orientation was also needed when running a program such as NGS since, as it happened, it was precisely this type of approach that had helped establish the NGS program in the first place.

19.4 Leveraging Opportunities for Establishing the NGS Program

Ensuring the sustainability of the NGS program was critical from the start. Visionary leadership, patience, and persistence were fundamental attributes of the NGS founders that enabled the programs establishment and, over time, elevated its internal and external visibility in ways that helped advance the program's goals.

In 2012, the year of the second cohort of the NGS program, Novartis was a global pharmaceutical leader with operations in 140 countries, discovering, developing, and delivering medicines, vaccines, diagnostics, and consumer health products to approximately 1.2 billion people. Headquartered in Basel, Switzerland, Novartis employed more than 120,000 people globally and generated sales of more than USD 55 billion (Novartis 2012).

Around the time NGS was established, Novartis was already actively committed to Diversity & Inclusion (D&I), traditionally understood as describing activities designed to foster an inclusive culture, i.e., including populations that had historically been negatively impacted by structural inequalities in society. Senior leadership supported its staff to explore how D&I could best be authentically incorporated into the company's culture to support the overall objective of discovering and developing new medicines that would reach patients everywhere who stood to benefit.

In a discussion with the Head of D&I at the Novartis research labs at the time, they brainstormed how they could maximize NGS impact:

> This is the right question to pose. Because in fact, our scientists here at Novartis would be surprised to hear how much the perspectives from scientists based in LMICs complement their own views and insights. How can we engineer a way to put them in touch so that they can explore this in-depth so as to get to the core of issues? This is an opportunity to go beyond

> being just another add-on D&I initiative, and should be integrated into the science of developing drugs. We will need the right skills and mindset to drive something like this if we want to achieve a lasting impact.

Colin clearly saw the opportunity arising in front of him. However, he needed to make a career choice: should he continue as head of an innovative and visible scientific group that was increasingly being sought out to guide critical drug development decisions with mathematical modeling and simulation—or should he consider a role that moved him away from direct scientific impact on the company's portfolio and into an unproven realm linked with D&I?

Colin accepted a newly created role as Head of D&I and Scientific Capability Building, thereby ensuring that both the research and the development organization of the company could pool their efforts for impact across the entire drug discovery and clinical development organization so as to support pioneering scientific capability-building programs.

Together with his counterpart in the Research Division, they brought together the initial eight-member Core Team that ultimately brought the NGS program to life. Strong diversity was represented even in there, with members from Africa, Asia, South America, and Europe. The Core Team engaged diverse scientific leaders around the company, especially those who had moved their careers from LMICs to the Novartis campus. Not surprisingly, these scientific leaders were readily convinced of the urgency and importance of a program such as the NGS, and specifically of the goals it pursued.

A central early step was visiting key partners in various parts of Africa (e.g. Ethiopia, Kenya, and South Africa) in order to test the concept and to gather local insights into real needs on-the-ground. Among others, the visit to Professor Kelly Chibale, Director of the Drug Discovery and Development Centre (H3-D) at the University of Cape Town, South Africa, provided a compass for what could be achieved with local support. Professor Chibale worked closely with the Core Team to identify projects that would help fill local technology and skills gaps. The 2012 Novartis Annual Report, a company publication to shareholders documenting its activities and finances, featured the program and included interviews with Professor Chibale:

> The attraction of the Next Generation scientist program goes beyond the individual intern; for us it's about building an institution, (...) simply sending people to Novartis or European universities provides no continuity when people return—what do they come back to? Interns returning to H3D continue to work on the same project and with some of the technical infrastructure they saw at Novartis. (Novartis 2012)

Starting from the launch of the pilot, the NGS program rapidly gained visibility inside and outside the company. For example, the Novartis Annual Report regularly[2] showcased

[2]Novartis Annual Reports (2012, 2016, 2017, 2018).

alumni from LMICs who had participated in the program, illustrating progress in their careers.

External recognition followed. The Access to Medicine Index (ATMi), organized by the Access to Medicine Foundation based in the Netherlands, provides an external benchmarking or report card tool to drive change in the pharmaceutical industry. The index identifies best practices, tracks progress, and suggests where critical action is needed to improve access to medicine for the poor. In the 2016 ATMi report, Novartis was placed as the overall leader in capacity-building: "Leader in capacity building, consistently addresses local needs" (ATMi 2016, p. 91). In an analysis on improving access to cancer care, they reported a year later:

> GSK, Eli Lilly, Novartis and Takeda are the only companies active in R&D capacity building for oncology in an LMC in scope: GSK through its Africa NCD Open Labs and South Africa MRC partnerships, Eli Lilly through its initiative for gynaecology oncology having founded an oncology research institute in Kenya, Novartis through its Next Generation Scientist programme, and Takeda with multiple partners in sub-Saharan Africa for paediatric cancer care. (ATMi 2017, p. 56)

19.5 Crisis Intervention

When Richard* shared his frank perceptions about his intern, Julia*, the NGS program was early in its genesis. The Core Team had already organized one formal touch-base meeting with the scientific mentors, before the arrival of the interns. They were now sitting through the first mid-way meeting, after the interns had already worked for 6 weeks as part of the mentors' teams. They collected feedback from their mentors, so that the Core Team could invest in mid-course corrections or offer support if needed. Given that the team already had multiple one-on-one meetings with each mentor and intern between the touch-base and the first mid-way meeting, the team was surprised about Richard's* outburst. They had not seen this coming, given that he had not mentioned any concerns previously.

After Richard's* statement, the tone of the meeting began to shift, from a convivial engagement toward other mentors also starting to take a more critical look at their own interns. In the end, the dominant voices in the room became those of the critics. Because of Richard's* complaint, the image of the program, indeed its very existence, suddenly felt to be standing on shaky grounds.

As Head of the NGS program, Colin called the Core Team together for an emergency session immediately after the meeting. Its goal was to determine a course of action to better understand Richard's* view and to prevent any misunderstandings that could result in Richard* or other mentors pulling out of the program. If that were to happen, it was conceivable that a chain of events could take place that would lead to the effective disappearance of the program. The Core Team decided to put together an approach playing on multiple registers.

Colin first turned to Henri. With his PhD in Contemporary History, Henri had joined the Diversity & Inclusion office of the Novartis research labs precisely because he would bring a differentiated perspective to a world dominated by the natural sciences. He did cut an unusual figure into the sphere of pharmaceutical fundamental research. His being recruited into the D&I team spoke volumes about the company's broad vision of D&I, one that focused on how the differences in thinking styles held reservoirs of creativity and original problem-solving. Also, Henri knew his way around the cultural codes in use in West Africa, in Southern Africa (he had completed his undergraduate studies in Cape Town), and in Europe, where he had spent a significant part of his life. Colin and Henri had the following exchange:

Colin:

*Please go speak with Richard**. *Make him understand what is at stake here. He might not be aware of what he has triggered with his comments.*

Henri:

I agree with you, Colin. Clearly, he spoke out of anger, and I think he lost sight of the venue where he was whilst speaking. Also, he might not be aware about the weight his voice carries, given that he himself is a scientist from an LMIC.

Colin:

*Have him appreciate this point. I know that you would know how to appeal to him, how to push the right buttons … Whilst you speak to him, I will talk to Julia** …*

Henri reached out to Richard*, just 2 h after the mid-way meeting. He walked into his lab without an appointment. He urged Richard* to withdraw into a quiet corner and said to him:

Henri:

*Richard**, *I appreciate the fact that you were frustrated over the performance of your intern. Yet I am sure you can remember your own early days in the lab, and they were not devoid of mistakes and faux pas, just like for all of us …*

Richard* [with quiet laughter]:

Oh … Yes, Henri, I can see that.

Henri:

I am glad you can see this. At the same time, Richard, you are a respected figure amongst the scientists here in the company . . .*

Richard*:

Thank you for saying this!

Henri:

You know it's the truth. And I respect you even more than the other staff members, Richard . . .*

Richard* paused for a second.

Richard*:

Now, what's with the flattery, Henri? What do you want from me?

Henri:

Nothing, Richard. This is no flattery at all. There is a reason to what I am saying. Unlike many of our colleagues here, I know the world you and I come from. I am aware of the odds you have had to face to emerge and become the scientist you are today. The power cuts in the labs, the strikes at university, the police charging, the political tensions . . . I know of all this, I was there, just like you. So I have a sense of what it takes to be able to achieve such high standards when emerging out of our world . . . This is where my respect stems from . . .*

Richard* was now listening intently. Henri continued:

Let's now consider your intern, Julia. I agree with you that it might not always be easy to work with her. But you understand, better than anyone else amongst the mentors here, where she comes from. And you know that things have gotten worse since the days when we were still studying . . . So here I am, asking you, on behalf of our common experiences, and out of a sense of duty toward the up-and-coming generation of African scientists, to please reconsider your tendency to pull out of the program. We, as Africans based out here in the West: we may not get to be on the ground on the continent of Africa, but we can do our bit. My commitment to this program is my part. You can't tell me that you didn't at least partly decide to be a mentor in the NGS for similar reasons, can you?*

There was a moment of silence. Then Richard* spoke:

Richard*:

Look, Henri, I hear what you are saying. I may have spoken out of anger earlier, at the meeting. I was tired, we are coming up with several deadlines now at the lab, everybody's stressed. Yet, this does not mean that what I said is not true. Having said this, I can see that I could have put it differently . . . I did not mean to harm the program as a whole . . .

Henri:

In fact, you created space for the mentors to come out with the issues they were faced with—which is also important for us to understand as the Core Team. But it could have gone quite wrong indeed . . .

Richard* concluded:

Okay. To be honest, I did not seriously think about withdrawing as Julia's mentor. I might want to reconsider the projects I put her on, and try and adapt to what she can effectively do at this point. You are right, Henri, to point out the special conditions out of which young scientists in our countries emerge. Let me have a meeting with her soon to discuss this.

As this conversation was taking place, Colin was speaking with Julia*. What followed was a highly constructive meeting between Richard* and Julia*, during which they agreed to redefine the scope of her work to be making considerable progress within the 6 weeks remaining for her stay in Basel.

The NGS program continues to operate each year, and interns to date have attributed important professional development to their experiences, which includes measures such as scientific publications. They use techniques learnt during their time at Novartis to engage in breakthrough discoveries and to help advance science in different parts of the world for the greater benefit of patients.

19.6 Capacity Development Programs and the Risk of a "Brain Drain"

A critical element of the NGS program is that it is not a talent recruitment program into Basel, but rather a program designed to help strengthen the science base in LMICs. From the selection stage, all applicants were clearly impressed that, if chosen to participate in the NGS, the emphasis was on supporting their return to their home institution to help further advance science in the setting they had come from—be it an independent lab, a hospital, or a university.

During a football game that the fellows attended together with some of the Core Team members, as part of a team-building exercise, Brian*, a mentee and clinician scientist from South Africa, remarked to Colin:

Brian*:

Hey Colin, what'd you say, I pack you in my suitcase and take you back home in it after the program is over.

Startled, Colin asked Brian* to elaborate.

Brian*:

You are such a brilliant clinical pharmacologist! We need your scientific skills back home! The country and the continent need such leadership.

Colin thanked Brian* for the compliment and carefully skirted the second part of the statement.

After the game, Henri went up to Colin and recalled the incident, telling him how Brian had already spoken to him in a similar tone. It was becoming clear to Colin and Henri that their message on the need to go back home to reinforce capacities was standing in glaring contradiction to their very presence as full-time employees of a multinational corporation based in Switzerland. In the eyes of some of the NGS fellows, Colin and Henri, citizens of South Africa and Côte d'Ivoire, were living examples of what they were claiming to be actively fighting against, namely, the "brain drain".

"Brain drain" is a term used to describe the professional exile of highly educated professionals from LMICs to jobs in high-income countries (HICs). This phenomenon stands as a marker of the inequalities between HICs and LMICs, for it underscores the fact that LMICs face challenges in recouping their investments in education, and are often deprived of their own intellectual resources, making any attempt to catch up technologically all the more illusory.

At a subsequent discussion session in the NGS program dedicated to leadership and communication skills training, Colin and Henri decided to facilitate a discussion on the topic with their fellows.

Colin:

It is not a mystery to Henri or me that as Africans, both with PhDs and working and living in Basel, we come across as being not too self-critical when addressing the issue of brain drain. What credibility can we have, standing in front of you as NGS fellows, telling you that you should go home after the program is over?

Henri then came in and confirmed that this was something they were both highly aware of.

Henri:

In fact, there is a clear connection between my choice of living and working in Europe and the fact that I've joined this team to passionately run a program such as the NGS. This connection was precisely that the NGS is our response to the brain drain situation. It was because of our awareness of the brain drain that we thought of structuring the NGS the way we have: How can we live in a world in which we can share knowledge and skills in a way that can be truly profitable to the places and communities which scientists came from? The NGS is a possible answer to such a challenging question.

Later, Colin and Henri continued the conversation alone—reiterating the tactics they had implemented:

- working with home supervisors like Kelly Chibale, who would find ways to ensure that what interns were learning in Basel would be of the highest relevance to the work they were going to perform after their return home;
- that the short duration of only 3 months was also a reminder that this had been a training program delivering sound scientific output and not an employment opportunity in Europe;
- consistent messaging that the goal was to strengthen scientists in LMICs versus recruitment into Basel; and
- that while the internship lasted 3 months, the opportunities for future research collaborations were long term.

While Colin and Henri argued that there was potential to become relevant to science and medicine back home without living there, both ultimately acknowledged the complex reasons behind migration and reminded each other to be more aware of the ethical and moral dilemmas associated with their own physical presence in Europe while their home countries were in need of their educational skills. The tactics seemed to work since the NGS program had a high retention of fellows in their home countries (>75%) (Pillai et al. 2018).

19.7 Success Does Not Ensure Longevity

In 2017, as the NGS program was about to hit its seventh year of existence, the company announced an organizational restructuring. Programs were identified that might be terminated for various reasons, including resource constraints.

The NGS program was identified as one of the programs that would potentially be cut. Colin, Henri, and the Core Team found themselves in discussions about this issue with multiple stakeholders across the broad spectrum of company teams. The future of the program was unclear.

At the same time, the Core Team was completing the final round of interviews with the interns who were expected to come to Basel the following summer. Their home institutions had received assurances that everything was going smoothly according to plan, and mentors in Basel were getting ready to receive their interns, arranging for their respective research projects.

In an effort to act decisively, to save the program, and to avert a potentially embarrassing situation involving partners who were already expecting to participate, Colin decided to take a bold step, reaching out directly to the Head of Development at Novartis at that time, who was a strong supporter of the program and a regular participant in the leadership development lecture series that saw Novartis' influential role models share a few hours of their time answering questions, dispensing mentoring tips and other useful anecdotes. His engagement with the interns had been a deep one, during which he recounted his years as a young physician working on finding concrete solutions to help curb the HIV/AIDS pandemic in various parts of Africa.

Remembering this episode, Colin made the following calculation: he strongly suspected that the company leader saw the role the NGS program played in supporting the company's long-term goals and the central mission of "reimagining medicine".

His bet paid off. Colin called the Core Team together so as to share elements of the motivating response he had received from the company leadership.

Colin:

Our leaders are impressed with what our team has done here. I have been informed that one of our leaders has in fact often been told about the NGS program by Ministers of Health in the various countries he visits. They thank him and ask how they might get their young scientists to become a part of it. In brief, his bottom-line message was that despite the hard times for the company, programs like ours will remind the associates what we are about as a business, and will affirm that the future of this company is to be a truly global company in which we commit to partnerships toward developing the science behind finding medicines for unmet needs. So let's get this program up and running . . .

Novartis continues with its commitment toward helping build scientific capacity in global settings, supporting multiple innovative global health programs like NGS that build authentic partnerships in order to gain a firsthand understanding of science and health systems in LMICs.

References

ATMi (2016). *Access to Medicine Index 2016*. Haarlem, the Netherlands: Access to Medicine Foundation.

ATMi (2017). *Improving access to cancer care – A first analysis of pharmaceutical company actions in low- and middle-income countries*. Retrieved from https://accesstomedicinefoundation.org/media/uploads/downloads/5bc5eddbf180e_Access-to-Medicine-Foundation_Cancer-care-study_22May2017.pdf

Novartis (2012). *Novartis Annual Report 2012*. Novartis: Switzerland.

Novartis (2016). *Novartis Annual Report 2016*. Novartis: Switzerland.

Novartis (2017). *Novartis Annual Report 2017*. Novartis: Switzerland.

Novartis (2018). *Novartis Annual Report 2018*. Novartis: Switzerland.

Pillai, G., Chibale, K., Constable, E.C., Keller, A.N., Gutierrez, M.M., Mirza, F., Sengstag, C., Masimirembwa, C., Denti, P., Maartens, G., Ramsay, M., Ogutu, B., Makonnen, E., Gordon, R., Ferreira, C.G., Goldbaum, F.A., Degrave, W.M.S., Spector, J., Tadmor, B., & Kaiser, H.J. (2018). The Next Generation Scientist program: Capacity-building for future scientific leaders in low- and middle-income countries. *BMC Medical Education*, 18*(233)*, https://doi.org/10.1186/s12909-018-1331-y

Building a Healthy Organization

20

Female Leadership Across Borders in Times of Crisis

Sylvie Oldenziel Scherrer and Ingo Stolz

20.1 Joining a Failing Organization

Sara*[1] looked around in the almost empty office space. Staff had left to take on new jobs in more promising and stable organizations. Sara had just recently joined the Swiss-based international aid organization as Program Manager and Deputy Executive Director, in a moment when the organization not only rapidly lost morale but was in debt by half a million Swiss francs. As a member of a newly recruited small team, her job was explicitly to fix the errors of the recent past.

The difficult financial situation has deepened the trenches between the headquarters in Switzerland and the local representatives organizing humanitarian aid and development programs in the respective target countries around the world, specifically in Africa. The

The case study represents a collection of real occurrences, written down, dramatized, and condensed in a way so as to illustrate leadership behaviors exhibited by the stakeholders involved.

[1] All names with an asterisk (*) are anonymized, with titles, country of origin and event settings altered in order to reduce the ability to connect with specific participants in the organization.

S. Oldenziel Scherrer (✉)
Centre for Family Entrepreneurship and Ownership, Jönköping University, Jönköping, Sweden
e-mail: sylvie.scherrer@ju.se

I. Stolz
Lucerne University of Applied Sciences and Arts – Business, Institute of Business and Regional Economics, Lucerne, Switzerland
e-mail: ingo.stolz@hslu.ch

I. Stolz, S. Oldenziel Scherrer (eds.), *International Leadership*, uniscope. Publikationen der SGO Stiftung, https://doi.org/10.1007/978-3-658-37306-1_20

local offices were disappointed with the financial management, but the headquarters saw the origin of financial troubles mostly in poorly managed country programs.

Sara knew that mutual blaming wouldn't help when—as a result of the financial troubles—the legitimacy of the NGO was being questioned by internal and also external stakeholders. Despite her little experience working in international aid organizations in the African context, and led by her female leadership instincts, Sara knew that they only could overcome the financial crisis as a united team.

Amid this fight for survival of the organization, another blow hit: the executive director of the organization suffered from severe health problems and was forced to step down shortly after the arrival of Sara. It was now ultimately up to Sara to expand her role as Deputy Executive Director to become the interim leader of the organization—without being formally promoted to Executive Director status—and to involve and organize support for the measures to be taken with the Board of Directors.

20.2 Tough Decisions in a Time When Giving Up Was No Option

With little central funds, the business model of the NGO relied on the local country offices raising funds to self-finance the projects they were running in their respective locations, i.e. sponsored mostly by institutional donors. However, not all country offices had been willing or able to assume this responsibility sufficiently in the past. Notably, one of the country offices in sub-Saharan Africa was generating a continuous loss of 20,000–30,000 CHF per month. In order to avoid a worsening of the financial situation, Sara realized that she would have to make some very tough decisions—there was no other viable option than to close the programs this country office was currently running:

> I almost had a nervous breakdown the night before my flight left for sub-Saharan Africa. To make matters considerably worse, just 20 kms away from the country office, violent rebel movements were threatening the security of the office staff. And I was about to go there to close their programs, and to lay them off for financial considerations. My family told me 'Don't go, don't go', but I had to. I knew that it needed to be done for the sake of our organization. We had run all the analyses, we had also tried on many occasions over the course of several weeks to work with them toward increasing their fundraising footprint. Without success, unfortunately. Ultimately, I knew that there was no other option—there was no chance we could turn the program around.

And so it came about: little more than a year after joining the organization, Sara indeed closed down the country office—which belonged to the DNA of the overall organization—for financial reasons and amid violent rebel movements.

20.3 Getting Back on Track or Not?

While executing decisions, Sara needed to secure new project funds so that programs and processes could be upheld. Yet, this undertaking proved to be an extremely difficult task. The organization's funding had relied heavily on institutional donors, mostly from the EU, the US, or Swiss governments, but they no longer trusted the overall financial viability of the organization.

> Each time I went to propose a project with one of our major donors, instead of explaining the project rationale, objectives, and activities, I had to defend the financial situation of the organization and explain all the measures the management had taken to get back on track. It was all about winning back the trust of long-term financial partners.

With persistence and transparency, Sara managed to regain some trust and to secure some funding that allowed for keeping existing programs and processes running at least for a little while. Even though the situation remained critical, Sara started to feel more optimistic: maybe they would really be able to turn the organization around?

Yet, in this situation of reemerging hope, another blow came for Sara:

> Just when we were starting to be hopeful again, we had a meeting with our accountant, and it was such a shock: apparently, there was an accounting error, and while we thought that the numbers started to look better, our financial situation was still very bad. Really bad. Because our overall running costs were higher than calculated so far. What a mess! This was such a setback!

Sara felt she needed to take care of the details, took on the challenge herself and dived into the world of accounting. She remembers:

> I had mainly been hired to run and develop our programs in sub-Saharan Africa, and suddenly I spent my days and many nights working through Excels, analyzing our financial data and trying to help clean up the mess in our accounting system. I felt I didn't have a choice.

Once again, the organization's bankruptcy was an imminent threat. In board meetings, even the dissolution of the organization was now discussed. Nevertheless, giving up was still no option for Sara:

> From my previous experience working in an African country, I knew that my driver supported almost 20 people with his salary. I couldn't stop thinking about all our staff in the country offices—how many people would lose their livelihood when our organization was shut down. And not to speak of the irreplaceable impact our programs had in the local geographies. I just had to put up one more fight!

Following the board discussion around the dissolution of the organization on the one hand, and motivating the country teams to move ahead and to acquire new projects on the other hand, Sara felt like on a tightrope: this was the leadership challenge of her lifetime!

20.4 Regaining Control and Legitimacy

Finally, the Board of Directors decided to go public and to make a transparent call to the supporters of the organization in Switzerland, investing in a final effort to save it. Sara said:

> It was hard to put the numbers out there so bluntly and to cry for help, but we just needed money. We were a tip away from losing everything, so we didn't have much more to lose anyway.

With the call for help now circulating publicly, Sara and a handful of trusted colleagues from the headquarters as well as from some country offices sat down to draw up a new vision and strategy for the organization. Sara felt:

> Our organization was too focused on providing humanitarian aid on the ground, we didn't pay attention to the management of our organization as a 'business'.

Thus, for the first time indeed since Sara had joined the organization, internal stakeholders collectively discussed not only how to run the multiple country aid programs but also management objectives and measures needed to sustain the organization. Under the slogan *Building a Healthy Organization*, Sara and her sparring partners developed the following cornerstones of what they had defined for themselves as a 'healthy organization':

- The financial management had to be professionalized. Solely securing new funds wasn't sufficient to bring the organization back to financial viability. This not only required the development of financial competence within the organization, but also increased governance efforts. Notably, a closer monitoring and continuous assessment of the country programs was needed. The first cornerstone of the new strategy therefore was **healthy finances**.
- The second cornerstone, building a **healthy organizational foundation**, was particularly important for Sara. She wanted to move beyond the clashes between the headquarters and the country offices, toward a collaborative culture characterized by interpersonal and participative leadership.
- Lastly, they understood that a small organization such as theirs is dependent on good cooperation with multiple stakeholders, notably with other NGOs and with institutional donors such as governments and transnational entities, such as the United Nations. Therefore, the organization would have to (re-)focus on (re-)establishing **healthy**

partnerships with the key stakeholders, characterized by collaboration, reliability, competence, and trust.

With this new vision and strategy, Sara convinced the Board of Directors. It approved this new approach and suggested to formally promote Sara to become the new Executive Director.

20.5 Stepping Up? Leading in the Background

Having taken the lead in this difficult crisis, Sara's appointment as Executive Director seemed to be a logical consequence. She knew that research on female leadership showed that in international organizations, such situations of crisis offer unique windows of opportunity for women to access leadership positions. They either legitimize women as suitable candidates or create *glass cliffs* that make positions unattractive to men. While Sara recognized the value of the opportunity, she nevertheless decided to avoid the *glass cliff* and—to the great surprise of the Board of Directors—declined the role of Executive Director:

> They wanted me to take over the role of the Executive Director, but I knew that at this point, we really needed somebody with a lot of experience in leading international organizations, namely in professionalizing an organically grown organization. I just knew that I didn't have this experience yet, and that if I assumed the role now, I would immediately run into a burn-out.

Declining the role of the Executive Director, however, didn't stop Sara from leading the organization in the background. She wanted a sparring partner and mentor from whom she could learn and develop while realizing the jointly developed new vision and strategy. She thus convinced the Board to invest in the recruitment and onboarding of a new Executive Director. Soon thereafter, Peter* started in this position. Looking back at a long and successful career in non-profit organizations, Peter was ready to take a leap of faith and to join Sara, and he indeed became an important mentor to her:

> Peter was my secure base and my mentor. I was not alone; he had my back, but he also did let me realize my vision, and my objectives. He always listened to my ideas and helped me implement them.

20.6 Further Consolidating the Value Streams

Sara and Peter knew that the organization was still in a fragile state, despite the fact that severe cost-saving measures helped overcome immediate threats. So they knew that additional and innovative steps needed to be taken.

> We again challenged our board. Ultimately, we now began telling them that we needed to invest money to raise funds; that we needed to recruit additional expertise and resources to run effective fundraising campaigns.

Sara also worked hard to push through the idea of installing transparent value streams at the level of the country offices: Every year, they were supposed to receive a certain percentage of the overall budget, to be spent freely on their country-specific needs.

> They receive some funds back from us—oftentimes this is rather symbolic. But implementing this formula was very important, because it showed them that we are listening to them, and as such, this measure was key in overcoming the divide between the headquarters and the country offices!

Concrete actions like these were important to open a continuous dialogue between the headquarters and the country offices, and to rebuild trust internally. However, expectations from the country offices toward the headquarters were still high:

> I still remember one visit to one of our offices in Africa. I arrived, and they literally grilled me with their questions and expectations! It was really uncomfortable to be heavily pressured by the country team without having much to offer.

Sara took time to explain the current state of the organization to this country team, and after many hours of tough discussions, she managed to have them lower their expectations. Only many months later she was told, in her recollection:

> The country representative told me that I am the connector between the country offices, the headquarters, and our Board of Directors. They called me an ambassador of the country offices. This made me happy, but I think that this is natural, because I could see it all—I spent time in the field with our country staff and I would sit in board meetings. So it felt natural, but I also felt that we needed to connect even more.

20.7 Broadening Horizons

Slowly, Sara was able to shift her focus away from immediate financial crisis management to what turned out to be her real passion: fostering collaboration across borders. Hereby, bilateral visits to the country offices weren't enough for Sara, she also wanted to foster collaboration amongst the different country offices, specifically in Africa:

> Our country representatives are the creators of the organization. In order to build a healthy organization, we really needed them to be aligned, to collaborate, we needed to decide collectively on how to move forward.

With the financial situation stabilized, Sara wanted to invite all country office leads to a senior management retreat in Switzerland. She needed the key persons to be involved and engaged in the process of building a healthy organization, and she even convinced Peter and the Board of Directors that such a senior management retreat needed to occur on regular basis from now on:

> Peter immediately agreed. But then he proposed to rent a house where we would work and live and cook together for a couple of days. Having lived in an African context before, where women literally chase their men out of the kitchen, I remember how I looked at him and thought he was crazy for wanting to put a group of African men into the kitchen! But we did it and it worked, even though some of them just opened cans! Only later I realized that this setting corresponded much better to the collective nature of their cultures than our Swiss understanding of professional management meetings in a nice hotel, and that it helped create a family spirit.

Ever since, the organization has rented a nice house and run senior management retreats on a regular basis. Slowly, this started to fill the trenches that had been opened by the financial crisis.

20.8 Finding One's Own Approach

While regaining the trust of the country teams, Sara's own approach to intercultural collaboration helped her a lot. She focused on being a careful observer, attentive listener, and humble sparring partner:

> I think that modesty is extremely important if you are a leader in different cultural settings. I always try to be humble—as a person, but also as a representative of a Swiss organization. I really see the country teams as the experts, and I see my role as the facilitator of their success. Therefore, it is very important that we interact at eye level and that we always develop down-to-earth approaches. I would never want to impose anything on them that doesn't make sense to them.

Even while she had to focus on the survival of the organization, Sara tried to carefully listen to the sorrows and the needs of the country representatives and their staff. Many of their concerns couldn't be addressed by Sara immediately, but listening to them still allowed her to develop a sound understanding of the country's specific habits and norms. Moreover, she relied on her experiences from having lived in multiple African countries before:

> Once, we were having lunch with the entire team at a local restaurant, and one staff member had to leave to attend a funeral for a close family member. I suddenly remembered that in many African countries, it is common to make a small financial contribution to major life events. When time came for him to leave, I accompanied him outside and gave him a little donation. Walking him out of the restaurant was just a small gesture, but it was really appreciated by the entire team. It is oftentimes the small things that help bond and create trust.

20.9 Tackling Issues Set Aside During the Crisis

Over the next few years, Sara made it a priority to push forward her vision of a healthy organization. Having intensively worked on stabilizing its financial situation and creating a more collaborative and professional organization, the time had also come to address issues which would hinder the organization's development in the long run, which had not been a priority during the crisis.

> We continued to have challenging discussions, but I was convinced that we needed honest conversations and clear decisions in order to be able to move forward as an organization. For example, one country program in Africa wasn't managed well. We tried to support and coach the country officer. We invested in his learning and development, but ultimately we needed to move forward. In this case, it meant we had to let the country officer go. It really hurts when you must let somebody go, especially if you like the person. It really hurt, but it was the right decision.

20.10 Fighting for Recognition and Jumping on Opportunities

After more than 5 years of struggling, fighting, and transforming, the organization was on stable ground again. While Sara still had many ideas on how to develop it further, she decided for once to fight for herself by asking for a promotion:

> It was clear to me that I wouldn't ask for a pay rise when we were struggling for financial survival, but once we were doing relatively well again, I wanted to be formally recognized for my work. I wanted the job title and the pay that matched my responsibilities. I got it very easily, but I still had to ask for it. You probably always need to be the one asking for this kind of recognition.

Another 3 years later, Sara didn't have to ask but instead was asked by Peter and the Board of Directors to follow in his footsteps as the Executive Director. Sara repeatedly declined, but she wanted to help hiring and onboarding a new Executive Director and then look for a new challenge outside the organization.

> We had already started the recruiting process when I participated in the general female strike in Switzerland in 2019. And then it hit me: here I was in the streets of Bern, fighting for equal pay and more women in higher management positions, but at the same time I turned down a unique opportunity. This didn't make any sense, so I called Peter and the Board of Directors. They immediately said: 'Please, take the role'.

Despite her ultimately passionate yes to her promotion, Sara felt terrible all the time from taking her decision until fully taking over as Executive Director some months later. She was ridden with doubts rather than confidence and excitement. She asked herself: why do I, why do women doubt, while men are often so confident and self-sufficient? However, once she effectively became Executive Director, the feeling changed:

> I realized that I very much liked to lead in the background and that I was afraid to be the public face of the organization. Sometimes, I still have to force myself to put myself out there, but I feel good now, it really feels good to have this role. I like it.

Since then, Sara has held full responsibility of the organization, as well as having overseen programs in seven countries, with a staff of 120 people and a yearly turnover of around USD8 million. During her tenure, the headquarters grew from 21 to 73 FTE, and she put her organization back on the Swiss scene of impactful NGOs in developmental aid. Nowadays, Sara focuses on promoting her collaborative spirit outside her organization, by fostering closer cooperation among likeminded NGOs—and still aims to build an even healthier organization:

> Sometimes, it feels like I have done my job here and that it is time to hand it over to a new person. At the same time, I still have many objectives that I feel we need to accomplish so as to realize our vision of a truly healthy organization. I want us to have a financial safety cushion, to considerably improve our internal quality assessments, and I also want to make sure that we do everything to keep our staff safe. We almost exclusively operate in high-risk countries; we need to focus on keeping our staff as healthy and safe as possible.

Acknowledgement The presentation of this business case would not have been possible without the contributions of Sara*, who decided to share in all honesty the ups and downs of her leadership journey. We would like to thank her for her openness and all the time and effort she has dedicated to this contribution.

MIX
Papier aus verantwortungsvollen Quellen
Paper from responsible sources
FSC® C105338

If you have any concerns about our products,
you can contact us on
ProductSafety@springernature.com

In case Publisher is established outside the EU,
the EU authorized representative is:
Springer Nature Customer Service Center GmbH
Europaplatz 3, 69115 Heidelberg, Germany

Printed by Libri Plureos GmbH
in Hamburg, Germany